Reading STREET

Grade 5, Unit 2

Doing the Right Thing

SCOTT FORESMAN

PEARSON
Scott Foresman

Editorial Offices: Glenview, Illinois • Parsippany, New Jersey • New York, New York
Sales Offices: Boston, Massachusetts • Duluth, Georgia • Glenview, Illinois
Coppell, Texas • Sacramento, California • Mesa, Arizona

scottforesman.com

We dedicate Reading Street to
Peter Jovanovich.

⁓

His wisdom, courage,
and passion for education
are an inspiration to us all.

Cover Greg Newbold

About the Cover Artist
Award-winning artist Greg Newbold began drawing and painting at age three—and never stopped. His illustrated books for children include *Spring Song* and *Winter Lullaby*. Mr. Newbold also does illustrations for magazines, motion pictures, and food products, such as catsup and jelly. He creates his illustrations in a studio next to his house, snuggled in the Rocky Mountains of Utah.

ISBN-13: 978-0-328-24386-0

ISBN-10:   0-328-24386-8

Copyright © 2008 Pearson Education, Inc.

All Rights Reserved. Printed in the United States of America. This publication is protected by Copyright, and permission should be obtained from the publisher prior to any prohibited reproduction, storage in a retrieval system, or transmission in any form by any means, electronic, mechanical, photocopying, recording, or likewise. For information regarding permission(s), write to: Permissions Department, Scott Foresman, 1900 East Lake Avenue, Glenview, Illinois 60025.

Many of the designations used by manufacturers and sellers to distinguish their products are claimed as trademarks. Where those designations appear in this book, and Scott Foresman was aware of a trademark claim, the designations have been printed with initial capitals and in cases of multiple usage have also been marked with either ® or ™ where they first appear.

2 3 4 5 6 7 8 9 10 11 V063 16 15 14 13 12 11 10 09 08 07
CC:N1

Reading STREET

Where the Love of Reading Begins

Reading Street Program Authors

Peter Afflerbach, Ph.D.
Professor, Department of
Curriculum and Instruction
University of Maryland at
College Park

Camille L.Z. Blachowicz, Ph.D.
Professor of Education
National-Louis University

Candy Dawson Boyd, Ph.D.
Professor, School of Education
Saint Mary's College of California

Wendy Cheyney, Ed.D.
Professor of Special Education
and Literacy, Florida
International University

Connie Juel, Ph.D.
Professor of Education, School of
Education, Stanford University

Edward J. Kame'enui, Ph.D.
Professor and Director, Institute for
the Development of Educational
Achievement, University of Oregon

Donald J. Leu, Ph.D.
John and Maria Neag Endowed
Chair in Literacy and Technology
University of Connecticut

Jeanne R. Paratore, Ed.D.
Associate Professor of Education
Department of Literacy
and Language Development
Boston University

P. David Pearson, Ph.D.
Professor and Dean,
Graduate School of Education
University of California, Berkeley

Sam L. Sebesta, Ed.D.
Professor Emeritus,
College of Education,
University of Washington, Seattle

Deborah Simmons, Ph.D.
Professor, College of Education
and Human Development
Texas A&M University
(Not pictured)

Sharon Vaughn, Ph.D.
H.E. Hartfelder/Southland
Corporation Regents Professor
University of Texas

Susan Watts-Taffe, Ph.D.
Independent Literacy Researcher
Cincinnati, Ohio

Karen Kring Wixson, Ph.D.
Professor of Education
University of Michigan

Components

Student Editions (1–6)

Teacher's Editions (PreK–6)

Assessment
Assessment Handbook (K–6)
Baseline Group Tests (K–6)
DIBELS™ Assessments (K–6)
ExamView® Test Generator CD-ROM (2–6)
Fresh Reads for Differentiated
Test Practice (1–6)
Online Success Tracker™ (K–6)*
Selection Tests Teacher's Manual (1–6)
Unit and End-of-Year
Benchmark Tests (K–6)

Leveled Readers
Concept Literacy Leveled Readers (K–1)
Independent Leveled Readers (K)
Kindergarten Student Readers (K)
Leveled Reader Teaching Guides (K–6)
Leveled Readers (1–6)
Listen to Me Readers (K)
Online Leveled Reader Database (K–6)*
Take-Home Leveled Readers (K–6)

Trade Books and Big Books
Big Books (PreK–2)
Read Aloud Trade Books (PreK–K)
Sing with Me Big Book (1–2)
Trade Book Library (1–6)

Decodable Readers
Decodable Readers (K–3)
Strategic Intervention
Decodable Readers (1–2)
Take-Home Decodable Readers (K–3)

Phonics and Word Study
Alphabet Cards in English and Spanish
(PreK–K)
Alphabet Chart in English and Spanish
(PreK–K)
Animal ABCs Activity Guide (K)
Finger Tracing Cards (PreK–K)
Patterns Book (PreK–K)
Phonics Activities CD-ROM (PreK–2)*
Phonics Activities Mats (K)
Phonics and Spelling Practice Book (1–3)
Phonics and Word-Building Board and Letters
(PreK–3)
Phonics Songs and Rhymes Audio CD (K–2)
Phonics Songs and Rhymes Flip Chart (K–2)
Picture Word Cards (PreK–K)
Plastic Letter Tiles (K)
Sound-Spelling Cards and Wall Charts (1–2)
Strategies for Word Analysis (4–6)
Word Study and Spelling Practice Book (4–6)

Language Arts
Daily Fix-It Transparencies (K–6)
Grammar & Writing Book and
Teacher's Annotated Edition, The (1–6)
Grammar and Writing Practice Book
and Teacher's Manual (1–6)
Grammar Transparencies (1–6)
Six-Trait Writing Posters (1–6)
Writing Kit (1–6)
Writing Rubrics and Anchor Papers (1–6)
Writing Transparencies (1–6)

Practice and Additional Resources
AlphaBuddy Bear Puppet (K)
Alphasaurus Annie Puppet (PreK)
Amazing Words Posters (K–2)
Centers Survival Kit (PreK–6)
Graphic Organizer Book (2–6)
Graphic Organizer Flip Chart (K–1)
High-Frequency Word Cards (K)
Kindergarten Review (1)
Practice Book and Teacher's Manual (K–6)
Read Aloud Anthology (PreK–2)
Readers' Theater Anthology (K–6)
Research into Practice (K–6)

Retelling Cards (K–6)
Scott Foresman Research Base (K–6)
Skill Transparencies (2–6)
Songs and Rhymes Flip Chart (PreK)
Talk with Me, Sing with Me Chart (PreK–K)
Tested Vocabulary Cards (1–6)
Vocabulary Transparencies (1–2)
Welcome to Reading Street (PreK–1)

ELL
ELL and Transition Handbook (PreK–6)
ELL Comprehensive Kit (1–6)
ELL Posters (K–6)
ELL Readers (1–6)
ELL Teaching Guides (1–6)
Ten Important Sentences (1–6)

Digital Components
AudioText CDs (PreK–6)
Background Building Audio CDs (3–6)
ExamView® Test Generator
CD-ROM (2–6)
Online Lesson Planner (K–6)
Online New Literacies Activities (1–6)*
Online Professional Development (1–6)
Online Story Sort (K–6)*
Online Student Editions (1–6)*
Online Success Tracker™ (K–6)*
Online Teacher's Editions (PreK–6)
Phonics Activities CD-ROM (PreK–2)*
Phonics Songs and Rhymes
Audio CD (K–2)
Sing with Me/Background Building
Audio CDs (PreK–2)
Songs and Rhymes Audio CD (PreK)

My Sidewalks Early Reading Intervention (K)

My Sidewalks Intensive Reading Intervention (Levels A–E)

Reading Street for the Guided Reading Teacher (1–6)

Unit 4
Adapting

Unit 5
Adventurers

Unit 6
The Unexpected

Unit 1
Meeting Challenges

Doing the Right Thing

What makes people
want to do the right thing?

Inside Out

A young boy helps a bully.

REALISTIC FICTION

connect to SOCIAL STUDIES

Paired Selection

Random Acts of Kindness

E-MAIL

Passage to Freedom

A man saves refugees from death.

BIOGRAPHY

connect to SOCIAL STUDIES

Paired Selection

I Wanted My Mother

AUTOBIOGRAPHY

The Ch'i-lin Purse

One act of kindness inspires another.

FOLK TALE

connect to SOCIAL STUDIES

Paired Selection

The Lion and the Mouse

FABLE

Jane Goodall's 10 Ways to Help Save Wildlife

A scientist helps save endangered species.

EXPOSITORY NONFICTION

connect to SCIENCE

Paired Selection

Why Some Animals Are Considered Bad or Scary

EXPOSITORY NONFICTION

The Midnight Ride of Paul Revere

A patriot warns citizens of a coming attack.

POEM

connect to SOCIAL STUDIES

Paired Selection

Revolutionary War Women

WEB SITE

Unit 2
Skills Overview

WEEK 1

146–161
**Inside Out/
Random Acts
of Kindness**
REALISTIC FICTION

*Why do people show
kindness?*

WEEK 2

166–185
**Passage to
Freedom/
I Wanted
My Mother**
BIOGRAPHY

*Why do we help others even
if there are risks?*

		WEEK 1	WEEK 2
Reading	**Comprehension**	**T** ⊙ **Skill** Compare and Contrast ⊙ **Strategy** Answer Questions **T** REVIEW **Skill** Author's Purpose	**T** ⊙ **Skill** Author's Purpose ⊙ **Strategy** Monitor and Fix Up **T** REVIEW **Skill** Sequence
	Vocabulary	**T** ⊙ **Strategy** Word Structure	**T** ⊙ **Strategy** Dictionary/Glossary
	Fluency	Characterization/Dialogue	Tone of Voice
Word Work	**Spelling and Phonics**	Digraphs *th, sh, ch, ph*	Irregular Plurals
Oral Language	**Speaking/Listening/ Viewing**	Persuasive Speech Listen to a Persuasive Speech	Oral Report Listen to Audio CD
Language Arts	**Grammar, Usage, and Mechanics**	**T** Regular and Irregular Plural Nouns	**T** Possessive Nouns
	Weekly Writing	Summary Writing Trait: Focus/Ideas	Story Review Writing Trait: Focus/Ideas
	Unit Process Writing	How-to Report	How-to Report
	Research and Study Skills	Reference Book	Parts of a Book
	Integrate Science and Social Studies Standards	*Time for* SOCIAL STUDIES Civic Values, Citizenship, Interactions	*Time for* SOCIAL STUDIES World War II, Holocaust, Government, Culture

 **Big Idea** *What makes people want to do the right thing?*

WEEK 3	WEEK 4	WEEK 5
190–207 **The Ch'i-lin Purse/The Lion and the Mouse** **FOLK TALE** *What are the rewards in helping others?*	**212–229** **Jane Goodall's 10 Ways to Help Save Wildlife/Why Some Animals Are Considered Bad or Scary** **EXPOSITORY NONFICTION** *What can people do to protect wild animals?*	**234–253** **The Midnight Ride of Paul Revere/Revolutionary War Women** **POEM** *How can people promote freedom?*
T **Skill** Compare and Contrast **Strategy** Predict **T** REVIEW **Skill** Sequence	**T** **Skill** Fact and Opinion **Strategy** Ask Questions **T** REVIEW **Skill** Compare and Contrast	**T** **Skill** Sequence **Strategy** Graphic Organizers **T** REVIEW **Skill** Setting and Theme
T **Strategy** Word Structure	**T** **Strategy** Context Clues	**T** **Strategy** Word Structure
Pitch	Phrasing	Tone of Voice
Vowel Sounds with *r*	Final Syllables *-en, -an, -el, -le, -il*	Final Syllables *er, ar, or*
Readers' Theater Analyze an Illustration	Debate Analyze Media	Radio Feature Story Listen to a CD
T Action and Linking Verbs	**T** Main and Helping Verbs	**T** Subject-Verb Agreement
News Story Writing Trait: Organization/Paragraphs	Rules Writing Trait: Word Choice	Interview Writing Trait: Organization/Paragraphs
How-to Report	How-to Report	How-to Report
Textbook/Trade Book	Technology: Electronic Media	Illustration/Caption
Time for SOCIAL STUDIES Cultures, Citizenship, Ancient Civilizations	**Time for Science** Habitats, Ecosystems, Environments, Ecology	**Time for SOCIAL STUDIES** Colonial America, U.S. History, American Revolution, American Patriots

Unit 2
Monitor Progress

Predictors of Reading Success	WEEK 1	WEEK 2	WEEK 3	WEEK 4
Fluency (WCPM)	Characterization/ Dialogue 110–116 WCPM	Tone of Voice 110–116 WCPM	Pitch 110–116 WCPM	Phrasing 110–116 WCPM
Vocabulary/ Concept Development (assessed informally)	homeless shelter volunteered	hiding officers poses	distress favor panic stranded	conservation naturalist wildlife
Lesson Vocabulary	**Strategy** Word Structure caterpillar cocoon disrespect emerge migrant sketched unscrewed	**Strategy** Dictionary/ Glossary agreement cable diplomat issue refugees representatives superiors visa	**Strategy** Word Structure astonished behavior benefactor distribution gratitude procession recommend sacred traditions	**Strategy** Dictionary/ Glossary conservation contribute enthusiastic environment investigation
Text Comprehension (Retelling)	**Skill** Compare and Contrast **Strategy** Answer Questions	**Skill** Author's Purpose **Strategy** Monitor and Fix Up	**Skill** Compare and Contrast **Strategy** Predict	**Skill** Fact and Opinion **Strategy** Ask Questions

◉ Target Skill   ✸ SuccessTracker/Unit 2 Benchmark Tested Skills

Make Data–Driven Decisions

Data Management
- Assess
- Diagnose
- Prescribe
- Disaggregate

Classroom Management
- Monitor Progress
- Group
- Differentiate Instruction
- Inform Parents

ONLINE CLASSROOM

WEEK 5

Tone of Voice

110–116 WCPM

battle
freedom
Monmouth

Strategy
Dictionary/
Glossary

fate
fearless
glimmer
lingers
magnified
somber
steed

Skill Sequence

Strategy
Graphic
Organizers

Manage Data

- Assign the Unit 2 Benchmark Test for students to take online.
- SuccessTracker records results and generates reports by school, grade, classroom, or student.
- Use reports to disaggregate and aggregate Unit 2 skills and standards data to monitor progress.
- Based on class lists created to support the categories important for AYP (gender, ethnicity, migrant education, English proficiency, disabilities, economic status), reports let you track adequate yearly progress every six weeks.

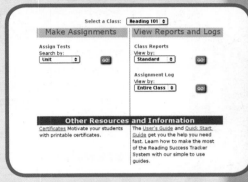

Group

- Use results from Unit 2 Benchmark Tests taken online through SuccessTracker to regroup students.
- Reports in SuccessTracker suggest appropriate groups for students based on test results.

Individualize Instruction

- Tests are correlated to Unit 2 tested skills and standards so that prescriptions for individual teaching and learning plans can be created.
- Individualized prescriptions target instruction and accelerate student progress toward learning outcome goals.
- Prescriptions include resources to reteach Unit 2 skills and standards.

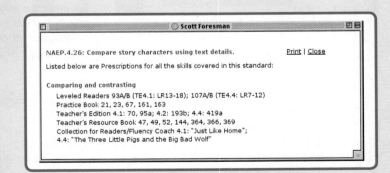

NAEP.4.26: Compare story characters using text details.   Print | Close

Listed below are Prescriptions for all the skills covered in this standard:

Comparing and contrasting
  Leveled Readers 93A/B (TE4.1: LR13-18); 107A/B (TE4.4: LR7-12)
  Practice Book: 21, 23, 67, 161, 163
  Teacher's Edition 4.1: 70, 95a; 4.2: 193b; 4.4: 419a
  Teacher's Resource Book 47, 49, 52, 144, 364, 366, 369
  Collection for Readers/Fluency Coach 4.1: "Just Like Home";
  4.4: "The Three Little Pigs and the Big Bad Wolf"

Unit 2
Grouping for AYP

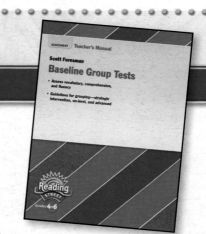

STEP 1

Diagnose and Differentiate

Diagnose
To make initial grouping decisions, use the Baseline Group Test or another initial placement test. Depending on students' ability levels, you may have more than one of each group.

Differentiate

If... student performance is **Below-Level** **then...** use the regular instruction and the daily Strategic Intervention lessons, pp. DI·2–DI·50.

If... student performance is **On-Level** **then...** use the regular instruction for On-Level learners throughout each selection.

If... student performance is **Advanced** **then...** use the regular instruction and the daily instruction for Advanced learners, pp. DI·3–DI·51.

Group Time

On-Level	Strategic Intervention	Advanced
• Explicit instructional routines teach core skills and strategies. • Independent activities provide practice for core skills and extension and enrichment options. • Leveled readers (LR1–45) provide additional reading and practice with core skills and vocabulary.	• Daily Strategic Intervention lessons provide more intensive instruction, more scaffolding, more practice with critical skills, and more opportunities to respond. • Reteach lessons (DI·52–DI·56) provide additional instructional opportunities with target skills. • Leveled readers instruction (LR1–45) builds background for the main selection and provides practice with target skills and vocabulary.	• Daily Advanced Lessons provide compacted instruction for accelerated learning, options for investigative work, and challenging reading content. • Leveled readers (LR1–45) provide additional reading tied to lesson concepts.

Additional opportunities to differentiate instruction:
- Reteach Lessons, pp. DI·52–DI·56
- Leveled Reader Instruction and Leveled Practice, LR1–45
- My Sidewalks on Scott Foresman Reading Street Intensive Reading Intervention Program

4–Step Plan for Assessment

1. Diagnose and Differentiate
2. Monitor Progress
3. Assess and Regroup
4. Summative Assessment

Monitor Progress

STEP 2

- **Guiding comprehension questions** and skill and strategy instruction during reading
- **Monitor Progress boxes** to check comprehension and vocabulary
- **Weekly Assessments** on Day 3 for comprehension, Day 4 for fluency, and Day 5 for vocabulary
- **Practice Book** pages at point of use
- **Weekly Selection Tests** or **Fresh Reads for Differentiated Test Practice**

Assess and Regroup

STEP 3

- **Days 3, 4, and 5 Assessments** Record results of weekly Days 3, 4, and 5 assessments in retelling, fluency, and vocabulary (pp. WA16–WA17) to track student progress.
- **Unit 2 Benchmark Test** Administer this test to check mastery of unit skills.
- Use weekly assessment information, Unit Benchmark Test performance, and the Unit 2 Assess and Regroup (p. WA18) to make regrouping decisions. See the time line below.

YOU ARE HERE
Begin Unit 2

SCOTT FORESMAN ASSESSMENT

Group Baseline Group Test → Assess → Regroup Units 1 and 2 (p. WA18) → Regroup Unit 3 → Regroup Unit 4 → Regroup Unit 5 → Assess

| Week | 1 | | 5 | | 10 | | 15 | | 20 | | 25 | | 30 |

END OF YEAR

OUTSIDE ASSESSMENT

Initial placement → Outside assessment for regrouping → Outside assessment for regrouping

Outside assessments (e.g., DIBELS) may recommend regrouping at other times during the year.

Summative Assessment

STEP 4

- **Benchmark Assessment** Use to measure a student's mastery of each unit's skills.
- **End-of-Year Benchmark Assessment** Use to measure a student's mastery of program skills covered in all six units.

Unit 2
Theme Launch

Discuss the Big Idea

As a class, discuss the Big Idea question, *What makes people want to do the right thing?*

Explain that we often have a choice whether or not to help others and do the right thing. Sometimes it is difficult to stand up for the rights of others, but doing so can make us feel good.

Ask students to give examples of what it might mean for people to "do the right thing."

A good example of a person doing the right thing is someone returning a lost wallet or purse to its owner. It may be tempting to keep any money found inside, but it belongs to someone else and should be returned.

Theme and Concept Connections

Weekly lesson concepts help students connect the reading selections and the unit theme. Theme-related activities throughout the week provide opportunities to explore the relationships among the selections, the lesson concepts, and the unit theme.

UNIT 2

Read Online
PearsonSuccess

Doing the Right Thing
What makes people want to do the right thing?

140

CONNECTING CULTURES

Use the following selections to help students learn more about living in another country and communicating with others.

Inside Out Have students discuss Francisco's struggles to communicate with others. They can also share ideas about making new students like Francisco feel welcomed.

Passage to Freedom Have students discuss how Hiroki was able to understand the problems of the children even though he could not speak their language. Students can also share their thoughts about being in a situation like Hiroki's.

Inside Out

A young boy helps a bully.
REALISTIC FICTION

connect to SOCIAL STUDIES

Paired Selection
Random Acts of Kindness
E-MAIL

Passage to Freedom

A man saves refugees from death.
BIOGRAPHY

connect to SOCIAL STUDIES

Paired Selection
I Wanted My Mother
AUTOBIOGRAPHY

The Ch'i-lin Purse

One act of kindness inspires another.
FOLK TALE

connect to SOCIAL STUDIES

Paired Selection
The Lion and the Mouse
FABLE

Jane Goodall's 10 Ways to Help Save Wildlife

A scientist helps save endangered species.
EXPOSITORY NONFICTION

connect to SCIENCE

Paired Selection
Why Some Animals Are Considered Bad or Scary
EXPOSITORY NONFICTION

The Midnight Ride of Paul Revere

A patriot warns citizens of a coming attack.
POEM

connect to SOCIAL STUDIES

Paired Selection
Revolutionary War Women
WEB SITE

141

Unit Inquiry Project

Doing the Right Thing

In the unit inquiry project, students each choose a charity or service group and research how it helps the community. They may use print or online resources as available.

The project assessment rubric can be found on p. 254a. Discuss the rubric's expectations before students begin the project. Rubric 4 3 2 1

PROJECT TIMETABLE

WEEK	ACTIVITY/SKILL CONNECTION
1	**IDENTIFY QUESTIONS** Each student chooses a local charity or service group and browses a few Web sites or print reference materials to develop an inquiry question about how it helps the community. If students need help identifying an organization, suggest they search the Internet using their town name and *volunteering* or *charity* as keywords.
2	**NAVIGATE/SEARCH** Students conduct effective information searches and look for text and images that can help them answer their questions.
3	**ANALYZE** Students explore Web sites or print materials. They analyze the information they have found to determine whether or not it will be useful to them. Students print or take notes on valid information.
4	**SYNTHESIZE** Students combine relevant information they've collected from different sources to develop answers to their inquiry questions from Week 1.

ASSESSMENT OPTIONS

5	**COMMUNICATE** Students present short speeches about local charities or service groups and how they help the community. Students may also make posters showing ways the organizations help others.

CONCEPT DEVELOPMENT

Unit 2
Doing the Right Thing

CONCEPT QUESTION

What makes people want to do the right thing?

Week 5

Expand the Concept
How can people promote freedom?

Connect the Concept

Literature

Develop Language
Battle, freedom, Monmouth

Teach Content
Boston, MA
Old North Church
Freedom Trail

Writing
Interview

Internet Inquiry
Promoting Freedom

Time for SOCIAL STUDIES

Week 4

Expand the Concept
What can people do to protect wild animals?

Connect the Concept

Literature

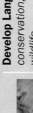
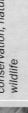

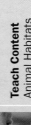

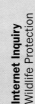

Develop Language
conservation, naturalist, wildlife

Teach Content
Animal Habitats
Roots and Shoots
Ecosystems

Writing
Rules

Internet Inquiry
Wildlife Protection

Time for Science

Week 3

Expand the Concept
What are the rewards in helping others?

Connect the Concept

Literature

Develop Language
distress, favor, panic, stranded

Teach Content
Chinese Family Customs
Jade
Aesop's Fables

Writing
News Story

Internet Inquiry
Good Deeds in Folk Tales

Time for SOCIAL STUDIES

Week 1

Expand the Concept
Why do people show kindness?

Connect the Concept

Literature

Develop Language
Homeless, shelter, volunteered

Teach Content
Migrant Workers
U.S. Constitution
World Kindness

Writing
Summary

Internet Inquiry
Kindness

Time for SOCIAL STUDIES

Week 2

Expand the Concept
Why do we help others even if there are risks?

Connect the Concept

Literature

Develop Language
hiding, officers, poses

Teach Content
World War II
Diplomacy

Writing
Story Review

Internet Inquiry
Taking Risks

Time for SOCIAL STUDIES

Unit 2
Doing the Right Thing

CONCEPT QUESTION
What makes people want to do the right thing?

Week 1
Why do people show kindness?

Week 2
Why do we help others even if there are risks?

Week 3
What are the rewards in helping others?

Week 4
What can people do to protect wild animals?

Week 5
How can people promote freedom?

EXPAND THE CONCEPT
Why do people show kindness?

CONNECT THE CONCEPT

▶ Build Background
homeless, shelter, volunteered

Concept Vocabulary Web

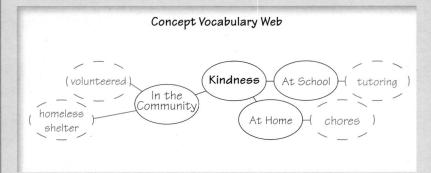

▶ Social Studies Content
Migrant Workers, U.S. Constitution, World Kindness

▶ Writing
Summary

▶ Internet Inquiry
Kindness

Preview Your Week

Why do people show kindness?

by Francisco Jiménez

Inside Out

illustrated by Raul Colon

Why does Francisco do what he does at the end of the story?

Genre

Realistic fiction deals with characters and actions that seem real but come from the author's imagination. As you read, notice how the author makes the setting and characters come to life.

Student Edition pages 146–157

Audio CD

Genre	Realistic Fiction
Vocabulary Strategy	Word Structure
Comprehension Skill	Compare and Contrast
Comprehension Strategy	Answer Questions

Paired Selection

Reading Across Texts
Identify a Random Act of Kindness

Genre
E-mail

Text Features
Headings

SOCIAL STUDIES

Social Studies in Reading

E-mails

Genre
- E-mail is short for "electronic mail."
- E-mails are messages sent on a computer over the Internet. They travel from sender to receiver in a matter of moments.

Text Features
- Each e-mail has a heading that tells who submitted it when.
- These e-mails are for a general audience. The sender is writing to anyone who visits the Web site to read about random acts of kindness.

Link to Social Studies
With your teacher's help, begin a Random Acts of Kindness File for your classroom. Think of times when you practiced kindness and write about them.

Random Acts of Kindness

These e-mails are from the Random Acts of Kindness Foundation Web site. This nonprofit organization encourages people to practice kindness whenever and wherever they can.

A Mother's Appreciation
SUBMITTED BY: HAYLEY'S MOTHER / DATE SUBMITTED: 3/18/2004

I want to acknowledge the kindness of Madison. She was so sweet to my daughter, Hayley, who is a kindergartener.

Hayley was having a very difficult morning after being dropped off at school. Madison, who is in the same class as Hayley's brother, saw Hayley crying and generously walked her to her class. She took her to her teacher and made her feel better by doing so.

A Student's Random Act of Kindness
SUBMITTED BY: FAITH / DATE SUBMITTED: 12/6/2003

A friend of mine seemed to be having a hard time, so I wrote her a note that told her how much of an inspiration she has been to me. I also told her to always follow her dreams and never give up hope.

I then decided to do this for others in my classes. Most of them I had never even talked to before, but they just looked lonely or sad.

I didn't sign my name, so it was really special watching as they smiled and looked around, wondering who could have written it. I know it wasn't much, but it made their day.

Just a Pencil
SUBMITTED BY: JIM / DATE SUBMITTED: 9/26/2003

On the first day of school, Mario said, "I have no pencil." The math teacher told him to use the one on the chalk tray. On the second day of school, Mario repeated his statement, and the teacher just pointed to the chalk tray.

The scenario went on until the first school day after the winter break. On that day Mario met with the teacher at the door, smiled, and said, "Mr. C., I now have a pencil for YOU." The teacher took the new pencil and read the inscription: "Thank you for being kind."

The teacher never hassled Mario about not having a pencil because he, too, came from a poor background and never forgot how embarrassing it was to be laughed at in school for not having school supplies.

At first, the pencil represented a small symbol of kindness, but soon it evolved into Mario's determination to pass math class. He voluntarily spent extra time in class. He always arrived early each morning to get a head start on his assignment.

Just a pencil?—not really. To Mario, the pencil meant someone cared, and this feeling gave him the desire to succeed in math class and be successful in his new American school.

Reading Across Texts
What was Francisco's random act of kindness?

Writing Across Texts Write a letter from Francisco to Curtis, explaining Francisco's random act of kindness.

Answer Questions Reread any e-mails you have questions about.

160

Student Edition pages 160–161

Audio CD

Read It
ONLINE
PearsonSuccessNet.com
- Student Edition
- Leveled Readers

Leveled Readers

◎ **Skill** Compare and Contrast

◎ **Strategy** Answer Questions

Lesson Vocabulary

JUAN'S JOURNEY
BY CAROL HERRERA
ILLUSTRATED BY CYNTHIA SEARS

Below-Level

Using Special Talents
by Sharon Franklin

On-Level

When the Disaster's Over
by Adam McClellan

Advanced

ELL Reader
- Concept Vocabulary
- Text Support
- Language Enrichment

Butterfly Garden

Time for SOCIAL STUDIES

Integrate Social Studies Standards
- Civic Values
- Citizenship
- Interactions

✓ **Read**

"Inside Out," pp. 146–157

"Random Acts of Kindness," pp. 160–161

Leveled Readers

Below-Level
• Support Concepts

On-Level
• Develop Concepts

Advanced
• Extend Concepts
• Social Studies Extension Activity

ELL Reader

Butterfly Garden

✓ **Build Concept Vocabulary**
Kindness, pp. 142l–142m

✓ **Teach Social Studies Concepts**
Migrant Workers, p. 149
U.S. Constitution, p. 155
World Kindness Movement, p. 161

✓ **Explore Social Studies Center**
Start a Journal, p. 142k

Weekly Plan

READING

45–90 minutes

TARGET SKILLS OF THE WEEK

Comprehension Skill
Compare and Contrast

Comprehension Strategy
Answer Questions

Vocabulary Strategy
Word Structure

DAY 1
PAGES 142l–144b, 161a, 161e–161k

Oral Language

QUESTION OF THE WEEK *Why do people show kindness?*

Read Aloud: "Dwaina Brooks," 142m
Build Concepts, 142l

Comprehension/Vocabulary

Comprehension Skill/Strategy Lesson, 142–143
 Compare and Contrast **T**
 Answer Questions
Build Background, 144a
Introduce Lesson Vocabulary, 144b
caterpillar, cocoon, disrespect, emerge, migrant, sketched, unscrewed **T**

Read Leveled Readers

Grouping Options 142f–142g

Fluency

Model Characterization/Dialogue, 142l–142m, 161a

DAY 2
PAGES 144–153, 161a, 161e–161k

Oral Language

QUESTION OF THE DAY *Why was Francisco grateful for the jacket from Mr. Sims?*

Comprehension/Vocabulary

Vocabulary Strategy Lesson, 144–145
 Word Structure **T**

Read "Inside Out," 146–153

Grouping Options
142f–142g

 Compare and Contrast **T**
 Answer Questions
REVIEW Author's Purpose **T**
Develop Vocabulary

Fluency

Echo Reading, 161a

LANGUAGE ARTS

30–60 minutes

Trait of the Week

Focus/Ideas

Grammar, 161e
Introduce Regular and Irregular Plural Nouns **T**

Writing Workshop, 161g
Introduce Summary
Model the Trait of the Week: Focus/Ideas

Spelling, 161i
Pretest for Digraphs *th, sh, ch, ph*

Internet Inquiry, 161k
Identify Questions

Grammar, 161e
Develop Regular and Irregular Plural Nouns **T**

Writing Workshop, 161g
Improve Writing with Eliminate Wordiness

Spelling, 161i
Teach the Generalization

Internet Inquiry, 161k
Navigate/Search

DAILY WRITING ACTIVITIES

Day 1 Write to Read, 142

Day 2 Words to Write, 145
Strategy Response Log, 146, 153

DAILY SOCIAL STUDIES CONNECTIONS

Day 1 Kindness Concept Web, 142l

Day 2 Time for Social Studies: Migrant Workers, 149
Revisit the Kindness Concept Web, 153

DAILY SUCCESS PREDICTORS
for Adequate Yearly Progress

Monitor Progress and Corrective Feedback

Vocabulary   Check Vocabulary, *142l*

RESOURCES FOR THE WEEK

- Practice Book, *pp. 51–60*
- Word Study and Spelling Practice Book, *pp. 21–24*
- Grammar and Writing Practice Book, *pp. 21–24*

- Selection Test, *pp. 21–24*
- Fresh Reads for Differentiated Test Practice, *pp. 31–36*
- The Grammar and Writing Book, *pp. 80–85*

Grouping Options for Differentiated Instruction

Turn the page for the small group lesson plan.

DAY 3 PAGES 154-159, 161a, 161e-161k

Oral Language

QUESTION OF THE DAY *Why do you think Miss Scalapino lets Francisco release the butterfly?*

Comprehension/Vocabulary

Read "Inside Out," 154–158

Grouping Options 142f–142g

- 🎯 Answer Questions
- 🎯 Word Structure **T**
- Develop Vocabulary

Reader Response

Selection Test

Fluency

Model Characterization/Dialogue, 161a

Grammar, 161f
Apply Regular and Irregular Plural Nouns in Writing **T**

Writing Workshop, 159, 161h
Write Now
Prewrite and Draft

Spelling, 161j
Connect Spelling to Writing

Internet Inquiry, 161k
Analyze Sources

Day 3 Strategy Response Log, 156
Look Back and Write, 158

Day 3 Time for Social Studies: U.S. Constitution, 155
Revisit the Kindness Concept Web, 157

DAY 4 PAGES 160-161a, 161e-161k

Oral Language

QUESTION OF THE DAY *Are humans naturally kind, or is kindness something that must be learned?*

Comprehension/Vocabulary

Read "Random Acts of Kindness," 160–161

Grouping Options 142f–142g

E-mails/Text Features
Reading Across Texts
Content-Area Vocabulary

Fluency

Partner Reading, 161a

Grammar, 161f
Practice Regular and Irregular Plural Nouns for Standardized Tests **T**

Writing Workshop, 161h
Draft, Revise, and Publish

Spelling, 161j
Provide a Strategy

Internet Inquiry, 161k
Synthesize Information

Day 4 Writing Across Texts, 161

Day 4 Time for Social Studies: World Kindness Movement, 161

DAY 5 PAGES 161a-161l

Oral Language

QUESTION OF THE WEEK *To wrap up the week, revisit the Day 1 question.*

Build Concept Vocabulary, 161c

Fluency

Read Leveled Readers

Grouping Options 142f–142g

Assess Reading Rate, 161a

Comprehension/Vocabulary

- 🎯 Reteach Compare and Contrast, 161b **T**
- Short Story, 161b
- 🎯 Review Word Structure, 161c **T**

Speaking and Listening, 161d
Persuasive Speech
Listen to a Persuasive Speech

Grammar, 161f
Cumulative Review

Writing Workshop, 161h
Connect to Unit Writing

Spelling, 161j
Posttest for Digraphs *th, sh, ch, ph*

Internet Inquiry, 161k
Communicate Results

Research/Study Skills, 161l
Reference Book

Day 5 Short Story, 161b

Day 5 Revisit the Kindness Concept Web, 161c

KEY 🎯 = Target Skill **T** = Tested Skill

Comprehension Check Retelling, *158*

Fluency Check Fluency WCPM, *161a*

Vocabulary Check Vocabulary, *161c*

SUCCESS PREDICTOR

Small Group Plan for Differentiated Instruction

Daily Plan
AT A GLANCE

Reading
Whole Group
- Oral Language
- Comprehension/Vocabulary

Group Time
Differentiated Instruction

Meet with small groups to provide:
- Skill Support
- Reading Support
- Fluency Practice

Read

This week's lessons for daily group time can be found behind the Differentiated Instruction (DI) tab on pp. DI·2–DI·11.

Whole Group
- Fluency

Language Arts
- Grammar
- Writing
- Spelling
- Research/Inquiry
- Speaking/Listening/Viewing

Use *My Sidewalks on Reading Street* for Tier III intensive reading intervention.

DAY 1

On-Level	Strategic Intervention	Advanced
Teacher-Led *Page DI·3*	**Teacher-Led** *Page DI·2*	**Teacher-Led** *Page DI·3*
• Develop Concept Vocabulary • **Read** On-Level Reader *Using Special Talents*	• Reinforce Concepts • **Read** Below-Level Reader *Juan's Journey*	• **Read** Advanced Reader *When the Disaster's Over* • Independent Extension Activity

(i) Independent Activities
While you meet with small groups, have the rest of the class...

- Visit the Reading/Library Center
- Listen to the Background Building Audio
- Finish Write to Read, p. 142
- Complete Practice Book pp. 53–54
- Visit Cross-Curricular Centers

DAY 2

On-Level	Strategic Intervention	Advanced
Teacher-Led *Pages 148–153*	**Teacher-Led** *Page DI·4*	**Teacher-Led** *Page DI·5*
• **Read** "Inside Out"	• Practice Lesson Vocabulary • Read Multisyllabic Words • **Read** or Listen to "Inside Out"	• Extend Vocabulary • **Read** "Inside Out"

(i) Independent Activities
While you meet with small groups, have the rest of the class...

- Visit the Reading/Library Center
- Listen to the AudioText for "Inside Out"
- Finish Words to Write, p. 145
- Complete Practice Book pp. 55–56
- Write in their Strategy Response Logs, pp. 146, 153
- Visit Cross-Curricular Centers
- Work on inquiry projects

DAY 3

On-Level	Strategic Intervention	Advanced
Teacher-Led *Pages 154–157*	**Teacher-Led** *Page DI·6*	**Teacher-Led** *Page DI·7*
• **Read** "Inside Out"	• Practice Compare and Contrast and Answer Questions • **Read** or Listen to "Inside Out"	• Extend Compare and Contrast and Answer Questions • **Read** "Inside Out"

(i) Independent Activities
While you meet with small groups, have the rest of the class...

- Visit the Reading/Library Center
- Listen to the AudioText for "Inside Out"
- Write in their Strategy Response Logs, p. 156
- Finish Look Back and Write, p. 158
- Complete Practice Book p. 57
- Visit Cross-Curricular Centers
- Work on inquiry projects

① Begin with whole class skill and strategy instruction.

② Meet with small groups to provide differentiated instruction.

③ Gather the whole class back together for fluency and language arts.

On-Level	Strategic Intervention	Advanced
Teacher-Led *Pages 160–161*	**Teacher-Led** *Page DI · 8*	**Teacher-Led** *Page DI · 9*
• **Read** "Random Acts of Kindness"	• Practice Retelling • **Read** or Listen to "Random Acts of Kindness"	• **Read** "Random Acts of Kindness" • Genre Study

DAY 4

ⓘ Independent Activities

While you meet with small groups, have the rest of the class...

- Visit the Reading/Library Center
- Listen to the AudioText for "Random Acts of Kindness"
- Visit the Writing/Vocabulary Center
- Finish Writing Across Texts, p. 161
- Visit Cross-Curricular Centers
- Work on inquiry projects

On-Level	Strategic Intervention	Advanced
Teacher-Led *Page DI · 11*	**Teacher-Led** *Page DI · 10*	**Teacher-Led** *Page DI · 11*
• **Reread** Leveled Reader *Using Special Talents* • Retell *Using Special Talents*	• **Reread** Leveled Reader *Juan's Journey* • Retell *Juan's Journey*	• **Reread** Leveled Reader *When the Disaster's Over* • Share Extension Activity

DAY 5

ⓘ Independent Activities

While you meet with small groups, have the rest of the class...

- Visit the Reading/Library Center
- Complete Practice Book pp. 58–60
- Visit Cross-Curricular Centers
- Work on inquiry projects

Grouping Place English language learners in the groups that correspond to their reading abilities in English.

Use the appropriate Leveled Reader or other text at students' instructional level.

TIP Send home the appropriate Multilingual Summary of the main selection on Day 1.

Take It to the NET™ ONLINE
PearsonSuccessNet.com

Edward Kame'enui
For an explanation of the techniques of direct instruction, see a summary of the book *Direct Instruction Reading* by Scott Foresman author Edward Kame'enui, D. Carnine, and J. Silbert.

TEACHER TALK

An **affix** is a prefix, suffix, or inflected ending attached to a base word.

Be sure to schedule time for students to work on the unit inquiry project "Doing the Right Thing." This week students choose charities or service groups and develop inquiry questions about how these organizations help their communities.

Looking Ahead

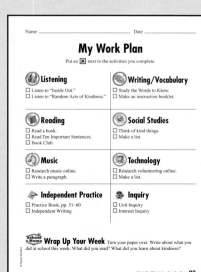

Name _____ Date _____
My Work Plan
Put an ☒ next to the activities you complete.

🎧 Listening
☐ Listen to "Inside Out."
☐ Listen to "Random Acts of Kindness."

✏ Writing/Vocabulary
☐ Study the Words to Know.
☐ Make an instruction booklet.

📖 Reading
☐ Read a book.
☐ Read Ten Important Sentences.
☐ Book Club

🌐 Social Studies
☐ Think of kind things.
☐ Make a list.

🎵 Music
☐ Research music online.
☐ Write a paragraph.

💻 Technology
☐ Research volunteering online.
☐ Make a list.

✍ Independent Practice
☐ Practice Book, pp. 51–60
☐ Independent Writing

🔍 Inquiry
☐ Unit Inquiry
☐ Internet Inquiry

🏠 Wrap Up Your Week Turn your paper over. Write about what you did at school this week. What did you read? What did you learn about kindness?

Unit 2 • Week 1 • *Inside Out* **23**

▲ **Group-Time Survival Guide** p. 23, Weekly Contract

✓ Customize Your Plan *by Stran*

ORAL LANGUAGE

SOCIAL STUDIES

Concept Development

Why do people show kindness?

CONCEPT VOCABULARY
homeless   shelter   volunteered

BUILD

❑ **Question of the Week** Introduce and discuss the question of the week. This week students will read a variety of texts and work on projects related to the concept *kindness.* Post the question for students to refer to throughout the week. DAY 1 *142d*

❑ **Read Aloud** Read aloud "Dwaina Brooks." Then begin a web to build concepts and concept vocabulary related to this week's lesson and the unit theme, Doing the Right Thing. Introduce the concept words *homeless, shelter,* and *volunteered* and have students place them on the web. Display the web for use throughout the week. DAY 1 *142l–142m*

DEVELOP

❑ **Question of the Day** Use the prompts from the Weekly Plan to engage students in conversations related to this week's reading and the unit theme. **EVERY DAY** *142d–142e*

❑ **Concept Vocabulary Web** Revisit the Kindness Concept Web and encourage students to add concept words from their reading and life experiences. DAY 2 *153,* DAY 3 *157*

CONNECT

❑ **Looking Back/Moving Forward** Revisit the Kindness Concept Web and discuss how it relates to this week's lesson and the unit theme. Then make connections to next week's lesson. DAY 5 *161c*

CHECK

❑ **Concept Vocabulary Web** Use the Kindness Concept Web to check students' understanding of the concept vocabulary words *homeless, shelter,* and *volunteered.* DAY 1 *142l,* **DAY 5** *161c*

VOCABULARY

STRATEGY WORD STRUCTURE
When you see an unfamiliar word, sometimes you can use prefixes to figure out the meaning. The meanings for prefixes can be found in a dictionary.

LESSON VOCABULARY
caterpillar   migrant
cocoon   sketched
disrespect   unscrewed
emerge

TEACH

❑ **Words to Know** Give students the opportunity to tell what they already know about this week's lesson vocabulary words. Then discuss word meaning. DAY 1 *144b*

❑ **Vocabulary Strategy Lesson** Use the vocabulary strategy lesson in the Student Edition to introduce and model this week's strategy, *word structure.* DAY 2 *144-145*

Vocabulary Strategy Lesson

PRACTICE/APPLY

❑ **Leveled Text** Read the lesson vocabulary in the context of leveled text. DAY 1 *LR1-LR9*

❑ **Words in Context** Read the lesson vocabulary and apply *word structure* in the context of "Inside Out." DAY 2 *146-153,* DAY 3 *154-158*

Leveled Readers

❑ **Writing/Vocabulary Center** Make a list of instructions for how to care for a pet. **ANY DAY** *142k*

Main Selection—Fiction

❑ **Homework** Practice Book pp. 54–55. DAY 1 *144b,* DAY 2 *145*

❑ **Word Play** Have small groups list five words with the prefixes *un-* and *dis-.* **ANY DAY** *161c*

ASSESS

❑ **Selection Test** Use the Selection Test to determine students' understanding of the lesson vocabulary words. DAY 3

RETEACH/REVIEW

❑ **Reteach Lesson** If necessary, use this lesson to reteach and review *word structure.* DAY 5 *161c*

① Use assessment data to determine your instructional focus. │ ② Preview this week's instruction by strand. │ ③ Choose instructional activities that meet the needs of your classroom.

COMPREHENSION

SKILL COMPARE AND CONTRAST To *compare* and *contrast* two or more things is to show how things are alike and different. Clue words such as *like, but,* and *however* may indicate that things are being compared and contrasted.

STRATEGY ANSWER QUESTIONS Answering questions can help you understand the text. Sometimes the answer to a question will be at one place in the text or in several places. Sometimes you must combine what you read with what you already know (prior knowledge).

TEACH

☐ **Skill/Strategy Lesson** Use the skill/strategy lesson in the Student Edition to introduce and model *compare and contrast* and *answer questions*. DAY 1 *142-143*

Skill/Strategy Lesson

☐ **Extend Skills** Teach short story. **ANY DAY** *161b*

PRACTICE/APPLY

☐ **Leveled Text** Apply *compare and contrast* and *answer questions* to read leveled text. DAY 1 *LR1-LR9*

Leveled Readers

☐ **Skills and Strategies in Context** Read "Inside Out," using the Guiding Comprehension questions to apply *compare and contrast* and *answer questions*. DAY 2 *146-153*, DAY 3 *154-158*

Main Selection—Fiction

☐ **Skills and Strategies in Context** Read "Random Acts of Kindness," guiding students as they apply *compare and contrast* and *answer questions*. Then have students discuss and write across texts. DAY 4 *160-161*

☐ **Homework** Practice Book pp. 53, 57, 58 DAY 1 *143*, DAY 3 *157*, DAY 5 *161b*

Paired Selection—Fiction

☐ **Fresh Reads for Differentiated Test Practice** Have students practice *compare and contrast* with a new passage. DAY 3

ASSESS

☐ **Selection Test** Determine students' understanding of the selection and their use of *compare and contrast*. DAY 3

☐ **Retell** Have students retell "Inside Out." DAY 3 *158-159*

RETEACH/REVIEW

☐ **Reteach Lesson** If necessary, reteach and review *compare and contrast*. DAY 5 *161b*

FLUENCY

SKILL CHARACTERIZATION/DIALOGUE Using the tone, pitch, or volume of your voice will make characters' dialogue more interesting and sound realistic.

TEACH

☐ **Read Aloud** Model fluent reading by rereading "Dwaina Brooks." Focus on this week's fluency skill, characterization/dialogue. DAY 1 *142l-142m, 161a*

PRACTICE/APPLY

☐ **Echo Reading** Read aloud selected paragraphs from "Inside Out," emphasizing the rhythm, expression, and emotion in your voice. Then practice as a class, doing three echo readings for the selected paragraphs. DAY 2 *161a*, DAY 3 *161a*

☐ **Partner Reading** Have partners practice reading, reading with expression and emotion, and offering each other feedback. As students reread, monitor their progress toward their individual fluency goals. DAY 4 *161a*

☐ **Listening Center** Have students follow along with the AudioText for this week's selections. **ANY DAY** *142j*

☐ **Reading/Library Center** Have students reread a selection of their choice. **ANY DAY** *142j*

☐ **Fluency Coach** Have students use Fluency Coach to listen to fluent readings or practice reading on their own. **ANY DAY**

ASSESS

☐ **Check Fluency** WCPM Do a one-minute timed reading, paying special attention to this week's skill—characterization/dialogue. Provide feedback for each student. DAY 5 *161a*

☑ Customize Your Plan *by Strand*

GRAMMAR

SKILL REGULAR AND IRREGULAR PLURAL NOUNS Plural nouns name more than one person, place, or thing. Adding -s or -es often forms plural nouns. Some nouns are exceptions when it comes to making them plural, and they are called irregular plural nouns. When irregular nouns become plural, their spelling changes in a different way, or it might not change at all.

TEACH

☐ **Grammar Transparency 6** Use Grammar Transparency 6 to teach regular and irregular plural nouns. DAY 1 *161e*

Grammar Transparency 6

PRACTICE/APPLY

☐ **Develop the Concept** Review the concept of regular and irregular plural nouns and provide guided practice. DAY 2 *161e*

☐ **Apply to Writing** Have students review something they have written and apply regular and irregular plural nouns. DAY 3 *161f*

☐ **Test Preparation** Examine common errors in regular and irregular plural nouns to prepare for standardized tests. DAY 4 *161f*

☐ **Homework** Grammar and Writing Practice Book pp. 21–23. DAY 2 *161e*, DAY 3 *161f*, DAY 4 *161f*

ASSESS

☐ **Cumulative Review** Use Grammar and Writing Practice Book p. 24. DAY 5 *161f*

RETEACH/REVIEW

☐ **Daily Fix-It** Have students find and correct errors in grammar, spelling, and punctuation. **EVERY DAY** *161e–161f*

☐ **The Grammar and Writing Book** Use pp. 80–83 of The Grammar and Writing Book to extend instruction for regular and irregular plural nouns. **ANY DAY**

The Grammar and Writing Book

WRITING

Trait of the Week

FOCUS/IDEAS Good writers focus on a main idea and develop this idea with strong supporting details. Having a purpose—whether it is to inform, to persuade, or to entertain—helps keep focus on the main idea.

TEACH

☐ **Writing Transparency 6A** Use the model to introduce and discuss the Trait of the Week. DAY 1 *161g*

☐ **Writing Transparency 6B** Use the transparency to show students how eliminating wordiness can improve their writing. DAY 2 *161g*

Writing Transparency 6A   **Writing Transparency 6B**

PRACTICE/APPLY

☐ **Write Now** Examine the model on Student Edition p. 159. Then have students write their own summary. DAY 3 *159, 161h*, DAY 4 *161h*

> **Prompt** "Inside Out" is a story that describes life at school for a boy who does not speak English. Think about a story you have read recently. Now write a summary of that story.

Write Now p. 159

☐ **Writing/Vocabulary Center** Make a list of instructions for how to care for a pet. **ANY DAY** *142k*

ASSESS

☐ **Writing Trait Rubric** Use the rubric to evaluate students' writing. DAY 4 *161h*

RETEACH/REVIEW

☐ **The Grammar and Writing Book** Use pp. 80–85 of The Grammar and Writing Book to extend instruction for regular and irregular plural nouns, eliminating wordiness, and summaries. **ANY DAY**

The Grammar and Writing Book

SPELLING

GENERALIZATION DIGRAPHS *TH, SH, CH, PH* Words can have two consonants together that are pronounced as one sound: *southern, shovel, chapter, hyphen.* Consonant digraphs are two consonants together that stand for one new sound.

TEACH

❑ **Pretest** Give the pretest for words with the digraphs *th, sh, ch, ph.* Guide students in self-correcting their pretests and correcting any misspellings. **DAY 1** *161i*

❑ **Think and Practice** Connect spelling to the phonics generalization for digraphs *th, sh, ch, ph* **DAY 2** *161i*

PRACTICE/APPLY

❑ **Connect to Writing** Have students use spelling words to write facts. Then review frequently misspelled words: *which, they, thought.* **DAY 3** *161j*

❑ **Homework** Word Study and Spelling Practice Book pp. 21–24. **EVERY DAY**

RETEACH/REVIEW

❑ **Review** Review spelling words to prepare for the posttest. Then provide students with a spelling strategy—problem parts. **DAY 4** *161j*

ASSESS

❑ **Posttest** Use dictation sentences to give the posttest for words with digraphs *th, sh, ch, ph.* **DAY 5** *161j*

Spelling Words

1. shovel	8. although	15. shiver*
2. southern	9. challenge	16. pharmacy
3. northern	10. approach	17. charity
4. chapter	11. astonish	18. china
5. hyphen	12. python	19. attach
6. chosen*	13. shatter	20. ostrich
7. establish	14. ethnic	

Challenge Words

21. emphasis	23. athlete	25. chimpanzee
22. sophomore	24. phenomenal	

*Word from the selection

RESEARCH AND INQUIRY

❑ **Internet Inquiry** Have students conduct an Internet inquiry on kindness. **EVERY DAY** *161k*

❑ **Reference Book** Review the features and terms associated with reference books and discuss how students can use these resources to find information. **DAY 5** *161l*

❑ **Unit Inquiry** Allow time for students to choose a charity or service group and develop inquiry questions about how that organization helps their community. **ANY DAY** *141*

SPEAKING AND LISTENING

❑ **Persuasive Speech** Have students give a speech to persuade others to perform an act of kindness. **DAY 5** *161d*

❑ **Listen to a Persuasive Speech** Have students listen to other students' persuasive speeches and answer questions. **DAY 5** *161d*

Resources for Differentiated Instruction

LEVELED READERS

▶ **Comprehension**
  - ◎ **Skill** Compare and Contrast
  - ◎ **Strategy** Answer Questions

▶ **Lesson Vocabulary**
  - ◎ Word Structure

migrant   cocoon   disrespect   emerge   sketched   caterpillar   unscrewed

▶ **Social Studies Standards**
  - • Civic Values
  - • Citizenship
  - • Interactions

Leveled Reader Database ONLINE
PearsonSuccessNet.com

Use the Online Database of over 600 books to
- • Download and print additional copies of this week's leveled readers.
- • Listen to the readers being read online.
- • Search for more titles focused on this week's skills, topic, and content.

On-Level

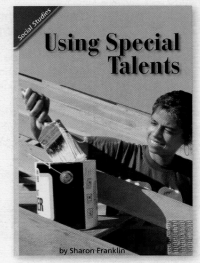

Social Studies
Using Special Talents
by Sharon Franklin

On-Level Reader

Name_____   Using Special Talents

Compare and Contrast
- • To **compare** is to tell how two or more things are alike.
- • To **contrast** is to tell how two or more things are different.

Directions Read the following sentence from *Using Special Talents*.

> In contrast to Annie, Miguel, and Lee, Hallanah is an experienced volunteer.

1. Think about all the different children you read about in *Using Special Talents*. What is one thing they all have in common?   **Possible responses given.**
   They all want to help others.
2. How does Hallanah differ from Annie, Miguel, and Lee?
   She has volunteered before.
3. What clue words tell that Hallanah is being compared to Annie, Miguel, and Lee?
   in contrast to
4. Make a list of your own interests and talents.
   Answers will vary.

5. Compare your list to the activities on the chart on page 11 of *Using Special Talents*. Based on your comparison, which activity would you like to do most. Why?
   Answers will vary but should show understanding of how talents and interests relate to the chosen volunteering activity.

On-Level Practice TE p. LR5

Name_____   Using Special Talents

Vocabulary
Directions Choose the word from the box that best matches each definition. Write the word on the line.

Check the Words You Know
___caterpillar   ___cocoon   ___disrespect   ___emerge
___migrant   ___sketched   ___unscrewed

1. **emerge** — to come out of
2. **disrespect** — the opposite of respect
3. **caterpillar** — an insect
4. **cocoon** — where a caterpillar turns into a butterfly
5. **migrant** — traveling from one place to another
6. **unscrewed** — past tense of twisting something off
7. **sketched** — something an artist might have done to make a quick drawing

Directions Write three sentences using one vocabulary word in each.
8. **Sentences will vary.**
9. _____
10. _____

On-Level Practice TE p. LR6

Strategic Intervention

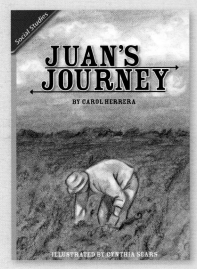

Social Studies
JUAN'S JOURNEY
BY CAROL HERRERA
ILLUSTRATED BY CYNTHIA SEARS

Below-Level Reader

Name_____   Juan's Journey

Compare and Contrast
- • To **compare** is to tell how two or more things are alike.
- • To **contrast** is to tell how two or more things are different.

Directions Fill in the following chart to compare what Juan wants to what Juan has. Circle the one thing Juan wanted and then got.   **Possible responses given.**

What Juan Wants	What Juan Has
to stay in one place	a life where he moves around
to have a big house for his parents	lives in a tent, trailer, or small houses
to have a big house next to his parents	old station wagon
to buy his parents a new red car	(gets a dog)
(a dog)	

Directions Look at your chart. Draw a picture of Juan leading the kind of life he would like to have.

Below-Level Practice TE p. LR2

Name_____   Juan's Journey

Vocabulary
Directions Find and circle the following words. All words go from left to right.

Check the Words You Know
___caterpillar   ___cocoon   ___disrespect   ___emerge
___migrant   ___sketched   ___unscrewed

C	O	C	O	O	N	A	T	Y	L	J	M	K	R	T
L	Y	M	C	E	M	E	R	G	E	T	C	A	T	P
M	T	I	E	N	Y	E	G	R	L	P	U	F	L	T
I	D	I	S	R	E	S	P	E	C	T	K	A	I	L
M	I	G	R	A	N	T	K	N	W	J	S	S	R	G
T	E	N	A	R	G	E	L	K	M	I	G	A	R	T
A	K	T	S	K	E	T	C	H	E	D	Y	T	C	M
C	O	C	O	R	U	N	S	C	R	E	W	E	D	Y
A	J	T	S	K	E	A	T	C	H	E	D	Y	L	O
D	I	T	C	A	T	E	R	P	I	L	L	A	R	T

Directions Use each vocabulary word in a sentence.
1. **Sentences will vary.**
2. _____
3. _____
4. _____
5. _____
6. _____
7. _____

Below-Level Practice TE p. LR3

Advanced

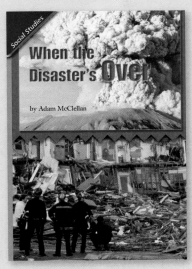

Advanced Reader

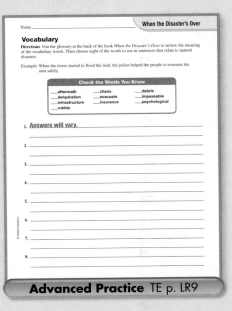

Advanced Practice TE p. LR8

Advanced Practice TE p. LR9

ELL Reader

ELL Poster 6

Teacher's Edition Notes

ELL notes throughout this lesson support instruction and reference additional resources at point of use.

Teaching Guide pp. 36–42, 222–223
- Multilingual summaries of the main selection
- Comprehension lesson
- Vocabulary strategies and word cards
- ELL Reader 5.2.1 lesson

ELL and Transition Handbook

Ten Important Sentences
- Key ideas from every selection in the Student Edition
- Activities to build sentence power

More Reading

Readers' Theater Anthology
- Fluency practice
- Five scripts to build fluency
- Poetry for oral interpretation

Leveled Trade Books

- Extended reading tied to the unit concept
- Lessons in the Trade Book Library Teaching Guide

School + Home

Homework
- Family Times Newsletter
- ELL Multilingual Selection Summaries

Take-Home Books
- Leveled Readers

Cross-Curricular Centers

Listen to the Selections

MATERIALS
CD player, headphones, AudioText CD, student book

`SINGLES`

LISTEN TO LITERATURE Listen to "Inside Out" and "Random Acts of Kindness" as you follow or read along in your book. Listen for similarities and differences between the acts of kindness described in both selections.

If there is anything you don't understand, you can listen again to any section.

Read it AGAIN!

MATERIALS
Collection of books for self-selected reading, reading logs, student book

`SINGLES`
`PAIRS`
`GROUPS`

Select a book you have already read. Record the title of the book in your reading log. You may want to read with a partner.

Choose from the following:

- **Leveled Readers**
- **ELL Readers**
- **Stories Written by Classmates**
- **Books from the Library**
- **"Inside Out"**

TEN IMPORTANT SENTENCES Read the Ten Important Sentences for "Inside Out." Then locate the sentences in the student book.

BOOK CLUB The characters and actions in "Inside Out" seem real, but they come from the author's imagination. Get together with a group and discuss the ways in which the author of this story makes the setting and characters seem real.

Think About Music

MATERIALS
Writing materials, Internet access

`SINGLES`
`PAIRS`

In "Inside Out," singing the traditional songs he used to hear on the car radio reminds Francisco of his old life in Mexico.

1. **Use a student-friendly search engine to find out about the music of another culture.**
2. **Write a paragraph describing the type of music you researched.**

EARLY FINISHERS Make a list of your top ten favorite songs or types of music. Think about what kind of mood each song puts you in.

 Corridos

Corridos are narrative songs that are sung in Mexico and parts of the U.S.

Scott Foresman Reading Street Centers Survival Kit

Use the *Inside Out* materials from the Reading Street Centers Survival Kit to organize this week's centers.

Writing/Vocabulary

Write About Pet Care

MATERIALS
Writing materials, research materials, Internet access

`SINGLES` `PAIRS`

In "Inside Out," Francisco cares for the caterpillar in his classroom. Think about what steps would be needed to care for a pet.

1. Make a list of instructions for how to care for a pet. If necessary, use the Internet and other resources to gather more information.
2. Create an instruction booklet using your list.

EARLY FINISHERS Draw an illustration for the cover of your booklet.

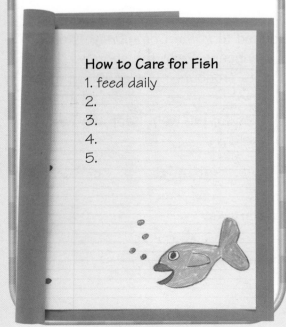

How to Care for Fish
1. feed daily
2.
3.
4.
5.

Social Studies

Start a JOURNAL

MATERIALS
Writing and art materials, journal

`SINGLES` `PAIRS`

Begin an "Acts of Kindness" journal.

1. Think of kind things that others have said to and done for you.
2. Make a list of these acts of kindness in your journal.
3. With your teacher's permission, add to the list in your journal each week.

EARLY FINISHERS Think about other ways that you could show kindness to people. Write a paragraph in your journal describing something you'd like to do to help someone you know.

Acts of Kindness

Technology

Get Involved

MATERIALS
Internet access, writing materials, e-mail program

`SINGLES`

Search how to become a volunteer.

1. Use a student-friendly search engine to find a Web site that focuses on volunteer opportunities in your community.
2. Make a list of two or three opportunities about which you would like more information.

EARLY FINISHERS Write an e-mail that you would send to your friends or family describing the information you found.

Search Engine
community volunteer

1. food drive
2.
3.

ALL CENTERS

Build Concepts

OBJECTIVES

- Build vocabulary by finding words related to the lesson concept.
- Listen to compare and contrast.

Concept Vocabulary

homeless without a home

shelter a temporary living place for poor or homeless people

volunteered offered services for free

Monitor Progress

Check Vocabulary

If...	then...
students are unable to place words on the web,	review the lesson concept. Place the words on the web and provide additional words for practice, such as *tutoring* and *chores*.

SUCCESS PREDICTOR

DAY 1 Grouping Options

Reading

Whole Group
Introduce and discuss the Question of the Week. Then use pp. 142l–144b.

Group Time
Differentiated Instruction
Read this week's Leveled Readers. See pp. 142h–142i for the small group lesson plan.

Whole Group
Use p. 161a.

Language Arts
Use pp. 161e–161k.

FLUENCY

MODEL CHARACTERIZATION/DIALOGUE As you read "Dwaina Brooks," model how to read the dialogue. Explain that people have unique pronunciations and rhythms to their speech depending on where they are from. Challenge students to read the dialogue phonetically to match the way Dwaina and her friends talk.

LISTENING COMPREHENSION

After reading "Dwaina Brooks," use the following questions to assess listening comprehension.

1. **Compare and contrast Dwaina's kitchen on Friday nights before and after her class came over.** (*Possible responses: Both Fridays were fun. They had only a few people working before; twenty-eight people after. They made much more food the Friday night her class came.*) **Compare and Contrast**

2. **Explain the steps Dwaina followed to get food to the shelter.** (*Purchased food, prepared food, delivered food.*) **Steps in a Process**

BUILD CONCEPT VOCABULARY

Start a web to build concepts and vocabulary related to this week's lesson and the unit theme.

- Draw the Kindness Concept Web.
- Read the sentence with the words *homeless shelter*. Ask students to pronounce them and discuss their meaning.
- Place *homeless shelter* in an oval attached to *In the Community*. Explain that *homeless shelter* is related to this concept. Read the sentence in which *volunteered* appears. Have students pronounce it, place it on the web, and provide reasons.
- Brainstorm additional words and categories for the web. Keep the web on display and add words throughout the week.

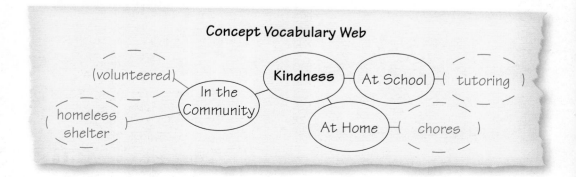

Concept Vocabulary Web

(volunteered) — In the Community — **Kindness** — At School — (tutoring)

(homeless shelter)

At Home — (chores)

DWAINA BROOKS

by Phillip Hoose

Dwaina Brooks and her family put together meals to take to a homeless shelter *in Dallas. One weekend, Dwaina gets her fifth grade class to help.*

Nearly every Friday night for a year, Dwaina and her mother and whatever sisters were around made food for shelters in Dallas. At first they took the food to the shelters themselves, but then their church volunteered to make the deliveries for them.

Always, Dwaina wanted to make more meals. That shelter had hundreds of people; she and her mom alone probably weren't feeding half of them. One Friday evening, she had an idea: she knew where she could get some extra help, and lots of it too.

The following Monday, she asked her fifth-grade teacher, Mr. Frost, if she could speak to the class while he took roll. Dwaina had been the class leader since the first day of school, when she had told a group of loud boys to shut up so she could hear her teacher. She could be tough or funny or kind. She always seemed to know exactly what would move them.

"Okay, y'all," she began. "We've been reading about the homeless in class, and I can tell you that for some reason it's getting worse and worse." Her eyes swept around the room. "Now my mama and I been makin' sandwiches this year till we got mayonnaise up to our elbows and we can't make enough. Why should we be up till midnight every Friday night when y'all ain't doin' a thing? Now, listen. I want you to come to my house this Friday night and help. Who'll be there?"

Twenty-three hands went up. When Dwaina excitedly reported this to her mother, Gail Brooks nearly passed out. "Twenty-three kids? Plus *our* family?"

"Yeah, Mama, isn't it great! Think how many meals we can make!"

Dwaina and Gail advised each participating family about where to get food cheaply. They made a central list of who would bring what and taped it to the refrigerator. All that week, parents drove boxes of food to the Brooks's small house. At school, the kids made bigger and bigger plans each day. Making food for the shelter was shaping up to be the social event of the year.

"Why don't y'all stay over?" asked Dwaina.

"I'll bring popcorn!" said Claire.

"What about boys?" said Christopher. "Can we sleep over too?"

"Sorry," came a chorus of girls. "Oh, maybe on the kitchen floor."

The next Friday night, twenty-eight people crowded into the Brooks's small kitchen. They set up one of the world's longest assembly lines, kicked the radio on to 100.3 FM-JAMS—the rap station—wrapped towels around their waists, and started in. By midnight, the boxes were filled with more than three hundred sacks.

Activate Prior Knowledge

Before students listen to the Read Aloud, ask them to share what they know about volunteering.

Set Purpose

Read aloud the title and have students predict what the selection will be about.

Read the introduction aloud. Have students listen to the compare and contrast of the food for shelters project before and after Dwaina asks her classmates to get involved.

Creative Response

Have students reenact the speech Dwaina gave to her class. They can practice with a partner to get suggestions to improve their speeches. *Drama*

Build Background Before students listen to the Read Aloud, explain that there are homeless shelters around the country for people who have no place to live. Tell them that meals are served to people who live there and to others who do not have enough money to buy food.

Homework Send home this week's Family Times newsletter.

SUCCESS PREDICTOR

BEFORE READING

SKILLS ⬌ STRATEGIES IN CONTEXT

Compare and Contrast
Answer Questions

OBJECTIVES

◎ Compare and contrast.

◎ Answer questions to compare and contrast.

Skills Trace
Compare and Contrast

Introduce/Teach	TE: 5.2 142–143, 186–187; 5.6 674–675
Practice	Practice Book: 36, 53, 57, 58, 73, 77, 78, 86, 273, 277, 278
Reteach/Review	TE: 5.1 101; 5.2 161b, 207b, 217, DI·52, DI·54; 5.6 699b, DI·54
Test	Selection Test: 21–24, 29–32, 109–112; Benchmark Test: Unit 2

INTRODUCE

Write the headings *Insects* and *Mammals* on the board. Ask students to tell how they are alike. *(Possible response: They are both animals.)* Then ask students to tell how they are different. *(Possible response: Insects have a hard outside covering. Mammals have body hair or fur.)*

Have students read the information on p. 142. Explain the following:

- To compare and contrast, readers notice how characters and other things in the story are alike and different.

- As you read, ask yourself, "How are these two things alike, and how are they different?" Answering the question will help you understand what you are reading.

Use Skill Transparency 6 to teach compare and contrast and ask questions.

Comprehension

Skill
Compare and Contrast

Strategy
Answer Questions

Compare and Contrast

- When writers compare and contrast things, they tell how those things are alike or different.

- Words such as *same, also, before, although,* and *however* are clues that things are being compared and contrasted.

- Sometimes writers do not use clue words when they compare and contrast things.

Before	After

Strategy: Answer Questions

Good readers know how to find the answers to questions such as, "How would you compare and contrast _____ and _____ ?" Sometimes you can find an answer in just one place. Other times you must search in several places to find all the information to answer a question.

Write to Read

1. Read "A New Home." Make a graphic organizer like the one above to compare and contrast life for some Mexican people before and after they come to the United States.

2. Write a comparison of how Mexicans celebrate holidays in Mexico and in the United States. Use information from your graphic organizer to help you.

142

Strategic Intervention

◎ **Compare and Contrast** Display two different writing tools, such as a pencil and chalk. To help students compare and contrast the items ask them to think about what the items look like and how they are used. Then have students work in pairs, comparing and contrasting the writing tools. Have pairs share their findings.

ELL

Access Content

Beginning/Intermediate For a Picture It! lesson on compare and contrast, see ELL Teaching Guide, pp. 36–37.

Advanced Have students write two sentences to practice using the skill of compare and contrast. The first sentence should tell something about life in their home country. The second should compare and contrast this with life in the United States.

142 Doing the Right Thing • Week 1

A NEW HOME

Thousands of people move from Mexico to the United States each year. Many come to find better-paying jobs and to provide better homes for their families.

The language of Mexico is Spanish. When adults move from Mexico to the United States, many continue to speak Spanish. Although learning a new language can be hard, their children usually learn English as well. They often speak Spanish at home and English at school. So, many Mexican American children speak two languages!

Some Mexican families come to towns where few other Mexicans live. However, many move to Mexican American neighborhoods. Some cities have large Mexican communities. In these communities, stores and restaurants have Spanish names and sell Mexican food, books, and clothing, the same as they do in Mexico. These neighborhoods can help make newcomers feel comfortable in their new country.

On May 5, Mexican Americans celebrate a Mexican holiday called Cinco de Mayo. On September 16, they celebrate Mexican Independence Day. Many Mexican Americans continue celebrating these holidays with parades, costumes, and special food. Of course they also enjoy celebrating American holidays, like the Fourth of July!

1 Skill There is no clue word here, but you can figure out a difference between life in Mexico and life in the United States for many people. Why would people come to the United States for jobs?

2 Strategy One sentence in this paragraph answers this question: How do many children's lives change when they come to the United States from Mexico?

3 Skill Which clue words in this paragraph call attention to a contrast and a comparison?

4 Strategy If someone asked you about the days on which Mexican and American holidays were celebrated, where would you find the answer?

143

Available as **Skill Transparency** 6

TEACH

1 SKILL Use paragraph 1 to model how to figure out a difference between life in Mexico and life in the United States.

Think Aloud **MODEL** From the last sentence in paragraph 1, I know that many Mexicans come to the United States to find better-paying jobs. This tells me that the jobs in Mexico don't pay as much as the jobs in the United States.

2 STRATEGY Use paragraph 2.

Think Aloud **MODEL** Mexican children are discussed in paragraph 2. After rereading the paragraph, I learned that many Mexican children speak two languages in the United States, whereas they only spoke one in Mexico.

PRACTICE AND ASSESS

3 SKILL Clue words: *however* and *same*.

4 STRATEGY The answer can be found in paragraph 4.

WRITE Have students complete steps 1 and 2 of the Write to Read activity. You might consider using this as a whole-class activity.

Monitor Progress
↻ Compare and Contrast

If... students are unable to complete **Write to Read** on p. 142,	then... use Practice Book p. 53 to provide additional practice.

Compare and Contrast

- To **compare** and **contrast** two or more things is to show how things are alike and different.
- Some clue words are: *as, like, but* and *however.*
- Sometimes writers do not use clue words when they compare and contrast things.

Directions Read the following passage. Fill in the columns below based on Alex's thoughts before and after he went to the kitchen at the shelter with his dad.

Alex had never gone with his father to the kitchen at the shelter where his dad volunteered. Alex figured it was just like an ordinary kitchen, just bigger. He imagined his dad and other people making and serving soup, but he never really thought about the people who ate at the soup kitchen. That all changed the first time he accompanied his dad to the shelter.

When he got to the shelter, Alex realized he had the wrong impression about what happened there. Volunteers like his dad were serving pancakes, oatmeal, and other breakfast items. Alex noticed a large dining area where many families were eating—moms, dads, and children. And he saw many people who reminded him of his grandparents.

Possible answers given.

Before	After
Alex figured it was an ordinary kitchen, just bigger.	1. The volunteers served breakfast items.
2. Alex thought his dad and other people made soup there.	3. Alex saw families eating there.
4. Alex never thought about the people who ate at the shelter.	5. Alex saw people like his grandparents there.

 **Home Activity** Your child compared and contrasted *before* and *after* details from a short passage. Discuss an event in your child's life and list your child's thoughts or feelings before and after the event.

Tech Files
ONLINE

Have students use the keyword *kindness* to search a student-friendly Web site. Be sure to follow classroom guidelines for Internet use.

ELL

Build Background Use ELL Poster 6 to build background and vocabulary for the lesson concept of kindness.

▲ **ELL Poster** 6

Build Background

ACTIVATE PRIOR KNOWLEDGE

BRAINSTORM what it's like to be a newcomer.

• Ask students to think about a time they were new to a group, a school, or a neighborhood.

• Have students brainstorm words and phrases to describe what it felt like to be a newcomer. Write these on the board.

• Now ask them to reverse roles and imagine a new student joining their class. What kinds of things could they do or say to make it easier on the newcomer?

BACKGROUND BUILDING AUDIO This week's audio explores overcoming challenges involved in moving to a new place. After students listen, discuss what they learned and what was most surprising to them.

Background Building Audio

Introduce Vocabulary

WORD DEFINITION MATCH

Write the vocabulary words on the board. Complete the following activities to introduce the vocabulary words to students.

Provide clues that are related to the definition of a particular vocabulary word. Students review vocabulary list and call out the word they think matches the clue. For example, you might ask:

Which word describes someone who moves around a lot? *(migrant)*

Which word names a colorful worm-like creature that is one part of the life cycle of a butterfly? *(caterpillar)*

Which word has a similar meaning as curling up and hiding or staying inside? *(cocoon)*

Which word means to "come out"? *(emerge)* **Activate Prior Knowledge**

Have students share where they may have seen some of these words.

Point out that two of this week's words, *sketched* and *unscrewed*, have *-ed* endings which tells us they are past tense verbs. **Word Endings**

Review with students at the end of the week by asking some of the same questions or by asking for another meaning for a particular word.

Have students use these steps for reading multisyllabic words. (See the Multisyllabic Word Routine on p. DI·1.)

1 **Look for Meaningful Word Parts** (base words, endings, prefixes, suffixes, roots) Think about the meaning of each part. Use the parts to read the word. Model: I see the prefix *dis-* in front of the word *disrespect*. *Respect* means "to show honor or esteem" or "to show politeness," and *dis-* means "not" or "lack of." Therefore, *disrespect* means "not to show honor" or "to show a lack of respect."

2 **Chunk Words with No Recognizable Parts** Say each chunk slowly. Then say the chunks fast to make a word. Model: *e, merge—emerge*.

Lesson Vocabulary

WORDS TO KNOW

T caterpillar the wormlike larvae of insects such as butterflies and moths

T cocoon case of silky thread spun by the larvae of various insects, to live in while they are developing into adults

T disrespect to show a lack of respect; to be rude

T emerge to come into view; come out; come up

T migrant worker, especially a farm worker, who travels from one area to another in search of work

T sketched drawn roughly and quickly

T unscrewed loosened or taken off by turning

MORE WORDS TO KNOW

gestured made a movement to help express an idea or a feeling

suspenders straps worn over the shoulders to hold up the trousers

T = Tested Word

Vocabulary

Directions Choose a word from the box that best matches each definition. Write the word on the line.

Check the Words You Know
__caterpillar
__cocoon
__disrespect
__emerge
__migrant
__sketched
__unscrewed

disrespect 1. lack of respect; to be rude

unscrewed 2. loosened or taken off by turning

migrant 3. someone who travels from one area to another in search of work

sketched 4. roughly drawn

emerge 5. to come into view or come out

Directions Choose the word from the box that best completes each sentence. Write the word on the line.

Janice found the 6. **caterpillar** sitting sleepily on a leaf in the yard. She brought it inside, 7. **unscrewed** the lid from a peanut-butter jar, and put it inside. She hoped to see it create a 8. **cocoon**. Her older sister had 9. **sketched** a beautiful picture of a caterpillar when she was younger. Janice planned to do the same while she watched the butterfly 10. **emerge** from its cocoon.

Write a Description
On a separate sheet of paper, write a description of an animal you have observed over time. It can be a house pet, or a common animal like a bird or squirrel. Use as many of the vocabulary words as you can to describe its changes.
Descriptions should be of an animal and include words from the vocabulary list.

School + Home Home Activity Your child identified and used vocabulary words from *Inside Out*. With your child, write a story about an act of kindness. Use as many vocabulary words as you can.

▲ **Practice Book** p. 54

Vocabulary Strategy

INTRODUCE

Discuss the strategy for word structure using the steps on p. 144.

TEACH

- Have students read "The Story of a Caterpillar," paying attention to how vocabulary is used.
- Model using word structure to determine the meaning of *unscrewed*.

Think Aloud **MODEL** I cover the prefix *un-* and see the base word *screw*. I know *screw* is "to turn or twist on." I know the prefix *un-* means "the opposite of." So, *unscrewed* must mean "to twist off."

Words to Know

- caterpillar
- sketched
- disrespect
- cocoon
- emerge
- migrant
- unscrewed

Remember

Try the strategy. Then, if you need more help, use your glossary or dictionary.

Vocabulary Strategy
for Prefixes

Word Structure Sometimes you can use prefixes to figure out the meaning of an unfamiliar word. The prefixes *un-* and *dis-* usually mean "the opposite of" or "to do the opposite," as in *untie* and *disappear*. Follow these steps.

1. Cover the prefix.
2. Look at the base word. See if you know what it means.
3. Ask: "How does the prefix change the meaning of the base word?"
4. Check to see if this new meaning makes sense in the sentence.

As you read "The Story of a Caterpillar," look for words that begin with the prefix *un-* or *dis-*. Use the prefixes to help you figure out the meanings of the words.

144

DAY 2 Grouping Options

Reading

Whole Group Discuss the Question of the Day. Then use pp. 144–147.

Group Time Differentiated Instruction
Read "Inside Out." See pp. 142h–142i for the small group lesson plan.

Whole Group Use p. 161a.

Language Arts
Use pp. 161e–161k.

Strategic Intervention

 Word Structure Have students work in pairs and follow the steps on p. 144 to find the meanings of *untie*, *disappear*, and *unscrewed*.

ELL

Access Content Use ELL Poster 6 to preteach vocabulary. Choose from the following to meet language proficiency levels.

Beginning Have students create a web with *Caterpillar* in the center oval and words that are related to caterpillars in the ovals around it.

Intermediate Point to the sentence with the word *disrespect*. Help students use the prefix to understand that *disrespect* means "not respect." Point out the double negative in the sentence. Have students create a new sentence that is positive (*We want to respect nature.*)

Advanced Teach the lesson on pp. 144–145. Have students find home-language terms for words that relate to caterpillars.

Resources for home-language words may include parents, bilingual staff members, bilingual dictionaries, or online translation sources.

The Story of a Caterpillar

During recess I like to poke around and see the finer details up close and personal. One day I discovered a caterpillar munching leaves on a bush. It had blue spots and yellowish lines and many stubby little legs. It moved by rippling its whole body along in waves. It looked so interesting that I sketched it in my notebook. I thought my teacher, who loves science, would be intrigued.

She said I could put it in a jar with air holes and lots of leaves to eat, but to do this carefully. "We must not hurt the caterpillar or make it suffer," she said. "We don't want to disrespect nature." We watched to see what would happen, but after many weeks, we wondered if anything ever would. Then one day we spied a white cocoon hanging from a twig! The caterpillar had wrapped itself up for a long nap.

For weeks we checked the jar every morning until the cocoon opened and a beautiful moth began to emerge. It sat on a twig opening and closing its wings. We looked up the moth in an insect book. It had come from an eastern tent caterpillar. The book also said that like a migrant worker, some moths and butterflies travel thousands of miles in a year. I unscrewed the jar so the moth's trip could begin.

Words to Write

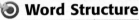

Be a science reporter. Write about the life cycle of a butterfly. Use as many words from the Words to Know list as you can.

145

PRACTICE AND ASSESS

- Have students identify other words in the selection with prefixes, and use word structure to determine the words' meanings.
- Point out to students that many dictionaries include entries that give the meanings of prefixes.
- As a follow-up to p. 144b, provide clues to students and see if they can match the clues to the vocabulary words. See if students are able to match more words this time.
- Have students complete Practice Book p. 55.

WRITE Writing should include vocabulary words that are related to the life cycle of a butterfly, such as *caterpillar, cocoon,* and *emerge.*

Monitor Progress

Word Structure

If… students need more practice with the lesson vocabulary,	then… use Tested Vocabulary Cards.

Vocabulary · Word Structure

- A **prefix** is added at the beginning of a base word to change its meaning.
- Sometimes you can use prefixes to figure out the meaning of an unfamiliar word.
- The prefixes *un–* and *dis–* usually mean "the opposite" or "to do the opposite."

Directions Read the following passage. Then answer the questions below. Look for prefixes in words to help determine their meaning.

Quietly, Rosa unscrewed the bottle of pickles. She was making a huge sandwich for her mom, who was busy in her office. "Try to be quiet," her mom had said. Rosa wanted to surprise her mom, because sometimes she worked so hard that she forgot to eat. For Rosa, it was unthinkable to miss a meal.

Rosa didn't want to show disrespect to her mom, but she couldn't help being excited about the sandwich she'd made. She came to the door and announced, "Lunch is served!" Her mom smiled and said, "How did you know I was hungry?" Rosa was relieved and pulled a chair to join her mom for lunch.

Possible answers given.
1. If *unscrewed* means "loosened by turning," what does its base word mean and why?
   The base word means "to tighten by turning;" Without the prefix you only have the meaning of the base word.
2. If *unthinkable* means "impossible to imagine," what does its base word mean and why?
   The base means "possible to imagine;" Without the prefix, you only have the meaning of the base word.
3. What word uses the prefix *dis–*? How does this prefix change the meaning of its base word?
   disrespect; *Dis–* changes "respect" to the opposite meaning.
4. Fill in the blank: If Rosa's mom wanted Rosa to make the sandwich again, she might say, "Rosa, can you **remake** this sandwich?"
5. Add prefixes to *pleased* and *excited* so each new word's meaning will be the opposite of the base word. Use one of the new words in a sentence.
   displeased, unexcited; I became displeased when I saw the final score of the game.

Home Activity Your child identified prefixes in words to understand their meanings. With your child, read a short selection. Ask your child to point out words that use prefixes and to explain how the prefixes change their meanings.

▲ **Practice Book** p. 55

Prereading Strategies

OBJECTIVES

- Compare and contrast to improve comprehension.
- Answer questions to compare and contrast.

GENRE STUDY

Realistic Fiction

"Inside Out" is realistic fiction. Explain that while fiction tells stories of imaginary people and events, realistic fiction tells a story that is possible. Plausible characters engage in actions that seem truthful and the story has a reasonable outcome.

PREVIEW AND PREDICT

Have students preview the story title and illustrations and discuss what might happen in this story. Have students use lesson vocabulary words as they discuss the possibilities.

Strategy Response Log

Activate Prior Knowledge Have students write in their strategy response logs about a time when they were the new kid in a group. Students will use this information when they do the Strategy Response Log activity on p. 153.

146

ELL

Access Content Lead a picture walk to introduce students to the main character, Francisco. Help them use the pictures to preview some of Francisco's actions as he interacts with other students.

Consider having students read the selection summary in English or in students' home languages. See the Multilingual Summaries in the ELL Teaching Guide, pp. 40–42.

by Francisco Jiménez

Inside Out

illustrated by Raul Colon

Why does Francisco do what he does at the end of the story?

Genre

Realistic fiction deals with characters and actions that seem real but come from the author's imagination. As you read, notice how the author makes the setting and characters come to life.

147

SET PURPOSE

Read the first page of the story aloud to students. Have them consider their preview discussion and talk about what they hope to find out as they read.

Remind students to compare and contrast as they read.

STRATEGY RECALL

Students have now used these before-reading strategies:

- preview the selection to be aware of its genre, features, and possible content;
- activate prior knowledge about that content and what to expect of that genre;
- make predictions;
- set a purpose for reading.

Remind students to be aware of and flexibly use the during-reading strategies they have learned:

- link prior knowledge to new information;
- summarize text they have read so far;
- ask clarifying questions;
- answer questions they or others pose;
- check their predictions and either refine them or make new predictions;
- recognize the text structure the author is using, and use that knowledge to make predictions and increase comprehension;
- visualize what the author is describing;
- monitor their comprehension and use fix-up strategies.

After reading, students will use these strategies:

- summarize or retell the text;
- answer questions they or others pose;
- reflect to make new information become part of their prior knowledge.

Audio CD   AudioText

Guiding Comprehension

1  **Compare and Contrast • Inferential**

Compare Francisco to Curtis.

Francisco is the smallest kid in class and he doesn't speak English. Curtis is big, strong, popular, and speaks English.

Monitor Progress
⊙ Compare and Contrast

If... students are unable to compare and contrast characters,	**then...** use the skill and strategy instruction on p. 149.

2 **Character • Critical**

What can you learn about Arthur from his friendship with Francisco?

Possible response: Arthur can relate to kids from different cultures and is a good friend.

148

ELL

Build Background Reread this sentence aloud: "His parents were migrant workers." Tell students that a migrant worker is a person who moves from place to place looking for work, often on a farm.

Francisco has come with his family from Mexico and speaks only Spanish. This is his first year in school in the United States. His parents are migrant workers. While Francisco is at school, they are out in the farm fields picking strawberries. Miss Scalapino is Francisco's teacher, and Roberto is his big brother. Right next to Francisco's desk is a caterpillar in a jar.

In time I learned some of my class-mates' names. The one I heard the most and therefore learned first was Curtis. Curtis was the biggest, strongest, and most popular kid in the class. Everyone wanted to be his friend and to play with him. He was always chosen captain when the kids formed teams. Since I was the smallest kid in the class and did not know English, I was chosen last.

1

I preferred to hang around Arthur, one of the boys who knew a little Span-ish. During recess, he and I played on the swings and I pretended to be a Mexican movie star, like Jorge Negrete or Pedro Infante, riding a horse and singing the *corridos* we often heard on the car radio. I sang them to Arthur as we swung back and forth, going as high as we could.

2

149

Migrant Workers

Time for SOCIAL STUDIES

In modern times, countries depend on each other economically. Migrant workers travel the U.S. to help farmers pick crops during the busy harvest time. When the work is finished, the workers move to another community to pick a different crop. This means their children must move from school to school.

 SKILLS ⟷ STRATEGIES IN CONTEXT

Compare and Contrast

TEACH

- Remind students that when writers compare and contrast things, they tell how those things are alike and different.
- Sometimes words act as clues that things are being compared and contrasted. Words that have *-est* added to them, like *saddest,* are sometimes used to compare characters.
- Model comparing characters on p. 149, paragraph 1.

Think Aloud **MODEL** The first paragraph compares two characters, Curtis and Francisco. Words used to describe Curtis are *biggest, strongest,* and *most popular.* The adjective used to describe Francisco is *small-est.* Also, the text says that Curtis is always chosen captain when teams are picked. But Francisco doesn't know English and is chosen last when the kids form teams.

PRACTICE AND ASSESS

Have students reread p. 149, paragraph 1. Ask which of the following adjectives best describes Francisco. *(Choice b)*

a) biggest
b) smallest
c) strongest

EXTEND SKILLS

Dialogue

Explain that dialogue is the conversation between two or more characters in a story. Dialogue usu-ally reveals information about characters and helps move the story forward. Have students look for examples of dialogue as they read.

Guiding Comprehension

3 **Author's Purpose • Critical**
Question the Author **Why do you think the author includes the scene where the teacher scolds Francisco for speaking Spanish?**

Possible response: To show how Francisco is made to feel different or out of place.

Monitor Progress

REVIEW Author's Purpose

If... students are unable to evaluate the author's purpose,	**then...** use the skill and strategy instruction on p. 151.

4 **Compare and Contrast • Inferential**
How is Francisco like the caterpillar?
Possible response: They are both hiding.

5 **Character • Inferential**
What have you learned about Francisco so far?
He likes to draw, likes butterflies, and has trouble communicating with others.

But when I spoke to Arthur in Spanish and Miss Scalapino heard me, she said "No!" with body and soul. Her head turned left and right a hundred times a second, and her index finger moved from side to side as fast as a windshield wiper on a rainy day. "English, English," she repeated. Arthur avoided me whenever she was around.

Often during recess I stayed with the caterpillar. Sometimes it was hard to spot him because he blended in with the green leaves and twigs. Every day I brought him leaves from the pepper and cypress trees that grew on the playground.

Just in front of the caterpillar, lying on top of the cabinet, was a picture book of caterpillars and butterflies. I went through it, page by page, studying all the pictures and running my fingers lightly over the caterpillars and the bright wings of the butterflies and the many patterns on them. I knew caterpillars turned into butterflies because Roberto had told me, but I wanted to know more. I was sure information was in the words written underneath each picture in large black letters. I tried to figure them out by looking at the pictures. I did this so many times that I could close my eyes and see the words, but I could not understand what they meant.

My favorite time in school was when we did art, which was every afternoon, after the teacher had read to us. Since I did not understand Miss Scalapino when she explained the art lesson, she let me do whatever I wanted. I drew all kinds of animals but mostly birds and butterflies. I sketched them in pencil and then colored them using every color in my crayon box. Miss Scalapino even tacked one of my drawings up on the board for everyone to see. After a couple of weeks it disappeared, and I did not know how to ask where it had gone.

150

Access Content Reread aloud the phrase "I was shivering" as you cross your arms across your chest and shake as if you were cold. Tell students that a person usually shivers because he or she is cold. Explain that it is also possible for a person to shiver with fear. Invite students to use gestures to act out "shivering with cold." Ask them to explain why Francisco was shivering.

One cold Thursday morning, during recess, I was the only kid on the playground without a jacket. Mr. Sims must have noticed I was shivering because that afternoon, after school, he took me to his office and pulled out a green jacket from a large cardboard box that was full of used clothes and toys. He handed it to me and gestured for me to try it on. It smelled like graham crackers. I put it on, but it was too big, so he rolled up the sleeves about two inches to make it fit. I took it home and showed it off to my parents. They smiled. I liked it because it was green, and it hid my suspenders.

151

Author's Purpose REVIEW

TEACH

- Explain that authors may have more than one reason for writing. Four common reasons are: to inform, to persuade, to entertain, and to express feelings or thoughts.

- Knowing the author's purpose can help a reader better understand a story.

 Think Aloud **MODEL** It must feel lonely and scary not to know the language and not to be allowed to speak your own language. I think the author wrote this page to express how Francisco feels isolated and as if he doesn't belong.

PRACTICE AND ASSESS

- Ask students to visualize the scenes as they reread pp. 150–151. Have them state the author's purpose in their own words.

- To assess, use Practice Book p. 56.

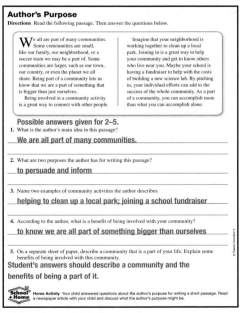

Author's Purpose

Directions Read the following passage. Then answer the questions below.

We all are part of many communities. Some communities are small, like our family, our neighborhood, or a soccer team we may be a part of. Some communities are larger, such as our town, our country, or even the planet we all share. Being part of a community lets us know that we are a part of something that is bigger than just ourselves.

Being involved in a community activity is a great way to connect with other people.

Imagine that your neighborhood is working together to clean up a local park. Joining in is a great way to help your community and get to know others who live near you. Maybe your school is having a fundraiser to help with the costs of building a new science lab. By pitching in, your individual efforts can add to the success of the whole community. As a part of a community, you can accomplish more than what you can accomplish alone.

Possible answers given for 2–5.

1. What is the author's main idea in this passage?
We are all part of many communities.

2. What are two purposes the author has for writing this passage?
to persuade and inform

3. Name two examples of community activities the author describes.
helping to clean up a local park; joining a school fundraiser

4. According to the author, what is a benefit of being involved with your community?
to know we are all part of something bigger than ourselves

5. On a separate sheet of paper, describe a community that is a part of your life. Explain some benefits of being involved with this community.
Student's answers should describe a community and the benefits of being a part of it.

School+Home **Home Activity** Your child answered questions about the author's purpose for writing a short passage. Read a newspaper article with your child and discuss what the author's purpose might be.

▲ **Practice Book** p. 56

Guiding Comprehension

6 **Cause and Effect • Inferential**

Why does Curtis attack Francisco?

Francisco is wearing the jacket that Curtis lost at the beginning of the year.

7 **Compare and Contrast • Inferential**

Compare the way Miss Scalapino responds to Francisco during the fight and how she responds to him later in the classroom.

She is more forceful when she breaks up the fight, grabbing Francisco by the collar. In the last paragraph she is gentler and allows him to be alone.

Monitor Progress	
Compare and Contrast	
If... students have difficulty comparing and contrasting,	**then...** use the skill and strategy instruction on p. 153.

152

ELL

Extend Language Explain that *embarrassed* means "uncomfortable or ashamed." Ask students to explain a situation where someone might feel embarrassed.

The next day I was on the playground wearing my new jacket and waiting for the first bell to ring when I saw Curtis coming at me like an angry bull. Aiming his head directly at me, and pulling his arms straight back with his hands clenched, he stomped up to me and started yelling. I did not understand him, but I knew it had something to do with the jacket because he began to pull on it, trying to take it off of me. The next thing I knew, he and I were on the ground wrestling. Kids circled us. I could hear them yelling Curtis's name and something else. He pulled on one of the sleeves so hard that it ripped at the shoulder. He pulled on the right pocket and it ripped. Then Miss Scalapino's face appeared above. She pushed Curtis off of me and grabbed me by the back of the collar and picked me up off the ground. It took all the power I had not to cry. **6**

On the way to the classroom Arthur told me that Curtis claimed the jacket was his, that he had lost it at the beginning of the year. He also said that the teacher told Curtis and me that we were being punished. We had to sit on the bench during recess for the rest of the week. I did not see the jacket again. Curtis got it but I never saw him wear it.

For the rest of the day, I could not even pretend I was paying attention to Miss Scalapino; I was so embarrassed. I laid my head on the top of my desk and closed my eyes. I kept thinking about what had happened that morning. I wanted to fall asleep and wake up to find it was only a dream. The teacher called my name but I did not answer. I heard her walk up to me. I did not know what to expect. She gently shook me by the shoulders. Again, I did not respond. Miss Scalapino must have thought I was asleep because she left me alone, even when it was time for recess and everyone left the room. **7**

153

Develop Vocabulary

PRACTICE LESSON VOCABULARY

Students orally respond *yes* or *no* to each question and provide a reason for each answer.

1. Does a *migrant* worker live in one place? *(No, workers who pick crops move from one community to another.)*

2. Would Francisco have *sketched* a robin? *(Yes, he liked to draw pictures of birds.)*

3. Did Francisco like *caterpillars*? *(Yes, he was interested in the small worm (larva) that could one day become a butterfly.)*

BUILD CONCEPT VOCABULARY

Review previous concept words with students. Ask if students have come across any words today in their reading that they would like to add to the Kindness Concept Web, such as *gently* and *noticed*.

 SKILLS ↔ STRATEGIES IN CONTEXT

Compare/Contrast Answer Questions

TEACH

Answering questions to compare and contrast characters will help students understand characters and their actions. Explain that the answer to a question can be in one or two sentences, or in several places.

Think Aloud **MODEL** At the end of the first paragraph on p. 153, it says Miss Scalapino grabbed Francisco by the collar. Then in the last paragraph it says she gently shook his shoulders and then left him alone. This shows how she treated Francisco differently at different times.

PRACTICE AND ASSESS

Ask students why they think Miss Scalapino treated Curtis and Francisco the same way immediately after the fight. *(She might not have known who started it or what happened.)*

Strategy Response Log

Monitor Comprehension Have students review their strategy response logs. (See p. 146.) Provide the following prompt: Has what you have learned about being the new kid in the group helped you to better understand this story?

If you want to teach this selection in two sessions, stop here.

Guiding Comprehension

If you are teaching the selection in two days, discuss any comparisons and contrasts so far and review the vocabulary.

8  **Vocabulary • Word Structure**

Have students use prefixes to determine the meaning of *disrespect* in paragraph 2 on p. 154.

The prefix *dis-* means "not," so *disrespect* means "not respect."

Monitor Progress

Word Structure

If... students have difficulty using prefixes to determine the meaning of *disrespect*,	**then...** use vocabulary strategy instruction on p. 155.

---

9 **Compare and Contrast • Critical**

When Francisco received the award, he said, "I was so proud I felt like bursting out of my skin." In what way is the author comparing Francisco to the cocoon?

Possible response: The caterpillar in the cocoon will burst out as a butterfly. Francisco is also getting ready to burst out of his cocoon.

DAY 3 Grouping Options

Reading
Whole Group Discuss the Question of the Day.

Group Time Differentiated Instruction
 "Inside Out." See pp. 142h–142i for the small group lesson plan.

Whole Group Discuss the Reader Response questions on p. 158. Then use p. 653a.

Language Arts
Use pp. 161e–161k.

Once the room was quiet, I slowly opened my eyes. I had them closed for so long that the sunlight coming through the windows blinded me. I rubbed my eyes with the back of my hands and then looked to my left at the jar. I looked for the caterpillar but could not see it. Thinking it might be hidden, I put my hand in the jar and lightly stirred the leaves. To my surprise, the caterpillar had spun itself into a cocoon and had attached itself to a small twig. It looked like a tiny cotton bulb, just like Roberto had said it would. I gently stroked it with my index finger, picturing it asleep and peaceful.

At the end of the school day, Miss Scalapino gave me a note to take home to my parents. Papa and Mama did not know how to read, but they did not have to. As soon as they saw my swollen upper lip and the scratches on my left cheek, they knew what the **8** note had said. When I told them what happened, they were very upset but relieved that I did not disrespect the teacher.

For the next several days, going to school and facing Miss Scalapino was harder than ever. However, I slowly began to get over what happened that Friday. Once I got used to the routine in school and I picked up some English words, I felt more comfortable in class.

On Wednesday, May 23, a few days before the end of the school year, Miss Scalapino took me by surprise. After we were all sitting down and she had taken roll, she called for everyone's attention. I did not understand what she said, but I heard her say my name as she held up a blue ribbon. She then picked up my drawing of the butterfly that had disappeared weeks before and held it up for everyone to see. She walked up to me and handed me the drawing and the silk blue ribbon that had the number one printed on it in gold. I knew then I had received first prize for my **9** drawing. I was so proud I felt like bursting out of my skin. My classmates, including Curtis, stretched their necks to see the ribbon.

154

ELL

Access Content Reread the phrase "Miss Scalapino took me by surprise." Explain that "to take someone by surprise" means to do or say something unexpected or unusual. Ask students to describe a time something took them by surprise.

Word Structure

TEACH

Remind students that prefixes are syllables added at the beginning of a base word to change its meaning. The prefixes *dis-* and *un-* both mean "the opposite of." The word *undone,* for example, means the opposite of *done;* it means "not done."

Read the last sentence in the second paragraph on p. 154. Model using prefixes to determine the meaning of *disrespect.*

Think Aloud **MODEL** The word *disrespect* has the base word *respect* and the prefix *dis-*. Since *dis-* means "the opposite of," the word *disrespect* means the opposite of *respect.* The sentence says, though, that Francisco did not *disrespect* the teacher; in other words, he did the opposite of *disrespect*; he showed respect for her.

PRACTICE AND ASSESS

Have students use their knowledge of prefixes to determine the meaning of *disappeared* in paragraph 4 on p. 154. *(not appeared)*

U.S. Constitution

Time for SOCIAL STUDIES

The Constitution of the United States is the supreme law of the land. Values basic to democracy include: individual rights and responsibilities, concern for the public good, the rule of law, justice, equality, diversity, and truth. Many of these values are embodied in the Bill of Rights, the first ten amendments to the U.S. Constitution. These rights include freedom of religion, freedom of speech, a free press, and the right to a speedy trial. In the story, Curtis did not show good citizenship when he attacked Francisco, and Francisco's individual rights were violated.

Guiding Comprehension

10  **Answer Questions • Inferential**

Why do you think Francisco is excited to see the butterfly emerge from the cocoon?

Possible answer: He has been watching it for a long time and waiting for this to happen.

11 Draw Conclusions • Inferential

Why do you think Francisco gives his drawing to Curtis?

Possible response: He wants to let Curtis know that all is forgiven and that they can be friends.

12 Summarize • Critical

Text to World **How does this story deepen your understanding of what it's like to be new to a school or neighborhood?**

Responses will vary, but should focus on students' experiences in new surroundings.

Strategy Response Log

Summarize When students finish reading the selection, provide this prompt: In "Inside Out," Francisco is the new student. Tell how he adjusts to the new classroom. In four or five sentences, explain the important points.

Tech Files
ONLINE

Several Web sites host ongoing or annual art contests for students. Have students use the keywords *art contests for kids* in a student-friendly search engine. Be sure to follow classroom guidelines for Internet use.

That afternoon, during our free period, I went over to check on the caterpillar. I turned the jar around, trying to see the cocoon. It was beginning to crack open. I excitedly cried out, "Look, look," pointing to it. The whole class, like a swarm of bees, rushed over to the counter. Miss Scalapino took the jar and placed it on top of a desk in the middle of the classroom so everyone could see it. For the next several minutes we all stood there watching the butterfly emerge from its cocoon, in slow motion.

At the end of the day, just before the last bell, Miss Scalapino picked up the jar and took the class outside to the playground. She placed the jar and on the ground and we all circled around her. I had a hard time seeing over the other kids, so Miss Scalapino called me and motioned for

156

ⒺⓁⓁ

Extend Language Reread aloud the sentence "The whole class, like a swarm of bees, rushed over to the counter." Explain that a swarm of bees moves together as a group, so in this case, the class moved together, as one large group, to the counter. Ask students to tell why the class moved "like a swarm of bees."

me to open the jar. I broke through the circle, knelt on the ground, and unscrewed the top. Like magic, the butterfly flew into the air, fluttering its wings up and down.

After school I waited in line for my bus in front of the playground. I proudly carried the blue ribbon in my right hand and the drawing in the other. Arthur and Curtis came up and stood behind me to wait for their bus. Curtis motioned for me to show him the drawing again. I held it up so he could see it.

"He really likes it, Francisco," Arthur said to me in Spanish.

"¿Como se dice 'es tuyo' en inglés?" I asked.

"It's yours," answered Arthur.

"It's yours," I repeated, handing the drawing to Curtis.

157

Develop Vocabulary

PRACTICE LESSON VOCABULARY

Students orally complete each statement.

1. Caterpillars spin themselves into (cocoons).

2. Francisco's parents did not want him to (disrespect) his teacher.

3. Did Francisco ever (emerge) from hiding?

4. Francisco (unscrewed) the top of the jar to set the butterfly free.

BUILD CONCEPT VOCABULARY

Review previous concept words with students. Ask if students have come across any words today in their reading that they would like to add to the Kindness Concept Web, such as *peaceful* and *relieved*.

STRATEGY SELF-CHECK

Answer Questions

Remind students that if they cannot find an answer to a question in just one sentence, they should search in several places to find all the information they need to answer it. Use Practice Book p. 57.

SELF-CHECK

Students can ask themselves these questions to assess their ability to use the strategy.

- Was I able to use the answering questions strategy to make comparisons and contrasts as I read?

- Was I able to locate information necessary to answer the questions?

Monitor Progress

Compare and Contrast

If... students have difficulty comparing and contrasting,	then... use the Reteach lesson on p. 161b.

Compare and Contrast

- When you **compare** and **contrast** two or more things, you show how they are alike and different.
- Clue words such as *like* or *as* show comparisons. Words such as *but* or *however* show contrasts.
- Sometimes, writers do not use clue words when they compare and contrast things.

Directions Read the following passage. Then answer the questions below.

Being involved in elections is an important way people can show good citizenship. Just about every year, there's some kind of election being held, either in your town, state, across the country, or maybe even in your school. A few people will serve their community by running for office. But running for office isn't for everyone. Some people volunteer their time to campaign for a candidate. They pass out flyers and buttons. Sometimes, they make phone calls to try and raise money for the campaign. They also help register people to vote.

Other people can get involved in a less direct way. They read newspapers and web sites, and talk to each other to learn about the issues. Learning about what's at stake in an election is an important part of being a good citizen, because it helps you decide how you want to vote. The one thing every citizen can do is vote.

Possible answers given for 1, 2, 5.

1. How can some people get directly involved in elections?
   Some people run for office or volunteer time to campaigns.

2. Name a less direct way people can get involved in an election.
   People can learn about the issues of an election.

3. What is one way all citizens can be involved in elections?
   They can vote.

4. Where do elections take place?
   Elections can take place in your town, your state, across the country, or in school.

5. Explain why you think voting is an important responsibility for every citizen.
   By voting, each citizen can be a part of the decision-making process.

Home Activity Your child answered compare-and-contrast questions about elections. Have your child think about a recent school election. Compare his or her voting choice with the outcome. Ask your child questions about the overall experience.

▲ **Practice Book** p. 57

Reader Response

Open for Discussion **Personal Response**

Think Aloud

MODEL Francisco probably needs a friend. I can invite him to join me during lunch and recess. I can help him learn my name and names of other things.

Comprehension Check **Critical Response**

1. Possible responses: Francisco doesn't speak English, so Miss Scalapino makes movements so he will understand. The author may describe the jacket to emphasize that it is used in order to set up Curtis's later claim that it is his. ***Author's Purpose***

2. Responses should include information that Francisco treats Curtis better than Curtis treats him. ⊙ ***Compare and Contrast***

3. Mr. Sims notices that Francisco is shivering. ⊙ ***Answer Questions***

4. Possible response: The *caterpillar* hides in a *cocoon*, like Francisco. Both *emerge* from their shells. ⊙ ***Vocabulary***

Look Back and Write For test practice, assign a 10–15 minute time limit. For assessment, see the Scoring Rubric at the right.

Retell

Have students retell "Inside Out."

Monitor Progress

Check Retelling Rubric 4 3 2 1

| If... students have difficulty retelling the story, | then... use the Retelling Cards and the Scoring Rubric for Retelling on p. 159 to assist fluent retelling. |

SUCCESS PREDICTOR

Check Retelling Have students use the art to guide their retellings. Go through the pictures with students, making sure they know the characters' names and words for items pictured. Let students listen to other retellings before attempting their own. For more ideas on assessing retellings, see the ELL and Transition Handbook.

Reader Response

Open for Discussion Imagine you are helping Miss Scalapino in her classroom. Your job is to help a new Spanish-speaking student named Francisco. Tell your plan.

1. Reread the descriptions of Miss Scalapino's movements at the top of page 150 and the green jacket on page 151. Why are they so specific? What do you think this author would say if you asked him this question? **Think Like an Author**

2. Compare and contrast how Curtis treats Francisco on page 153 with how Francisco treats Curtis on page 157. Which character do you admire and why? **Compare and Contrast**

3. Why does Mr. Sims give Francisco the jacket? Explain, including details from page 151 in your answer. **Answer Questions**

4. How does the caterpillar help Francisco adjust to his new school? Tell about it using words from the Words to Know list and the story. **Vocabulary**

TEST PRACTICE

Look Back and Write
Francisco and the caterpillar seem to have something in common. Look back at page 154, where Francisco receives first prize, and read on about the caterpillar. Then write a comparison of what happens to the two of them.

Meet author Francisco Jiménez on page 768.

158

Scoring Rubric **Look Back and Write**

Top-Score Response A top-score response will use details from the selection to show how Francisco's changing state of mind parallels the changing condition of the butterfly.

Example of a Top-Score Response Francisco and the butterfly both change. Both are hidden. The butterfly is wrapped in a cocoon. Francisco is quiet and no one pays him much attention. When the butterfly bursts from its cocoon and then flies away, it is free. When he wins the prize, Francisco is so proud he could burst out of his skin. Everyone admires him. He shows his feeling of freedom by giving his drawing to Curtis.

For additional rubrics, see p. WA10.

Write Now

Summary

Prompt

"Inside Out" is a story that describes life at school for a boy who does not speak English.

Think about a story you have read recently. Now write a summary of that story.

Writing Trait

A story summary **focuses** on main **ideas** and the most important details in the story.

Student Model

Summary focuses on the most important ideas in the story.

Story being summarized is identified in opening sentence.

Summary is written in present tense.

In _Thunder Rose_, Jerdine Nolen tells a tall tale about a girl with special talents. Rose is born on a stormy night, and the storm's power gets into the baby. She is smart and strong, and her parents give her the nickname "Thunder Rose."

Rose is pretty and sweet, but she is also tough. She can twist metal any way she likes and wrestle steers to a halt.

When a drought comes, Rose lassos a cloud to squeeze out rain. This action sets the clouds to churning, and they turn into a twister that tries to catch Rose. She calms those storms with her sweet, powerful song.

Use the model to help you write your own summary.

159

Write Now

Look at the Prompt Explain that each sentence in the prompt has a purpose.

- Sentence 1 presents a topic.
- Sentence 2 suggests students think about the topic.
- Sentence 3 tells what to write—a summary.

Strategies to Develop Focus/Ideas

Have students

- read their summary to a partner who can identify any unnecessary information.
- rewrite wordy sentences to sharpen focus.

NO: Carrie asked and got permission from Pa to go to town in order to buy a book.

YES: Carrie got Pa's permission to go to town to buy a book.

For additional suggestions and rubric, see pp. 161g–161h.

Writer's Checklist

☑ **Focus** Could unimportant details be eliminated?
☑ **Organization** Do transitions connect ideas?
☑ **Support** Is enough information included?
☑ **Conventions** Are punctuation and spelling correct?

Scoring Rubric | Narrative Retelling

Rubric 4 3 2 1	4	3	2	1
Connections	Makes connections and generalizes beyond the text	Makes connections to other events, stories, or experiences	Makes a limited connection to another event, story, or experience	Makes no connection to another event, story, or experience
Author's Purpose	Elaborates on author's purpose	Tells author's purpose with some clarity	Makes some connection to author's purpose	Makes no connection to author's purpose
Characters	Describes the main character(s) and any character development	Identifies the main character(s) and gives some information about them	Inaccurately identifies some characters or gives little information about them	Inaccurately identifies the characters or gives no information about them
Setting	Describes the time and location	Identifies the time and location	Omits details of time or location	Is unable to identify time or location
Plot	Describes the problem, goal, events, and ending using rich detail	Tells the problem, goal, events, and ending with some errors that do not affect meaning	Tells parts of the problem, goal, events, and ending with gaps that affect meaning	Retelling has no sense of story

Retelling Plan

☑ **This week assess Strategic Intervention students.**
☐ **Week 2** Assess Advanced students.
☐ **Week 3** Assess Strategic Intervention students.
☐ **Week 4** Assess On-Level students.
☐ **Week 5** Assess any students you have not yet checked during this unit.

Use the Retelling Chart on p. TR16 to record retelling.

Selection Test To assess with "Inside Out," use Selection Tests, pp. 21–24.

Fresh Reads for Differentiated Test Practice For weekly leveled practice, use pp. 31–36.

Social Studies in Reading

OBJECTIVES

- Examine features of e-mails.
- Practice a test-taking strategy.
- Compare and contrast across texts.

PREVIEW/USE TEXT FEATURES

As students preview "Random Acts of Kindness," have them look at the headings on the e-mails. After they preview ask:

- **How do the e-mail headings help the reader?** *(They provide hints about the topic.)*

Link to Social Studies

Brainstorm students' ideas about random acts of kindness they have performed or received.

E-MAILS

Use the sidebar on p. 160 to guide discussion.

- Explain that e-mail is an informal, quick form of communication that is sent electronically.
- Point out that each e-mail includes a heading that tells who sent it, when it was sent, and what the subject is.
- Use the headings on pp. 160–161 to discuss acts of kindness the e-mails might tell about.

DAY 4 Grouping Options

Reading

Whole Group Discuss the Question of the Day.

Group Time Differentiated Instruction
Read "Random Acts of Kindness." See pp. 142h–142i for the small group lesson plan.

Whole Group Use p. 161a.

Language Arts
Use pp. 161e–161k.

Social Studies in Reading

E-mails

Genre

- E-mail is short for "electronic mail."

- E-mails are messages sent on a computer over the Internet. They travel from sender to receiver in a matter of minutes.

Text Features

- Each e-mail has a heading that tells who submitted it when.

- These e-mails are for a general audience. The sender is writing to anyone who visits this Web site.

Link to Social Studies

With your teacher's help, begin a Random Acts of Kindness File for your classroom. Think of times when you practiced kindness and write about them.

160

Random Acts of Kindness

These e-mails are from the Random Acts of Kindness Foundation Web site. This nonprofit organization encourages people to practice kindness whenever and wherever they can.

A Mother's Appreciation
SUBMITTED BY: HAYLEY'S MOTHER / DATE SUBMITTED: 3/10/2004

I want to acknowledge the kindness of Madison. She was so sweet to my daughter, Hayley, who is a kindergartener.

Hayley was having a very difficult morning after being dropped off at school. Madison, who is in the same class as Hayley's brother, saw Hayley crying and generously walked her to her class. She took her to her teacher and made her feel better by doing so.

A Student's Random Act of Kindness
SUBMITTED BY: FAITH / DATE SUBMITTED: 12/4/2003

A friend of mine seemed to be having a hard time, so I wrote her a note that told her how much of an inspiration she has been to me. I also told her to always follow her dreams and never give up hope.

I then decided to do this for others in my classes. Most of them I had never even talked to before, but they just looked lonely or sad.

I didn't sign my name, so it was really special watching as they smiled and looked around, wondering who could have written it. I know it wasn't much, but it made their day.

Content-Area Vocabulary | Social Studies

represented	stood for
symbol	something that stands for or represents something else

 AudioText

Just a Pencil

SUBMITTED BY: JIM / DATE SUBMITTED: 9/26/2003

On the first day of school, Mario said, "I have no pencil." The math teacher told him to use the one on the chalk tray. On the second day of school, Mario repeated his statement, and the teacher just pointed to the chalk tray.

The scenario went on until the first school day after the winter break. On that day Mario met with the teacher at the door, smiled, and said, "Mr. C., I now have a pencil for YOU." The teacher took the new pencil and read the inscription: "Thank you for being kind."

The teacher never hassled Mario about not having a pencil because he, too, came from a poor background and never forgot how embarrassing it was to be laughed at in school for not having school supplies.

At first, the pencil represented a small symbol of kindness, but soon it evolved into Mario's determination to pass math class. He voluntarily spent extra time in class. He always arrived early each morning to get a head start on his assignment.

Just a pencil?—not really. To Mario, the pencil meant someone cared, and this feeling gave him the desire to succeed in math class and be successful in his new American school.

Reading Across Texts

What was Francisco's random act of kindness?

Writing Across Texts Write a letter from Francisco to Curtis, explaining Francisco's random act of kindness.

Answer Questions Reread any e-mails you have questions about.

161

Strategies for Nonfiction

USE HEADINGS Headings let readers know what information they will be reading. Use headings to locate information for test questions. Provide this strategy.

Use the Strategy

1. Read the question and locate a key word.
2. Look for matches in the headings.
3. When you find a match, read the information to answer the test question.

GUIDED PRACTICE Have students discuss how they would use the strategy to answer the following question.

How would lending someone a pencil be an act of kindness?

INDEPENDENT PRACTICE After students answer the following test question, discuss the process they used to find information.

Who e-mails the Foundation's Web site?

Answer Questions

Ask students to state questions they have about the e-mails and then answer them by rereading.

CONNECT TEXT TO TEXT

Reading Across Texts

Discuss "Inside Out" with students, and recall Francisco's act of kindness. Talk about how it was an act of kindness and what the results might be.

Writing Across Texts Have students put themselves in Francisco's place as they write.

World Kindness Movement

Time for SOCIAL STUDIES

The Random Acts of Kindness Foundation was started in 1995. Its mission is to inspire people to do acts of kindness for others. This foundation is part of a larger organization called "World Kindness Movement," which includes other nations. The Random Acts of Kindness Foundation has a Web site that provides teachers, students, youth organizations, individuals, community groups, and the workplace with ideas about how to get involved and incorporate kindness in their surroundings.

CHARACTERIZATION/DIALOGUE
Fluency

Fluency Assessment Plan

- ☑ **This week assess Advanced students.**
- ☐ **Week 2** Assess Strategic Intervention students.
- ☐ **Week 3** Assess On-Level students.
- ☐ **Week 4** Assess Strategic Intervention students.
- ☐ **Week 5** Assess any students you have not yet checked during this unit.

Set individual goals for students to enable them to reach the year-end goal.
- Current Goal: 110–116 wcpm
- Year-End Goal: 140 wcpm

For English language learners, reading aloud song lyrics, favorite poems, and very short, engaging stories provides good opportunities to increase oral reading fluency.

To develop fluent readers, use Fluency Coach.

DAY 5 **Grouping Options**

Reading
Whole Group
Revisit the Question of the Week.

Group Time
Differentiated Instruction
Reread this week's Leveled Readers. See pp. 142h–142i for the small group lesson plan.

Whole Group
Use p. 161b–161c.

Language Arts
Use pp. 161d–161l.

DAY 1

Model Reread "Dwaina Brooks" on p. 142m. Explain that you will use your voice to bring the characters "alive" in the selection. Model for students as you read.

DAY 2

Echo Reading Read aloud the first paragraph on p. 156. Have students notice how you use your voice to show Francisco's excitement and then everyone's curiosity when they gather quietly to watch the butterfly emerge. Have students practice as a class doing three echo readings of this paragraph.

DAY 3

Model Read aloud p. 157, starting with the first complete paragraph. Have students notice how you read the dialogue to reveal how the characters are feeling. Practice as a class by doing three echo readings.

DAY 4

Partner Reading Partners practice reading p. 157, three times, starting with the first complete paragraph. They should read the text as if they were the characters.

Monitor Progress   Check Fluency WCPM

As students reread, monitor their progress toward their individual fluency goals. Current Goal: 110–116 words correct per minute. End-of-Year Goal: 140 words correct per minute.

If... students cannot read fluently at a rate of 110–116 words correct per minute,
then... make sure students practice with text at their independent level. Provide additional fluency practice, pairing nonfluent readers with fluent readers.

If... students already read at 140 words correct per minute,
then... they do not need to reread three to four times.

SUCCESS PREDICTOR

DAY 5

Assessment
Individual Reading Rate Use the Fluency Assessment Plan and do a one-minute timed reading of either selection from this week to assess students in Week 1. Pay special attention to this week's skill, characterization/dialogue. Provide corrective feedback for each student.

RETEACH

Compare and Contrast

TEACH

Review the definitions for *compare* and *contrast* on p. 142. Students can complete Practice Book p. 58 on their own, or you can complete it as a class. Point out that the information to complete the sentences under "Before" can be found in the first paragraph of the passage.

ASSESS

Have partners reread pp. 160–161 in their books to compare and contrast two e-mail messages: "A Mother's Appreciation" and "Just a Pencil." *(Comparison: Both describe acts of kindness towards students who are having problems at school. Contrast: One act of kindness was done by a student and the other by a teacher.)*

For additional instruction on compare and contrast, see DI·52.

EXTEND SKILLS

Short Story

TEACH

A short story is a concise piece of fiction that focuses on only one character or a few characters and describes a single event or a closely related series of events.

- A short story contains all of the story elements — setting, characters, plot, and theme.
- The main difference between a short story and a novel is its length.

Have students work in small groups to determine if "Inside Out" is a short story. First, have students write a list of questions to ask, such as, "Is the story fiction?" or "Is it short?" "Is a single event described?"

ASSESS

Have students write a descriptive paragraph about whether they think "Random Acts of Kindness" is or is not a short story. Pose the following questions before writing:

1. Is "Random Acts of Kindness" fiction? If not, what is it? *(nonfiction)*

2. Does "Random Acts of Kindness" tell about a related series of events? *(yes)*

OBJECTIVES

- Compare and contrast.
- Identify short stories and recognize their elements.

Skills Trace
Compare and Contrast

Introduce/Teach	TE: 5.2 142–143, 186–187; 5.6 674–675
Practice	Practice Book: 36, 53, 57, 58, 73, 77, 78, 86, 273, 277, 278
Reteach/Review	TE: 5.1 101; 5.2 161b, 207b, 217, DI•52, DI•54; 5.6 699b, DI•54
Test	Selection Test: 21–24, 29–32, 109–112; Benchmark Test: Unit 2

ELL

Access Content Reteach the skill by reviewing the Picture It! lesson on compare and contrast in the ELL Teaching Guide, pp. 36–37.

Compare and Contrast

- When you **compare** and **contrast** two or more things, you show how they are alike and different.
- Clue words such as *but* or *however* show contrasts. The clue words *like* and *as* show comparisons.
- Sometimes, writers do not use clue words when they compare and contrast things.

Directions Read the following passage. Fill in the columns below based on Jorge and Ed's friendship before and after the tornado touched down.

Jorge and Ed grew up on opposite ends of the same street. They went to the same school, and they were sometimes in the same classroom. They were always friendly to each other, but Jorge and Ed didn't really know each other very well.
On the night the tornado touched down, things changed between Jorge and Ed. The roof of Ed's house was blown off. Jorge and his parents were the first people there to help Ed's family. They worked together all night to help clean up Ed's house. That night, Jorge and Ed began to know each other a lot better. They became good friends.

Before	After
1. They lived **on the same street.**	2. They worked **together all night.**
3. They were sometimes **in the same classroom.**	4. They became **good friends.**

5. On a separate sheet of paper, compare and contrast one of your friendships now with what it was like at the beginning. How has it changed? How has it remained the same?
Students should include both comparisons and contrasts in their answers.

School + Home Home Activity Your child compared and contrasted before and after details from a short passage. Read a favorite story with your child. Identify an important event in the story and compare and contrast what happened before and after that event.

▲ **Practice Book** p. 58

Vocabulary and Word Study

VOCABULARY STRATEGY
🎯 Word Structure

PREFIXES Remind students that they can use prefixes to figure out the meanings of unfamiliar words. Introduce the prefixes in the chart. Challenge students to find the prefixes in the words listed below and tell what a new word means. Remind them to check the word meanings by looking them up in a dictionary.

Word	Prefix/Meaning	Meaning
repay	re- means "again or back"	pay back
preplan		
inconsiderate		

Words With Un- or Dis-

The prefixes un- and dis- can be added to many other base words. Remind students that un- and dis- mean "not" or "the opposite of." Challenge small groups to list five words with un- and dis-. Remind them to check a dictionary for accuracy. When finished, ask groups to compare their lists and discuss word meanings.

Un-	Dis-
1. unscrewed	1. disrespect
2.	2.
3.	3.
4.	4.
5.	5.

BUILD CONCEPT VOCABULARY
Kindness

LOOKING BACK Remind students of the question of the week: Why do people show kindness? Discuss how this week's Concept Web of vocabulary words relates to the theme of doing the right thing. Ask students if they have any words or categories to add. Discuss if words and categories are appropriately related to the concept.

MOVING FORWARD Preview the title of the next selection, *Passage to Freedom*. Ask students which Concept Web words might apply to the new selection based on the title alone.

Put a star next to these words on the web.

Display the Concept Web and revisit the vocabulary words as you read the next selection to check predictions.

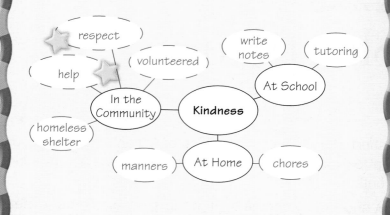

Monitor Progress
Check Vocabulary

If... students suggest words or categories that are not related to the concept,	then... review the words and categories on the Concept Web and discuss how they relate to the lesson concept.

SUCCESS PREDICTOR

Speaking and Listening

SPEAKING

Persuasive Speech

SET-UP Have students recall the act of kindness Francisco does at the end of "Inside Out." Tell students they will give speeches to persuade others to perform acts of kindness too.

PLANNING Offer these suggestions to students:

- Make a list of as many reasons to do acts of kindness as you can think of.
- Choose the best ideas to include in your speech.
- Give examples and results of acts of kindness.
- End with one statement that summarizes reasons why others should do acts of kindness.

ORGANIZATION Tell students they may want to open with an interesting question or example. Then they can include details and examples to support or reinforce their points. Have them conclude their speeches with their best persuasive reason for doing acts of kindness.

Delivery Tips
- Be comfortable with your material. Be sincere.
- Make eye contact with your audience.
- Speak in a loud, clear voice.
- Use persuasive language.

LISTENING

Listen to a Persuasive Speech

Have students listen to other students' persuasive speeches. They can answer these questions individually in writing.

1. **What is the speaker's point of view?**
2. **What details does the speaker include to support his or her ideas or opinions?**
3. **Do you agree or disagree with the speaker's point of view? Why or why not?**

Encourage students to listen for persuasive speeches on television or radio programs.

Support Vocabulary Use the following to review and extend vocabulary and to explore lesson concepts further:
- ELL Poster 6, Days 3–5 instruction
- Vocabulary Activities and Word Cards in ELL Teaching Guide, pp. 38–39

Assessment For information on assessing students' speaking and listening, see the ELL and Transition Handbook.

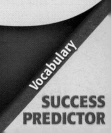

Vocabulary

SUCCESS PREDICTOR

Grammar — Regular and Irregular Plural Nouns

OBJECTIVES

- Define and identify regular and irregular plural nouns.
- Use regular and irregular plural nouns in writing.
- Become familiar with regular and irregular plural nouns on high-stakes tests.

Monitor Progress

Grammar

If... students have difficulty spelling plural nouns correctly,	then... provide additional instruction and practice in The Grammar and Writing Book pp. 80–83.

DAILY FIX-IT

This week use Daily Fix-It Transparency 6.

Spiral REVIEW

Support Grammar See the Grammar Transition lessons in the ELL and Transition Handbook.

▲ **The Grammar and Writing Book**
For more instruction and practice, use pp. 80–83.

DAY 1 — Teach and Model

DAILY FIX-IT

1. Students put their sack lunchs in a row on the tabel. *(lunches; table)*
2. Does the cafeteria serves hot food. *(serve; food?)*

READING-GRAMMAR CONNECTION

Write this sentence beginning from *Inside Out* on the board:

- *I knew caterpillars turned into butterflies. . . .*

Explain that *caterpillars* and *butterflies* are **plural nouns.** Most nouns form the plural by adding -s, but there are exceptions. The *y* in *butterfly* is changed to an *i*, and -*es* is added.

Display Grammar Transparency 6. Read aloud the definitions, rules, and examples. Work through the items.

Regular and Irregular Plural Nouns

Plural nouns name more than one person, place, or thing.
- Add -s to form the plural of most nouns.
  picture/pictures   wing/wings   pattern/patterns
- Add -es to nouns ending in ch, sh, x, z, s, and ss.
  bunch/bunches   wish/wishes   box/boxes   class/classes
- If a noun ends in a vowel and y, add -s.
  day/days   boy/boys
- If a noun ends in a consonant and y, change y to i and add -es.
  city/cities   lady/ladies
- Some nouns have **irregular plural** forms. They change spelling.
  man/men   mouse/mice   goose/geese   foot/feet   child/children
- For most nouns that end in f or fe, change f to v and add -es.
  leaf/leaves   knife/knives   calf/calves
- Some nouns have the same singular and plural forms.
  sheep   deer   moose   headquarters   series

Directions Write the plural form of each noun. Use a dictionary if you need help.

1. twig — **twigs**
2. team — **teams**
3. field — **fields**
4. Tuesday — **Tuesdays**
5. lunch — **lunches**
6. fox — **foxes**
7. woman — **women**
8. half — **halves**
9. cracker — **crackers**
10. goose — **geese**

Directions Write the plural forms of the underlined singular nouns.

11. Migrant worker pick many crop and work long hour.
   workers, crops, hours
12. They filled many box with orange, strawberry, and peach.
   boxes, oranges, strawberries, peaches
13. Sometimes they must trim leaf from plant with sharp knife.
   leaves, plants, knives
14. Migrant child miss class on day when they must help their parent at work.
   children, classes, days, parents
15. Other workers herd sheep and cow while riding horse.
   sheep, cows, horses

Unit 2 Inside Out   Grammar **6**

▲ **Grammar Transparency** 6

DAY 2 — Develop the Concept

DAILY FIX-IT

3. The children wor warm coats and scarfs. *(wore; scarves)*
4. That cold wind make me siver. *(makes; shiver)*

GUIDED PRACTICE

Review the concept of regular and irregular plural nouns.

- **Plural nouns** name more than one person, place, or thing.
- Most plural nouns are formed by adding -s. Nouns ending in *ch, sh, x, z, s,* and *ss* add -es to form the plural. For nouns ending in consonant -y, change the *y* to *i* and add -es.
- Nouns with **irregular plurals** change spelling or have the same singular and plural forms.

HOMEWORK Grammar and Writing Practice Book p. 21. Work through the first two items with the class.

Regular and Irregular Plural Nouns

Plural nouns name more than one person, place, or thing.
- Add -s to form the plural of most nouns.
  swing/swings   animal/animals
- Add -es to nouns ending in ch, sh, x, z, s, and ss.
  fox/foxes   bush/bushes   church/churches
- If a noun ends in a vowel and y, add -s.
  monkey/monkeys   toy/toys
- If a noun ends in a consonant and y, change y to i and add -es.
  blueberry/blueberries   pony/ponies   penny/pennies
- Some nouns have **irregular plural** forms. They change spelling.
  woman/women   tooth/teeth   ox/oxen
- For most nouns that end in f or fe, change f to v and add -es.
  wife/wives   wolf/wolves   thief/thieves
- Some nouns have the same singular and plural forms.
  salmon   trout   sheep

Directions Underline the plural nouns in each sentence.

1. Caterpillars eat leaves constantly.
2. This one looks beautiful with its bright yellow stripes.
3. Those leaves come from maples, cherries, and oaks.
4. It looks as though it has many feet.
5. Bristles stick up on its back like little brooms.

Directions Cross out each incorrectly spelled plural noun. Write the correct spelling above the word you crossed out.

6. Nature makes many intricate patterns in bright colors.
7. From the oceans to the skies, we find swirls, zig-zags, circles, and arches of color.
8. In autumn leaves turn vivid colors and stand like brushes full of paint against the sky.

Home Activity Your child learned about regular and irregular plural nouns. Take a walk and have your child identify people, places, animals, and things in groups. Ask him or her to spell these plural nouns correctly.

▲ **Grammar and Writing Practice Book** p. 21

DAY 3 — Apply to Writing

DAILY FIX-IT

5. A butterflys wings astonis me. *(butterfly's; astonish)*

6. The migrating insects travel thousands of mile to a suthern country. *(miles; southern)*

WRITE PLURALS CORRECTLY

Explain that specific nouns help build interesting descriptions. Plural nouns should be spelled correctly so that they do not distract from the picture painted with words.

- Have students review something they have written. They may be able to improve it by making sure plural nouns are spelled correctly.

HOMEWORK Grammar and Writing Practice Book p. 22.

Regular and Irregular Plural Nouns

Directions Write a sentence using the plural form of each noun. Possible answers:

1. woman **Women need to exercise their bodies as well as their minds.**

2. foot **My feet flew over the ground during the race.**

3. monkey **In the wild, monkeys play and learn much like humans.**

4. deer **We saw several deer run across the playground.**

5. leaf **They left no tracks on the carpet of leaves.**

Directions Write the paragraph on the lines. Write the plural form of each noun in ( ). Add a word of your own to describe each plural noun. Write your own ending sentence for the paragraph.

Our scout troop collected ___ (coat) and (glove) for ___ (child). We made ___ (poster) and knocked on ___ (door). Many people gave ___ (donation). Sometimes ___ (family) searched their ___ (closet) to help us. We took ___ (bunch) of winter wear to the Salvation Army.

Possible answer: Our scout troop collected winter coats and warm gloves for needy children. We made colorful posters and knocked on countless doors. Many people gave generous donations. Sometimes entire families searched their jam-packed closets to help us. We took impressive bunches of winter wear to the Salvation Army. We were proud of ourselves and our neighbors for making life better for others.

 Home Activity Your child learned how to use plural nouns in writing. Have your child point out plural nouns on packages and labels and explain the rule for forming each plural.

▲ **Grammar and Writing Practice Book** p. 22

DAY 4 — Test Preparation

DAILY FIX-IT

7. The story is a chater from a longer book about a migrant family. *(chapter; migrant)*

8. Francisco have trouble at school because him does not speak English. *(has; he does)*

STANDARDIZED TEST PREP

Test Tip

Do not confuse plural nouns with possessive nouns or singular forms of verbs. Possessives have an apostrophe and show ownership.

Plural: She packed two dresses.

Possessive: The dress's buttons are white.

Singular verb form: He dresses well.

HOMEWORK Grammar and Writing Practice Book p. 23.

Regular and Irregular Plural Nouns

Directions Mark the letter of the word that correctly completes each sentence.

1. Dad found caterpillars eating his beloved rose ___
   A bushs
   B bush's
   C bushes
   D bushies

2. Put two caterpillars in a jar with some ___
   A leafs
   B leaves
   C leafes
   D leavs

3. I punched many ___ in the lid of the jar.
   A holes
   B hols
   C hole
   D holez

4. The caterpillars were soft as ___
   A bunnys
   B bunnyes
   C bunnies
   D bunny

5. I had to gather ___ of grass and leafy twigs.
   A bunches
   B bunnies
   C bunchen
   D bunchs

6. One morning I was sure ___ had stolen them.
   A thief
   B thiefs
   C thiefes
   D thieves

7. Then I saw cottony ___ attached to twigs.
   A capsules
   B capsulies
   C capsuls
   D capsulen

8. They had sewn their ___ into cushions called pupas.
   A body
   B bodys
   C bodeys
   D bodies

9. Soon they would be winged ___
   A creature
   B creatures
   C creatuares
   D creaturies

10. Their wings would have brilliant ___ of color.
   A patchs
   B patchies
   C patches
   D patch

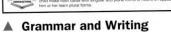 **Home Activity** Your child prepared for taking tests on regular and irregular plural nouns. Have your child make flash cards with singular and plural forms of nouns on opposite sides. Use the cards to help him or her learn plural forms.

▲ **Grammar and Writing Practice Book** p. 23

DAY 5 — Cumulative Review

DAILY FIX-IT

9. Did the girls wipe there feets? *(their feet)*

10. Curtis and adam plays football at recess. *(Adam; play)*

ADDITIONAL PRACTICE

Assign pp. 80–83 in The Grammar and Writing Book.

EXTRA PRACTICE Grammar and Writing Practice Book p. 127.

TEST PREPARATION Grammar and Writing Practice Book pp. 153–154.

ASSESSMENT

CUMULATIVE REVIEW Grammar and Writing Practice Book p. 24.

Regular and Irregular Plural Nouns

Directions Write the plural forms of the underlined singular nouns.

1. Are you good at drawing picture or painting scene?
   pictures, scenes

2. Latoya loves art and has taken many art class.
   classes

3. An artist must consider the line, space, color, and texture of a painting.
   lines, spaces, colors, textures

4. A portrait artist paints pictures of lady and gentleman.
   ladies, gentlemen

Directions Cross out each incorrectly spelled plural noun. Write the correct spelling above the word you crossed out.

5. These ~~kindes~~ **kinds** of ~~paintings~~ **paintings** are called still life.

6. I will draw a picture of this bowl of ~~peachs, pears~~ **peaches pears**, and bananas.

7. Unfortunately, they only look like ~~circles, ovals~~ **circles crescents**, and ~~crescentes~~.

8. Janelle draws ~~horse, sheeps,~~ **horses sheep pigs** and ~~pigss~~ well.

Directions Write each sentence. Write the plural forms of the nouns in ( ). Add your own describing word for each plural noun.

9. Some artists make ___ (craft) such as ___ (quilt) and ___ (pot).
   Some artists make useful crafts such as patchwork quilts and glazed pots.

10. ___ (dish) and ___ (tablecloth) can be ___ (work) of art.
   Hand-painted dishes and embroidered tablecloths can be original works of art.

 **Home Activity** Your child reviewed regular and irregular plural nouns. Ask your child to list things you have in your kitchen and write the plural form for each noun.

▲ **Grammar and Writing Practice Book** p. 24

Writing Workshop Summary

OBJECTIVES

- Identify qualities of a summary.
- Understand how to eliminate wordiness from writing.
- Focus on focus/ideas.
- Use a rubric.

Genre Summary
Writer's Craft Eliminate Wordiness
Writing Trait Focus/Ideas

ELL

Focus/Ideas Talk with English learners about what they plan to write. Record ideas and help them generate language for support. Help them tighten their focus by eliminating unrelated details. See more writing support in the ELL and Transition Handbook.

Writing Traits

FOCUS/IDEAS Summary includes all the main events in the plot of the story.

ORGANIZATION/PARAGRAPHS Events in the plot are mentioned in order. Transitions connect events.

VOICE Writer is objective but clearly engaged in summarizing the story.

WORD CHOICE Writer uses precise words to capture main ideas about story. *(They fight and both boys are punished.)* No irrelevant or unnecessary words are used.

SENTENCES Use of an appositive and compound and complex sentences adds variety and interest.

CONVENTIONS There is excellent control and accuracy, including the spelling of plural nouns.

DAY 1 Model the Trait

READING-WRITING CONNECTION

- "Inside Out" describes the struggles at school of a boy who does not speak English.
- The story focuses on his adjustment and a conflict with a bully.
- Students will write a **summary of a story** focusing on main ideas and eliminating unneeded words.

MODEL VOICE Discuss Writing Transparency 6A. Then discuss the model and the writing trait of focus/ideas.

 Think Aloud The writer gives a brief description of story events in his own words. Paragraph 2 summarizes two pages of the story: The principal gives Francisco a coat. Curtis attacks Francisco for stealing it. Francisco feels terrible. These details focus on the most important actions and feelings.

Summary

A summary highlights the main ideas from an article or a story. Because a summary is brief, it does not include minor details, repeated words or thoughts, or unimportant ideas. Write a summary in your own words, but do not include your opinions.

Story Summary: Inside Out

First sentence tells story title, author, and main idea.

In "Inside Out," Francisco Jiménez shows what life at school is like for a boy who does not speak English. Francisco has only one friend, Arthur, a classmate who speaks some Spanish. Francisco does not understand what his teacher and other students are saying, but he loves watching the caterpillar in a jar by his desk. He also loves art class, when he draws pictures of birds and butterflies.

Important ideas are in writer's own words.

When the principal sees Francisco shivering, he gives the boy a coat from the lost and found. A popular boy named Curtis angrily attacks Francisco because he thinks Francisco has stolen his coat. They fight and both boys are punished. Francisco feels humiliated and ashamed.

One page of action is summarized in a few sentences.

Observing the caterpillar helps make life more bearable for Francisco. He watches it turn into a pupa. Near the end of the school year, Francisco wins a blue ribbon for one of his drawings. That same day, the butterfly emerges from its cocoon. Francisco sees that Curtis really likes the drawing and gives it to him as a gesture of friendship.

Unit 2 Inside Out   Writing Model **6A**

▲ **Writing Transparency** 6A

DAY 2 Improve Writing

WRITER'S CRAFT
Eliminate Wordiness

Display Writing Transparency 6B. Read the directions and work together to correct wordy statements and state ideas succinctly.

 Think Aloud **STATE IMPORTANT IDEAS BRIEFLY** Tomorrow, we will write a **story summary**. I could summarize the *Island of the Blue Dolphins*. How can I paraphrase the story beginning? I might write, "Alone on the island, Karana first searched for the best place to build a shelter, near water and food and safe from wild dogs." Including details about the wild dogs or island features would make the summary too wordy.

GUIDED WRITING Some students may need more help with eliminating wordiness. Provide example sentences with two endings. Have students choose the more precise, succinct ending.

Eliminate Wordiness

Express your ideas clearly and directly. To **eliminate wordiness**, delete words that repeat or are unnecessary. Replace wordy phrases with specific words.
Wordy   He was often late and not on time.
Improved   He was often late.
Wordy   He wore a coat that had many different kinds of colors.
Improved   He wore a colorful coat.

Directions Read each sentence. Cross out words that repeat or are unnecessary.
1. Fighting ~~or otherwise engaging in physical conflict~~ on the playground is forbidden.
2. All people disagree at times, ~~and those times can occur at any hour~~.
3. Frequently a miscommunication ~~or failure to communicate~~ causes the conflict.
4. We need to learn to resolve our differences ~~and mend our fences~~ with words rather than fists.

Directions Each underlined part is wordy. Think of a shorter, clearer way to say this part. Rewrite the sentence on the line. **Possible answers:**
5. How do you create a friendly, warm relationship with someone you previously did not know?
   How do you make friends with someone new?
6. A friendly smile and a wave of the hand or a "Hi. How are you?" are a good beginning.
   A friendly smile and greeting are a good beginning.
7. Show an interest in the person by throwing out ideas in the form of queries.
   Show an interest in the person by asking questions.
8. Then really listen—give the person the benefit of every ounce of concentrated brain power as he or she answers. Then really listen—give the person your full attention as he or she answers.
9. To keep a friend, be considerate and refrain from any actions that may be seen as disloyal.
   To keep a friend, be considerate and loyal.
10. In happy times or times that are the exact opposite of happy, you can always count on a good friend. In happy times or sad times, you can always count on a good friend.

Unit 2 Inside Out   Writer's Craft **6B**

▲ **Writing Transparency** 6B

DAY 3 Prewrite and Draft

READ THE WRITING PROMPT

on page 159 in the Student Edition.

"Inside Out" is a story that describes life at school for a boy who does not speak English.

Think about a story you have read recently.

Now write a summary of that story.

Writing Test Tips

- Write the author's purpose for writing, or the point you think he or she was trying to make.
- Look over the story again. Write a sentence summarizing each new event that happens.
- Look over your notes and delete any unimportant details or unnecessary words.

GETTING STARTED Students can do any of the following:

- Order story events in a graphic organizer such as a sequence chart.
- Consider the main character's experiences and changes. Jot down what they think these things illustrate.
- Brainstorm transition words that show how one event leads to another.

DAY 4 Draft and Revise

EDITING/REVISING CHECKLIST

- ☑ Are there any unnecessary or repeated words I should eliminate?
- ☑ Have I used the correct plural forms of nouns?
- ☑ Have I spelled words with the digraphs *th, sh, ch,* and *ph* correctly?

See *The Grammar and Writing Book,* pp. 80–85.

Revising Tips

Focus/Ideas

- Eliminate any information that is not important or includes minor details.
- Write broad statements that show the overall meaning of what happened in an event.
- Use connecting words and combine sentences where possible to make the summary flow smoothly.

PUBLISHING Students can compile their work in a class book of story summaries for reference. Some students may wish to revise their work later.

ASSESSMENT Use the scoring rubric to evaluate students' work.

DAY 5 Connect to Unit Writing

How-to Report	
Week 1	Summary 161g–161h
Week 2	Story Review 185g–185h
Week 3	News Story 207g–207h
Week 4	Rules 229g–229h
Week 5	Interview 253g–253h

PREVIEW THE UNIT PROMPT

Write a report explaining how to make or do something that is familiar to you. Choose words that make your report interesting to read and easy to understand. Explain all the steps and materials needed.

APPLY

- A how-to report explains the steps for making or doing something.
- A how-to report should not include any unnecessary words or details.

Writing Trait Rubric

	4	3	2	1
Focus/Ideas	Excellent focus with many vivid supporting details; no unnecessary details	Clear focus with some supporting details; no unnecessary details	Limited focus with a few supporting details; some unrelated details	Unfocused with little support and many unrelated details
	Excellent summary with interesting, well-supported main idea	Good summary with adequately supported main idea	Sharper focus on main idea needed in summary	Summary with no clear focus or main idea

Spelling & Phonics Digraphs *th, sh, ch, ph*

OBJECTIVE

- Spell words with consonant digraphs *th, sh, ch, ph.*

Generalization

Connect to Phonics Words can have two consonants together that are pronounced as one sound: *southern, shovel, chapter, hyphen.* Consonant digraphs are two consonants together that stand for one new sound.

Spelling Words

1. shovel	11. astonish
2. southern	12. python
3. northern	13. shatter
4. chapter	14. ethnic
5. hyphen	15. shiver*
6. chosen*	16. pharmacy
7. establish	17. charity
8. although	18. china
9. challenge	19. attach
10. approach	20. ostrich

Challenge Words

21. emphasis	24. phenomenal
22. sophomore	25. chimpanzee
23. athlete	

* Words from the selection

ELL

Spelling/Phonics Support See the ELL and Transition Handbook for spelling support.

DAY 1 Pretest and Sort

PRETEST

Use the Dictation Sentences from Day 5 to administer the pretest. Read the word, read the sentence, and then read the word again. Guide students in self-correcting their pretests and correcting any misspellings.

Monitor Progress

Spelling

If...	then...
If... students misspell more than 5 pretest words,	**then...** use words 1–10 for Strategic Intervention.
If... students misspell 1–5 pretest words,	**then...** use words 1–20 for On-Level practice.
If... students correctly spell all pretest words,	**then...** use words 1–25 for Advanced Learners.

HOMEWORK Spelling Practice Book, p. 21.

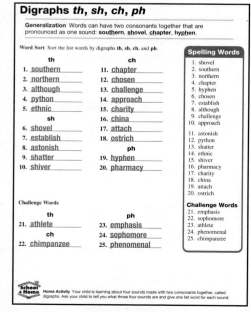

▲ **Spelling Practice Book** p. 21

DAY 2 Think and Practice

TEACH

Consonant digraphs consist of two letters that stand for one sound. Write *pharmacy* on the board. Underline *ph.* Explain that the letters *ph* stand for one sound, /f/. Write *python, shiver,* and *chosen.* Underline and pronounce the consonant digraphs.

> *pharmacy*

MISSING LETTERS Have students copy the list words, replacing the consonant digraphs with two blank lines. Tell them to trade lists with another student and fill in the missing letters.

HOMEWORK Spelling Practice Book, p. 22.

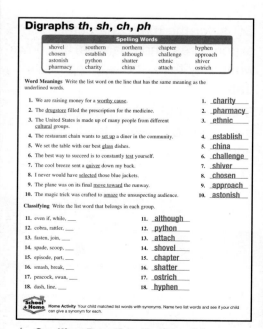

▲ **Spelling Practice Book** p. 22

DAY 3 — Connect to Writing

WRITE FACTS

Ask students to use at least four spelling words to write a paragraph that tells important facts about something they learned on their own or in another class.

Frequently Misspelled Words

which   they

thought

These words may seem easy to spell, but they are often misspelled by fifth-graders. Alert students to these frequently misspelled words. Point out the digraphs. Discuss the unusual spellings of the vowel sounds in *they* and *thought*.

HOMEWORK Spelling Practice Book, p. 23.

Digraphs *th, sh, ch, ph*

Proofread a Poster Circle five spelling errors. Find one sentence with a punctuation error. Write the corrections on the lines.

Come to the charaty auction for the new recreation center.

Help dig the building site. Buy a chance to shovle some earth.

Bid and buy, wonderful prizes from around the world!

Challange yourself in contests and games.

Bid on lovely china figures and platters.

Sample delicious northurn and southern cooking!

Time: Saturday, from 9 A.M. to 6 P.M.

Place: The old pharmecy building

Spelling Words
shovel
southern
northern
chapter
hyphen
chosen
establish
although
challenge
approach
astonish
python
shatter
ethnic
shiver
pharmacy
charity
china
attach
ostrich

1. charity   2. shovel
3. Challenge   4. northern
5. pharmacy
6. Bid and buy wonderful prizes from around the world!

Proofread Words Circle the correct spelling of the word.

7. The ending of the book will ____ you.
   astonish   astonesh   astonash
8. I need a stapler to ____ the poster to the bulletin board.
   attach   attach   atach
9. Music is my ____ field of study.
   chosen   chozen   choicen
10. I want to read a ____ a day.
    chaptar   shapter   chapter
11. Numbers, such as sixty-five, are written with a ____.
    hiphen   hyphen   hipfen
12. The ____ in the zoo was 12 feet long.
    pythn   python   pithon

Frequently Misspelled Words
which
they
thought

Home Activity Your child identified misspelled list words. Select words with two different digraph sounds and ask your child to spell them.

▲ **Spelling Practice Book** p. 23

DAY 4 — Review

REVIEW DIGRAPHS *th, sh, ch, ph*

Have students use at least ten list words to make a word search puzzle. Use graph paper if available. Have students solve each other's puzzles.

Spelling Strategy
Problem Parts

We all have words that are hard for us to spell.

Step 1: Ask yourself: Which part of the word gives me a problem?

Step 2: Underline the problem part.

Step 3: Picture the word. Focus on the problem part.

HOMEWORK Spelling Practice Book, p. 24.

Digraphs *th, sh, ch, ph*

Spelling Words				
shovel	southern	northern	chapter	hyphen
chosen	establish	although	challenge	approach
astonish	python	shatter	ethnic	shiver
pharmacy	charity	china	attach	ostrich

Word Search Circle the ten list words below that are hidden in the puzzle. They are across, down, and diagonal. Write the words.

although	chosen	pharmacy	challenge	hyphen
attach	ethnic	approach	establish	southern

1. establish
2. pharmacy
3. attach
4. hyphen
5. chosen
6. southern
7. approach
8. ethnic
9. challenge
10. although

Words in Context Finish the story with list words.

The money we raised at the (11) ____ auction will (12) ____ you. We were able to (13) ____ last year's record amount of $585.00. People bid on items such as an (14) ____ egg and a book about snakes with a (15) ____ on the cover. One (16) ____ cup fetched $25.00! An antique (17) ____ brought in $20.00. Auctions are exciting. Each time the gavel sounded, a (18) ____ of joy went down my spine.

11. charity
12. astonish
13. shatter
14. ostrich
15. python
16. china
17. shovel
18. shiver

Home Activity Your child has learned to read, write, and spell combined consonants, called digraphs. Have your child underline the digraphs in each word and then say the word.

▲ **Spelling Practice Book** p. 24

DAY 5 — Posttest

DICTATION SENTENCES

1. Tom dug a hole with the <u>shovel</u>.
2. The <u>southern</u> states have a warmer climate.
3. Maine is a <u>northern</u> state.
4. Read the book's first <u>chapter</u>.
5. Use a <u>hyphen</u> to divide the word.
6. Al was <u>chosen</u> for our team.
7. Let's <u>establish</u> a plan for getting the work done.
8. <u>Although</u> it was cold, we had fun.
9. I <u>challenge</u> you to a race.
10. Never <u>approach</u> a wild animal.
11. Did the surprise <u>astonish</u> you?
12. A <u>python</u> crawled down the trail.
13. The glass will <u>shatter</u> if you drop it.
14. Each <u>ethnic</u> group has special customs.
15. The icy rain made us <u>shiver</u>.
16. The doctor sent us to the <u>pharmacy</u>.
17. A <u>charity</u> helps people in need.
18. Some dishes are made of fine <u>china</u>.
19. Can you <u>attach</u> the nametag with a pin?
20. An <u>ostrich</u> is a bird that cannot fly.

CHALLENGE

21. Our <u>emphasis</u> is on safety.
22. My brother is a <u>sophomore</u> in high school.
23. Phyllis is a talented <u>athlete</u>.
24. The outfielder made a <u>phenomenal</u> catch.
25. A <u>chimpanzee</u> swung through the trees.

OBJECTIVES

- Formulate an inquiry question that is connected to this week's lesson focus.
- Effectively and efficiently find, evaluate, and communicate information related to an inquiry question using electronic sources.

New Literacies	
Day 1	**Identify Questions**
Day 2	**Navigate/Search**
Day 3	**Analyze**
Day 4	**Synthesize**
Day 5	**Communicate**

NEW LITERACIES
Internet Inquiry Activity
EXPLORE KINDNESS

Use the following 5-day plan to help students conduct this week's Internet inquiry activity on kindness. Remind students to follow classroom rules when using the Internet.

DAY 1

Identify Questions Discuss the lesson focus question: *Why do people show kindness?* Brainstorm ideas for specific inquiry questions about acts of kindness. For example, students might enjoy reading about charities or volunteering to help people in need. Have students work individually, in pairs, or in small groups to write inquiry questions they want to answer.

DAY 2

Navigate/Search Explain that a search engine is like an electronic index for all the subjects covered on the Internet. When using a search engine, just as when you use an index, use keywords related to the topic to find information. Invite students to use keywords like *charities* or *volunteering* in a student-friendly search engine to find Web sites containing information they need to answer their inquiry questions.

DAY 3

Analyze Have students skim and scan the Web sites they identified on Day 2 to look specifically for Web sites that would be relevant for students their age in their community. They can do this by reading the brief summaries, finding the publisher and how recently the site was updated. Encourage students to take notes from the best sites or, if appropriate, print out and highlight relevant information.

DAY 4

Synthesize Have students synthesize information by combining relevant ideas from the sites they found to develop answers to their inquiry questions. Suggest that they document their sources by recording information on the writer, publisher, and copyright date of each site.

DAY 5

Communicate Have students share their inquiry results. They can use a word processing program to create numbered lists of ways they can be kind and help people in their community.

RESEARCH/STUDY SKILLS
Reference Book

TEACH

Ask students what they could do if they couldn't remember whether they should use *lay* or *lie* in a sentence, or if they weren't sure whether a noun should be singular or plural. Students will probably mention grammar textbooks and may need prompting to mention handbooks or manuals. Show a grammar manual to students and explain these terms:

- A **manual** and a **handbook** are reference books that are meant to be kept "at hand," and convenient to carry around. Both contain instructions on how to do something.

- A **grammar reference book** is a type of manual. It provides grammar instructions and rules for writing that can be looked up easily.

- A grammar manual is usually divided into **sections** or **chapters** according to the grammar skill.

Have students work in pairs, and give each pair a grammar manual. Then, discuss these questions:

1. **Identify the parts contained in the grammar manual.** *(Possible response: table of contents; chapters on nouns, pronouns, verbs, adverbs, and adjectives; index)*

2. **If you wanted to find out if you should use the pronoun *I* or *me*, where would you look?** *(Possible response: chapter on pronouns.)*

Verbs

Mistaken Verbs	Meanings
leave	go away
let	allow
raise	lift
rise	get up
sit	to be seated
set	to place something

Grammar Handbook for Students

ASSESS

As students work with the grammar reference book, check to see if they use the table of contents, the index, and chapter heads to locate information.

For more practice or to assess students, use Practice Book pp. 59–60.

OBJECTIVES

- Review the terms *manual, handbook,* and *reference.*
- Use a grammar reference book or manual to look up grammar rules.

Reference Book

A **reference book** is a type of **manual.** Manuals usually contain instructions, either for immediate use or for reference. A grammar reference book is a manual for using language. Like other manuals, it usually has a table of contents, an index, sections, illustrations, and explanations. Be sure to consult a grammar reference book whenever you have questions about grammar.

Directions Use the following selection from a grammar book to answer the questions below.

> **The Apostrophe**
> Use an apostrophe
> 1. to show possession
> *John's dad collects bottle caps.*
> 2. with *s* to show the plural of letters
> *b's   j's   t's*
> 3. to show the omissions of a letter, letters, or numbers
> *We'll   class of '05   won't*
> Study the following contractions and notice the letter or letters that have been omitted to form the contraction.
> *they're — they are   she'll — she will*
> *we've — we have   let's — let us*
> *o'clock — of the clock   aren't — are not*

1. How many ways is an apostrophe used?
   <u>Apostrophes can be used in three different ways.</u>
2. Which of the ways the apostrophe is used would apply if you were describing ownership of something?
   <u>The apostrophe in that case shows possession.</u>
3. How would you use an apostrophe to contract the words "must" and "not"?
   <u>mustn't</u>
4. What numbers are omitted in the recent class of '05?
   <u>20</u>
5. Insert apostrophes where needed in the following sentence: *Ill take my moms casserole over to the neighbors house at 6 oclock.*
   <u>I'll take my mom's casserole over to the neighbor's house at</u>
   <u>6 o'clock.</u>

▲ **Practice Book** p. 59

Directions Use the following table of contents from a grammar book to answer the questions below.

Possible answers given for 7, 8, 10.
6. Which chapter would you look in for usage question about the word *theirs*?
   <u>Chapter 3</u>
7. Why do you think grammar books are organized by individual parts of speech?
   <u>Organizing them by individual parts of speech helps make them</u>
   <u>easier to use and makes the content easier to absorb.</u>
8. What kind of words might you find in the section on "Personal Pronouns"?
   <u>I, me, mine, you, yours</u>
9. If you were having trouble writing a word that showed ownership, in which section of the grammar book would you look?
   <u>Possessive Form of Nouns</u>
10. Why might the short essays at the end of each chapter be included in a grammar book?
    <u>The essays may provide helpful tips on how to use particular</u>
    <u>parts of the language.</u>

Home Activity Your child answered questions about grammar reference books and manuals. With your child, find a manual to an item in your house (computer, refrigerator, television, phone, etc.) and read through the table of contents to see how it is organized. Does it make sense? Could you easily find an answer to a question or a problem by using the manual?

▲ **Practice Book** p. 60

Assessment Checkpoints *for the Week*

Selection Assessment

Use pp. 21–24 of Selection Tests to check:

 Selection Understanding

 Comprehension Skill
Compare and Contrast

 Selection Vocabulary

caterpillar	migrant
cocoon	sketched
disrespect	unscrewed
emerge	

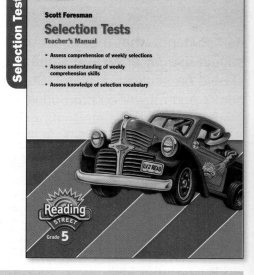

Selection Tests

ASSESSMENT

Scott Foresman
Selection Tests
Teacher's Manual

• Assess comprehension of weekly selections
• Assess understanding of weekly comprehension skills
• Assess knowledge of selection vocabulary

Reading STREET
Grade 5

Leveled Assessment

On-Level

Strategic Intervention

Advanced

Use pp. 31–36 of Fresh Reads for Differentiated Test Practice to check:

 Comprehension Skill
Compare and Contrast

 REVIEW Comprehension Skill
Author's Purpose

 Fluency *Words Correct Per Minute*

ASSESSMENT   Teacher's Manual

Scott Foresman
Fresh Reads
for Differentiated Test Practice

Leveled passages—strategic intervention, on-level, and advanced—for
• Fluency checks
• Practice and application of weekly comprehension skills
• Answer key for all practice pages

Fresh Reads for Differentiated Test Practice

Reading STREET
Grade 5

Managing Assessment

Use Assessment Handbook for:

 Observation Checklists

 Record-Keeping Forms

 Portfolio Assessment

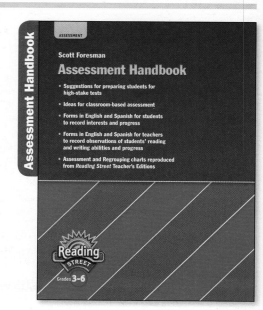

Assessment Handbook

ASSESSMENT

Scott Foresman
Assessment Handbook

• Suggestions for preparing students for high-stake tests
• Ideas for classroom-based assessment
• Forms in English and Spanish for students to record interests and progress
• Forms in English and Spanish for teachers to record observations of students' reading and writing abilities and progress
• Assessment and Regrouping charts reproduced from *Reading Street* Teacher's Editions

Reading STREET
Grades 3-6

Unit 2
Doing the Right Thing

CONCEPT QUESTION
What makes people want to do the right thing?

Week 1

Why do people show kindness?

Week 2

Why do we help others even if there are risks?

Week 3

What are the rewards in helping others?

Week 4

What can people do to protect wild animals?

Week 5

How can people promote freedom?

EXPAND THE CONCEPT
Why do we help others even if there are risks?

CONNECT THE CONCEPT

▶ **Build Background**

hiding, officers, poses

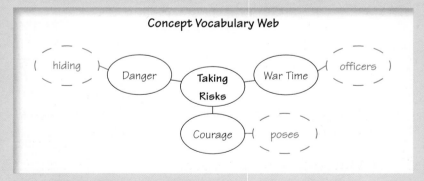

Concept Vocabulary Web

▶ **Social Studies Content**
World War II
Diplomacy

▶ **Writing**
Story Review

▶ **Internet Inquiry**
Taking Risks

Preview Your Week

Why do we help others even if there are risks?

PASSAGE TO FREEDOM
The Sugihara Story

by Ken Mochizuki   illustrated by Dom Lee
Afterword by Hiroki Sugihara

What makes Mr. Sugihara decide to help the refugees?

Genre A **biography** is the true story of a person's life, written by someone else. As you read, notice how Mr. Sugihara's life changes.

166

Student Edition pages 166–177

Audio CD

Genre	Biography
Vocabulary Strategy	Dictionary/Glossary
Comprehension Skill	Author's Purpose
Comprehension Strategy	Monitor and Fix Up

Paired Selection

Reading Across Texts
Compare How People Feel About Helping Others

Genre
Autobiography

Text Features
First-Person Point of View
Order of Events

Social Studies in Reading

Autobiography

Genre
- An autobiography is the story of a person's life, or a single incident in it, told by that person.
- An autobiography tells about real places, people, and events in the author's life and how the author feels about them.

Text Features
- An autobiography is written from the first-person point of view, so the narrator refers to herself as *I*.
- Events in an autobiography are usually presented in chronological order.
- Scan the first few words of the paragraphs. Some begin with a phrase such as "by now" to show that time is passing.

Link to Social Studies
Read other autobiographies of people who lived in Europe during World War II. How were their experiences like Deborah Biron's? How were they different?

I Wanted my Mother
BY DEBORA BIRON

During World War II, Debora Biron lived in Lithuania. Her family was Jewish, and the invading Germans were killing Jews. So Debora, about seven at this time, and her mother went to live with the Karashkas, a non-Jewish family who hid them on their farm. Natasha, a friend of the Karashkas, also helped. They also hid Herman, a friend of Debora's mother. Then one day the Germans began closing in.

By now the Germans were everywhere. It got so dangerous, we could no longer live upstairs and instead moved into the cellar under the kitchen. But Herman thought that wasn't safe either and decided we should build a bunker next to the cellar, where the Germans were less likely to look. He and Mr. Karashka designed the room.

It was seven feet long and very narrow. To get in and out, they made a trap door that opened into the hallway. It had wooden planks on top that matched the flooring. Underneath it was insulated with blankets and cotton so it wouldn't sound hollow when someone walked on it.

Author's Purpose Is the author trying to inform you or entertain you?

180

Student Edition pages 180–185

Audio CD

Read It
ONLINE
PearsonSuccessNet.com
- Student Edition
- Leveled Readers

Leveled Readers

○ **Skill** Author's Purpose
○ **Strategy** Monitor and Fix Up
Lesson Vocabulary

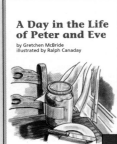

Below-Level

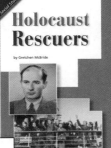

On-Level

Advanced

ELL Reader
- Concept Vocabulary
- Text Support
- Language Enrichment

Time for SOCIAL STUDIES

Integrate Social Studies Standards
- World War II
- Holocaust
- Government
- Culture

✓ Read

Passage to Freedom, pp. 166–177

"I Wanted My Mother," pp. 180–185

Leveled Readers

Below-Level   **On-Level**   **Advanced**
- Support Concepts   • Develop Concepts   • Extend Concepts
- Social Studies Extension Activity

ELL Reader

✓ Build Concept Vocabulary
Taking Risks, pp. 162l–162m

✓ Teach Social Studies Concepts
World War II, pp. 169, 181
Diplomacy, p. 175

✓ Explore Social Studies Center
Map Distances, p. 162k

Weekly Plan

READING

45–90 minutes

TARGET SKILLS OF THE WEEK

- **Comprehension Skill**
  Author's Purpose
- **Comprehension Strategy**
  Monitor and Fix Up
- **Vocabulary Strategy**
  Dictionary/Glossary

LANGUAGE ARTS

30–60 minutes

Trait of the Week

Focus/Ideas

DAY 1
PAGES 162l–164b, 185a, 185e–185k

Oral Language

QUESTION OF THE WEEK *Why do we help others even if there are risks?*

Read Aloud: "Number the Stars," 162m
Build Concepts, 162l

Comprehension/Vocabulary

Comprehension Skill/Strategy Lesson, 162–163
  - Author's Purpose **T**
  - Monitor and Fix Up

Build Background, 164a

Introduce Lesson Vocabulary, 164b
agreement, cable, diplomat, issue, refugees, representatives, superiors, visa **T**

Read Leveled Readers

Grouping Options 162f–162g

Fluency

Model Tone of Voice, 162l–162m, 185a

Grammar, 185e
Introduce Possessive Nouns **T**

Writing Workshop, 185g
Introduce Story Review
Model the Trait of the Week: Focus/Ideas

Spelling, 185i
Pretest for Irregular Plurals

Internet Inquiry, 185k
Identify Questions

DAY 2
PAGES 164–173, 185a, 185e–185k

Oral Language

QUESTION OF THE DAY *Why did Mr. Sugihara ask the family members what he should do?*

Comprehension/Vocabulary

Vocabulary Strategy Lesson, 164–165
  - Dictionary/Glossary **T**

Read *Passage to Freedom,* 166–173

Grouping Options
162f–162g

  - Author's Purpose **T**
  - Dictionary/Glossary **T**
  - **REVIEW** Sequence **T**
  Develop Vocabulary

Fluency

Choral Reading, 185a

Grammar, 185e
Develop Possessive Nouns **T**

Writing Workshop, 185g
Improve Writing with Support Your Ideas

Spelling, 185i
Teach the Generalization

Internet Inquiry, 185k
Navigate/Search

DAILY WRITING ACTIVITIES

Day 1 Write to Read, 162

Day 2 Words to Write, 165
Strategy Response Log, 166, 173

DAILY SOCIAL STUDIES CONNECTIONS

Day 1 Taking Risks Concept Web, 162l

Day 2 Time for Social Studies: World War II, 169
Revisit the Taking Risks Concept Web, 173

DAILY SUCCESS PREDICTORS
for Adequate Yearly Progress

Monitor Progress and Corrective Feedback

Vocabulary Check Vocabulary, *162l*

RESOURCES FOR THE WEEK

- Practice Book, *pp. 61–70*
- Word Study and Spelling Practice Book, *pp. 25–28*
- Grammar and Writing Practice Book, *pp. 25–28*
- Selection Test, *pp. 25–28*
- Fresh Reads for Differentiated Test Practice, *pp. 37–42*
- The Grammar and Writing Book, *pp. 86–91*

Grouping Options for Differentiated Instruction

Turn the page for the small group lesson plan.

DAY 3
PAGES 174–179, 185a, 185e–185k

Oral Language

QUESTION OF THE DAY *Why was Mr. Sugihara's help to the refugees so important?*

Comprehension/Vocabulary

Read *Passage to Freedom, 174–178*

Grouping Options 162f–162g

🎯 Author's Purpose **T**

🎯 Monitor and Fix Up

Develop Vocabulary

Reader Response

Selection Test

Fluency

Model Tone of Voice, 185a

Grammar, 185f
Apply Possessive Nouns in Writing **T**

Writing Workshop, 179, 185h
Write Now
Prewrite and Draft

Spelling, 185j
Connect Spelling to Writing

Internet Inquiry, 185k
Analyze Sources

Day 3 Strategy Response Log, 176
Look Back and Write, 178

Day 3 Time for Social Studies: Diplomacy, 175
Revisit the Taking Risks Concept Web, 177

DAY 4
PAGES 180–185a, 185e–185k

Oral Language

QUESTION OF THE DAY *For what possible reasons might someone risk death or bodily injury to help another person?*

Comprehension/Vocabulary

Read "I Wanted My Mother," 180–185

Grouping Options 162f–162g

Autobiography/Text Features

Reading Across Texts

Content-Area Vocabulary

Fluency

Partner Reading, 185a

Grammar, 185f
Practice Possessive Nouns for Standardized Tests **T**

Writing Workshop, 185h
Draft, Revise, and Publish

Spelling, 185j
Provide a Strategy

Internet Inquiry, 185k
Synthesize Information

Day 4 Writing Across Texts, 185

Day 4 Time for Social Studies: World War II, 181

DAY 5
PAGES 185a–185l

Oral Language

QUESTION OF THE WEEK *To wrap up the week, revisit the Day 1 question.*
Build Concept Vocabulary, 185c

Fluency

Read Leveled Readers

Grouping Options 162f–162g

Assess Reading Rate, 185a

Comprehension/Vocabulary

🎯 Reteach Author's Purpose, 185b **T**
Point of View, 185b
🎯 Review Dictionary/Glossary, 185c **T**

Speaking and Listening, 185d
Oral Report/Oral Book Reports
Listen to Audio CD

Grammar, 185f
Cumulative Review

Writing Workshop, 185h
Connect to Unit Writing

Spelling, 185j
Posttest for Irregular Plurals

Internet Inquiry, 185k
Communicate Results

Research/Study Skills, 185l
Parts of a Book

Day 5 Point of View, 185b

Day 5 Revisit the Taking Risks Concept Web, 185c

KEY 🎯 = Target Skill **T** = Tested Skill

Comprehension — Check Retelling, *178*

Fluency — Check Fluency WCPM, *185a*

Vocabulary — Check Vocabulary, *185c*

SUCCESS PREDICTOR

Small Group Plan *for Differentiated Instruction*

Daily Plan AT A GLANCE

Reading
Whole Group
- Oral Language
- Comprehension/Vocabulary

Group Time
Differentiated Instruction

Meet with small groups to provide:
- Skill Support
- Reading Support
- Fluency Practice

Read

This week's lessons for daily group time can be found behind the Differentiated Instruction (DI) tab on pp. DI·12–DI·21.

Whole Group
- Fluency

Language Arts
- Grammar
- Writing
- Spelling
- Research/Inquiry
- Speaking/Listening/Viewing

Use *My Sidewalks on Reading Street* for Tier III intensive reading intervention.

DAY 1

On-Level	Strategic Intervention	Advanced
Teacher-Led *Page DI · 13*	**Teacher-Led** *Page DI · 12*	**Teacher-Led** *Page DI · 13*
• Develop Concept Vocabulary • **Read** On-Level Reader *Holocaust Rescuers*	• Reinforce Concepts • **Read** Below-Level Reader *A Day in the Life of Peter and Eve*	• **Read** Advanced Reader *A Safe Haven* • Independent Extension Activity

ⓘ Independent Activities
While you meet with small groups, have the rest of the class...

- Visit the Reading/Library Center
- Listen to the Background Building Audio
- Finish Write to Read, p. 162
- Complete Practice Book pp. 63–64
- Visit Cross-Curricular Centers

DAY 2

On-Level	Strategic Intervention	Advanced
Teacher-Led *Pages 168–173*	**Teacher-Led** *Page DI · 14*	**Teacher-Led** *Page DI · 15*
• **Read** *Passage to Freedom*	• Practice Lesson Vocabulary • Read Multisyllabic Words • **Read** or Listen to *Passage to Freedom*	• Extend Vocabulary • **Read** *Passage to Freedom*

ⓘ Independent Activities
While you meet with small groups, have the rest of the class...

- Visit the Reading/Library Center
- Listen to the AudioText for *Passage to Freedom*
- Finish Words to Write, p. 165
- Complete Practice Book pp. 65–66
- Write in their Strategy Response Logs, pp. 166, 173
- Visit Cross-Curricular Centers
- Work on inquiry projects

DAY 3

On-Level	Strategic Intervention	Advanced
Teacher-Led *Pages 174–177*	**Teacher-Led** *Page DI · 16*	**Teacher-Led** *Page DI · 17*
• **Read** *Passage to Freedom*	• Practice Author's Purpose and Monitor and Fix Up • **Read** or Listen to *Passage to Freedom*	• Extend Author's Purpose and Monitor and Fix Up • **Read** *Passage to Freedom*

ⓘ Independent Activities
While you meet with small groups, have the rest of the class...

- Visit the Reading/Library Center
- Listen to the AudioText for *Passage to Freedom*
- Write in their Strategy Response Logs, p. 176
- Finish Look Back and Write, p. 178
- Complete Practice Book p. 67
- Visit Cross-Curricular Centers
- Work on inquiry projects

① Begin with whole class skill and strategy instruction.

② Meet with small groups to provide differentiated instruction.

③ Gather the whole class back together for fluency and language arts.

DAY 4

On-Level
Teacher-Led
Pages 180–185
- **Read** "I Wanted My Mother"

Strategic Intervention
Teacher-Led
Page DI · 18
- Practice Retelling
- **Read** or Listen to "I Wanted My Mother"

Advanced
Teacher-Led
Page DI · 19
- **Read** "I Wanted My Mother"
- Genre Study

ⓘ Independent Activities

While you meet with small groups, have the rest of the class...

- Visit the Reading/Library Center
- Listen to the AudioText for "I Wanted My Mother"
- Visit the Writing/Vocabulary Center
- Finish Writing Across Texts, p. 185
- Visit Cross-Curricular Centers
- Work on inquiry projects

DAY 5

On-Level
Teacher-Led
Page DI · 21
- **Reread** Leveled Reader *Holocaust Rescuers*
- Retell *Holocaust Rescuers*

Strategic Intervention
Teacher-Led
Page DI · 20
- **Reread** Leveled Reader *A Day in the Life of Peter and Eve*
- Retell *A Day in the Life of Peter and Eve*

Advanced
Teacher-Led
Page DI · 21
- **Reread** Leveled Reader *A Safe Haven*
- Share Extension Activity

ⓘ Independent Activities

While you meet with small groups, have the rest of the class...

- Visit the Reading/Library Center
- Complete Practice Book pp. 68–70
- Visit Cross-Curricular Centers
- Work on inquiry projects

ELL

Grouping Place English language learners in the groups that correspond to their reading abilities in English.

Use the appropriate Leveled Reader or other text at students' instructional level.

TiP Send home the appropriate Multilingual Summary of the main selection on Day 1.

Take It to the NET
ONLINE
PearsonSuccessNet.com

Sharon Vaughn
For ideas and activities for English language learners, see the article "Storybook Reading" by Scott Foresman author S. Vaughn, P. Hickman, and S. Pollard-Durodola.

TEACHER TALK

Fluency is the ability to read words and connected text rapidly, accurately, and smoothly. Fluency may be measured in words correct per minute.

Looking Ahead

Be sure to schedule time for students to work on the unit inquiry project "Doing the Right Thing." This week students conduct searches to find information that helps answer their inquiry questions about charities or service groups.

Name _____ Date _____

My Work Plan
Put an ☒ next to the activities you complete.

Listening
☐ Listen to *Passage to Freedom.*
☐ Listen to "I Wanted My Mother."

Writing/Vocabulary
☐ Study the Words to Know.
☐ Write a newspaper article.

Reading
☐ Read a book.
☐ Read Ten Important Sentences.
☐ Book Club

Social Studies
☐ Locate cities on a map.
☐ Measure distance.

Drama
☐ Look for character clues.
☐ Write and perform a skit.

Technology
☐ Research heroes online.
☐ Write a biography.

Independent Practice
☐ Practice Book, pp. 61–70
☐ Independent Writing

Inquiry
☐ Unit Inquiry
☐ Internet Inquiry

Wrap Up Your Week Turn your paper over. Write about what you did at school this week. What did you read? What did you learn about taking risks?

24 Unit 2 • Week 2 • *Passage to Freedom*

▲ **Group-Time Survival Guide** p. 24, Weekly Contract

☑ Customize Your Plan *by Strand*

ORAL LANGUAGE

Concept Development

Why do we help others even if there are risks?

CONCEPT VOCABULARY
poses   officers   hiding

BUILD

❑ **Question of the Week** Introduce and discuss the question of the week. This week students will read a variety of texts and work on projects related to the concept *taking risks*. Post the question for students to refer to throughout the week. **DAY 1** *162d*

❑ **Read Aloud** Read aloud " Number the Stars." Then begin a web to build concepts and concept vocabulary related to this week's lesson and the unit theme, Doing the Right Thing. Introduce the concept words *poses, officers,* and *hiding* and have students place them on the web. Display the web for use throughout the week. **DAY 1** *162l–162m*

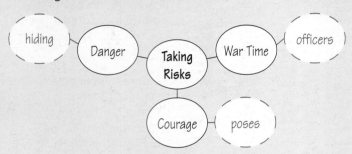

DEVELOP

❑ **Question of the Day** Use the prompts from the Weekly Plan to engage students in conversations related to this week's reading and the unit theme. **EVERY DAY** *162d–162e*

❑ **Concept Vocabulary Web** Revisit the Taking Risks Concept Web and encourage students to add concept words from their reading and life experiences. **DAY 2** *173*, **DAY 3** *177*

CONNECT

❑ **Looking Back/Moving Forward** Revisit the Taking Risks Concept Web and discuss how it relates to this week's lesson and the unit theme. Then make connections to next week's lesson. **DAY 5** *185c*

CHECK

❑ **Concept Vocabulary Web** Use the Taking Risks Concept Web to check students' understanding of the concept vocabulary words *poses, officers,* and *hiding*. **DAY 1** *162l*, **DAY 5** *185c*

VOCABULARY

STRATEGY DICTIONARY/GLOSSARY
Sometimes you come across an unfamiliar word, and the sentences around the word do not help with understanding the meaning; you should then look the word up in a dictionary or glossary. A dictionary lists all words, in alphabetical order, and gives their meanings and pronunciations. A glossary is a list of important words in a book and their meanings.

LESSON VOCABULARY
agreement   refugees
cable   representatives
diplomat   superiors
issue   visa

TEACH

❑ **Words to Know** Give students the opportunity to tell what they already know about this week's lesson vocabulary words. Then discuss word meaning. **DAY 1** *164b*

❑ **Vocabulary Strategy Lesson** Use the vocabulary strategy lesson in the Student Edition to introduce and model this week's strategy, *dictionary/glossary*. **DAY 2** *164–165*

Vocabulary Strategy Lesson

PRACTICE/APPLY

❑ **Leveled Text** Read the lesson vocabulary in the context of leveled text. **DAY 1** *LR10–LR18*

❑ **Words in Context** Read the lesson vocabulary and apply *dictionary/glossary* in the context of *Passage to Freedom*. **DAY 2** *166–173*, **DAY 3** *174–178*

Leveled Readers

❑ **Writing/Vocabulary Center** Imagine that you are a newspaper reporter covering a story. Make up a headline and write an article. **ANY DAY** *162k*

Main Selection—Nonfiction

❑ **Homework** Practice Book pp. 64–65. **DAY 1** *164b*, **DAY 2** *165*

❑ **Word Play** Have partners locate three words from *Passage to Freedom* that have more than one meaning. Have them record the words, parts of speech, and their meanings on a chart. **ANY DAY** *185c*

ASSESS

❑ **Selection Test** Use the Selection Test to determine students' understanding of the lesson vocabulary words. **DAY 3**

RETEACH/REVIEW

❑ **Reteach Lesson** If necessary, use this lesson to reteach and review *dictionary/glossary*. **DAY 5** *185c*

❶ Use assessment data to determine your instructional focus.

❷ Preview this week's instruction by strand.

❸ Choose instructional activities that meet the needs of your classroom.

COMPREHENSION

🎯 **SKILL AUTHOR'S PURPOSE** The author's purpose is the reason or reasons the author has for writing. An author may write to persuade, to inform, to entertain, or to express himself or herself.

🎯 **STRATEGY MONITOR AND FIX UP** Good readers check their understanding as they read. Pace your reading rate depending on the author's purpose. If the author is informing you and you want to understand every detail, slow down. If the author is entertaining you, you can read a little faster.

TEACH

☐ **Skill/Strategy Lesson** Use the skill/strategy lesson in the Student Edition to introduce and model *author's purpose* and *monitor and fix up*. **DAY 1** 162-163

☐ **Extend Skills** Teach point of view. **ANY DAY** 185b

Skill/Strategy Lesson

PRACTICE/APPLY

☐ **Leveled Text** Apply *author's purpose* and *monitor and fix up* to read leveled text. **DAY 1** LR10-LR18

☐ **Skills and Strategies in Context** Read *Passage to Freedom*, using the Guiding Comprehension questions to apply *author's purpose* and *monitor and fix up*. **DAY 2** 166-173, **DAY 3** 174-178

Leveled Readers

☐ **Skills and Strategies in Context** Read "I Wanted My Mother," guiding students as they apply *author's purpose* and *monitor and fix up*. Then have students discuss and write across texts. **DAY 4** 180-185

Main Selection—Nonfiction

☐ **Homework** Practice Book pp. 63, 67, 68. **DAY 1** 163, **DAY 3** 177, **DAY 5** 185b

Paired Selection—Nonfiction

☐ **Fresh Reads for Differentiated Test Practice** Have students practice *author's purpose* with a new passage. **DAY 3**

ASSESS

☐ **Selection Test** Determine students' understanding of the selection and their use of *author's purpose*. **DAY 3**

☐ **Retell** Have students retell *Passage to Freedom*. **DAY 3** 178-179

RETEACH/REVIEW

☐ **Reteach Lesson** If necessary, reteach and review *author's purpose*. **DAY 5** 185b

FLUENCY

SKILL TONE OF VOICE Tone of voice is the ability to add emotion to words. By changing your tone you can bring words to life, create the mood, and make the reading lively.

TEACH

☐ **Read Aloud** Model fluent reading by rereading "Number the Stars." Focus on this week's fluency skill, tone of voice. **DAY 1** 162l-162m, 185a

PRACTICE/APPLY

☐ **Choral Reading** Read aloud selected paragraphs from *Passage to Freedom*, emphasizing the inflections in your voice. Then practice as a class, doing three choral readings of the selected paragraphs. **DAY 2** 185a, **DAY 3** 185a

☐ **Partner Reading** Have partners practice reading aloud, reading with changing inflections to reflect different characters' voices and offering each other feedback. As students reread, monitor their progress toward their individual fluency goals. **DAY 4** 185a

☐ **Listening Center** Have students follow along with the AudioText for this week's selections. **ANY DAY** 162j

☐ **Reading/Library Center** Have students reread a selection of their choice. **ANY DAY** 162j

☐ **Fluency Coach** Have students use Fluency Coach to listen to fluent readings or practice reading on their own. **ANY DAY**

ASSESS

☐ **Check Fluency** WCPM Do a one-minute timed reading, paying special attention to this week's skill—tone of voice. Provide feedback for each student. **DAY 5** 185a

☑ Customize Your Plan *by Strand*

GRAMMAR

SKILL POSSESSIVE NOUNS A *possessive noun* shows ownership. *Singular possessive nouns* show one person, place, or thing has or owns something. *Plural possessive nouns* show that more than one person, place, or thing has or owns something.

TEACH

☐ **Grammar Transparency 7** Use Grammar Transparency 7 to teach possessive nouns. DAY 1 *185e*

Grammar Transparency 7

PRACTICE/APPLY

☐ **Develop the Concept** Review the concept of possessive nouns and provide guided practice. DAY 2 *185e*

☐ **Apply to Writing** Have students review something they have written and apply possessive nouns. DAY 3 *185f*

☐ **Test Preparation** Examine common errors in possessive nouns to prepare for standardized tests. DAY 4 *185f*

☐ **Homework** Grammar and Writing Practice Book pp. 25–27
DAY 2 *185e*, DAY 3 *185f*, DAY 4 *185f*

ASSESS

☐ **Cumulative Review** Use Grammar and Writing Practice Book p. 28.
DAY 5 *185f*

RETEACH/REVIEW

☐ **Daily Fix-It** Have students find and correct errors in grammar, spelling, and punctuation. **EVERY DAY** *185e-185f*

☐ **The Grammar and Writing Book** Use pp. 86–89 of The Grammar and Writing Book to extend instruction for possessive nouns. **ANY DAY**

The Grammar and Writing Book

WRITING

Trait of the Week

FOCUS/IDEAS Good writers focus on a main idea and develop this idea with strong supporting details. Having a purpose—whether it is to inform, to persuade, or to entertain—helps keep focus on the main idea.

☐ **Writing Transparency 7A** Use the model to introduce and discuss the Trait of the Week. DAY 1 *185g*

☐ **Writing Transparency 7B** Use the transparency to show students how supporting their ideas can improve their writing. DAY 2 *185g*

Writing Transparency 7A   **Writing Transparency 7B**

PRACTICE/APPLY

☐ **Write Now** Examine the model on Student Edition p. 179. Then have students write their own story review. DAY 3 *179, 185h*, DAY 4 *185h*

> **Prompt** *Passage to Freedom* is a powerful story about decisions a family makes. Think about another story you have read recently. Now write a story review telling what you liked or did not like about the story.

Write Now p. 179

☐ **Writing/Vocabulary Center** Imagine that you are a newspaper reporter covering a story. Make up a headline and write an article. **ANY DAY** *162k*

ASSESS

☐ **Writing Trait Rubric** Use the rubric to evaluate students' writing. DAY 4 *185h*

RETEACH/REVIEW

☐ **The Grammar and Writing Book** Use pp. 86–91 of The Grammar and Writing Book to extend instruction for possessive nouns, supporting ideas, and story reviews. **ANY DAY**

The Grammar and Writing Book

❶ Use assessment data to determine your instructional focus.

❷ Preview this week's instruction by strand.

❸ Choose instructional activities that meet the needs of your classroom.

SPELLING

GENERALIZATION IRREGULAR PLURALS Sometimes plurals are formed in irregular ways: shel_ves_, echo_es_. Regular plurals follow the rules. Irregular plurals often have base word changes. Some irregular plurals are the same as the singular form.

TEACH

❑ **Pretest** Give the pretest for words with irregular plurals. Guide students in self-correcting their pretests and correcting any misspellings. **DAY 1** *185i*

❑ **Think and Practice** Connect spelling to the phonics generalization for irregular plurals. **DAY 2** *185i*

PRACTICE/APPLY

❑ **Connect to Writing** Have students use spelling words to write opinions. Then review frequently misspelled words: *no, know, new, knew*. **DAY 3** *185j*

❑ **Homework** Word Study and Spelling Practice Book pp. 25–28. **EVERY DAY**

RETEACH/REVIEW

❑ **Review** Review spelling words to prepare for the posttest. Then provide students with a spelling strategy—memory tricks. **DAY 4** *185j*

ASSESS

❑ **Posttest** Use dictation sentences to give the posttest for words with irregular plurals. **DAY 5** *185j*

Spelling Words

1. staffs
2. ourselves
3. pants
4. scissors
5. loaves
6. volcanoes
7. chiefs
8. buffaloes
9. flamingos
10. beliefs
11. echoes
12. shelves
13. quizzes
14. sheriffs
15. dominoes
16. thieves
17. measles
18. avocados
19. chefs
20. pianos

Challenge Words

21. bailiffs
22. wharves
23. mosquitoes
24. armadillos
25. desperadoes

*Word from the selection

RESEARCH AND INQUIRY

❑ **Internet Inquiry** Have students conduct an Internet inquiry on taking risks in dangerous times. **EVERY DAY** *185k*

❑ **Parts of a Book** Review the terms that name parts of a book and discuss how students can use parts of a book to locate information. **DAY 5** *185l*

❑ **Unit Inquiry** Allow time for students to conduct searches to find information that helps them answer their inquiry questions about charities or service groups. **ANY DAY** *141*

SPEAKING AND LISTENING

❑ **Oral Report** Have students present an oral report on people who risked their lives to help others during World War II. **DAY 5** *185d*

❑ **Oral Book Reports** Have students choose, read, and present reports on fiction or nonfiction books about people who do the right things or who take risks helping others. **DAY 5** *185d*

❑ **Listen to Audio CD** Have students listen to the AudioText of *Passage to Freedom* and answer questions. **DAY 5** *185d*

Resources for
Differentiated Instruction

LEVELED READERS

▶ **Comprehension**
- ◎ **Skill** Author's Purpose
- ◎ **Strategy** Monitor/Fix Up

▶ **Lesson Vocabulary**
- ◎ Dictionary/Glossary

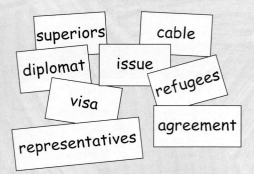

superiors · cable · diplomat · issue · refugees · visa · representatives · agreement

▶ **Social Studies Standards**
- World War II
- Holocaust
- Government
- Culture

Leveled Reader Database ONLINE

PearsonSuccessNet.com

Use the Online Database of over 600 books to
- Download and print additional copies of this week's leveled readers.
- Listen to the readers being read online.
- Search for more titles focused on this week's skills, topic, and content.

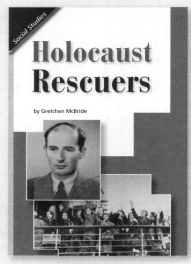

Social Studies

Holocaust Rescuers

by Gretchen McBride

On-Level Reader

Name _____ Holocaust Rescuers

Author's Purpose
- An **author's purpose** is the reason an author writes something. Some purposes an author may have are to persuade, to inform, to entertain, and to express a mood or feeling.
- An author may have more than one purpose in writing a particular selection.

Directions Refer to the selection and answer the questions below.
Possible responses given.
1. What do you think is the author's purpose for writing *Holocaust Rescuers*?
She wants to inform the reader about some of the people who took risks to help Jews escape the Nazi Holocaust.

2. Why do you think the author includes the section entitled "Did people know?" (pages 5–7)?
She wants the reader to understand why Hitler was able to kill so many Jews during the Holocaust and why more people did not step forward to help Jews and stop the Nazis.

3. The author starts page 16 with this sentence: "More than anyone else, Raoul Wallenberg is remembered for saving Jewish people from the Holocaust." Why does she write this about Wallenberg? Use details from the selection to explain your answer.
She wants to persuade the reader that Wallenberg was a great hero. She supports her argument by telling how he saved thousands of Jews by having them live in "Swedish houses"; how he climbed on train cars to hand out protective passes to Jews; and how he threatened a German general.

4. How does the last section entitled "Remembering: Yad Vashem" support the author's purpose?
It informs the reader of one way that Holocaust rescuers have been recognized for the risks they took.

◎ **On-Level Practice** TE p. LR14

Name _____ Holocaust Rescuers

Vocabulary
Directions Use the vocabulary words above to complete the following sentences. Not all words will be used.

Check the Words You Know
___agreement ___cable ___diplomat ___issue
___refugees ___representatives ___superiors ___visa

1. Many ___refugees___ from various countries fled to foreign countries and became citizens in their new lands.
2. My friend and I are in ___agreement___ that the Holocaust was a terrible time in history.
3. The work of a ___diplomat___ must be interesting and exciting, since you travel and meet people from many other countries.
4. Without a ___visa___, it is difficult to enter some foreign countries.
5. When she was growing up, Grandma says, people feared receiving a ___cable___ because it almost always meant bad news.

Directions For each word below, use a thesaurus to find as many synonyms as you can that relate to the meaning of the word as it is used in *Holocaust Rescuers*. Possible responses given.
6. allot ___provide, distribute, allot___
7. representatives ___legislators, elected officials___
8. superiors ___bosses, managers, chiefs___

Directions Write two sentences using the words *diplomat* and *refugees*.
9. ___Responses will vary.___

10. _____

◎ **On-Level Practice** TE p. LR15

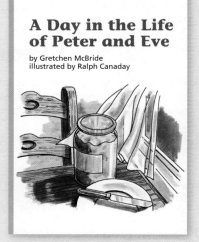

A Day in the Life of Peter and Eve

by Gretchen McBride
illustrated by Ralph Canaday

Below-Level Reader

Name _____ Peter and Eve

Author's Purpose
- An **author's purpose** is the reason an author writes something. Some purposes an author may have are to persuade, to inform, to entertain, and to express a mood or feeling.
- An author may have more than one purpose in writing a particular selection.

Directions Refer to *A Day in the Life of Peter and Eve* and answer the questions below. Use complete sentences.
1. What is the author's purpose in describing what it was like for Peter, Eve, and their mother to sleep in the basement?
Possible response: She wants the reader to imagine the sacrifices that Peter's family, and maybe other families, had to make to survive the war.

2. What are some of the ways the author lets the reader know that Fräulein Mann does not agree with Hitler and the Nazis?
Possible responses: She is uncomfortable repeating the salute to Hitler; she bows her head during the presentation by the councilmen; she has a cousin and knows other people who helped Jews

3. What images of the war does the author demonstrate through Carl's letter?
Possible responses: The food eaten by German soldiers is often spoiled; the fighting is terrible; soldiers don't often get to visit families back home

4. Why does the author have their mother wait until they are in the cellar before she tells Peter and Eve her feelings about the Nazis?
Possible response: She doesn't want anyone to overhear her say bad things about the Nazis. Not all people agree with her, and she might be punished for her opinions.

◎ **Below-Level Practice** TE p. LR11

Name _____ Peter and Eve

Vocabulary
Directions Draw a line from the vocabulary word to its correct definition.

Check the Words You Know
___agreement ___cable ___diplomat ___issue
___refugees ___representative ___superiors ___visa

1. agreement — a. a message sent through wires by electric current or electronic signals
2. cable — b. an official signature or endorsement upon a passport that gives someone permission to enter a foreign country
3. issue — c. an understanding reached by two or more persons or groups
4. superiors — d. people of higher position, rank, or ability
5. visa — e. to send out; put forth

Directions For each of the following characters from the story, write the vocabulary word from the box that best describes him or her.
6. Herr Karp ___refugee___
7. Herr Meitzel ___diplomat___
8. Fräulein Mann's cousin Thomas ___representative___
9. Peter's friend Hans Karp ___refugee___
10. Herr Lutz ___representative___

Directions Choose three of the vocabulary words and write a sentence for each word.
11. ___Sentences will vary.___

12. _____

13. _____

◎ **Below-Level Practice** TE p. LR12

Advanced

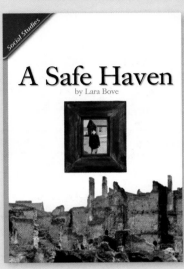

A Safe Haven
by Lara Bove

Advanced Reader

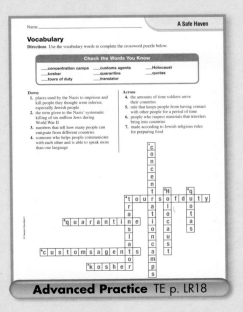

Advanced Practice TE p. LR17

Advanced Practice TE p. LR18

ELL

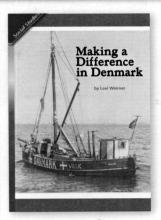

Making a Difference in Denmark
by Levi Weimer

ELL Reader

ELL Poster 7

Teacher's Edition Notes

ELL notes throughout this lesson support instruction and reference additional resources at point of use.

Teaching Guide pp. 43–49, 224–225

- Multilingual summaries of the main selection
- Comprehension lesson
- Vocabulary strategies and word cards
- ELL Reader 5.2.2 lesson

ELL and Transition Handbook

Ten Important Sentences

- Key ideas from every selection in the Student Edition
- Activities to build sentence power

More Reading

Readers' Theater Anthology

- Fluency practice
- Five scripts to build fluency
- Poetry for oral interpretation

Leveled Trade Books

- Extended reading tied to the unit concept
- Lessons in the Trade Book Library Teaching Guide

School + Home

Homework

- Family Times Newsletter
- ELL Multilingual Selection Summaries

Take-Home Books

- Leveled Readers

Cross-Curricular Centers

 Listening

Listen to the Selections

MATERIALS
CD player, headphones, AudioText CD, student book

`SINGLES`

LISTEN TO LITERATURE Listen to *Passage to Freedom* and "I Wanted My Mother" as you follow or read along in your book. Listen to identify what the author's purpose was in writing each story.

If there is anything you don't understand, you can listen again to any section.

 Reading/Library

Read It Again!

MATERIALS
Collection of books for self-selected reading, reading logs, student book

`SINGLES`
`PAIRS`
`GROUPS`

Select a book you have already read. Record the title of the book in your reading log. You may want to read with a partner.

Choose from the following:

- **Leveled Readers**
- **ELL Readers**
- **Stories Written by Classmates**
- **Books from the Library**
- *Passage to Freedom*

TEN IMPORTANT SENTENCES
Read the Ten Important Sentences from *Passage to Freedom*. Then locate the sentences in the student book.

BOOK CLUB Look at "Meet Authors" on p. 763 of the student book to help you set up an author study of Ken Mochizuki. Read other books by Mochizuki, or other biographies, and get together with a group to share your favorites.

 Drama

Create a Scene

MATERIALS
Writing materials

`GROUPS`

Write a short skit in which Mr. Sugihara and his family discuss what he should do about the refugees who are desperate for his help.

1. **Look for clues about each character so you can write dialogue that sounds authentic.**
2. **Think about how the characters' feelings might translate into words and actions.**
3. **Write the dialogue.**
4. **Be prepared to perform your skit with classmates at a later time if your teacher suggests it.**

EARLY FINISHERS Make a list of the props and costumes that you would use during a performance of your skit.

"I wish there was something I could do."

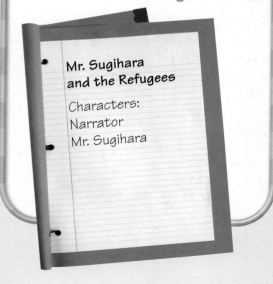

Mr. Sugihara and the Refugees

Characters:
Narrator
Mr. Sugihara

Scott Foresman Reading Street Centers Survival Kit

Use the *Passage To Freedom* materials from the Reading Street Centers Survival Kit to organize this week's centers.

Writing/Vocabulary

Write an *Article*

MATERIALS
Writing materials

[SINGLES] [PAIRS]

Imagine that you are a newspaper reporter covering the story of the refugees gathered outside Mr. Sugihara's house.

1. Use the following headline or make up your own: "Refugees Plead for Help."
2. Use details from the story to write a brief article.
3. Remember to address some or all of the 5 W's (who, what, when, where, why).

EARLY FINISHERS Add an interview with Mr. Sugihara or one of the refugees. Role play the interview with a partner.

Refugees Plead for Help

Kaunas, Lithuania

Social Studies

Map Distances

MATERIALS
Atlas with legend, writing materials, ruler

[SINGLES] [PAIRS]

Measure the distance between cities.

1. Locate Kaunas, Lithuania, on a map.
2. Locate a major city in one of the countries mentioned in the selection (Germany, Japan, Poland).
3. Measure the distance between these cities using the map's legend.

EARLY FINISHERS Use this number to measure north, south, east, and west from your hometown. Write where you end up.

Technology

Find a Hero

MATERIALS
Internet access, writing materials

[SINGLES] [PAIRS] [GROUPS]

Find out more about another historical hero from the World War II era.

1. Use a student-friendly search engine to find sources related to a World War II hero.
2. Choose a site that gives you the best summary of his or her contributions to the war effort.
3. Take brief notes about the information you find and prepare a biography to share with your class.

EARLY FINISHERS Look for more background information about the person you researched. Be prepared to share that information.

ALL CENTERS

OBJECTIVES

- Build vocabulary by finding words related to the lesson concept.
- Listen for clues to author's purpose.

Concept Vocabulary

poses pretends to be something
officers members of the armed forces who command others
hiding putting or keeping out of sight

Monitor Progress

Check Vocabulary

If...	then...
students are unable to place words on the web,	...review the lesson concept. Place the words on the web and provide additional words for practice, such as *detained* and *soldiers*.

SUCCESS PREDICTOR

DAY 1   Grouping Options

Reading

Whole Group
Introduce and discuss the Question of the Week. Then use pp. 162l–164b.

Group Time
Differentiated Instruction
Read this week's Leveled Readers. See pp. 162h–162i for the small group lesson plan.

Whole Group
Use p. 185a.

Language Arts
Use pp. 185e–185k.

Build Concepts

FLUENCY

MODEL TONE OF VOICE As you read "Number the Stars," use your tone of voice to model reading with expression that conveys the feelings of fear, anger, and relief in the story, such the officer laughing scornfully.

LISTENING COMPREHENSION

After reading "Number the Stars," use the following questions to assess listening comprehension.

1. **Is the author writing to entertain, to inform, to persuade, or to express her opinion?** *(Answers may vary, but should demonstrate that students are aware that authors often have more than one purpose for writing.)* **Author's Purpose**

2. **What happened before Papa gave the photographs to the German officers?** *(Possible response: The officer was questioning the relation of the dark-haired girl to the others.)* **Sequence**

BUILD CONCEPT VOCABULARY

Start a web to build concepts and vocabulary related to this week's lesson and the unit theme.

- Draw the Taking Risks Concept Web.
- Read the sentence with the word *poses* again. Ask students to pronounce *poses* and discuss its meaning.
- Place *poses* in an oval attached to *Courage*. Explain that *poses* is related to this concept. Read the sentences in which *hiding* and *officers* appear. Have students pronounce the words, place them on the web, and provide reasons.
- Brainstorm additional words and categories for the web. Keep the web on display and add words throughout the week.

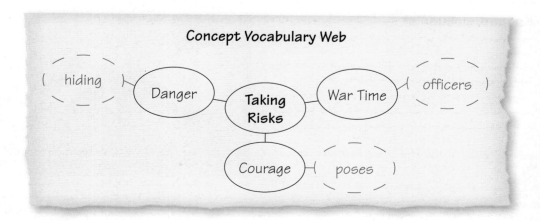

Concept Vocabulary Web

Number the Stars

By Lois Lowry

On September 29, 1943, Jewish people in Denmark were rounded up by Nazi soldiers, and then sent to death camps. In this passage a Jewish girl named Ellen Rosen poses as the sister of her best friend, Annemarie Johansen, as the Nazi soldiers search for Jews.

"Get up!" he ordered. "Come out here!"

Trembling, the two girls rose from the bed and followed him, brushing past the two remaining officers in the doorway, to the living room.

These men were older and their faces were set with anger.

"Your names?" the officer barked.

"Annemarie Johansen. And this is my sister — "

"Quiet! Let her speak for herself. Your name?" He was glaring at Ellen.

Ellen swallowed. "Lise," she said, and cleared her throat. "Lise Johansen."

The officer stared at them grimly.

"Now," Mama said in a strong voice, "you have seen that we are not hiding anything. May my children go back to bed?"

The officer ignored her. Suddenly he grabbed a handful of Ellen's hair. Ellen winced.

He laughed scornfully. "You have a blond child sleeping in the other room. And you have this blond daughter—" He gestured toward Annemarie with his head. "Where did you get the dark-haired one?"

For a moment no one spoke. Then Annemarie, watching in panic, saw her father move swiftly to the small bookcase and take out a book. She saw that he was holding the family photograph album. Very quickly he searched through its pages, found what he was looking for, and tore out three pictures from three separate pages.

He handed them to the German officer, who released Ellen's hair.

"You will see each of my daughters, each with her name written on the photograph," Papa said.

Annemarie knew instantly which photographs he had chosen. The album had many snapshots — all the poorly focused pictures of school events and birthday parties. But it also contained a portrait, taken by a photographer, of each girl as a tiny infant. Mama had written, in her delicate handwriting, the name of each baby daughter across the bottom of those photographs.

She realized too, with an icy feeling, why Papa had torn them from the book. At the bottom of each page, below the photograph itself, was written the date. And the real Lise Johansen had been born twenty-one years earlier.

"Kirsten Elisabeth," the officer read, looking at Kirsti's baby picture. He let the photograph fall to the floor.

"Annemarie," he read next, glanced at her, and dropped the second photograph.

(Continued on TR1.)

SKILLS ⟷ STRATEGIES IN CONTEXT

Author's Purpose Monitor/Fix Up

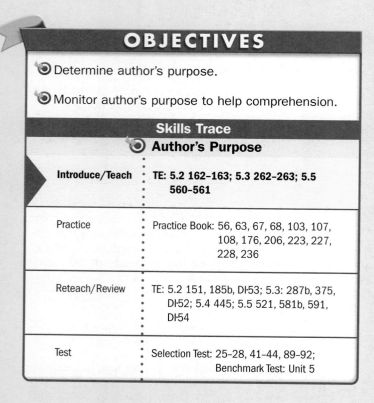

OBJECTIVES

◎ Determine author's purpose.

◎ Monitor author's purpose to help comprehension.

Skills Trace
◎ Author's Purpose

Introduce/Teach	TE: 5.2 162–163; 5.3 262–263; 5.5 560–561
Practice	Practice Book: 56, 63, 67, 68, 103, 107, 108, 176, 206, 223, 227, 228, 236
Reteach/Review	TE: 5.2 151, 185b, DI·53; 5.3: 287b, 375, DI·52; 5.4 445; 5.5 521, 581b, 591, DI·54
Test	Selection Test: 25–28, 41–44, 89–92; Benchmark Test: Unit 5

INTRODUCE

Write the heading *About Me* and add the following information on the board: *I wrote my first book at thirteen. I was born in London, England. I like to watch horror movies.* Ask what might be the author's purpose in an article with this title and information. *(to inform)*

Have students read the information on p. 162. Explain the following:

• Author's purpose is the reason an author has for writing.

• Knowing an author's purpose can help you monitor your comprehension and determine the rate at which you should read the selection.

Use Skill Transparency 7 to teach author's purpose and monitor and fix up.

Comprehension

Skill
Author's Purpose

Strategy
Monitor and Fix Up

 ## Author's Purpose

• An author may write to persuade, to inform, to entertain, or to express himself or herself.

• You can infer an author's purpose from the text features and specific language the author chose.

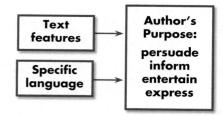

Strategy: Monitor and Fix Up

Good readers check their understanding as they read. Pace your reading depending on the author's purpose. If the author is informing you and you want to understand every detail, slow down. If the author is entertaining you, you can read a little faster.

Write to Read

1. Before you read "The Job of a Diplomat," preview the article. Make a graphic organizer like the one above to predict the author's purpose.

2. As you read, check your understanding. Make a second graphic organizer to see if the author's purpose is the same as you predicted.

162

Strategic Intervention

◎ **Author's Purpose** To help determine author's purpose, have pairs of students read the article on p. 163. Suggest they answer these four questions: *Is the author trying to entertain me? persuade me to believe one thing or another? share ideas or feelings with me? provide me with information?*

ELL

Access Content

Beginning/Intermediate For a Picture It! lesson on author's purpose, see ELL Teaching Guide, pp. 43–44.

Advanced Before students read "The Job of a Diplomat," have volunteers tell what they know about diplomats. Read the title aloud and help students use it to determine that the author's purpose is to inform.

The Job of a DIPLOMAT

The world has nearly 200 countries. How can we keep peace among so many groups? One way is through persons called diplomats. A country sends diplomats to foreign countries to speak for it.

Ambassadors The chief diplomat is often the ambassador. An ambassador is chosen by the president or other government leader. He or she lives in a foreign country and meets with its leaders. The spaces where ambassadors live and work are protected. The police or army of the foreign country may not enter these spaces.

Other diplomats Besides the ambassador, other diplomats serve in foreign countries. They must pass a government test to become a diplomat. In college they study subjects such as languages and world history that will help them understand other nations. They speak the language of the country where they are sent.

Diplomats report to their home government about the country in which they serve. They help travelers from their home country. They issue papers that allow people to come to their home country. In all these ways, diplomats help the countries of the world get along.

1 Skill Look at the title, headings, and some of the language. Is the author writing to persuade, inform, entertain, or express?

2 Strategy Pause after this first paragraph to check your understanding. Do you need to read more slowly? More quickly?

3 Strategy Check your understanding of the author's purpose. Has your understanding changed?

4 Skill Do you think the author achieved her purpose? Why or why not?

163

Available as **Skill Transparency** 7

TEACH

1 SKILL Use the title, headings, and some of the language to model how to determine the author's purpose.

Think Aloud **MODEL** From previewing the article, I can tell that it provides information about diplomats, such as how they are selected and what they do. Since the article provides information, the author's purpose is to inform.

2 STRATEGY Model how to monitor comprehension.

Think Aloud **MODEL** After reading the first paragraph, I can tell that this article is going to provide me with information about diplomats. I will need to read this article slowly so I don't miss any of the important details.

PRACTICE AND ASSESS

3 STRATEGY Possible response: No, my understanding is still that the author's purpose is to inform.

4 SKILL Possible response: Yes, because the article provides a lot of information about diplomats.

WRITE Have students complete steps 1 and 2 of the Write to Read activity. You might consider using this as a whole-class activity.

Monitor Progress
🔎 **Author's Purpose**

| If... students are unable to complete **Write to Read** on p. 162, | then... use Practice Book p. 63 to provide additional practice. |

Author's Purpose

- The **author's purpose** is the reason or reasons the author has for writing.
- An author may write to persuade, to inform, to entertain, or to express himself or herself.

Directions Read the following passage.

Levi Coffin was an abolitionist. He helped people who had been enslaved head north to find freedom. Levi was part of the Underground Railroad for many years. A few thousand enslaved people passed through his home in Indiana on their way to Canada. Levi was able to give them supplies for their journey. Eventually, people called Levi the "President of the Underground Railroad." Although it was illegal at the time to help people escape slavery, Levi took a risk to do what he knew was right.

Directions Complete the diagram by answering the questions about the author's purpose.

Questions	Answers
What information is the author providing you with?	1. The author gives information about Levi Coffin's life as an abolitionist.
For what purpose did the author write this passage?	2. The author wrote this to provide information about Coffin's life.
How do you know?	3. Possible answer: The author uses facts about Coffin to tell his story.
Why did the author not use "I" in the passage?	4. Possible answer: This is a story about someone else's life, not the author's.
What idea is the author trying to convey in the last sentence?	5. Sometimes people have to take risks to help other people.

School + Home Home Activity: Your child analyzed the author's purpose in a nonfiction passage. Look at an article in a newspaper or magazine. Read the article with your child and discuss what you each think is the author's purpose.

BEFORE READING

Tech Files ONLINE

Have students use a student-friendly search engine to find out more information about the Holocaust. Be sure to follow classroom rules for Internet use.

ELL

Build Background Use ELL Poster 7 to build background and develop vocabulary for the lesson concept of risks people took helping others during WWII.

▲ ELL Poster 7

Build Background

ACTIVATE PRIOR KNOWLEDGE

BEGIN A KWL CHART about the Holocaust.

- Give students a KWL chart and allow them two to three minutes to brainstorm what they know about the Holocaust. Record what they know in the first column of the chart.

- Give students two to three more minutes to ask questions they would like answered about the Holocaust. Record the questions in the second column of the chart.

Topic	The Holocaust		
K	**W**	**L**	
Happened during World War II Six million people died	Why did the Nazis dislike Jewish people?		

▲ **Graphic Organizer** 4

BACKGROUND BUILDING AUDIO This week's audio builds background about World War II. Students will find out how Hiroki Sugihara's father helped Jewish refugees escape from Lithuania during World War II. After students listen, discuss what they found out and what surprised them most about the selection.

Background Building Audio

164a Doing the Right Thing • Week 2

Introduce Vocabulary

WORD RATING CHART

Create word knowledge rating charts using the categories *Know, Have Seen,* and *Don't Know.*

Word Rating Chart

Word	Know	Have Seen	Don't Know
agreement			
cable			
diplomat			✓
issue			
refugees			
representatives	✓		
superiors			
visa			

▲ **Graphic Organizer** 5

- Read each word to students and have them place it in one of the three columns: *Know* (know and can use); *Have Seen* (have seen or heard the word; don't know meaning); *Don't Know* (don't know the word). ***Activate Prior Knowledge***

- Discuss the words in each column. For *Don't Know* words, have students use a dictionary to look up word meanings.

- Have students share where they may have seen some of these words. Point out that some of this week's words will be unfamiliar or have multiple meanings *(issue* and *cable),* and students may learn new definitions for these words. (For additional practice with multiple meaning words, see p. 185c.) ***Unfamiliar Words • Multiple-Meaning Words***

Use the Multisyllabic Word Routine on p. DI·1 to help students read multisyllabic words.

Lesson Vocabulary

Words to Know

T agreement harmony in feeling or opinion

T cable message sent through wires by electric current; also called a telegram

T diplomat person whose work is to manage relations between nations

T issue to send out; put forth

T refugees people who flee to another country for safety

T representatives people appointed or elected to act or speak for others

T superiors people who are higher in rank or position

T visa official signature or endorsement upon passport or document, showing it has been examined and approved

More Words to Know

Hanukkah a yearly Jewish festival lasting eight days, celebrating the rededication of the temple in Jerusalem

Nazis members of the National Socialist Party, a fascist political party in Germany led by Adolf Hitler

Soviets persons belonging to or fighting for the former Soviet Union

T = Tested Word

Vocabulary

Directions Choose the word from the box that best matches each definition. Write the word on the line shown to the left.

refugees   1. people who flee to another country for safety

issue   2. to distribute officially

visa   3. official signature or endorsement on a passport or document

representatives   4. people appointed or elected to act or speak for others

agreement   5. harmony in feeling or opinion

Check the Words You Know
___agreement
___cable
___diplomat
___issue
___refugees
___representatives
___superiors
___visa

Directions Choose the word from the box that best matches the clue.

6. These people are in a higher position or rank.
s u p e r i o r s

7. You might need this to travel to another country.
v i s a

8. Today we might use e-mail instead of this to send a message.
c a b l e

9. A person who manages the relationship between countries.
d i p l o m a t

10. This is the opposite of conflict.
a g r e e m e n t

Write a Newspaper Article
On a separate sheet of paper write an imaginary newspaper article about people helping refugees come to a new country. Use as many vocabulary words as you can.
Articles should include details about providing aid to refugees.

Home Activity Your child identified and used vocabulary words from *Passage to Freedom*. With your child, discuss the meaning of each word from the vocabulary list. Help your child use each word in a sentence.

▲ **Practice Book** p. 64

Vocabulary Strategy

INTRODUCE

Discuss the strategy for using a dictionary or glossary to find meanings of unfamiliar words by following the steps on p. 164.

TEACH

• Have students read "Foreign Service," paying attention to how vocabulary is used.

• Model using a dictionary to determine the meaning of *diplomat.*

Think Aloud **MODEL** I read the sentence that says, "Diplomats must know this language well." I'm not sure what *diplomat* means, so I look up the word in a dictionary. I go to the D section and then I use the guide words at the top of the page to find where *diplomat* would be. I see *diplomat* means "a person who manages the relations between his or her nation and other nations." That definition makes sense here.

DAY 2 Grouping Options

Reading

Whole Group Discuss the Question of the Day. Then use pp. 164–167.

Group Time Differentiated Instruction
Read *Passage to Freedom.* See pp. 162h–162i for the small group lesson plan.

Whole Group Use p. 185a.

Language Arts
Use pp. 185e–185k.

Words to Know

| diplomat |
| representatives |
| visa |
| issue |
| refugees |
| agreement |
| superiors |
| cable |

Vocabulary Strategy
for Unfamiliar Words

Dictionary/Glossary Sometimes the sentences around an unfamiliar word don't have context clues to help you find its meaning. Then you should look up the word in a dictionary or glossary. Follow these steps.

1. Look to see whether the book has a glossary. If not, then use a dictionary.

2. Find the word entry. If the pronunciation is given, read it aloud. You may recognize the word when you hear yourself say it.

3. Look over all the meanings listed in the entry. Try each meaning in the sentence with the unfamiliar word.

4. Choose the meaning that makes sense in your sentence.

As you read "Foreign Service," follow the steps above to help you find the meanings of unfamiliar words.

164

Strategic Intervention

 Dictionary/Glossary To reinforce meanings, have students work in pairs to use these words in sentences: *visa, refugee, superiors,* and *cable.* Encourage them to use a dictionary to verify word meanings.

ELL

Access Content Use ELL Poster 7 to preteach vocabulary. Choose from the following to meet language proficiency levels.

Beginning/Intermediate Point out the vocabulary words listed on page 164. Ask students which letter each word will be listed under. Ask if there are any words listed under the same letter. Have students list the words in alphabetical order to make finding them easier.

Advanced Teach the lesson on pp. 164–165. Have students use each of the Words to Know in a sentence. Students may want to translate each of these words into their home languages.

FOREIGN SERVICE

A U.S. diplomat works for the United States government in another country, the host country. He or she must be able to talk to the people of this country in their own language. Diplomats must know this language well. Imagine all the time diplomats would waste if they had to wait for everyone's words to be translated.

As representatives of the United States, diplomats have important duties. They may have to help Americans who want to travel to the host country or who are already there. For example, if visitors need a visa to enter the country, government officials may make certain demands before they issue this paper. In that case, a diplomat could help clear up any problems.

Refugees from the host country may want to live in the United States. Generally, there is an agreement between the two countries about refugees. This agreement outlines what the diplomat can and cannot do to help. If there is a question, the diplomat will call his or her superiors back in the United States for advice. Years ago, this meant sending a wire, or cable. Getting an answer could take hours, or even days. Today, a cell phone means instant contact.

Words to Write

Look at the pictures in *Passage to Freedom*. Choose one to describe in words. Use as many words from the Words to Know list as you can.

165

PRACTICE AND ASSESS

- Have students use a dictionary to find the meanings of other unfamiliar words from the passage.
- Remind students that some words have several meanings and that they should find the meaning for each word that makes sense in this story.
- Have students complete Practice Book p. 65.

WRITE Do a picture walk of the illustrations on pp. 166–177 with students. Choose an illustration to write about. Writing should include vocabulary words as well as other related words.

Monitor Progress

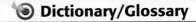

Dictionary/Glossary

If... students need more practice with the lesson vocabulary,	then... use Tested Vocabulary Cards.

Vocabulary · Dictionary/Glossary

- Dictionaries and glossaries provide alphabetical lists of words and their meanings.
- A dictionary is a book of words and their meanings, and a glossary is a short dictionary at the back of some books.
- An **entry** shows the spelling of a word and comes before the definition.

Directions Read the following passage. Then answer the questions below using a dictionary or your glossary.

Ayako's father is a diplomat, sent to our country by his homeland. Last week I went home with Ayako after school and her mother was crying so I could understand. Her father's superiors had called and told them that it was not safe to return to their homeland. Now Ayako and her family are refugees. Her father is not sure what job he can get. Ayako's little brother asks every day when they will be able to see their friends and relatives back home, but nobody knows the answer. Her family has made an agreement that they will try to be brave and to wait patiently for things to change. Someday, they will go home again.

Possible answers given for 1, 4, 5.

1. What is the definition of *diplomat*? Put it in your own words.
   a person who makes sure countries can work together

2. What entry do you have to look at in the dictionary to find the meaning for *translated*? What does *translated* mean?
   translate; changed from one language to another

3. What does *superiors* mean? What part of speech is it?
   people who are higher in position or rank; noun

4. What is the meaning of *agreement*? Use it in an original sentence.
   harmony in feeling or opinion; We made an agreement never to see that movie again.

5. Explain why a dictionary would give more complete information for an entry than a glossary.
   A dictionary may include more parts of speech for the word than the glossary.

School + Home Home Activity Your child used a dictionary to find out the meanings of unfamiliar words. Choose a few words that your child does not know. Have your child use a dictionary to find their meanings.

▲ **Practice Book** p. 65

Prereading Strategies

GENRE STUDY

Biography

Passage to Freedom is a biography. Explain that a biography is a selection about a real person's life that is written by another person. A biography may cover a person's whole life or only part of it.

PREVIEW AND PREDICT

Have students look at the selection title, question, and illustration. Have students identify the subject of the biography and predict who the people in the illustration might be. Have students use lesson vocabulary words in their discussion.

Strategy Response Log

Ask Questions Have students write two questions about the selection in their strategy response logs. Students will answer their questions in the Strategy Response Log activity on p. 173.

PASSAGE TO FREEDOM

The Sugihara Story

by Ken Mochizuki illustrated by Dom Lee

Afterword by Hiroki Sugihara

What makes Mr. Sugihara decide to help the refugees?

Genre A **biography** is the true story of a person's life, written by someone else. As you read, notice how Mr. Sugihara's life changes.

166

Access Content Preview the story by pointing to each picture and helping students talk about what they see. Provide story information as needed.

Consider having students read the selection summary in English or in students' home languages. See the Multilingual Summaries in the ELL Teaching Guide, pp. 47–49.

Vocabulary Support

Kaunus (KOW nuhs) city in Lithuania where the Sugiharas lived.

SET PURPOSE

Read the first page of the selection aloud to students. Have them consider the preview discussion and the questions they wrote for the Strategy Response Log and share what they hope to find out as they read. Have students use this to set a purpose for reading.

Remind students to think about what the author's purpose was for writing the selection.

STRATEGY RECALL

Students have now used these before-reading strategies:

- preview the selection to be aware of its genre, features, and possible content;
- activate prior knowledge about that content and what to expect of that genre;
- make predictions;
- set a purpose for reading.

Remind students that, as they read, they should monitor their own comprehension. If they realize something does not make sense, they can regain their comprehension by using fix-up strategies they have learned, such as:

- use phonics and word structure to decode new words;
- use context clues or a dictionary to figure out meanings of new words;
- adjust their reading rate—slow down for difficult text, speed up for easy or familiar text, or skim and scan just for specific information;
- reread parts of the text;
- read on (continue to read for clarification);
- use text features such as headings, subheadings, charts, illustrations, and so on as visual aids to comprehension;
- make a graphic organizer or a semantic organizer to aid comprehension;
- use reference sources, such as an encyclopedia, dictionary, thesaurus, or synonym finder.

After reading, students will use these strategies:

- summarize or retell the text;
- answer questions they or others pose;
- reflect to make new information become part of their prior knowledge.

AudioText

Guiding Comprehension

1  **Author's Purpose • Inferential**

Reread p. 168, paragraph 3. Is the author writing to entertain, to inform, to persuade, or to express his opinion?

The author is writing to inform. He's telling us about the members of his family and where they lived.

Monitor Progress

 **Author's Purpose**

If... students are unable to determine the author's purpose,	**then...** use the skill and strategy instruction on p. 169.

---

2 **Draw Conclusions • Inferential**

What do the narrator and his brother know about Germans? What clue does the narrator give you?

Possible response: They think of Germans as military people. Clue: They play with toy German soldiers.

Tech Files
ONLINE

Students should use a student-friendly research engine and the keywords *World War II* and *Lithuania* to search for information about the setting of the selection. Be sure to follow classroom Internet guidelines.

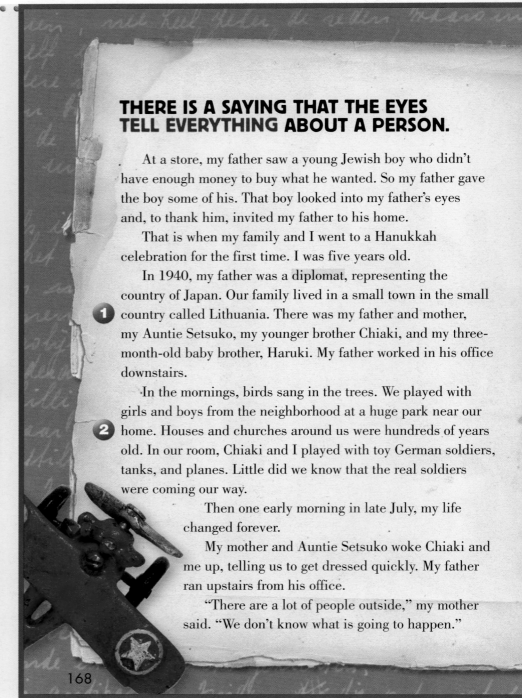

THERE IS A SAYING THAT THE EYES TELL EVERYTHING ABOUT A PERSON.

At a store, my father saw a young Jewish boy who didn't have enough money to buy what he wanted. So my father gave the boy some of his. That boy looked into my father's eyes and, to thank him, invited my father to his home.

That is when my family and I went to a Hanukkah celebration for the first time. I was five years old.

1 In 1940, my father was a diplomat, representing the country of Japan. Our family lived in a small town in the small country called Lithuania. There was my father and mother, my Auntie Setsuko, my younger brother Chiaki, and my three-month-old baby brother, Haruki. My father worked in his office downstairs.

In the mornings, birds sang in the trees. We played with girls and boys from the neighborhood at a huge park near our **2** home. Houses and churches around us were hundreds of years old. In our room, Chiaki and I played with toy German soldiers, tanks, and planes. Little did we know that the real soldiers were coming our way.

Then one early morning in late July, my life changed forever.

My mother and Auntie Setsuko woke Chiaki and me up, telling us to get dressed quickly. My father ran upstairs from his office.

"There are a lot of people outside," my mother said. "We don't know what is going to happen."

168

ELL

Access Content Reread the sentence, "In 1940, my father was a diplomat, representing the country of Japan." Explain that the father lived in Lithuania and handled relationships between the two countries.

In the living room, my parents told my brother and me not to let anybody see us looking through the window. So, I parted the curtains a tiny bit. Outside, I saw hundreds of people crowded around the gate in front of our house.

The grown-ups shouted in Polish, a language I did not understand. Then I saw the children. They stared at our house through the iron bars of the gate. Some of them were my age. Like the grown-ups, their eyes were red from not having slept for days. They wore heavy winter coats—some wore more than one coat, even though it was warm outside. These children looked as though they had dressed in a hurry. But if they came from somewhere else, where were their suitcases?

"What do they want?" I asked my mother.

"They have come to ask for your father's help," she replied. "Unless we help, they may be killed or taken away by some bad men."

169

SKILLS ⟷ STRATEGIES IN CONTEXT

Author's Purpose

TEACH

- Remind students that authors write for many reasons: to entertain, to explain or inform, to express opinions, or to persuade.
- Model finding the author's purpose on p. 168, paragraph 3.

Think Aloud **MODEL** This paragraph seems to be filled with details like what year it was, who the father was, and where they lived. This makes me think that the author is trying to tell or inform me about something.

PRACTICE AND ASSESS

Have students reread p. 169, paragraph 2. Ask students to identify the author's purpose for the paragraph. *(Choice a)*

a) to inform

b) to entertain

c) to express an opinion

World War II

Time for **SOCIAL STUDIES**

In 1939, German forces invaded Poland. This event prompted Britain and France to declare war on Germany. In 1940, Soviet troops occupied Lithuania. By mid-1941, Lithuania fell under the control of Nazi Germany. In late 1941, the United States then joined Britain and France against Germany after Japan bombed Pearl Harbor, Hawaii.

Guiding Comprehension

3  **Vocabulary • Unfamiliar Words**

Use a dictionary to learn what _translated_ means on p. 170, paragraph 2.

Translated means "changed from one language to another."

Monitor Progress

Unfamiliar Words

If... students have difficulty using a dictionary to define _translated_,	then... use the vocabulary strategy instruction on p. 171.

---

4 **Main Idea • Inferential**

What is the main idea of the selection so far?

Possible response: Jewish refugees beg Mr. Sugihara, a Japanese diplomat posted in Lithuania, to issue them visas so they could escape the Nazis during World War II.

Some of the children held on tightly to the hands of their fathers, some clung to their mothers. One little girl sat on the ground crying.

I felt like crying too. "Father," I said, "please help them."

My father stood quietly next to me, but I knew he saw the children. Then some of the men in the crowd began climbing over the fence, Borislav and Gudje, two young men who worked for my father, tried to keep the crowd calm.

My father walked outside. Peering through the curtains, I saw him standing on the steps. Borislav translated what **3** my father said: He asked the crowd to choose five people to come inside and talk.

My father met downstairs with the five men. My father could speak Japanese, Chinese, Russian, German, French, and English. At this meeting, everyone spoke Russian.

I couldn't help but stare out the window and watch the crowd, while downstairs, for two hours, my father listened to frightening stories. These people were refugees—people who ran away from their homes because, if they stayed, they would be killed. They were Jews from Poland, escaping from the Nazi soldiers who had taken over their country.

The five men had heard my father could give them visas—official written permission to travel through another country. The hundreds of Jewish refugees outside hoped to travel east through the Soviet Union and end up in Japan. Once in Japan, they could go to another country. Was it true? the men asked. Could my father give them visas? If he did not, the Nazis **4** would soon catch up with them.

170

ELL

Extend Language Read aloud the last sentence on p. 170. Tell students that "to catch up with" is a phrase often used about a race; for example, "I caught up with Billy just before the finish line." Ask students to act out "catching up with."

My father answered that he could issue a few, but not hundreds. To do that, he would have to ask for permission from his government in Japan.

That night, the crowd stayed outside our house. Exhausted from the day's excitement, I slept soundly. But it was one of the worst nights of my father's life. He had to make a decision. If he helped these people, would he put our family in danger? If the Nazis found out, what would they do?

But if he did not help these people, they could all die.

My mother listened to the bed squeak as my father tossed and turned all night.

171

VOCABULARY STRATEGY

Unfamiliar Words

TEACH

Dictionaries are books with thousands of words and definitions. Glossaries are smaller and are usually found at the end of books. Explain that both are good sources for finding definitions of unfamiliar words. Model using a dictionary to find the meaning of an unfamiliar word.

 Think Aloud

MODEL On p. 170, it says, "Borislav translated what my father said..." I don't know what *translated* means, so, I look it up in the dictionary. It says: "changed from one language to another." It makes sense that Borislav had to change what the father said, because the father didn't speak their language.

PRACTICE

- Have students use a dictionary to find the meanings of these words on pp. 170–171: *clung*, *peering*, and *exhausted*. Remind them to look for the definition that makes the most sense in the selection. *(clung:* "held fast to something"; *peering:* "looking closely"; *exhausted:* "very tired")*

EXTEND SKILLS

Mood

Explain that mood is the atmosphere or feeling of a story. Discuss the mood on pp. 170–171. Ask students how it makes them feel and how the author creates the mood.

Guiding Comprehension

5 Sequence • Inferential

Find the clue words in the first sentence on p. 172 that tell you when the father sent the cable to his government.

The clue words "The next day" tell you when the father sent the cable.

Monitor Progress

REVIEW Sequence

If... students have difficulty finding clue words to understand sequence,	then... use the skill and strategy instruction on p. 173.

6 Author's Craft • Inferential

Question the Author **What is the author trying to tell you when he says "My father cabled his superiors a third time, and I knew the answer by the look in his eyes?"**

Possible response: He is trying to convey his father's disappointment and frustration.

7 Details• Critical

Text to Self **What lesson did the author's mother and aunt remind him about when they decided they had to stay and help the refugees? Did you ever learn a lesson like this?**

Possible response: That it was more important to think about others than yourself and to imagine if you were in their shoes.

5   The next day, my father said he was going to ask his government about the visas. My mother agreed it was the right thing to do. My father sent his message by cable. Gudje took my father's written message down to the telegraph office.

I watched the crowd as they waited for the Japanese government's reply. The five representatives came into our house several times that day to ask if an answer had been received. Any time the gate opened, the crowd tried to charge inside.

Finally, the answer came from the Japanese government. It was "no." My father could not issue that many visas to Japan. For the next two days, he thought about what to do.

Hundreds more Jewish refugees joined the crowd. My father sent a second message to his government, and again the answer was "no." We still couldn't go outside. My little brother Haruki cried often because we were running out of milk.

172

Context Clues Explain that *dis-* is a suffix that means not, so *disobey* means "not to obey," or "not to follow orders or instructions." Ask students to tell how the boy's father will disobey his government.

I grew tired of staying indoors. I asked my father constantly, "Why are these people here? What do they want? Why do they have to be here? Who are they?"

My father always took the time to explain everything to me. He said the refugees needed his help, that they needed permission from him to go to another part of the world where they would be safe.

"I cannot help these people yet," he calmly told me. "But when the time comes, I will help them all that I can."

My father cabled his superiors yet a third time, and I knew the answer by the look in his eyes. That night, he said to my mother, "I have to do something. I may have to disobey my government, but if I don't, I will be disobeying my conscience."

The next morning, he brought the family together and asked what he should do. This was the first time he ever asked all of us to help him with anything.

My mother and Auntie Setsuko had already made up their minds. They said we had to think about the people outside before we thought about ourselves. And that is what my parents had always told me—that I must think as if I were in someone else's place. If I were one of those children out there, what would I want someone to do for me?

I said to my father, "If we don't help them, won't they die?"

With the entire family in agreement, I could tell a huge weight was lifted off my father's shoulders. His voice was firm as he told us, "I will start helping these people."

Outside, the crowd went quiet as my father spoke, with Borislav translating.

"I will issue visas to each and every one of you to the last. So, please wait patiently."

173

Develop Vocabulary

PRACTICE LESSON VOCABULARY

Students orally respond *true* or *false* to each question and provide a reason for each answer that is false

1. A *diplomat* is the leader of a nation. *(False; a diplomat manages relations between nations.)*

2. *Superiors* are people of a higher rank than others. *(True)*

3. *Representatives* act and speak for others. *(True)*

BUILD CONCEPT VOCABULARY

Review previous concept words with students. Ask if students have come across any words today in their reading or elsewhere that they would like to add to the Taking Risks Concept Web, such as *disobey* and *conscience*.

Sequence REVIEW

TEACH

- Sequence is the order of events. Clue words can alert you to sequence.
- Model using clue words to tell you when the father sent a cable to his government.

Think Aloud **MODEL** In the first sentence on p. 172, it says "The next day, my father said he was going to ask his government about the visas." The clue words "The next day" tell me when this happened.

PRACTICE AND ASSESS

- Have students locate, on p. 172, the actions his father did after the Japanese government denied his request for more visas. *(He thought about what he could do to help.)*
- To assess, use Practice Book p. 66.

Strategy Response Log

Answer Questions Have students answer the questions they posed at the beginning of the selection. (See p. 166.) Then have them write two more questions.

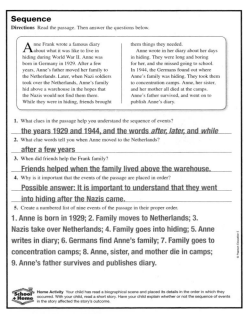

▲ **Practice Book** p. 66

If you want to teach this selection in two sessions, stop here.

Guiding Comprehension

If you are teaching the selection in two days, discuss the author's purpose so far and review the vocabulary.

8 🎯 **Vocabulary • Unfamiliar Words**

Use a dictionary to find the meaning of *embraced* on p. 174.

Meaning: hugged

9 **Sequence • Literal**

What does Mr. Sugihara do after he finishes each visa?

He looks into the eyes of the person receiving it and says, "Good luck."

10 🎯 **Author's Purpose • Inferential**

What is the author trying to tell you when he describes the Sugihara children playing with the refugee children?

Possible response: He wants to show that even though the children don't speak the same language, they can still be friends.

Monitor Progress

🎯 Author's Purpose

If... students have difficulty determining the author's purpose,	then... use the skill and strategy instruction on page 175.

DAY 3 Grouping Options

Reading

Whole Group Discuss the Question of the Day.

Group Time Differentiated Instruction

Read *Passage to Freedom.* See pp. 162h–162i for the small group lesson plan.

Whole Group Discuss the Reader Response questions on p. 178. Then use p. 185a.

Language Arts
Use pp. 185e–185k.

The crowd stood frozen for a second. Then the refugees burst into cheers. Grown-ups embraced each other, and some reached to the sky. Fathers and mothers hugged their children. I was especially glad for the children.

My father opened the garage door and the crowd tried to rush in. To keep order, Borislav handed out cards with numbers. My father wrote out each visa by hand. After he finished each one, he looked into the eyes of the person receiving the visa and said, "Good luck."

Refugees camped out at our favorite park, waiting to see my father. I was finally able to go outside.

Chiaki and I played with the other children in our toy car. They pushed as we rode, and they rode as we pushed. We chased each other around the big trees. We did not speak the same language, but that didn't stop us.

For about a month, there was always a line leading to the garage. Every day, from early in the morning till late at night, my father tried to write three hundred visas. He watered down the ink to make it last. Gudje and a young Jewish man helped out by stamping my father's name on the visas.

My mother offered to help write the visas, but my father insisted he be the only one, so no one else could get into trouble. So my mother watched the crowd and told my father how many were still in line.

One day, my father pressed down so hard on his fountain pen, the tip broke off. During that month, I only saw him late at night. His eyes were always red and he could hardly talk. While he slept, my mother massaged his arm, stiff and cramped from writing all day.

174

ⒺⓁⓁ

Extend Language Reread the phrase "the Soviets came from the east and took over Lithuania." Tell students that *took over* is the past tense of *take over*, which means "to take charge of." Explain that the verb *take* is an irregular verb and it has an irregular past *(took)* and past participle *(taken)*.

Soon my father grew so tired, he wanted to quit writing the visas. But my mother encouraged him to continue. "Many people are still waiting," she said. "Let's issue some more visas and save as many lives as we can."

While the Germans approached from the west, the Soviets came from the east and took over Lithuania. They ordered my father to leave. So did the Japanese government, which re-assigned him to Germany. Still, my father wrote the visas until we absolutely had to move out of our home. We stayed at a hotel for two days, where my father still wrote visas for the many refugees who followed him there.

Then it was time to leave Lithuania. Refugees who had slept at the train station crowded around my father. Some refugee men surrounded my father to protect him. He now just issued permission papers—blank pieces of paper with his signature.

175

Author's Purpose Monitor / Fix Up

TEACH

Remind students that authors write for many reasons: to entertain, to explain or inform, to express opinions, or to persuade. When reading, students should consider what words the author uses. Students should also consider what the author wants the reader to think or feel.

 Think Aloud

MODEL When I read paragraph 4 on p. 174 about the Sugihara children playing with the refugee children, I wonder why the author included this in the story. I think it's to show that people with different backgrounds can be friends and that all people are alike in some ways.

PRACTICE AND ASSESS

Have students reread the last paragraph on p. 175. Why did the author include this sentence: "Some refugee men surrounded my father to protect him"? *(To show how much they cared for him and appreciated his kindness and generosity.)*

Diplomacy

Time for SOCIAL STUDIES

Diplomacy is a way to resolve conflicts and maintain peace between nations through dialogue and negotiation, rather than violence or war. In cases when a necessary war is waged, diplomacy is still an important tool in negotiating an end to war and building peace between warring nations.

Guiding Comprehension

11 🔊 **Author's Purpose • Critical**

What does the author want you to think about his father?

Possible responses: He was kind, courageous, and had compassion for the refugees. He was a man of conscience and a hero.

12 **REVIEW** **Sequence • Literal**

What happened to the Sugiharas after they left Lithuania and before they returned to Japan?

They were imprisoned in a Soviet internment camp for eighteen months.

13 **Compare and Contrast • Critical**

Text to World **Mr. Sugihara had the courage to put the needs of the refugees ahead of his own and was willing to face the consequences. Tell about someone you know or another historical figure who has done a similar thing.**

Possible response: Dr. Martin Luther King Jr. dedicated his life to improving the rights of African Americans. He went to jail and risked his life for what he believed to be right.

Strategy Response Log

Summarize When students finish reading the selection, provide this prompt: Describe what *Passage to Freedom* is about in a few sentences.

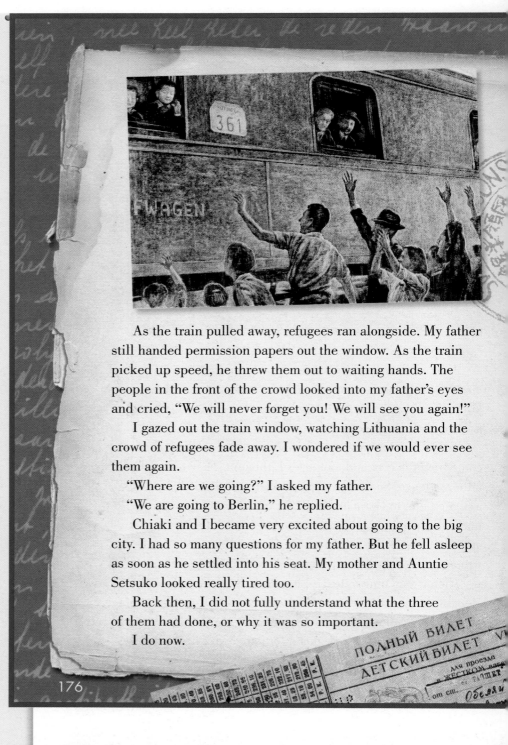

As the train pulled away, refugees ran alongside. My father still handed permission papers out the window. As the train picked up speed, he threw them out to waiting hands. The people in the front of the crowd looked into my father's eyes and cried, "We will never forget you! We will see you again!"

I gazed out the train window, watching Lithuania and the crowd of refugees fade away. I wondered if we would ever see them again.

"Where are we going?" I asked my father.

"We are going to Berlin," he replied.

Chiaki and I became very excited about going to the big city. I had so many questions for my father. But he fell asleep as soon as he settled into his seat. My mother and Auntie Setsuko looked really tired too.

Back then, I did not fully understand what the three of them had done, or why it was so important.

I do now.

176

ELL

Fluency Help students chunk words into meaningful phrases. For example, the second sentence on p. 177, paragraph 3, can be separated this way to support comprehension:

Finally, in the 1960s / he started hearing from "Sugihara survivors," / many of whom had kept their visas / and considered the worn pieces of paper to be family treasures.

AFTERWORD

Each time that I think about what my father did at Kaunas, Lithuania, in 1940, my appreciation and understanding of the incident continues to grow. In fact, it makes me very emotional to realize that his deed saved thousands of lives, and that I had the opportunity to be a part of it.

I am proud that my father had the courage to do the right thing. **11** Yet, his superiors in the Japanese government did not agree. The years after my family left Kaunas were difficult ones. We were imprisoned for eighteen months in a Soviet internment camp; and when we **12** finally returned to Japan, my father was asked to resign from diplomatic service. After holding several different jobs, my father joined an export company, where he worked until his retirement in 1976.

My father remained concerned about the fate of the refugees, and at one point left his address at the Israeli Embassy in Japan. Finally, in the 1960s, he started hearing from "Sugihara survivors," many of whom had kept their visas, and considered the worn pieces of paper to be family treasures.

In 1969, my father was invited to Israel, where he was taken to the famous Holocaust memorial, Yad Vashem. In 1985, he was chosen to receive the "Righteous Among Nations" Award from Yad Vashem. He was the first and only Asian to have been given this great honor.

In 1992, six years after his death, a monument to my father was dedicated in his birthplace of Yaotsu, Japan, on a hill that is now known as the Hill of Humanity. In 1994, a group of Sugihara survivors traveled to Japan to rededicate the monument in a ceremony that was attended by several high officials of the Japanese government.

The story of what my father and my family experienced in 1940 is an important one for young people today. It is a story that I believe will inspire you to care for all people and to respect life. It is a story that proves that one person can make a difference. **13**

Thank you. *Hiroki Sugihara*

177

Develop Vocabulary

PRACTICE LESSON VOCABULARY

As a class, have students complete the following sentences orally.

1. Mr. Sugihara sent messages to Japan by *(cable)*, or telegram.

2. Mr. Sugihara asked for five *(representatives)* from the crowd of refugees to come meet with him.

3. *(Refugees)* from wars are cared for by neighboring countries.

BUILD CONCEPT VOCABULARY

Review previous concept words with students. Ask if students have come across any words today in their reading or elsewhere that they would like to add to the Taking Risks Concept Web, such as *imprisoned* and *internment.*

STRATEGY SELF-CHECK

Monitor and Fix Up

Ask students to identify the author's purpose in the selection. Remind students that authors can have more than one reason for writing. Discuss how identifying author's purposes as they read help students understand the story. Use Practice Book p. 67.

SELF-CHECK

Students can ask themselves these questions to assess their ability to use the skill and strategy.

- Did I identify author's purpose as I read *Passage to Freedom?*
- Did I monitor the author's purpose to help me understand the story?

Monitor Progress

Author's Purpose

If... students have difficulty monitoring to understand author's purpose,	then... use the Reteach lesson on p. 185b.

Author's Purpose

- The **author's purpose** is the reason or reasons the author has for writing.
- An author may write to persuade, to inform, to entertain, or to express himself or herself.

Directions Read the following passage. Then answer the questions below.

Tom stood outside the school office, not knowing what to do. He should have been excited about the class pizza party. He loved pizza. But he wasn't excited. Tom's class won the pizza party when three of his classmates entered the best guess for the number of marbles it took to fill up a jar. The problem was, Tom knew that his classmates had cheated. They had found the principal's notes, which told exactly how many marbles had been used, and had copied the number down. A group of third-graders had come within fifteen marbles all by themselves, just by estimating. Even though he loved pizza, Tom didn't think it was fair to enjoy the party that the third-graders had earned. If he did nothing, Tom would feel dishonest. He took a deep breath, and went into the office to talk to the principal.

Possible answers given.

1. Why do you think the author wrote this passage?
   The author wrote this passage to entertain and to persuade the reader that cheating is wrong.

2. Do you think the author met his or her purpose for writing? Why or why not?
   Yes, because the character told the truth even though it was hard.

3. Why do you think the author wrote the passage from Tom's point of view?
   The author wrote it from Tom's point of view to show what Tom was feeling.

4. Why does the author tell a story instead of simply writing an essay about why cheating is wrong?
   The author wrote a story to make the events seem more real.

5. Did you need to change your normal reading pace to understand it? Why or why not?
   I read it a little faster than normal, because the author didn't use difficult words or lots of information to tell the story.

School + Home **Home Activity** Your child analyzed the author's purpose in a passage, and monitored his or her understanding of it. Read a persuasive piece such as a newspaper editorial with your child and discuss how the author persuades the reader.

▲ **Practice Book** p. 67

Passage to Freedom **177**

Reader Response

Open for Discussion Personal Response

MODEL Mr. Sugihara thought about his family's safety and his obligation to Japan and the refugees. I hope I would have the courage to do the same.

Comprehension Check Critical Response

1. Possible response: Examples should include the children playing with toys. This shows the innocence of the children involved in this difficult time. **Author's Purpose**

2. Possible response: The author wants to inform readers of the dangers his family faced and to express feelings about helping the refugees. **Author's Purpose**

3. Mr. Sugihara wrote each visa by hand, working from early in the morning until late at night. **Monitor and Fix Up**

4. Responses will vary but should be in friendly letter form and include words such as *refugees, visa,* and *issue.* **Vocabulary**

Look Back and Write For test practice, assign a 10–15 minute time limit. For assessment, see the Scoring Rubric at the right.

Retell

Have students retell *Passage to Freedom.*

Monitor Progress

Check Retelling Rubric 4 3 2 1

If... students have difficulty retelling the selection,	**then...** use the Retelling Cards and the Scoring Rubric for Retelling on p. 179 to assist fluent retelling.

SUCCESS PREDICTOR

ELL

Check Retelling As students retell the selection, focus on their comprehension rather than on their mistakes with English. For more ideas on assessing students' retellings, see the ELL and Transition Handbook.

Reader Response

Open for Discussion Sometimes it is hard to figure out the right thing to do. What was Mr. Sugihara's difficulty in deciding what to do? How did he make his decision? What would you have done? Explain why.

1. *Passage to Freedom* is told through the eyes of a child. Discuss how this point of view adds to the report of events. Select examples for support. Think Like an Author

2. Is the purpose of the author to entertain the reader, inform the reader, or express how he felt? Find examples from pages 168–169 to justify your answer. Author's Purpose

3. How hard did Mr. Sugihara have to work to help the refugees? Reread page 174 and discuss all the things he had to do. Monitor and Fix Up

4. Pretend you are one of the refugees Mr. Sugihara helped. Write him a letter of gratitude. Use words from the Words to Know list and the selection. Vocabulary

Look Back and Write Mr. Sugihara was honored for his work in several ways. Look back at page 177 to write about how he was honored.

Meet author **Ken Mochizuki on page 763 and** illustrator **Dom Lee on page 774.**

178

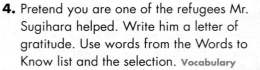
Scoring Rubric | **Look Back and Write**

Top-Score Response A top-score response will use details from p. 177 to list ways Mr. Sugihara was honored for bravely saving the lives of so many refugees.

Example of a Top-Score Response Mr. Sugihara received several honors from the Jewish people. In 1969, he was invited to the Holocaust memorial in Israel. In 1985, he was given the "Righteous Among Nations" award. The Japanese honored him in 1992 with a memorial in his birthplace. Top government officials and Jewish survivors attended the rededication in 1994.

For additional rubrics, see p. WA10.

Write Now

Story Review

Prompt

Passage to Freedom is a powerful story about decisions a family makes.

Think about another story you have read recently.

Now write a story review telling what you liked or did not like about the story.

Writing Trait

Discussing only a few key **ideas** will help make your story review more **focused.**

Student Model

First paragraph tells about story's main character and plot.

Writer **focuses** on **idea** from story that is valued.

Idea is supported by evidence from story.

Ending states why writer values idea.

> In "Inside Out," Francisco Jiménez shows what life at school is like for a boy who does not speak English. Francisco does not understand what his teacher and other students say. He finds comfort in watching a caterpillar in a jar near his desk. He also loves to draw birds and butterflies.
>
> What I liked about this story is that as Francisco's confidence grows, he does not lose his ability to be kind, even when others are not kind to him. When he wins the art prize and earns the respect of his teacher and his classmates, he could have bragged. Instead, he chooses to be friends with the boy who fought with him. This story provides a good lesson about courage for everyone.

Use the model to help you write your own story review.

179

Write Now

Look at the Prompt Have students identify and discuss key words and phrases in the prompt. *(story you have read recently, summary)*

Strategies to Develop Focus/Ideas

Have students

- write their opinion of the story using specific words.

NO: The story was very good.

YES: The story was action-packed.

- list details from the story that support their opinion.

NO: I liked the ending.

YES: Al, believed dead, opened the door.

- reread their drafts, stopping to ask, "Does this support my main idea?"

For additional suggestions and rubric, see pp. 185g–185h.

Hints for Better Writing

- Carefully read the prompt.
- Use a graphic organizer to plan your writing.
- Support your ideas with information and details.
- Use words that help readers understand.
- Proofread and edit your work.

Scoring Rubric   Expository Retelling

Rubric 4 3 2 1	4	3	2	1
Connections	Makes connections and generalizes beyond the text	Makes connections to other events, texts, or experiences	Makes a limited connection to another event, text, or experience	Makes no connection to another event, text, or experience
Author's Purpose	Elaborates on author's purpose	Tells author's purpose with some clarity	Makes some connection to author's purpose	Makes no connection to author's purpose
Topic	Describes the main topic	Identifies the main topic with some details early in retelling	Identifies the main topic	Retelling has no sense of topic
Important Ideas	Gives accurate information about events, steps, and ideas using details and key vocabulary	Gives accurate information about events, steps, and ideas with some detail and key vocabulary	Gives limited or inaccurate information about events, steps, and ideas	Gives no information about events, steps, and ideas
Conclusions	Draws conclusions and makes inferences to generalize beyond the text	Draws conclusions about the text	Is able to draw few conclusions about the text	Is unable to draw conclusions or make inferences about the text

Retelling Plan

- ☑ **Week 1** Assess Strategic Intervention students.
- ☑ **This week assess Advanced students.**
- ☐ **Week 3** Assess Strategic Intervention students.
- ☐ **Week 4** Assess On-Level students.
- ☐ **Week 5** Assess any students you have not yet checked during this unit.

Use the Retelling Chart on p. TR17 to record retelling.

Selection Test To assess with *Passage to Freedom*, use Selection Tests, pp. 25–28.

Fresh Reads for Differentiated Test Practice For weekly leveled practice, use pp. 37–42.

SUCCESS PREDICTOR

Social Studies in Reading

- Examine features of an autobiography.
- Practice a test-taking strategy.
- Compare and contrast across texts.

PREVIEW/USE TEXT FEATURES

As students preview "I Wanted My Mother" have them look at the title and scan the paragraphs. After they preview ask:

- **Who is this selection about? How do you know?** *(Debora Biron; Debora Biron is the author, and the story is written in the first-person point of view.)*

- **What do you think this selection is about?** *(Debora Biron's escape from the Germans during World War II.)*

Link to Social Studies

Have students complete a Venn diagram to help them make comparisons and contrasts between Debora Biron and another person who lived in Europe during World War II.

DAY 4 — Grouping Options

Reading

Whole Group Discuss the Question of the Day.

Group Time Differentiated Instruction
Read "I Wanted My Mother." See pp. 162h–162i for the small group lesson plan.

Whole Group Use p. 185a.

Language Arts
Use pp. 185e–185k.

Social Studies in Reading

Autobiography

Genre
- An autobiography is the story of a person's life, or a single incident in it, told by that person.
- It tells about real places, people, and events in the author's life.

Text Features
- An autobiography is written from the first-person point of view, so the narrator refers to herself as *I*.
- Events in an autobiography are usually presented in chronological order.
- Note that some paragraphs begin with phrases such as "by now" to show that time is passing.

Link to Social Studies
Read other autobiographies of people who lived in Europe during World War II. How were their experiences like Debora Biron's? How were they different?

180

I Wanted my Mother

BY DEBORA BIRON

During World War II, Debora Biron lived in Lithuania. Her family was Jewish, and the invading Germans were killing Jews. So Debora, about seven at this time, and her mother went to live with the Karashkas, a non-Jewish family who hid them on their farm. Natasha, a friend of the Karashkas, also helped. They also hid Herman, a friend of Debora's mother. Then one day the Germans began closing in.

Content-Area Vocabulary	Social Studies
ghetto	a part of a city in Europe where Jews were required to live
kerosene	a thin oil obtained from petroleum; used as a fuel in lamps, stoves, and some engines

Access Content Lead a picture walk to reinforce vocabulary, such as *bunker* (p. 181) *forked stick* and *kerosene lamp* (p. 182). Use the picture on p. 183 to explain where the people were hiding. As students read, have them refer to the pictures for additional support.

By now the Germans were everywhere. It got so dangerous, we could no longer live upstairs and instead moved into the cellar under the kitchen. But Herman thought that wasn't safe either and decided we should build a bunker next to the cellar, where the Germans were less likely to look. He and Mr. Karashka designed the room.

It was seven feet long and very narrow. To get in and out, they made a trap door that opened into the hallway. It had wooden planks on top that matched the flooring. Underneath it was insulated with blankets and cotton so it wouldn't sound hollow when someone walked on it.

Author's Purpose Is the author trying to inform you or entertain you?

181

DURING READING

AUTOBIOGRAPHY

Use the sidebar on p. 180 to guide discussion.

- Explain to students that an autobiography is nonfiction and provides information about a person's life as told by that person.
- Tell students that an autobiography is written in the first-person point of view.
- Discuss with students the pronouns they might find in a selection that would lead them to believe that it is an autobiography. *(I, we, me, us, my, mine, our, ours)*

 AudioText

Author's Purpose

Possible response: The sequence and serious tone of the selection indicate that the author is trying to inform.

World War II

Time for **SOCIAL STUDIES**

In 1933, Adolf Hitler (1889–1945) became leader of Germany. He also led the National Socialist German Workers' party, whose members were called Nazis. Once in control of Germany, Hitler began to seize control of Europe, one country at a time. His goal was to dominate the world and get rid of all peoples the Nazis deemed inferior. When the German army invaded Poland in 1939, Britain and France declared war. The war raged in Europe until Germany surrendered in May 1945.

TEST PRACTICE

Strategies for Nonfiction

USE TIME PHRASES Explain to students that an autobiography usually presents the information in chronological order. Words and phrases such as *after, at last, while, for one week, finally,* and *by then,* provide clues to when the events took place. Students can use the chronological clue words to help answer test questions. Provide the following strategy.

Use the Strategy

1. Read the test question carefully.
2. If the question is looking for information concerning the sequence or length of events, scan the selection looking for chronological clue words.
3. Then read the information to find an answer to the test question.

GUIDED PRACTICE Have students discuss how they would use the strategy to answer the following question.

When did Herman close the bunker trap door?

INDEPENDENT PRACTICE After students answer the following test question, discuss the process they used to find information.

What did the people in the bunker do after the Russian troops arrived?

For one week we all helped build the bunker, sleeping in the day and digging at night. Hour after hour we shoveled earth into bags which Mr. Karashka emptied onto his field. Finally the bunker was finished. It was tiny, dark, and uncomfortable. Although we each had a quilt and a wooden board to sleep on, the earthen floor was always damp, so our clothing and blankets smelled musty.

Because there was hardly any fresh air in the bunker, we kept the trap door braced open with a forked stick. At night the adults took turns being on guard to alert us if there was trouble.

Once we moved into the bunker, the Karashkas said we could go upstairs only to use the bathroom. But since they had told people I was their cousin and had an excuse for my living with the family, they said I could also go up to the kitchen to get food for myself and the others. I was proud that they trusted me. And I was happy to get away from the cramped, smelly bunker, even if only for a little while.

I hated living so tightly together with grown-ups who were irritable and constantly arguing. They fought if someone snored too loud, and they fussed over who should sleep in which bed. It got so bad, they began to tell one another to leave.

The worst was when they started talking about what they thought was happening to the Jews. That scared me. All I wanted was to lie in my mother's arms and listen to her read to me by the kerosene lamp.

Soon the Russians were bombing our area, always in the middle of the night. There was shelling in the forest next to our house. I was terrified, but I never complained. I didn't want to cause any extra problems. Besides, I thought this was what life was supposed to be like.

182

Test Practice Help students understand some of the chronological clue words or phrases found in this selection. Point them out in the selection and write them on the board: *while, for one week, finally, soon, by then, a moment before, afterward, one more month, a few days later.* Discuss the meanings and how they indicate sequence.

By then the Germans were searching for men to send to labor camps. Mr. Karashka moved into the bunker with us while Mrs. Karashka and Gruzia, the Karashkas' daughter, slept in the cellar under the kitchen to escape the bombing.

One hot summer night we all woke up to the sound of thumping on the floor above. I recognized that sound from the ghetto. It was the boots of German soldiers, and it meant something bad.

Herman, who had been on guard, heard it first and quickly started to close the trap door. With each step above, he carefully moved the forked stick a tiny bit, not wanting to grab it fast, or the door would have slammed shut. Each second the tramping upstairs came nearer. If the trap door didn't close soon the soldiers would find us.

Monitor & Fix Up You may have to reread paragraphs carefully.

183

Monitor and Fix-Up

Remind students that if they don't understand what they read or have trouble recalling events, they should reread parts of the selection.

Access Content Point to the word *ghetto*. Tell students that generally a *ghetto* refers to a part of a city where people of the same race or nationality live. Explain that in Europe during World War II, *ghetto* specifically referred to a part of the city where Jews were forced to live.

USE TEXT FEATURES

Discuss with students the first-person point of view used in the selection. Point out that the author tells the story from her point of view and uses the pronoun *I* to refer to herself. Then ask:

- **What effect does the first-person narrative have on your reading of the selection?** *(Possible response: It makes me feel more connected to the narrator.)*

- **How would the selection be different if it was told from someone else's point of view?** *(Possible response: If it was told from Mrs. Karashkas' point of view, it might tell about how scary it was to help her friends and why she did.)*

Suddenly the house was silent. The soldiers were standing right above us. A moment before, the trap door had closed.

"Who's down there?" a soldier shouted.

"It's only my child and me," Mrs. Karashka called from the cellar under the kitchen.

"Where is your husband?" he yelled.

"He's at the front," she said.

The soldier went downstairs and took a look for himself. None of us dared to breathe. When the soldier was satisfied with what he saw, he and the others left.

184

Extend Language Point to the word *front*. Explain that this word has two meanings. Help students name the more common meaning *(the part that faces forward)*. Tell them that *the front* also refers to a "battle front, or the place where a battle is being fought." Ask students why Mrs. Karashka tells the soldiers that her husband is at the front.

Afterward that's all we talked about. Over and over we relived what had happened. We couldn't believe we had survived to tell the story.

Now I could better understand how the Karashkas were protecting us. All along Natasha and my mother told me what wonderful people they were, and although I liked them a lot, I didn't realize until that night how they were risking their lives for us.

We stayed in the bunker for one more month. Then in August 1944 Russian troops marched through our village, and the Germans were finally gone. When it seemed safe, we crawled out of the bunker. A few days later we said good-bye to the Karashkas. After being in their house for a year, I was so happy to leave it. I wanted to get as far away from that place as possible.

Reading Across Texts

How do the Karashkas and Mr. Sugihara feel about helping people in trouble?

Writing Across Texts Make a list of reasons why a person should help someone in trouble.

Ⓒ **Monitor & Fix Up** Where do you learn the Karashkas are risking their lives?

185

CONNECT TEXT TO TEXT

Reading Across Texts

Have students tell what the Karashkas and Mr. Sugihara did to help people who were in trouble. Discuss the dangers that were involved. Then have students tell what they think the Karashkas and Mr. Sugihara would say about helping people who are in trouble.

Writing Across Texts Encourage students to think about times they've helped friends or neighbors and why they did.

Ⓒ **Monitor and Fix Up**

Possible response: At the end, when the German soldiers come and search the Karashkas's home and the cellar, I learn that if the others had been found, they all would've been in danger.

Fluency

Fluency Assessment Plan

☑ **Week 1** Assess Advanced students.

☑ **This week assess Strategic Intervention students.**

☐ **Week 3** Assess On-Level students.

☐ **Week 4** Assess Strategic Intervention students.

☐ **Week 5** Assess any students you have not yet checked during this unit.

Set individual goals for students to enable them to reach the year-end goal.
- Current Goal: 110–116 wcpm
- Year-End Goal: 140 wcpm

Read intresting sentences aloud to English language learners frequently, adding think-aloud comments to explain how cues such as letter patterns in words, phrases and other "chunks" of words, and punctuation can help you understand and read fluently.

To develop fluent readers, use Fluency Coach.

DAY 5 Grouping Options

Reading
Whole Group
Revisit the Question of the Week.

Group Time
Differentiated Instruction
Reread this week's Leveled Readers. See pp. 162h–162i for the small group lesson plan.

Whole Group
Use pp. 185b–185c.

Language Arts
Use pp. 185d–185l.

DAY 1

Model Reread "Number the Stars" on p. 162m. Tell students you will use different tones of voice to show emotions as you read the selection. Model for students how expressing a word in a certain manner lets the reader feel emotions as the author intends.

DAY 2

Choral Reading Read aloud p. 169. Have students notice how you pause at dashes and change the expressiveness of your voice for the different characters. Have students practice as a class doing three choral readings of p. 169.

DAY 3

Model Read aloud the first four paragraphs on p. 173. Have students notice how you pause at commas and how your voice changes when you read questions. Practice as a class by doing three choral readings.

DAY 4

Partner Reading Partners practice reading aloud the first four paragraphs on p. 173, three times. Students should read with proper expression and offer each other feedback.

Monitor Progress | Check Fluency WCPM

As students reread, monitor their progress toward their individual fluency goals. Current Goal: 110–116 words correct per minute. End-of-Year Goal: 140 words correct per minute.

If... students cannot read fluently at a rate of 110–116 words correct per minute,
then... make sure students practice with text at their independent level. Provide additional fluency practice, pairing nonfluent readers with fluent readers.

If... students already read at 140 words correct per minute,
then... they do not need to reread three to four times.

SUCCESS PREDICTOR

DAY 5

Assessment
Individual Reading Rate Use the Fluency Assessment Plan and do a one-minute timed reading of either selection from this week to assess students in Week 2. Pay special attention to this week's skill, tone of voice. Provide corrective feedback for each student.

RETEACH

◎ Author's Purpose

TEACH

Review the definition of *author's purpose* on p. 162. Students can complete Practice Book p. 68 on their own, or you can complete it as a class. Point out that students need to complete the answers in the graphic organizer after reading the information about Varian Fry in the passage.

ASSESS

Have students work with partners to determine author's purpose for writing the afterword on p. 177. Remind them that authors can have more than one reason for writing. *(Possible response: The author is writing to inform readers about what happened after the story ends and to express his feelings about his father.)*

For additional instruction on author's purpose, see DI·53.

EXTEND SKILLS

Point of View

TEACH

The author's point of view is the way an author presents the actions and characters of a story. In *Passage to Freedom,* Hiroki Sugihara tells the story from a personal, first-person point of view.

• Identify the point of view of a selection by thinking about who is telling it.

Have students consider how *Passage to Freedom* might be different it were told from a third-person point of view, or by someone else other than the person who actually experienced it.

ASSESS

Have students write a sentence about something that happened to them from a first-person point of view. Then have them write about the same thing from a third-person point of view and compare the two.

Look at the pronouns used to describe the characters such as *I, he, she, we,* and *they.*

OBJECTIVES

◎ Determine author's purpose.

● Understand point of view.

Skills Trace	
◎ Author's Purpose	
Introduce/Teach	TE: 5.2 162–163; 5.3 262–263; 5.5 560–561
Practice	Practice Book: 56, 63, 67, 68, 103, 107, 108, 176, 206, 223, 227, 228, 236
Reteach/Review	**TE: 5.2 151, 185b, DI•53; 5.3: 287b, 375, DI•52; 5.4 445; 5.5 521, 581b, 591, DI•54**
Test	Selection Test: 25–28, 41–44, 89-92; Benchmark Test: Unit 5

Access Content Reteach the skill by reviewing the Picture It! lesson on author's purpose in the ELL Teaching Guide, p. 43–44.

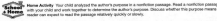

▲ **Practice Book** p. 68

Vocabulary and Word Study

VOCABULARY STRATEGY

Dictionary/ Glossary

UNFAMILIAR WORDS Remind students that they can use a dictionary or glossary to determine the correct meaning of an unfamiliar word. Remind students that some words have more than one meaning. Have students list unfamiliar words from *Passage to Freedom* and "I Wanted My Mother," look up their meanings, and write the definitions that most closely match the meanings in the selections.

Word	Best Dictionary Definition
tanks	heavily armored combat vehicles
parted	
monument	

Multiple Meanings

Multiple-meaning words are words that have several meanings depending upon how they are used in a sentence. Challenge partners to find three words from *Passage to Freedom* or "I Wanted My Mother" that have more than one meaning. Have them record the words, parts of speech, and meanings.

Multiple-Meaning Words	
1. safe	*adjective:* free from harm; *noun:* steel or iron box for storing money, jewels, etc.
2.	
3.	

BUILD CONCEPT VOCABULARY

Taking Risks

LOOKING BACK Remind students of the question of the week: Why do we help others even if there are risks? Discuss how this week's Concept Web of vocabulary words relates to the theme of taking risks. Ask students if they have any words or categories to add. Discuss if words and categories are appropriately related to the concept.

MOVING FORWARD Preview the title of the next selection, "The Ch'i-lin Purse." Ask students which Concept Web words might apply to the new selection based on the title alone.

Put a star next to these words on the web.

Display the Concept Web and revisit the vocabulary words as you read the next selection to check predictions.

Monitor Progress
Check Vocabulary

If... students suggest words or categories that are not related to the concept,	**then...** review the words and categories on the Concept Web and discuss how they relate to the lesson concept.

SUCCESS PREDICTOR

Speaking and Listening

Oral Report

SET-UP Have students research people who risked their lives to help others during World War II. Working in pairs or individually, have them present an oral report on the persons they chose.

RESEARCH Guide students to appropriate library resources to conduct their research. Once they choose subjects for their reports, suggest that students focus on whom the subjects helped, how they helped, and the risks involved.

ORGANIZATION Suggest students tell the story from the subject's point of view. While most students will structure their report in chronological order, point out that they could also consider using a cause-and-effect structure or a compare-and-contrast structure. They should begin by drawing in their audience with compelling statements describing the dangers the subjects put themselves in to help others. Then students should provide further information, detailing the ways in which the subjects helped and giving examples of the dangers involved. Have students conclude with final, brief notes summarizing the subjects' heroism.

Planning Tips

- Keep in mind when you must complete your report.
- Use an outline to organize your information according to your purpose.
- Practice your presentation.
- Provide visual aids if available.
- Consider your audience when planning your report.

ELL

Support Vocabulary Use the following to review and extend vocabulary and to explore lesson concepts further:
- ELL Poster 7, Days 3–5 instruction
- Vocabulary Activities and Word Cards in ELL Teaching Guide, pp. 45–46

Assessment For information on assessing students' speaking and listening, see the ELL and Transition Handbook.

Listen to Audio CD

Have students listen to the AudioText of *Passage to Freedom*. With partners, have students answer these questions orally or in writing.

1. **Did you learn new information from listening to the selection that you didn't pick up while reading it?**

2. **What is one advantage of hearing the selection read out loud? What is one disadvantage?** *(Responses will vary but students may describe what they like about hearing a selection read out loud, such as understanding information they didn't get from reading it themselves, and what they don't like about hearing a selection read out loud.)*

3. **Did your perception of any of the characters change after hearing the selection read out loud?**

Book Reports

SET-UP Have students find and read a fiction or nonfiction book of their choice about a person who does the right thing. They will present oral book reports to the class.

ORGANIZATION Help students organize their reports. Reports should tell the title and author, genre, a summary of events, a critique of the book, and a recommendation.

REPORT Students should use an outline or note cards to guide their reports. Remind students to speak clearly. Classmates will listen as they take turns reporting.

Vocabulary

SUCCESS PREDICTOR

Grammar Possessive Nouns

Monitor Progress

Grammar

If... students have difficulty identifying and using possessive nouns correctly,	then... provide additional instruction and practice in The Grammar and Writing Book pp. 86–89.

DAILY FIX-IT

This week use Daily Fix-It Transparency 7. **Spiral REVIEW**

ELL

Support Grammar See the Grammar Transition lessons in the ELL and Transition Handbook.

▲ **The Grammar and Writing Book**
For more instruction and practice, use pp. 86–89.

DAY 1 Teach and Model

DAILY FIX-IT

1. The childrens eyes were sad? *(children's; sad.)*

2. Them fled from the nazis. *(They; Nazis)*

READING-GRAMMAR CONNECTION

Write this sentence from *Passage to Freedom* on the board:

That boy looked into my father's eyes.

Explain that *father's* is a **possessive noun**. To make a singular noun show possession, add an apostrophe (') and an *-s*.

Display Grammar Transparency 7. Read aloud the definitions and example sentences. Work through the items.

Possessive Nouns

A **possessive noun** shows ownership. A **singular possessive noun** shows that one person, place, or thing has or owns something. A **plural possessive noun** shows that more than one person, place, or thing has or owns something.

- To make a singular noun show possession, add an apostrophe (') and -s.
  the baby's crib
- To make a plural noun that ends in -s show possession, add an apostrophe (').
  the soldiers' uniforms
- To make a plural noun that does not end in -s show possession, add an apostrophe (') and -s.
  the men's shoes

Directions Write the possessive form of each singular and plural noun.

1.	family	family's	11.	families	families'
2.	brother	brother's	12.	brothers	brothers'
3.	suitcase	suitcase's	13.	suitcases	suitcases'
4.	child	child's	14.	children	children's
5.	government	government's	15.	governments	governments'
6.	pen	pen's	16.	pens	pens'
7.	train	train's	17.	trains	trains'
8.	tree	tree's	18.	trees	trees'
9.	woman	woman's	19.	women	women's
10.	refugee	refugee's	20.	refugees	refugees'

Directions Circle the correct possessive noun in ( ) to complete each sentence.

21. A (pen's/pens') point can be sharp.
22. This (author's/authors') story is powerful.
23. The (Nazi's/Nazis') goal was to destroy or drive out all Jews.
24. Most (refugee's/refugees') stories were heartbreaking.
25. A Japanese (family's/families') compassion saved many lives.

Unit 2 Passage to Freedom   Grammar **7**

▲ **Grammar Transparency** 7

DAY 2 Develop the Concept

DAILY FIX-IT

3. The many travelers belongings were left behine. *(travelers'; behind)*

4. Thay could not save theirself. *(They; themselves)*

GUIDED PRACTICE

Review the concept of possessive nouns.

- **Singular possessive nouns** show that one person, place, or thing has or owns something. Add an apostrophe and *-s* to form singular possessive nouns.

- **Plural possessive nouns** show that more than one person, place, or thing has or owns something. Add an apostrophe to a plural noun ending in *-s* to form the possessive. If the plural noun does not end in *-s*, add an apostrophe and *-s*.

HOMEWORK Grammar and Writing Practice Book p. 25.

Possessive Nouns

A **possessive noun** shows ownership. A **singular possessive noun** shows that one person, place, or thing has or owns something. A **plural possessive noun** shows that more than one person, place, or thing has or owns something.

- To make a singular noun show possession, add an apostrophe (') and -s.
  a bird's song
- To make a plural noun that ends in -s show possession, add an apostrophe (').
  several weeks' work
- To make a plural noun that does not end in -s show possession, add an apostrophe (') and -s.
  the women's papers

Directions Write each noun as a possessive noun. Write S if the possessive noun is singular. Write P if the possessive noun is plural.

1.	friends	friends'	P
2.	story	story's	S
3.	freedom	freedom's	S
4.	mornings	mornings'	P
5.	children	children's	P
6.	milk	milk's	S

Directions Add an apostrophe (') or an apostrophe (') and -s to make each underlined word possessive. Write the sentence on the line.

7. A diplomat life requires travel.
   A diplomat's life requires travel.

8. Would democracy followers win the struggle?
   Would democracy's followers win the struggle?

Home Activity Your child learned about possessive nouns. Have your child look at some sale ads and make up sentences about them using possessive nouns.

▲ **Grammar and Writing Practice Book** p. 25

DAY 3 — Apply to Writing

5. Two mens' clothing stores had its windows broken. *(men's; their)*

6. Brave citizens hided refugees in several house. *(hid; houses)*

WRITE CORRECT POSSESSIVES

Explain that possessive nouns reduce wordiness so that writing flows more smoothly.

Wordy: the eyes of my father

Not Wordy: my father's eyes

- Have students review something they have written. They may be able to improve it by using possessive nouns in place of prepositional phrases.

HOMEWORK Grammar and Writing Practice Book p. 26.

Possessive Nouns

Directions Make each sentence less wordy by replacing the underlined words with a possessive noun phrase. Write the sentence on the line.

1. The pride of a son in his father can inspire him all his life.
   A son's pride in his father can inspire him all his life.

2. The rights of fathers are strong in Japanese society.
   Fathers' rights are strong in Japanese society.

3. The wishes of a father should always be respected by his family.
   A father's wishes should always be respected by his family.

4. The status of an elderly relative is highest of all.
   An elderly relative's status is highest of all.

5. What is more, the commands of government officials must be obeyed by all.
   What is more, government officials' commands must be obeyed by all.

6. The wants of an individual are less important than the well-being of the nation.
   An individual's wants are less important than the nation's well-being.

Directions Write a paragraph describing some of the traits of people in your family. Use possessive nouns to make your writing smooth and less wordy. **Possible answer:**
My family's heritage includes curly hair and big feet. My father's shoes are size 13, and my mother's are size 9. Both my sisters' hair is tight with curls. Jenny's feet are already size 9, but Melissa's are only size 8 even though she is older. Both grandmas' feet are large too. They joke about big feet running in our family.

School-Home Connection **Home Activity** Your child learned how to use possessive nouns in writing. Have your child make labels for the belongings of different family members using possessive nouns.

▲ **Grammar and Writing Practice Book** p. 26

DAY 4 — Test Preparation

7. The boy had no belt for he pantz. *(his pants)*

8. If she had a pare of scisors, Mama would fix them. *(pair; scissors)*

STANDARDIZED TEST PREP

Test Tip

Remember that an apostrophe shows ownership or relationship. Do not use an apostrophe to make a noun plural.

Plural: Two girls left their coats.

Possessive: Two girls' coats were left.

HOMEWORK Grammar and Writing Practice Book p. 27.

Possessive Nouns

Directions Mark the letter of the word that correctly completes each sentence.

1. _____ Jews fled from the German soldiers.
   A Polands
   B Poland's
   C Polands'
   D Polands's

2. American _____ efforts helped win the war.
   A soldiers
   B soldier's
   C soldiers'
   D soldiers's

3. A _____ shoes wore out quickly.
   A soldiers
   B soldier's
   C soldiers'
   D soldiers's

4. Success often depended on the _____ food supply.
   A armies
   B armie's
   C armys'
   D army's

5. Soldiers carried several _____ cold rations.
   A days
   B day's
   C days'
   D days's

6. Many _____ stomachs were often empty.
   A refugees
   B refugee's
   C refugees'
   D refugees's

7. A _____ kindness kept them alive another day.
   A strangers
   B stranger's
   C strangers'
   D strangers's

8. Money might be sewn into _____ coat linings.
   A women's
   B woman's
   C womens'
   D womans'

9. Worry haunted the refugee _____ eyes.
   A childrens
   B children's
   C childrens'
   D childrens's

10. _____ stories seemed unbelievable.
    A Survivors
    B Survivor's
    C Survivors'
    D Survivors's

School-Home Connection **Home Activity** Your child prepared for taking tests on possessive nouns. Have your child write several sentences describing a favorite toy or game using possessive nouns (such as *the bear's nose* or *the pieces' shapes*).

▲ **Grammar and Writing Practice Book** p. 27

DAY 5 — Cumulative Review

9. Poland was attacked, by the german army. *(attacked by; German)*

10. Ain't it a shame people cant' get along? *(Isn't; can't)*

ADDITIONAL PRACTICE

Assign pp. 86–89 in The Grammar and Writing Book.

EXTRA PRACTICE Grammar and Writing Practice Book p. 128.

TEST PREPARATION Grammar and Writing Practice Book pp. 153–154.

ASSESSMENT

CUMULATIVE REVIEW Grammar and Writing Practice Book p. 28.

Possessive Nouns

Directions Write each sentence. Change the underlined phrase to show possession.

1. The honesty of children is refreshing.
   Children's honesty is refreshing.

2. The comment of one little boy was especially moving.
   One little boy's comment was especially moving.

3. The eyes of the grown-ups were red from lack of sleep.
   The grown-ups' eyes were red from lack of sleep.

4. Did they sleep on the benches of the park?
   Did they sleep on the park's benches?

Directions Cross out each incorrect possessive noun. Write the correct possessive form above the word you crossed out.

5. Some children held their ~~fathers~~ hands. **fathers'**

6. One little ~~girls'~~ coat was too small for her. **girl's**

7. The little girl looked warm and happy in ~~Sukios'~~ coat. **Sukio's**

8. Small acts of kindness made the ~~outcast's~~ lives better. **outcasts'**

Directions Write a paragraph describing a refugee family that the Sugiharas might have helped. Use possessive nouns correctly. **Possible answer:**
The family's clothes were torn and dirty. The man's bare hands were stiff and gray. The parents' concern for their children was urgent. What would become of them if they could not leave Poland? Yet their eyes' expression was not hopeless. They had not given up.

School-Home Connection **Home Activity** Your child reviewed possessive nouns. Ask your child to write sentences telling what he or she appreciates about home, family, school, and friends. Ask your child to try to use a possessive noun in each sentence.

▲ **Grammar and Writing Practice Book** p. 28

Writing Workshop Story Review

OBJECTIVES

- Identify qualities of a story review or critique.
- Understand how to support ideas in a review.
- Focus on focus/ideas.
- Use a rubric.

Genre Story Review
Writer's Craft Support Your Ideas
Writing Trait Focus/Ideas

ELL

Focus/Ideas Write the following sentences on sheets of paper, one to a sheet. Work with English learners to identify the sentence that doesn't belong: Books can be about anything. Libraries have many books. We will swim after lunch. I read many books this summer.

Writing Traits

FOCUS/IDEAS Review summarizes story setting, characters, and theme and includes reaction to story.

ORGANIZATION/PARAGRAPHS Basic story information is followed by opinions and support. Conclusion wraps up review.

VOICE Writing is interesting. Writer's feelings about the story are communicated clearly.

WORD CHOICE Specific nouns (visas, diplomat, refugees) and verbs (crowd, inspired) are used. Connecting words tie thoughts together.

SENTENCES Sentences are varied in length and complexity.

CONVENTIONS There is excellent control and accuracy. Possessive nouns are used correctly.

READING-WRITING CONNECTION

- *Passage to Freedom* is about a Japanese diplomat's efforts to save Jewish refugees.
- The story focuses on the refugee crisis and supports the idea that it took heroic effort and courage to defy the Nazis.
- Students will write a **story review** focused on theme and characters, supported by plot details.

MODEL FOCUS/IDEAS Discuss Writing Transparency 7A. Then discuss the model and the writing trait of focus/ideas.

Think Aloud The writer focuses on what the story is about in the first sentence. This is the main idea on which the rest of the review is built. The next sentences summarize the setting and plot. Mr. Sugihara's job and the wartime situation make it clear that the diplomat's decision means life or death.

Story Review

A story review tells readers about a story's theme, setting, and characters and gives a brief summary of its plot. A review is also a critique because it tells the writer's thoughts and opinions about the story. These ideas should be supported by details and quotes from the story.

Story Review

First sentence gives story name, author, and main idea.

In "Passage to Freedom," Ken Mochizuki tells the story of a family's decision that saved thousands of lives during World War II. The Sugihara family is living in Lithuania in 1940. Mr. Sugihara is a diplomat who represents Japan. When Jewish refugees from Poland crowd the Sugihara home, Mr. Sugihara must make a decision. Should he go against his government's order and give the refugees visas to escape the Nazis?

Writer outlines setting and plot for readers.

What I love about this story is the way the whole family helps Mr. Sugihara decide to do the right thing. When his superiors in Japan refuse his request to give visas, Mr. Sugihara turns to his family and asks what he should do. Five-year-old Hiroki, the story's narrator, asks, "If we don't help them, won't they die?" The family makes up its mind to save as many people as possible by writing visas. The children help by playing with refugee children. Mrs. Sugihara helps by encouraging Mr. Sugihara when he is exhausted and by massaging his cramped hand and arm.

Story details support writer's opinions on story's strong points.

This story inspired me. It showed how much courage and strength it took to save others when risking personal danger.

Unit 2 Passage to Freedom   Writing Model **7A**

▲ **Writing Transparency** 7A

WRITER'S CRAFT
Support Your Ideas

Display Writing Transparency 7B. Read the directions and work together to identify sentences that provide support for opinions.

 PROVIDE GOOD SUPPORT FOR IDEAS Tomorrow we will write a **story review.** How can I support my opinion that the immigrants in *Shutting Out the Sky* showed determination in New York City? I might point out how they shared cramped rooms to save money. I might describe how they worked hard and long at humble jobs such as peddling. Details like these show their determination to beat the odds.

GUIDED WRITING Some students may need more help with supporting ideas. Have them find main idea sentences in the story and point out details that support those ideas.

Support Your Ideas

When you give an opinion about a story, you should **support your ideas** with facts and details. These details can include examples and quotes from the story or descriptions of characters or actions.

Directions Read each opinion. Circle the sentences that help support this opinion.
1. The refugees had been pushed to a state of desperation.
   - A Their eyes were red from lack of sleep.
   - B They shoved and pushed to get into the Sugihara house.
   - C The children played in the park.
   - D Children clung to their mothers.

2. Mr. Sugihara is torn between obeying his superiors and his conscience.
   - A His arm is stiff from writing visas.
   - B He tosses and turns all night.
   - C He explains the situation carefully to his son.
   - D He sends three cables to his government.

3. Mrs. Sugihara feels strongly that the refugees must be saved.
   - A She keeps the children indoors.
   - B She offers to help write the visas.
   - C She massages her husband's cramped, sore arm.
   - D She encourages him to continue when he wants to quit.

4. The refugees were very grateful to the Sugiharas.
   - A They cried, "We will never forget you!"
   - B They sent letters.
   - C Mr. Sugihara received the "Righteous Among Nations" Award.
   - D They traveled to Japan to rededicate a monument to Mr. Sugihara.

Directions Write your opinion about an important idea in a story you have read. List at least three pieces of evidence from the story that support your opinion. **Possible answers:**

My Opinion: Karana, the young Native American girl in *Island of the Blue Dolphins,* solves problems in a practical and ingenious way.

Supporting Evidence:
A A She chooses to make her home on the headland because the noise from the sea elephants is too deafening. B She uses strong, curved whale bones for a fence to keep out the wild dogs. C She makes a
B cooking pot by grinding a depression in a big stone.
C

Unit 2 Passage to Freedom   Writer's Craft **7B**

▲ **Writing Transparency** 7B

DAY 3 — Prewrite and Draft

READ THE WRITING PROMPT

on page 179 in the Student Edition.

Passage to Freedom is a power-ful story about a decision a family makes.

Think about another story you have read recently.

Now write a story review telling what you liked or did not like about the story.

Writing Test Tips

- Think of your reader as a friend to whom you are telling a story.
- Write a sentence telling the title, the author, and what you think the author's purpose was for telling the story.
- Write the main feeling or opinion you get from the story. Then list details from the story that make you think or feel this way.

GETTING STARTED Students can do any of the following:

- Make a story chart with these heads: *Main Characters, Setting, Plot Details, Main Idea Behind Story.* Then fill in the chart information.
- Write an opinion statement and list reasons for it in a word web.
- List examples and quotes from the story that support the opinion.

DAY 4 — Draft and Revise

EDITING/REVISING CHECKLIST

- ☑ Have I supported my opinion of the story with details from the story?
- ☑ Have I used the correct possessive forms of nouns?
- ☑ Have I spelled irregular plurals such as words that end in *f* and *o* correctly?

See *The Grammar and Writing Book,* pp. 86–91.

Revising Tips

Focus/Ideas

- Begin by introducing story title, author, setting, characters, and author's purpose for writing.
- Make your statements of opinion clear.
- Follow an opinion with supporting evidence from the story.

PUBLISHING Students can share their story reviews in a small group and offer listeners a chance to ask questions about the story.

ASSESSMENT Use the scoring rubric to evaluate students' work.

DAY 5 — Connect to Unit Writing

How-to Report	
Week 1	Summary 161g–161h
Week 2	Story Review 185g–185h
Week 3	News Story 207g–207h
Week 4	Rules 229g–229h
Week 5	Interview 253g–253h

PREVIEW THE UNIT PROMPT

Write a report explaining how to make or do something that is familiar to you. Choose words that make your report interesting to read and easy to understand. Explain all the steps and materials needed.

APPLY

- A how-to report explains the steps for making or doing something.
- A how-to report should include specific, clear supporting details for each step.

Writing Trait Rubric

	4	3	2	1
Focus/Ideas	Excellent focus with many vivid supporting details; no unnecessary details	Clear focus with some supporting details; no unnecessary details	Limited focus with a few supporting details; some unrelated details	Unfocused with little support and many unrelated details
	Excellent review with interesting, well-supported main idea	Good review with adequately supported main idea	Sharper focus on main idea needed in review	Review with no clear focus or main idea

Spelling & Phonics Irregular Plurals

OBJECTIVE

● Spell irregular plural words.

Generalization

Connect to Phonics Sometimes plurals are formed in irregular ways: *shelves*, *echoes*. Regular plurals follow the rules. Irregular plurals often have base word changes. Some irregular plurals are the same as the singular form.

Spelling Words

1. staffs	11. echoes
2. ourselves	12. shelves
3. pants	13. quizzes
4. scissors	14. sheriffs
5. loaves	15. dominoes
6. volcanoes	16. thieves
7. chiefs	17. measles
8. buffaloes	18. avocados
9. flamingos	19. chefs
10. beliefs	20. pianos

Challenge Words

21. bailiffs	24. armadillos
22. wharves	25. desperadoes
23. mosquitoes	

ELL

Spelling/Phonics Support See the ELL and Transition Handbook for spelling support.

PRETEST

Use the Dictation Sentences from Day 5 to administer the pretest. Read the word, read the sentence, and then read the word again. Guide students in self-correcting their pretests and correcting any misspellings.

Monitor Progress

Spelling

If... students misspell more than 5 pretest words,	**then...** use words 1–10 for Strategic Intervention.
If... students misspell 1–5 pretest words,	**then...** use words 1–20 for On-Level practice.
If... students correctly spell all pretest words,	**then...** use words 1–25 for Advanced Learners.

HOMEWORK Spelling Practice Book, p. 25.

▲ **Spelling Practice Book** p. 25

TEACH

Many irregular plurals do not seem to follow any rules. Write *chief* and *thief*. Model how to make *chief* plural by adding *s*. Model how to make *thief* plural by changing *f* to *v* and adding *-es*. Explain that some irregular plurals just need to be memorized.

> chief/chiefs
> thief/thieves

USE THE DICTIONARY Explain that the plurals of words that end in *o* may be formed by adding *-s* or *-es*. Model how to find plural forms in a dictionary. Have students look up the plural forms of the list words that end in *o* and other words such as *video, hero, banjo, patio, cargo,* and *tornado.*

HOMEWORK Spelling Practice Book, p. 26.

▲ **Spelling Practice Book** p. 26

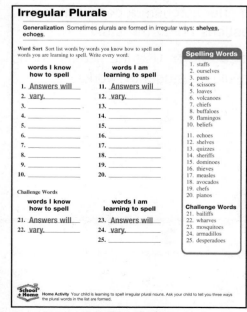

DAY 3 — Connect to Writing

WRITE OPINIONS

Ask students to use at least four spelling words to write sentences about things they liked and did not like about a movie or television show.

Frequently Misspelled High-Frequency Words

no	new
know	knew

Some students might still have difficulty spelling high-frequency words. Alert students to these frequently misspelled words. Point out that the letters *kn* stand for one sound, /n/. Review that *ow* can stand for the long *o* sound and *ew* can stand for the long *u* sound. Also alert students that the examples given are homophones, words that have the same pronunciation but have different spellings and meanings. Students can master words like these using memorization games, word lists, or a word wall.

HOMEWORK Spelling Practice Book, p. 27.

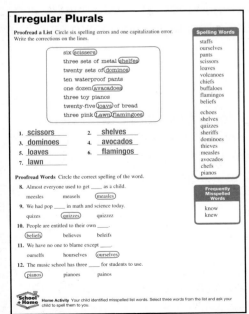

▲ **Spelling Practice Book** p. 27

DAY 4 — Review

REVIEW IRREGULAR PLURALS

Have pairs of students write the list words on note cards and sort them according to how the plural was formed. Have students compare and explain their sorts.

Spelling Strategy
Memory Tricks

Some words seem so tricky to spell that we need to outsmart them with tricks of our own.

Step 1: Mark the letters that give you a problem.

Step 2: Find words you know with the same letters.

Step 3: Use your problem words and the word you know in a phrase or sentence.

Example:

Hard word: domin<u>oes</u>

Memory trick: We pushed the domin<u>oes</u> with our <u>toes</u>.

HOMEWORK Spelling Practice Book, p. 28.

Irregular Plurals

Spelling Words				
staffs	ourselves	pants	scissors	loaves
volcanoes	chiefs	buffaloes	flamingos	beliefs
echoes	shelves	quizzes	sheriffs	dominoes
thieves	measles	avocados	chefs	pianos

Alphabetize Write the ten list words in the box below in alphabetical order.

1. beliefs
2. buffaloes
3. chefs
4. chiefs
5. loaves
6. measles
7. ourselves
8. pants
9. scissors
10. volcanoes

ourselves	scissors
volcanoes	pants
chiefs	measles
buffaloes	chefs
beliefs	loaves

Related Words Write the list word that is the plural of each word below.

11. echo	echoes	12. piano	pianos
13. quiz	quizzes	14. shelf	shelves
15. domino	dominoes	16. flamingo	flamingos
17. thief	thieves	18. avocado	avocados
19. staff	staffs	20. sheriff	sheriffs

Home Activity Your child has learned to read, write, and spell words with irregular plurals. Have your child underline the irregular ending in each word.

▲ **Spelling Practice Book** p. 28

DAY 5 — Posttest

DICTATION SENTENCES

1. The <u>staffs</u> at each company donated money for the victims.
2. We gave <u>ourselves</u> plenty of time.
3. Both boys tore their <u>pants</u> on the fence.
4. All the <u>scissors</u> are in that bin.
5. We need two <u>loaves</u> of bread.
6. Active <u>volcanoes</u> can be deadly.
7. Three fire <u>chiefs</u> raced to the fire.
8. Many <u>buffaloes</u> once covered the plains.
9. Pink <u>flamingos</u> wade in the pond.
10. I always try to act on my <u>beliefs</u>.
11. The <u>echoes</u> grew fainter.
12. The <u>shelves</u> are filled with cans.
13. I have three <u>quizzes</u> on Friday.
14. Two <u>sheriffs</u> worked on the case.
15. John put the <u>dominoes</u> in the box.
16. The <u>thieves</u> were soon arrested.
17. All the children have <u>measles</u>.
18. We need two <u>avocados</u> for this dish.
19. Both <u>chefs</u> host cooking shows.
20. Grand <u>pianos</u> take up lots of space.

CHALLENGE

21. The judges appointed new <u>bailiffs</u>.
22. The <u>wharves</u> were lined with boats.
23. Buzzing <u>mosquitoes</u> kept me awake.
24. I saw many <u>armadillos</u> when I lived in Texas.
25. The posse chased the <u>desperadoes</u>.

OBJECTIVES

- Formulate an inquiry question that is connected to this week's lesson focus.
- Effectively and efficiently find, evaluate, and communicate information related to an inquiry question using electronic sources.

New Literacies	
Day 1	Identify Questions
Day 2	Navigate/Search
Day 3	Analyze
Day 4	Synthesize
Day 5	Communicate

NEW LITERACIES

Internet Inquiry Activity

EXPLORE TAKING RISKS

Use the following 5-day plan to help students conduct this week's Internet inquiry activity on taking risks in dangerous times. Remind students to follow classroom rules when using the Internet.

DAY 1

Identify Questions Discuss the lesson focus question: *Why do we help others even if there are risks?* Brainstorm ideas for specific inquiry questions about taking risks for other people in dangerous times. Have students work individually, in pairs, or in small groups to write inquiry questions they want to answer.

DAY 2

Navigate/Search Explain how to conduct a simple Internet search about people performing risky, heroic acts using a student-friendly search engine. Have students determine keywords related to their inquiry questions. Discuss how to monitor their results to identify helpful Web sites. Remind students to think about why the Web site was created, and by whom.

DAY 3

Analyze Have students explore the Web sites they identified on Day 2. Tell them to scan each site for information that helps answer their inquiry questions. Students should analyze information for updated sources and usefulness. They can take notes from the sites, or if appropriate, print out and highlight relevant information.

DAY 4

Synthesize Have students synthesize information from Day 3. Remind them that when they synthesize, they combine relevant ideas and information from different sources to develop answers to their inquiry questions. Have students determine the best ways to communicate the results they have found.

DAY 5

Communicate Have students share their inquiry results. They can create fact sheets listing the reasons why someone might choose a career that could be dangerous.

RESEARCH/STUDY SKILLS

Parts of a Book

TEACH

Ask students for ideas about how to decide if a particular reference book is appropriate for a research report they are working on. They may need prompting to mention parts of a book, such as the title page, table of contents, and index. Hold up a social studies or science book and define these features.

- A **title page** gives the title, author, and publisher of the book, and sometimes, the name of the illustrator and date and place of publication.

- A **copyright page** tells the year a book was published, who is the copyright holder (having the rights to the text or illustrations), and the publisher.

- A **table of contents** is a list of chapters, articles, or stories in a book. It shows the page on which each chapter or selection begins.

- A **chapter title** often appears in both the Table of Contents and at the beginning of each chapter, and tells what the chapter will be about.

- A **glossary** is a list of words at the back of a book. Glossaries contain only words that are found in the book in which they appear.

- An **index** is an alphabetical listing of topics covered in a book followed by the page number or numbers where the topic can be found.

- An **appendix** provides more information and is found at the back of some books.

Have students work in pairs, and give each pair a science or social studies textbook. Have them locate the parts defined above. Then, discuss these questions:

1. **Where would you look to determine if this book gives information about Japanese schools?** (table of contents, index)

2. **Who is the publisher of the book and when was it published?** (Possible response: Scott Foresman; 2007)

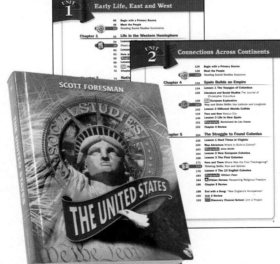

ASSESS

As students work with textbooks, check that they are able to identify various parts of the book and use the parts of the book to locate information.

For more practice or to assess students, use Practice Book pp. 69–70.

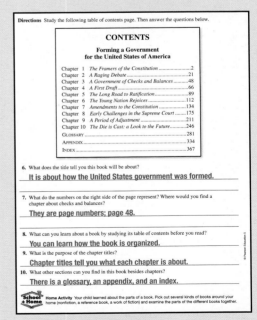

▲ **Practice Book** p. 69

▲ **Practice Book** p. 70

Assessment Checkpoints *for the Week*

Selection Assessment

Use pp. 25–28 of Selection Tests to check:

- [x] **Selection Understanding**
- [x] **Comprehension Skill** *Author's Purpose*
- [x] **Selection Vocabulary**

agreement	refugees
cable	representatives
diplomat	superiors
issue	visa

Leveled Assessment

Strategic Intervention
Advanced

Use pp. 37–42 of Fresh Reads for Differentiated Test Practice to check:

- [x] **Comprehension Skill** *Author's Purpose*
- [x] **REVIEW** **Comprehension Skill** *Sequence*
- [x] **Fluency** *Words Correct Per Minute*

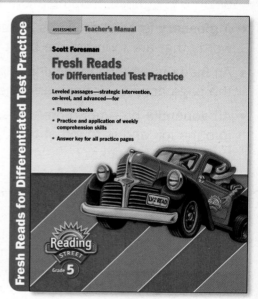

Managing Assessment

Use Assessment Handbook for:

- [x] **Observation Checklists**
- [x] **Record-Keeping Forms**
- [x] **Portfolio Assessment**

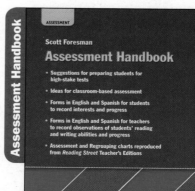

Unit 2
Doing the Right Thing

CONCEPT QUESTION
What makes people want to do the right thing?

Week 1
Why do people show kindness?

Week 2
Why do we help others even if there are risks?

Week 3
What are the rewards in helping others?

Week 4
What can people do to protect wild animals?

Week 5
How can people promote freedom?

EXPAND THE CONCEPT
What are the rewards in helping others?

Time for SOCIAL STUDIES

The Ch'i-lin Purse
RETOLD BY LINDA FANG
ILLUSTRATED BY ED YOUNG

How does the story show that one good deed deserves another?

CONNECT THE CONCEPT

▶ **Build Background**
distress, favor, panic, stranded

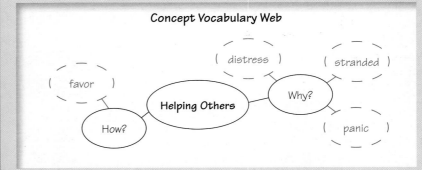

Concept Vocabulary Web

- distress
- stranded
- favor
- Helping Others
- Why?
- How?
- panic

▶ **Social Studies Content**
Chinese Family Customs, Jade, Aesop's Fables

▶ **Writing**
News Story

▶ **Internet Inquiry**
Good Deeds in Folk Tales

Preview Your Week

What are the rewards in helping others?

The Ch'i-lin Purse

RETOLD BY LINDA FANG
ILLUSTRATED BY ED YOUNG

How does the story show that one good deed deserves another?

Genre Folk tales are stories or legends that are told over and over from one generation to the next. As you read, imagine that someone is sitting next to you telling you the story.

Student Edition pages 190–203

Audio CD

Genre	Folk Tale
◉ **Vocabulary Strategy**	Word Structure
◉ **Comprehension Skill**	Compare and Contrast
◉ **Comprehension Strategy**	Predict

Paired Selection

Reading Across Texts
Compare Actions of Main Characters

Genre
Fable

Folk Literature

Fable

Genre
- A fable is a brief story that states a moral or lesson at the end. The action in the story shows the moral in action.
- Many fables have been passed by word of mouth from generation to generation until someone has written them down.
- Characters in fables are often animals.
- Animals in fables usually talk and behave like humans.

Link to Writing
Read other fables and make a list of the morals from each one. In your own words, write what each moral means.

The Lion and the Mouse

BY AESOP

A lion was sleeping in his lair one hot afternoon when a mouse ran over his nose and woke him up. The lion snarled and was just about to crush the mouse with his huge paw when:

"Oh spare me, my lord," cried the mouse. "I am really not worth killing. I mean you no harm—and I don't even taste nice."

The lion snarled sleepily.

"Besides," the mouse squeaked, "perhaps I can do something for you one day if you spare me now."

The lion gave a great roar of laughter, but he lifted his paw, and the mouse skipped out of reach. Still laughing, the lion sank back to his dreams.

206

Not long after, the lion was hunting in the woods when he fell into a trap. Some hunters had stretched a trip rope across one of his favorite paths. They had suspended a huge net above the path and had fixed it so that when the lion fell over the rope, the net would fall down and cover him, holding him prisoner until morning.

The lion twisted and turned and scratched and bit, but the more he struggled the more tightly he seemed to be held in the net. Soon he could not move at all. With no hope of escape, he began to roar, and his mighty voice echoed through every corner of the forest.

Now it happened that the mouse was also out hunting that night. Of course he quickly recognized the lion's voice, and he ran as fast as he could to the spot. He saw at a glance what the situation was and pausing only to say "Don't worry, sir, I'll have you out in no time," and "Keep still, sir, please," he began to gnaw and nibble the thick cords of the net. In a very short time the lion's front paws were free; then his head and mane; then his back legs and finally his tail.

The little mouse had done something for the great lion, just as he had promised.

In fact, he had saved his life.

Do not judge people's abilities by their appearance.

Reading Across Texts
How are the actions of the main characters in "The Ch'i-lin Purse" and "The Lion and the Mouse" alike?

Writing Across Texts Make a list of how the characters' actions are alike.

ⓒ **Predict** Do the illustrations help you predict what will happen?

Student Edition pages 206–207

Audio CD

Read It
ONLINE
PearsonSuccessNet.com
- Student Edition
- Leveled Readers

Leveled Readers

⊙ **Skill** Compare and Contrast

⊙ **Strategy** Predict

Lesson Vocabulary

Below-Level

On-Level

Advanced

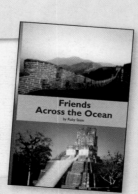

ELL Reader
- Concept Vocabulary
- Text Support
- Language Enrichment

Integrate Social Studies Standards

- **Cultures**
- **Citizenship**
- **Ancient Civilizations**

✓ **Read**

"The Ch'i-lin Purse," pp. 190–203

"The Lion and the Mouse," pp. 206–207

Leveled Readers

Below-Level

On-Level

Advanced

- Support Concepts
- Develop Concepts
- Extend Concepts

ELL Reader

✓ **Build Concept Vocabulary**
  Helping Others, pp. 186l–186m

✓ **Teach Social Studies Concepts**
  Chinese Family Customs, p. 195
  Jade, p. 201
  Aesop's Fables, p. 207

✓ **Explore Social Studies Center**
  Explore Traditions, p. 186k

Weekly Plan

READING

45–90 minutes

TARGET SKILLS OF THE WEEK

🎯 **Comprehension Skill**
Compare and Contrast

🎯 **Comprehension Strategy**
Predict

🎯 **Vocabulary Strategy**
Word Structure

DAY 1   PAGES 186l–188b, 207a, 207e–207k

Oral Language

QUESTION OF THE WEEK *What are the rewards in helping others?*

Read Aloud: "The Call of the Sea," 186m
Build Concepts, 186l

Comprehension/Vocabulary

Comprehension Skill/Strategy Lesson, 186–187
🎯 Compare and Contrast **T**
🎯 Predict
Build Background, 188a
Introduce Lesson Vocabulary, 188b
astonished, behavior, benefactor, distribution, gratitude, procession, recommend, sacred, traditions **T**

Read Leveled Readers

Grouping Options 186f–186g

Fluency

Model Pitch, 186l–186m, 207a

DAY 2   PAGES 188–197, 207a, 207e–207k

Oral Language

QUESTION OF THE DAY *Why does Hsiang-ling help the poor bride?*

Comprehension/Vocabulary

Vocabulary Strategy Lesson, 188–189
🎯 Word Structure **T**

Read "The Ch'i-lin Purse," 190–197

Grouping Options 186f–186g

🎯 Compare and Contrast **T**
🎯 Predict
🎯 Word Structure **T**
Develop Vocabulary

Fluency

Choral Reading, 207a

LANGUAGE ARTS

30–60 minutes

Trait of the Week

Organization/Paragraphs

DAY 1

Grammar, 207e
Introduce Action and Linking Verbs **T**

Writing Workshop, 207g
Introduce News Story

Model the Trait of the Week:
Organization/Paragraphs

Spelling, 207i
Pretest for Vowel Sounds with *r*

Internet Inquiry, 207k
Identify Questions

DAY 2

Grammar, 207e
Develop Action and Linking Verbs **T**

Writing Workshop, 207g
Improve Writing with Answer 5 Ws and How

Spelling, 207i
Teach the Generalization

Internet Inquiry, 207k
Navigate/Search

DAILY WRITING ACTIVITIES

Day 1 Write to Read, 186

Day 2 Words to Write, 189
Strategy Response Log, 190, 197

DAILY SOCIAL STUDIES CONNECTIONS

Day 1 Helping Others Concept Web, 186l

Day 2 Time for Social Studies: Chinese Family Customs, 195
Revisit the Helping Others Concept Web, 197

DAILY SUCCESS PREDICTORS ➤
for Adequate Yearly Progress

Monitor Progress and Corrective Feedback

Vocabulary   Check Vocabulary, *186l*

RESOURCES FOR THE WEEK

- Practice Book, *pp. 71–80*
- Word Study and Spelling Practice Book, *pp. 29–32*
- Grammar and Writing Practice Book, *pp. 29–32*
- Selection Test, *pp. 29–32*
- Fresh Reads for Differentiated Test Practice, *pp. 43–48*
- The Grammar and Writing Book, *pp. 92–97*

Grouping Options for Differentiated Instruction

Turn the page for the small group lesson plan.

DAY 3 PAGES 198–205, 207a, 207e–207k

Oral Language

QUESTION OF THE DAY *What happened as a result of Hsiang-ling's kindness?*

Comprehension/Vocabulary

Read "The Ch'i-lin Purse," 198–204

Grouping Options 186f–186g

- ◉ Compare and Contrast **T**
- ◉ Predict
- **REVIEW** Sequence **T**
- Develop Vocabulary

Reader Response

Selection Test

Fluency

Model Pitch, 207a

Grammar, 207f
Apply Action and Linking Verbs in Writing **T**

Writing Workshop, 205, 207h
Write Now
Prewrite and Draft

Spelling, 207j
Connect Spelling to Writing

Internet Inquiry, 207k
Analyze Sources

Day 3 Strategy Response Log, 202
Look Back and Write, 204

Day 3 Time for Social Studies: Jade, 201
Revisit the Helping Others Concept Web, 203

DAY 4 PAGES 206–207a, 207e–207k

Oral Language

QUESTION OF THE DAY *What feelings or emotions do people experience after helping others?*

Comprehension/Vocabulary

Read "The Lion and the Mouse," 206–207

Grouping Options 186f–186g

Fable
Reading Across Texts

Fluency

Partner Reading, 207a

Grammar, 207f
Practice Action and Linking Verbs for Standardized Tests **T**

Writing Workshop, 207h
Draft, Revise, and Publish

Spelling, 207j
Provide a Strategy

Internet Inquiry, 207k
Synthesize Information

Day 4 Writing Across Texts, 207

Day 4 Time for Social Studies: Aesop's Fables, 207

DAY 5 PAGES 207a–207l

Oral Language

QUESTION OF THE WEEK *To wrap up the week, revisit the Day 1 question.*

Build Concept Vocabulary, 207c

Fluency

Read Leveled Readers

Grouping Options 186f–186g

Assess Reading Rate, 207a

Comprehension/Vocabulary

- ◉ Reteach Compare and Contrast, 207b **T**
- Illustrator's Craft, 207b
- ◉ Review Word Structure, 207c **T**

Speaking and Viewing, 207d
Readers' Theater
Analyze an Illustration

Grammar, 207f
Cumulative Review

Writing Workshop, 207h
Connect to Unit Writing

Spelling, 207j
Posttest for Vowel Sounds with *r*

Internet Inquiry, 207k
Communicate Results

Research/Study Skills, 207l
Textbook/Trade Book

Day 5 Illustrator's Craft, 207b

Day 5 Revisit the Helping Others Concept Web, 207c

KEY ◉ = Target Skill **T** = Tested Skill

Comprehension — Check Retelling, *204*

Fluency — Check Fluency WCPM, *207a*

Vocabulary — Check Vocabulary, *207c*

SUCCESS PREDICTOR

Small Group Plan *for Differentiated Instruction*

Daily Plan
AT A GLANCE

Reading
Whole Group
- Oral Language
- Comprehension/Vocabulary

Group Time
Differentiated Instruction
Meet with small groups to provide:
- Skill Support
- Reading Support
- Fluency Practice

Read

This week's lessons for daily group time can be found behind the Differentiated Instruction (DI) tab on pp. DI·22–DI·31.

Whole Group
- Fluency

Language Arts
- Grammar
- Writing
- Spelling
- Research/Inquiry
- Speaking/Listening/Viewing

Use *My Sidewalks on Reading Street* for Tier III intensive reading intervention.

DAY 1

On-Level	Strategic Intervention	Advanced
Teacher-Led *Page DI·23*	**Teacher-Led** *Page DI·22*	**Teacher-Led** *Page DI·23*
• Develop Concept Vocabulary • **Read** On-Level Reader *The Gift*	• Reinforce Concepts • **Read** Below-Level Reader *China: Now and Then*	• **Read** Advanced Reader *Making Friends in Mali* • Independent Extension Activity

(i) Independent Activities
While you meet with small groups, have the rest of the class...

- Visit the Reading/Library Center
- Listen to the Background Building Audio
- Finish Write to Read, p. 186
- Complete Practice Book pp. 73–74
- Visit Cross-Curricular Centers

DAY 2

On-Level	Strategic Intervention	Advanced
Teacher-Led *Pages 192–197*	**Teacher-Led** *Page DI·24*	**Teacher-Led** *Page DI·25*
• **Read** "The Ch'i-lin Purse"	• Practice Lesson Vocabulary • Read Multisyllabic Words • **Read** or Listen to "The Ch'i-lin Purse"	• Extend Vocabulary • **Read** "The Ch'i-lin Purse"

(i) Independent Activities
While you meet with small groups, have the rest of the class...

- Visit the Reading/Library Center
- Listen to the AudioText for "The Ch'i-lin Purse"
- Finish Words to Write, p. 189
- Complete Practice Book, pp. 75-76
- Write in their Strategy Response Logs, pp. 190, 197
- Visit Cross-Curricular Centers
- Work on inquiry projects

DAY 3

On-Level	Strategic Intervention	Advanced
Teacher-Led *Pages 198–203*	**Teacher-Led** *Page DI·26*	**Teacher-Led** *Page DI·27*
• **Read** "The Ch'i-lin Purse"	• Practice Compare and Contrast and Predict • **Read** or Listen to "The Ch'i-lin Purse"	• Extend Compare and Contrast and Predict • **Read** "The Ch'i-lin Purse"

(i) Independent Activities
While you meet with small groups, have the rest of the class...

- Visit the Reading/Library Center
- Listen to the AudioText for "The Ch'i-lin Purse"
- Write in their Strategy Response Logs, p. 202
- Finish Look Back and Write, p. 204
- Complete Practice Book p. 77
- Visit Cross-Curricular Centers
- Work on inquiry projects

① Begin with whole class skill and strategy instruction.

② Meet with small groups to provide differentiated instruction.

③ Gather the whole class back together for fluency and language arts.

DAY 4

On-Level	Strategic Intervention	Advanced
Teacher-Led *Pages 206–207*	**Teacher-Led** *Page DI · 28*	**Teacher-Led** *Page DI · 29*
• **Read** "The Lion and the Mouse"	• Practice Retelling • **Read** or Listen to "The Lion and the Mouse"	• **Read** "The Lion and the Mouse" • Genre Study

i Independent Activities

While you meet with small groups, have the rest of the class...

- Visit the Reading/Library Center
- Listen to the AudioText for "The Lion and the Mouse"
- Visit the Writing/Vocabulary Center
- Finish Writing Across Texts, p. 207
- Visit Cross-Curricular Centers
- Work on inquiry projects

DAY 5

On-Level	Strategic Intervention	Advanced
Teacher-Led *Page DI · 31*	**Teacher-Led** *Page DI · 30*	**Teacher-Led** *Page DI · 31*
• **Reread** Leveled Reader *The Gift* • Retell *The Gift*	• **Reread** Leveled Reader *China: Now and Then* • Retell *China: Now and Then*	• **Reread** Leveled Reader *Making Friends in Mali* • Share Extension Activity

i Independent Activities

While you meet with small groups, have the rest of the class...

- Visit the Reading/Library Center
- Complete Practice Book pp. 78–80
- Visit Cross-Curricular Centers
- Work on inquiry projects

Grouping Place English language learners in the groups that correspond to their reading abilities in English.

Use the appropriate Leveled Reader or other text at students' instructional level.

TiP Send home the appropriate Multilingual Summary of the main selection on Day 1.

Take It to the NET ONLINE
PearsonSuccessNet.com

Karen Wixson For ideas on teaching reading strategies, see the article "Becoming a Strategic Reader" by S. G. Paris, M. Y. Lipson, and Scott Foresman author Karen Wixson.

TEACHER TALK

Keywords are one or more words a researcher uses to explore a topic in an encyclopedia, index, or search engine.

Be sure to schedule time for students to work on the unit inquiry project "Doing the Right Thing." This week students analyze the information they gathered about charities or service groups.

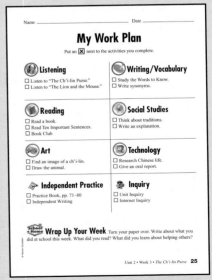

▲ **Group-Time Survival Guide** p. 25, Weekly Contract

The Ch'i-lin Purse 186g

☑ Customize Your Plan *by Strand*

ORAL LANGUAGE

SOCIAL STUDIES

Concept Development

What are the rewards in helping others?

CONCEPT VOCABULARY

distress   favor   panic   stranded

BUILD

☐ **Question of the Week** Introduce and discuss the question of the week. This week students will read a variety of texts and work on projects related to the concept *helping others*. Post the question for students to refer to throughout the week. DAY 1 *186d*

☐ **Read Aloud** Read aloud "The Call of the Sea." Then begin a web to build concepts and concept vocabulary related to this week's lesson and the unit theme, Doing the Right Thing. Introduce the concept words *distress, favor, panic,* and *stranded* and have students place them on the web. Display the web for use throughout the week. DAY 1 *186l–186m*

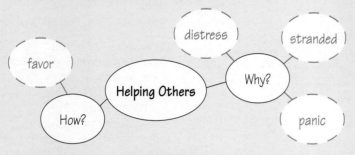

DEVELOP

☐ **Question of the Day** Use the prompts from the Weekly Plan to engage students in conversations related to this week's reading and the unit theme. **EVERY DAY** *186d–186e*

☐ **Concept Vocabulary Web** Revisit the Helping Others Concept Web and encourage students to add concept words from their reading and life experiences. DAY 2 *197*, DAY 3 *203*

CONNECT

☐ **Looking Back/Moving Forward** Revisit the Helping Others Concept Web and discuss how it relates to this week's lesson and the unit theme. Then make connections to next week's lesson. DAY 5 *207c*

CHECK

☐ **Concept Vocabulary Web** Use the Helping Others Concept Web to check students' understanding of the concept vocabulary words *distress, favor, panic,* and *stranded*. DAY 1 *186l*, **DAY 5** *207c*

VOCABULARY

STRATEGY WORD STRUCTURE When you see an unfamiliar word, sometimes you can check if there is a familiar root within it. Greek and Latin roots are used in many English words. Using a root can help you figure out the meaning of an unknown word.

LESSON VOCABULARY

astonished   procession
behavior   recommend
benefactor   sacred
distribution   traditions
gratitude

TEACH

☐ **Words to Know** Give students the opportunity to tell what they already know about this week's lesson vocabulary words. Then discuss word meaning. DAY 1 *188b*

☐ **Vocabulary Strategy Lesson** Use the vocabulary strategy lesson in the Student Edition to introduce and model this week's strategy, *word structure*. DAY 2 *188–189*

Vocabulary Strategy Lesson

PRACTICE/APPLY

☐ **Leveled Text** Read the lesson vocabulary in the context of leveled text. DAY 1 *LR19–LR27*

Leveled Readers

☐ **Words in Context** Read the lesson vocabulary and apply *word structure* in the context of "The Ch'i-lin Purse." DAY 2 *190–197*, DAY 3 *198–204*

☐ **Writing/Vocabulary Center** Make a chart listing vocabulary words. Write two synonyms for each word. **ANY DAY** *186k*

Main Selection—Fiction

☐ **Homework** Practice Book pp. 74–75. DAY 1 *188b*, DAY 2 *189*

☐ **Word Play** Provide students with a list of common Latin roots and their definitions. Have students refer to the list to determine the meanings of the following words: *benediction, dictator, contradict,* and *prediction*. **ANY DAY** *207c*

ASSESS

☐ **Selection Test** Use the Selection Test to determine students' understanding of the lesson vocabulary words. DAY 3

RETEACH/REVIEW

☐ **Reteach Lesson** If necessary, use this lesson to reteach and review *word structure*. DAY 5 *207c*

1 Use assessment data to determine your instructional focus.

2 Preview this week's instruction by strand.

3 Choose instructional activities that meet the needs of your classroom.

COMPREHENSION

SKILL COMPARE AND CONTRAST To compare is to describe how two ideas or concepts are similar or alike. To contrast is to describe how ideas or concepts are different.

STRATEGY PREDICT The ability to think about what is going to happen next is predicting. Good readers look for clues and combine those clues with what they already know to tell what is going to happen next. Predicting can help you become a better reader and writer.

TEACH

☐ **Skill/Strategy Lesson** Use the skill/strategy lesson in the Student Edition to introduce and model *compare and contrast* and *predict*. **DAY 1** *186-187*

Skill/Strategy Lesson

☐ **Extend Skills** Teach illustrator's craft. **ANY DAY** *207b*

PRACTICE/APPLY

☐ **Leveled Text** Apply *compare and contrast* and *predict* to read leveled text. **DAY 1** *LR19-LR27*

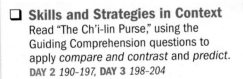

Leveled Readers

☐ **Skills and Strategies in Context** Read "The Ch'i-lin Purse," using the Guiding Comprehension questions to apply *compare and contrast* and *predict*. **DAY 2** *190-197*, **DAY 3** *198-204*

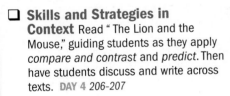

Main Selection—Fiction

☐ **Skills and Strategies in Context** Read " The Lion and the Mouse," guiding students as they apply *compare and contrast* and *predict*. Then have students discuss and write across texts. **DAY 4** *206-207*

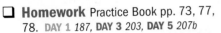

Paired Selection—Fiction

☐ **Homework** Practice Book pp. 73, 77, 78. **DAY 1** *187*, **DAY 3** *203*, **DAY 5** *207b*

☐ **Fresh Reads for Differentiated Test Practice** Have students practice *compare and contrast* with a new passage. **DAY 3**

ASSESS

☐ **Selection Test** Determine students' understanding of the selection and their use of *compare and contrast*. **DAY 3**

☐ **Retell** Have students retell "The Ch'i-lin Purse." **DAY 3** *204-205*

RETEACH/REVIEW

☐ **Reteach Lesson** If necessary, reteach and review *compare and contrast*. **DAY 5** *207b*

FLUENCY

SKILL PITCH Pitch is the ability to add expression to your voice. By raising or lowering the pitch in your voice, the reading will be more lively and enjoyable to the listener.

TEACH

☐ **Read Aloud** Model fluent reading by rereading "The Call of the Sea." Focus on this week's fluency skill, pitch. **DAY 1** *186l-186m, 207a*

PRACTICE/APPLY

☐ **Choral Reading** Read aloud selected paragraphs from "The Ch'i-lin Purse," emphasizing the change in pitch. Then practice as a class, doing three choral readings of the selected paragraphs. **DAY 2** *207a*, **DAY 3** *207a*

☐ **Partner Reading** Have partners practice reading aloud, reading with varying pitch and offering each other feedback. As students reread, monitor their progress toward their individual fluency goals. **DAY 4** *207a*

☐ **Listening Center** Have students follow along with the AudioText for this week's selections. **ANY DAY** *186j*

☐ **Reading/Library Center** Have students reread a selection of their choice. **ANY DAY** *186j*

☐ **Fluency Coach** Have students use Fluency Coach to listen to fluent readings or practice reading on their own. **ANY DAY**

ASSESS

☐ **Check Fluency** WCPM Do a one-minute timed reading, paying special attention to this week's skill—pitch. Provide feedback for each student. **DAY 5** *207a*

Customize Your Plan *by Strand*

GRAMMAR

SKILL ACTION AND LINKING VERBS An action verb tells what the subject does. It can express physical or mental action. A linking verb tells what the subject is or is like. It links, or joins, the subject to a word or words in the predicate.

TEACH

☐ **Grammar Transparency 8** Use Grammar Transparency 8 to teach action and linking verbs. DAY 1 *207e*

Grammar Transparency 8

PRACTICE/APPLY

☐ **Develop the Concept** Review the concept of action and linking verbs and provide guided practice. DAY 2 *207e*

☐ **Apply to Writing** Have students review something they have written and apply action and linking verbs. DAY 3 *207f*

☐ **Test Preparation** Examine common errors in action and linking verbs to prepare for standardized tests. DAY 4 *207f*

☐ **Homework** Grammar and Writing Practice Book pp. 29–31. DAY 2 *207e*, DAY 3 *207f*, DAY 4 *207f*

ASSESS

☐ **Cumulative Review** Use Grammar and Writing Practice Book p. 32. DAY 5 *207f*

RETEACH/REVIEW

☐ **Daily Fix-It** Have students find and correct errors in grammar, spelling, and punctuation. EVERY DAY *207e-207f*

☐ **The Grammar and Writing Book** Use pp. 92–95 of The Grammar and Writing Book to extend instruction for action and linking verbs. ANY DAY

The Grammar and Writing Book

WRITING

Trait of the Week

ORGANIZATION/PARAGRAPHS Good writers have organization to their writing. Their ideas are written in an order that helps readers with understanding, and that shows connections among them. The ideas can be organized from general to specific, most important to least important, or in the opposite order.

TEACH

☐ **Writing Transparency 8A** Use the model to introduce and discuss the Trait of the Week. DAY 1 *207g*

☐ **Writing Transparency 8B** Use the transparency to show students how the 5 Ws and How can improve their writing. DAY 2 *207g*

Writing Transparency 8A **Writing Transparency 8B**

PRACTICE/APPLY

☐ **Write Now** Examine the model on Student Edition p. 205. Then have students write their own news stories. DAY 3 *205, 207h*, DAY 4 *207h*

> **Prompt** "The Ch'i-lin Purse" tells about important events in a young woman's life. Think about a real or fictional person or event. Now write a news story telling about that person or event.

Write Now p. 205

☐ **Writing/Vocabulary Center** Make a chart listing vocabulary words. Write two synonyms for each word. ANY DAY *186k*

ASSESS

☐ **Writing Trait Rubric** Use the rubric to evaluate students' writing. DAY 4 *207h*

RETEACH/REVIEW

☐ **The Grammar and Writing Book** Use pp. 92–97 of The Grammar and Writing Book to extend instruction for action and linking verbs, the 5 Ws and How, and news stories. ANY DAY

The Grammar and Writing Book

❶ Use assessment data to determine your instructional focus.

❷ Preview this week's instruction by strand.

❸ Choose instructional activities that meet the needs of your classroom.

SPELLING

GENERALIZATION VOWEL SOUNDS WITH r The vowel sound /ôr/ can be spelled *or* and *ore*: rep*or*t, sn*ore*. The vowel sound /ir/ can be spelled *ear* and *eer*: app*ear*, pion*eer*. The vowel sound /âr/ can be spelled *are* and *air*: aw*are*, ch*air*. Vowels and vowel digraphs have a slightly different sound when followed by *r*. Vowels followed by *r* are called *r*-controlled vowels.

TEACH

❏ **Pretest** Give the pretest for words with vowel sounds with *r*. Guide students in self-correcting their pretests and correcting any misspellings. **DAY 1** *207i*

❏ **Think and Practice** Connect spelling to the phonics generalization for vowel sounds with *r*. **DAY 2** *207i*

PRACTICE/APPLY

❏ **Connect to Writing** Have students use spelling words to write about a real event. Then review frequently misspelled words: *caught, there's*. **DAY 3** *207j*

❏ **Homework** Word Study and Spelling Practice Book pp. 29–32. **EVERY DAY**

RETEACH/REVIEW

❏ **Review** Review spelling words to prepare for the posttest. Then provide students with a spelling strategy—rhyming helpers. **DAY 4** *207j*

ASSESS

❏ **Posttest** Use dictation sentences to give the posttest for words with vowel sounds with *r*. **DAY 5** *207j*

Spelling Words

1. snore	8. prepare	15. ignore
2. tornado	9. pioneer	16. order
3. spare	10. chair*	17. engineer
4. appear	11. beware	18. resort
5. career	12. smear	19. volunteer
6. square	13. repair	20. declare
7. report	14. sword	

Challenge Words

21. impair	23. hardware	25. porpoise
22. directory	24. clearance	

*Word from the selection

RESEARCH AND INQUIRY

❏ **Internet Inquiry** Have students conduct an Internet inquiry on good deeds in folk tales. **EVERY DAY** *207k*

❏ **Textbook/Trade Book** Review the features of textbooks or trade books and discuss how students can use these resources to find information. **DAY 5** *207l*

❏ **Unit Inquiry** Allow time for students to analyze the information they gathered about charities or service groups. **ANY DAY** *141*

SPEAKING AND VIEWING

❏ **Readers' Theater** Have students work in small groups to perform a dramatic reading from "The Ch'i-lin Purse." **DAY 5** *207d*

❏ **Analyze an Illustration** Have students study the illustration on p. 196 and answer questions. **DAY 5** *207d*

Resources for
Differentiated Instruction

▶ **Comprehension**
- ◎ **Skill** Compare and Contrast
- ◎ **Strategy** Predict

▶ **Lesson Vocabulary**
- ◎ Word Structure

sacred • behavior • benefactor • distribution • procession • gratitude • astonished • recommend • traditions

▶ **Social Studies Standards**
- • Cultures
- • Citizenship
- • Ancient Civilizations

Leveled Reader Database
ONLINE
PearsonSuccessNet.com

Use the Online Database of over 600 books to
- • Download and print additional copies of this week's leveled readers.
- • Listen to the readers being read online.
- • Search for more titles focused on this week's skills, topic, and content.

On-Level

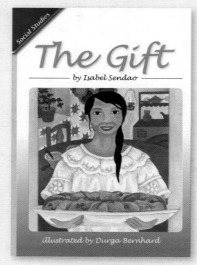

The Gift
by Isabel Sendao
illustrated by Durga Bernhard

On-Level Reader

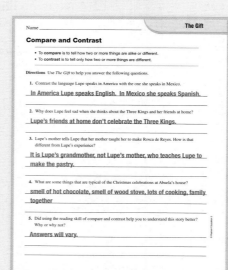

Name _____ The Gift

Compare and Contrast
- • To **compare** is to tell how two or more things are alike or different.
- • To **contrast** is to tell only how two or more things are different.

Directions Use *The Gift* to help you answer the following questions.

1. Contrast the language Lupe speaks in America with the one she speaks in Mexico.
In America Lupe speaks English. In Mexico she speaks Spanish.

2. Why does Lupe feel sad when she thinks about the Three Kings and her friends at home?
Lupe's friends at home don't celebrate the Three Kings.

3. Lupe's mother tells Lupe that her mother taught her to make Rosca de Reyes. How is that different from Lupe's experience?
It is Lupe's grandmother, not Lupe's mother, who teaches Lupe to make the pastry.

4. What are some things that are typical of the Christmas celebrations at Abuela's house?
smell of hot chocolate, smell of wood stove, lots of cooking, family together

5. Did using the reading skill of compare and contrast help you to understand this story better? Why or why not?
Answers will vary.

◎ **On-Level Practice** TE p. LR23

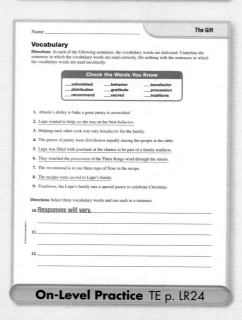

Name _____ The Gift

Vocabulary
Directions In each of the following sentences, the vocabulary words are italicized. Underline the sentences in which the vocabulary words are used correctly. Do nothing with the sentences in which the vocabulary words are used incorrectly.

Check the Words You Know
astonished | behavior | benefactor
distribution | gratitude | procession
recommend | sacred | traditions

1. Abuela's ability to bake a great pastry is *astonished*.
2. Lupe wanted to help, so she was on her best *behavior*.
3. Helping each other cook was very *benefactor* for the family.
4. The pieces of pastry were *distribution* equally among the people at the table.
5. Lupe was filled with *gratitude* at the chance to be part of a family tradition.
6. They watched the *procession* of the Three Kings wind through the streets.
7. The *recommend* is to use three cups of flour in the recipe.
8. The recipes were *sacred* to Lupe's family.
9. *Traditions*, the Lupe's family eats a special pastry to celebrate Christmas.

Directions Select three vocabulary words and use each in a sentence.

10. Responses will vary.
11. _____
12. _____

◎ **On-Level Practice** TE p. LR24

Strategic Intervention

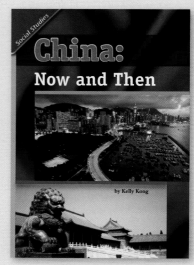

China: Now and Then
by Kelly Kong

Below-Level Reader

Name _____ China: Now and Then

Compare and Contrast
- • To **compare** is to tell how two or more things are alike or different.
- • To **contrast** is to tell only how two or more things are different.

Directions Use *China: Now and Then* to help you complete this page.

1. In the past China was ruled by emperors ; China's government today is communist

2. In contrast to a democratic country, people in a communist country do not elect their officials

3. The ancient Chinese did activities such as paper cutting, painting, writing poetry and going to the Peking Opera In addition to doing many of these same activities, modern Chinese go to the movies

4. In ancient times, the sports popular in China were hunting horseback riding and archery Today, the athletic activities that are popular in China are soccer, basketball, swimming and diving

5. How are Chinese bicycles different from American bicycles?
They are designed for transportation, not for sport. They have a rack behind the seat for carrying things.

6. How does Chinese writing differ from English writing?
In Chinese, each word is a picture. In English, words are made up of letters.

◎ **Below-Level Practice** TE p. LR20

Name _____ China: Now and Then

Vocabulary
Directions Fill in each blank with a word from the box that matches the definition.

Check the Words You Know
astonished | behavior | benefactor
distribution | gratitude | procession
recommend | sacred | traditions

1. holy sacred
2. thankfulness gratitude
3. a line or sequence of people or things procession
4. way of acting behavior
5. the act of giving out distribution
6. very surprised astonished
7. person who gives money or kindly help benefactor
8. to suggest recommend
9. customs traditions

Directions Write a paragraph about *China: Now and Then* using as many vocabulary words as you can.
Responses will vary.

◎ **Below-Level Practice** TE p. LR21

Advanced

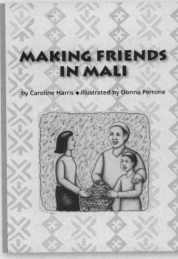

MAKING FRIENDS IN MALI

by Caroline Harris ◆ illustrated by Donna Perrone

Advanced Reader

Name_____   **Making Friends in Mali**

Compare and Contrast

- To **compare** is to tell how two or more things are alike or different.
- To **contrast** is to tell only how two or more things are different.

Directions Use *Making Friends in Mali* to help you answer the questions below.

1–2. Compare Georgia and her father. How is Georgia like her father? How is she different?

Both are ambitious; both like to improve things; both like working
with chickens and agriculture. Georgia wants to improve things in
a place that needs it more than where she lives.

3. Contrast Georgia's home in Mali with her home in Maine.

Unlike her home in Maine, Georgia's home in Mali is made out of
mud, is very small, and has no electricity.

4–5. Contrast the Zeroulias' garden center when they first bought it with the way it is now.

When they bought it, the garden center had been a tumbledown
place with a sagging greenhouse and a barn with a hole in the roof.
Now, customers come from all over to buy their flowers.

6–7. Compare Moussa and Georgia.

Both are go-getters; both have big plans. Moussa is Muslim; Georgia
is not.

8. How are Ibrahim and Charlie alike?

Both are the same age; both notice things around them.

Advanced Practice TE p. LR26

Name_____   **Making Friends in Mali**

Vocabulary

Directions Use a word from the box to complete each sentence below.

Check the Words You Know			
___ambition	___efficiency	___moped	___rummaging
___simplicity	___thriving	___volunteer	

1. Georgia started ___rummaging___ through the photographs looking for her favorite picture of Charlie crowing.
2. Many people love the ___simplicity___ of life in developing countries.
3. Georgia was impressed with the ___efficiency___ with which Ibrahim made the bricks.
4. A characteristic that both Moussa and Georgia's father had in common was ___ambition___.
5. Costa had built an old barn and greenhouse into a popular, ___thriving___ business.
6. Georgia had become a ___volunteer___ worker for the Peace Corps.
7. Georgia hopped on the ___moped___ behind Moussa.

Directions Underline the word does not belong in each set.

8. volunteer, tradesperson, professional
9. waste, effectiveness, efficiency
10. rummaging, selling, searching
11. book, moped, magazine
12. simplicity, difficulty, complexity
13. ambition, laziness, drive
14. prospering, failing, thriving

Advanced Practice TE p. LR27

ELL

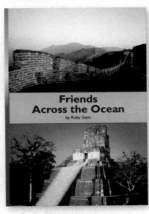 

ELL Reader   **ELL Poster 8**

Teacher's Edition Notes

ELL notes throughout this lesson support instruction and reference additional resources at point of use.

Teaching Guide pp. 50–56, 226–227

- Multilingual summaries of the main selection
- Comprehension lesson
- Vocabulary strategies and word cards
- ELL Reader 5.2.3 lesson

ELL and Transition Handbook

Ten Important Sentences

- Key ideas from every selection in the Student Edition
- Activities to build sentence power

More Reading

Readers' Theater Anthology

- Fluency practice
- Five scripts to build fluency
- Poetry for oral interpretation

Leveled Trade Books

- Extended reading tied to the unit concept
- Lessons in the Trade Book Library Teaching Guide

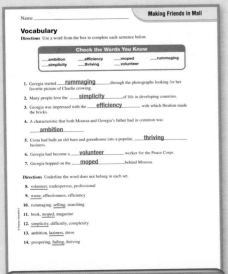

School + Home

Homework

- Family Times Newsletter
- ELL Multilingual Selection Summaries

Take-Home Books

- Leveled Readers

Cross-Curricular Centers

Listening

Listen to the Selections

MATERIALS `SINGLES`
CD player, headphones, AudioText CD, student book

LISTEN TO LITERATURE Listen to "The Ch'i-lin Purse" and "The Lion and the Mouse" as you follow or read along in your book. Listen for similarities and differences between the folk tale and the fable.

If there is anything you don't understand, you can listen again to any section.

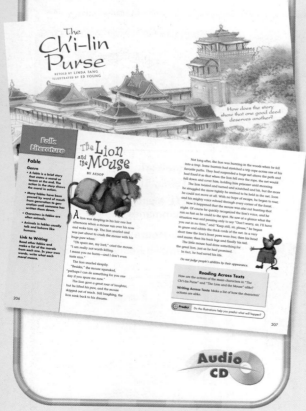

Reading/Library

Read It AGAIN!

MATERIALS `SINGLES` `PAIRS` `GROUPS`
Collection of books for self-selected reading, reading logs, student book

Select a book you have already read. Record the title of the book in your reading log. You may want to read with a partner.

Choose from the following:

- Leveled Readers
- ELL Readers
- Stories Written by Classmates
- Books from the Library
- "The Ch'i-lin Purse"

TEN IMPORTANT SENTENCES
Read the Ten Important Sentences from "The Ch'i-lin Purse". Then locate the sentences in the student book.

BOOK CLUB Discuss the common themes in "The Ch'i-lin Purse" and "The Lion and the Mouse." Compare and contrast this story with other folk tales and fables. Get together with a group to share your favorites.

Art

Sketch a Ch'i-lin

MATERIALS `SINGLES`
Internet access, Chinese art history resources, writing and art materials

Research the ch'i-lin or other legendary animals from Chinese art history.

1. Use a student-friendly search engine or other Chinese art history resources to search for an image of the ch'i-lin or other legendary animals.
2. Draw and label a pencil sketch of the animal you choose.

EARLY FINISHERS Write a paragraph about your sketch describing the animal and the legend associated with it.

Ch'i-lin

Scott Foresman Reading Street Centers Survival Kit

Use *The Ch'i-lin Purse* materials from the Reading Street Centers Survival Kit to organize this week's centers.

Writing/Vocabulary

Find
Synonyms

MATERIALS
Writing materials, copy of chart below, index cards

`SINGLES`
`PAIRS`

Find synonyms for the lesson vocabulary.

1. List the vocabulary words for both stories in the first column of the chart.
2. Find two synonyms for each word. Use a thesaurus if needed.
3. Write the synonyms in the second and third columns.

EARLY FINISHERS Write the words from the chart on index cards. Play a matching game with a partner.

Word	Synonym	Synonym
Sacred	Valued	Revered

Social Studies

Explore
Traditions

MATERIALS
Writing and art materials

`SINGLES`

Explore a tradition from your family or culture.

1. Think about some traditions that your family has or that you've read about. What do they symbolize?
2. Write a brief explanation of one tradition and how it began.

EARLY FINISHERS Illustrate a traditional celebration that you enjoy.

My Family's Annual Fourth of July Picnic

Technology

Research
China

MATERIALS
Word processing program, Internet access, index cards

`SINGLES`

Research life in modern-day China.

1. Choose a topic about modern-day Chinese life to research, such as family life, education, or sports.
2. Follow classroom rules for using the Internet. Use a student-friendly search engine to find two sources for your topic.
3. Take notes from the sources on index cards.
4. Be prepared to share your findings in the form of an oral report.

EARLY FINISHERS Using your word processing program, write one or two paragraphs summarizing your findings.

Search Engine

sports in China

China's gymnastics team...

ALL CENTERS

OBJECTIVES

- Build vocabulary by finding words related to the lesson concept.
- Listen to compare and contrast.

Concept Vocabulary

distress anxiety or trouble

favor act of kindness

panic caused by unreasoning, terror, or haste

stranded 1. left in a helpless position; 2. run aground

Monitor Progress

Check Vocabulary

If...	then... review the
students are unable to place words on the web,	lesson concept. Place the words on the web and provide additional words for practice, such as *wreckage* and *drowning*.

SUCCESS PREDICTOR

DAY 1 Grouping Options

Reading
Whole Group
Introduce and discuss the Question of the Week. Then use pp. 186l–188b.

Group Time
Differentiated Instruction
Read this week's Leveled Readers. See pp. 186h–186i for the small group lesson plan.

Whole Group
Use p. 207a.

Language Arts
Use pp. 207e–207k.

Build Concepts

FLUENCY

MODEL PITCH As you read "The Call of the Sea," model how to vary the pitch of your voice. For example, you might use a high voice when the mermaid speaks and a lower voice for Joseph. Both of their voices should be higher when they are in distress.

LISTENING COMPREHENSION

After reading "The Call of the Sea," use the following questions to assess listening comprehension.

1. **How were things different for Joseph after he helped the mermaid?** *(He was able to call on her when he needed help.)* **Compare and Contrast**

2. **What invented word does the author use to describe the mermaid's hair, and what does it mean?** *(salt-spangled; her hair sparkles with the salt from the sea.)* **Imagery**

BUILD CONCEPT VOCABULARY

Start a web to build concepts and vocabulary related to this week's lesson and the unit theme.

- Draw the Helping Others Concept Web.
- Read the sentence with the word *stranded* again. Ask students to pronounce *stranded* and discuss its meaning.
- Place *stranded* in an oval attached to *Why?* Explain that *stranded* is related to this concept. Read the sentences in which *favor, panic,* and *distress* appear. Have students pronounce the words, place them on the web, and provide reasons.
- Brainstorm additional words and categories for the web. Keep the web on display and add words throughout the week.

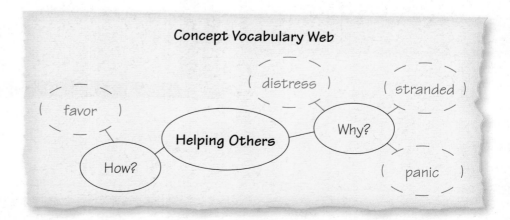
Concept Vocabulary Web

THE CALL OF THE SEA

by Geraldine McCaughrean

This is a legend from the Channel Islands about a man who helped a stranded mermaid get back out to sea. She returns the favor when he calls her with a special comb.

When the tide goes out in Bonuit Bay, it leaves rock pools studded with limpets and starry with sea urchins. Joseph Rolande, after a day's fishing, would often stroll along the beach…watching the sunset tinge the red sea. One evening he found more than peace and tranquility. A woman lay up to her waist in one of the tide pools…crying bitterly into hands of her long salt-spangled hair. She called out in panic: "Please! Don't go! Help me! I stayed too long! The tide went out and left me stranded here. Carry me down to the sea or I shall die!" As she reached out toward him, he glimpsed the ripple of scales and a huge tail fin.

"Oh, no! Oh, no!" said Joseph, backing away. "You're a mermaid, and I've heard what you mermaids do! I've heard how you'll lure a man down into your own world and drown him there!"

"I'll die if I dry!" she sobbed.

Joseph was a good man. So lifting her in his arms…he carried her past the third wave, where she spilled out of his arms like a shining salmon.

Something sharp pricked his palm. She had slid the amber comb from her hair and was pressing it into his hand—a gift, a thank-you present. "If you ever need my help, pass this three times through the water and I will come." With a thrash of a gleaming tail, she was gone.

One night, the rain beat on Joseph's roof like a thousand galloping hooves. A storm worse than anyone could remember rived the sea to a frenzy of leaping waves. It drove a ship onto the Bonuit rocks, and the Bonuit distress rockets went up.

Every soul who lived in the bay ran to the shore and peered through the downpour. All but one of the little boats lying along the shore was overturned and smashed. The screams of the sailors clinging to the wreckage on the rocks were all but washed away. "It's hopeless. No one can get to them," said one of the men watching.

"Help me launch my boat!" shouted…Joseph Rolande.

He and his boat disappeared beyond the mountainous waves into…Bonuit Bay. Only when the lightning flashed could those onshore glimpse the little rowing boat and the pounded wreck with its sad clutch of crew.

The lightning burst and faded…But surely they could not *all* have been mistaken? There was someone else besides Joseph out there…a gigantic fish? A drowning woman? "You called me with the comb and I came, Joseph. At last you called me!"

"Help me save these men!" he shouted back, his mouth full of rain.

And she did. She caught up each sailor washed off the wreck, and swam with them to Joseph's boat.

SKILLS ⬌ STRATEGIES IN CONTEXT

Compare/Contrast Predict

OBJECTIVES

- Compare and contrast.

- Use comparisons and contrasts to predict what will happen next.

Skills Trace

Compare and Contrast

Introduce/Teach	TE: 5.2 142–143, 186–187; 5.6 674–675
Practice	Practice Book: 36, 53, 57, 58, 73, 77, 78, 86, 273, 277, 278
Reteach/Review	TE: 5.1 101; 5.2 161b, 207b, 217, DI-52, DI-54; 5.6 699b, DI-54
Test	Selection Test: 21–24, 29–32, 109–112; Benchmark Test: Unit 2

INTRODUCE

Write the headings *Summer* and *Winter* on the board. Ask students to tell how they are alike. *(Possible response: They are both seasons of the year.)* Then ask students to tell how they are different. *(Possible response: Summer is warmer than winter.)*

Have students read the information on p. 186. Explain the following:

- Comparisons and contrasts can be made between things in the text, and between something in the text and what you already know.

- Recognizing comparisons and contrasts can help you understand the text and help you make predictions.

Use Skill Transparency 8 to teach compare and contrast, and predict.

Comprehension

Skill
Compare and Contrast

Strategy
Predict

Compare and Contrast

- When you compare and contrast things you tell how they are alike or different.

- Sometimes clue words point out comparisons and contrasts, but not always.

- You can compare and contrast different things you read about with one another, and also with what you already know.

Similarities in Text	Differences in Text	Compared with What I Know

Strategy: Predict

Good readers predict what will come next in a story or article. You can use the author's ideas and clue words to predict what the author will write about next. For example, if you have read an author's comparisons of things, you might predict you will next read about contrasts.

Write to Read

1. Read "Wedding Traditions." Make a graphic organizer like the one above to compare and contrast the wedding traditions in the article.

2. Write about two wedding traditions you know of. Tell how they are similar to and different from the traditions in the article.

186

Strategic Intervention

Compare and Contrast Remind students that when you compare and contrast things, you tell how the things are alike and different. Read "Wedding Traditions" with students. Then using the callouts as a guide, record the comparisons and contrasts on a graphic organizer similar to the one shown on p. 186.

ELL

Access Content

Beginning/Intermediate For a Picture It! lesson on compare and contrast, see ELL Teaching Guide, pp. 50–51.

Advanced Have students write two sentences to practice using the skill of compare and contrast. The first sentence should tell something about wedding traditions in their home country. The second should compare and contrast these traditions with wedding traditions in the United States.

Wedding Traditions

Every day, all around the world, people get married. Marriage is special, so couples in different countries follow special wedding traditions.

One common tradition is to give money. In England a bride may receive a coin to put in her shoe on her wedding day. In Jordan and some other Muslim countries, the bride and her family get money or other gifts from the groom himself.

However, in many countries, the bride's family must pay money to the groom's family. This payment is called a dowry. In Greece, the dowry is often a piece of land.

Another common tradition is for the bride to wear something special for good luck. In Germany a bride may wear a gown that has been in her family for years, as well as a special wedding crown. In Ireland a bride may wear lace at the bottom of her dress, but in England, she might carry a lace handkerchief.

What about the United States? Perhaps you have heard this advice, which many brides follow: "Wear something old, something new, something borrowed, and something blue."

1 **Strategy** The word *different* can be a clue. What do you predict the author will compare and contrast?

2 **Skill** The word *common* can be a clue. Look for one similar wedding tradition in many countries described in the text. As you read, compare and contrast what you know about weddings with what you are reading.

3 **Skill** What contrast is signaled by the word *however*?

4 **Strategy** What do you predict the author will compare and contrast in this paragraph?

187

Available as **Skill Transparency** 8

Compare and Contrast

- When you **compare and contrast** things you tell how they are similar and how they are different.
- Sometimes clue words point out comparisons and contrasts, but not always.
- You can compare and contrast different things you read about with one another and also with what you already know.

Directions Read the following passage.

> In Japan during the Middle Ages, samurai warriors followed a code of honor called bushido. Following the code meant being a fierce fighter, an athlete, a kind and honest person, and living a simple life. During the same time in Europe, knights were expected to follow the code of chivalry. Chivalry meant you were loyal to a lord (the landowner who hired the knight), brave in battle, and honorable in all deeds. They wore different armor. Samurai primarily wore protective leather gear, and knights wore heavy metal armor.

Possible answers given.

Directions Complete the following graphic organizer. List similarities and differences between *chivalry* and *bushido*. Then compare them with a code with which you are familiar.

Similarities in Text	Differences in Text	Compared with What I Know
1. Both had to be honorable.	3. Samurai lived in Asia; knights lived in Europe.	4. Our school honor code forbids cheating.
2. Both were fierce fighters.	Samurai wore leather gear, and knights wore metal armor.	5. Our school has school colors.

School + Home Home Activity Your child read a short passage and made comparisons and contrasts. Read two of your child's favorite stories and compare and contrast the main characters.

▲ **Practice Book** p. 73

TEACH

1 **STRATEGY** Use paragraph 1 to model how to predict what the author will compare and contrast.

Think Aloud **MODEL** From the title, I know that the article is about wedding traditions. I see the clue word *different* in paragraph 1. This clue word leads me to think that the author will compare and contrast wedding traditions in different countries.

2 **SKILL** Use paragraph 2 to compare.

Think Aloud **MODEL** The word *common* in paragraph 2 tells me that the author is going to describe something that is similar or alike. As I read the paragraph, I see that giving money is a tradition that is similar in many countries. I know that the bride and groom often receive gifts of money in the United States.

PRACTICE AND ASSESS

3 **SKILL** Instead of receiving money, in some countries a bride's family must give money to the groom's family.

4 **STRATEGY** Possible response: items a bride wears for good luck.

WRITE Have students complete steps 1 and 2 of the Write to Read activity. You might consider using this as a whole-class activity.

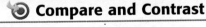

Monitor Progress

Compare and Contrast

If... students are unable to complete **Write to Read** on p. 186,	then... use Practice Book p. 73 to provide additional practice.

Tech Files ONLINE

Have students use the keywords *Chinese history* or *Chinese culture* in a student-friendly search engine to learn more about the setting of this story. Be sure to follow classroom guidelines for Internet use.

ELL

Build Background Use ELL Poster 8 to build background and develop vocabulary for the lesson concept of interacting with others can be a reward in itself.

▲ **ELL Poster** 8

Build Background

ACTIVATE PRIOR KNOWLEDGE

BEGIN A T-CHART about China.

- Tell students the story they will read is set in China. Have students work together to brainstorm a list of what they already know about China. Record what students already know in the left column of a T-chart.

- Provide a world map or globe and challenge students to find China on it.

- Tell students that, as they read, they should look for new information about China to add to the chart.

What I Know About China	What I Learned About China
Ruled by emperors in the past	
Great Wall of China	
Dragon parades	

▲ **Graphic Organizer** 25

BACKGROUND BUILDING AUDIO This week's audio explores wedding customs and traditions. After students listen, discuss what information they learned about these traditions.

 **Background Building Audio**

Introduce Vocabulary

SYNONYM ANALOGIES

Write the vocabulary words and this analogy on the board:

Astonished is to surprised as gratitude is to _____.

Have students identify vocabulary words in the analogy. Help them understand how analogies work by pointing out that the first two words are synonyms. They are to complete the analogy by finding a synonym for *gratitude.* Allow students to use a thesaurus if needed. Have students work with partners to write their own synonym analogies using another vocabulary word. Discuss if time allows. ***Activate Prior Knowledge***

Other possible analogies:

Traditions are to customs as benefactor is to helper.

Recommend is to suggest as sacred is to holy.

Procession is to parade as distribution is to ration.

Check word meanings at the end of the week by naming a vocabulary word and asking students to provide a synonym for it.

Use the Multisyllabic Word Routine on p. DI·1 to help students read multisyllabic words.

Lesson Vocabulary

WORDS TO KNOW

T astonished surprised greatly; amazed

T behavior manner of behaving; way of acting

T benefactor person who has given money or kindly help

T distribution act or process of giving some of to each; dividing and giving out in shares

T gratitude kindly feeling because of a favor received; desire to do a favor in return; thankfulness

T procession something that moves forward; persons marching or riding

T recommend to speak in favor of; suggest favorably

T sacred worthy of reverence

T traditions customs or beliefs handed down from generation to generation

MORE WORDS TO KNOW

footmen uniformed male servants who answer the bell, wait on tables, go with a car or carriage to open the door, etc.

matchmaker person who arranges, or tries to arrange, marriages for others

pavilion a light building, usually somewhat open, used for shelter, pleasure, etc.

T = Tested Word

Vocabulary

Directions Draw a line to connect each word on the left with its definition on the right.

1. astonished — thankfulness
2. procession — to suggest favorably
3. behavior — surprised greatly
4. gratitude — way of acting
5. recommend — something that moves forward

Check the Words You Know
___astonished
___behavior
___benefactor
___distribution
___gratitude
___procession
___recommend
___sacred
___traditions

Directions Choose a word from the box that best completes each sentence. Write the word on the line to the left.

distribution — 6. The unequal ____ of food caused some people to be hungry.

benefactor — 7. Without the generosity of his ____, Guillermo would not be able to afford to go to art school.

sacred — 8. In some cultures, animals are highly valued and considered ____.

traditions — 9. Our family's holiday____ are passed from generation to generation.

astonished — 10. I was surprised by the contest results, but the winner was truly ____.

Write a Thank-You Note
On a separate sheet of paper, write a thank you note to someone who has helped you in some way. Use as many vocabulary words as you can.
Thank-you notes should include words from the vocabulary list and specify the helpful gesture that was done.

School Home Home Activity Your child identified and used vocabulary words from the story *The Ch'i-lin Purse.* With your child, read a story about someone who performed an act of kindness. Look for words in the story that describe that person.

▲ **Practice Book** p. 74

Vocabulary Strategy

OBJECTIVE

⊙ Use word structure to identify Greek and Latin roots in unknown words.

INTRODUCE

Discuss the strategy for word structure using the steps on p. 188.

TEACH

- Have students read "The Meaning of Tales," paying attention to how vocabulary is used.
- Model using word structure to find Greek and Latin roots to determine the meaning of *bene-factor.*

Think Aloud **MODEL** The word *benefactor* has the Latin root *bene-*, which means "well" or "good." Other words I know with this root are *benefit* and *beneficial,* which both mean something that is good. That makes sense in this selection, so *benefactor* must mean "a person who does good things."

Words to Know

traditions
behavior
sacred
benefactor
astonished
gratitude
procession
distribution
recommend

Remember

Try the strategy. Then, if you need more help, use your glossary or dictionary.

Vocabulary Strategy
for Greek and Latin Roots

Word Structure When you find a word you cannot read, see if there is a familiar root within it. Greek and Latin roots are used in many English words. For example, the Latin root *bene-* means "well" or "good." This root is used in *benefit, benefactor,* and *beneficial.* You can use roots to figure out the meaning of an unknown word.

1. See if you recognize a root in an unknown word. If you do, think about the words you know that also have this root.

2. See whether the root meaning of the known words gives you a clue about the meaning of the unknown word.

3. Then check to see if this meaning makes sense in the sentence.

As you read "The Meaning of Tales," look for roots in unfamiliar words to try and figure out their meaning.

188

DAY 2 Grouping Options

Reading

Whole Group Discuss the Question of the Day. Then use pp. 188–191.

Group Time Differentiated Instruction
Read "The Ch'i-lin Purse." See pp. 186h–186i for the small group lesson plan.

Whole Group Use p. 207a.

Language Arts
Use pp. 207e–207k.

Strategic Intervention

⊙ **Word Structure** Give students these Greek word parts: *auto*— "self"; *graph*—"write; recording"; *photo*—"light"; *tele*—"at a distance." Have them find the meanings of *autograph, photograph,* and *telegraph.*

Access Content Use ELL Poster 8 to preteach vocabulary. Choose from the following to meet language proficiency levels.

Beginning/Intermediate Discuss the meanings of the words *traditions, procession,* and *recommend.* Have students talk about related words from their home languages. For example, the Spanish cognates are *tradiciones, procesíon,* and *recomendar.*

Advanced Teach the lesson on pp. 188–189. Have students use T-charts labeled *word* and *synonym* to organize the vocabulary words.

Resources for home-language words may include parents, bilingual staff members, bilingual dictionaries, or online translation sources.

The Meaning of Tales

Myths, fairy tales, and folk tales are time-honored traditions in many countries. Before people could write, they told stories to make each other laugh, cry, or shake with fear. These stories do more than just entertain. They preserve the earliest ideas and imaginings of a people. A myth may explain why something happens in nature. It may tell what causes the seasons, for example. A tale may show us the rewards for our behavior and teach us a lesson. Often, both myths and tales are tied to what people in earlier times found sacred and mysterious.

Fairy tales reach into the world of fancy. A poor girl finds a benefactor, such as a fairy godmother. A handsome prince discovers the girl and is astonished by her beauty. They fall in love. Someone evil tears them apart, and they suffer great misery. A magic being helps them defeat the evil. They feel a joyful gratitude. They celebrate their triumph in a grand procession through the kingdom.

The distribution of these stories all over the world shows how important they are to all people. Do you want to understand the nature of people? I recommend that you study tales.

Words to Write

Write a myth or tale of your own that explains something or teaches a lesson about life. Use as many of the words from the Words to Know list as you can.

189

PRACTICE AND ASSESS

- Have students use Greek or Latin roots to figure out the meanings of *geography*, *telescope*, and *migrate*.
- Explain that if students don't recognize a root or aren't familiar with the root's meaning, they can refer to a dictionary for help. Many dictionary entries include information about the word origins, or etymologies, and roots.
- If you began discussing synonym analogies (p. 188b), have students try to think of more synonyms for vocabulary words. Students may also create new analogies and have partners solve them.
- Have students complete Practice Book p. 75.

WRITE Writing should include any of the vocabulary words that students can use in their tales. Writing should reflect what students learned in "The Meaning of Tales."

Monitor Progress

Word Structure

If... students need more practice with the lesson vocabulary,	**then**... use Tested Vocabulary Cards.

Vocabulary · Word Structure

- **Greek and Latin roots** are used in many English words.
- When you find a word you don't know, recognizing the root can help you figure out its meaning.
- The Latin word *bene* means "well" or "good," as in *beneficial, benefit,* and *benefactor*.
- The Latin word *gratus* means "pleasing," as in *gratitude* and *grateful*.

Directions Read the following passage. Then answer the questions below.

I always wanted to be a singer, and I worked very hard. I was grateful to be able to do something that I loved. However, it was difficult to make enough money to pay for lessons. One day, I was singing in a procession to celebrate the holidays. Afterwards, my mother found me and she was very excited. "This is Mrs. Kazarian. She is a benefactor for young artists and wants to pay for your lessons at the school of music," my astonished mother said. "I'd like to recommend a teacher who works with young singers," Mrs. Kazarian told us. A month later, I was practicing with my new teacher. Each day, I am filled with gratitude that I am the beneficiary of Mrs. Kazarian's generosity. Without her support, I would not have had this chance.

Possible answers given.

1. What is the Latin root in *grateful*? How does the root help you understand its meaning? *gratus;* **The root lets you know that the word has to do with something that is pleasing.**

2. What is the Latin root in *benefactor*? How does the root help you understand its meaning? *bene;* **The root lets you know that the word has to do with something that is good.**

3. What do you think *beneficiary* means? How does the root help you understand its meaning? **It probably means someone who receives something good, because** *bene* **means "good."**

4. How does the root in *gratitude* help you understand its meaning? **The root means "pleasing," so it means being pleased.**

5. Write a sentence using a new word with either the root *bene* or *gratus*. **Exercising every day benefits your health.**

Home Activity Your child read a short passage and identified the meanings of unfamiliar words using Latin roots. Look in a dictionary with your child to find other words that use the Latin roots *bene* and *gratus*.

▲ **Practice Book** p. 75

Prereading Strategies

OBJECTIVES

◉ Compare and contrast people, events, and cultures.

◉ Use compare and contrast to predict what will happen next in a story.

GENRE STUDY

Folk Tale

"The Ch'i-lin Purse" is a Chinese folk tale. Explain that the author is unknown and that folk tales often have different versions. These stories are passed down through generations over many centuries.

PREVIEW AND PREDICT

Have students preview the story title and illustrations, discuss the setting, and predict what the story might be about. Have students use lesson vocabulary words in their discussion.

Strategy Response Log

Ask Questions Have students write two questions about life in ancient China in their strategy response logs. Students will answer their questions in the Strategy Response Log activity on p. 197.

The Ch'i-lin Purse

RETOLD BY LINDA FANG

ILLUSTRATED BY ED YOUNG

Genre

Folk tales are stories or legends that are told over and over from one generation to the next. As you read, imagine that someone is sitting next to you telling you the story.

190

ELL

Access Content Lead a picture walk to reinforce vocabulary, such as *tradition* (p. 192), *procession* (pp. 194, 196), *distribution* (p. 197), and *behavior* (p. 198).

Consider having students read the selection summary in English or in students' home languages. See the Multilingual Summaries in the ELL Teaching Guide, pp. 54–56.

How does the story show that one good deed deserves another?

191

SET PURPOSE

Have students use a story prediction chart and fill out the first two columns before they read.

Remind students to look for things to compare and contrast as they read.

STRATEGY RECALL

Students have now used these before-reading strategies:

- preview the selection to be aware of its genre, features, and possible content;
- activate prior knowledge about that content and what to expect of that genre;
- make predictions;
- set a purpose for reading.

Remind students to be aware of and flexibly use the during-reading strategies they have learned:

- link prior knowledge to new information;
- summarize text they have read so far;
- ask clarifying questions;
- answer questions they or others pose;
- check their predictions and either refine them or make new predictions;
- recognize the text structure the author is using, and use that knowledge to make predictions and increase comprehension;
- visualize what the author is describing;
- monitor their comprehension and use fix-up strategies.

After reading, students will use these strategies:

- summarize or retell the text;
- answer questions they or others pose;
- reflect to make new information become part of their prior knowledge.

Audio CD **AudioText**

Guiding Comprehension

1 🎯 **Compare and Contrast • Critical**

How is Hsiang-ling's life similar to your life? In what ways is it different?

Possible response: Hsiang-ling has a mother. But she lives in ancient China, gets married at age 16, receives a dowry, wears traditional Chinese clothing, has a servant, and rides in a *hua-chiao*.

Monitor Progress

🎯 **Compare and Contrast**

If... students are unable to compare and contrast,	then... use the skill and strategy instruction on p. 193.

---

2 **Literary Devices • Literal**

Describe and explain the symbol on the purse.

The figure is a *ch'i-lin*, a legendary animal from ancient times. It had scales all over its body and a single horn on its head. It is the symbol of promising male offspring.

Tech Files
ONLINE

Have students use a student-friendly search engine to learn more about ancient Chinese family traditions by using the keywords *Ancient Chinese traditions* in quotations to receive more specific results.

It is said that many years ago in China, in a small town called Teng-chou, there lived a wealthy widow, Mrs. Hsüeh. She had only one daughter, Hsüeh Hsiang-ling. Hsiang-ling was beautiful and intelligent, and her mother loved her dearly. But since everything Hsiang-ling wanted was given to her, she became rather spoiled.

When Hsiang-ling was sixteen years old, her mother decided that it was time for her to marry. Through a matchmaker, Hsiang-ling was engaged to a young man from a wealthy family in a neighboring town.

1 Mrs. Hsüeh wanted to prepare a dowry for Hsiang-ling that no girl in town could match. But Hsiang-ling was hard to please. Almost everything her mother bought for her was returned or exchanged at least two or three times.

When the dowry was finally complete, Mrs. Hsüeh decided to add one more item to it. It was the Ch'i-lin Purse, a red satin bag embroidered on both sides with a *ch'i-lin*, a legendary animal from ancient times. The *ch'i-lin* had scales all over its body and a single horn on its head. In the old Chinese tradition, the **2** *ch'i-lin* is the symbol of a promising male offspring. Mrs. Hsüeh wanted to give Hsiang-ling the purse because she hoped that her daughter would give birth to a talented son.

When the purse Mrs. Hsüeh had ordered was ready, a family servant brought it home. But Hsiang-ling was not satisfied at all. "I don't like the pattern, take it back!" she said.

192

ELL

Context Clues Reread aloud the sentence: "But since everything Hsiang-ling wanted was given to her, she became rather spoiled." Help students use the context of the sentence to determine the meaning of *spoiled*. (getting one's way so much that his or her character is harmed) Ask students to tell why Hsiang-ling's mother spoiled her.

The servant returned to the store and ordered another. But when it was brought home, Hsiang-ling merely glanced at it and said, "The colors of the *ch'i-lin* are too dark, take it back!"

The servant went to place another order, but the new purse still did not please her. This time the servant broke down in tears.

"I won't go back again, young mistress. The people in the store laugh at me. They say I am hard to please. This is not true. You are the one who is hard to please. If you don't want this purse, I am going to leave you and work for someone else."

Although Hsiang-ling was spoiled, she was not a mean-spirited person. She somehow began to feel sorry for the old man, who had been with her family for more than forty years. So she looked at the purse and said, "All right, I will have this one. You may go and pay for it." The servant went back to the store, paid for the purse, and gave it to Mrs. Hsüeh.

Hsiang-ling's wedding fell on the eighteenth day of the sixth month according to the lunar calendar. It was the day Hsiang-ling had longed for since her engagement. She was very excited and yet a bit sad, because she knew she was leaving her mother and the home she had lived in for sixteen years.

Hsiang-ling wore a red silk dress and a red silk veil over her head. As she sat in her *hua-chiao*, a sedan chair draped with red satin, and waited to be carried to her new home, her mother came to present her with the Ch'i-lin Purse.

"My dear child," she said as she lifted up the satin curtain in front, "this is your *ta-hsi-jih-tzu*, your big, happy day. I am delighted to see you get married even though I will miss you terribly. Here is the Ch'i-lin Purse. I have put some wonderful things in it. But don't open it now. Wait until you are in your new home, and you will feel that I am with you."

193

SKILLS ←→ STRATEGIES IN CONTEXT

Compare and Contrast

TEACH

- Explain that when you compare and contrast, you tell how things are alike and different.
- Model comparing and contrasting Hsiang-ling's life with modern-day American girls' lives on p. 192, paragraphs 1–3.

Think Aloud

MODEL First I'll look for contrasts. First of all, she lived in China a long time ago. She got married at age 16 and her mother gave her a dowry. She had a servant, wore traditional Chinese clothing, and rode in a *hua-chiao*. Now I'll look for comparisons. Hsiang-ling had a mother. She got married, like some modern-day American girls do.

PRACTICE AND ASSESS

Ask students to find the statement below that provides a contrast between Hsiang-ling and her servant. *(Choice c)*

a) Both are from the same household.

b) Hsiang-ling and her servant are Chinese.

c) The servant works for the family.

EXTEND SKILLS

Symbolism

A symbol is something that stands for something else. The *ch'i-lin* is a Chinese symbol of promising male offspring. Why might this be important? *(Having male children was highly valued.)* What might the purse symbolize? *(money or wealth)*

The Ch'i-lin Purse   **193**

Guiding Comprehension

3 👁 Vocabulary • Word Structure
Two Latin roots were used to form the word *procession*: *pro* means "before" or "forward," and *cede* means "to go." Use these clues to define the word.

Procession means something going forward or proceeding.

Monitor Progress

👁 **Word Structure**

If... students have difficulty using Latin roots to determine word meaning,	then... use the vocabulary strategy instruction on p. 195.

---

4 Character • Inferential
What does Hsiang-ling do that lets the reader know that she is a kind person?

She gives the Ch'i-lin purse to a poor bride.

5 Compare and Contrast • Critical
Text to Self **Describe a tradition in your own family or culture. Compare and contrast it with the Chinese traditions described in this story.**

Answers will vary but responses should include descriptions of family or cultural traditions, and at least one similarity and difference.

Hsiang-ling was hardly listening. She was thinking about the wedding and wondering about her husband-to-be, whom she had never met. She took the purse and laid it on her lap. A few minutes later, four footmen came. Picking up the *hua-chiao*, they placed it on their shoulders, and the wedding procession began.

As the procession reached the road, it started to rain. Soon it was pouring so heavily that the footmen could not see well enough to continue. The wedding procession came to a halt, and the *hua-chiao* was carried into a pavilion that stood alongside the road.

There was another *hua-chiao* in the pavilion. It was shabby, with holes in the drapes. Hsiang-ling could hear a girl sobbing inside. This annoyed her, because she believed that a person crying on her wedding day could bring bad luck. So she told her maid to go and find out what was wrong.

194

ELL

Access Content Point to the word *shabby* in the third paragraph on p. 194. Explain that *shabby* means "worn-out and faded." Ask students why they think the other girl rode in a *shabby hua-chiao*.

"The bride is very sad," the maid said when she returned. "She is poor and has nothing to take to her new home."

Hsiang-ling couldn't help feeling sorry for the girl. Then her eyes fell on the Ch'i-lin Purse in her lap. She realized that she was lucky to have so many things, while this girl had nothing. Since she wasn't carrying any money with her, she handed the Ch'i-lin Purse to her maid. "Give this to the girl, but don't mention my name."

So the maid went over and gave the purse to the other bride. The girl stopped crying at once. Hsiang-ling had given away her mother's wedding gift without ever finding out what was inside.

195

Chinese Family Customs

Traditionally in China, a male was head of the household. The head of the household selected mates for his children, since they were considered too inexperienced to make a proper choice. Because the family was built on the male line, boys were treated better than girls, who would leave the family some day to be married and become part of another family.

VOCABULARY STRATEGY

Word Structure

TEACH

Read the last sentence of the second paragraph on page 194. Model using Latin roots to determine the meaning of *procession*.

Think Aloud — **MODEL** The last sentence in the first paragraph on p. 194 says, "…and the wedding procession began." I'm not sure what *procession* means, but it looks like the word *proceed*. When I look up *proceed* in the dictionary, I see that it is made up of two Latin roots meaning "to move forward." So, I think a *procession* is "something that moves forward."

PRACTICE AND ASSESS

Read the fourth sentence on p. 192, paragraph 4, that contains the word *tradition*. Have students look up *tradition* in the dictionary to find out its Latin roots. To assess, have students explain how the meanings of the original Latin roots relate to the modern meaning of *tradition*.

The Ch'i-lin Purse 195

Guiding Comprehension

6 🔄 **Compare and Contrast • Inferential**

How has Hsiang-ling's life changed? Why did it change?

Possible responses: She is now poor and alone. A flood destroyed their home and everything they owned. Hsiang-ling became separated from her husband and son in the crowds.

7 **Vocabulary • Context Clues**

What is a food-distribution shack? How do you know?

A temporary shelter set up to hand out food to people in need, such as after a flood. The clue words "hungry" and "help the flood victims" helped me determine the meaning.

8 🔄 **Predict • Inferential**

Based on the selection, what do you think will happen next?

Answers will vary but responses should be based on the changes in Hsiang-ling's life.

A few minutes later, the rain stopped, the footmen picked up Hsiang-ling's *hua-chiao*, and the procession continued on its way. In an hour, Hsiang-ling arrived at her new home. She was happily married that evening, and to her delight she found her husband to be a wonderful and handsome young man. In a year's time, when she became the mother of a little boy, she felt she was the happiest woman in the world.

But six years later, there came a terrible flood. Hsiang-ling and her family lost their home and everything they owned. When they were fleeing their town, Hsiang-ling became separated from her husband and young son in the crowds of other townspeople. After searching for them in vain, Hsiang-ling followed a group of people to another town called Lai-chou. She had given up hope that she would ever see her husband **6** and child again.

196

ELL

Point to the word *flood* on p. 196, paragraph 2. Explain that a flood is a powerful flow of water often caused by things like heavy rain, broken dams, or melting snow. Ask them to predict what would happen to their town if there was a flood.

As Hsiang-ling sat, exhausted and alone, at the side of the road leading to Lai-chou, a woman came up to her and said, "You must be hungry. Don't you know that a *li* (one-third of a mile) down the road there is a food-distribution shack? Yüan-wai Lu has opened it to help the flood victims. Talk to his butler. I am sure you can get something to eat there."

Hsiang-ling thanked the woman, followed her directions, and found the place. A long line of people with bowls in their hands was waiting to get a ration of porridge. Hsiang-ling had never done such a thing in her life. As she stood in line holding a bowl and waiting her turn, she felt distraught enough to cry, but she forced herself to hold back the tears.

Finally, when it was her turn, Yüan-wai Lu's butler scooped the last portion of porridge into her bowl and said to the rest of the people in line, "Sorry, no more porridge left. Come back early tomorrow."

The person behind Hsiang-ling began to sob. Hsiang-ling turned around and saw a woman who reminded her of her mother, except that she was much older. Without a word, she emptied her porridge into the woman's bowl and walked away.

The butler was surprised at what Hsiang-ling had done. Just as she had made her way back to the road, he caught up with her and said, "Young lady, I don't understand. Why did you give away your porridge—are you not hungry?"

"I am hungry," said Hsiang-ling, "but I am young and I can stand hunger a bit longer."

"You are very unselfish," said the man. "I would like to help you. My master, Yüan-wai Lu, is looking for someone to take care of his little boy. If you are interested, I would be happy to recommend you."

Hsiang-ling gratefully accepted his offer and was brought to the house where Yüan-wai Lu and his wife lived.

197

Develop Vocabulary

PRACTICE LESSON VOCABULARY

Students orally respond *yes* or *no* to each question and provide a reason.

1. Are *traditions* something parents pass on to their children? (*Yes, traditions are special customs within families and cultures.*)

2. Does *recommend* mean to insist? (*No, it means to suggest.*)

3. Does a *procession* mean a fast race? (*No, a procession means an orderly line moving forward.*)

BUILD CONCEPT VOCABULARY

Review previous concept words with students. Ask if students have come across any new words today in their reading or elsewhere that they would like to add to the Helping Others Concept Web, such as *distraught* and *humbled.*

STRATEGY SELF-CHECK

Predict

Remind students that they should periodically stop to check the predictions they made on p. 191. Have students fill out the third column on their story prediction charts for events that have already happened.

Students can compare and contrast Hsiang-ling as a young bride to the woman she became. They can use this information to add more clues to the story prediction chart. Have students refine their predictions.

SELF-CHECK

Students can ask themselves these questions to assess their ability to use the strategy.

- Did I check the predictions I made?
- Did I compare and contrast the young Hsiang-ling to the woman she is today?
- How did this help me refine my story predictions?

Monitor Progress	
Predict	
If... students have difficulty contrasting the young bride to Hsiang-ling today or refining their predictions,	**then...** revisit the skill lesson on pp. 186–187. Reteach as necessary.

Answer Questions Ask students to answer the two questions about life in ancient China that they wrote in their strategy response logs. (See p. 190.) Then have them ask another question about the rest of the selection.

If you want to teach this selection in two sessions, stop here.

Guiding Comprehension

If you are teaching the selection in two days, discuss students' predictions so far and review vocabulary.

9 **Sequence • Literal**

What happens before Hsiang-ling goes into Pearl Hall?

The ball she and the boy are playing with goes through a window into Pearl Hall.

Monitor Progress

REVIEW **Sequence**

If... students have difficulty understanding sequence,	**then...** use skill and strategy instruction on p. 199.

---

10 **Literary Device • Critical**

In what ways is the Ch'i-lin Purse a symbol for Hsiang-ling? In what ways is it a symbol for the Lu family?

Possible responses: For Hsiang-ling, it is a symbol of her marriage, husband, son, and happy former life. For the Lu family, it could be a symbol of the kindness of a stranger, good luck, and/or wealth.

DAY 3 Grouping Options

Reading
Whole Group Discuss the Question of the Day.

Group Time **Differentiated Instruction**
Read "The Ch'i-lin Purse." See pp. 186h–186i for the small group lesson plan.

Whole Group Discuss the Reader Response questions on p. 204. Then use p. 207a.

Language Arts
Use pp. 207e–207k.

Yüan-wai Lu, a man in his early thirties, was impressed by Hsiang-ling's graceful bearing, and he agreed to hire her. "My wife's health is very delicate and she seldom leaves her room. Your job is to take care of our son. You may play with him anywhere in the garden, but there is one place you must never go. That is the Pearl Hall, the house that stands by itself on the east side of the garden. It is a sacred place, and if you ever go in there, you will be dismissed immediately."

So Hsiang-ling began her life as a governess. The little boy in her care was very spoiled. Whenever he wanted anything, he wanted it right away, and if he didn't get it, he would cry and cry until he got it. Hsiang-ling was saddened by his behavior; it reminded her of how spoiled she had been as a child.

One day, Hsiang-ling and the little boy were in the garden. Suddenly, the ball they were playing with disappeared through the window of the Pearl Hall. The boy began to wail, "I want my ball, I want my ball! Go and get my ball."

"Young Master, I cannot go into the Pearl Hall," said Hsiang-ling. "Your father doesn't allow it. I will be dismissed if I do."

But the little boy only cried louder, and finally Hsiang-ling decided that she had no choice. She walked over to the east side of the garden and looked around. No one was in sight. She quickly walked up the steps that led to the Pearl Hall and again made sure that no one was watching. Then **9** she opened the door and stepped in.

198

Access Content After the flood, Hsiang-ling becomes a governess. Explain that a governess is a woman who works in a private home to educate and train the family's children.

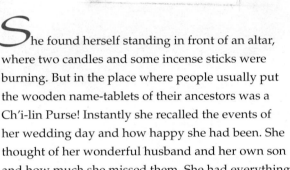
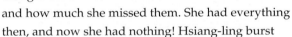

She found herself standing in front of an altar, where two candles and some incense sticks were burning. But in the place where people usually put the wooden name-tablets of their ancestors was a Ch'i-lin Purse! Instantly she recalled the events of her wedding day and how happy she had been. She thought of her wonderful husband and her own son and how much she missed them. She had everything then, and now she had nothing! Hsiang-ling burst into tears.

Suddenly, she felt a hand on her shoulder. When she turned around she found herself face-to-face with Mrs. Lu, her mistress, and a young maid.

"What are you doing here?" Mrs. Lu asked angrily.

"Young Master told me to come here and pick up his ball," Hsiang-ling replied.

199

Sequence REVIEW

TEACH

- Remind students that sequence is the order in which things happen.
- Clue words can help clarify the sequence of events in a story.

Think Aloud **MODEL** The ball Hsiang-ling and the little boy are playing with goes into Pearl Hall. The last sentence on p. 198 says, "Then she opened the door and stepped in." *Then* is a clue word. Hsiang-ling goes into Pearl Hall after the ball flies through the window.

PRACTICE AND ASSESS

- Have students put these events in the correct order. *(c, a, b)*
  a) Hsiang-ling starts to cry.
  b) Mrs. Lu gets angry at Hsiang-ling.
  c) Hsiang-ling sees the Ch'i-lin Purse in Pearl Hall.
- To assess, use Practice Book p. 76.

Sequence
Directions Read the following article. Then answer the questions below.

Mary had volunteered for a community organization that built homes for those in need. Mary learned that there are many steps to putting up a wall. First, she put up the wall frame. To do this, she measured and remeasured boards, cut them using a table saw, and screwed and nailed them into place. When the wall frame was up, she learned how to staple the insulation onto it, cutting around the electrical sockets and switches so that she did not cover them. She helped with the drywalling too. She nailed the drywall boards to the wall frame and learned how to tape the seams. By the end of the day, she was exhausted, but she had completed her wall.

Possible answers given for 2–5.
1. Which does Mary do first, staple the insulation or "tape" the seams?
   She staples the insulation first.
2. What would happen if Mary nailed the drywall before she stapled the insulation?
   She couldn't add the insulation after the drywall was up.

3. Summarize the steps Mary followed to build her wall.
   First, Mary put up the wall frame. Then she stapled the insulation. Last, she nailed the drywall and taped the seams.
4. Explain why the sequence of steps is important to building a wall.
   The sequence is important because steps that occur later depend on earlier steps being completed.
5. Explain the sequence of steps in a something you did for the first time.
   First, I preheated the oven. Second, I measured the ingredients. Third, I mixed the batter. Fourth, I put the batter into a pan. Last, I baked the cake.

School +Home **Home Activity** Your child read a short passage and answered questions about sequence. With your child, write down the sequence of events that occur at home before school begins.

▲ **Practice Book** p. 76

Guiding Comprehension

11 Visualize • Critical

The picture on p. 200 shows Pearl Hall. How did you picture Pearl Hall in your mind before you saw this picture? Compare and contrast what you saw with the picture.

Answers will vary but should show that students are able to compare the image they had with the illustration in the story.

12 Illustrator's Craft • Critical

Ask the Illustrator **How does the artist illustrate Hsiang-ling's sadness in this picture?**

Possible response: The artist shows Hsiang-ling bent over and crying.

13 ◎ Compare and Contrast • Critical

Think about Hsiang-ling's behavior at the beginning of the story. Compare and contrast it with how she acts and feels at this point in the story.

Possible response: At the beginning, Hsiang-ling acted spoiled but not mean-spirited. At this point, she is sad and humbled.

200

Monitor Progress	
◎ **Compare and Contrast**	
If... students have difficulty comparing and contrasting,	**then...** use the skill and strategy instruction on p. 201.

201

 SKILLS ←→ **STRATEGIES IN CONTEXT**

Compare/Contrast Predict

TEACH

Compare and contrast the picture of Hsiang-ling on pp. 200–201 with the picture of her on p. 192. What do you notice? *(She is no longer rich with a servant but is poor and a servant herself.)* Model how to predict how Hsiang-ling's life might be at the end of the story.

 MODEL Hsiang-ling's life has had ups and downs. First, she was rich and spoiled. Then she lost everything and was poor. Now she has found the ch'i-lin purse. Perhaps Mrs. Lu is the one to whom she gave the purse. I think her life might improve once again if Mrs. Lu finds out that Hsiang-ling is the woman who gave her the purse.

PRACTICE AND ASSESS

Have students work in pairs to evaluate the comparisons they've made so far. Have them use this information to predict what will happen in the rest of the story.

Time for SOCIAL STUDIES

Jade

Jade is a green shiny stone that the Chinese used to make tools, weapons, utensils, and decorative items. For centuries, jade has symbolized love and power. In ancient China, only wealthy aristocrats were allowed to own jade items. It was and continues to be honored as a royal gemstone in Chinese culture.

Guiding Comprehension

14 Cause and Effect • Inferential

Why does Mrs. Lu move Hsiang-ling to a stool, then to a chair on her left, then to a middle seat?

She wants to honor her as she discovers that Hsiang-ling was her benefactor.

15 ⊙ Predict • Critical

Which, if any, of the predictions you made earlier were accurate?

Answers will vary but responses should compare predictions made earlier to events in the story and tell which of the predictions came true.

16 Theme • Inferential

Text to Self **What lesson can you learn from reading this folk tale?**

Possible response: It reminds me that if I have a chance to do a good deed, I should do it, and happiness might come back to me.

Strategy Response Log

Summarize When students finish reading the selection, provide this prompt: Think about the different places where Hsiang-ling lives in "The Ch'i-lin Purse." Write a sentence telling what happens at each place.

EXTEND SKILLS

Foreshadowing

Tell students that foreshadowing is a literary device used to give hints or clues about events to come in a story. Have students notice that each improvement of Hsiang-ling's position foreshadows another improvement. Explain how these techniques make the story more interesting as a whole.

"Then why are you weeping at the altar?"

"Because I saw the purse which once belonged to me."

Mrs. Lu looked startled. "Where are you from?" she asked, as she took the purse from the altar and sat down on a chair that leaned against a long table. There was a tremble in her voice.

"I am from Teng-chou."

"Bring her a stool," said Mrs. Lu, motioning to her maid. Not wanting to wait on another servant, the maid grudgingly brought a stool and put it to Mrs. Lu's right. "You may sit down," said Mrs. Lu. Somewhat confused, Hsiang-ling sat down.

"What was your maiden name?"

"Hsüeh Hsiang-ling."

"When were you married?"

"On the eighteenth day of the sixth moon, six years ago."

"Bring her a chair and put it to my left," Mrs. Lu ordered the maid. Hsiang-ling was told to move to the chair. She was surprised to see herself treated as a guest of honor.

"Tell me how you lost the purse," said Mrs. Lu.

"It was a gift from my mother. My wedding procession was stopped on the road because of a storm, and my *hua-chiao* was carried into a pavilion. There was another *hua-chiao* in it, and the bride was crying."

"Move her chair to the middle and move mine to the right side," ordered Mrs. Lu. The chairs were switched, and once again Hsiang-ling **14** was told to sit down. She was astonished to find herself sitting in the middle seat—the place of the highest honor.

"Please continue," said Mrs. Lu.

"I gave the bride my purse. I never saw it again, and I have no idea how it got here."

Mrs. Lu dropped to her knees in front of Hsiang-ling and cried, **15** "You are my benefactor! All these years I have been praying here for your well-being. When I got to my new home, I opened the purse and found it full of valuables, including this." She opened the purse and

202

ELL

Access Content Mrs. Lu says that Hsiang-ling is her benefactor. Point to the word *benefactor* and explain that a benefactor is someone who gives money or other aid to another person. Ask students why Mrs. Lu considered Hsiang-ling her benefactor.

took out a piece of jade. "My husband and I were able to pawn it for a large sum of money. Using the money, we started a business and have now become very wealthy. So I reclaimed the jade and have kept it here in the purse since. We also built the Pearl Hall to house the purse and to honor you.

"I knew that you lived in the Teng-chou area, so when I heard about the flood I prayed day and night in that direction, begging Buddha to protect you from harm. I was hoping that one day I would find you and show you my gratitude. And here you are, taking care of my son! I know what we must do. We shall divide our property and give you half of it. That will make us all very happy."

Hsiang-ling was speechless as Mrs. Lu placed the purse in her hands. That same day, Yüan-wai Lu sent out servants in all directions to look for Hsiang-ling's husband and son. Soon they were found, in a village not far from Teng-chou.

A great friendship developed between the two families. Later, whenever Hsiang-ling told people about her purse, she would always end the tale by saying, "If you have a chance to do something good, be sure to do it. Happiness will come back to you."

203

Develop Vocabulary

PRACTICE LESSON VOCABULARY

Students orally respond *true* or *false* to each question and provide a reason for each false answer.

1. **Pencils are *sacred* things.** (False. Pencils are not worthy of honor.)
2. **A *benefactor* could help a poor student go to college.** (True)
3. **A person should show *gratitude* when receiving a gift.** (True)
4. **You would be not be *astonished* if a friend called you.** (True)

BUILD CONCEPT VOCABULARY

Review previous concept words with students. Ask if students have come across any new words today in their reading or elsewhere that they would like to add to the Helping Others Concept Web, such as *unselfish* and *recommend*.

Predict

Have students review their predictions and use them to compare and contrast the changes in Hsiang-ling's life. Use Practice Book p. 77.

SELF-CHECK

Students can ask themselves these questions to assess their ability to use the skill and strategy.

- Did I compare and contrast to keep track of the changes in Hsiang-ling's life?
- Was I able to use story clues to help me predict?

Monitor Progress	
Compare and Contrast	
If... students have difficulty comparing and contrasting to make predictions,	**then...** use the Reteach lesson on p. 207b.

Compare and Contrast

- When you **compare and contrast** things you tell how they are similar and different.
- Sometimes clue words point out comparisons and contrasts, but not always.
- You can compare and contrast different things you read about with one another and also with what you already know.

Directions Read the following passage. Then answer the questions below.

Bill was the head ranger for the town's parks. He had a difficult choice. Two local organizations wanted permits to use River Park at the same time on the very same day. The local middle school wanted to use it for its annual family picnic, and the soccer league wanted to use it for its playoff games.

Bill supported both groups. The picnic brought the school community together. The soccer playoffs had more participants than the middle school picnic, and Bill knew that the teams were a source of pride for the whole town. He didn't know what to do.

1. Which two groups want to schedule an event at River Park?
   The middle school and the soccer league want to schedule events.
2. What do the events have in common?
   Both groups want to hold an event on the same day and at the same time.
3. Name a benefit each offers the community.
   The school picnic helps teachers and parents work together. The playoffs brings pride to the community.
4. What major differences does Bill see between the events?
   The soccer playoffs involve more participants.
5. Predict how you think Bill will solve this issue.
   Possible answer: He will let the soccer team have it because they have more participants.

Home Activity Your child read a short passage and answered compare-and-contrast questions. With your child, discuss a current issue. Compare and contrast two opinions about the issue. Make a prediction about how the issue will be resolved.

▲ **Practice Book** p. 77

Reader Response

Open for Discussion Personal Response

Think Aloud **MODEL** I'd compare Hsiang-ling before and after she was married as well as when she was working for the Lus.

Comprehension Check Critical Response

1. Responses will vary, but should mention the lesson about helping others. **Author's Purpose**

2. Possible response: Hsiang-ling gives her purse to Mrs. Lu but unknowingly gives away valuables. Mrs. Lu intentionally gives Hsiang-ling half her property as a reward. **Compare and Contrast**

3. Possible response: A man tells her she's unselfish and gives her a job. **Predict**

4. Possible responses: wedding *procession*, *tradition* of using a matchmaker, *pavilion* on side of road, dowry, *ch'i-lin* legend, *hua-chiao*, switching chairs to show honor. **Vocabulary**

Look Back and Write For test practice, assign a 10–15 minute time limit. For assessment, see the Scoring Rubric at the right.

Retell

Have students retell "The Ch'i-Lin Purse."

Monitor Progress
Check Retelling Rubric 4 3 2 1

If... students have difficulty retelling the story,	then... use the Retelling Cards and the Scoring Rubric for Retelling on p. 205 to assist fluent retelling.

SUCCESS PREDICTOR

 ELL

Check Retelling Have students use the selection illustrations to guide their retellings. Focus on comprehension rather than on mistakes in English. For more ideas on assessing students' retellings, see the ELL and Transition Handbook.

Reader Response

Open for Discussion Tell about all the changes that happe in this story. Don't forget the changes in Hsiang-ling herself.

1. In ancient times, someone told or wrote or painted this story. Then it was handed down for generations. Why? What do you find in "The Ch'i-lin Purse" to explain its long life? **Think Like an Author**

2. Look back at pages 194–195 and 202–203. Compare and contrast what the two women did for one another and why they did it. **Compare and Contrast**

3. Find clues on page 197 that lead you to predict that Hsiang-ling's life is going to get better. **Predict**

4. This story is called an ancient Chinese story. What traditions of ancient China did you read about? Make a list, using some of the Words to Know list words and words from the story. **Vocabulary**

Look Back and Write Early in the story there is a clue that Hsiang-ling is not as selfish as she seems. Look back at page 193 to find that clue. Write what the clue is and why it is important.

Meet author **Linda Fang** on page 764.

204

Scoring Rubric Look Back and Write

Top-Score Response A top-score response will use details from p. 193 of the selection to explain that Hsiang-ling shows kindness to her servant and will relate her action to her unselfish acts later in the story.

Example of a Top-Score Response Hsiang-ling sees that a servant is suffering because she is being overly picky about the purse. She feels sorry for her servant and accepts the purse. This act is important because it suggests the unselfishness and kindness she shows to the bride who was poor and didn't have anything.

For additional rubrics, see p. WA10.

Write Now

News Story

Prompt

"The Ch'i-lin Purse" tells about important events in a young woman's life. Think about a real or fictional person or event. Now write a news story telling about that person or event.

Student Model

Lead grabs readers' attention and sets up the story.

> The heroic actions of a Japanese diplomat helped save the lives of thousands of refugees fleeing from the Nazis. The diplomat, Mr. Sugihara, was living in Lithuania when the Nazis invaded that country. Refugees who were Jews from Poland needed visas to escape to safe countries.

Writer provides necessary background information.

> Mr. Sugihara is credited with writing exit visas for the many refugees who came to him for help. He did this even though he disobeyed his government and risked his job and his life. Finally, he was reassigned to Germany.

The final **paragraph** provides closure to the news story.

> "I am proud that my father had the courage to do the right thing," said Hiroki Sugihara, the diplomat's son.

Use the model to help you write your own news story.

205

Write Now

Write Now

Look at the Prompt Explain that each sentence in the prompt has a purpose.

- Sentence 1 presents a topic.
- Sentence 2 suggests students think about the topic.
- Sentence 3 tells what to write—a news story.

Strategies to Develop Organization/Paragraphs

Have students

- make an outline to help organize ideas in the appropriate order for a news story.
- use transitions such as *in addition, for example,* and *however* to connect ideas, sentences, and paragraphs.
- tell the events in the order in which they happened, from first to last.

For additional suggestions and rubric, see pp. 207g–207h.

Writer's Checklist

☑ **Focus** Does the article focus on one person or event?

☑ **Organization** Does the story have a lead? Are events told in time order?

☑ **Support** Are events described with action words?

☑ **Conventions** Are all the words spelled correctly?

Scoring Rubric — Narrative Retelling

Rubric 4 3 2 1	4	3	2	1
Connections	Makes connections and generalizes beyond the text	Makes connections to other events, stories, or experiences	Makes a limited connection to another event, story, or experience	Makes no connection to another event, story, or experience
Author's Purpose	Elaborates on author's purpose	Tells author's purpose with some clarity	Makes some connection to author's purpose	Makes no connection to author's purpose
Characters	Describes the main character(s) and any character development	Identifies the main character(s) and gives some information about them	Inaccurately identifies some characters or gives little information about them	Inaccurately identifies the characters or gives no information about them
Setting	Describes the time and location	Identifies the time and location	Omits details of time or location	Is unable to identify time or location
Plot	Describes the problem, goal, events, and ending using rich detail	Tells the problem, goal, events, and ending with some errors that do not affect meaning	Tells parts of the problem, goal, events, and ending with gaps that affect meaning	Retelling has no sense of story

Retelling Plan

☑ **Week 1** Assess Strategic Intervention students.

☑ **Week 2** Assess Advanced students.

☑ **Week 3 This week assess Strategic Intervention students.**

☐ **Week 4** Assess On-Level students.

☐ **Week 5** Assess any students you have not yet checked during this unit.

Use the Retelling Chart on p. TR16 to record retelling.

Selection Test To assess with "The Ch'i-lin Purse" use Selection Tests, pp. 29–32.

Fresh Reads for Differentiated Test Practice For weekly leveled practice, use pp. 43–48.

SUCCESS PREDICTOR

Folk Literature

OBJECTIVES

- Examine features of a fable.
- Practice a test-taking strategy.
- Compare and contrast across texts.

PREVIEW

Ask students to preview "The Lion and the Mouse" by reading the title and author and by looking at the pictures. After they preview ask:

- **What do you think will happen between the mouse and the lion?** *(Accept all reasonable answers.)*

Link to Writing

Have students explain in their own words the moral of "The Lion and the Mouse." Record students' suggestions on chart paper.

FABLE

Use the sidebar on p. 206 to guide discussion.

- Explain to students that a fable is a very brief story, usually with animal characters, that points clearly to a moral or lesson.
- Ask students to think about a lesson a lion and a mouse could learn from each other.

DAY 4 Grouping Options

Reading

Whole Group Discuss the Question of the Day.

Group Time Differentiated Instruction
Read "The Lion and the Mouse." See pp. 186h–186i for the small group lesson plan.

Whole Group Use p. 207a.

Language Arts
Use pp. 207e–207k.

Folk Literature

Fable

Genre

- A fable is a brief story that states a moral or lesson at the end. The action in the story shows the moral in action.
- Many fables have been passed by word of mouth from generation to generation until someone has written them down.
- Characters in fables are often animals.
- Animals in fables usually talk and behave like humans.

Link to Writing

Read other fables and make a list of the morals from each one. In your own words, write what each moral means.

206

The Lion and the Mouse

BY AESOP

A lion was sleeping in his lair one hot afternoon when a mouse ran over his nose and woke him up. The lion snarled and was just about to crush the mouse with his huge paw when:

"Oh spare me, my lord," cried the mouse. "I am really not worth killing. I mean you no harm—and I don't even taste nice."

The lion snarled sleepily.

"Besides," the mouse squeaked, "perhaps I can do something for you one day if you spare me now."

The lion gave a great roar of laughter, but he lifted his paw, and the mouse skipped out of reach. Still laughing, the lion sank back to his dreams.

Vocabulary Support

Aesop (EE sop) Greek writer who often used animals in his stories to show how people should behave

 **AudioText**

Not long after, the lion was hunting in the woods when he fell into a trap. Some hunters had stretched a trip rope across one of his favorite paths. They had suspended a huge net above the path and had fixed it so that when the lion fell over the rope, the net would fall down and cover him, holding him prisoner until morning.

The lion twisted and turned and scratched and bit, but the more he struggled the more tightly he seemed to be held in the net. Soon he could not move at all. With no hope of escape, he began to roar, and his mighty voice echoed through every corner of the forest.

Now it happened that the mouse was also out hunting that night. Of course he quickly recognized the lion's voice, and he ran as fast as he could to the spot. He saw at a glance what the situation was and pausing only to say "Don't worry, sir, I'll have you out in no time," and "Keep still, sir, please," he began to gnaw and nibble the thick cords of the net. In a very short time the lion's front paws were free; then his head and mane; then his back legs and finally his tail.

The little mouse had done something for the great lion, just as he had promised.

In fact, he had saved his life.

Do not judge people's abilities by their appearance.

Reading Across Texts

How are the actions of the main characters in "The Ch'i-lin Purse" and "The Lion and the Mouse" alike?

Writing Across Texts Make a list of how the characters' actions are alike.

Predict Do the illustrations help you predict what will happen?

207

Aesop's Fables

Time for **SOCIAL STUDIES**

No one is sure if there ever was a real person named Aesop. Many, many years ago someone claimed that Aesop was a slave. Someone else claimed that he was an adviser to a king. In addition to conflicting information about who Aesop was, there is also contradictory information about where he came from. So we don't know for sure whether Aesop, who is given credit for writing a huge collection of fables that bear his name, was an actual person or a name used to describe ancient fables whose authors are unknown.

TEST PRACTICE

Strategies for Fiction

USE THEME The moral or lesson in a fable is also its theme. The theme is the reason for the story, or the "big idea." Students can use a fable's moral to answer test questions. Provide this strategy.

Use the Strategy

1. Read the test question.
2. Ask yourself if the question is about the theme.
3. Locate the moral and see if it provides information that will help you answer the question.

GUIDED PRACTICE Have students discuss how they would use the strategy to answer the following question.

Why do you think this story was written?

INDEPENDENT PRACTICE After students answer the following test question, discuss the process they used to find information.

What lesson can the reader learn from this fable?

Predict

Accept students' reasonable responses.

CONNECT TEXT TO TEXT

Reading Across Texts

Provide list topics for students to use to compare, such as attitude, changes, and acts of kindness.

Writing Across Texts Help students begin their lists by having the class generate one way the characters' actions are alike.

Fluency Assessment Plan

- ☑ **Week 1** Assess Advanced students.
- ☑ **Week 2** Assess Strategic Intervention students.
- ☑ **This week assess On-Level students.**
- ☐ **Week 4** Assess Strategic Intervention students.
- ☐ **Week 5** Assess any students you have not yet checked during this unit.

Set individual goals for students to enable them to reach the year-end goal.
- Current Goal: 110–116 wcpm
- Year-End Goal: 140 wcpm

English learners benefit from assisted reading, with modeling by the teacher or by a skilled classmate. When the English learner reads the passage aloud, the more proficient reader assists by providing feedback and encouragement.

To develop fluent readers, use Fluency Coach.

DAY 5 Grouping Options

Reading
Whole Group
Revisit the Question of the Week.

Group Time
Differentiated Instruction
Reread this week's Leveled Readers. See pp. 186h–186i for the small group lesson plan.

Whole Group
Use pp. 207b–207c.

Language Arts
Use pp. 207d–207l.

PITCH

Fluency

DAY 1

Model Reread "The Call of the Sea" on p. 186m. Explain that you will use a different pitch, high or low, for the mermaid and for Joseph, and that your voice will rise when the speaker is afraid. Model for students as you read.

DAY 2

Choral Reading Read aloud the first three paragraphs on p. 193. Have students notice how the pitch changes at an exclamation point and when the servant is talking to Hsiang-ling. Have students practice as a class doing three choral readings of these paragraphs.

DAY 3

Model Read aloud paragraphs 3 and 4 on p. 198. Have students notice the pitch you use for the boy and Hsiang-ling. Practice as a class by doing three choral readings.

DAY 4

Partner Reading Partners practice reading paragraphs 3 and 4 on p. 198, three times. Encourage them to vary pitch according to who is speaking.

Monitor Progress | Check Fluency WCPM

As students reread, monitor their progress toward their individual fluency goals. Current Goal: 110–116 words correct per minute. End-of-Year Goal: 140 words correct per minute.

If... students cannot read fluently at a rate of 110-116 words correct per minute,
then... make sure students practice with text at their independent level. Provide additional fluency practice, pairing nonfluent readers with fluent readers.

If... students already read at 140 words correct per minute,
then... they do not need to reread three to four times.

SUCCESS PREDICTOR

DAY 5

Assessment
Individual Reading Rate Use the Fluency Assessment Plan and do a one-minute timed reading of either selection from this week to assess students in Week 3. Pay special attention to this week's skill, pitch. Provide corrective feedback for each student.

RETEACH

Compare and Contrast

TEACH

Review the definition of *compare* and *contrast* on p.186. Have students work in pairs to complete Practice Book p.78. Make sure students know that they tell how things are alike in the first column and how they are different in the second column.

ASSESS

Have students reread pp. 193–195 to compare and contrast characteristics of the two brides. *(Comparisons: Both had the same wedding day; both are transported in hua-chiaos and stop inside the pavilion. Contrasts: Hsiang-ling's hua-chiao was fancy, the other bride's was shabby; Hsiang-ling was happy, the other bride was crying.)*

For additional instruction on compare and contrast, see DI·54.

EXTEND SKILLS

Illustrator's Craft

TEACH

An illustrator is someone who creates the art that appears in a book.

• Illustrators choose what to illustrate. An illustrator may choose to show a person or object to help the reader understand more about it.

• An illustrator may choose a certain style of art to let the reader know more about the story's setting or mood.

Ask students to explain how the illustration of the *hua-chiao* on pp. 194–195 helps them better understand what it is. *(It shows that it is a small box with windows that provides a place for someone to sit.)*

ASSESS

Have students study the illustration on p. 192, and write a response to the following question:

1. What does the illustration tell you about Hsiang-ling? *(Possible response: She has a servant and looks disappointed with him.)*

OBJECTIVES

• Compare and contrast.

• Understand and describe illustrator's craft.

Skills Trace	
Compare and Contrast	
Introduce/Teach	TE: 5.2 142–143, 186–187; 5.6 674–675
Practice	Practice Book: 36, 53, 57, 58, 73, 77, 78, 86, 273, 277, 278
Reteach/Review	**TE: 5.1 101; 5.2 161b, 207b, 217, DI·52, DI·54; 5.6 699b, DI·54**
Test	Selection Test: 21–24, 29–32, 109–112; Benchmark Test: Unit 2

Access Content Reteach the skill by reviewing the Picture It! lesson on compare and contrast in the ELL Teaching Guide, p. 50–51.

Compare and Contrast

• When you **compare** and **contrast** things you tell how they are similar or different.
• Sometimes clue words point out comparisons and contrasts, but not always.
• You can compare and contrast different things you read about with one another and also with what you already know.

Directions Read the following passage.

Serena thought the holidays were the best of both worlds. She loved giving people presents, and she loved receiving them as well. She and her brother usually gave each other gifts of the same value. They both enjoyed making gifts for each other. Serena always asked her brother what he wanted, although he seldom asked her. Serena carefully wrapped her gifts so that the wrapping gave her brother a clue as to what was inside. Her brother would often present his gift to her in a paper bag or wrapped in newspaper. His unusually wrapped gifts always made her smile.

Possible answers given for 4, 5.
Directions Complete the following graphic organizer. List similarities and differences between Serena and her brother. Then compare them with your experience of gift giving.

Similarities in Text	Differences in Text	Compared with What I Know
1. Serena and her brother gave gifts of **the same value.**	3. Serena always asked her brother what he wanted, but he **did not ask her.**	4. **Jan and I always give each other balloons on our birthdays.**
2. They both enjoyed **making gifts.**	Serena carefully wrapped her gifts, and her brother did not.	5. **I bring my balloons to school, but Jan leaves them at home.**

School + Home Home Activity Your child read a short passage and made comparisons and contrasts. With your child, compare and contrast details of two activities that your child likes to do.

▲ **Practice Book** p. 78

Vocabulary and Word Study

VOCABULARY STRATEGY
Word Structure

GREEK AND LATIN ROOTS Remind students that they can use Greek and Latin roots to figure out the meanings of unfamiliar words. Have students look up these words from "The Ch´i-lin Purse" and tell how the meanings of the Latin root relates to the modern meanings of the words: *direction, distribution.*

Word	Greek/Latin Root	Root Meaning	Modern Meaning
direction	directum	led straight	course along which something moves
distribution			

Words With Latin Roots

Provide students with these definitions of common Latin roots: *bene* means "well or good" and *dict* means "to say." Have them work with partners to figure out the meaning of these words.

Words with Latin Roots

Word	Meaning
benediction	to say something good
dictator	
contradict	
prediction	

BUILD CONCEPT VOCABULARY
Helping Others

LOOKING BACK Remind students of the question of the week: *What are the rewards in helping others?* Discuss how this week's Concept Web of vocabulary words relates to the theme of doing the right thing. Ask students if they have any words or categories to add. Discuss whether the words and categories are appropriately related to the concept.

MOVING FORWARD Preview the title of the next selection, "Jane Goodall's 10 Ways to Help Save Wildlife." Ask students which Concept Web words might apply to the new selection based on the title alone.

Put a star next to these words on the web.

Display the Concept Web and revisit the vocabulary words as you read the next selection to check predictions.

Speaking and Viewing

SPEAKING

Readers' Theater

SET-UP Have students use the dialogue between Hsiang-ling and Mrs. Lu that begins on p. 199 and finishes on p. 203 to create a dramatic reading.

PLANNING Have students work in groups of three, each student playing the role of Hsiang-ling, Mrs. Lu, or the narrator. Have each group create a script from the dialogue and descriptions on pp. 199–203. They should cut out tag phrases, such as "Mrs. Lu asked angrily." Remind them to decide how much descriptive text to include for the narrator's part. Suggest that students make copies of their scripts and mark their own parts so they can be easily found. Have them practice until they have their lines nearly memorized and have found the pace and tone of voice they want to use.

Delivery Tips
- Be comfortable with your lines.
- Pay attention to and interpret cues from other performers so you know when it's your turn to speak.
- Say your lines so they express the emotions the characters are feeling.

VIEWING

Analyze an Illustration

Have students view the illustration from "The Ch'i-Lin Purse" on p. 196. With partners, they can answer these questions orally or in writing.

1. **What is the initial impact of the picture?** *(Possible response: It expresses the emotions of Hsiang-ling and the woman who helps her.)*

2. **How does the artist show how Hsiang-ling feels in the picture?** *(The artist shows her kneeling with face uplifted. She looks like she is needy and grateful.)*

3. **What is your emotional reaction to the picture?** *(Possible response: I feel sorry for Hsiang-ling.)*

Have students look at the illustration again for details. Discuss how viewing the illustration gives a better understanding of the recording.

A few minutes later, the rain stopped, the footmen picked up Hsiang-ling's *hua-chiao*, and the procession continued on its way. In an hour, Hsiang-ling arrived at her new home. She was happily married that evening, and to her delight she found her husband to be a wonderful and handsome young man. In a year's time, when she became the mother of a little boy, she felt she was the happiest woman in the world.

But six years later, there came a terrible flood. Hsiang-ling and her family lost their home and everything they owned. When they were fleeing their town, Hsiang-ling became separated from her husband and young son in the crowds of other townspeople. After searching for them in vain, Hsiang-ling followed a group of people to another town called Lai-chou. She had given up hope that she would ever see her husband and child again.

6

196

ELL

Support Vocabulary Use the following to review and extend vocabulary and to explore lesson concepts further:
- ELL Poster 8, Days 3–5 instruction
- Vocabulary Activities and Word Cards in ELL Teaching Guide, pp. 52–53

Assessment For information on assessing students' speaking, listening, and viewing, see the ELL and Transition Handbook.

Vocabulary

SUCCESS PREDICTOR

Grammar Action and Linking Verbs

OBJECTIVES

- Define and identify action and linking verbs.
- Use action and linking verbs in writing.
- Become familiar with action and linking verbs on high-stakes tests.

Monitor Progress

Grammar

If... students have difficulty identifying action and linking verbs,	then... provide additional instruction and practice in The Grammar and Writing Book pp. 92–95.

DAILY FIX-IT

This week use Daily Fix-It Transparency 8.

Spiral REVIEW

ELL

Support Grammar See the Grammar Transition lessons in the ELL and Transition Handbook.

▲ **The Grammar and Writing Book**
For more instruction and practice, use pp. 92–95.

DAY 1 Teach and Model

DAILY FIX-IT

1. Six years ago, she gives away her weding gift. *(gave; wedding)*
2. Were that girl mean or just spoiled. *(Was; spoiled?)*

READING-GRAMMAR CONNECTION

Write this sentence from "The Ch'i-lin Purse" on the board:

Hsiang-ling was beautiful and intelligent, and her mother loved her dearly.

Explain that *was* is a **linking verb.** It tells what the subject *(Hsiang-ling)* was like. *Loved* is an **action verb.** It tells what the subject *(mother)* did.

Display Grammar Transparency 8. Read aloud the definitions and sample sentences. Work through the items.

▲ **Grammar Transparency 8**

DAY 2 Develop the Concept

DAILY FIX-IT

3. Today families spends years planning a childs' wedding. *(spend; child's)*
4. Ever detail should be prefect. *(Every; perfect)*

GUIDED PRACTICE

Review the concept of action and linking verbs.

- The main word in the predicate is a verb.
- An **action verb** tells what the subject does. It can express physical or mental action.
- A **linking verb** tells what the subject is or is like. It links, or joins, the subject to a word or words in the predicate.

HOMEWORK Grammar and Writing Practice Book p. 29. Work through the first two items with the class.

▲ **Grammar and Writing Practice Book** p. 29

DAY 3 — Apply to Writing

DAILY FIX-IT

5. A purse are a bag for mony. *(is; money)*

6. Today most women carried a purse for small ojects. *(carry; objects)*

USE SPECIFIC ACTION VERBS

Good writers use action verbs that tell exactly what the subject does. *The boy wailed* is more precise than *The boy cried. Wailed* shows that his crying was loud and pained. Specific action verbs make writing clear and lively.

• Have students review something they have written. They may be able to improve it by replacing general action verbs with specific ones.

HOMEWORK Grammar and Writing Practice Book p. 30.

Action and Linking Verbs

celebrate	drink	ring
write	sways	dress

Directions Use an action verb from the box to complete each sentence. Write the sentence.

1. People from around the world _____ the new year.
People from around the world celebrate the new year.

2. In China, some people _____ as dragons.
In China, some people dress as dragons.

3. The dragon's tail _____ as it parades down the street.
The dragon's tail sways as it parades down the street.

4. Children in Belgium _____ letters to parents on decorated paper. **Children in Belgium write letters to parents on decorated paper.**

5. In the United States, people _____ a toast to the new year. **In the United States, people drink a toast to the new year.**

6. Bells _____ out at midnight.
Bells ring out at midnight.

Directions Write a paragraph describing a celebration. Use vivid action verbs and appropriate linking verbs. **Possible answer:**
We always have a tree trimming party on the first Sunday of December. We invite Aunt Lindy, Uncle Bill, and friends and neighbors. Everyone trims the tree and listens to holiday music. Mom climbs on a ladder to put the star on top. I tie a bow on Sam's collar. This is my favorite holiday event.

 Home Activity Your child learned how to use action and linking verbs in writing. Ask your child to write a description of dinnertime at your home using action verbs and linking verbs.

▲ **Grammar and Writing Practice Book** p. 30

DAY 4 — Test Preparation

DAILY FIX-IT

7. Purses is often made of manufactured materiels or fabric. *(are; materials)*

8. A plastic handbag may appeer to be made of lether. *(appear; leather)*

STANDARDIZED TEST PREP

Test Tip

Most linking verbs are forms of the verb *to be (am, is, are, was, were).* However, some other verbs can be linking verbs. The word *feel* can be a linking verb: I feel happy. When *feel* is used as a linking verb, follow it with an adjective, not an adverb.

No: I feel well. I feel badly.

Yes: I feel good. I feel bad.

HOMEWORK Grammar and Writing Practice Book p. 31.

Action and Linking Verbs

Directions Mark the letter of the phrase that correctly identifies the underlined word in the sentence.

1. In ancient China, the Three Letters custom <u>was</u> important to a marriage.
  A action verb (physical)
  B action verb (mental)
  Ⓒ linking verb
  D not a verb

2. The Betrothal Letter formally <u>announced</u> the engagement.
  Ⓐ action verb (physical)
  B action verb (mental)
  C linking verb
  D not a verb

3. After that, a Gift Letter was <u>necessary</u>.
  A action verb (physical)
  B action verb (mental)
  C linking verb
  Ⓓ not a verb

4. The letter <u>listed</u> gifts for the wedding.
  Ⓐ action verb (physical)
  B action verb (mental)
  C linking verb
  D not a verb

5. She <u>approved</u> the proposed marriage.
  A action verb (physical)
  Ⓑ action verb (mental)
  C linking verb
  D not a verb

6. The Wedding Letter <u>was</u> the third formal document.
  A action verb (physical)
  B action verb (mental)
  Ⓒ linking verb
  D not a verb

7. The groom's family <u>presented</u> this letter to the bride's family.
  Ⓐ action verb (physical)
  B action verb (mental)
  C linking verb
  D not a verb

8. It formally <u>accepted</u> the bride into the groom's family.
  A action verb (physical)
  Ⓑ action verb (mental)
  C linking verb
  D not a verb

9. The bride usually <u>brought</u> a dowry of jewels and furniture.
  A action verb (physical)
  B action verb (mental)
  C linking verb
  Ⓓ not a verb

10. Today, these wedding customs <u>seem</u> unusual.
  A action verb (physical)
  B action verb (mental)
  Ⓒ linking verb
  D not a verb

 **Home Activity** Your child prepared for taking tests on action and linking verbs. With your child, read a newspaper article. Have your child circle action verbs and underline linking verbs in the article.

▲ **Grammar and Writing Practice Book** p. 31

DAY 5 — Cumulative Review

DAILY FIX-IT

9. Yesterday the bride sitted on a sedan chare. *(sat; chair)*

10. Everyone celebrated at the Grand feast? *(grand feast.)*

ADDITIONAL PRACTICE

Assign pp. 92–95 in The Grammar and Writing Book.

EXTRA PRACTICE Grammar and Writing Practice Book p. 129.

TEST PREPARATION Grammar and Writing Practice Book pp. 153–154.

ASSESSMENT

CUMULATIVE REVIEW Grammar and Writing Practice Book p. 32.

Action and Linking Verbs

Directions Underline the verb in each sentence. Write *A* on the line if the verb is an action verb. Write *L* if it is a linking verb.

1. A governess <u>raises</u> a child in a private home.   **A**
2. She <u>is</u> important to the family.   **L**
3. She <u>teaches</u> the child his or her lessons.   **A**
4. However, a governess <u>is</u> much more than a teacher.   **L**
5. She <u>shares</u> playtime and mealtime with children.   **A**
6. She soon <u>seems</u> like one of the family.   **L**

Directions Match the verb with the phrase that correctly identifies the verb. Write the letter of the phrase on the line.

B 7. marries   A. linking verb
A 8. becomes   B. action verb (physical)
D 9. wonders   C. not a verb
C 10. happy   D. action verb (mental)

Directions Rewrite each sentence. Add your own verb to make the sentence clear and interesting.
Possible answers:
11. People _____ candles and incense for different reasons.
People burn candles and incense for different reasons.

12. Candlelight _____ a soft, mysterious mood.
Candlelight creates a soft, mysterious mood.

13. Fragrant incense _____ pleasant.
Fragrant incense smells pleasant.

14. The pleasing light and scent _____ into the air.
The pleasing light and scent rise into the air.

15. In this way, people _____ holy beings.
In this way, people honor holy beings.

Home Activity Your child reviewed action and linking verbs. Ask your child to write a letter to a friend or family member using some vivid action verbs and some linking verbs.

▲ **Grammar and Writing Practice Book** p. 32

Writing Workshop News Story

- Identify qualities of a news story.
- Answer 5 Ws and How for a news story.
- Focus on organization/paragraphs.
- Use a rubric.

Genre News Story
Writer's Craft Answer 5 Ws and How
Writing Trait Organization/ Paragraphs

Organization/Paragraphs Explain that transition words make order clear in writing. Write *however, therefore, as a result, after, finally,* and *since* on index cards, one to a card, and model their meaning and use. Help language learners use these transition words in their writing. Display cards for reference.

Writing Traits

FOCUS/IDEAS Story focuses on one theme. All details support that idea.

ORGANIZATION/PARAGRAPHS Interesting lead is followed by strong elaboration and short paragraphs. Final sentence provides closure.

VOICE Writer is engaged in story but objective.

WORD CHOICE Language is concrete and specific (*forced to flee; filled with valuables*). Details are descriptive and uncluttered (*found herself alone in Lai-chou*). Transitions tie story together.

SENTENCES Most sentences are simple and direct. Sentence lengths vary.

CONVENTIONS There is excellent control and accuracy. Strong action verbs (*lost, regained*) and linking verbs add clarity.

DAY 1 Model the Trait

READING-WRITING CONNECTION

- "The Ch'i-lin Purse" follows fortunate and unfortunate events in a young woman's life.
- The story is organized around family life and clearly expresses setting, characters, and motives.
- Students will write a **news story** with strong organization and comprehensive content.

MODEL ORGANIZATION/PARAGRAPHS

Discuss Writing Transparency 8A. Then discuss the model and the writing trait of organization/paragraphs.

Think Aloud The writer begins the story with a paragraph that summarizes the important information. It tells who (a wife and mother), where (Lai-chou), when (June), what (regained lost family), why and how (through a local couple). The other paragraphs are short and tell the details of the story in order.

Writing Transparency 8A

> **News Story**
>
> A **news story** gives the facts about an event. It focuses on answering these six questions: *Who? What? Where? When? Why?* and *How?* A good news story begins with a lead that grabs readers' attention and sets up the story. The body of the news story explains and supports the lead with specific details and examples.
>
> **Lost Woman's Acts of Kindness Bring Reward**
>
> Lead grabs attention and sets up the story.
> This June in Lai-chou, a wife and mother who had lost her family and home, regained it all, thanks to a local couple.
>
> Sentences are plain, objective, and specific.
> Hsiang-ling was forced to flee her home during the spring floods. She soon became separated from her husband and son and found herself alone in Lai-chou. But her luck changed when she visited a local food distribution center run by Yuan-wai Lu.
>
> When Hsiang-ling gave her ration of food to an elder, Yuan-wai Lu's butler noticed her act. He helped Hsiang-ling become governess to Mr. Lu's young son.
>
> Transitions clarify time order of events.
> While working as governess, Hsiang-ling discovered that she had a link with her employers. Six years ago Hsiang-ling had given a poor bride a ch'i-lin purse filled with valuables. That bride was Mrs. Lu.
>
> Quotes engage readers and reveal motives.
> Said Yuan-wai Lu, "We owe all our wealth and happiness to this kind, generous woman. We will give her half of all we possess."
>
> Hsiang-ling is now reunited with her husband and son in Teng-chou. In a recent interview she said, "No good deed goes unnoticed."
>
> Unit 2 Ch'i-lin Purse   Writing Model **8A**

▲ **Writing Transparency** 8A

DAY 2 Improve Writing

WRITER'S CRAFT
Answer 5 Ws and How

Display Writing Transparency 8B. Read the directions and work together to identify the 5 Ws and How in a story.

Think Aloud **WRITE A LEAD PARAGRAPH** Tomorrow we will write a **news story.** I could write a story about our class play. What information would I want to put in my lead paragraph? The who and what include Ms. Pearson's fifth-grade class and the play, *Leave It to Bart.* The when and where include Friday, March 10, at 3 P.M. in the gym. The why and how include raising money for charity and a $5 donation per person.

GUIDED WRITING Some students may need more help with answering 5 Ws and How. Have them answer these questions about a familiar story.

Writing Transparency 8B

> **Answer 5 Ws and How**
>
> A news story gives key information about an event. It answers a set of questions called the **5 Ws and How:** *Who? What? Where? When? Why? How?* This essential information informs readers about the event in direct, concrete, and objective sentences.
>
> **Directions** Read the news story lead. Write answers to the 5 Ws and How.
>
> Three brothers and local builders, the Porkson brothers of Curly Tale Lane, narrowly avoided being eaten by well-known predator B. B. Wolf yesterday. Wolf blew down the houses of Porky and Dorky Porkson, which were made of straw and wood, respectively. The pair escaped to brother Gorky's brick home. The determined Wolf crawled down Gorky's chimney. However, the attacker was killed when he fell into a pot of boiling water.
>
> Who? Porky, Dorky, and Gorky Porkson and B. B. Wolf (*or* three little pigs and big bad wolf)
> What? escaped being eaten by wolf; killed wolf in boiling water
> Where? at Porkson brothers homes on Curly Tale Lane
> When? yesterday
> Why? wolf wanted a meal; pigs wanted to live
> How? wolf blew down two houses; pigs set boiling pot of water in chimney
>
> **Directions** Rewrite the basic information (5 Ws and How) of a fairy tale or well-known story as a news story. Possible answer:
> A local girl broke into the home of the Bear family of Cozy Nook in North Woods yesterday. The bears had taken a short walk while their breakfast cooled. They returned to find their breakfasts eaten and their chairs and beds damaged. The suspect, whom the Bears described as a young female with blonde hair, escaped. She is still at large.
>
> Unit 2 Ch'i-lin Purse   Writer's Craft **8B**

▲ **Writing Transparency** 8B

DAY 3 Prewrite and Draft

READ THE WRITING PROMPT

on page 205 in the Student Edition.

"The Ch'i-lin Purse" tells about important events in a young woman's life.

Think about a real or fictional person or event.

Now write a news story telling about that person or event.

Writing Test Tips

- First answer the question *What is the story about?*
- Introduce main events in the lead paragraph by answering the questions *Who? What? Where? When? Why?* and *How?*
- Write short paragraphs relating the sequence of events. Connect the paragraphs with transitions.

GETTING STARTED Students can do any of the following:

- Fill in a chart answering the questions *Who? What? Where? When? Why?* and *How?*
- Brainstorm a list of precise nouns and verbs relevant to the story.
- Write the story's main idea. Include only details that support the main idea.

DAY 4 Draft and Revise

EDITING/REVISING CHECKLIST

☑ Did I tell what the story is about in my first paragraph?

☑ Have I answered the 5 Ws and How about the story?

☑ Have I used action and linking verbs effectively?

☑ Have I spelled words with /ir/, /or/, and /ar/ correctly?

See *The Grammar and Writing Book,* pp. 92–97.

Revising Tips

Organization/ Paragraphs

- Put essential information in the lead paragraph.
- Delete unnecessary words to help paragraph flow.
- Use transitions to move smoothly from paragraph to paragraph.

PUBLISHING Students can compile a fun newspaper of their news stories. Some students may wish to revise their work later.

ASSESSMENT Use the scoring rubric to evaluate students' work.

DAY 5 Connect to Unit Writing

How-to Report	
Week 1	Summary 161g–161h
Week 2	Story Review 185g–185h
Week 3	News Story 207g–207h
Week 4	Rules 229g–229h
Week 5	Interview 253g–253h

PREVIEW THE UNIT PROMPT

Write a report explaining how to make or do something that is familiar to you. Choose words that make your report interesting to read and easy to understand. Explain all the steps and materials needed.

APPLY

- A how-to report explains the steps for making or doing something.
- A how-to report should give information telling who, what, where, when, why, and how.

Writing Trait Rubric

	4	3	2	1
Organization/ Paragraphs	Ideas well developed from beginning to end; strong closure	Ideas that progress from beginning to end; good closure	Some sense of movement from beginning to end; weak closure	No sense of movement from beginning to end; no closure
	News story organized with exceptional logic	News story organized adequately	News story not clearly organized	News story not organized

Spelling & Phonics Vowel Sounds with *r*

OBJECTIVE

- Spell words with *r*-controlled vowels.

Generalization

Connect to Phonics The vowel sound /ôr/ can be spelled *or* and *ore*: <u>re**por**t</u>, <u>**snore**</u>. The vowel sound /ir/ can be spelled *ear* and *eer*: <u>ap**pear**</u>, <u>pio**neer**</u>. The vowel sound /âr/ can be spelled *are* and *air*: <u>a**ware**</u>, <u>**chair**</u>. Vowels and vowel digraphs have a slightly different sound when they are followed by *r*. Vowels followed by *r* are called *r*-controlled vowels.

Spelling Words

1. snore	11. beware
2. tornado	12. smear
3. spare	13. repair
4. appear	14. sword
5. career	15. ignore
6. square	16. order
7. report	17. engineer
8. prepare	18. resort
9. pioneer	19. volunteer
10. chair*	20. declare

Challenge Words

21. impair	24. clearance
22. directory	25. porpoise
23. hardware	

* Word from the selection

ELL

Spelling/Phonics Support See the ELL and Transition Handbook for spelling support.

PRETEST

Use the Dictation Sentences from Day 5 to administer the pretest. Read the word, read the sentence, and then read the word again. Guide students in self-correcting their pretests and correcting any misspellings.

Monitor Progress

Spelling

If... students misspell more than 5 pretest words,	then... use words 1–10 for Strategic Intervention.
If... students misspell 1–5 pretest words,	then... use words 1–20 for On-Level practice.
If... students correctly spell all pretest words,	then... use words 1–25 for Advanced Learners.

HOMEWORK Spelling Practice Book, p. 29.

▲ **Spelling Practice Book** p. 29

TEACH

Vowels and vowel digraphs that are followed by *r* are called *r*-controlled vowels because the *r* changes the vowel sound. Write *chain* and *chair*. Underline *ain* and *air* and say both words as students listen for the vowel sound. Have students say the following words and listen for the vowel sound: *report, snore, smear, career,* and *spare.*

chain
chair

GUESS MY WORD Have pairs of students give each other sound and meaning clues for the words, following this model:

Which word has *ore* and is something you do when you sleep?

HOMEWORK Spelling Practice Book, p. 30.

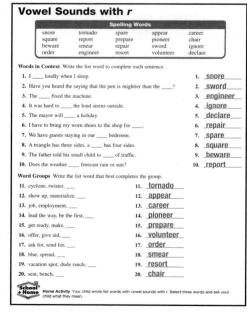

▲ **Spelling Practice Book** p. 30

DAY 3 Connect to Writing

WRITE ABOUT A REAL EVENT

Ask students to use at least four spelling words to write about a true event that appeared in the news.

Frequently Misspelled Words

caught   there's

These words may seem easy to spell, but they are often misspelled by fifth-graders. Alert students to these frequently misspelled words. Point out the *augh* pattern in *caught*. Elicit that *there's* is a contraction that can replace the words *there is* or *there has*.

HOMEWORK Spelling Practice Book, p. 31.

Vowel Sounds with *r*

Proofread a Story Ramon wrote this story about sharing a room with his brother. Circle six spelling errors. Find one sentence with a punctuation error. Write the corrections on the lines.

My Brother

Our mother asked my brother and me to *voluntier* to give up our rooms for our visiting grandparents. So, we're sharing the *spair* attic room, but it's no fun. My brother snores and it's hard to *ignoure* it. Just as I was I threw my pillow at him. It knocked over the lamp which hit the *chare* with a loud pop. This did not *apear* to disturb him at all. I gave up and slept in the hallway as a last resort.

Spelling Words
snore
tornado
spare
appear
career
square
report
prepare
pioneer
chair

beware
smear
repair
sword
ignore
order
engineer
resort
volunteer
declare

1. volunteer   2. spare
3. ignore   4. tornado
5. chair   6. appear
7. That was it!

Proofread Words Circle the correct spelling of the word.

8. A _____ is someone who leads the way for others.
(pioneer)   pioner   pieneer

9. The knight wore a brightly polished _____ on his hip.
sword   (sword)   sworde

10. The _____ is a wind funnel.
(tornado)   tornardo   tornadoe

11. Be careful or you'll _____ the fresh paint.
(smear)   smere   smeer

12. I asked the bike shop to _____ my flat tire.
ripare   (repair)   repare

Frequently Misspelled Words
caught
there's

School + Home Home Activity Your child identified misspelled list words in a paragraph. Ask your child to tell you the six patterns used in the list words to spell vowel sounds with r.

▲ **Spelling Practice Book** p. 31

DAY 4 Review

REVIEW VOWEL SOUNDS WITH *R*

Distribute graph paper, and have students create a crossword puzzle with at least five spelling words. Tell students to write a clue for each word and then exchange papers and solve each other's puzzles.

Spelling Strategy
Rhyming Helpers

Use rhymes to help spell. Rhyming helpers are spelled the same at the end. Watch out! Rhyming words are not always good helpers. *Career* and *volunteer* are rhyming helpers, but *appear* is not.

HOMEWORK Spelling Practice Book, p. 32.

Vowel Sounds with *r*

Spelling Words

snore	tornado	spare	appear	career
square	report	prepare	pioneer	chair
beware	smear	repair	sword	ignore
order	engineer	resort	volunteer	declare

Categorize Write the list word that completes each group.

1. weather, wind, prairie, _____   1. tornado
2. interest, study, job, _____   2. career
3. sleep, nose, exhale, _____   3. snore
4. vacation, travel, hotel, _____   4. resort
5. octagon, hexagon, pentagon, _____   5. square
6. explorer, frontier, first, _____   6. pioneer
7. be careful, look out, _____   7. beware
8. spread, blur, smudge, _____   8. smear
9. announce, say, claim, _____   9. declare
10. handle, blade, sheath, _____   10. sword

Word Scramble Unscramble the list words and write them on the lines.

11. espra   11. spare
12. hrcia   12. chair
13. perria   13. repair
14. rrdoe   14. order
15. tvlunoere 15. volunteer
16. riengene 16. engineer
17. grnioe   17. ignore
18. peaapr   18. appear

School + Home Home Activity Your child has learned to use patterns to spell vowel sounds followed by r. Look in a book or magazine with your child and find two other words that use one of these patterns.

▲ **Spelling Practice Book** p. 32

DAY 5 Posttest

DICTATION SENTENCES

1. Many people snore in their sleep.
2. Take cover when you hear a tornado warning.
3. The spare tire is in the trunk.
4. The twins will appear in the play.
5. Ann plans a career as a doctor.
6. Put it in the square box.
7. Max wrote a report about tigers.
8. It is time to prepare dinner now.
9. The pioneer family moved west.
10. The cat slept on the arm of the chair.
11. Beware of barking dogs.
12. The wet paint will smear if you touch it.
13. Mom can repair the broken toy.
14. The blade of the sword is sharp.
15. Try to ignore the noise and go to sleep.
16. The waiter took our lunch order.
17. An engineer drives a train.
18. We spent our vacation at a resort.
19. Who will volunteer to help out?
20. She is about to declare that she will run for office.

CHALLENGE

21. The wrong glasses may impair your vision.
22. The address is in the directory.
23. The hardware store sells tools.
24. The store held a clearance sale.
25. We saw a porpoise at the zoo.

OBJECTIVES

- Formulate an inquiry question that is connected to this week's lesson focus.
- Effectively and efficiently find, evaluate, and communicate information related to an inquiry question using electronic sources.

New Literacies	
Day 1	Identify Questions
Day 2	Navigate/Search
Day 3	Analyze
Day 4	Synthesize
Day 5	Communicate

NEW LITERACIES

Internet Inquiry Activity

EXPLORE GOOD DEEDS IN FOLK TALES

Use the following 5-day plan to help students conduct this week's Internet inquiry activity on good deeds in folk tales. Remind students to follow classroom rules when using the Internet.

DAY 1

Identify Questions Discuss the lesson focus question: *What are the rewards in helping others?* Tell students that frequently in folk tales such as "The Ch'i-Lin Purse," and sometimes in real life, good deeds are rewarded. Brainstorm specific inquiry questions about folk tales. For example, students might ask, "What are some other folk tales in which good deeds are rewarded?" Have students work individually, in pairs, or in small groups to write inquiry questions they want to answer.

DAY 2

Navigate/Search As students explore a student-friendly search engine for information on their topics, demonstrate how to bookmark a Web site so they can return to it quickly at a later time.

DAY 3

Analyze Have students skim and scan the Web sites they identified on Day 2. Point out that some of the sites may be commercial ones that aim to sell published folk tales. Encourage them to eliminate those and look for ones that include the folk tales themselves.

DAY 4

Synthesize Have students read the folk tales they found and think about which ones provide the best examples of good deeds being rewarded. Encourage them to think about the best ways to share the folk tales they found with the rest of the class.

DAY 5

Communicate Have students share their inquiry results. They can provide oral or written summaries of folk tales they found or create posters illustrating the key events of the folk tales. Their presentations should emphasize the good deeds in the folk tales and how the characters were rewarded.

RESEARCH/STUDY SKILLS
Textbook/Trade Book

TEACH

Ask students to produce samples of textbooks, and show them samples of trade books. Compare and contrast the books.

- A **textbook** is a book used to teach a certain subject. It is written to be used in a classroom or home school, and is often accompanied by additional materials, such as tests and workbooks.

- A **trade book** is any book that is not a textbook, magazine, or reference book, such as a collection of short stories or a nonfiction book about Franklin D. Roosevelt. Trade books can be read for pleasure or to seek information.

- Both textbooks and trade books may have the same parts: title and copyright page, table of contents, divisions such as chapters or units, graphic aids such as maps and photos, a glossary, and an index.

- Previewing a textbook or trade book before reading will help the reader understand the material contained in it and its purpose.

Have students work in small groups to compare and contrast features of trade books and textbooks in the classroom. They can divide the books by category. Members of the group can skim each book to look for its parts.

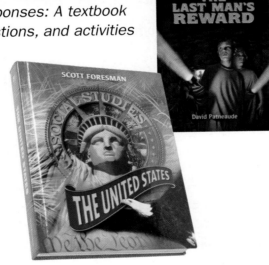

1. **What if any differences did you find between trade books and textbooks?** (Possible responses: A textbook has notes to students, lessons, questions, and activities for students to complete. It often has many authors and editors. A trade book has more information about a main topic.)

2. **How could you use a textbook and a trade book for a research report?** (Possible response: I could use my textbook to find basic information and a trade book to find more detailed information.)

ASSESS

As students work on the activity, check that they are able to distinguish between a trade book and a textbook, and identify features and purposes of each.

For more practice or to assess students, use Practice Book pp. 79–80.

OBJECTIVES

- Review the terms *textbook* and *trade book*.

- Identify features of textbooks and trade books.

Textbook/Trade Book

A **textbook** usually teaches one subject, such as social studies or math. Textbooks contain **chapter titles, headings, subheadings, and vocabulary words**. A **trade book** is any book that is not a textbook, a periodical, or a reference book.

Directions Study the following table of contents from a textbook. Then answer the questions below.

1. What subject do you think this textbook is for? Why?
   The textbook is about social studies because the chapters are about events in history.
2. Based on the table of contents, how are the sections of this textbook organized?
   The book is organized into chapters and subsections.
3. In what chapter and section can you learn about the city of Tokyo?
   You can find out about Tokyo in Chapter 19, Section 1.
4. In what section would you find a summary of the whole chapter?
   You can find summaries in the sections called *Chapter in Review*.
5. What do you think is included in the sections in italics? How can you tell?
   The sections in italics include graphic sources because they have words like *Map* and *Art* in their title.

▲ **Practice Book** p. 79

Directions Read the back cover of this trade book. Then answer the questions below.

The Chinatown Dragon
The Day My Little Sister Was Eaten by a Paper Dragon

THE UPDATED AND EXPANDED TENTH ANNIVERSARY EDITION

It has been ten years since Lori Liu first gave us her collection of stories about her childhood growing up in San Francisco's Chinatown. That edition let people from all over the world get a close up glimpse of a Chinatown few outsiders are able to see. Readers eagerly immersed themselves in sights and sounds, like the time her little sister ran straight into the mouth of a block-long paper dragon during a parade!

Since then, Ms. Liu has captured new tales full of music, action, humor, and good food to add to the original collection. This edition celebrates the original collection and expands it in a way that will delight her long-time readers.

"Lori Liu's stories are full of the laughter and tears common to everyone's childhood."
—Mario Michelin, *San Jose Post*

"If you have ever enjoyed an afternoon's visit to Chinatown, you will love Lori Liu's collection of stories, *The Chinatown Dragon*. You will feel like a resident rather than a visitor."
—Beatrice Kelly, *San Francisco News*

6. What kind of book is this?
   It is a collection of stories.
7. What is the book's title? What do you think the subtitle, which is in italics, means?
   The Chinatown Dragon; It is the name of one of the stories.
8. What is special about this edition of the book?
   This is the tenth anniversary edition and contains new stories.
9. Why are quotes included on the back cover?
   The quotes are meant to convince people to buy the book.
10. If you wanted to look up information about the history of Chinese New Year, would you look in a textbook or a trade book? Why?
   I'd look in a textbook because they tend to focus on facts.

Home Activity Your child read a short passage and then answered questions about textbooks and trade books. With your child, look at a trade book and a textbook. Ask your child to explain the difference between the two types of books.

▲ **Practice Book** p. 80

Assessment Checkpoints *for the Week*

Selection Assessment

Use pp. 29–32 of Selection Tests to check:

 Selection Understanding

 Comprehension Skill
Compare and Contrast

 Selection Vocabulary

astonished	procession
behavior	recommend
benefactor	sacred
distribution	traditions
gratitude	

ASSESSMENT
Scott Foresman
Selection Tests
Teacher's Manual
• Assess comprehension of weekly selections
• Assess understanding of weekly comprehension skills
• Assess knowledge of selection vocabulary

Selection Tests

Reading STREET
Grade 5

Leveled Assessment

On-Level
Strategic Intervention
Advanced

Use pp. 43–48 of Fresh Reads for Differentiated Test Practice to check:

 Comprehension Skill
Compare and Contrast

 REVIEW **Comprehension Skill** *Sequence*

 Fluency *Words Correct Per Minute*

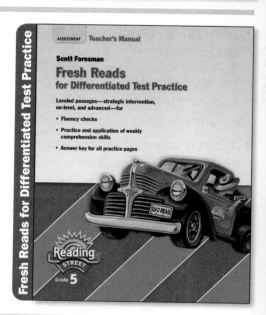

ASSESSMENT Teacher's Manual
Scott Foresman
Fresh Reads
for Differentiated Test Practice
Leveled passages—strategic intervention, on-level, and advanced—for
• Fluency checks
• Practice and application of weekly comprehension skills
• Answer key for all practice pages

Fresh Reads for Differentiated Test Practice

Reading STREET
Grade 5

Managing Assessment

Use Assessment Handbook for:

 Observation Checklists

 Record-Keeping Forms

 Portfolio Assessment

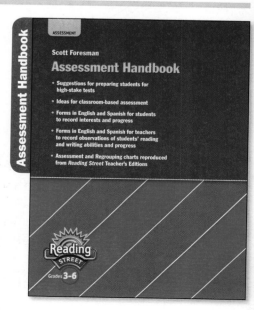

ASSESSMENT
Scott Foresman
Assessment Handbook
• Suggestions for preparing students for high-stake tests
• Ideas for classroom-based assessment
• Forms in English and Spanish for students to record interests and progress
• Forms in English and Spanish for teachers to record observations of students' reading and writing abilities and progress
• Assessment and Regrouping charts reproduced from *Reading Street Teacher's Editions*

Assessment Handbook

Reading STREET
Grades 3–6

Unit 2
Doing the Right Thing

CONCEPT QUESTION
What makes people want to do the right thing?

Week 1

Why do people show kindness?

Week 2

Why do we help others even if there are risks?

Week 3

What are the rewards in helping others?

Week 4

What can people do to protect wild animals?

Week 5

How can people promote freedom?

EXPAND THE CONCEPT
What can people do to protect wild animals?

CONNECT THE CONCEPT

▶ **Build Background**
conservation, naturalist, wildlife

Concept Vocabulary Web

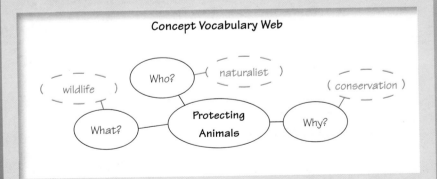

▶ **Science Content**
Animal Habitats, Roots and Shoots, Ecosystems

▶ **Writing**
Rules

▶ **Internet Inquiry**
Wildlife Protection

Preview Your Week

What can people do to protect wild animals?

from National Geographic for Kids

Jane Goodall's
10 Ways to Help Save Wildlife

by Jane Goodall

212

How does Jane Goodall feel about wild animals?

Genre — **Expository nonfiction** explains a person, a thing, or an idea. As you read, notice how the author gives both facts and opinions based on those facts.

Student Edition pages 212–223

Audio CD

Genre	Expository Nonfiction
Vocabulary Strategy	Context Clues
Comprehension Skill	Fact and Opinion
Comprehension Strategy	Ask Questions

Paired Selection

Reading Across Texts

Expand List of Suggestions

Genre

Expository Nonfiction

Text Features

Title

Pictures

Preview Questions

Science in Reading

Expository Nonfiction

Genre
- Expository nonfiction gives you facts and, sometimes, opinions about real-life people, places, and things.
- Some expository non-fiction focuses on a single topic about those people, places, and things.

Text Features
- Sometimes the title gives the reader a hint about the topic of the selection. Here the title states the topic directly.
- Pictures show what the selection is about.
- Read the first paragraph. Notice the questions the selection will answer.

Link to Science
Choose one of the animals in the selection and research more about it. Then write an explanation telling a small child why he or she should not be afraid of that animal.

from Sandiegozoo.org

Why Some Animals Are Considered BAD or SCARY

illustrated by John Manders

You've heard the stories and seen the movies. Wolves gather in the woods to attack helpless people, especially girls (remember Little Red Riding Hood?). Bats with huge fangs seek you out to suck your blood. Snakes deliberately find peo-ple to attack. Toads give you warts. Actually, none of these things are true. So why do humans have so many fears and superstitions about certain animals? Why do people think some animals are evil?

Most of the time it's because of ignorance, not knowing the facts about an animal or not understanding what its behavior is for. Humans tend to fear what they don't know or understand. So if someone sees a vampire bat sucking a cow's blood, he might assume that all bats do that, and that they will do it to anything they can. Stories are made up and rumors start, and the next thing you know, people believe that all bats attack deliberately and suck blood. But this isn't based on fact. There are thousands of bat species, and most of them eat fruit or insects and are very important to the environment. Only a few bats suck blood—they are small and not aggressive, and they hang around livestock and nip at their heels to get blood. They don't ravenously attack, and they are just an annoyance to the cows and horses—they don't kill them.

Ask Questions What additional questions are you asking yourself?

226

Student Edition pages 226–229

Audio CD

Read It
ONLINE
PearsonSuccessNet.com
- Student Edition
- Leveled Readers

Leveled Readers

◉ **Skill** Fact and Opinion

◉ **Strategy** Ask Questions

Lesson Vocabulary

Below-Level

On-Level

Advanced

ELL Reader
- Concept Vocabulary
- Text Support
- Language Enrichment

Integrate Science Standards
- Habitats
- Ecosystems
- Environments
- Ecology

✓ Read

"Jane Goodall's 10 Ways to Help Save Wildlife," pp. 212–223

"Why Some Animals Are Considered Bad or Scary," pp. 226–229

Leveled Readers

Below-Level   On-Level   Advanced

- Support Concepts
- Develop Concepts
- Extend Concepts
- Science Extension Activity

ELL Reader

 Build Concept Vocabulary
Protecting Animals, pp. 208l–208m

 Teach Science Concepts
Animal Habitats, p. 215
Roots & Shoots, p. 221
Ecosystems, p. 227

✓ **Explore Science Center**
Research Predators, p. 208k

Jane Goodall's 10 Ways to Help Save Wildlife

Weekly Plan

READING

45–90 minutes

TARGET SKILLS OF THE WEEK

- **Comprehension Skill**
  Fact and Opinion
- **Comprehension Strategy**
  Ask Questions
- **Vocabulary Strategy**
  Context Clues

LANGUAGE ARTS

30–60 minutes

Trait of the Week

Word Choice

DAY 1
PAGES 208l–210b, 229a, 229e–229k

Oral Language

QUESTION OF THE WEEK *What can people do to protect wild animals?*

Read Aloud: "Jane Goodall," 208m
Build Concepts, 208l

Comprehension/Vocabulary

Comprehension Skill/Strategy Lesson, 208–209
- Fact and Opinion **T**
- Ask Questions
Build Background, 210a
Introduce Lesson Vocabulary, 210b
conservation, contribute, enthusiastic, environment, investigation **T**

Read Leveled Readers

Grouping Options 208f–208g

Fluency

Model Phrasing, 208l–208m, 229a

Grammar, 229e
Introduce Main and Helping Verbs **T**

Writing Workshop, 229g
Introduce Rules
Model the Trait of the Week: Word Choice

Spelling, 229i
Pretest for Final Syllables *-en, -an, -el, -le, -il*

Internet Inquiry, 229k
Identify Questions

DAY 2
PAGES 210–219, 229a, 229e–229k

Oral Language

QUESTION OF THE DAY *What examples from her life does Jane Goodall give to illustrate the first three suggestions?*

Comprehension/Vocabulary

Vocabulary Strategy Lesson, 210–211
- Context Clues **T**

Read "Jane Goodall's 10 Ways to Help Save Wildlife," 212–219

Grouping Options 208f–208g

- Fact and Opinion **T**
- Context Clues **T**
- **REVIEW** Compare and Contrast **T**
Develop Vocabulary

Fluency

Choral Reading, 229a

Grammar, 229e
Develop Main and Helping Verbs **T**

Writing Workshop, 229g
Improve Writing with Know Your Purpose

Spelling, 229i
Teach the Generalization

Internet Inquiry, 229k
Navigate/Search

DAILY WRITING ACTIVITIES

Day 1 Write to Read, 208

Day 2 Words to Write, 211
Strategy Response Log, 212, 219

DAILY SCIENCE CONNECTIONS

Day 1 Protecting Animals Concept Web, 208l

Day 2 Time for Science: Animal Habitats, 215
Revisit the Protecting Animals Concept Web, 219

DAILY SUCCESS PREDICTORS

for Adequate Yearly Progress

Monitor Progress and Corrective Feedback

Vocabulary — Check Vocabulary, *208l*

RESOURCES FOR THE WEEK

- Practice Book, *pp. 81–90*
- Word Study and Spelling Practice Book, *pp. 33–36*
- Grammar and Writing Practice Book, *pp. 33–36*
- Selection Test, *pp. 33–36*
- Fresh Reads for Differentiated Test Practice, *pp. 49–54*
- The Grammar and Writing Book, *pp. 98–103*

Grouping Options for Differentiated Instruction

Turn the page for the small group lesson plan.

DAY 3 PAGES 220-225, 229a, 229e-229k

Oral Language

QUESTION OF THE DAY *How has Jane Goodall's lifelong work with chimpanzees affected her thinking?*

Comprehension/Vocabulary

Read "Jane Goodall's 10 Ways to Help Save Wildlife," 220–224

Grouping Options 208f–208g

- Fact and Opinion **T**
- Ask Questions
- Develop Vocabulary

Reader Response

Selection Test

Fluency

Model Phrasing, 229a

Grammar, 229f
Apply Main and Helping Verbs in Writing **T**

Writing Workshop, 225, 229h
Write Now
Prewrite and Draft

Spelling, 229j
Connect Spelling to Writing

Internet Inquiry, 229k
Analyze Sources

Day 3 Strategy Response Log, 222
Look Back and Write, 224

Day 3 Time for Science: Roots and Shoots, 221
Revisit the Protecting Animals Concept Web, 223

DAY 4 PAGES 226-229a, 229e-229k

Oral Language

QUESTION OF THE DAY *Why do you think it is a good idea to protect endangered animals?*

Comprehension/Vocabulary

Read "Why Some Animals Are Considered Bad or Scary," 226–229

Grouping Options 208f–208g

Expository Nonfiction/Text Features
Reading Across Texts
Content-Area Vocabulary

Fluency

Partner Reading, 229a

Grammar, 229f
Practice Main and Helping Verbs for Standardized Tests **T**

Writing Workshop, 229h
Draft, Revise, and Publish

Spelling, 229j
Provide a Strategy

Internet Inquiry, 229k
Synthesize Information

Day 4 Writing Across Texts, 229

Day 4 Time for Science: Ecosystems, 227

DAY 5 PAGES 229a-229l

Oral Language

QUESTION OF THE WEEK *To wrap up the week, revisit the Day 1 question.*

Build Concept Vocabulary, 229c

Fluency

Read Leveled Readers

Grouping Options 208f–208g

Assess Reading Rate, 229a

Comprehension/Vocabulary

- Reteach Fact and Opinion, 229b **T**
- Author's Viewpoint/Bias, 229b
- Review Context Clues, 229c **T**

Speaking and Viewing, 229d
Debate/Panel Discussion
Analyze Film Media

Grammar, 229f
Cumulative Review

Writing Workshop, 229h
Connect to Unit Writing

Spelling, 229j
Posttest for Final Syllables *-en, -an, -el, -le, -il*

Internet Inquiry, 229k
Communicate Results

Research/Study Skills, 229l
Electronic Media

Day 5 Author's Viewpoint/Bias, 229b

Day 5 Revisit the Protecting Animals Concept Web, 229c

KEY ◎ = Target Skill   **T** = Tested Skill

Comprehension Check Retelling, *224*

Fluency Check Fluency WCPM, *229a*

Vocabulary Check Vocabulary, *229c*

SUCCE
PREDICT

Small Group Plan *for Differentiated Instruction*

Daily Plan AT A GLANCE

Reading
Whole Group
- Oral Language
- Comprehension/Vocabulary

Group Time
Differentiated Instruction

Meet with small groups to provide:
- Skill Support
- Reading Support
- Fluency Practice

Read

This week's lessons for daily group time can be found behind the Differentiated Instruction (DI) tab on pp. DI·32–DI·41.

Whole Group
- Fluency

Language Arts
- Grammar
- Writing
- Spelling
- Research/Inquiry
- Speaking/Listening/Viewing

Use *My Sidewalks on Reading Street* for Tier III intensive reading intervention.

DAY 1

On-Level
Teacher-Led
Page DI·33
- Develop Concept Vocabulary
- **Read** On-Level Reader *Habitats In Need of Help*

Strategic Intervention
Teacher-Led
Page DI·32
- Reinforce Concepts
- **Read** Below-Level Reader *Endangered Animals*

Advanced
Teacher-Led
Page DI·33
- **Read** Advanced Reader *Saving Endangered Species*
- Independent Extension Activity

ⓘ Independent Activities
While you meet with small groups, have the rest of the class...

- Visit the Reading/Library Center
- Listen to the Background Building Audio
- Finish Write to Read, p. 208
- Complete Practice Book pp. 83–84
- Visit Cross-Curricular Centers

DAY 2

On-Level
Teacher-Led
Pages 214–219
- **Read** "Jane Goodall's 10 Ways to Help Save Wildlife"

Strategic Intervention
Teacher-Led
Page DI·34
- Practice Lesson Vocabulary
- Read Multisyllabic Words
- **Read** or Listen to "Jane Goodall's 10 Ways to Help . . ."

Advanced
Teacher-Led
Page DI·35
- Extend Vocabulary
- **Read** "Jane Goodall's 10 Ways to Help Save Wildlife"

ⓘ Independent Activities
While you meet with small groups, have the rest of the class...

- Visit the Reading/Library Center
- Listen to the AudioText for "Jane Goodall's 10 Ways to Help Save Wildlife"
- Finish Words to Write, p. 211
- Complete Practice Book pp. 85–86
- Write in their Strategy Response Logs, pp. 212, 219
- Visit Cross-Curricular Centers
- Work on inquiry projects

DAY 3

On-Level
Teacher-Led
Pages 220–223
- **Read** "Jane Goodall's 10 Ways to Help Save Wildlife"

Strategic Intervention
Teacher-Led
Page DI·36
- Practice Fact and Opinion and Ask Questions
- **Read** or Listen to "Jane Goodall's 10 Ways to Help . . ."

Advanced
Teacher-Led
Page DI·37
- Extend Fact and Opinion and Ask Questions
- **Read** "Jane Goodall's 10 Ways to Help Save Wildlife"

ⓘ Independent Activities
While you meet with small groups, have the rest of the class...

- Visit the Reading/Library Center
- Listen to the AudioText for "Jane Goodall's 10 Ways to Help Save Wildlife"
- Write in their Strategy Response Logs, p. 222
- Finish Look Back and Write, p. 224
- Complete Practice Book p. 87
- Visit Cross-Curricular Centers
- Work on inquiry projects

① Begin with whole class skill and strategy instruction.

② Meet with small groups to provide differentiated instruction.

③ Gather the whole class back together for fluency and language arts.

DAY 4

On-Level
Teacher-Led
Pages 226–229
- **Read** "Why Some Animals Are Considered Bad or Scary"

Strategic Intervention
Teacher-Led
Page DI·38
- Practice Retelling
- **Read** or Listen to "Why Some Animals Are Considered Bad or Scary"

Advanced
Teacher-Led
Page DI·39
- **Read** "Why Some Animals Are Considered Bad or Scary"
- Genre Study

ⓘ Independent Activities

While you meet with small groups, have the rest of the class...

- Visit the Reading/Library Center
- Listen to the AudioText for "Why Some Animals Are Considered Bad or Scary"
- Visit the Writing/Vocabulary Center

- Finish Writing Across Texts, p. 229
- Visit Cross-Curricular Centers
- Work on inquiry projects

DAY 5

On-Level
Teacher-Led
Page DI·41
- **Reread** Leveled Reader *Habitats In Need of Help*
- Retell *Habitats In Need of Help*

Strategic Intervention
Teacher-Led
Page DI·40
- **Reread** Leveled Reader *Endangered Animals*
- Retell *Endangered Animals*

Advanced
Teacher-Led
Page DI·41
- **Reread** Leveled Reader *Saving Endangered Species*
- Share Extension Activity

ⓘ Independent Activities

While you meet with small groups, have the rest of the class...

- Visit the Reading/Library Center
- Complete Practice Book pp. 88–90

- Visit Cross-Curricular Centers
- Work on inquiry projects

Grouping Place English language learners in the groups that correspond to their reading abilities in English.

Use the appropriate Leveled Reader or other text at students' instructional level.

TIP Send home the appropriate Multilingual Summary of the main selection on Day 1.

Take It to the NET™ ONLINE
PearsonSuccessNet.com

Donald Leu
For ideas and activities to build new literacies, see the article "The New Literacies" by Scott Foresman author Donald Leu.

TEACHER TALK

Generating Questions is an effective way for students to engage with and comprehend text. Teach students to ask good questions about important text information as they read.

Be sure to schedule time for students to work on the unit inquiry project "Doing the Right Thing." This week students combine the relevant information they have collected to help them answer their inquiry questions.

Looking Ahead

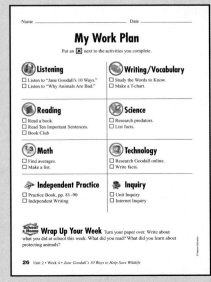

Name _____ Date _____
My Work Plan
Put an ☒ next to the activities you complete.

Listening
☐ Listen to "Jane Goodall's 10 Ways."
☐ Listen to "Why Animals Are Bad."

Writing/Vocabulary
☐ Study the Words to Know.
☐ Make a T-chart.

Reading
☐ Read a book.
☐ Read Ten Important Sentences.
☐ Book Club

Science
☐ Research predators.
☐ List facts.

Math
☐ Find averages.
☐ Make a list.

Technology
☐ Research Goodall online.
☐ Write facts.

Independent Practice
☐ Practice Book, pp. 81–90
☐ Independent Writing

Inquiry
☐ Unit Inquiry
☐ Internet Inquiry

Wrap Up Your Week Turn your paper over. Write about what you did at school this week. What did you read? What did you learn about protecting animals?

26 Unit 2 • Week 4 • *Jane Goodall's 10 Ways to Help Save Wildlife*

▲ **Group-Time Survival Guide**
p. 26, Weekly Contract

☑ Customize Your Plan *by Strand*

 Science

Concept Development

What can people do to protect wild animals?

CONCEPT VOCABULARY
conservation   naturalist   wildlife

BUILD

☐ **Question of the Week** Introduce and discuss the question of the week. This week students will read a variety of texts and work on projects related to the concept *protecting animals*. Post the question for students to refer to throughout the week. **DAY 1** *208d*

☐ **Read Aloud** Read aloud "Jane Goodall." Then begin a web to build concepts and concept vocabulary related to this week's lesson and the unit theme, Doing the Right Thing. Introduce the concept words *conservation, naturalist,* and *wildlife* and have students place them on the web. Display the web for use throughout the week. **DAY 1** *208l–208m*

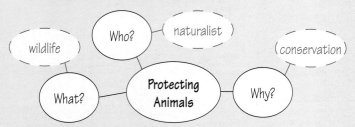

DEVELOP

☐ **Question of the Day** Use the prompts from the Weekly Plan to engage students in conversations related to this week's reading and the unit theme. **EVERY DAY** *208d–208e*

☐ **Concept Vocabulary Web** Revisit the Protecting Animals Concept Web and encourage students to add concept words from their reading and life experiences. **DAY 2** *219*, **DAY 3** *223*

CONNECT

☐ **Looking Back/Moving Forward** Revisit the Protecting Animals Concept Web and discuss how it relates to this week's lesson and the unit theme. Then make connections to next week's lesson. **DAY 5** *229c*

CHECK

☐ **Concept Vocabulary Web** Use the Protecting Animals Concept Web to check students' understanding of the concept vocabulary words *conservation, naturalist,* and *wildlife*. **DAY 1** *208l*, **DAY 5** *229c*

STRATEGY CONTEXT CLUES
Context means the words and sentences near the unfamiliar word. Good readers use context clues to figure out the meaning of a new word.

LESSON VOCABULARY
conservation   environment
contribute   investigation
enthusiastic

TEACH

☐ **Words to Know** Give students the opportunity to tell what they already know about this week's lesson vocabulary words. Then discuss word meaning. **DAY 1** *210b*

☐ **Vocabulary Strategy Lesson** Use the vocabulary strategy lesson in the Student Edition to introduce and model this week's strategy, *context clues*. **DAY 2** *210–211*

Vocabulary Strategy Lesson

PRACTICE/APPLY

☐ **Leveled Text** Read the lesson vocabulary in the context of leveled text. **DAY 1** *LR28–LR36*

Leveled Readers

☐ **Words in Context** Read the lesson vocabulary and apply *context clues* in the context of "Jane Goodall's 10 Ways to Help Save Wildlife." **DAY 2** *212–219*, **DAY 3** *220–224*

☐ **Writing/Vocabulary Center** Make a pro and con T-chart for one of the "scary" animals you read about this week. **ANY DAY** *208k*

Main Selection—NonFiction

☐ **Homework** Practice Book pp. 84–85. **DAY 1** *210b*, **DAY 2** *211*

☐ **Word Play** Have partners make lists of proper nouns from "Jane Goodall's 10 Ways to Help Save Wildlife," and then alphabetize the proper nouns in a list. **ANY DAY** *229c*

ASSESS

☐ **Selection Test** Use the Selection Test to determine students' understanding of the lesson vocabulary words. **DAY 3**

RETEACH/REVIEW

☐ **Reteach Lesson** If necessary, use this lesson to reteach and review *context clues*. **DAY 5** *229c*

1 Use assessment data to determine your instructional focus.

2 Preview this week's instruction by strand.

3 Choose instructional activities that meet the needs of your classroom.

COMPREHENSION

SKILL FACT AND OPINION A *statement of fact* can be proved true or false. A *statement of opinion* tells what someone thinks or feels.

STRATEGY ASK QUESTIONS Asking questions is a strategy that good readers use. Asking questions *before* you read will help you connect what you will read to what you already know (prior knowledge). Asking questions *as* you read helps you understand what you are reading. Asking questions *after* you read helps you remember important information.

TEACH

Skill/Strategy Lesson

☐ **Skill/Strategy Lesson** Use the skill/strategy lesson in the Student Edition to introduce and model *fact and opinion* and *ask questions*. **DAY 1** *208–209*

☐ **Extend Skills** Teach author's viewpoint/bias. **ANY DAY** *229b*

PRACTICE/APPLY

☐ **Leveled Text** Apply *fact and opinion* and *ask questions* to read leveled text. **DAY 1** *LR28–LR36*

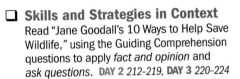

Leveled Readers

☐ **Skills and Strategies in Context** Read "Jane Goodall's 10 Ways to Help Save Wildlife," using the Guiding Comprehension questions to apply *fact and opinion* and *ask questions*. **DAY 2** *212–219*, **DAY 3** *220–224*

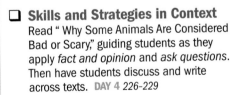

Main Selection—NonFiction

☐ **Skills and Strategies in Context** Read "Why Some Animals Are Considered Bad or Scary," guiding students as they apply *fact and opinion* and *ask questions*. Then have students discuss and write across texts. **DAY 4** *226–229*

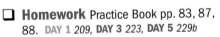

Paired Selection—Nonfiction

☐ **Homework** Practice Book pp. 83, 87, 88. **DAY 1** *209*, **DAY 3** *223*, **DAY 5** *229b*

☐ **Fresh Reads for Differentiated Test Practice** Have students practice *fact and opinion* with a new passage. **DAY 3**

ASSESS

☐ **Selection Test** Determine students' understanding of the selection and their use of *fact and opinion*. **DAY 3**

☐ **Retell** Have students retell "Jane Goodall's 10 Ways to Help Save Wildlife." **DAY 3** *224–225*

RETEACH/REVIEW

☐ **Reteach Lesson** If necessary, reteach and review *fact and opinion*. **DAY 5** *229b*

FLUENCY

SKILL PHRASING Phrasing is grouping related words, such as prepositional phrases, verbal phrases, and other clauses, to reinforce meaning and make the text sound smooth and like natural language. Phrasing allows the reader and listener to better understand the text.

TEACH

☐ **Read Aloud** Model fluent reading by rereading "Jane Goodall." Focus on this week's fluency skill, phrasing. **DAY 1** *208l–208m, 229a*

PRACTICE/APPLY

☐ **Choral Reading** Read aloud selected paragraphs from "Jane Goodall's 10 Ways to Help Save Wildlife," placing emphasis on grouping related words together. Then practice as a class, doing three choral readings of the selected paragraphs. **DAY 2** *229a*, **DAY 3** *229a*

☐ **Partner Reading** Have partners practice reading aloud, reading with careful phrasing, and offering each other feedback. As students reread, monitor their progress toward their individual fluency goals. **DAY 4** *229a*

☐ **Listening Center** Have students follow along with the AudioText for this week's selections. **ANY DAY** *208j*

☐ **Reading/Library Center** Have students reread a selection of their choice. **ANY DAY** *208j*

☐ **Fluency Coach** Have students use Fluency Coach to listen to fluent readings or practice reading on their own. **ANY DAY**

ASSESS

☐ **Check Fluency** **WCPM** Do a one-minute timed reading, paying special attention to this week's skill—phrasing. Provide feedback for each student. **DAY 5** *229a*

☑ Customize Your Plan *by Strand*

GRAMMAR

SKILL MAIN AND HELPING VERBS Verbs that are made up of more than one word are verb phrases. In a verb phrase, the *main verb* names the action. The *helping verb* helps tell the time of the action.

TEACH

❑ **Grammar Transparency 9** Use Grammar Transparency 9 to teach main and helping verbs. **DAY 1** *229e*

Grammar Transparency 9

PRACTICE/APPLY

❑ **Develop the Concept** Review the concept of main and helping verbs and provide guided practice. **DAY 2** *229e*

❑ **Apply to Writing** Have students review something they have written and apply main and helping verbs. **DAY 3** *229f*

❑ **Test Preparation** Examine common errors in main and helping verbs to prepare for standardized tests. **DAY 4** *229f*

❑ **Homework** Grammar and Writing Practice Book pp. 33–35. **DAY 2** *229e*, **DAY 3** *229f*, **DAY 4** *229f*

ASSESS

❑ **Cumulative Review** Use Grammar and Writing Practice Book p. 36. **DAY 5** *229f*

RETEACH/REVIEW

❑ **Daily Fix-It** Have students find and correct errors in grammar, spelling, and punctuation. **EVERY DAY** *229e–229f*

❑ **The Grammar and Writing Book** Use pp. 98–101 of The Grammar and Writing Book to extend instruction for main and helping verbs. **ANY DAY**

The Grammar and Writing Book

WRITING

Trait of the Week

WORD CHOICE Good writers choose their words carefully. Strong verbs, specific nouns, and vivid adjectives help writers elaborate on their ideas. Well-chosen and exact words make writing precise, clear, and lively.

TEACH

❑ **Writing Transparency 9A** Use the model to introduce and discuss the Trait of the Week. **DAY 1** *229g*

❑ **Writing Transparency 9B** Use the transparency to show students how to know your purpose can improve their writing. **DAY 2** *229g*

Writing Transparency 9A **Writing Transparency 9B**

PRACTICE/APPLY

❑ **Write Now** Examine the model on Student Edition p. 225. Then have students write their own rules. **DAY 3** *225, 229h*, **DAY 4** *229h*

> **Prompt** "Jane Goodall's 10 Ways to Help Save Wildlife" lists rules for protecting animals. Think about another situation where rules are helpful. Now write rules that people can follow in that situation.

Write Now p. 225

❑ **Writing/Vocabulary Center** Make a pro and con T-chart for one of the "scary" animals you read about this week. **ANY DAY** *208k*

ASSESS

❑ **Writing Trait Rubric** Use the rubric to evaluate students' writing. **DAY 4** *229h*

RETEACH/REVIEW

❑ **The Grammar and Writing Book** Use pp. 98–103 of The Grammar and Writing Book to extend instruction for main and helping verbs, know your purpose, and rules. **ANY DAY**

The Grammar and Writing Book

SPELLING

GENERALIZATION FINAL SYLLABLES -EN, -AN, -EL, -LE, -IL
Vowels in final syllables often sound alike even when they are spelled differently: cancel, chuckle, fossil, veteran, wooden. Vowels in unaccented syllables often stand for the same sound, /ə/.

TEACH

❑ **Pretest** Give the pretest for words with final syllables -en, -an, -el, -le, -il. Guide students in self-correcting their pretests and correcting any misspellings. DAY 1 229i

❑ **Think and Practice** Connect spelling to the phonics generalization for final syllables -en, -an, -el, -le, -il. DAY 2 229i

PRACTICE/APPLY

❑ **Connect to Writing** Have students use spelling words to write about the environment. Then review frequently misspelled words: Mom, Dad's, heard. DAY 3 229j

❑ **Homework** Word Study and Spelling Practice Book pp. 33–36. EVERY DAY

RETEACH/REVIEW

❑ **Review** Review spelling words to prepare for the posttest. Then provide students with a spelling strategy—problem parts. DAY 4 229j

ASSESS

❑ **Posttest** Use dictation sentences to give the posttest for words with final syllables -en, -an, -el, -le, -il. DAY 5 229j

Spelling Words

1. example	8. wooden	15. veteran
2. level	9. double	16. chisel
3. human*	10. travel*	17. suburban
4. quarrel	11. cancel	18. single
5. scramble	12. chuckle	19. sudden
6. evil	13. fossil	20. beagle
7. oxygen	14. toboggan	

Challenge Words

21. obstacle	23. abdomen	25. enlighten
22. kindergarten	24. pummel	

*Word from the selection

RESEARCH AND INQUIRY

❑ **Internet Inquiry** Have students conduct an Internet inquiry on wildlife protection. EVERY DAY 229k

❑ **Electronic Media** Review the different types of electronic media and the features. Discuss how students can use these resources to find information. DAY 5 229l

❑ **Unit Inquiry** Allow time for students to combine the relevant information they have collected to help them answer their inquiry questions. ANY DAY 141

SPEAKING AND VIEWING

❑ **Debate** Have students work in pairs to evaluate "Jane Goodall's 10 Ways to Help Save Wildlife" in a debate. DAY 5 229d

❑ **Panel Discussion** Have students work in groups researching, investigating, and discussing environmental or societal issues.

❑ **Analyze Film Media** Discuss with students, or arrange to show, a scene from a movie or TV program that focuses on wild animals, and answer questions. DAY 5 229d

Resources for Differentiated Instruction

LEVELED READERS

▶ **Comprehension**
  🎯 **Skill** Fact and Opinion
  🎯 **Strategy** Ask Questions

▶ **Lesson Vocabulary**
  🎯 **Context Clues**

conservation   contribute
environment
enthusiastic   investigation

▶ **Science Standards**
  • Habitats
  • Ecosystems
  • Environments
  • Ecology

Leveled Reader Database
ONLINE
PearsonSuccessNet.com

Use the Online Database of over 600 books to
- Download and print additional copies of this week's leveled readers.
- Listen to the readers being read online.
- Search for more titles focused on this week's skills, topic, and content.

On-Level

On-Level Reader

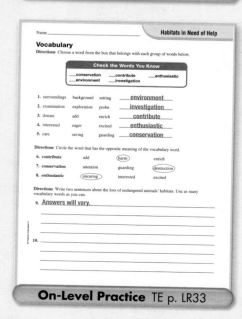

Name _____ | Habitats in Need of Help

Fact and Opinion

- A statement of **fact** can be proven true or false by reading, observing, or asking an expert.
- A statement of **opinion** is a judgment or belief. It cannot be proven true or false but can be supported or explained.

Directions Read the following passage. Decide which sentences are facts and which sentences are opinions. Then complete the chart below by listing three statements of fact and two statements of opinion.

The habitat of orangutans is at risk of disappearing. Orangutans are large, funny-looking apes. They live on the island of Borneo and the neighboring Indonesian island of Sumatra. An orangutan can weigh from sixty to three hundred pounds and requires large areas of forest in which to roam. But today, due to humans having taken over land for mining, logging, and various types of farming, less than 20 percent of the orangutans' original habitat remains. Some researchers estimate that there are fewer than thirty thousand orangutans on the islands today. Losing even one of these amazing apes would be a big tragedy.

Possible responses given.

Statements of Fact	Statements of Opinion
1. Orangutans live on the island of Borneo and the neighboring Indonesian island of Sumatra.	4. Orangutans are large, funny-looking apes.
2. An orangutan can weigh from sixty to three hundred pounds and requires large areas of forest in which to roam.	5. Losing even one of these amazing apes would be a big tragedy.
3. Due to humans having taken over land for mining, logging, and various types of farming, less than 20 percent of the orangutan's original habitat remains.	

🎯 **On-Level Practice** TE p. LR32

Name _____ | Habitats in Need of Help

Vocabulary
Directions Choose a word from the box that belongs with each group of words below.

Check the Words You Know
conservation   contribute   enthusiastic
environment   investigation

1. surroundings   background   setting   **environment**
2. examination   exploration   probe   **investigation**
3. donate   add   enrich   **contribute**
4. interested   eager   excited   **enthusiastic**
5. care   saving   guarding   **conservation**

Directions Circle the word that has the opposite meaning of the vocabulary word.

6. **contribute**   add   (harm)   enrich
7. **conservation**   attention   guarding   (destruction)
8. **enthusiastic**   (uncaring)   interested   excited

Directions Write two sentences about the loss of endangered animals' habitats. Use as many vocabulary words as you can.

9. **Answers will vary.**
10. _____

🎯 **On-Level Practice** TE p. LR33

Strategic Intervention

Below-Level Reader

Name _____ | Endangered Animals

Fact and Opinion

- A statement of **fact** can be proven true or false by reading, observing, or asking an expert.
- A statement of **opinion** is a judgment or belief. It cannot be proven true or false but can be supported or explained.

Directions Read the following passage. Decide which sentences are facts and which sentences are opinions. Then complete the chart below.

A law called the Endangered Species Act protects endangered and threatened species. It is one of the most important laws in America. Under the Endangered Species Act, endangered species of animals are listed by the government. Then plans are made to keep the species from becoming extinct. The government must try to protect the animal habitats from being destroyed and may breed young animals in captivity for release in the wild. Hunting and fishing for endangered animals might be limited by the government.

Some people's jobs or businesses are affected by these rules. But saving endangered species is worth the sacrifice. Without protection, many animals will disappear from the Earth forever.

Possible responses given.

Statements of Fact	Statements of Opinion
1. A law called the Endangered Species Act protects endangered and threatened species.	4. The Endangered Species Act is one of the most important laws in America.
2. Under the Endangered Species Act, endangered species of animals are listed by the government.	5. Saving endangered species is worth the sacrifice.
3. Some people's jobs or businesses are affected because of the Endangered Species Act.	

🎯 **Below-Level Practice** TE p. LR29

Name _____ | Endangered Animals

Vocabulary
Directions Write the word from the box that best completes each sentence.

Check the Words You Know
conservation   contribute   enthusiastic
environment   investigation

1. Our class will **contribute** cupcakes to the school bake sale.
2. The police are conducting an **investigation** of the robbery.
3. A hot, dry desert is the perfect **environment** for a camel.
4. I love animals, so I am **enthusiastic** about my job at the pet store.
5. The **conservation** of habitats will help save endangered animals.

Directions Circle the word that has the same meaning as the vocabulary word.

6. **contribute**   neglect   harm   (help)
7. **conservation**   waste   (guarding)   destruction
8. **enthusiastic**   (excited)   disinterested   uncaring
9. **environment**   people   object   (setting)
10. **investigation**   (examination)   test   routine

Directions Write a sentence of your own for each vocabulary word.

11. **Sentences will vary.**
12. _____
13. _____
14. _____
15. _____

🎯 **Below-Level Practice** TE p. LR30

Advanced

Advanced Reader

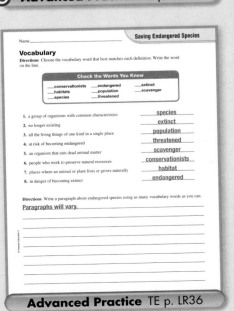

Advanced Practice TE p. LR35

Advanced Practice TE p. LR36

ELL

ELL Reader

ELL Poster 9

Teacher's Edition Notes

ELL notes throughout this lesson support instruction and reference additional resources at point of use.

Teaching Guide
pp. 57–63, 228–229

- Multilingual summaries of the main selection
- Comprehension lesson
- Vocabulary strategies and word cards
- ELL Reader 5.2.4 lesson

ELL and Transition Handbook

Ten Important Sentences

- Key ideas from every selection in the Student Edition
- Activities to build sentence power

More Reading

Readers' Theater Anthology

- Fluency practice
- Five scripts to build fluency
- Poetry for oral interpretation

Leveled Trade Books

- Extended reading tied to the unit concept
- Lessons in the Trade Book Library Teaching Guide

School + Home

Homework

- Family Times Newsletter
- ELL Multilingual Selection Summaries

Take-Home Books

- Leveled Readers

Cross-Curricular Centers

Listening

Listen to the Selections

MATERIALS — SINGLES

CD player, headphones, AudioText CD, student book

LISTEN TO LITERATURE Listen to "Jane Goodall's 10 Ways to Help Save Wildlife" and "Why Some Animals are Considered Bad or Scary" as you follow or read along in your book. Listen to identify the statements of fact and the opinion in each selection.

If there is anything you don't understand, you can listen again to any section.

Reading/Library

Read It Again!

MATERIALS — SINGLES / PAIRS / GROUPS

Collection of books for self-selected reading, reading logs, student book

Select a book you have already read. Record the title of the book in your reading log. You may want to read with a partner.

Choose from the following:

- **Leveled Readers**
- **ELL Readers**
- **Stories Written by Classmates**
- **Books from the Library**
- **"Jane Goodall's 10 Ways to Help Save Wildlife"**

TEN IMPORTANT SENTENCES

Read the Ten Important Sentences for "Jane Goodall's 10 Ways to Help Save Wildlife." Then locate the sentences in the student book.

BOOK CLUB Look at "Meet Authors" on p. 766 of the student book. Read other books about Jane Goodall and the work she has done with chimpanzees.

Math

Find Averages

MATERIALS — SINGLES

Writing materials, copy of chart below, graph paper

Use the chart below to find the average weights of primates.

1. Add the primate's lightest and heaviest weights together. Divide the sum by 2. Include the label *pounds* in each average.
2. List the primates from lightest to heaviest using your averages.

EARLY FINISHERS Make a bar graph showing the average weight of each primate.

Primate	Weight Range in lbs.
Bonobo	55–110
Guenon	5–15
Chimpanzee (male)	90–120
Gorilla (female)	150–200
Mangabey	7–44

Writing/ Vocabulary

Make a *List*

MATERIALS `SINGLES`
Writing materials, research materials.

Make a pro and con T-chart for one of the "scary" animals you read about this week.

1. Choose an animal from the selections.
2. Find out more about the animal.
3. Use a T-chart to make a pro and con list that summarizes the good and bad points you found.

EARLY FINISHERS Write a persuasive essay about the good points of the animal and why it deserves our respect.

My Animal: Sharks

Pros	Cons
Sharks help control fish populations.	Sharks bite.

 ## Science

Research **Predators**

MATERIALS `SINGLES`
Books on predators, Internet access, writing and art materials, index cards

Research the behavior of predators.

1. Choose a predator to research.
2. Find out more about the behaviors and habits of this animal. Use a student-friendly research engine or books.
3. List at least five facts about the animal on index cards.
4. Be prepared to share with your class.

EARLY FINISHERS Use the information you find to make and illustrate a poster informing others about the animal.

Lion Facts
1. Groups are called prides

 ## Technology

Learn about *Jane Goodall*

MATERIALS `SINGLES` `GROUPS`
Internet access, writing materials, e-mail program

Use the Internet to search for new facts about Jane Goodall.

1. Type the keywords *Jane Goodall* into a student-friendly search engine, following classroom rules.
2. Explore a few sources and select one that you find interesting.
3. Find an interesting fact about the naturalist that you didn't already know and write it down.
4. Be prepared to share your fact with the rest of the class.

EARLY FINISHERS With your teacher's permission write and send an e-mail to a friend or family member telling them some of the interesting facts you've learned about Jane Goodall.

Search Engine
Jane Goodall

Facts about Jane Goodall
1. She was born in England.

 **ALL CENTERS**

OBJECTIVES

- Build vocabulary by finding words related to the lesson concept.
- Listen for statements of fact and opinion.

Concept Vocabulary

conservation preservation from harm or decay

naturalist a person who studies living things

wildlife wild animals and plants

Monitor Progress

Check Vocabulary

If...	then... review the
students are	lesson concept.
unable to	Place the words on
place words	the web and provide
on the web,	additional words for
	practice, such as
	observation and
	donation.

SUCCESS PREDICTOR

DAY 1 Grouping Options

Reading
Whole Group
Introduce and discuss the Question of the Week. Then use pp. 208l–210b.

Group Time
Differentiated Instruction
Read this week's Leveled Readers. See pp. 208h–208i for the small group lesson plan.

Whole Group
Use p. 229a.

Language Arts
Use pp. 229e–229k.

Build Concepts

FLUENCY

MODEL PHRASING As you read aloud "Jane Goodall," group together groups of related words to model phrasing. The introduction and first paragraph, especially, have a number of prepositional phrases well suited for modeling.

LISTENING COMPREHENSION

After reading "Jane Goodall," use the following questions to assess listening comprehension.

1. **Is the introductory sentence a statement of fact or opinion? Explain.** *(Possible response: It's a statement of fact because you could do research to verify if Goodall is considered an expert in her field.)* **Fact and Opinion**

2. **What was the effect of Jane's visit to her friend's family in Kenya when she was twenty-three?** *(Jane decided she wanted to return there someday to do her work.)* **Cause and Effect**

BUILD CONCEPT VOCABULARY

Start a web to build concepts and vocabulary related to this week's lesson and the unit theme.

- Draw the Protecting Animals Concept Web.
- Read the sentence with the word *wildlife.* Ask students to pronounce *wildlife* and discuss its meaning.
- Place *wildlife* in an oval attached to *What?* Explain that *wildlife* is related to this concept. Read the sentences in which *conservation* and *naturalist* appear. Have students pronounce the words, place them on the web, and provide reasons.
- Brainstorm additional words and categories for the web. Keep the web on display and add words throughout the week.

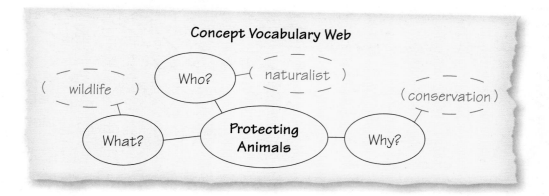

Concept Vocabulary Web

Jane Goodall

by Jeannine Atkins

Jane Goodall is one of the world's foremost authorities on wildlife and nature conservation.

Jane Goodall loved to watch spiders scramble, beetles scatter, and worms slither. At age five, she was used to hearing her mother call, "Jane! Where are you?" But the panic in her mother's eyes when she found her one day was unusual. "I was in the hen house," Jane said. She liked to sift through the straw for the warm, smooth eggs, then carry them home as carefully as if she held treasures. But that afternoon she hadn't been collecting eggs.

"I was about to call the police!" her mother said. "What on earth were you doing?"

"I wanted to see the hen lay an egg," Jane confessed.

"But you were gone all afternoon!"

Jane nodded. She knew chickens rushed off if followed, so she had hidden hours before and sat so quietly that she hadn't been spotted.

"And you saw a hen lay an egg?" When Jane smiled, her mother smiled, too. She didn't scold Jane for making her worry. Instead, she pulled her close and said, "Tell me about it."

With a knack for quiet, concentrated observation—and an understanding mother—five-year-old Jane was well on her way to a career as a naturalist. Her grandmother was a careful watcher, too. When she noticed how often Jane climbed a beech tree in her yard, she gave her the tree as her own. And seeing that Jane had checked a Doctor Doolittle book out of the library several times, her grandmother gave her the book for Christmas. Jane liked to wander through the meadows pretending that she, too, could talk to African animals. She carefully watched insects and squirrels, while dreaming that someday she, like Tarzan, would hear nothing but wind in the trees and animals calling to each other. Jane started a nature club with her younger sister and two friends. She named it the Alligator Club, even though she knew she wouldn't find alligators in England! The four girls started a magazine which included nature notes, sketches of insects, and quizzes. They set up a museum.

Jane made her little sister ask passersby to visit, then collected a donation to a society that protected old horses. The visitors admired the pressed flowers and bird eggs, held seashells to their ears, and petted the guinea pigs. The most famous exhibit was a human skeleton donated by Jane's uncle who had studied to be a doctor.

When she was twenty-three, a friend invited her to visit her family's new farm in Kenya. Jane moved back home to save money, took a job as a waitress, learned to balance a dozen plates of food at once, and saved her tips. In 1957, she headed off to Africa.

Activate Prior Knowledge

Before students listen to the Read Aloud, ask them what they know about nature and animals.

Set Purpose

Read aloud the title and have students predict what the selection will be about.

Read the introduction aloud. Have students listen for statements of fact and think about how they can be verified.

Creative Response

Have students create and perform charades that show Jane Goodall as a budding naturalist. *Drama*

Access Content Before reading, share this summary: Jane Goodall loves to watch animals. She climbs trees, and watches squirrels and insects. She even hides so she can see a hen lay an egg. When she is older she will go to Africa to study wildlife.

Homework Send home this week's Family Times newsletter.

SUCCESS PREDICTO

SKILLS ←→ STRATEGIES IN CONTEXT

Fact and Opinion
Ask Questions

- Identify statements of fact and opinion.

- Ask questions to differentiate statements of fact and opinion.

Skills Trace
Fact and Opinion

Introduce/Teach	TE: 5.2 208–209; 5.3 316–317; 5.6 700–701
Practice	Practice Book: 83, 87, 88, 123, 127, 128, 136, 283, 287, 288
Reteach/Review	TE: 5.2 229b, DI·55; 5.3 301, 345b, 355, DI·54; 5.6 725b, DI·55
Test	Selection Test: 33–36, 49–52, 113–116; Benchmark Test: Unit 3

INTRODUCE

Write this statement on the board: *This is an interesting lesson.* Have students classify the statement as fact or opinion. Have them identify the clue word that they used. *(Statement: opinion; Clue word: interesting)*

Have students read the information on p. 208. Explain the following:

- To tell whether a sentence contains a statement of fact or opinion, you can ask yourself if the statement can be proved true or false.

- You can verify statements of fact and interpret statements of opinion by asking yourself questions as you read.

Use Skill Transparency 9 to teach fact and opinion and ask questions.

Comprehension

Skill
Fact and Opinion

Strategy
Ask Questions

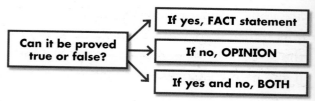 Fact and Opinion

- A statement of fact can be proved true or false. A statement of opinion tells what someone thinks or feels.

- Statements of opinion often contain words that make judgments, such as *interesting* or *beautiful*.

- A single sentence might contain both a statement of fact and a statement of opinion.

Can it be proved true or false?	→	If yes, FACT statement
	→	If no, OPINION
	→	If yes and no, BOTH

Strategy: Ask Questions

Good readers ask themselves questions. As you read statements, ask yourself, "Is this a statement of fact? If so, how do I know whether it's true or false? Or is it a statement of opinion? Is the author trying to convince me of something?"

Write to Read

1. Make a graphic organizer like the one above. As you read "Chimps," write three sentences in the correct boxes: a statement of fact, a statement of opinion, and one with both.

2. Using a graphic organizer, find another statement of opinion. Write about why it is a statement of opinion, whether or not you agree with it, and why.

208

Strategic Intervention

Fact and Opinion Write on the board statements of fact and opinion about the same topic. *(For example, My coat is red; My coat is beautiful; My coat is two years old.)* Have students apply the first two bulleted definitions on page 208 to each statement to tell whether it is a statement of fact or opinion. Then have students work in pairs to generate their own statements of fact and opinion about the same topic.

ELL

Access Content

Beginning/Intermediate For a Picture It! lesson on fact and opinion, see ELL Teaching Guide, pp. 57–58.

Advanced Have students preview the article by reading the first sentence in each paragraph. Help them determine whether the sentence contains a statement of fact, a statement of opinion, or both.

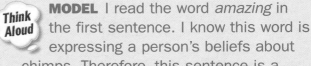

Chimps

Chimpanzees, or "chimps" for short, are amazing animals. They look and act in ways that sometimes remind us of ourselves.

Chimpanzees are hairy animals. Long dark hair covers most of their bodies, except their faces, which are bald. They grow to be from 3 to 5.5 feet tall and can weigh as much as 130 pounds. Chimpanzees have long arms and large ears, and they can make the funniest faces you've ever seen.

Chimpanzees spend time on the ground but are often in trees. It must be fun to swing from branch to branch the way they do. They also like to eat and sleep in trees, building nests from branches and leaves.

Chimpanzees are social animals. They live in groups. Chimps regularly groom each other's fur. They communicate using facial expressions, gestures, screams, hoots, and even roars.

Unfortunately, many chimpanzees are dying because people hunt them or destroy the forests where they live. It is important for us to learn as much as we can about these fascinating animals. We must make sure this endangered species does not become extinct.

① Skill A word in this first sentence gives a clue about whether it is a statement of fact or opinion.

② Strategy Here's a good place to ask yourself, "Which sentences in this paragraph contain facts? Which contain opinions?"

③ Skill Remember that a sentence can contain both a statement of fact and of opinion. One sentence in this paragraph has both.

④ Strategy What questions could you ask yourself about the statements in this paragraph to help you decide whether they are facts or opinions?

209

Available as **Skill Transparency** 9

TEACH

① SKILL Use the first sentence to model how to differentiate statements of fact and opinion.

Think Aloud **MODEL** I read the word *amazing* in the first sentence. I know this word is expressing a person's beliefs about chimps. Therefore, this sentence is a statement of opinion.

② STRATEGY Ask questions to tell statements of fact from statements of opinion.

Think Aloud **MODEL** To tell whether the sentences in paragraph 2 are statements of fact, I ask myself if the statements can be proved. All but one statement can. To identify statements of opinion, I ask myself if there are any words that express a person's feelings, beliefs, or judgments. The word *funniest* in the second part of the last sentence tells me that this part of the sentence is a statement of opinion.

PRACTICE AND ASSESS

③ SKILL The second sentence contains both. The first part of the sentence is a statement of opinion; the second part is a statement of fact.

④ STRATEGY Can the statements be proved true or false? Is the author trying to persuade me of something?

WRITE Have students complete steps 1 and 2 of the Write to Read activity. You might consider using this as a whole-class activity.

Fact and Opinion

- A **statement of fact** can be proved true or false. A **statement of opinion** tells what someone thinks or feels.
- Statements of opinion often contain words that make judgments, such as *interesting* or *beautiful*.
- A single sentence might contain both a statement of fact and a statement of opinion.

Directions Read the following passage.

Dirty beaches are disgusting. I hate to see the shore of a lake, or ocean dotted with candy wrappers or soda bottles or other bits of garbage. Garbage on beaches is more than an eyesore, though. It also kills wildlife. Animals such as fish and turtles may try to eat drifting garbage they find in the water. If they do, they may choke. The plastic six-pack yokes from soda cans are dangerous to birds. Birds often become tangled in the plastic and die. To help keep beaches clean, volunteer on clean-up days. People who clean beaches help protect the environment and deserve the best places to sit when they visit the shore.

Directions Fill in the diagram below based on the passage.

Statement	Can it be proved true or false?	Fact? Opinion? Or both?
Dirty beaches are disgusting.	1. no	2. opinion
The plastic yokes from soda cans are dangerous to birds.	3. yes	4. fact
5. People who clean beaches help protect the environment and deserve the best places to sit when they visit the shore.	The first part can be proved true or false, but not the second part.	contains both fact and opinion

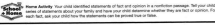 **Home Activity** Your child identified statements of fact and opinion in a nonfiction passage. Tell your child a series of statements about your family and have your child determine whether they are fact or opinion. For each fact, ask your child how the statements can be proved true or false.

Tech Files
ONLINE

Students can learn more about additional ways to help save wildlife by searching the Internet using a student-friendly search engine with the keywords *Jane Goodall*. Be sure to follow classroom guidelines for Internet use.

ELL

Build Background Use ELL Poster 9 to build background and vocabulary for the lesson concept of humans better understanding nature.

▲ **ELL Poster** 9

Build Background

ACTIVATE PRIOR KNOWLEDGE

BEGIN A KWL CHART about protecting animals.

- Give students two to three minutes to write as many things as they can about how people can help protect animals. Record what students know on a KWL chart.

- Give students two minutes to write three questions they would like to find out about helping wildlife. Record questions on the KWL chart. Add a question of your own.

- Tell students that, as they read, they should look for the answers to their questions and note any new information to add to the chart.

Topic _____ Protecting Animals

K	W	L
Don't hunt endangered species. Stay away from animals that could hurt you.	Does hunting help overpopulated species? What's a safe way to observe animals in the wild?	

▲ **Graphic Organizer** 4

BACKGROUND BUILDING AUDIO This week's audio explores wildlife and ways to protect wildlife. After students listen, discuss new information they learned about protecting wildlife.

Background Building Audio

Introduce Vocabulary

WORD/DEFINITION MATCH

Share the lesson vocabulary with students. Give students clues, such as the following, to the definition of each vocabulary word. Have students review their vocabulary list and call out the word they think matches the clue.

- **Which word has to do with the temperature outside?** *(environment)*
- **Which word describes a way to assist?** *(contribute)*
- **Which word has to do with a quest for information?** *(investigation)*
- **Which word describes feeling excited?** *(enthusiastic)*
- **Which word has to do with preventing pollution?** *(conservation)*

You may wish to extend this activity by having students write questions of their own using the More Words to Know.

Follow up on this activity by asking these questions at the end of the week.

Use the Multisyllabic Word Routine on p. DI·1 to help students read multisyllabic words.

Lesson Vocabulary

WORDS TO KNOW

T conservation preservation from harm or decay; protection from loss or from being used up

T contribute to help bring about

T enthusiastic eagerly interested

T environment condition of the air, water, soil, etc.

T investigation a careful search

MORE WORDS TO KNOW

humane not cruel or brutal; kind

loggers people whose work is cutting down trees

tapeworms long, flat worms that live as a parasite in the intestines of humans and animals

T = Tested Word

Vocabulary

Directions Choose a word from the box that best matches each clue. Write the word on the line.

conservation _____ 1. preservation from harm

environment _____ 2. surroundings

enthusiastic _____ 3. full of eager interest

contribute _____ 4. give money, help, or time

investigation _____ 5. detailed, thorough examination

Check the Words You Know
___conservation
___contribute
___enthusiastic
___environment
___investigation

Directions Choose the word from the box that best completes each sentence. Write the word on the line.

Migrating birds, like the Canada goose, travel twice each year to a new

6. **environment** _____ Scientists who study these annual moves are interested in

7. **conservation** _____ of bird habitats. These 8. **enthusiastic** _____

scientists 9. **contribute** _____ greatly to the safety of birds. Through

10. **investigation** _____ research, and observation, environmental scientists serve

an important role in preserving nature.

Write an Opinion

On a separate sheet of paper, write your opinion on what people should do to help endangered animals. Explain why you feel the way you do. Use as many vocabulary words as you can.

Students should explain the reasoning behind their opinions and use words from the vocabulary list.

Home Activity Your child identified and used vocabulary words from *Jane Goodall's 10 Ways to Help Save Wildlife.* With your child, find out information on endangered plants or animals in your area. Use the vocabulary words to discuss them.

▲ **Practice Book** p. 84

Vocabulary Strategy

OBJECTIVE

⊙ Use context clues to determine word meaning.

INTRODUCE

Discuss the strategy for context clues using the steps on p. 210.

TEACH

- Have students read "Young People Helping the Environment," paying attention to how vocabulary is used.

- Model using context clues to determine the meaning of *contribute*.

 Think Aloud

MODEL The author uses *contribute* to contrast plants and animals (who do not pollute) with people (who do). The sentences that come after make me think that to *contribute* to the problem of pollution means to "help bring it about."

Words to Know

environment

contribute

conservation

enthusiastic

investigation

Remember 📖

Try the strategy. Then, if you need more help, use your glossary or dictionary.

Vocabulary Strategy
for Unfamiliar Words

Context Clues As you read, you will find unfamiliar words. See if you can use context to figure out the meaning of a new word. *Context* means the words and sentences near the unfamiliar word.

1. Reread the sentence with the unfamiliar word. The author may include a synonym or other context clue to the word's meaning.

2. If you need more help, read the surrounding sentences. You may spot examples or explanations that give you clues to the word's meaning.

3. Add up the clues and decide on the meaning of the word.

4. Check to see that this meaning makes sense in the sentence.

As you read "Young People Helping the Environment," look for context clues to help you figure out the meanings of unfamiliar words.

210

DAY 2 Grouping Options

Reading

Whole Group Discuss the Question of the Day. Then use pp. 210–213.

Group Time **Differentiated Instruction**
Read "Jane Goodall's 10 Ways to Help Save Wildlife." See pp. 208h–208i for the small group lesson plan.

Whole Group Use p. 229a.

Language Arts
Use pp. 229e–229k.

Strategic Intervention

⊙ **Context Clues** Have students work in pairs to define *migrating*, using the steps on p. 210. Tell them to look for context clues in the sentence with the unfamiliar word and the one after.

 ELL

Access Content Use ELL Poster 9 to preteach vocabulary. Choose from the following to meet language proficiency levels.

Beginning Point out clues on p. 211 that show that *enthusiastic* means "eagerly" and "cheerfully."

Intermediate Before reading, have students choose a vocabulary word and use it to complete a vocabulary frame.

Advanced Teach the lesson on pp. 210–211. Have students determine whether any of the tested words have cognates in their home languages. Resources for home-language words may include parents, bilingual staff members, bilingual dictionaries, or online translation sources.

YOUNG PEOPLE Helping the Environment

This well-known line first appeared in a comic strip called *Pogo:* "We have met the enemy and he is us." Let's face it. When it comes to the environment, people are the enemy! Pollution has become a problem that worries people all over the world. Plants and animals do not contribute to the problem in any way. A migrating bird is not like a vacationing family. Birds do not send exhaust into the air or throw out bags full of trash. A growing number of people understand that conservation is necessary. We must protect our air, water, soil, plants, and animals.

We have no other home but Earth, so we had better make it last. Once young people understand this, they become enthusiastic about cleaning up. They will work long, hard, and cheerfully to help. They begin all sorts of projects, such as recycling paper and picking up trash. They may call attention to a problem so that a news station begins an investigation.

Young people like action. They like the feeling of accomplishing something good. The successes of young people can be inspirational. If you inspire adults to act in favor of the environment, think how much help the Earth can get.

Words to Write

Be a reporter. Write a news story about a group of young people who are helping the environment. Use the photos on pages 212 to 223 for ideas. Use as many words from the Words to Know list as you can.

211

PRACTICE AND ASSESS

- Have students determine the meanings of the remaining words and explain the context clues they used.
- Point out that context doesn't work with every word. Students may have to use the glossary or a dictionary to tell word meaning.
- Return to the word/definition match (p. 210b), and have students explain what more they have learned about each word. *(Possible response: how to use enthusiastic correctly, examples of conservation)*
- Have students complete Practice Book p. 85.

WRITE News stories should include vocabulary words that describe young environmentalists and their efforts.

Monitor Progress

Context Clues

If... students need more practice with the lesson vocabulary,	then... use Tested Vocabulary Cards.

Vocabulary · Context Clues

As you read, you will find unfamiliar words. You can use context clues to figure out the meaning of a new word. **Context clues** are found in the words and sentences around an unfamiliar word.

Directions Read the following passage. Then answer the questions below. Look for context clues around unfamiliar words to determine their meaning.

The U.S. Fish and Wildlife Service (USFWS) is one of our country's most enthusiastic protectors of endangered species. When the environment, or home, of one of our nation's species is threatened, the USFWS tries to protect it as best they can. They will begin with an investigation of the threat, and when they discover what is causing it they will act to repair the damage. Conservation of wetlands, prairies, and other geographically sensitive areas is an important part of the preservation goals of the USFWS. We can all help save endangered species by being responsible citizens and making sure we don't litter or contribute to the destruction of these sensitive lands.

1. What does the word *enthusiastic* mean?
   It means "showing eager interest."
2. What context clues can help you understand the meaning of the word *environment*?
   "or home"
3. Look at the sentence before the word *conservation*. How does this sentence give a clue to the meaning of *conservation*?
   It talks about investigating a threat to plants or animals and then repairing any damage.
4. What does *contribute* mean as it is used in this passage?
   It means "to play a part in."
5. What is the meaning of *investigation*? How do you know?
   It means "to look into something closely"; The sentence says that the investigation leads to understanding the cause of the threat.

School + Home Home Activity Your child answered questions about unfamiliar words in a nonfiction passage by using context clues. Explain a process to your child, like making a complicated meal, using unfamiliar words and help your child figure out what the new words mean by their context.

▲ **Practice Book** p. 85

Prereading Strategies

OBJECTIVES

- ⊙ Recognize statements of fact and opinion to improve comprehension.
- ⊙ Ask questions to distinguish between fact and opinion and verify facts.

GENRE STUDY

Expository Nonfiction

"Jane Goodall's 10 Ways to Help Save Wildlife" is expository nonfiction. Explain that expository nonfiction provides information about real-life persons, objects, or ideas.

PREVIEW AND PREDICT

Have students preview text features that signal important information, such as numbered sub-heads and large type. Have students use lesson vocabulary words as they discuss what they expect to learn.

Strategy Response Log

Ask Questions Have students write two questions about Jane Goodall's suggestions for protecting animals. Students will answer their questions in the Strategy Response Log activity on p. 219.

from
National Geographic for Kids

Jane Goodall's

10 Ways to Help Save Wildlife

by Jane Goodall

212

ⒺⓁⓁ

Access Content Lead students on a picture walk to reinforce the animal names, such as *snake* (p. 214), *shark* (p. 215), *chimpanzee* (p. 217), *iguana* (p. 218), *butterfly* (p. 219), and *frog* (p. 221).

Consider having students read the selection summary in English or in students' home languages. See the Multilingual Summaries in the ELL Teaching Guide, pp. 61–63.

How does Jane Goodall feel about wild animals?

213

SET PURPOSE

Read the headnote on p. 214 aloud to students. Have them consider their preview discussion and tell what they hope to learn as they read.

Remind students to pay attention to places where the author gives facts and where she gives opinions based on those facts.

STRATEGY RECALL

Students have now used these before-reading strategies:

- preview the selection to be aware of its genre, features, and possible content;
- activate prior knowledge about that content and what to expect of that genre;
- make predictions;
- set a purpose for reading.

Remind students that, as they read, they should monitor their own comprehension. If they realize something does not make sense, they can regain their comprehension by using fix-up strategies they have learned, such as:

- use phonics and word structure to decode new words;
- use context clues or a dictionary to figure out meanings of new words;
- adjust their reading rate—slow down for difficult text, speed up for easy or familiar text, or skim and scan just for specific information;
- reread parts of the text;
- read on (continue to read for clarification);
- use text features such as headings, subheadings, charts, illustrations, and so on as visual aids to comprehension;
- make a graphic organizer or a semantic organizer to aid comprehension;
- use reference sources, such as an encyclopedia, dictionary, thesaurus, or synonym finder;
- use another person, such as a teacher, a peer, a librarian, or an outside expert, as a resource.

After reading, students will use these strategies:

- summarize or retell the text;
- answer questions they or others pose;
- reflect to make new information become part of their prior knowledge.

AudioText

Guiding Comprehension

1 Author's Purpose • Inferential

Reread the headnote on p. 214. What is the author's purpose for writing?

The author is writing to inform—to tell young people how they can help protect wildlife.

2 ⊙ Fact and Opinion • Inferential

Explain whether the statement "tapeworms are simply too revolting to love" is a fact or opinion.

The statement is an opinion because it tells what the author feels, and it cannot be proved.

Monitor Progress	
⊙ Fact and Opinion	
If... students are unable to distinguish between statements of fact and opinion,	**then...** use the skill and strategy instruction on p. 215.

3 Draw Conclusions • Critical

Question the Author **Suppose you ask the author why she did not get hurt by an animal during all her years in the forest. What might she say?**

Possible response: She might say that she learned the habits of animals that can hurt people and stayed out of the animals' way.

Chimpanzees are our closest living relatives. I have been lucky enough to spend most of my life studying these fascinating creatures. Now I travel the world teaching about wildlife conservation. Along the way, I've met thousands of caring young people who are enthusiastic about helping protect animals and who want to know what they can do to help. Here **1** are ten suggestions:

1 Respect all life.

It's true that bees sting and sharks bite, so it's smart to **2** be cautious. And tapeworms are simply too revolting to love. But we don't need to love a creature to respect it. And you can control your fear by learning about an animal's habits and staying out of its way. In all my years in the forest, not once did any leopard, buffalo, **3** snake, or scorpion hurt me.

214

Access Content The author warns that it is "smart to be cautious." Tell students that *cautious* means careful. Ask students why the author suggests that they be careful.

215

Fact and Opinion

TEACH

- Remind students that a statement of fact tells something that can be proved true or false.
- A statement of fact may be correct or incorrect.
- Model checking the statement of fact that makes up the first sentence on p. 214.

 Think Aloud **MODEL** Goodall says that chimpanzees are our closest living relatives. I don't know enough about chimpanzees to tell if this statement of fact is correct. But I could ask a reference librarian to help me find a book with the information that I need to check it.

PRACTICE AND ASSESS

Have students identify another statement of fact in the headnote on p. 214. Ask how they could check to see if it is true. *(The second and third sentences contain statements of fact. To check them, students could search for information about Goodall in a biographical dictionary or other reference book. Students could also do a web search using the keywords Jane Goodall.)*

TIME FOR Science

Animal Habitats

Scorpions, snakes, and leopards are native to the forests bordering Lake Tanganyika, where Goodall conducts her research. The venom of scorpions is poisonous and can be deadly. Some snakes' bites can also be lethal. Leopards generally avoid humans and are likely to become aggressive only if provoked or threatened. Goodall wisely urges not only learning wild animals' habits but also using caution when visiting their homes.

EXTEND SKILLS

Magazine Article

Explain that this selection was taken from an online magazine article. Usually magazine articles give information about current events or issues. Have students identify text and organizational features that help them distinguish this as a magazine article. One example is the numbered subheads, which are often used in articles.

Jane Goodall's 10 Ways to Help Save Wildlife **215**

Guiding Comprehension

4 Draw Conclusions • Inferential

Why were other scientists shocked when the author gave names to the chimpanzees that she was studying?

Possible response: At the time, few scientists thought of animals as individuals.

5 Compare and Contrast • Inferential

In what way does the author see animals and people as alike?

The author sees both animals and people as thinking, feeling individuals.

Monitor Progress

REVIEW Compare and Contrast

If... students have difficulty identifying the author's comparison,	then... use the skill and strategy instruction on p. 217.

6 Graphic Sources • Critical

How do the photos help support Jane Goodall's belief that animals are thinking, feeling individuals?

Possible response: One photo shows an adult and a young chimpanzee hugging. They look like a mother and child who love each other.

2 Think of animals as individuals.

When I first began writing reports about my "study subjects" and referred to them by name, scientists were shocked! They thought I should give chimpanzees like Flo and David Greybeard identifying numbers instead of names. But names are important; they make animals special. Once I was giving a speech and a fly flew into the room. I had just been talking about the need to respect all life. Oh, no, I thought. Somebody is going to swat that fly. So I said, "Do you see that fly who has come in through the window? I think her name is Elizabeth." And nobody swatted that fly! By naming the fly Elizabeth, I helped people see her as more than just another insect. Elizabeth had become an individual.

3 Dare to admit that humans aren't the only thinking, feeling beings on the planet.

How do I know? When I was 12 years old, I had a marvelous teacher—a small black dog named Rusty. Rusty was so intelligent that if I caught him stealing food off the table, he'd roll over on his back and act guilty. But if I scolded him for doing something he didn't realize was bad, he sulked! Rusty would go over to the wall and sit with his nose almost touching it. Even if I offered him walks or nibbles, he wouldn't budge. Only when I went down on my knees and apologized to him would Rusty stop sulking.

216

ELL

Access Content The author uses several verbs to describe Rusty's behavior. Point to the word *scold* and act out scolding a dog. Explain that *scold* means "to speak sharply to." Repeat this with *sulked*; tell students that *sulked* means "became angry and silent."

217

SKILLS ←→ STRATEGIES IN CONTEXT

Compare and Contrast REVIEW

TEACH

- Remind students that comparisons tell how things are alike.
- Explain that sometimes comparisons are stated indirectly, or *implied*. In that case, the reader must detect the comparison.

Think Aloud **MODEL** As I read about Goodall's dog, Rusty, I see that she is explaining how her dog acts like a human. Rusty sulks like a child after he is punished unfairly. His behavior shows that animals have feelings similar to ours.

PRACTICE AND ASSESS

Have students compare Rusty's behavior when he is scolded for something he knows is wrong and something he doesn't know is wrong. *(Rusty acts guilty when he knows that he has misbehaved but demands an apology when he is unfairly punished.)*

To assess, use Practice Book p. 86.

Compare and Contrast
Directions Read the article. Then answer the questions below.

The vast majority of frogs eat a diet of insects and worms. A frog's long tongue can strike out at a passing fly in a split second, scooping up its prey and pulling it back into its mouth faster than the human eye can see. This diet partly explains why so many species of frogs live near water. There are always plenty of insects to be found in and around a water source.

But some frogs eat more than insects and worms. Some frogs eat other frogs, mice, snakes, and even turtles! This is only seen among very large frogs, such as the North American bullfrog. They still use their lightning-fast, sticky tongues to grab their prey. However, the bullfrog's large size gives it the power to capture and eat such large meals.

1. What do the majority of frogs eat?
   The majority eat insects and worms.

2. What does a North American bullfrog sometimes eat that most frogs do not?
   Possible answer: Bullfrogs sometimes eat mice, snakes, other frogs, and turtles.

3. Why do you think a North American bullfrog would need to eat a mouse?
   North American bullfrogs are very large, so they have bigger appetites and need more food to satisfy them.

4. What do both small and large frogs use to catch their prey?
   They both have their fast and sticky tongues.

5. On a separate sheet of paper, compare what you eat during a meal to what an older relative eats. What is the same and what is different?
   Responses should include examples of different foods and should compare and contrast the portions and types of food.

School + Home **Home Activity** Your child has compared and contrasted information about frogs in a nonfiction passage. Discuss with your child the differences and similarities of two kinds of animals, such as birds and fish. How are they alike? How are they different?

▲ **Practice Book** p. 86

Jane Goodall's 10 Ways to Help Save Wildlife   **217**

Guiding Comprehension

218

7  **Vocabulary • Context Clues**

How could you use a context clue to help figure out the meaning of the word *migrating*?

Possible response: You can find context clues in the same sentence as the word. The sentence says that some *migrating* animals navigate across thousands of miles. That tells you that *migrating* involves moving from one place to another. To find the word's exact meaning, you might need to use a dictionary.

Monitor Progress

Context Clues

If... students have difficulty using context to infer the meaning of *migrate*,	**then...** use vocabulary strategy instruction on p. 219.

---

8 **Draw Conclusions • Critical**

Text to Text **Have you read any other books about animals doing amazing things?**

Answers may vary. Students may tell of other books about pets alerting owners to possible dangers or traveling long distances to return home.

Context Clues Help students understand that a *tomcat* is a male cat. Ask students what clues are given in Rule 5 on p. 219. (The cat is referred to as *he*.)

4 Get to know animals.

Avoid taming any creature (such as a deer) that might later be captured or shot because you've made it trust people. But if it (and you!) will be safe, try setting out food for the animal to eat. Then sit quietly a little distance away and observe. Take notes and try to imagine what the animal's life is like. You can do the same with a pet—yours or someone else's.

5 Be willing to learn from animals.

Many possess mysterious powers that humans lack. I am in awe of migrating birds, butterflies, and salmon, which all manage to navigate across thousands of miles of unfamiliar territory. And I am amazed when I hear about pets like Ninja, a tomcat who traveled 850 miles to get to his old home. Soon after moving with his owners from Utah to Washington State, Ninja disappeared. He showed up again a year later—back at their old house in Utah! How did he find it?

7

8

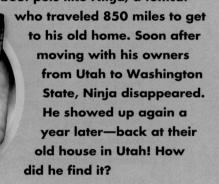

219

VOCABULARY STRATEGY

VOCABULARY STRATEGY
Context Clues

TEACH

Remind students that context clues are words or information that can help them figure out the meaning of an unfamiliar word.

Read the first two sentences in suggestion five. Model using context clues to determine the meaning of an unfamiliar word, *migrating*.

Think Aloud **MODEL** The sentence with *migrating* includes the phrase: "navigate across thousands of miles of unfamiliar territory." This is a context clue that tells me *migrating* must mean "moving from one place to another."

PRACTICE AND ASSESS

Have students use context clues to determine the meaning of *mysterious* in the first sentence in suggestion 5 *(not able to be understood, inexplicable)*. Clues may be found in the sentence with the unfamiliar word and other sentences. They include *that humans lack* and the examples of mysterious powers that Goodall gives.

Strategy Response Log

Answer Questions Provide the following prompt: Did you find answers to your questions? (See p. 212.) Record the answers and write one new question that you think may be answered in the rest of the selection.

Develop Vocabulary

PRACTICE LESSON VOCABULARY

Students orally respond to each question.

1. What does your *environment* include? *(Possible response: Trees, flowers, people, birds, and dogs.)*

2. Name a kind of *conservation*, and give a suggestion for practicing it. *(Possible response: Water conservation. Take shorter showers.)*

3. What makes you *enthusiastic*? *(Possible response: Sports, seeing my friends, summer vacations.)*

BUILD CONCEPT VOCABULARY

Review previous concept words with students. Ask if students have come across any new words today in their reading or elsewhere that they would like to add to the Protecting Animals Concept Web, such as *individuals* and *naming*.

If you want to teach this selection in two sessions, stop here.

Guiding Comprehension

If you are teaching the selection in two days, discuss any statements of fact or opinion so far and review the vocabulary.

9 🔵 **Fact and Opinion • Critical**

Reread the last two sentences of suggestion 6 on p. 220. Do they state a fact or an opinion? How do you know?

They state an opinion because the first sentence says, "Caitlin feels sure."

Monitor Progress
🔵 Fact and Opinion

If... students have difficulty distinguishing fact from opinion,	then... use the skill and strategy instruction on p. 221.

10 **Vocabulary • Word Structure**

How can you use suffixes to tell what the words *production* and *inspirational* (suggestion 6) mean?

You can cover the suffix *-ion* in *production* to figure out that it means "the act of producing or creating something." You can cover the suffix *-al* in *inspirational* to figure out that it means something "that inspires or influences someone or something."

DAY 3 Grouping Options

Reading
Whole Group Discuss the Question of the Day.

Group Time Differentiated Instruction
Read "Jane Goodall's 10 Ways to Help Save Wildlife." See pp. 208h–208i for the small group lesson plan.

Whole Group Discuss the Reader Response questions on p. 224. Then use p. 229a.

Language Arts
Use pp. 229e–229k.

6 Speak up for what you believe.
Caitlin Alegre, 13, of Oakland, California, hated how some cosmetic companies put guinea pigs, rabbits, and mice through misery in order to test the safety of their products. So she pinned posters to trees and handed out informational leaflets. Now 16, she writes inspirational songs for her band, the Envirochicks.

9 Once people know which companies are humane and which are not, Caitlin feels sure that most will buy only from humane companies. Then the other companies will change their ways.

7 Use less paper, gasoline, and red meat.
These are three products that **contribute** to reasons the rain forest homes of many animals are being destroyed. And it's easy to conserve. Simply reusing, recycling, and using less paper means loggers will cut down fewer trees. You can even help preserve rain forests by riding bikes, walking, and eating more veggie burritos than hamburgers. Saving gas and eating less beef can help reduce the need to clear rain forest land for oil production and **10** grazing cattle.

220

ELL

Extend Language Reread suggestion 5 aloud, "Be willing to learn from animals." Explain that to be *willing* means to be "wanting or ready" to do something.

Fact and Opinion Ask Questions

TEACH

Tell students that asking questions can often help them distinguish statements of fact from statements of opinion.

Model asking questions to identify the first sentence of suggestion seven on p. 220 as either fact or opinion.

Think Aloud **MODEL** The first sentence says that paper, gasoline and red meat contribute to rain forest destruction. If I ask if this statement can be proven, I realize that the answer is yes. If I did some research I could confirm if this statement is true, therefore it must be a fact.

PRACTICE AND ASSESS

Have students work in pairs, asking questions about the other statements in suggestion 7, to determine if they are facts or opinions.

221

Roots and Shoots

TIME FOR Science

Roots and Shoots began in 1991 when 16 students met with Jane Goodall on her porch in Dar es Salaam, Tanzania. The program's guiding principle states that "knowledge leads to compassion, which inspires action." All Roots and Shoots participants work in local groups, identifying and implementing projects that benefit humans, animals, the environment, or all three. A Roots and Shoots group might clean up a park, volunteer at an animal shelter, or hold a food or clothing drive. Roots and Shoots groups are found in schools (pre-K to college and university), faith communities, zoos, foster care centers, and many other places.

EXTEND SKILLS

Author's Viewpoint/Bias

An author's viewpoint is his or her attitude toward a subject. An author may show bias when he or she shows strong feeling for or against something. In this selection, Jane Goodall makes no attempt to hide her love and respect for animals. In fact, she actively tries to persuade her readers to feel the way she does and to take care, as she says on p. 223, "not to harm the environment, animals, or each other."

Guiding Comprehension

11  **Vocabulary • Multiple-Meaning Words**

Define the meaning of the word *bear* in the second sentence of suggestion 8.

In this sentence the word *bear* means "to put up with, or to endure."

12 Draw Conclusions • Critical

Text to Self **How can you use Goodall's suggestions in your own life to help save wildlife?**

Possible responses: I could form a Roots and Shoots group; find opportunities to get to know animals and learn from them; choose vegetarian foods more often; walk or ride bicycles instead of using cars.

Strategy Response Log

Summarize When students finish reading the selection, provide this prompt: In four or five sentences, explain the most important points that Jane Goodall makes in "Jane Goodall's 10 Ways to Help Save Wildlife."

Tech Files
ONLINE

Students can type the keywords *Roots and Shoots* in a student-friendly search engine to learn more about forming a group in their community. Be sure to follow classroom guidelines for Internet use.

222

8 Be inspired by the work of others.

Not many of us could bear to do what 16-year-old Lisa Thomas does. There are so many stray dogs in her hometown of Johannesburg, South Africa, that the local animal shelter regularly puts some to sleep. On those difficult days, Lisa visits the shelter and spends ten minutes petting and talking to each doomed animal. That way every dog experiences at least some love in its life and dies knowing human caring.

9 Join Roots and Shoots.

This is a program I started to help young people learn about animals and nature. As of today, groups have sprung up in more than 70 countries, and they're accomplishing wonderful things. One group, in Chicago, launched an investigation when a water bottling company suggested building a new plant at the head of a stream. The group's research showed that the factory would cause serious environmental harm, so the entire project was put on hold!

10 Have hope.

Believe that what you do matters. Yes, you're only one person out of more than six billion people living on this planet. And yes, a lot of damage has been done. But just think. If you and I and everyone else who reads this takes care not to harm the environment, animals, or each other—what a difference it will make! Together we can change the world.

223

Develop Vocabulary

PRACTICE LESSON VOCABULARY

Students orally respond *true* or *false* to each question. Students should provide an explanation for false responses.

1. Animal shelter volunteers *contribute* their time. (*True.*)
2. A crime *investigation* attempts to solve a mystery. (*True.*)
3. An *inspirational* speech is a boring speech. (*False, it is speech that makes you think or feel something.*)

BUILD CONCEPT VOCABULARY

Review previous concept words with students. Ask if students have come across any new words today in their reading or elsewhere that they would like to add to the Protecting Animals Concept Web, such as *caring*, *investigation*, and *accomplishing*.

STRATEGY SELF-CHECK

Ask Questions

Have students ask questions to identify the following statements in suggestion 10 as fact, opinion, or both: *Yes, you're only one person out of more than six billion people living on this planet. And yes, a lot of damage has been done.*

SELF-CHECK

Students can ask themselves these questions to assess their ability to use the skill and strategy.

- Could I tell facts from opinions as I read "Jane Goodall's 10 Ways to Help Save Wildlife"?
- Could I think of ways to tell if the statements of fact are true or false?
- Was I able to ask questions to help me?

Monitor Progress

Fact and Opinion

If... students have difficulty distinguishing facts and opinions or asking questions,	then... use the Reteach lesson on p. 229b.

Fact and Opinion

- A **statement of fact** can be proved true or false. A **statement of opinion** tells what someone thinks or feels.
- Statements of opinion often contain words that make judgments, such as *interesting* or *beautiful*.
- A single sentence might contain both a statement of fact and a statement of opinion.

Directions Read the following passage. Then answer the questions below.

Some people prefer cats to dogs as house pets. Fans of cats say they are just as friendly as dogs and that they are equally loving. We know from studies that cats sleep a bit more than dogs; a majority of a cat's day is spent napping. We also know that cats are preferable in pet-therapy situations because they are smaller and easier to handle for elderly or handicapped persons. For the past few years, polls have found that more people have cats as pets than dogs. But cats are hunters, and if let outside, a house cat will hunt birds, mice, and other small mammals. Some people say they are more frightened of cats than dogs. For some reason, they say, dogs seem friendlier.

1. What takes up most of a cat's day?
   A majority of a cat's day is spent napping.
2. Give one example of a statement of opinion found in the passage.
   Possible answer: Cats are as friendly and loving as dogs.
3. How do you know that your example is a statement of opinion?
   It is a statement of opinion because it cannot be proved true or false.
4. Give one example of a statement of fact in the passage.
   Possible answer: Cats sleep eighty percent of the day.
5. On a separate sheet of paper, give your opinion of cats and dogs. Which would you prefer to have as a pet?
   Answers should include statements of opinion.

School + Home Home Activity Your child answered questions about facts and opinions based on a passage. Read a newspaper or magazine article with your child and discuss which parts are statements of fact and which ones are statements of opinion.

▲ **Practice Book** p. 87

Reader Response

Open for Discussion Personal Response

MODEL I'd start by describing Goodall's background and experience. Afterwards, I'd ask for questions.

Comprehension Check Critical Response

1. Possible response: Yes. It's useful in an article that provides a list of suggestions or gives steps in a process. **Author's Purpose**

2. Facts: "bees sting," "sharks bite," "Goodall was never hurt;" Opinions: "it's smart to be cautious," "tapeworms are too revolting," "we need not love to respect," "fear can be controlled" The facts can be proved to be true. **Fact and Opinion**

3. Responses will vary but should be based on and answered in the text. **Ask Questions**

4. Responses will vary but should include at least two lesson vocabulary words and show an understanding of their meaning as used in the selection. **Vocabulary**

Look Back and Write For test practice, assign a 10–15 minute time limit. For assessment, see the Scoring Rubric at the right.

Retell
Have students retell "Jane Goodall's 10 Ways to Help Save Wildlife."

Monitor Progress

Check Retelling Rubric 4 3 2 1

If... students have difficulty retelling the selection,	then... use the Retelling Cards and the Scoring Rubric for Retelling on p. 225 to assist fluent retelling.

SUCCESS PREDICTOR

Check Retelling Have students use the numbered points and illustrations to guide their retellings of the selection. For more ideas on assessing students' retellings, see the ELL and Transition Handbook.

Reader Response

Open for Discussion If you were introducing Jane Goodall to an audience, what would you say to help prepare them to listen to her message? What would you say or do afterward to help make the message effective?

1. Jane Goodall numbers her points and discusses each one before moving on to the next. Do you find this a useful way of organizing? When might it be most useful? **Think Like an Author**

2. Look back at the section called "Respect All Life" on page 214. Identify some facts and some opinions you see there. How did you distinguish the facts from the opinions? **Fact and Opinion**

3. Write two test questions about this selection. What are the answers and on which pages would you find them? **Ask Questions**

4. Create a way of your own to help save wildlife or protect the environment. Plan a poster. Use words from the Words to Know list or the selection. **Vocabulary**

Look Back and Write Look at page 216 to learn Jane Goodall's reason for giving personal names to wildlife. Write her reason. Then write about whether she has convinced you to think in the same way.

Meet author **Jane Goodall on page 766.**

224

Scoring Rubric **Look Back and Write**

Top-Score Response A top-score response will use details from p. 216 of the selection to explain that Jane Goodall named animals to set them apart as individuals and will analyze why the writer agrees or disagrees with Goodall's rationale.

Example of a Top-Score Response Jane Goodall gives a name to each animal she works with to make it a special individual. She thinks this makes people look at animals with more respect. I agree with her because people who have pets usually name them. I think people will care more about and not hurt animals when they have names.

For additional rubrics, see p. WA10.

Write Now

Rules

Prompt

"Jane Goodall's 10 Ways to Help Save Wildlife" lists rules for protecting animals. Think about another situation where rules are helpful.

Now write rules that people can follow in that situation.

Writing Trait

Exact **word choice** helps make rules precise and clear.

Student Model

Rules are stated as brief commands followed by explanations.

Exact, vivid <u>word</u> <u>choice</u> makes points clear to readers.

Details give logical reasons to follow rules.

Rules for the Writing Club

1. Be polite and kind when people share.
   We want to help each other become better writers. When someone shares an original story or poem, focus on what you liked about it before saying anything negative.

2. Step up and share your writing.
   We're here because we like to write. Be brave and share what you have written. This gives others the chance to enjoy and learn from your work. It also gives them the chance to help you become a better writer.

3. Listen and be open to suggestions.
   Be open-minded to new ideas and willing to revise your work.

Use the model to help you write your own rules.

Write Now

Look at the Prompt Have students identify and discuss key words in the prompt. *(situation where rules are helpful, rules that people can follow)*

Strategies to Develop Word Choice

Have students

- rewrite negative rules so they are positive.

NO: Don't come late or you'll miss something.

YES: Be on time to see everything.

- replace general words with specific ones.

NO: Be nice.

YES: Treat others with kindness.

- Avoid wordiness.

NO: Obey each and every rule.

YES: Obey all rules.

For additional suggestions and rubric, see pp. 229g–229h.

Hints for Better Writing

- Carefully read the prompt.
- Use a graphic organizer to plan your writing.
- Support your ideas with information and details.
- Use words that help readers understand.
- Proofread and edit your work.

225

Scoring Rubric — Expository Retelling

Rubric 4 3 2 1	4	3	2	1
Connections	Makes connections and generalizes beyond the text	Makes connections to other events, texts, or experiences	Makes a limited connection to another event, text, or experience	Makes no connection to another event, text, or experience
Author's Purpose	Elaborates on author's purpose	Tells author's purpose with some clarity	Makes some connection to author's purpose	Makes no connection to author's purpose
Topic	Describes the main topic	Identifies the main topic with some details early in retelling	Identifies the main topic	Retelling has no sense of topic
Important Ideas	Gives accurate information about events, steps, and ideas using details and key vocabulary	Gives accurate information about events, steps, and ideas with some detail and key vocabulary	Gives limited or inaccurate information about events, steps, and ideas	Gives no information about events, steps, and ideas
Conclusions	Draws conclusions and makes inferences to generalize beyond the text	Draws conclusions about the text	Is able to tell some learnings about the text	Is unable to draw conclusions or make inferences about the text

Retelling Plan

- ☑ **Week 1** Assess Strategic Intervention students.
- ☑ **Week 2** Assess Advanced students.
- ☑ **Week 3** Assess Strategic Intervention students.
- ☑ **This week assess On-Level students.**
- ☐ **Week 5** Assess any students you have not yet checked during this unit.

Use the Retelling Chart on p. TR17 to record retelling.

Retelling

Selection Test To assess with "Jane Goodall's 10 Ways to Help Save Wildlife," use Selection Tests, pp. 33–36.

Fresh Reads for Differentiated Test Practice For weekly leveled practice, use pp. 49–54.

SUCCESS PREDICTO

Science in Reading

- Examine features of expository nonfiction.
- Practice a test-taking strategy.
- Compare and contrast across texts.

PREVIEW/USE TEXT FEATURES

As students preview "Why Some Animals Are Considered Bad or Scary," have them read the title and look at the illustrations. Then ask:

- **What do you think the selection will be about?** (Answers will vary.)

- **Cartoon animals are used to illustrate the article instead of photographs. What does that suggest to you about the article?** (Possible response: The article might have a light tone or even be amusing instead of being a "heavy" read.)

Link to Science

Encourage students to research an animal they are interested in or don't know much about. Help students brainstorm appropriate sources for information.

DAY 4 Grouping Options

Reading
Whole Group Discuss the Question of the Day.

Group Time Differentiated Instruction
Read "Why Some Animals Are Considered Bad or Scary." See pp. 208h–208i for the small group lesson plan

Whole Group Use p. 229a.

Language Arts
Use pp. 229e–229k.

Science in Reading

Expository Nonfiction

Genre
- Expository nonfiction gives you facts and, sometimes, opinions about real-life people, places, and things.
- Some expository nonfiction focuses on a single topic about those people, places, and things.

Text Features
- The title states the topic of the selection directly.
- Pictures help show what the selection is about.
- The first paragraph. Notice the questions the selection will answer.

Link to Science
Choose one of the animals in the selection and research more about it. Then write an explanation telling a small child why he or she should not be afraid of that animal.

226

from Sandiegozoo.org

Why Some Animals Are Considered BAD or SCARY

illustrated by John Manders

You've heard the stories and seen the movies. Wolves gather in the woods to attack helpless people, especially girls (remember Little Red Riding Hood?). Bats with huge fangs seek you out to suck your blood. Snakes deliberately find people to attack. Toads give you warts. Actually, none of these things are true. So why do humans have so many fears and superstitions about certain animals? Why do people think some animals are evil?

Content-Area Vocabulary	Science
adapted	changed to fit different conditions; adjusted
carnivores	animals that eat meat
prey	animals hunted and killed for food by other animals
species	a set of related living things that all have certain characteristics

Most of the time it's because of ignorance, not knowing the facts about an animal or not understanding what its behavior is for. Humans tend to fear what they don't know or understand. So if someone sees a vampire bat sucking a cow's blood, he might assume that all bats do that, and that they will do it to anything they can. Stories are made up and rumors start, and the next thing you know, people believe that all bats attack deliberately and suck blood. But this isn't based on fact. There are thousands of bat species, and most of them eat fruit or insects and are very important to the environment. Only a few bats suck blood—they are small and not aggressive, and they hang around livestock and nip at their heels to get blood. They don't ravenously attack, and they are just an annoyance to the cows and horses—they don't kill them.

Ask Questions What additional questions are you asking yourself?

227

Ecosystems

An ecosystem is made up of all the living and non-living things in an area. The different components of an ecosystem all interact together. Some interactions benefit both members. For example, the Egyptian plover is a bird that feeds on leeches in the Nile crocodile's mouth. The Egyptian plover gets food from this interaction. The Nile crocodile gets its teeth cleaned.

Use the sidebar on p. 226 to guide discussion.

EXPOSITORY NONFICTION

- Remind students that expository nonfiction gives factual information about a topic. Some expository nonfiction selections also include opinions.

- Inform students that many expository nonfiction articles, such as "Why Some Animals Are Considered Bad or Scary" include illustrations to support the text.

- Discuss with students the kinds of facts and opinions they think this selection will provide.

 **AudioText**

Ask Questions

Possible response: What animals am I afraid of? Why?

Jane Goodall's 10 Ways to Help Save Wildlife **227**

Strategies for Nonfiction

USE INTRODUCTIONS AND CONCLUSIONS
Remind students that writers use introductions and conclusions to present and summarize information. Students can often use the beginning and end of a selection (the introduction and conclusion) to answer test questions. Provide the following strategy.

Use the Strategy

1. Read the test question carefully.
2. If the question asks something about the whole selection, reread the introduction and conclusion.
3. See if information given in the introduction or conclusion answers the test question.

GUIDED PRACTICE Have students discuss how they would use the strategy to answer the following question.

What types of fears and superstitions does this selection talk about?

INDEPENDENT PRACTICE After students answer the following test question, discuss the process they used to find information.

Based on the selection, how can people disprove rumors that some animals are "bad"?

Sometimes people's fears about animals are based on instinctive reactions from a long time ago. Thousands of years ago when humans didn't have houses and roads and cars, they did have reason to be frightened of some animals, especially big carnivores, because people could be hunted for dinner just like other prey animals. That's why the roar of a lion, the snarl of a jaguar, or the howl of wolves can send chills up our spines—instinctively, we remember when we were prey. And we still can be frightened—a tiger or a killer whale could certainly decide to eat you if it wanted to. But that's where knowledge comes in. If you researched the animal's behavior, you'd find out it probably wouldn't want to eat you. Humans are not a "natural" prey source for any of the top carnivores. They have many other regular sources of food that they'd rather eat. If they can't find their regular food and they are starving, or if a human intrudes upon them and makes them defensive, they will kill people, but it's not a common occurrence.

228

Test Practice Discuss with students the location and purpose of an introduction and a conclusion. Have students locate and reread the introduction and conclusion in "Why Some Animals Are Considered Bad or Scary."

Doing the Right Thing • Week 4

Some people believe that animals think the same way some people do, and that they are deliberately trying to hurt us or hunt us down—that they have evil intentions. That just isn't the case. Animals behave the way they do to survive. If a carnivore is hungry, it will kill something— but not because it is "evil," just because it will die if it doesn't eat. Venomous snakes don't hunt people down to bite them just because they feel like it—they only strike in order to defend themselves. Animals are wonderfully adapted to look and act the way they need to in order to live in their habitat and circumstances. They're just being themselves and going about their business. It's up to us to learn about them and understand them, rather than just thinking they are "bad."

So the next time you hear something strange about an animal, such as bats who zero in on you to get tangled in your hair, or hyenas who eat young children for fun, don't assume it's true. Do some research and find out what that animal is really like!

Reading Across Texts

Look over Jane Goodall's 10 points. What is another point that could be added to that list, based on "Why Some Animals Are Considered Bad or Scary"?

Writing Across Texts   Write your point #11 and explain it.

 **Fact & Opinion**   How can you tell the author's opinions?

229

CONNECT TEXT TO TEXT

Reading Across Texts

List Jane Goodall's 10 suggestions on chart paper. Have students explain each suggestion in their own words. Discuss with students what they learned from "Why Some Animals Are Considered Bad or Scary" that could be added to the list of suggestions.

Writing Across Texts Point out the text feature from the Jane Goodall selection in which the suggestion and its number is printed in larger letters than the explanation. Have students replicate this style when they record their suggestion and explanation.

Fact and Opinion

Possible response: They are statements that can't be checked.

Fluency Assessment Plan

- ☑ **Week 1** Assess Advanced students.
- ☑ **Week 2** Assess Strategic Intervention students.
- ☑ **Week 3** Assess On-Level students.
- ☑ **This week assess Strategic Intervention students.**
- ☐ **Week 5** Assess any students you have not yet checked during this unit.

Set individual goals for students to enable them to reach the year-end goal.

- Current Goal: 110–116 wcpm
- Year-End Goal: 140 wcpm

Provide opportunities for students to read aloud from their books as they follow an audio recording of the text. As students gain fluency with text, they can read and reread it independently.

To develop fluent readers, use Fluency Coach.

DAY 5 Grouping Options

Reading
Whole Group
Revisit the Question of the Week.

Group Time
Differentiated Instruction
Reread this week's Leveled Readers. See pp. 208h–208i for the small group lesson plan.

Whole Group
Use pp. 229b–229c.

Language Arts
Use pp. 229d–229l.

PHRASING

Fluency

DAY 1

Model Reread "Jane Goodall" on p. 208m. Explain that you will group words together as you read, making the text sound smooth and like natural language. Model for students as you read.

DAY 2

Choral Reading Read aloud suggestion 1 on p. 214. Have students notice how you group chunks of words together in meaningful units. Have students practice as a class doing three choral readings of suggestion 1.

DAY 3

Model Read aloud suggestion 3 on p. 216. Have students notice how you group related words to add emphasis. Practice as a class by doing three choral readings.

DAY 4

Partner Reading Partners practice reading suggestion 3 on p. 216, three times. Students should use appropriate phrasing and offer each other feedback.

Monitor Progress | Check Fluency WCPM

As students reread, monitor their progress toward their individual fluency goals. Current Goal: 110–116 words correct per minute. End-of-Year Goal: 140 words correct per minute.

If... students cannot read fluently at a rate of 110–116 words correct per minute,
then... make sure students practice with text at their independent level. Provide additional fluency practice, pairing nonfluent readers with fluent readers.

If... students already read at 140 words correct per minute,
then... they do not need to reread three to four times.

SUCCESS PREDICTOR

DAY 5

Assessment
Individual Reading Rate Use the Fluency Assessment Plan and do a one-minute timed reading of either selection from this week to assess students in Week 4. Pay special attention to this week's skill, phrasing. Provide corrective feedback for each student.

RETEACH
Fact and Opinion

TEACH

Review the definitions of *fact* and *opinion* on p. 208. Students can complete Practice Book p. 88 on their own, or you can complete it as a class. Point out that they need to complete the table and that two correct answers are provided.

ASSESS

Have students reread p. 223, suggestion 9, in their books. Ask them if this paragraph is a statement of opinion. Why or why not? *(No, it is not an opinion because it tells about something that can be proved true or false.)*

For additional instruction on fact and opinion, see DI·55.

EXTEND SKILLS

Author's Viewpoint/Bias

TEACH

An author's viewpoint is the way an author looks at the subject he or she is writing about. Biased writing is writing that shows an author's strong feeling for or against something.

- You can learn about an author's viewpoint by asking youself questions about the author's beliefs and assumptions as you read.
- You can determine whether writing is biased by evaluating the evidence that an author gives to support his or her viewpoint.

Discuss Jane Goodall's viewpoint as expressed in suggestion 10 on p. 223. Talk about the optimistic tone of the paragraph which provides a clue that her view is that the environment can be preserved.

ASSESS

Have students reread suggestion 7 on p. 220. Have them write a paragraph that expresses the author's viewpoint on the suggestion given.

OBJECTIVES

- Recognize statements of fact and opinion.
- Identify author's viewpoint.

Skills Trace
Fact and Opinion

Introduce/Teach	TE: 5.2 208–209; 5.3 316–317; 5.6 700–701
Practice	Practice Book: 83, 87, 88, 123, 127, 128, 136, 283, 287, 288
Reteach/Review	TE: 5.2 229b, DI·55; 5.3 301, 345b, 355, DI·54; 5.6 725b, DI·55
Test	Selection Test: 33–36, 49–52, 113–116; Benchmark Test: Unit 3

Access Content Reteach the skill by reviewing the Picture It! lesson on fact and opinion in the ELL Teaching Guide, pp. 57–58.

Fact and Opinion

- A **statement of fact** can be proved true or false. A **statement of opinion** tells what someone thinks or feels.
- Statements of opinion often contain words that make judgments, such as *interesting* or *beautiful*.
- A single sentence might contain both a statement of fact and a statement of opinion.

Directions Read the following passage about penguins. Fill in the diagram below.

Molting is a process during which an animal sheds an outer layer of protection and grows a new one. When humans do this, it involves tiny amounts of skin or hair at a time. We should feel sorry for molting penguins, though, because molting is a difficult time for them. While penguins molt each year, they cannot go into the water. Penguins eat fish and other sea life, so while a penguin is molting, it cannot eat. A molting penguin also looks strange. Molting penguins migrate to a communal molting site, usually in a sheltered area. Depending on the size of the penguin, molting can take anywhere from two weeks to a full month! Maybe penguins think of molting as a way to diet.

Statement	Can it be proved true or false?	Fact? Opinion? Or both?
Molting penguins isolate themselves from other penguins.	1. yes	2. fact
We should feel sorry for molting penguins, though, because molting is a difficult time for them.	The first part cannot be proved true or false, but the second part can.	3. both
4. A molting penguin also **looks strange.**	5. no	Opinion

School + Home Home Activity Your child answered questions about facts and opinions in a nonfiction passage. Read a magazine article with your child and ask him or her to identify facts and opinions in the text.

▲ **Practice Book** p. 88

SUCCES PREDICTO

Vocabulary and Word Study

VOCABULARY STRATEGY
Context Clues

UNFAMILIAR WORDS Remind students that they can use context clues to determine the meaning of unfamiliar words. Have students list any unfamiliar words from "Jane Goodall's 10 Ways to Help Save Wildlife" or "Why Some Animals Are Considered Bad or Scary," and write the context clues and the word meanings.

Word	Context Clues	Meaning
sulked	scolded; acted guilty; wouldn't budge	silent or bad-tempered

Proper Nouns

Proper nouns, such as *Jane Goodall*, name a specific person, place, thing, or idea. (By contrast, a common noun, such as *naturalist*, names any person, place, thing, or idea.) Have partners make lists of proper nouns from "Jane Goodall's 10 Ways to Help Save Wildlife," then alphabetize the nouns in a list.

Proper Nouns

1. Caitlin Alegre
2. California
3. Chicago
4. _____
5. _____

BUILD CONCEPT VOCABULARY
Protecting Animals

LOOKING BACK Remind students of the question of the week: *What can people do to protect wild animals?* Discuss how this week's Concept Web of vocabulary words relates to the theme of protecting animals. Ask students if they have any words or categories to add. Discuss whether the words and categories are appropriately related to the concept.

MOVING FORWARD Preview the title of the next selection, *The Midnight Ride of Paul Revere.* Ask students which Concept Web words might apply to the new selection based on the title alone.

Put a star next to these words on the web.

Display the Concept Web and revisit the vocabulary words as you read the next selection to check predictions.

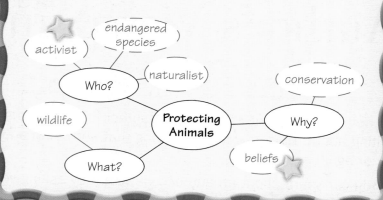

Monitor Progress

Check Vocabulary

If... students suggest words or categories that are not related to the concept,	then... review the words and categories on the Concept Web and discuss how they relate to the lesson concept.

SUCCESS PREDICTOR

Speaking and Viewing

SPEAKING

Debate

SET-UP Have students evaluate "Jane Goodall's 10 Ways to Help Save Wildlife" in a debate. Students should work in pairs or small teams for this activity.

TOPICS You may wish to assign one or two of Goodall's ten points to each team. Encourage students to use the text as a springboard to explore the issues and evaluate the strategies that Goodall presents. Each team should phrase a debate topic; for example, *Resolved: People should use less paper.* Then one or two students should represent the affirmative side and one or two others should represent the negative side.

PRESENTATION Students should plan their presentations carefully in advance. After each side has presented, allow time for rebuttal. Appoint a timekeeper to keep speeches within a reasonable limit.

Listening Tips

- Tell students to make visual contact with speakers to demonstrate attention, interest, and/or appreciation.
- Advise students to listen carefully to what the opposing side says.
- Make judgements about the information being presented.
- Draw conclusions based on these inferences.

ELL

Support Vocabulary Use the following to review and extend vocabulary and to explore lesson concepts further:
- ELL Poster 9, Days 3–5 instruction
- Vocabulary Activities and Word Cards in ELL Teaching Guide, pp. 59–60

Assessment For information on assessing students' speaking, listening, and viewing, see the ELL and Transition Handbook.

VIEWING

Analyze Film Media

Discuss with students any television shows or movies they have seen that focus on wild animals. Have students answer these questions orally, in groups, or individually in writing.

1. Compare the way animals are depicted in the film to the way they are depicted in "Why Some Animals are Considered Bad or Scary."
2. What feelings toward wild animals do you have as you view the program?
3. What techniques does the program use to engage your emotions?

SPEAKING

Panel Discussion

SET-UP Divide the class into groups of three or four. Review the dynamics of working in a group. Define the roles and responsibilities of each member as leader, facilitator, and recorder. Each group will present a panel discussion on an environmental or societal issue in front of the class.

RESEARCH Have groups investigate an issue such as rain forests, the declining population of fish, or pollution. Group leaders should help teams choose an issue to research, discuss, and present. Have students focus their research on ways to minimize, prevent, or solve the problem.

TEAM PRESENTATION Have the designated leader introduce the topic and describe the causes for the problem. The leader should pose this stem: What are the ten best ways to…? Students should take turns presenting, listening to other members.

SUCCESS PREDICTO

Grammar Main and Helping Verbs

OBJECTIVES

- Define and identify main and helping verbs.
- Use main and helping verbs in writing.
- Become familiar with main and helping verbs on high-stakes tests.

Monitor Progress

Grammar

If... students have difficulty identifying main and helping verbs,	then... provide additional instruction and practice in The Grammar and Writing Book pp. 98–101.

DAILY FIX-IT

This week use Daily Fix-It Transparency 9.

Spiral REVIEW

ELL

Support Grammar See the Grammar Transition lessons in the ELL and Transition Handbook.

▲ **The Grammar and Writing Book** For more instruction and practice, use pp. 98–101.

DAY 1 Teach and Model

DAILY FIX-IT

1. Wild animals is having a hard time living with humens. *(are having; humans)*

2. Many has becomed endangered. *(have become)*

READING-GRAMMAR CONNECTION

Write this sentence from "Jane Goodall's 10 Ways to Help Save Wildlife" on the board:

Once I was giving a speech and a fly flew in the room.

Explain that *was giving* is a **verb phrase.** It is made up of a main verb *(giving)* that tells the action and a helping verb *(was)* that helps tell the time of the action.

Display Grammar Transparency 9. Read aloud the definitions and sample sentences. Work through the items.

Main and Helping Verbs

Verbs that are made up of more than one word are **verb phrases**. In a verb phrase, the **main verb** names the action. The **helping verb** helps tell the time of the action. Some common helping verbs are *has, have, had, am, is, are, was, were, do, does, did, can, could, will, would,* and *should*.

- The main verb is always the last word in a verb phrase. (Animals *are losing* habitats.)
- There may be more than one helping verb in a verb phrase. (We *should have saved* more wetland habitats.)
- Helping verbs such as *is* and *are* show that action is happening in the present. (Forests *are cut* down for wood.) *Was* and *were* tell that the action happened in the past. (Once millions of acres of forest *were standing* in this area.) *Will* tells that the action is happening in the future. (Trees *will disappear* if we don't conserve them.)

Directions Underline the verb phrase in each sentence.

1. For years, people <u>have given</u> names to their pets.
2. Our dog is <u>named</u> Groucho.
3. Pets <u>can perform</u> fascinating tricks.
4. Groucho <u>has entertained</u> us for years.
5. He <u>could have been</u> a standup comic.
6. Sometimes he <u>will walk</u> on his hind legs.
7. You <u>should see</u> his stubby tail.
8. No one <u>can resist</u> his floppy ears.

Directions Find the verb phrase in each sentence. Write the helping verb on the first line and the main verb on the second line.

9. We should respect wild animals.
   <u>should</u>   <u>respect</u>
10. They are sharing the planet with us.
    <u>are</u>   <u>sharing</u>
11. They can frighten us at times.
    <u>can</u>   <u>frighten</u>
12. Most of them are frightened by us too.
    <u>are</u>   <u>frightened</u>

Unit 2 Jane Goodall's 10 Ways to Help Save Wildlife   Grammar **9**

▲ **Grammar Transparency** 9

DAY 2 Develop the Concept

DAILY FIX-IT

3. The scouts is clening up the river. *(are cleaning)*

4. This be a good way to hep animals. *(is; help)*

GUIDED PRACTICE

Review the concept of main and helping verbs.

- Verbs that are made up of more than one word are **verb phrases.**
- In a verb phrase, the **main verb** names the action.
- The **helping verb** helps tell the time of the action.

HOMEWORK Grammar and Writing Practice Book p. 33. Work through the first two items with the class.

Main and Helping Verbs

Verbs that are made up of more than one word are **verb phrases**. In a verb phrase, the **main verb** names the action. The **helping verb** helps tell the time of the action. Some common helping verbs are *has, have, had, am, is, are, was, were, do, does, did, can, could, will, would,* and *should*.

- The main verb is always the last word in a verb phrase. (A bird *is looking* at me.)
- There may be more than one helping verb in a verb phrase. (She *has been* studying animals a long time.)
- Helping verbs such as *is* and *are* show that action is happening in the present. (Annamae *is reading* about ecosystems.) *Was* and *were* tell that the action happened in the past. (The class *was reading* about animals last month.) *Will* tells that the action is happening in the future. (We *will study* extinct animals next week.)

Directions Underline the verb phrase in each sentence. Put one line under each helping verb and two lines under the main verb.

1. I <u>have watched</u> animals for years.
2. Right now I <u>am watching</u> birds at the feeder.
3. Some birds <u>will visit</u> the feeder dozens of times.
4. The chickadees <u>have eaten</u> all the thistle seeds.
5. A bright red cardinal <u>is singing</u> cheerfully.
6. Within two days, the birds <u>will have emptied</u> the feeder.
7. I <u>can tell</u> that moment.
8. The birds <u>will be sitting</u> on bushes by my window.
9. They <u>are reminding</u> me of their hunger.
10. Bird watchers <u>should fill</u> the feeder often.

Home Activity Your child learned about main and helping verbs. Have your child model an activity such as making a sandwich. Ask him or her to explain the job using sentences with verb phrases.

▲ **Grammar and Writing Practice Book** p. 33

DAY 3 Apply to Writing

DAILY FIX-IT

5. We shuld plant trees to replace the wons we cut down. *(should; ones)*

6. Loss of trees increases the level, of carbon dioxide in the air? *(level of; air.)*

SHOW TIME OF ACTION

Explain that a verb phrase tells when an action takes place. *Is, are, do, does, has,* and *have* show present time. *Was, were, did,* and *had* show past time. *Will* shows future time. The main verb may change to show time too *(is walking; had walked).*

- Have students review something they have written to see if they can show when events occurred more accurately by using verb phrases.

HOMEWORK Grammar and Writing Practice Book p. 34.

Main and Helping Verbs

Directions Underline the verbs and verb phrases in each paragraph. Circle the verb phrase that expresses the wrong time. Write the correct verb phrase on the line.

1. We are eating more fruits and vegetables these days. For example, for lunch I am having a veggie burger. It smells great. Cheese was melting on the top of it now.
   is melting

2. Last week we drove to a state park. Dad had been studying forest plants. He had brought along his plant identification book. Soon we are looking for ferns. Bobbie yelled. He had fallen in a stream!
   were looking

3. This winter our family will visit a coral reef. Shelly may test her scuba gear. I will snorkel in the clear ocean water. We did marvel at the colorful fish and coral formations.
   will marvel

4. I am teaching the dog a trick. She loves her treats. She is getting a treat for her trick. She sits at the mere sight of the box. Was she learning? What do you think?
   is learning

Directions Write a paragraph about an animal you have watched. Use some verb phrases.
   Possible answer: One day last week I was watching some squirrels in the park. A gray squirrel was chasing a brown squirrel all over the place. Both were chattering angrily. The brown squirrel must have invaded the gray squirrel's territory. Suddenly, they were both scolding me! I wondered if squirrels are always so crabby.

Home Activity Your child learned how to express time correctly using verb phrases. Ask your child to use to use verbs with action verbs to make up sentences about something he or she did in the past, is doing now, and will do in the future.

▲ **Grammar and Writing Practice Book** p. 34

DAY 4 Test Preparation

DAILY FIX-IT

7. We once had a beagel named obiwan. *(beagle; Obiwan)*

8. That dog aten more than i did. *(ate; I)*

STANDARDIZED TEST PREP

Test Tip

A test may ask you to tell whether a word such as *are* is a helping verb or a linking verb. To answer, check how the word is used in a sentence. A helping verb is part of a verb phrase and is followed by a verb. A linking verb is usually followed by a noun or an adjective.

Helping Verb: They are traveling.

Linking Verb: They are excited.

HOMEWORK Grammar and Writing Practice Book p. 35.

Main and Helping Verbs

Directions Mark the letter of the words that correctly identify the underlined word or words in the sentence.

1. People should drive less.
   - **A** helping verb
   - B main verb
   - C verb phrase
   - D not a verb

2. Exhaust fumes are polluting the environment.
   - A helping verb
   - B main verb
   - **C** verb phrase
   - D not a verb

3. Certain chemicals will kill fish.
   - A helping verb
   - **B** main verb
   - C verb phrase
   - D not a verb

4. Runoff from farms may contain these chemicals.
   - A helping verb
   - B main verb
   - **C** verb phrase
   - D not a verb

5. Oil tankers have spilled millions of gallons of oil.
   - A helping verb
   - B main verb
   - **C** verb phrase
   - D not a verb

6. Fish, birds, and mammals are coated with the oil.
   - A helping verb
   - B main verb
   - C verb phrase
   - D not a verb

7. Without help they soon will die.
   - A helping verb
   - B main verb
   - **C** verb phrase
   - D not a verb

8. Many towns are putting garbage in landfills.
   - A helping verb
   - B main verb
   - C verb phrase
   - **D** not a verb

9. Plastics do not break down easily.
   - **A** helping verb
   - B main verb
   - C verb phrase
   - D not a verb

10. We are poisoning ourselves slowly.
   - A helping verb
   - **B** main verb
   - C verb phrase
   - D not a verb

Home Activity Your child prepared for taking tests on main and helping verbs and verb phrases. Have your child write sentences about his or her day's activities using verb phrases and point out main and helping verbs.

▲ **Grammar and Writing Practice Book** p. 35

DAY 5 Cumulative Review

DAILY FIX-IT

9. Jane goodall has spent she life educating the world about animals. *(Goodall; her life)*

10. She is a great exampel of how to treat Wildlife. *(example; wildlife)*

ADDITIONAL PRACTICE

Assign pp. 98–101 in The Grammar and Writing Book.

EXTRA PRACTICE Grammar and Writing Practice Book p. 130.

TEST PREPARATION Grammar and Writing Practice Book pp. 153–154.

ASSESSMENT

CUMULATIVE REVIEW Grammar and Writing Practice Book p. 36.

Main and Helping Verbs

Directions Choose a helping verb from the box to complete each sentence. Write the sentence on the line. Underline the verb phrase.

| could | should | has | was | had | did |

1. Jane Goodall _____ studied African animals for decades.
   Jane Goodall has studied African animals for decades.

2. She _____ raised in England.
   She was raised in England.

3. Even as a little girl, she _____ always loved animals.
   Even as a little girl, she had always loved animals.

4. In the jungle, Jane _____ watch chimpanzees for hours.
   In the jungle, Jane could watch chimpanzees for hours.

5. She _____ not notice the hours passing.
   She did not notice the hours passing.

6. We _____ admire such devotion to animals.
   We should admire such devotion to animals.

Directions Find the verb phrases. Underline each helping verb. Circle each main verb.

7. A wildlife refuge may provide the only safe habitat for some animals.

8. Many animals have been hunted too much.

9. Scientists have predicted the extinction of some species.

10. Animals in trouble are described as endangered.

11. Many groups are working to protect endangered animals.

12. Without our help, these animals will disappear like the dodo.

Home Activity Your child reviewed main and helping verbs. Ask your child to make up sentences using verb phrases to describe an animal's past, present, and future actions.

▲ **Grammar and Writing Practice Book** p. 36

AFTER READING

Writing Workshop Rules

OBJECTIVES

- Identify characteristics of well-written rules.
- State and follow a purpose for writing.
- Focus on word choice.
- Use a rubric.

Genre Rules
Writer's Craft Know Your Purpose
Writing Trait Word Choice

Word Choice Pair an English learner with a proficient English speaker to discuss pictures in books or magazines. Have them list colorful words from the discussion to use in writing, such as *friendly, picnic, caterpillar, broken, snowstorm,* and *furry.*

Writing Traits

FOCUS/IDEAS Rules focus on key aspects of saving the environment.

ORGANIZATION/PARAGRAPHS Paragraphs are developed logically and smoothly with supporting details and reasons.

VOICE The writer is engaged and compelling in logical persuasion.

WORD CHOICE Strong verbs and nouns state rules clearly and forcefully. Vivid language persuades readers to follow rules.

SENTENCES Strong commands are used for rules. Supporting sentences vary in length and kind.

CONVENTIONS There is excellent control and accuracy. Verb phrases are used effectively.

DAY 1 Model the Trait

READING-WRITING CONNECTION

- "Jane Goodall's 10 Ways to Help Save Wildlife" lists rules and reasons for saving animals.
- The rules use vivid, active words to persuade.
- Students will write **rules** using clear, forceful words that make their purpose clear.

MODEL WORD CHOICE Discuss Writing Transparency 9A. Then discuss the model and the writing trait of word choice.

 Think Aloud Each rule begins with a strong verb. *Recycle* tells readers exactly what they should do. Vivid adjectives persuade and create word pictures. Because our natural resources are *precious,* we should save them. *Paper, glass, metal,* and *plastic* are precise nouns that let me picture the things to recycle.

Rules

Some writing assignments will ask you to support your ideas with **rules.** Make sure that each rule is stated clearly and concisely and supports your main idea. Rules may consist of a simple list, or they may be developed in paragraphs with persuasive details.

Rules to Save the Environment

Rules are expressed as brief commands using specific verbs.

1. Recycle everything you can.

Think of all the paper, glass, metal, and plastic you throw out every week in the trash. These precious natural resources could be used again instead of being buried in a landfill. As garbage, they take up room and can pollute the land. If we recycle them, we will need to cut fewer trees, dig less ore, and pump less oil.

Writer addresses reader personally. Details give compelling, logical reasons to follow rules.

2. Conserve water every way you can.

Clean fresh water is essential to life. Earth has an enormous population of humans and a limited supply of water. When you run water needlessly, you waste our most precious resource. Take a brief shower instead of a long one. Flush the toilet less often. Fix leaky faucets. You'll be surprised how many thousands of gallons of water you save over time!

Exact, vivid words drive home the point and persuade readers.

Unit 2 Jane Goodall's 10 Ways to Help Save Wildlife   Writing Model **9A**

▲ **Writing Transparency** 9A

DAY 2 Improve Writing

WRITER'S CRAFT
Know Your Purpose

Display Writing Transparency 9B. Work with students to identify details that support a writer's purpose.

Think Aloud **SUPPORT YOUR PURPOSE FOR WRITING** Tomorrow we will write **rules.** I could write safety rules for using an escalator. My purpose would be to persuade riders to act responsibly and safely. I might write "Stand still and hold the escalator railing." To support this rule, I could explain that if you lose your balance and fall, your clothing could get caught and you would be injured.

GUIDED WRITING Some students may need more help with understanding purposes of explaining rules. Work with them to find sentences in the selection that made them want to obey Goodall's rules.

Know Your Purpose

Authors write for different **purposes.** They might want to inform, persuade, or entertain their readers. Before writing, have your purpose firmly in mind. For example, when you explain rules, your purpose is to persuade readers to follow them. To motivate your readers to act, give them reasons, facts and well-supported opinions.

Directions Read each rule and the sentences that follow it. Mark the sentences that help support the rule.
Avoid overly packaged, "disposable" products.
- ✓ 1. Plastic and plastic foam packaging will not break down and is not often recycled.
- 2. Marketers make packaging colorful and appealing.
- ✓ 3. "Disposable" products have to be thrown away, so they waste resources.
- ✓ 4. Some of the packaging materials, such as plastic foam, harm the environment.

Compost natural wastes.
- ✓ 5. Leaves and other yard waste add to the richness of the soil.
- ✓ 6. Putting this waste in the trash uses landfill space.
- 7. Burning this waste contributes to air pollution.
- 8. Bird feeders and birdhouses will make your yard an attractive habitat.

Directions Think of your own rule for saving the environment. Write at least three pieces of evidence (facts, opinions, examples, logical arguments) to show why the rule is a good one.
Rule: Give your time and effort to conservation projects.
Support for rule: Possible answer:
1. You will learn about wise use of our resources.
2. One person really can make a difference. If every person volunteered, think what could be done.
3. Your good example will encourage your family, friends, and neighbors to save resources too.

Unit 2 Jane Goodall's 10 Ways to Help Save Wildlife   Writer's Craft **9B**

▲ **Writing Transparency** 9B

229g Doing the Right Thing • Week 4

DAY 3 Prewrite and Draft

READ THE WRITING PROMPT

on page 225 in the Student Edition.

"Jane Goodall's 10 Ways to Help Save Wildlife" lists rules for protecting animals.

Think about another situation where rules are helpful.

Now write rules that people can follow in that situation.

Writing Test Tips

- Brainstorm a list of safety or health issues about the situation.
- Write rules as brief, specific commands that tell exactly how to behave.
- Choose descriptive words with precise meanings to persuade readers to follow rules.

GETTING STARTED Students can do any of the following:

- Make a word web for each rule. Around it list reasons that the rule is helpful.
- Brainstorm a list of precise and vivid words to explain these rules.
- Research the facts to make your explanations persuasive.

DAY 4 Draft and Revise

EDITING/REVISING CHECKLIST

- ☑ Do my rules and explanations accomplish my purpose?
- ☑ Have I used main and helping verbs effectively?
- ☑ Have I spelled words with final syllables *-en, -an, -el, -le,* and *-il* correctly?

See *The Grammar and Writing Book,* pp. 98–103.

Revising Tips

Word Choice

- Support each rule using strong verbs.
- Include specific nouns to make each rule clear.
- Make reasons persuasive with vivid words that create moods and word pictures.

PUBLISHING Students can make a bulletin board or hallway display of their rules, with explanations placed around them in balloons. Some students may wish to revise their work later.

ASSESSMENT Use the scoring rubric to evaluate students' work.

DAY 5 Connect to Unit Writing

How-to Report	
Week 1	Summary 161g–161h
Week 2	Story Review 185g–185h
Week 3	News Story 207g–207h
Week 4	Rules 229g–229h
Week 5	Interview 253g–253h

PREVIEW THE UNIT PROMPT

Write a report explaining how to make or do something that is familiar to you. Choose words that make your report interesting to read and easy to understand. Explain all the steps and materials needed.

APPLY

- A how-to report explains the steps for making or doing something.
- The purpose of the report should be clearly stated in the introduction.

Writing Trait Rubric

	4	3	2	1
Word Choice	Vivid style created by use of exact nouns, strong verbs, exciting adjectives, and clear figurative language	Some style created by strong and precise words	Little style created by strong, precise words; some lack of clarity	Word choice vague or incorrect
	Uses strong, specific words that make rules clear, lively, and energetic	Uses some specific words that make rules clear and vivid at times	Needs more precise word choice to create style and clarity in rules	Rules made dull or unclear by poor word choice

Spelling & Phonics — Final Syllables -*en*, -*an*, -*el*, -*le*, -*il*

OBJECTIVE

● Spell words with final syllables -*en*, -*an*, -*el*, -*le*, -*il*.

Generalization

Connect to Phonics Vowels in final syllables often sound alike even when they are spelled differently: canc*el*, chuck*le*, foss*il*, veter*an*, wood*en*. Vowels in unaccented syllables often stand for the same sound, /ə/.

Spelling Words

1. example	11. cancel
2. level	12. chuckle
3. human*	13. fossil
4. quarrel	14. toboggan
5. scramble	15. veteran
6. evil	16. chisel
7. oxygen	17. suburban
8. wooden	18. single
9. double	19. sudden
10. travel*	20. beagle

Challenge Words

21. obstacle	24. pummel
22. kindergarten	25. enlighten
23. abdomen	

* Words from the selection

ELL

Spelling/Phonics Support See the ELL and Transition Handbook for spelling support.

DAY 1 — Pretest and Sort

PRETEST

Use the Dictation Sentences from Day 5 to administer the pretest. Read the word, read the sentence, and then read the word again. Guide students in self-correcting their pretests and correcting any misspellings.

Monitor Progress

Spelling

If...	then...
If... students misspell more than 5 pretest words,	**then...** use words 1–10 for Strategic Intervention.
If... students misspell 1–5 pretest words,	**then...** use words 1–20 for On-Level practice.
If... students correctly spell all pretest words,	**then...** use words 1–25 for Advanced Learners.

HOMEWORK Spelling Practice Book, p. 33.

Final Syllables -*en*, -*an*, -*el*, -*le*, -*il*

Generalization Vowels in final syllables often sound alike even when they are spelled differently: **cancel, chuckle, fossil, veteran, wooden.**

Word Sort Sort words by the way in which the final syllable is spelled.

Spelling Words
1. example
2. level
3. human
4. quarrel
5. scramble
6. evil
7. oxygen
8. wooden
9. double
10. travel
11. cancel
12. chuckle
13. fossil
14. toboggan
15. veteran
16. chisel
17. suburban
18. single
19. sudden
20. beagle

-en
1. oxygen
2. wooden
3. sudden

-an
4. human
5. toboggan
6. veteran
7. suburban

-el
8. level
9. quarrel
10. travel
11. cancel
12. chisel

-le
13. example
14. scramble
15. double
16. chuckle
17. single
18. beagle

-il
19. evil
20. fossil

Challenge Words
21. obstacle
22. kindergarten
23. abdomen
24. pummel
25. enlighten

-en
21. kindergarten
22. abdomen
23. enlighten

-el
24. pummel

-le
25. obstacle

Home Activity Your child is learning to spell words with final syllables -en, -an, -el, -le, and -il. Ask your child to tell you an ending sound and two ways it can be spelled.

▲ **Spelling Practice Book** p. 33

DAY 2 — Think and Practice

TEACH

Because different vowels may have the same sound when they appear in the final syllable of a two-syllable word, it often impossible to sound out these words to spell them. Write *sudden* and *human*. Underline the *en* and *an* as you say /ən/. Write *chisel, single,* and *evil*. Have students say and spell the final sounds in each word.

> sudd*en*
> hum*an*

FINISH THE WORD Have pairs of students take turns reading and spelling the list words. Tell the readers to read a word and spell all but the last two letters. Have the other partner finish spelling the word and say it again.

HOMEWORK Spelling Practice Book, p. 34.

Final Syllables -*en*, -*an*, -*el*, -*le*, -*il*

Spelling Words

example	level	human	quarrel	scramble
evil	oxygen	wooden	double	travel
cancel	chuckle	fossil	toboggan	veteran
chisel	suburban	single	sudden	beagle

Word Clues Write the list word that matches each clue.

1. a kind of laugh — 1. chuckle
2. not urban or rural — 2. suburban
3. a kind of sled — 3. toboggan
4. a gas we breathe — 4. oxygen
5. something made of oak or maple — 5. wooden
6. something that has been preserved in stone — 6. fossil
7. a small argument — 7. quarrel
8. two of something — 8. double
9. only one — 9. single
10. a kind of hound dog — 10. beagle

Synonyms Write a list word that has the same meaning as the underlined word.

11. I found a perfect model of my favorite color. — 11. example
12. Did you mix the eggs for me? — 12. scramble
13. The sculptor had to carefully carve the marble bit by bit. — 13. chisel
14. One of my goals is to journey around the world. — 14. travel
15. The ground was flat and then it dropped down steeply. — 15. level
16. The wicked queen tried to poison her enemy. — 16. evil
17. Every person makes a mistake at some time. — 17. human
18. The politician was an old hand at running elections. — 18. veteran
19. I had to call off my dentist appointment today. — 19. cancel
20. The storm was swift and unexpected. — 20. sudden

Home Activity Your child matched list words to meanings. Ask your child to tell you the meaning of three list words.

▲ **Spelling Practice Book** p. 34

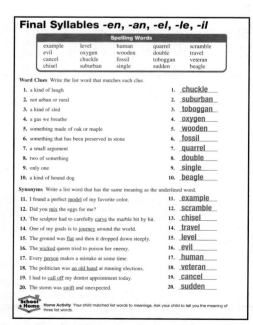

DAY 3 Connect to Writing

WRITE ABOUT THE ENVIRONMENT

Ask students to use at least four spelling words to write about an environmental problem.

Frequently Misspelled Words

Mom   Dad's
heard

These words may seem easy to spell, but they are often misspelled by fifth-graders. Alert students to these frequently misspelled words. Explain that when *Mom* and *Dad* are used as names, both words are capitalized. When they are preceded by a word such as *my,* they are not capitalized. Discuss the possessive form of *Dad's,* and remind students that *heard* is the past tense of *hear* so it is spelled with *ear.*

HOMEWORK Spelling Practice Book, p. 35.

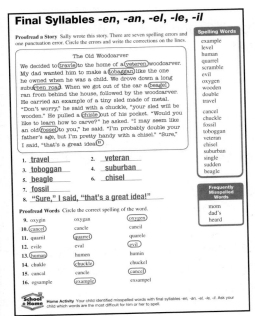

▲ **Spelling Practice Book** p. 35

DAY 4 Review

REVIEW WORDS WITH FINAL SYLLABLES -en, -an, -el, -le, -il

Have pairs of students write *-en, -an, -el, -le,* and *-il* on note cards and turn the cards face down. Tell the partners to take turns drawing a card and naming and spelling a word that ends with the letters on the card.

Spelling Strategy Problem Parts

We all have words that are hard for us to spell.
Step 1: Ask yourself: Which part of the word gives me a problem?
Step 2: Underline the problem part.
Step 3: Picture the word. Focus on the problem part.

HOMEWORK Spelling Practice Book, p. 36.

▲ **Spelling Practice Book** p. 36

DAY 5 Posttest

DICTATION SENTENCES

1. See the example at the top of the page.
2. Rain made the water level rise.
3. The parrot sounds almost human.
4. The friends made up soon after their quarrel.
5. When the bell rang, there was a scramble for the door.
6. The actor had an evil grin.
7. Fire will not burn without oxygen.
8. Dad carved a wooden toy.
9. Two puppies are double the fun.
10. Will you travel by car or by bus?
11. We may cancel the trip if it snows.
12. Tim's joke made me chuckle.
13. The fossil shows a fern leaf.
14. Our toboggan slid down the hill.
15. The veteran returned from the war.
16. He hit the chisel with a hammer.
17. We moved to a suburban home.
18. Not a single person knew the answer.
19. The sudden storm surprised us.
20. The beagle wagged its tail.

CHALLENGE

21. The mouse ran through the obstacle course.
22. Most kindergarten students can tie their shoes.
23. Sit-ups tone muscles in the abdomen.
24. Boxers pummel each other.
25. These books will enlighten us about our topic.

Jane Goodall's 10 Ways to Help Save Wildlife   **229j**

OBJECTIVES

- Formulate an inquiry question that is connected to this week's lesson focus.
- Effectively and efficiently find, evaluate, and communicate information related to an inquiry question using electronic sources.

New Literacies

Day 1	**Identify Questions**
Day 2	**Navigate/Search**
Day 3	**Analyze**
Day 4	**Synthesize**
Day 5	**Communicate**

NEW LITERACIES

Internet Inquiry Activity

EXPLORE WILDLIFE PROTECTION

Use the following 5-day plan to help students conduct this week's Internet inquiry activity on wildlife protection. Remind students to follow classroom rules when using the Internet.

DAY 1

Identify Questions Discuss the lesson focus question: *What can people do to protect wild animals?* Brainstorm ideas for specific inquiry questions about wildlife protection. For example, students might want to find out about efforts to protect an endangered species like the red fox or the bald eagle. Have students work individually, in pairs, or in small groups to write inquiry questions they want to answer.

DAY 2

Navigate/Search Review using keywords to conduct a search using a student-friendly search engine. More than one keyword, for example, *wildlife protection,* can sometimes yield results based on each individual word rather than the two words together. Have students evaluate the sites for text based on facts and opinions, then gather and record information using three or more sources.

DAY 3

Analyze Have students skim and scan the Web sites they identified on Day 2. Students should analyze information for credibility and timeliness. To do this, they can check an author's background in the subject area and look to see when a site was last updated.

DAY 4

Synthesize Have students synthesize information from Day 3 and think about how they will present their information to the class. Explain that graphic organizers like charts, graphs, or time lines can be helpful in summarizing factual information.

DAY 5

Communicate Have students share their inquiry results. They can use a word processing or simple graphing program to present their data visually in the form of charts, graphs, or time lines.

RESEARCH/STUDY SKILLS
Electronic Media

TEACH

Ask students about the types of sources they could use to find an interview with Jane Goodall for information on how to help save endangered animals. Lead students to recognize different types of electronic media. Discuss electronic media they are familiar with and how they are used. Show examples of various types of electronic media (audiotape, DVD, CD-ROM) and discuss these terms.

- **Electronic media** includes both computer and non-computer means of communication.

- **Computer media** includes software, CD-ROMs, and the Internet.

- **Non-computer media** includes audiotapes, videotapes, DVDs, films, TV, and radio.

- To use computer sources such as CD-ROMs and the Internet, a keyword search is usually best for finding information. A **keyword** is a word that defines the information you are looking for.

Have students work in pairs or small groups, as classroom resources allow. Have groups examine different types of electronic media. For instance, students can choose to view Internet sites, part of a TV documentary, or listen to an audio file. Then, discuss these questions:

1. **What source(s) might you use to find information about chimpanzee behavior?** *(Possible response: Internet site, TV documentary)*

2. **How would you begin a search on the Internet for information about endangered species?** *(Possible response: I would begin with the keywords* endangered species.*)*

ASSESS

As students work with electronic media, be sure they can identify different types of media, can demonstrate an understanding of the purposes and value of the different types of media, and are able to use keywords to search the Internet.

For more practice or to assess students, use Practice Book pp. 89–90.

- Review types of electronic media.
- Evaluate electronic media.

Electronic Media

- There are two types of **electronic media**—computer and non-computer. Computer sources include computer software, CD-ROMs, and the Internet. Non-computer sources include audiotapes, videotapes, films, filmstrips, television, and radio.
- To find information on the Internet, use a search engine and type in your keywords. Be specific. It's a good idea to use two or more keywords as well as typing "AND" between keywords. To go to a Web page that's listed in your search results, click on the underlined link.

Directions Use the following list of electronic media to answer the questions below.

- *Monkey-ing Around* (Public Television documentary about captive monkey behavior)
- *Monkey Project* (Internet site for an international primate organization)
- *Field Recordings: Monkeys of Gambia* (CD of natural monkey sounds recorded in Gambia in 1998)
- "Jane Goodall's Quest" (Taped interview with Jane Goodall)
- *World Wildlife Fund's Annual Report 2003* (CD-ROM with annual assessment of endangered species and habitats)
- *One World* (Internet site about wild animal habitats that are endangered)

1. Which source would be most helpful in writing a report on Jane Goodall?
   "Jane Goodall's Quest" would be the most helpful.
2. How would you access information from the *World Wildlife Fund's Annual Report 2003*?
   You would have to use the CD-ROM at a computer.
3. If you were doing an Internet search, what keywords would you type into the search engine to find the Web site *One World*?
   Use keywords wild animals and habitats and endangered.
4. Which source would be most helpful if you wanted to learn about the sounds monkeys make?
   Field Recordings: Monkeys of Gambia would the be most useful.
5. Which source would you start with if you were investigating primates in your local zoo?
   You would start with Monkey-ing Around.

▲ **Practice Book** p. 89

Directions Use the following Internet search results found on a search engine to answer the questions below.

Search Results
Prairie Shores
   State of Illinois' official site for prairie habitat information. Northern Illinois prairies adjacent to Lake Michigan. Flora, fauna, ecosystems, wildlife habitats.
Federally Protected Ecosystems
   U.S. Department of the Interior. Based on annual assessment, site lists all federally protected ecosystems by state, region, ecosystem type, EPA ranking, etc.
Our Backyard
   Waukegan community organization site to protect Amber Prairie. Updates on preservation effort, fundraising efforts, state and federal decision deadlines.
Habitat and Ecosystem Interdependence
   University of Northern Illinois three-year study on development impact on Amber Prairie and its ecosystems, habitats, and indigenous species.

6. What does the information below the underlined links tell you?
   It tells you more specific information about the site.
7. What key words might have been used to get these search results?
   Possible answers: ecosystems, Amber Prairie, habitats.
8. Which sites are the official government sources regarding this prairie?
   Prairie Shores and Federally Protected Ecosystems
9. Which site would be the least reliable if you were doing a report for school?
   Our Backyard would be the least reliable.
10. Why might the *Habitat and Ecosystem Interdependence* site be valuable if you were doing a report?
   Possible answer: Because it was done by a university and may be less biased than the others.

Home Activity Your child answered questions about electronic media. With your child, look around your house and see how many different types of electronic media you have on hand. Talk with your son or daughter about how each of the various electronic media sources could be valuable in his or her studies.

▲ **Practice Book** p. 90

Assessment Checkpoints *for the Week*

Selection Assessment

Use pp. 33–36 of Selection Tests to check:

 Selection Understanding

 Comprehension Skill *Fact and Opinion*

 Selection Vocabulary
conservation
contribute
enthusiastic
environment
investigation

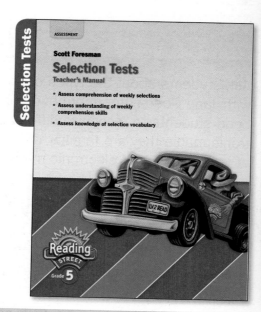

Leveled Assessment

Use pp. 49–54 of Fresh Reads for Differentiated Test Practice to check:

 Comprehension Skill *Fact and Opinion*

 REVIEW Comprehension Skill *Compare and Contrast*

 Fluency *Words Correct Per Minute*

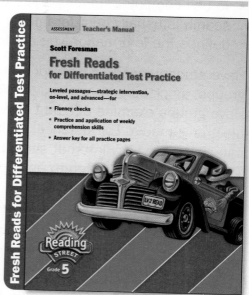

Managing Assessment

Use Assessment Handbook for:

 Observation Checklists

 Record-Keeping Forms

 Portfolio Assessment

Unit 2
Doing the Right Thing

CONCEPT QUESTION
What makes people want to do the right thing?

Week 1

Why do people show kindness?

Week 2

Why do we help others even if there are risks?

Week 3

What are the rewards in helping others?

Week 4

What can people do to protect wild animals?

Week 5

How can people promote freedom?

Week 5

EXPAND THE CONCEPT
How can people promote freedom?

CONNECT THE CONCEPT

▶ **Build Background**
battle, freedom, Monmouth

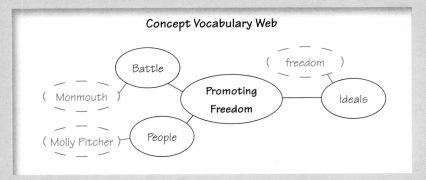

Concept Vocabulary Web

▶ **Social Studies Content**
Boston, MA; Old North Church; Freedom Trail

▶ **Writing**
Interview

▶ **Internet Inquiry**
Promoting Freedom

The Midnight Ride of Paul Revere **230a**

Preview Your Week

How can people promote freedom?

How does Paul Revere feel during his ride?

THE MIDNIGHT RIDE OF PAUL REVERE

by
Henry
Wadsworth
Longfellow

graved and painted by
Christopher Bing

Genre A **poem** is a composition arranged in lines. Some poems have rhyme, some have rhythm, and some have both. As you read this narrative poem—a long poem that tells a story—notice the rhyme and rhythm.

234

Student Edition pages 234–247

Audio CD

Genre	Poem
◉ **Vocabulary Strategy**	Word Structure
◉ **Comprehension Skill**	Sequence
◉ **Comprehension Strategy**	Graphic Organizers

Paired Selection

SOCIAL STUDIES

Reading Across Texts
Compare Lessons Learned

Genre
Web Page

Text Features
Links

Reading Online
Editorial: PearsonSuccessNet.com

Web Site

Genre
• Web pages are found on Internet Web sites.
• A Web page contains information about a topic or topics.

Text Features
• Often this information is broken down into subtopics. Each subtopic is a link.
• The links on this page are in blue and underlined. When you click on a link, you move to another page.

Link to Social Studies
Do research to find out more about women in the Revolutionary War. Share what you find with the class.

Revolutionary War Women

Let's say you want to learn about women in the Revolutionary War. You find this page at a Web site created by a fifth-grade social studies class:

WOMEN IN THE REVOLUTION

Men alone did not win the American Revolution. Women helped make life easier for soldiers, and some of them even fought on the front lines. Many women stayed with their husbands during the American Revolution. Some women even brought their children.

We had fun researching women of this time period. We hope you enjoy our reports and illustrations.

• Deborah Sampson
• Betsy Ross
• Phillis Wheatley
• Nancy Morgan Hart
• Molly Pitcher
• Abigail Adams

You click your mouse on the link for Deborah Sampson, and a new page pops up on your computer screen:

For more practice
Take It to the Net

250

ⓒ **Sequence** What steps has the writer taken so far?

Student Edition pages 250–253

Audio CD

Read It
ONLINE
PearsonSuccessNet.com
- Student Edition
- Leveled Readers

Leveled Readers

- **Skill** Sequence
- **Strategy** Graphic Organizers
- **Lesson Vocabulary**

Below-Level

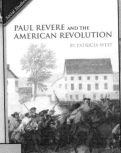

On-Level

Advanced

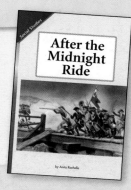

ELL Reader
- Concept Vocabulary
- Text Support
- Language Enrichment

Time for SOCIAL STUDIES

Integrate Social Studies Standards
- Colonial America
- U.S. History
- American Revolution
- American Patriots

✓ Read

The Midnight Ride of Paul Revere,
pp. 234–247

"Revolutionary War Women,"
pp. 250–253

Leveled Readers

Below-Level • Support Concepts
On-Level • Develop Concepts
Advanced • Extend Concepts
• Social Studies Extension Activity

ELL Reader

 Build Concept Vocabulary
Promoting Freedom,
pp. 230l–230m

✓ **Teach Social Studies Concepts**
Boston, MA, p. 237
Old North Church, p. 239
Freedom Trail, p. 245

 Explore Social Studies Center
Make a Map, p. 230k

The Midnight Ride of Paul Revere **230c**

Weekly Plan

My Lesson Planner
ONLINE
PearsonSuccessNet.com

READING

45-90 minutes

TARGET SKILLS OF THE WEEK

Comprehension Skill
Sequence

Comprehension Strategy
Graphic Organizers

Vocabulary Strategy
Word Structure

DAY 1
PAGES 230I–232b, 253a, 253e–253k

Oral Language

QUESTION OF THE WEEK *How can people promote freedom?*

Read Aloud: "Molly Pitcher," 230m
Build Concepts, 230I

Comprehension/Vocabulary

Comprehension Skill/Strategy Lesson, 230–231
Sequence **T**
Graphic Organizers
Build Background, 232a
Introduce Lesson Vocabulary, 232b
fate, fearless, glimmer, lingers, magnified, somber, steed **T**

Read Leveled Readers

Grouping Options 230f–230g

Fluency

Model Tone of Voice, 230I–230m, 253a

DAY 2
PAGES 232–241, 253a, 253e–253k

Oral Language

QUESTION OF THE DAY *What risks did Paul Revere and his friend face that night?*

Comprehension/Vocabulary

Vocabulary Strategy Lesson, 232–233
Word Structure **T**

Read *The Midnight Ride of Paul Revere,* 234–241

Grouping Options 230f–230g

Sequence **T**
Graphic Organizers
REVIEW Setting and Theme **T**
Develop Vocabulary

Fluency

Echo Reading, 253a

LANGUAGE ARTS

30-60 minutes

Trait of the Week

Organization/Paragraphs

Grammar, 253e
Introduce Subject-Verb Agreement **T**

Writing for Tests, 253g
Introduce Interview

Model the Trait of the Week:
Organization/Paragraphs

Spelling, 253i
Pretest for Final Syllables *er, ar, or*

Internet Inquiry, 253k
Identify Questions

Grammar, 253e
Develop Subject-Verb Agreement **T**

Writing Workshop, 253g
Improve Writing with Organization

Spelling, 253i
Teach the Generalization

Internet Inquiry, 253k
Navigate/Search

DAILY WRITING ACTIVITIES

Day 1 Write to Read, 230

Day 2 Words to Write, 233
Strategy Response Log, 234, 241

DAILY SOCIAL STUDIES CONNECTIONS

Day 1 Promoting Freedom Concept Web, 230I

Day 2 Time for Social Studies: Boston, MA, 237; Old North Church, 239; Revisit the Promoting Freedom Concept Web, 241

DAILY SUCCESS PREDICTORS
for Adequate Yearly Progress

Monitor Progress and Corrective Feedback

Vocabulary — Check Vocabulary, *230I*

RESOURCES FOR THE WEEK

- Practice Book, *pp. 91–100*
- Word Study and Spelling Practice Book, *pp. 37–40*
- Grammar and Writing Practice Book, *pp. 37–40*
- Selection Test, *pp. 37–40*
- Fresh Reads for Differentiated Test Practice, *pp. 55-60*
- The Grammar and Writing Book, *pp. 104–109*

Grouping Options for Differentiated Instruction

Turn the page for the small group lesson plan.

DAY 3 — PAGES 242-249, 253a, 253e–253k

Oral Language

QUESTION OF THE DAY *How did Paul Revere promote freedom?*

Comprehension/Vocabulary

Read *The Midnight Ride of Paul Revere,* 242–248

Grouping Options 230f–230g

- Sequence **T**
- Graphic Organizers
- Word Structure **T**
- Develop Vocabulary

Reader Response

Selection Test

Fluency

Model Tone of Voice, 253a

Grammar, 253f
Apply Subject-Verb Agreement in Writing **T**

Writing Workshop, 249, 253h
Write Now
Prewrite and Draft

Spelling, 253j
Connect Spelling to Writing

Internet Inquiry, 253k
Analyze Sources

Day 3 Strategy Response Log, 246
Look Back and Write, 248

Day 3 Time for Social Studies: Freedom Trail, 245
Revisit the Promoting Freedom Concept Web, 247

DAY 4 — PAGES 250-253a, 253e–253k

Oral Language

QUESTION OF THE DAY *What is your definition of freedom?*

Comprehension/Vocabulary

Read "Revolutionary War Women," 250–253

Grouping Options 230f–230g

Web Site/Text Features
Reading Across Texts

Fluency

Partner Reading, 253a

Grammar, 253f
Practice Subject-Verb Agreement for Standardized Tests **T**

Writing Workshop, 253h
Draft, Revise, and Publish

Spelling, 253j
Provide a Strategy

Internet Inquiry, 253k
Synthesize Information

Day 4 Writing Across Texts, 253

Day 4 Social Studies Center: Make a Map, 230k

DAY 5 — PAGES 253a–253l

Oral Language

QUESTION OF THE WEEK *To wrap up the week, revisit the Day 1 question.*
Build Concept Vocabulary, 253c

Fluency

Read Leveled Readers

Grouping Options 230f–230g

Assess Reading Rate, 253a

Comprehension/Vocabulary

- Reteach Sequence, 253b **T**
- Personification, 253b
- Review Word Structure, 253c **T**

Speaking and Listening, 253d
Radio Feature Story
Listen to a CD

Grammar, 253f
Cumulative Review

Writing Workshop, 253h
Connect to Unit Writing

Spelling, 253j
Posttest for Final Syllables *er, ar, or*

Internet Inquiry, 253k
Communicate Results

Research/Study Skills, 253l
Illustration/Caption

Day 5 Personification, 253b

Day 5 Revisit the Promoting Freedom Concept Web, 253c

KEY ◎ = Target Skill **T** = Tested Skill

Comprehension — Check Retelling, *248*

Fluency — Check Fluency WCPM, *253a*

Vocabulary — Check Vocabulary, *253c*

SUCCESS PREDICTOR

Small Group Plan *for Differentiated Instruction*

Daily Plan
AT A GLANCE

Reading
Whole Group
- Oral Language
- Comprehension/Vocabulary

Group Time

Differentiated Instruction

Meet with small groups to provide:
- Skill Support
- Reading Support
- Fluency Practice

Read

This week's lessons for daily group time can be found behind the Differentiated Instruction (DI) tab on pp. DI·42–DI·51.

Whole Group
- Fluency

Language Arts
- Grammar
- Writing
- Spelling
- Research/Inquiry
- Speaking/Listening/Viewing

Use *My Sidewalks on Reading Street* for Tier III intensive reading intervention.

DAY 1

On-Level	Strategic Intervention	Advanced
Teacher-Led Page DI·43	**Teacher-Led** Page DI·42	**Teacher-Led** Page DI·43
• Develop Concept Vocabulary • **Read** On-Level Reader *Paul Revere and the American Revolution*	• Reinforce Concepts • **Read** Below-Level Reader *Paul Revere's Midnight Ride*	• **Read** Advanced Reader *The National Guard: ...* • Independent Extension Activity

(i) Independent Activities

While you meet with small groups, have the rest of the class...

- Visit the Reading/Library Center
- Listen to the Background Building Audio
- Finish Write to Read, p. 230
- Complete Practice Book pp. 93–94
- Visit Cross-Curricular Centers

DAY 2

On-Level	Strategic Intervention	Advanced
Teacher-Led Pages 236–241	**Teacher-Led** Page DI·44	**Teacher-Led** Page DI·45
• **Read** *The Midnight Ride of Paul Revere*	• Practice Lesson Vocabulary • Read Multisyllabic Words • **Read** or Listen to *The Midnight Ride of Paul Revere*	• Extend Vocabulary • **Read** *The Midnight Ride of Paul Revere*

(i) Independent Activities

While you meet with small groups, have the rest of the class...

- Visit the Reading/Library Center
- Listen to the AudioText for *The Midnight Ride of Paul Revere*
- Finish Words to Write, p. 233
- Complete Practice Book pp. 95–96
- Write in their Strategy Response Logs, pp. 234, 241
- Visit Cross-Curricular Centers
- Work on inquiry projects

DAY 3

On-Level	Strategic Intervention	Advanced
Teacher-Led Pages 242–247	**Teacher-Led** Page DI·46	**Teacher-Led** Page DI·47
• **Read** *The Midnight Ride of Paul Revere*	• Practice Sequence and Graphic Organizers • **Read** or Listen to *The Midnight Ride of Paul Revere*	• Extend Sequence and Graphic Organizers • **Read** *The Midnight Ride of Paul Revere*

(i) Independent Activities

While you meet with small groups, have the rest of the class...

- Visit the Reading/Library Center
- Listen to the AudioText for *The Midnight Ride of Paul Revere*
- Write in their Strategy Response Logs, p. 246
- Finish Look Back and Write, p. 248
- Complete Practice Book p. 97
- Visit Cross-Curricular Centers
- Work on inquiry projects

① Begin with whole class skill and strategy instruction.

② Meet with small groups to provide differentiated instruction.

③ Gather the whole class back together for fluency and language arts.

DAY 4

On-Level	Strategic Intervention	Advanced
Teacher-Led Pages 250–253	**Teacher-Led** Page DI · 48	**Teacher-Led** Page DI · 49
• **Read** "Revolutionary War Women"	• Practice Retelling • **Read** or Listen to "Revolutionary War Women"	• **Read** "Revolutionary War Women" • Genre Study

ⓘ Independent Activities

While you meet with small groups, have the rest of the class…

• Visit the Reading/Library Center
• Listen to the AudioText for "Revolutionary War Women"
• Visit the Writing/Vocabulary Center

• Finish Writing Across Texts, p. 253
• Visit Cross-Curricular Centers
• Work on inquiry projects

DAY 5

On-Level	Strategic Intervention	Advanced
Teacher-Led Page DI · 51	**Teacher-Led** Page DI · 50	**Teacher-Led** Page DI · 51
• **Reread** Leveled Reader *Paul Revere and the American Revolution* • Retell *Paul Revere and the American Revolution*	• **Reread** Leveled Reader *Paul Revere's Midnight Ride* • Retell *Paul Revere's Midnight Ride*	• **Reread** Leveled Reader *The National Guard: Modern Minutemen* • Share Extension Activity

ⓘ Independent Activities

While you meet with small groups, have the rest of the class…

• Visit the Reading/Library Center
• Complete Practice Book pp. 98–100

• Visit Cross-Curricular Centers
• Work on inquiry projects

Grouping Place English language learners in the groups that correspond to their reading abilities in English.

Use the appropriate Leveled Reader or other text at students' instructional level.

Tip Send home the appropriate Multilingual Summary of the main selection on Day 1.

Take It to the NET™ ONLINE
PearsonSuccessNet.com

Peter Afflerbach
For analysis of think-aloud studies and what they show about comprehension, see a summary of the book *Verbal Protocols of Reading* by M. Pressley and Scott Foresman author P. Afflerbach.

TEACHER TALK

New literacies are skills and strategies needed to successfully use information technologies, such as CD-ROMs, the Internet, and e-mail.

Looking Ahead

Be sure to schedule time for students to work on the unit inquiry project "Doing the Right Thing." This week students present speeches about the information they have learned about how charities or service groups help the communities they serve.

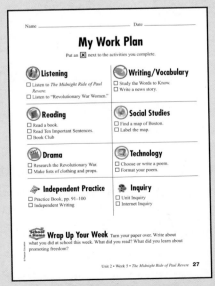

Name _____	Date _____

My Work Plan

Put an ☒ next to the activities you complete.

🎧 Listening
☐ Listen to *The Midnight Ride of Paul Revere*.
☐ Listen to "Revolutionary War Women."

✏️ Writing/Vocabulary
☐ Study the Words to Know.
☐ Write a news story.

📖 Reading
☐ Read a book.
☐ Read Ten Important Sentences.
☐ Book Club

🌎 Social Studies
☐ Find a map of Boston.
☐ Label the map.

🎭 Drama
☐ Research the Revolutionary War.
☐ Make lists of clothing and props.

💻 Technology
☐ Choose or write a poem.
☐ Format your poem.

✍️ Independent Practice
☐ Practice Book, pp. 91–100
☐ Independent Writing

🔍 Inquiry
☐ Unit Inquiry
☐ Internet Inquiry

🏠 Wrap Up Your Week Turn your paper over. Write about what you did at school this week. What did you read? What did you learn about promoting freedom?

Unit 2 • Week 5 • *The Midnight Ride of Paul Revere* **27**

▲ **Group-Time Survival Guide** p. 27, Weekly Contract

The Midnight Ride of Paul Revere **230g**

☑ Customize Your Plan *by Strand*

ORAL LANGUAGE

Concept Development

SOCIAL STUDIES

How can people promote freedom?

CONCEPT VOCABULARY
battle   freedom   Monmouth

BUILD

☐ **Question of the Week** Introduce and discuss the question of the week. This week students will read a variety of texts and work on projects related to the concept *promoting freedom*. Post the question for students to refer to throughout the week. **DAY 1** *230d*

☐ **Read Aloud** Read aloud "Molly Pitcher." Then begin a web to build concepts and concept vocabulary related to this week's lesson and the unit theme, Doing the Right Thing. Introduce the concept words *battle, freedom,* and *Monmouth* and have students place them on the web. Display the web for use throughout the week. **DAY 1** *230l–230m*

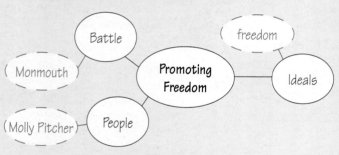

DEVELOP

☐ **Question of the Day** Use the prompts from the Weekly Plan to engage students in conversations related to this week's reading and the unit theme. **EVERY DAY** *230d–230e*

☐ **Concept Vocabulary Web** Revisit the Promoting Freedom Concept Web and encourage students to add concept words from their reading and life experiences. **DAY 2** *241,* **DAY 3** *247*

CONNECT

☐ **Looking Back** Revisit the Promoting Freedom Concept Web and discuss how it relates to this week's lesson and the unit theme. **DAY 5** *253c*

CHECK

☐ **Concept Vocabulary Web** Use the Promoting Freedom Concept Web to check students' understanding of the concept vocabulary words *battle, freedom, and Monmouth.*
DAY 1 *230l,* **DAY 5** *253c*

VOCABULARY

STRATEGY WORD STRUCTURE
The inflected endings *-s, -ed,* and *-ing* may be added to a verb to help you figure out the meaning of unfamiliar verbs.

LESSON VOCABULARY
fate   magnified
fearless   somber
glimmer   steed
lingers

TEACH

☐ **Words to Know** Give students the opportunity to tell what they already know about this week's lesson vocabulary words. Then discuss word meaning. **DAY 1** *232b*

☐ **Vocabulary Strategy Lesson** Use the vocabulary strategy lesson in the Student Edition to introduce and model this week's strategy, *word structure.*
DAY 2 *232-233*

Vocabulary Strategy Lesson

PRACTICE/APPLY

☐ **Leveled Text** Read the lesson vocabulary in the context of leveled text. **DAY 1** *LR37-LR45*

☐ **Words in Context** Read the lesson vocabulary and apply *word structure* in the context of *The Midnight Ride of Paul Revere.* **DAY 2** *234-241,* **DAY 3** *242-248*

Leveled Readers

☐ **Writing/Vocabulary Center** Write a headline and lead paragraph about the midnight ride of Paul Revere. **ANY DAY** *230k*

Main Selection—Poetry

☐ **Homework** Practice Book pp. 94–95. **DAY 1** *232b,* **DAY 2** *233*

☐ **Word Play** Have students work with partners to choose three words from *The Midnight Ride of Paul Revere* and brainstorm as many rhyming words as they can for each word. **ANY DAY** *253c*

ASSESS

☐ **Selection Test** Use the Selection Test to determine students' understanding of the lesson vocabulary words. **DAY 3**

RETEACH/REVIEW

☐ **Reteach Lesson** If necessary, use this lesson to reteach and review *word structure.* **DAY 5** *253c*

① Use assessment data to determine your instructional focus.

② Preview this week's instruction by strand.

③ Choose instructional activities that meet the needs of your classroom.

COMPREHENSION

SKILL SEQUENCE The sequence of events is the order in which they take place, from first to last. Clue words such as *first, next,* and *then* may show sequence in a story or article.

STRATEGY GRAPHIC ORGANIZERS Creating charts, making lists, or setting up a time line can help you organize your thoughts as you read. Using graphic organizers can help you keep track of the sequence of events.

TEACH

❑ **Skill/Strategy Lesson** Use the skill/strategy lesson in the Student Edition to introduce and model *sequence* and *graphic organizers.* **DAY 1** 230-231

❑ **Extend Skills** Teach personification. **ANY DAY** 253b

Skill/Strategy Lesson

PRACTICE/APPLY

❑ **Leveled Text** Apply *sequence* and *graphic organizers* to read leveled text. **DAY 1** LR37-LR45

❑ **Skills and Strategies in Context** Read *The Midnight Ride of Paul Revere,* using the Guiding Comprehension questions to apply *sequence* and *graphic organizers.* **DAY 2** 234-241, **DAY 3** 242-248

Leveled Readers

❑ **Skills and Strategies in Context** Read "Revolutionary War Women," guiding students as they apply *sequence* and *graphic organizers.* Then have students discuss and write across texts. **DAY 4** 250-253

Main Selection—Poetry

❑ **Homework** Practice Book pp. 93, 97, 98. **DAY 1** 231, **DAY 3** 247, **DAY 5** 253b

Paired Selection—Poetry

❑ **Fresh Reads for Differentiated Test Practice** Have students practice *sequence* with a new passage. **DAY 3**

ASSESS

❑ **Selection Test** Determine students' understanding of the selection and their use of *sequence.* **DAY 3**

❑ **Retell** Have students retell *The Midnight Ride of Paul Revere.* **DAY 3** 248-249

RETEACH/REVIEW

❑ **Reteach Lesson** If necessary, reteach and review *sequence.* **DAY 5** 253b

FLUENCY

SKILL TONE OF VOICE Adjusting your tone of voice gives you the ability to show different emotions as you read. Emotions such as desperation or suspense or other emotions are easily conveyed through a changing tone of voice.

TEACH

❑ **Read Aloud** Model fluent reading by rereading "Molly Pitcher." Focus on this week's fluency skill, tone of voice. **DAY 1** 230l-230m, 253a

PRACTICE/APPLY

❑ **Echo Reading** Read aloud selected paragraphs from *The Midnight Ride of Paul Revere,* emphasizing how your voice changes as you move from narrative to dialogue to description. Then practice as a class by doing three echo readings of the selected paragraphs. **DAY 2** 253a, **DAY 3** 253a

❑ **Partner Reading** Have partners practice reading aloud, reading with changing inflections to reflect different characters' emotions, and offering each other feedback. As students reread, monitor their progress toward their individual fluency goals. **DAY 4** 253a

❑ **Listening Center** Have students follow along with the AudioText for this week's selections. **ANY DAY** 230j

❑ **Reading/Library Center** Have students reread a selection of their choice. **ANY DAY** 230j

❑ **Fluency Coach** Have students use Fluency Coach to listen to fluent readings or practice reading on their own. **ANY DAY**

ASSESS

❑ **Check Fluency** WCPM Do a one-minute timed reading, paying special attention to this week's skill—tone of voice. Provide feedback for each student. **DAY 5** 253a

☑ Customize Your Plan *by Strand*

GRAMMAR

SKILL SUBJECT-VERB AGREEMENT The subject and verb of a sentence must work together, or agree in number. When a singular subject takes a present tense verb, that verb usually ends in *-s* or *-es*. When a plural subject takes a present tense verb, that verb usually does not end in *-s* or *-es*.

TEACH

☐ **Grammar Transparency 10** Use Grammar Transparency 10 to teach subject-verb agreement. **DAY 1** *253e*

Grammar Transparency 10

PRACTICE/APPLY

☐ **Develop the Concept** Review the concept of subject-verb agreement and provide guided practice. **DAY 2** *253e*

☐ **Apply to Writing** Have students review something they have written and apply subject-verb agreement. **DAY 3** *253f*

☐ **Test Preparation** Examine common errors in subject-verb agreement to prepare for standardized tests. **DAY 4** *253f*

☐ **Homework** Grammar and Writing Practice Book pp. 37–39. **DAY 2** *253e*, **DAY 3** *253f*, **DAY 4** *253f*

ASSESS

☐ **Cumulative Review** Use Grammar and Writing Practice Book p. 40. **DAY 5** *253f*

RETEACH/REVIEW

☐ **Daily Fix-It** Have students find and correct errors in grammar, spelling, and punctuation. **EVERY DAY** *253e-253f*

☐ **The Grammar and Writing Book** Use pp. 104–107 of The Grammar and Writing Book to extend instruction for subject-verb agreement. **ANY DAY**

The Grammar and Writing Book

WRITING

Trait of the Week

ORGANIZATION/PARAGRAPHS Good writers have organization to their writing. Their ideas are written in an order that helps readers with understanding and that shows connections among those ideas.

TEACH

☐ **Writing Transparency 10A** Use the model to introduce and discuss the Trait of the Week. **DAY 1** *253g*

☐ **Writing Transparency 10B** Use the transparency to show students how organization can improve their writing. **DAY 2** *253g*

Writing Transparency 10A **Writing Transparency 10B**

PRACTICE/APPLY

☐ **Write Now** Examine the model on Student Edition p. 249. Then have students write their own interview. **DAY 3** 249, *253h*, **DAY 4** 253h

> **Prompt** *The Midnight Ride of Paul Revere* tells about a famous American. Think about another famous American. Now write an interview with that person.

Write Now p. 249

☐ **Writing/Vocabulary Center** Write a headline and lead paragraph about the midnight ride of Paul Revere. **ANY DAY** *230k*

ASSESS

☐ **Writing Trait Rubric** Use the rubric to evaluate students' writing. **DAY 4** *253h*

RETEACH/REVIEW

☐ **The Grammar and Writing Book** Use pp. 104–109 of The Grammar and Writing Book to extend instruction for subject-verb agreement, organization, and interviews. **ANY DAY**

The Grammar and Writing Book

SPELLING

GENERALIZATION FINAL SYLLABLES ER, AR, OR Final syllables *er*, *ar*, and *or* often sound alike even when they are spelled differently: *danger, tractor, dollar.* Some sounds can be spelled in different ways.

TEACH

❑ **Pretest** Give the pretest for words with final syllables *er, ar, or.* Guide students in self-correcting their pretests and correcting any misspellings. **DAY 1** *253i*

❑ **Think and Practice** Connect spelling to the phonics generalization for using final syllables *er, ar, or.* **DAY 2** *253i*

PRACTICE/APPLY

❑ **Connect to Writing** Have students use spelling words to write facts about an historic person. Then review frequently misspelled words: *another, we're.* **DAY 3** *253j*

❑ **Homework** Word Study and Spelling Practice Book pp. 37–40. **EVERY DAY**

RETEACH/REVIEW

❑ **Review** Review spelling words to prepare for the posttest. Then provide students with a spelling strategy—steps for spelling new words. **DAY 4** *253j*

ASSESS

❑ **Posttest** Use dictation sentences to give the posttest for words with final syllables *er, ar, or.* **DAY 5** *253j*

Spelling Words

1. danger	8. surrender	15. caterpillar
2. wander*	9. solar	16. rumor
3. tractor	10. sticker	17. glimmer
4. dollar	11. locker	18. linger
5. harbor	12. helicopter	19. sensor
6. eager*	13. pillar	20. alligator
7. eraser	14. refrigerator	

Challenge Words

21. numerator	23. ancestor	25. denominator
22. collector	24. counselor	

*Word from the selection

RESEARCH AND INQUIRY

❑ **Internet Inquiry** Have students conduct an Internet inquiry on promoting freedom. **EVERY DAY** *253k*

❑ **Illustration/Caption** Review the purposes of illustrations and captions and discuss how students can use these resources to better understand text. **DAY 5** *253l*

❑ **Unit Inquiry** Allow time for students to present the information they have learned about how charities or service groups help the communities they serve. **ANY DAY** *141*

SPEAKING AND LISTENING

❑ **Radio Feature Story** Have students write a biographical feature story on one main event in a person's life. Stress that the biographical feature story will be retold from the subject's point of view to put a new spin on the story that will capture their audience's attention. **DAY 5** *253d*

❑ **Listen to a CD** Have students listen to the audio CD of *The Midnight Ride of Paul Revere* and answer questions. **DAY 5** *253d*

Resources for
Differentiated Instruction

LEVELED READERS

▶ **Comprehension**
- ◎ **Skill** Sequence
- ◎ **Strategy** Graphic Organizers

▶ **Lesson Vocabulary**
- ◎ Word Structure

fate · fearless · glimmer · lingers · magnified · somber · steed

▶ **Social Studies Standards**
- Colonial America
- U.S. History
- American Revolution
- American Patriots

Leveled Reader Database
ONLINE
PearsonSuccessNet.com

Use the Online Database of over 600 books to
- Download and print additional copies of this week's leveled readers.
- Listen to the readers being read online.
- Search for more titles focused on this week's skills, topic, and content.

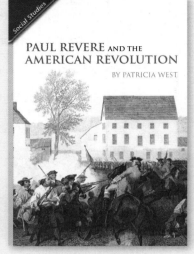

On-Level Reader

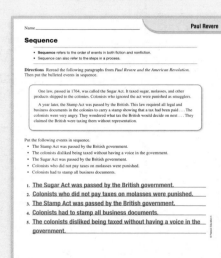

On-Level Practice TE p. LR41

Paul Revere

Sequence
- **Sequence** refers to the order of events in both fiction and nonfiction.
- Sequence can also refer to steps in a process.

Directions Reread the following paragraphs from *Paul Revere and the American Revolution.* Then put the bulleted events in sequence.

One law, passed in 1764, was called the Sugar Act. It taxed sugar, molasses, and other products shipped to the colonies. Colonists who ignored the act were punished as smugglers.

A year later, the Stamp Act was passed by the British. This law required all legal and business documents in the colonies to carry a stamp showing that a tax had been paid . . . The colonists were very angry. They wondered what tax the British would decide on next . . . They claimed the British were taxing them without representation.

Put the following events in sequence.
- The Stamp Act was passed by the British government.
- The colonists disliked being taxed without having a voice in the government.
- The Sugar Act was passed by the British government.
- Colonists who did not pay taxes on molasses were punished.
- Colonists had to stamp all business documents.

1. The Sugar Act was passed by the British government.
2. Colonists who did not pay taxes on molasses were punished.
3. The Stamp Act was passed by the British government.
4. Colonists had to stamp all business documents.
5. The colonists disliked being taxed without having a voice in the government.

Paul Revere

Vocabulary
Directions Draw a line from each word to its synonym.

Check the Words You Know
fate · fearless · glimmer · lingers · magnified · somber · steed

1. fate — increased
2. fearless — unafraid
3. glimmer — uncontrolled event
4. lingers — horse
5. magnified — faint light
6. somber — stays
7. steed — solemn

Directions Write a paragraph about the beginning of the American Revolution. Use as many vocabulary words as you can.

Possible response: Maybe it was *fate* that led the colonists and the British to fight against one another. Their early battles over taxation ended up being *magnified* to the point where one *fearless* soldier was pitted against the other—the British on his *steed*, and the colonist often on foot. The colonists took the *somber* news of taxation badly, because they did not even have the *glimmer* of a voice in the British government. The memory of their hard-won battle *lingers*, as we remember their contribution.

On-Level Practice TE p. LR42

Below-Level Reader

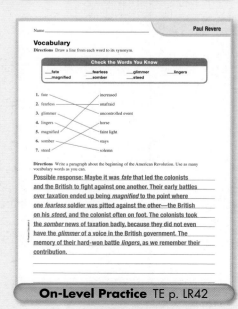

Below-Level Practice TE p. LR38

Paul Revere's Ride

Sequence
- **Sequence** refers to the order of events in both fiction and nonfiction.
- Sequence can also refer to steps in a process.

Directions Reread the following paragraphs from *Paul Revere's Midnight Ride.* Then put the bulleted events in sequence.

Revere woke Adams and Hancock and told them about the British. Hearing the news, the two men planned to return to Boston within a few hours.

Then Revere met with William Dawes to decide what to do next. They both would ride on to Concord. There they would be able to help in the fight against the British. Along the way, Revere and Dawes met Dr. Samuel Prescott. Dr. Prescott joined them, and the three men rode on together.

- Adams and Hancock decided to go to Boston.
- Dawes and Revere started their trip to Concord.
- Revere woke Adams and Hancock.
- Revere met with William Dawes.
- Dr. Prescott met Dawes and Revere on their way.

1. Revere woke Adams and Hancock.
2. Adams and Hancock decided to go to Boston.
3. Revere met with William Dawes.
4. Dawes and Revere started their trip to Concord.
5. Dr. Prescott met Dawes and Revere on their way.

Paul Revere's Ride

Vocabulary
Directions Draw a line from each word to its definition.

Check the Words You Know
fate · fearless · glimmer · lingers · magnified · somber · steed

1. fate — lasts; stays around or near
2. fearless — solemn or serious; sad
3. glimmer — something that cannot be controlled
4. lingers — made to appear larger
5. magnified — shine with a faint light
6. somber — not afraid; brave
7. steed — horse or other riding animal

Directions Write a paragraph about Paul Revere's ride. Use as many vocabulary words as you can.
Possible response given.
It was Paul Revere's *fate* to end up riding his way into the history books. He took his responsibility to help our nation with a *somber* attitude, realizing that the *glimmer* of liberty rested partly on his shoulders. With a *fearless* manner, he rode into the night to warn American leaders. Riding on his *steed*, he spread the word that the British were on their way. Although his legend has been *magnified* by the passing of time, the importance of his ride *lingers* even today.

Below-Level Practice TE p. LR39

Advanced

The National Guard: Modern Minutemen
by Patricia Walsh

Advanced Reader

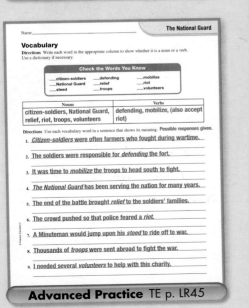

Advanced Practice TE p. LR44

Advanced Practice TE p. LR45

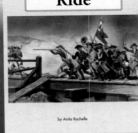

After the Midnight Ride
by Anita Rochelle

ELL Reader

ELL Poster 10

Teacher's Edition Notes
ELL notes throughout this lesson support instruction and reference additional resources at point of use.

Teaching Guide
pp. 64–70, 230–231
- Multilingual summaries of the main selection
- Comprehension lesson
- Vocabulary strategies and word cards
- ELL Reader 5.2.5 lesson

ELL and Transition Handbook

Ten Important Sentences
- Key ideas from every selection in the Student Edition
- Activities to build sentence power

More Reading

Readers' Theater Anthology
- Fluency practice
- Five scripts to build fluency
- Poetry for oral interpretation

Leveled Trade Books

- Extended reading tied to the unit concept
- Lessons in the Trade Book Library Teaching Guide

School + Home

Homework
- Family Times Newsletter
- ELL Multilingual Selection Summaries

Take-Home Books
- Leveled Readers

The Midnight Ride of Paul Revere

Cross-Curricular Centers

Listening

Listen to the
Selections

MATERIALS | SINGLES
CD player, headphones, AudioText CD, student book

LISTEN TO LITERATURE Listen to *The Midnight Ride of Paul Revere* and "Revolutionary War Women" as you follow or read along in your book. Pay special attention to the sequence of events in both selections.

If there is anything you don't understand, you can listen again to any section.

Reading/Library

Read It
Again!

MATERIALS | SINGLES PAIRS GROUPS
Collection of books for self-selected reading, reading logs, student book

Select a book you have already read. Record the title of the book in your reading log. You may want to read with a partner.

Choose from the following:

- **Leveled Readers**
- **ELL Readers**
- **Stories Written by Classmates**
- **Books from the Library**
- *The Midnight Ride of Paul Revere*

TEN IMPORTANT SENTENCES
Read the Ten Important Sentences for *The Midnight Ride of Paul Revere*. Then locate the sentences in the student book.

BOOK CLUB Look at "Meet Authors" on p. 771 of the student book to set up an author study of Henry Wadsworth Longfellow. Read other poems by Longfellow and get together with a group to share your favorites.

Drama

Set the
Stage

MATERIALS | PAIRS GROUPS
Writing and art materials, books about the Revolutionary War, Internet access

Imagine that the poem *The Midnight Ride of Paul Revere* is being performed as a play. You are responsible for costumes and props.

1. Search the Internet using a student-friendly research engine or use other research materials for images of people from the Revolutionary War period.
2. List the items of clothing you'll need for your actors.
3. List ten props you'll need for the play.

EARLY FINISHERS Sketch a scene from the play featuring props and costume.

Props
1. Lantern
2.
3.
4.
5.
6.
7.
8.
9.
10.

Scott Foresman Reading Street Centers Survival Kit

Use *The Midnight Ride* materials from the Reading Street Centers Survival Kit to organize this week's centers.

Writing/ Vocabulary

Write a News Story

MATERIALS — SINGLES PAIRS
Writing materials

Imagine you are a newspaper reporter breaking the big story about the midnight ride of Paul Revere.

1. Write an attention-grabbing headline for your article. Think about the most important message you want to convey.
2. Write the lead paragraph for the article that addresses some of the 5 Ws: who, what, when, where, why.

EARLY FINISHERS With a partner, role-play interviewing Paul Revere, a British soldier, or a colonist reacting to the midnight ride.

The British Are Coming

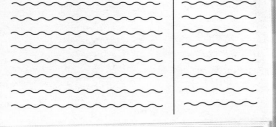

Social Studies

Make a Map

MATERIALS — PAIRS
Map of greater Boston area, writing and art materials

Work with a partner to make a map of Paul Revere's famous ride.

1. Find a map of the present-day greater Boston area.
2. Label the map with key events and locations of Paul Revere's ride.
3. Display the map in your classroom.

EARLY FINISHERS Illustrate your map with pictures representing key events from the poem.

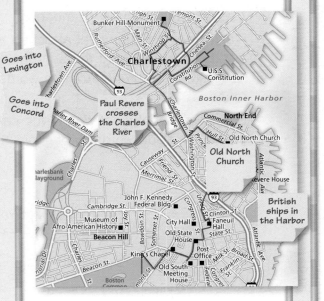

Technology

Format a Poem

MATERIALS — SINGLES
Word processing program, printer

Experiment with formats for publishing a poem.

1. Choose a favorite poem or write a short poem of your own.
2. Use a word processing program to write the poem using your standard format.
3. Change the margin widths, type font, size, and line breaks until you create an image with your words that reflects the poem.
4. Print your poem with your teacher's permission.

EARLY FINISHERS Print another version of your poem formatted differently. Compare the two versions to see which you prefer.

My Favorite Tree

My favorite tree
was full and green, with leaves
clustered together, no space in
between. Then in autumn, when
the air turned cold, the leaves
they changed from green to gold.
And they began to fall,
until
none,
were
left,
at all.

ALL CENTERS

OBJECTIVES

- Build vocabulary by finding words related to the lesson concept.
- Listen to understand sequence.

Concept Vocabulary

battle a fight between opposing armed forces

freedom power to do, say, or think as you please

Monmouth New Jersey site of an important Revolutionary War battle

Monitor Progress

Check Vocabulary

If...	then... review the
students are unable to place words on the web,	lesson concept. Place the words on the web and provide additional words for practice, such as *gunner* and *soldier*.

SUCCESS PREDICTOR

DAY 1 Grouping Options

Reading

Whole Group
Introduce and discuss the Question of the Week. Then use pp. 230l–232b.

Group Time
Differentiated Instruction
Read this week's Leveled Readers. See pp. 230h–230i for the small group lesson plan.

Whole Group
Use p. 253a.

Language Arts
Use pp. 253e–253k.

Build Concepts

FLUENCY

MODEL TONE OF VOICE As you read "Molly Pitcher," use your tone of voice to model reading with expression. Show desperation or other emotions in places like the quotation in the first paragraph.

LISTENING COMPREHENSION

After reading "Molly Pitcher," use the following questions to assess listening comprehension.

1. **Which of these events happened first: Molly hears the cries of fallen soldiers or Molly gives the thirsty soldiers water to drink?** *(Molly hears cries of fallen soldiers.)* **Sequence**

2. **What characteristic do Molly and the soldiers have in common?** *(Possible response: Both are brave.)* **Compare and Contrast**

BUILD CONCEPT VOCABULARY

Start a web to build concepts and vocabulary related to this week's lesson and the unit theme.

- Draw the Promoting Freedom Concept Web.

- Read the sentence with the word *freedom* again. Ask students to pronounce *freedom* and discuss its meaning.

- Place *freedom* in an oval attached to Ideals. Explain that *freedom* is related to this concept. Read the sentences in which *battle* and *Monmouth* appear. Have students pronounce the words, place them on the web, and provide reasons.

- Brainstorm additional words and categories for the web. Keep the web on display and add words throughout the week.

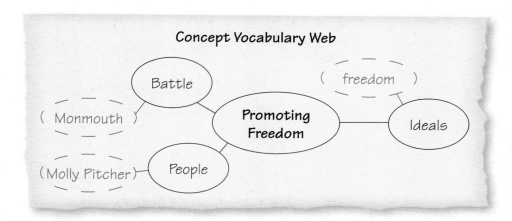

Concept Vocabulary Web

Battle — freedom — Monmouth — Promoting Freedom — Ideals — Molly Pitcher — People

Molly Pitcher

by Jan Gleiter

On one hot June day in 1778 American soldiers were ordered to attack resting British troops in Monmouth, New Jersey. A young woman named Molly traveled with the American troops, working at their camps. The following passage describes a battlefield in the Revolutionary War and tells how one woman found a way to help fight for the freedom of her beloved country.

In between the sounds of battle, Molly could hear cries. "Water! Water!" Men were falling, falling from the heat.

Molly wasn't a gunner. She wasn't a soldier of any kind. But she was as brave as any of them, and she knew when she was needed.

Picking up her long skirts, she ran. She grabbed up a pitcher and raced through the trees to a spring. She filled the pitcher with cold, clear water and hurried back toward the fighting.

Molly ran out onto the battlefield. The air was thick with the smell of gunpowder. A musket ball whizzed past her ear. But all she heard was the cry for water.

A soldier kneeled in the dirt, pouring gunpowder into his musket. His hair stuck to his forehead, and his throat was dry with dust. Suddenly a woman knelt beside him. She held a pitcher of cool water to his lips. He drank deeply, looking into the steady eyes so close to his own. And then, before he could even thank her, she was gone. He watched her move ahead, crouching and running to another thirsty soldier, and another.

Molly moved quickly. She could tell at a glance which men were most in need, and she went to them first.

Time and again, she ran back to the spring. The safety of the trees called to her. She needed to stop. She needed to be safe for awhile. But she could not, not while American soldiers were fighting for American freedom. Not while American men needed the bravery of an American woman.

Now, at the Battle of Monmouth, Molly was more a part of the fight than she had ever been before. Once, a cannonball slammed into a wagon. A flying piece of broken wood knocked her to the ground. Jumping to her feet, she snatched up the pitcher. She hardly noticed the fall except that it had spilled her precious water. She raced, again, for the spring.

Activate Prior Knowledge

Before listening to the Read Aloud, have students discuss ways people have fought for their freedom and the reasons that they have done so.

Set Purpose

Read aloud the title and have students predict what the selection will be about.

Read the introduction. Have students listen to determine the author's purpose and to evaluate how well the author meets his purpose.

Creative Response

Have students create and perform monologues in which Molly looks back on the Revolutionary War and describes her experiences. *Drama*

Access Content Before reading, share this summary: Molly traveled with the American troops during the Revolutionary War. During a battle, the troops were hot and thirsty. Molly risked her life filling a pitcher of water for the soldiers.

Note to the Teacher During the Revolutionary War, the many women who helped on the battlefield were often referred to as "Molly Pitcher." It is possible that the stories of these brave women have been combined into the tale of one courageous woman at the Battle of Monmouth.

Homework Send home this week's Family Times newsletter.

SKILLS ⟷ STRATEGIES IN CONTEXT

Sequence Graphic Organizers

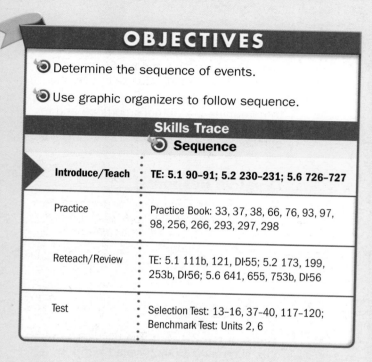

OBJECTIVES

- Determine the sequence of events.
- Use graphic organizers to follow sequence.

Skills Trace
Sequence

Introduce/Teach	TE: 5.1 90–91; 5.2 230–231; 5.6 726–727
Practice	Practice Book: 33, 37, 38, 66, 76, 93, 97, 98, 256, 266, 293, 297, 298
Reteach/Review	TE: 5.1 111b, 121, DI·55; 5.2 173, 199, 253b, DI·56; 5.6 641, 655, 753b, DI·56
Test	Selection Test: 13–16, 37–40, 117–120; Benchmark Test: Units 2, 6

INTRODUCE

Write the following on the board: *Snapped on my skis. Put on some warm socks. Headed for the ski slope. Slipped my feet into my boots.*

Have students order the events. *(Put on some warm socks. Slipped my feet into my boots. Snapped on my skis. Headed for the ski slope.)*

Have students read the information on p. 230. Explain the following:

- Sequence is the order in which events happen. Keeping track of the sequence of events will help you better understand what you read.
- Graphic organizers, such as time lines and story sequence charts, can help you keep track of the sequence of events.

Use Skill Transparency 10 to teach sequence and graphic organizers.

Comprehension

Skill
Sequence

Strategy
Graphic Organizers

Sequence

- The sequence of events is the order in which they take place, from first to last.
- Clue words such as *first*, *next*, and *then* may show sequence in a story or article, but not always. Other clues are dates and time of day.
- Two events can happen at the same time. *While* and *at the same time* are clue words.

Strategy: Graphic Organizers

Active readers often create graphic organizers to help them understand and remember what they read. A time line like the one below can help you keep track of the sequence of events.

Date			Date
First Event	Second Event	Third Event	Final Event

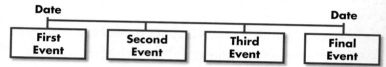

Write to Read

1. Read "Before the Midnight Ride." Make a graphic organizer like the one above to show the sequence of events in the article.

2. Jot down three questions about the sequence of events. Look for answers in the article and do library research. Write your questions and answers.

230

Strategic Intervention

Sequence Write several sequence clue words, such as *now*, *then*, *first*, *during*, *next*, *after*, *while*, *finally*, on the board. Invite volunteers to tell in order what they did upon arriving at school today. Ask them to use clue words to help the other students keep track of the sequence. Suggest that students use a time line to record the events.

Access Content

Beginning/Intermediate For a Picture It! lesson on sequence, see the ELL Teaching Guide, pp. 64–65.

Advanced Before students read "Before the Midnight Ride," have them skim the selection and jot down the dates on a time line. As they read, ask them to write what happened on each date. Then students can use the time line to retell the story in sequence.

Before the Midnight Ride

Paul Revere was born in December of 1734 in Boston, Massachusetts. He went to school at the North Writing School. His childhood was much like that of other boys at the time.

When Paul was a teenager, he was paid to ring the bells at a church. At the same time, his father was teaching him to work with silver. Paul was a silversmith until he joined the army in 1756. After his army service, Paul married Sarah Orne and returned to silverworking. He became one of the best-known silversmiths in America.

In the 1760s and 1770s, trouble arose between the American colonies and England, and Paul became involved. He joined a group called the Sons of Liberty. They believed that the colonies should be free from England. In December of 1773 he helped throw tea into the harbor because the tea was taxed by England. This protest became known as the Boston Tea Party.

After that, Paul Revere became an express rider for the Massachusetts government. He rode a horse to bring news from Boston to the other colonies. He was at this job on that day in 1775, when his most famous ride took place.

1 Skill What should be the first event on a time line about Paul Revere?

2 Strategy Here's a good spot to ask yourself: "What two things were going on in Paul's life when he was a teenager?"

3 Skill Dates in this paragraph are clues to events you can put on your time line.

4 Strategy Ask yourself: "What were all the important events in Paul Revere's life? Which events were happening at the same time as others?"

231

Available as **Skill Transparency** 10

Sequence

- The **sequence** of events is the order in which they take place, from first to last.
- Clue words such as *first, next,* and *then* may show sequence in a story or article, but not always. Other clues are dates and times of day.
- Sometimes two events happen at the same time. Clue words that show this are *meanwhile* and *in that same year.*

Directions Read the following passage and complete the time line below.

The Reverend Martin Luther King Jr. is one of the heroes of freedom in America. In 1948, at the age of 19, King graduated from Morehouse College. He is best known, however, for his role in the civil rights movement. In 1955, he helped organize the Montgomery Bus Boycott. In 1963, he led the Freedom March on Washington, D.C. Because of his frequent participation in civil rights protests, he was arrested 30 times. In 1964, he was awarded the Nobel Peace Prize. Dr. King was assassinated in 1968.

Events in Martin Luther King's Life

1. King became a minister
2. graduated from Morehouse College
3. Montgomery Bus Boycott
4. led Freedom March
5. won Nobel Peace prize
6. Dr. King assassinated

Date   1948   1955   1963   1964   1968

5. Which two events happened at nearly the same time? How can you tell?
The first two events both occurred in 1948; The passage uses the words "That same year."

School + Home Home Activity Your child read a short passage and made a time line of key events in the life of Dr. Martin Luther King Jr. Talk with your child about some of the important events in your own life. Create a time line to show the sequence of those events.

▲ **Practice Book** p. 93

TEACH

1 SKILL Determine the first event in the sequence of Paul Revere's life.

 MODEL From the first paragraph, I know that this article is about Paul Revere's life. His birth in December 1734, is the very first event of his life. This is what I will record in the first spot on a time line.

2 STRATEGY Model how self-questioning can help determine where events should be recorded on a time line.

 MODEL In paragraph 2, the phrase *At the same time* tells me two things are happening at once. I ask myself, "What two things are happening?" I reread to find out that as a teenager, Paul rings the church bells and learns to be a silversmith. I will record both these events on the time line.

PRACTICE AND ASSESS

3 SKILL There are several dates in the third paragraph. Help students see how they can use these dates to identify the order of events in Paul Revere's life.

4 STRATEGY Students should use their time lines to recount the important events in Paul Revere's life. The time lines will make it easy to see which events happened at the same time.

WRITE Have students complete steps 1 and 2 of the Write to Read activity. You might consider using this as a whole class activity.

Monitor Progress

🎯 Main Idea

If... students are unable to complete **Write to Read** on p. 230,	then... use Practice Book p. 93 to provide additional practice.

The Midnight Ride of Paul Revere

ELL

Build Background Use ELL Poster 10 to build background and vocabulary for the lesson concept of American patriots.

▲ **ELL Poster** 10

Build Background

ACTIVATE PRIOR KNOWLEDGE

BEGIN A WORD WEB about Independence Day.

- Ask students to brainstorm words or phrases associated with Independence Day, or the Fourth of July. Use a word web and write "Fourth of July" in the center oval.

- Encourage students to discuss the meaning of the day and discuss ways that they celebrate the holiday. Prompt them to discuss what the Revolutionary War has to do with the Fourth of July. List their ideas on the web and add more ovals if needed.

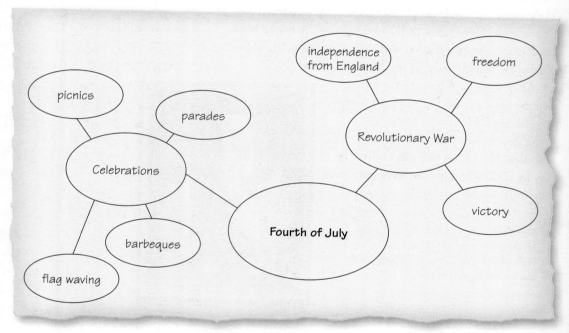

▲ **Graphic Organizer** 16

BACKGROUND BUILDING AUDIO This week's audio is an interview with an expert from the Paul Revere Historic House in Boston. After students listen, discuss with them what they found most interesting.

Background Building Audio

Introduce Vocabulary

USE CONTEXT CLUES

Present the following diary entry to students with words in context:

Dear Diary,
   Father asked me to take the *steed* to the barn after dinner. Our horse, Belle, always *lingers* near the house at sunset. Belle waits there, hoping for some extra grain. Just then, I could see the sun *glimmer* near the horizon. I tried to sneak up on Belle so she wouldn't run off, but the sound of my walking was *magnified* by the new heels on my boots. The minute Belle heard me coming, she galloped away into the *somber* dusk. I yelled a warning for her to stop, but Belle is *fearless* with me. Despite my shouts, she just looked at me as if to say, "Ha! Ha!"
   Just wait until Father comes out for her. Then her *fate* will be sealed!

Read the entry to students and ask them to listen for the seven vocabulary words. ***Activate Prior Knowledge***

Ask students to number a sheet 1–7. Then reread one or two sentences at a time. Encourage students to pay attention to how each vocabulary word is used. Have them write down a synonym or meaning for each vocabulary word. Invite volunteers to explain what context clue helped them figure out each word meaning. ***Context Clues***

Have students keep these word lists. At the end of the week, ask them to revise any word meanings if needed.

Use the Multisyllabic Word Routine on p. DI·1 to help students read multisyllabic words.

Lesson Vocabulary

WORDS TO KNOW

T fate what becomes of someone or something

T fearless without fear; afraid of nothing

T glimmer a faint, unsteady light

T lingers stays on; goes slowly, as if unwilling to leave

T magnified caused something to look larger than it actually is

T somber having deep shadows; dark; gloomy

T steed a horse, especially a riding horse

MORE WORDS TO KNOW

belfry a space in a tower in which bells may be hung

grenadiers members of a specially chosen unit of foot soldiers

stealthy done in a secret manner

T = Tested Word

Vocabulary

Directions Choose the word from the box that best completes each sentence. Write the word on the line.

steed _____ 1. a high-spirited horse

magnified _____ 2. made something look larger

fearless _____ 3. not afraid

glimmer _____ 4. a faint, unsteady light

somber _____ 5. dark or gloomy

Check the Words You Know

___ fate
___ fearless
___ glimmer
___ lingers
___ magnified
___ somber
___ steed

Directions Choose a word from the box that best matches each clue. Write the word on the line.

Some have fought for freedom in a **6. fearless** _____ and inspiring way.

The founding fathers **7. magnified** _____ this kind of commitment when they fought against the British and, some would say, **8. fate** _____ itself.

The **9. glimmer** _____ of hope they felt eventually became reality when they defeated the English King's forces. That dedication to the fight for freedom

10. lingers _____ in all Americans to this day.

Write a Conversation

On a separate sheet of paper, write a short conversation between two members of the colonial army in 1775. Use as many vocabulary words as you can.

Conversations should include words from the vocabulary list and details about colonial life around the time of the Revolutionary War.

Home Activity Your child identified and used vocabulary words from the poem *The Midnight Ride of Paul Revere*. With your child, look up information about Paul Revere and his activities as a colonist in the 1700s. Discuss the information, using as many vocabulary words as possible.

▲ **Practice Book** p. 94

Vocabulary Strategy

INTRODUCE

Discuss the strategy for word structure to determine the meanings of verbs using the steps on p. 232.

TEACH

- Have students read "War Heroes in Stone," paying attention to how vocabulary is used.

- Model how to use word structure to determine the meaning of *lingers.*

Think Aloud

MODEL First, I cover up the ending and read *linger.* I know that *linger* means "to last or stay on." I read the sentence, and the meaning "to last or stay on" makes sense.

Words to Know

somber
fate
steed
fearless
magnified
glimmer
lingers

Remember

Try the strategy. Then, if you need more help, use your glossary or dictionary.

Vocabulary Strategy
for Endings

Word Structure The endings *-s, -ed,* and *-ing* may be added to verbs to change the tense, person, or usage of the verbs. You can use these endings to help you figure out the meanings of unfamiliar verbs.

1. Cover the ending and read the base form of the word.

2. Reread the sentence and make sure the word is a verb, that it shows action. (Nouns can also end in *-s.*)

3. Now look in the sentence for clues about what the word may mean.

4. See if your meaning makes sense in the sentence.

As you read "War Heroes in Stone," look for verbs that end with *-s, -ed, or -ing.* Think about the endings and the way the words are used to help you figure out their meanings.

232

DAY 2 **Grouping Options**

Reading
Whole Group Discuss the Question of the Day. Then use pp. 232–235.

Group Time Differentiated Instruction
Read *The Midnight Ride of Paul Revere.* See pp. 230h–230i for the small group lesson plan.

Whole Group Use p. 253a.

Language Arts
Use pp. 253e–253k.

Strategic Intervention

◉ **Word Structure** Have partners work together to follow the steps on p. 232 to figure out the meaning of *fearless.*

Access Content Use ELL Poster 10 to preteach vocabulary. Choose from the following to meet language proficiency levels.

Beginning Use the Multilingual Lesson Vocabulary list in the ELL Teaching Guide, pp. 272–283, and other home-language resources to provide translations of the tested words.

Intermediate Use a three-column chart to organize the vocabulary. Label the columns "noun," "verb," and "adjective."

Advanced Teach the lesson on pp. 232–233. Have students determine whether any of the tested words have cognates in their home languages.

Resources for home-language words may include parents, bilingual staff members, bilingual dictionaries, or online translation sources.

War Heroes in Stone

Monuments to war heroes have a noble feeling. Artists who make statues to honor the war dead seem to understand their job. Soldiers who died in battle gave their lives for country and freedom. The somber job of the artist is to honor these heroes. Artists also want us to feel proud of what these heroes did. The artists' work is one way of giving thanks to those who met their fate on the field of battle.

Often the statue shows a general sitting on his steed, sword raised overhead. The marble forms are beautiful, powerful, and larger than life. In addition, the statue sits high on a pedestal so that visitors must look up. Both horse and man are a study in fearless forward motion. In this way, their bravery and patriotism are magnified and set in stone.

Have you ever seen such a statue at night? Imagine the white stone looming in the dark. Then a glimmer of moonlight brings it to life. The effect is strange to see. You feel you can almost hear the tread of troops marching down a dusty road. The distant sound of marching lingers in the air. You send a silent word of thanks to those who fought to keep your country free.

Words to Write

Choose one of the illustrations from the next selection. Write a paragraph describing it. Use as many words from the Words to Know list as you can.

233

Connect to Phonics

Word Study/Decoding Point out that the spelling of the base word often changes before adding an inflected ending. Model identifying the inflected ending and base word using *magnified* from p. 233, paragraph 2. Have students suggest other words they know with the inflected endings *-s*, *-ed*, and *-ing*. Have them identify the inflected ending and base in each word. Then have them identify the meaning of each word with and without the inflected ending.

PRACTICE AND ASSESS

- Ask students to find the meanings of the remaining lesson vocabulary words and explain how word structure helped them figure out the meanings.
- Point out that if students don't know the meaning of a base word, they may need to refer to a dictionary or glossary for help.
- Return to the lists students made of lesson vocabulary meanings (232b), and have them revise their meanings if necessary. Encourage them to write new sentences using each vocabulary word.
- Have students complete Practice Book p. 95.

WRITE Writing should include lesson vocabulary that describes or explains events taking place.

Monitor Progress

Word Structure

If... students need more practice with the lesson vocabulary,	then... use Tested Vocabulary Cards.

Vocabulary · Word Structure

- An **ending** is a letter or letters added to the end of a base word.
- *-s* or *-es* can be added to a singular noun to make it plural, and *-ed*, *-ing*, and *-s* can be added to a verb to change its tense.

Directions Read the following passage. Then answer the questions below.

A colonist's life was filled with hard work, especially when compared with our lives. Many of these differences can be connected to a single fact: in the 1700s, there were no cars. Traveling from place to place was particularly difficult. A colonist without a good horse often had to walk. Once outside of town, many miles separated settlements—and there were no sidewalks, few roads, and no street lights. Lingering on the trail after dark was risky.

1. *Compared* and *connected* both have the same ending. What are their base words? How does *-ed* change the meaning of their base words?
   compare and connect; Both verbs take their past-tense forms.

2. *Lives* and *differences* both have the same ending. What are their base words? How does *-s* change the meaning of their base words?
   life and difference; Both words become plural.

3. *Traveling* and *lingering* both have the same ending. What are their base words? How does *-ing* change the meaning of their base words?
   travel and linger; The verbs become nouns.

4. What is the difference between *-s* at the end of *lingers* and *-s* at the end of *sidewalks*?
   Lingers is a verb. Adding -s makes it third-person singular.
   Sidewalks is a noun. Adding -s makes it plural.

5. Choose a noun or a verb from the passage. What is its base word? Add a new ending to it. How has the meaning of the word changed?
   Possible answer: Fact becomes plural when an -s is added to it.

Home Activity Your child identified and answered questions about word endings. Change the word endings of common words your child knows. Ask your child how these new words are different from the original words in spelling and meaning.

▲ **Practice Book** p. 95

The Midnight Ride of Paul Revere   233

Prereading Strategies

OBJECTIVES

- Sequence events to improve comprehension.
- Use graphic organizers to understand the sequence of events.

GENRE STUDY

Poetry

The Midnight Ride of Paul Revere is a poem. Explain that poetry is an arrangement of words in lines having rhythm. Sometimes those lines rhyme, as in this narrative poem.

PREVIEW AND PREDICT

Have students look at the poem title and illustrations. Have students identify the subject of the poem and predict why the ride was made. Have students use lesson vocabulary words in their discussion.

Strategy Response Log

Ask Questions Have students write two questions about Paul Revere's ride in their strategy response logs. Students will answer their questions in the Strategy Response Log activity on p. 241.

How does Paul Revere feel during his ride?

Genre A **poem** is a composition arranged in lines. Some poems have rhyme, some have rhythm, and some have both. As you read this narrative poem—a long poem that tells a story—notice the rhyme and rhythm.

234

ELL

Access Content Use the pictures to preview the events in this selection. Point to each picture and ask students to tell what they see. Summarize the action that takes place on each page of text and use the picture to support it.

Consider having students read the selection summary in English or in students' home languages. See the Multilingual Summaries in the ELL Teaching Guide, pp. 68–70.

THE MIDNIGHT RIDE OF
PAUL
REVERE

by
Henry
Wadsworth
Longfellow

graved and painted by
Christopher Bing

235

SET PURPOSE

Read the first page of the selection aloud to students. Have them consider the two questions they wrote about Paul Revere's ride for their Strategy Response Logs and share what they hope to learn about it.

Remind students to notice which event happens first, next, and so on as they read. Suggest using a time line to track these events.

STRATEGY RECALL

Students have now used these before-reading strategies:

• preview the selection to be aware of its genre, features, and possible content;
• activate prior knowledge about that content and what to expect of that genre;
• make predictions;
• set a purpose for reading.

Remind students to be aware of and flexibly use the during-reading strategies they have learned:

• link prior knowledge to new information;
• summarize text they have read so far;
• ask clarifying questions;
• answer questions they or others pose;
• check their predictions and either refine them or make new predictions;
• recognize the text structure the author is using, and use that knowledge to make predictions and increase comprehension;
• visualize what the author is describing;
• monitor their comprehension and use fix-up strategies.

After reading, students will use these strategies:

• summarize or retell the text;
• answer questions they or others pose;
• reflect to make new information become part of their prior knowledge.

Audio CD **AudioText**

Guiding Comprehension

1 Setting • Literal

What is the poem's setting? Identify the time of the events in the poem.

The events take place on the night of April 18, 1775.

Monitor Progress

REVIEW Setting

If... students are unable to identify the setting and theme,	**then...** use the skill and strategy instruction on p. 237.

2 Main Idea • Inferential

Reread the second stanza. Name the main idea and one supporting detail.

Main Idea: If Paul Revere sees the lantern(s), he will let everyone know of the British plans to march. Supporting detail: One lantern means they are coming by land, two lanterns mean they are coming by sea.

3 Theme • Inferential

Based on the first page, what do you think the theme, or the big idea, of the poem will be?

Possible response: I think the theme will have to do with patriotism and the importance of fighting and taking risks for your freedom.

Tech Files ONLINE

Encourage students to type the keywords *Paul Revere's ride* into a student-friendly search engine to find out information about the poem, legend, and facts about the ride. Be sure to follow classroom guidelines for Internet use.

LISTEN, MY CHILDREN, AND YOU SHALL HEAR

1 Of the midnight ride of Paul Revere,
On the eighteenth of April, in Seventy-Five,
Hardly a man is now alive
Who remembers that famous day and year.

He said to his friend, "If the British march
By land or sea from the town tonight,
Hang a lantern aloft in the belfry arch
Of the North Church tower as a signal light—
2 One, if by land, and two, if by sea;
And I on the opposite shore will be,
Ready to ride and spread the alarm
Through every Middlesex village and farm,
For the country folk to be up and to arm."

Then he said, "Good night!"
    and with muffled oar
Silently rowed to the Charlestown shore,
Just as the moon rose over the bay,
Where swinging wide at her moorings lay
The *Somerset,* British man-of-war;
3 A phantom ship, with each mast and spar
Across the moon like a prison bar,
And a huge black hulk, that was magnified
By its own reflection in the tide.

236

Fluency Help students chunk words into meaningful phrases to help emphasize rhyme and rhythm and support comprehension. For example: One if by land, / and two, if by sea; / And I on the opposite shore / will be ready to ride and spread the alarm / through every Middlesex village and farm, / For the country folk to be up and to arm.

237

Setting and Theme REVIEW

TEACH

- Setting is the time and place the events in a story or poem occur.
- Theme is the big idea of a selection.
- Model how to determine the setting, using the poem's first two stanzas.

 Think Aloud **MODEL** I see that the first stanza gives clues about the time: "midnight," "eighteenth of April, in Seventy-Five." The second stanza gives clues about place: "North Church," "by sea," "Middlesex village." I put these clues together and I know that the time is an April night in 1775 and the place is somewhere near a village and sea.

PRACTICE AND ASSESS

- Have students reread the last stanza. Ask which clues reinforce the correct setting. *(Choice a)*

  a) Charlestown shore, bay, moon

  b) "Goodnight," prison bar, reflection

- To assess, use Practice Book p. 96.

Boston, MA

Time for
SOCIAL STUDIES

In 1775, Boston, Massachusetts, was the largest city in the British American colonies with nearly 15,000 people. People communicated with each other by word of mouth, by letters, and by using signals. Most people in Massachusetts colony were farmers, but fishing, shipbuilding, and trading were growing industries. Boston's big harbor was busy. The city was America's trading capital.

Literary Elements · Setting and Theme

Directions Read the article. Then answer the questions below.

Patrick Henry was one of the many interesting characters in the American Revolution. He provided us with one of the great sayings in American history. As a young man, he tried and failed at being a farmer and shopkeeper. He eventually educated himself and became a lawyer. Patrick Henry became a famous activist in the fight against British control of the colonies. He spoke out against English rule early and often. He urged fellow colonists to revolt. He challenged the British over their restrictions upon American liberty. In 1775, at a meeting of colonial leaders, he spoke his most famous line: "I know not what course others may take, but as for me, give me liberty or give me death." This was the theme of his adult life.

Possible answers given for 2–4.
1. When and where did Patrick Henry live?
   Patrick Henry lived in the American colonies in the 1700s.

2. How do you know Patrick Henry was outspoken?
   He spoke often in favor of revolution.

3. How did Patrick Henry feel about British rule of the colonies?
   He strongly disapproved of it.

4. Why do you think Patrick Henry said, "Give me liberty or give me death"?
   Patrick Henry would risk his life for freedom.

5. On a separate sheet of paper, describe something you feel so strongly about that you would say something like what Patrick Henry said.
   Students' responses should express a strong feeling about a specific topic.

School + Home Home Activity Your child read a short passage and answered questions about setting and theme. Discuss the setting of one of your child's favorite places. Ask your child: What does it look like? What do you see there?

▲ **Practice Book** p. 96

Guiding Comprehension

4 🎯 **Sequence • Literal**

What was Paul Revere's friend doing *before* he heard the British soldiers marching to their boats?

He was walking through town checking whether the British soldiers planned to march that night.

238

Monitor Progress	
🎯 **Sequence**	
If... students have difficulty determining sequence,	**then...** use the skill and strategy instruction on p. 239.

5 **Cause and Effect • Inferential**

What caused Paul Revere's friend to climb the tower of Old North Church?

He was getting ready to hang lanterns as a signal for Paul Revere that the British were marching.

6 **Draw Conclusions • Critical**

Why do you think Paul Revere's friend feels "secret dread"?

Possible response: He may be worrying about what will happen and how many men will die when the British march.

ELL

Build Background Point to the words *barrack* and *grenadiers* in the first verse on p. 239. Explain that both these words relate to the army. Barracks are the buildings where soldiers live. Grenadiers were British soldiers fighting for the Royal Army. Ask students what Paul Revere's friend hears. *(the sound of arms, men's feet)*

Meanwhile, his friend, through alley and street,
Wanders and watches, with eager ears,
Till in the silence around him he hears
The muster of men at the barrack door,
The sound of arms, and the tramp of feet,
And the measured tread of the grenadiers,
Marching down to their boats on the shore.

4

Then he climbed the tower
  of the Old North Church,
By the wooden stairs, with stealthy tread,
To the belfry-chamber overhead,
And startled the pigeons from their perch
On the somber rafters, that round him made
Masses and moving shapes of shade—
By the trembling ladder, steep and tall,
To the highest window in the wall,
Where he paused to listen and look down
A moment on the roofs of the town,
And the moonlight flowing over all.

5

Beneath the churchyard, lay the dead,
In the night-encampment on the hill,
Wrapped in silence so deep and still
That he could hear, like a sentinel's tread,
The watchful night-wind, as it went
Creeping along from tent to tent,
And seeming to whisper, "All is well!"
A moment only he feels the spell
Of the place and the hour, the secret dread
Of the lonely belfry and the dead;
For suddenly all his thoughts are bent
On a shadowy something far away,

6

239

Old North Church

The Old North Church is Boston's oldest church
building. It was built in 1723. The church's giant
steeple guided ships into Boston Harbor. In 1744, eight
bells were hung in the belfry. On April 18, 1775, Sexton Robert
Newman hung two lanterns there. They signaled to the colonists that
British troops were setting out for Concord, Massachusetts, to seize
colonial weapons.

Time for **SOCIAL STUDIES**

SKILLS ↔ STRATEGIES IN CONTEXT

Sequence

TEACH

- Sequence is the order in which events take place.
- Clue words like *first*, *next*, *then*, *last*, *until*, and *meanwhile* sometimes signal a new event.
- If there are no clue words, the reader has to figure out the correct order.

Think Aloud **MODEL** In the first stanza, I see the words *meanwhile* and *till*. Both words signal a new event. The first event is that Paul Revere's friend wanders through the streets, checking on the British. The next event is that his friend hears the sounds of the soldiers getting ready to march.

PRACTICE AND ASSESS

Have students reread the second stanza to find the clue word and to determine what event it signals.

Then; at the opening, the word signals the start of an event: Paul Revere's friend climbing the tower and looking down.

EXTEND SKILLS

Rhythm/Cadence

In poetry, rhythm can be as important as rhyme. The flow of words contributes to how the poem makes the reader feel. A fast rhythm can add lightness, while a very slow rhythm can reinforce fear, worry, or sadness.

The Midnight Ride of Paul Revere   **239**

Guiding Comprehension

7 **Metaphor • Inferential**

What does the phrase "a line of black that bends and floats" in the first verse on p. 240 mean?

It refers to the way the river looks at night.

8 **Graphic Organizers • Inferential**

What events could you add to a time line to help identify the order of events?

Possible responses: Paul Revere asks his friend to signal; his friend checks on the British.

9 **Summarize • Inferential**

Text to Self **Summarize the facts you've learned from the poem so far and think about the impact this event has had on your life.**

Paul Revere's ride took place on April 18, 1775. Signal lights were hung in the Old North Church. Paul Revere waited on the Charlestown shore for the signal. Two lights was the signal the British were coming by sea. This event reminds me that we would not have the freedoms we enjoy today if this historic event had not taken place.

Where the river widens to meet the bay–
A line of black that bends and floats
7 On the rising tide, like a bridge of boats.

Meanwhile, impatient to mount and ride,
Booted and spurred, with a heavy stride
On the opposite shore walked Paul Revere.
Now he patted his horse's side,
Now gazed on the landscape far and near,
Then, impetuous, stamped the earth,
And turned and tightened his saddle girth;
But mostly he watched with eager search
The belfry tower of the Old North Church,
As it rose above the graves on the hill,
Lonely and spectral and somber and still.

And lo! as he looks, on the belfry's height
A glimmer, and then a gleam of light!
He springs to the saddle, the bridle he turns,
But lingers and gazes, till full on his sight
A second lamp in the belfry burns!

A hurry of hoofs in a village street,
A shape in the moonlight, a bulk in the dark,
And beneath, from the pebbles,
    in passing, a spark
Struck out by a steed flying fearless and fleet:
That was all! And yet,
    through the gloom and the light,
8 The fate of a nation was riding that night;
And the spark struck out
    by that steed, in his flight,
9 Kindled the land into flame with its heat.

240

ELL

Access Content In the verse beginning "Meanwhile..." on p. 240, the poet uses three words to describe Paul Revere: *impatient, impetuous,* and *eager.* Explain the meaning of each word and ask students what Paul Revere was eager to see *(the lanterns in the belfry).*

241

STRATEGY SELF-CHECK

Graphic Organizers

TEACH

Have students ask questions about the order of events in the poem so far, such as "What happened first, next, and last?" Use a story sequence chart to list the sequence of events in order. (*Paul Revere asks his friend to signal if the British march. His friend wanders around town, checking on the British. He hears the British begin to march, and then climbs the tower. Paul Revere waits for a signal from his friend. He sees a signal in the tower.*)

SELF-CHECK

Students can ask themselves these questions to assess their ability to use the skill and strategy.

- Was I able to identify the important events while I read?
- Was I able to identify events in the correct order?
- Did I use graphic organizers to help me correctly identify the sequence of events?

Monitor Progress	
Sequence	
If... students have difficulty using graphic organizers to identify the sequence of events,	then... revisit the skill lesson on pp. 230–231. Reteach as necessary.

Strategy Response Log

Answer Questions Have students answer the two questions they posed at the beginning of the poem. (See p. 234.) Then have them write two or more questions about the rest of the selection

If you want to teach this poem in two sessions, stop here.

Develop Vocabulary

PRACTICE LESSON VOCABULARY

Students orally respond *yes* or *no* to each question and provide a reason for each answer.

1. Is a soldier *somber* when marching off to war? (*Yes; it is a very serious occasion.*)

2. Would a *steed* ever race across a field? (*Yes; a horse sometimes races across a field.*)

3. Would a *fearless* soldier be afraid? (*No; he would be brave.*)

BUILD CONCEPT VOCABULARY

Review previous concept words with students. Ask if students have come across any words today in their reading or elsewhere to add to the Promoting Freedom Concept Web, such as *barrack, grenadiers,* and *arms.*

The Midnight Ride of Paul Revere **241**

Guiding Comprehension

If you are teaching the poem in two days, discuss the sequence of events so far and review the vocabulary.

10 Draw Conclusions • Inferential

How do you think Paul Revere is feeling at this point in the poem?

Possible response: He is feeling nervous, determined, focused, responsible.

11 Graphic Organizers • Inferential

What events during the start of Paul Revere's ride could you add to a time line?

Possible responses: Paul Revere leaves the village; he crosses the bridge into Medford.

12 Sequence • Literal

What does Paul Revere do right before he comes into Medford town?

He crosses a bridge.

Monitor Progress
Sequence

If... students have difficulty determining sequence,	then... use the skill and strategy instruction on p. 243.

DAY 3 Grouping Options

Reading
Whole Group Discuss the Question of the Day.

Group Time Differentiated Instruction
Read *The Midnight Ride of Paul Revere.* See pp. 230h–230i for the small group lesson plan.

Whole Group Discuss the Reader Response questions on p. 248. Then use p. 253a.

Language Arts
Use pp. 253e–253k.

242

ELL

Extend Language Reread aloud the phrase "under the alders that skirt its edge" on p. 243. Point to the word *skirt*. Explain that this word has two meanings. Help students name the more common meaning (an article of women's clothing). Tell them that *skirt* can also mean to "lie along the edge or border of something."

He has left the village and mounted the steep,
And beneath him, tranquil and broad and deep,
Is the Mystic, meeting the ocean tides;   **10**
And under the alders that skirt its edge,
Now soft on the sand, now loud on the ledge,
Is heard the tramp of his steed as he rides.

It was twelve by the village clock,
When he crossed the bridge   **11**
    into Medford town.   **12**
He heard the crowing of the cock,
And the barking of the farmer's dog,
And felt the damp of the river fog,
That rises after the sun goes down.

243

SKILLS ⟷ STRATEGIES IN CONTEXT

Sequence Graphic Organizers

TEACH

Ask students to reread the first stanza and tell the correct order of the following places where Paul Revere rode: ledge, steep, sand. *(steep, sand, ledge)* Use this information to model how using a time line can help determine the sequence of events.

Think Aloud **MODEL** As I read, I ask myself where Paul Revere rides first, and where he goes after that. I try to visualize each step of the way. I call then add these events in the correct sequence on a time line

PRACTICE AND ASSESS

Have students reread the second paragraph on p. 243. Ask them to tell what time and place words give clues about sequence. *(time: twelve by the village clock; place: bridge, Medford town)*

Guiding Comprehension

13 🎯 **Vocabulary • Word Structure: Endings**

Identify the base word and ending of _galloped_ in the first sentence. What is the meaning of the word?

Base word is _gallop._ Ending is _-ed._ Meaning: raced.

Monitor Progress

🎯 **Word Structure**

If... students have difficulty using endings to determine word meaning,	**then...** use the vocabulary strategy instruction on p. 245.

---

14 Mood • Critical

How would you describe the mood, or feeling, of the poem at this point? Does it reflect Paul Revere's mood?

Possible response: The mood is serious and somber. It is similar to Paul Revere's mood.

15 Author's Viewpoint • Critical

What do you think the author's opinion is of the farmers of Concord?

Question the Author Possible response: The author admires them for returning fire upon the well-armed British Regulars.

244

ⒺⓁⓁ

Fluency Ask students to echo read the first verse on p. 245. Read aloud the last word in the first line: _clock._ Ask students to find the word at the end of another line that rhymes with it. Then point to the words _passed_ and _aghast_ as you say them aloud. Discuss rhyming words. Some have similar spellings and others have very different spellings. Point out _bare / glare_ and _trees / breeze._

It was one by the village clock,
When he galloped into Lexington.
He saw the gilded weathercock
Swim in the moonlight as he passed,
And the meeting-house windows,
    blank and bare,
Gaze at him with a spectral glare,
As if they already stood aghast
At the bloody work they would look upon.

It was two by the village clock,
When he came to the bridge in Concord town.
He heard the bleating of the flock,
And the twitter of birds among the trees,
And felt the breath of the morning breeze
Blowing over the meadows brown.
And one was safe and asleep in his bed
Who at the bridge would be first to fall,
Who that day would be lying dead,
Pierced by a British musket-ball.

You know the rest. In the books you have read
How the British Regulars fired and fled—
How the farmers gave them ball for ball,
From behind each fence and farmyard wall,
Chasing the red-coats down the lane,
Then crossing the fields to emerge again
Under the trees at the turn of the road
And only pausing to fire and load.

13

14

15

245

 VOCABULARY STRATEGY

Word Structure

TEACH

Read the third line of the second stanza. Model how to use word ending to help determine the meaning of *bleating*.

 Think Aloud

MODEL To figure out the meaning of *bleating*, I cover up the ending and see *bleat*. I know that sheep bleat, or cry, so *bleating* must mean crying. That makes sense because Paul Revere hears the bleating, or crying, of the flock.

PRACTICE AND ASSESS

Have students identify the ending and meaning of *blowing* (verse 2, line 6), and *fired* (verse 3, line 2). *blowing: -ing;* meaning: "gusting, moving"; *fired: -ed;* meaning: "shot."

Freedom Trail

Time for SOCIAL STUDIES

The Freedom Trail is a walking tour of sixteen historic sites in Boston, including Old North Church and Paul Revere's house. It was set up around 1950 to introduce visitors to Colonial Revolutionary Boston. Today, a red brick path or painted lines connect the sites, and visitors can walk from one to the other. The tour takes from two to three hours, or even longer if a visitor chooses to spend extra time at one or more of the stops.

Guiding Comprehension

16 🔄 **Sequence • Inference**

How much time has passed during the ride?

It lasts through the night, until Paul Revere has spread his message through every village in the colony.

17 Compare and Contrast • Critical

Text to Text **How is this poem different from other stories you have read about the Revolutionary War? Why do you think Longfellow chose to tell this story as a poem?**

Possible response: The poem is more personal and emotional with some factual background, whereas other things I've read on the subject, like nonfiction history books or articles, concentrate just on facts and information.

Strategy Response Log

Summarize When students finish reading the selection, provide this prompt: Suppose you were babysitting a younger friend, brother, or sister, and it was bedtime. In a few sentences, tell the story of *The Midnight Ride of Paul Revere*.

16 So through the night rode Paul Revere,
And so through the night went his cry of alarm
To every Middlesex village and farm—
A cry of defiance and not of fear,
A voice in the darkness, a knock at the door,
And a word that shall echo for evermore!
For, borne on the night-wind of the Past,
Through all our history, to the last,
In the hour of darkness and peril and need,
The people will waken and listen to hear
The hurrying hoof-beats of that steed,
And the midnight message of Paul Revere.

17

246

ELL

Access Content Reread aloud "a cry of defiance and not of fear" on p. 246. Tell students that *defiance* means "bold resistance to an opposing force." Ask students what Paul Revere's cry of defiance was about. *(It was a warning to stand strong and be prepared.)*

247

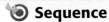 STRATEGY SELF-CHECK

Graphic Organizers

Have students complete the story sequence chart they began earlier. Remind them to ask questions to help them identify the sequence of events in the poem, such as "What happened first, next, last? Where did Paul Revere go first, next, last?"

SELF-CHECK

Students can ask themselves these questions to assess their understanding of the selection.

- Did I keep track of the sequence of events as I read *The Midnight Ride of Paul Revere*?
- How did graphic organizers help me keep track of the events?

Monitor Progress	
Sequence	
If... students have difficulty sequencing events or using graphic organizers,	**then...** use the Reteach lesson on p. 253b.

Develop Vocabulary

PRACTICE LESSON VOCABULARY

As a class, have students answer the following questions orally.

1. If an image is *magnified*, how does it look? (It looks larger than it actually is.)

2. What does it mean if a rainstorm *lingers* for days? (It stays around and doesn't go away.)

3. What did Paul Revere see *glimmer* from the belfry? (He saw the lantern shine unsteadily, when his friend put it in the window.)

BUILD CONCEPT VOCABULARY

Review previous concept words with students. Ask if they have come across any words today in their reading or elsewhere they would like to add to the Promoting Freedom Concept Web, such as *musket-ball*.

Sequence

- The **sequence** of events is the order in which they take place, from first to last.
- Clue words such as *first*, *next*, and *then* may show sequence in a story or article, but not always. Other clues are dates and times of day.
- Sometimes two events happen at the same time. Clue words that show this are *meanwhile* and *in that same year*.

Directions Read the following passage. Then answer the questions below.

In 1773, American colonists in Boston raided three British ships in Boston Harbor. They dumped more than 300 crates of British tea into the water. They were protesting England's taxes on the American colonies. Eight months earlier, the British government had created a tax on all tea shipped from England to America. The colonists were furious. On the night of December 16, 1773, Samuel Adams led approximately 100 colonists and stormed the British ships waiting to unload their tea. By dumping the tea into the harbor, the colonists let the King know that they would not stand for his high taxation.

1. What did the British do that angered the American colonists? What year did they do it?
   The British put taxes on tea in 1773.
2. How long did it take for the colonists to take action?
   eight months
3. Why did the colonists dump the tea into Boston Harbor?
   They dumped tea to protest the British taxes on tea sent to the colonies.
4. Why is knowing that the colonists were angry at the British important to the sequence of events?
   Possible answer: Knowing the source of the colonists' anger helps you understand the cause of their actions.
5. Imagine that you have been asked to give a history presentation on the Boston Tea Party. On a separate sheet of paper, list at least five questions you might try to answer in your presentation.
   Students' questions should be logical research questions relevant to the Boston Tea Party.

Home Activity Your child read a short passage and answered questions about the sequence of events described in it. Read a newspaper or magazine article with your child and discuss the sequence of events it describes.

▲ **Practice Book** p. 97

The Midnight Ride of Paul Revere **247**

Reader Response

Open for Discussion Personal Response

MODEL I'd describe the movie in a suspenseful way to let my friend know how high the stakes were for Paul Revere and the colonists.

Comprehension Check Critical Response

1. Responses will vary, but should reflect students' efforts to bring feeling and rhythm to their readings. *Author's Purpose*

2. Possible responses: *then, just as, meanwhile, till, suddenly,* and *now.* **Sequence**

3. Responses will vary but webs should include words like *soldiers, arms, muskets, firepower, grenadiers* **Graphic Organizers**

4. Possible responses: *Somber* describes the tower of the Old North Church; *fearless* describes Paul Revere's steed, or horse; *huge, black, hulk* describes the British ship. **Vocabulary**

Look Back and Write For text practice, assign a 10–15 minute time limit. For assessment, see the Scoring Rubric at the right.

Retell

Have students retell *The Midnight Ride of Paul Revere.*

Monitor Progress	
Check Retelling Rubric [4][3][2][1]	
If... students have difficulty retelling the poem,	**then...** use the Retelling Cards and the Scoring Rubric for Retelling on p. 249 to assist fluent retelling.

SUCCESS PREDICTOR

Check Retelling Review the illustrations with students, making sure they can identify Paul Revere, his friend, the British soldiers, and key words from the selection. Then have them use the illustrations to retell the story. For more ideas on assessing students' retellings, see the ELL and Transition Handbook.

Reader Response

Open for Discussion What if *The Midnight Ride of Paul Revere* were a movie? Imagine that you saw it. Tell about it, scene by scene, to your best friend. Remember, this is a spy movie with a stealthy, fast ride.

1. Read your favorite stanza aloud. Get the gallop into the rhythm as you read. Make the spoken words reveal the scene. Report your results. **Think Like an Author**

2. Identify clue words and phrases in the poem that signal the sequence of events. Make a list. **Sequence**

3. What makes the ride a dangerous one? Make a graphic organizer, a web with the word *danger* in the center, to answer the question. **Graphic Organizers**

4. Longfellow's descriptions help us see and hear this historic ride. What do *somber* and *fearless* describe? Find other examples of adjectives the poet uses to describe things. **Vocabulary**

Look Back and Write Who is the audience for this poem? Look back at the first stanza for clues. Based on those clues, who seems to be the speaker of the poem? Write your answers to these questions.

Meet author Henry Wadsworth Longfellow on page 771 and illustrator Christopher Bing on page 772.

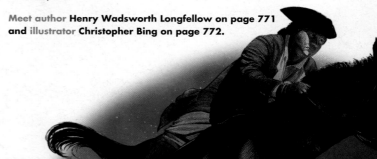

248

Scoring Rubric Look Back and Write

Top-Score Response A top-score response will use details from p. 236 of the selection and inferential thinking to identify the audience as younger generations and the speaker as an older patriot who has vivid memories of the historic events of 1775.

Example of a Top-Score Response The speaker addresses the audience as "my children." He also says that most people who lived through that time have died. These words suggest that he is very old and wants young people to know about this historic event and be proud of their country. He is probably talking to future generations.

For additional rubrics, see p. WA10.

Write Now

Interview

Prompt

The Midnight Ride of Paul Revere tells about a famous American.
Think about another famous American.
Now write an interview with that person.

Writing Trait

Interviews are **organized** as questions and answers in **paragraphs.**

Student Model

First question focuses on circumstances that made person famous.

Q: Ms. Tubman, what made you want to get involved with the Underground Railroad?

A: Call me Harriet. My family and I were slaves. Then the plantation owner decided to sell us. We might have ended up in the awful sugarcane fields farther south. We ran away instead. Folks helped us along the Underground Railroad. After I got to freedom, I hated the thought that others were still suffering. Later, I went back to help them.

Q: Were you ever afraid, Harriet?

A: Sure I was, many times. We were hunted as criminals for helping people get to freedom, but you can't let fear keep you from doing what's right.

Sequence words clarify order of events.

Questions and answers are **organized** in separate **paragraphs**.

Use the model to help you write your own interview.

249

Write Now

Look at the Prompt Explain that each sentence in the prompt has a purpose.

- Sentence 1 presents a topic.
- Sentence 2 suggests students think about the topic.
- Sentence 3 tells what to write—an interview.

Strategies to Develop Organization/Paragraphs

Have students

- write question/answer pairs on note cards to sort information in a logical way.
- add sequence words to connect ideas.

NO: I broke Mom's vase. I regretted it. I told her what I'd done.

YES: I broke Mom's vase. Later, I regretted it, so I told her what I had done.

For additional suggestions and rubric, see pp. 253g–253h.

Writer's Checklist

☑ **Focus** Do questions focus on an event or theme?

☑ **Organization** Are questions and answers in separate paragraphs?

☑ **Support** Do details answer the questions?

☑ **Conventions** Are questions punctuated correctly?

Scoring Rubric — Narrative Retelling

Rubric 4 3 2 1	4	3	2	1
Connections	Makes connections and generalizes beyond the text	Makes connections to other events, stories, or experiences	Makes a limited connection to another event, story, or experience	Makes no connection to another event, story, or experience
Author's Purpose	Elaborates on author's purpose	Tells author's purpose with some clarity	Makes some connection to author's purpose	Makes no connection to author's purpose
Characters	Describes the main character(s) and any character development	Identifies the main character(s) and gives some information about them	Inaccurately identifies some characters or gives little information about them	Inaccurately identifies the characters or gives no information about them
Setting	Describes the time and location	Identifies the time and location	Omits details of time or location	Is unable to identify time or location
Plot	Describes the problem, goal, events, and ending using rich detail	Tells the problem, goal, events, and ending with some errors that do not affect meaning	Tells parts of the problem, goal, events, and ending with gaps that affect meaning	Retelling has no sense of story

Retelling Plan

☑ **Week 1** Assess Strategic Intervention students.

☑ **Week 2** Assess Advanced students.

☑ **Week 3** Assess Strategic Intervention students.

☑ **Week 4** Assess On-Level students.

☑ **This week assess any students you have not yet checked during this unit.**

Use the Retelling Chart on p. TR16 to record retelling.

Selection Test To assess with *The Midnight Ride of Paul Revere*, use Selection Tests, pp. 37–40.

Fresh Reads for Differentiated Test Practice For weekly leveled practice, use pp. 55–60.

Retelling

SUCCESS PREDICTO

Reading Online

OBJECTIVES

- Examine the features of a Web page.
- Compare and contrast across texts.

PREVIEW/USE TEXT FEATURES

Have students preview "Revolutionary War Women." Ask:

- **What is the main topic of the Web page shown on p. 251, and what are the sub-topics?** *(The main topic is "Women in the Revolution" and the subtopics are each of the specific women whose lives were researched.)*

- **Why are the women's names on p. 251 underlined?** *(They are links to other Web pages.)*

If students have trouble understanding how to navigate using links, use the Technology Tools.

Link to Social Studies

Suggest that students do their research using an online encyclopedia or search engine. Brainstorm keywords with students, modeling how to narrow a broad topic.

DAY 4 Grouping Options

Reading
Whole Group Discuss the Question of the Day.

Group Time Differentiated Instruction
Read "Revolutionary War Women." See pp. 230h–230i for the small group lesson plan.

Whole Group Use p. 253a.

Language Arts
Use pp. 253e–253k.

Reading Online

New Literacies: PearsonSuccessNet.com

Revolutionary War Women

Web Site

Genre
- Web pages are found on Internet Web sites.
- A Web page contains information about a topic or topics.

Text Features
- Often this information is broken down into subtopics. Each subtopic is a link.
- The links on this page are in blue and underlined. When you click on a link, you move to another page.

Link to Social Studies
Do research to find out more about women in the Revolutionary War. Share what you find with the class.

Let's say you want to learn about women in the Revolutionary War. You find this page at a Web site created by a fifth-grade social studies class:

For more practice

Take It to the Net
PearsonSuccessNet.com

250

TECHNOLOGY TOOLS

Web Page

Web Page A Web page is found on an Internet Web site. It contains information about a topic or topics.

Link A link allows you to move quickly and easily from one Web page to another. You can usually identify a link because it looks different from the other words on a Web page. Words that are links may be highlighted, underlined, or shown on a button. Icons such as arrows might also be used as links. For example, an arrow pointing to the right may mean, "click here for the next page."

Mouse The mouse allows you to position the cursor over words, icons, or other links. When a link is active, you can navigate to another page of the Web site by clicking on the link using the mouse.

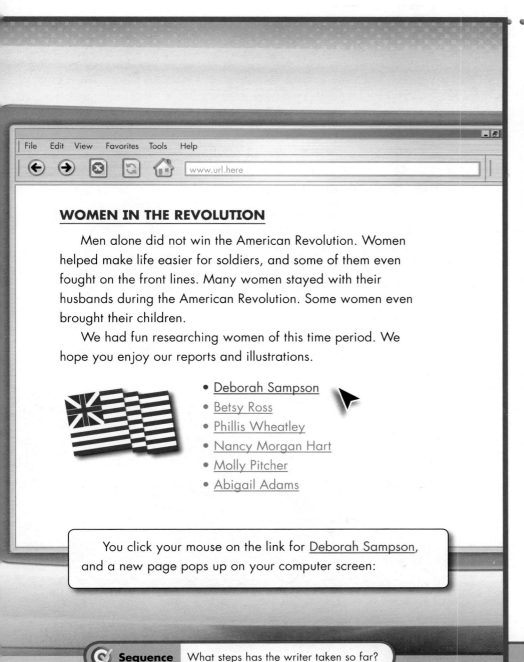

WOMEN IN THE REVOLUTION

Men alone did not win the American Revolution. Women helped make life easier for soldiers, and some of them even fought on the front lines. Many women stayed with their husbands during the American Revolution. Some women even brought their children.

We had fun researching women of this time period. We hope you enjoy our reports and illustrations.

- <u>Deborah Sampson</u>
- <u>Betsy Ross</u>
- <u>Phillis Wheatley</u>
- <u>Nancy Morgan Hart</u>
- <u>Molly Pitcher</u>
- <u>Abigail Adams</u>

You click your mouse on the link for <u>Deborah Sampson</u>, and a new page pops up on your computer screen:

Sequence What steps has the writer taken so far?

251

NEW LITERACIES: WEB SITE

Use the sidebar on p. 250 to guide discussion.

- Web sites contain information about a topic or topics. There are thousands of Web pages on the Internet. Individuals and companies buy space to post their information there. Each site is made up of any number of Web pages.

- The information on a Web page is often organized by a main topic broken down into subtopics. Subtopics often appear as links (here they are in blue and underlined). Each link takes you to a different page where you can find more information.

- Ask students what the subtopics are. Discuss strategies for navigating the page, including using the mouse to position the cursor and to activate the links.

 **AudioText**

Sequence

Possible response: The writer has found a Web site that focuses on women in the Revolutionary War.

Build Background Have students look at the computer screen and keyboard on p. 251. Explain that what they see on the screen is a Web page. Ask volunteers to point to the site address (here represented by *www.url. here*) and the cursor. Read aloud the caption on p. 251. Have students point to the new Web pages on pp. 252 and 253.

- Ask students to use the pictures on the Web pages to identify Deborah Sampson and to make predictions about her role in the Revolutionary War.

WEB-IQUETTE

Web Sites

Tell students that, while using Web sites can be a quick and efficient way to find information, there are rules of etiquette they should follow:

- Be aware of how much time you are spending online. If you are sharing computer time, sign off promptly when your time is up.
- Use your time efficiently by using only those Web pages that have the most useful and factual information.
- Use good judgment in choosing which sites to visit. Avoid sites that have inappropriate or inaccurate content, that are poorly designed, or that are unreliable.

Strategies for Navigation

USE THE *FIND* FEATURE Some Web sites contain a lot of information. Rather than reading all of the text on a Web page, find exactly what you need by using the "find on this page" feature. Note that this feature works on individual pages but does not search an entire Web site.

Use the Strategy

1. The next time you are looking for specific information on a Web site, try using the *Find* feature. Look for *Find* under the *Edit* menu or in another menu at the top of the screen. Click on it.

2. When a box appears, type the keyword or phrase you're looking for into the box.

3. Press *Enter* or click on the *Find* button. The words you are looking for will appear highlighted in color on the screen.

PRACTICE Think about the ways you use the *Find* feature at home and at school.

When planning a report, list the keywords that you might use to search for information using the *Find* feature.

The next time you access a Web page, use the *Find* feature. Try using different keywords to locate specific information.

www.url.here

Deborah Sampson By Michael Z.

Deborah Sampson was born in Plypton, Massachusetts. She was born on December 17, 1760. She died in 1827. She read a copy of Tom Paine's *Common Sense*, and decided to make herself some men's clothing and disguise herself as a man and fight in the Revolutionary War as a soldier. She went to Medway, Massachusetts, and enlisted in the army as Robert Shirtliff.

252

Guided Practice If there is time, have students log on to the Internet. Show them how to use the *Find* feature. Help students make connections between the steps they are doing and related vocabulary terms.

It is not certain how long Deborah served in the army, but she was wounded twice. The first time she got a sword slash on her head during a skirmish with Loyalist soldiers near Tarrytown, New York. A few months later she was shot in the shoulder with a musket ball. It was not discovered that she was a woman when she got medical help.

Her true identity was not revealed until she got sick with yellow fever in Philadelphia. When she rejoined her troop, her doctor gave her commanding officer a letter telling them the truth. The officers were shocked, but Deborah had earned their respect. Instead of the punishment she expected, she received an honorable discharge from the army.

Reading Across Texts

Think about the two selections and what lessons you learn from reading about Paul Revere and Deborah Sampson.

Writing Across Texts Imagine that you are explaining the lessons you learned to a friend. Write down what you would say.

🎯 **Graphic Organizers** | What organizer would best show facts about Sampson?

253

CONNECT TEXT TO TEXT

Reading Across Texts

Discuss the ways that Paul Revere and Deborah Sampson responded to the challenges of war, and how their responses were affected by the time period in which they lived. Think about what you would do if faced with similar challenges.

Have students make a cause-and-effect chart to show what each person did, and why.

Writing Across Texts Before writing, students may want to review their cause-and-effect charts in order to understand better how the actions of Paul Revere and Deborah Sampson may have helped others.

🎯 **Graphic organizers**

Possible response: time line

Fluency Assessment Plan

- ☑ **Week 1** Assess Advanced students.
- ☑ **Week 2** Assess Strategic Intervention students.
- ☑ **Week 3** Assess On-Level students.
- ☑ **Week 4** Assess Strategic Intervention students.
- ☑ **This week assess any students you have not yet checked during this unit.**

Set individual goals for students to enable them to reach the year-end goal.

- Current Goal: 110–116 wcpm
- Year-End Goal: 140 wcpm

Provide opportunities for English language learners to read aloud to younger children. This allows them to practice their oral reading and improve their fluency.

To develop fluent readers, use Fluency Coach.

 DAY 5 **Grouping Options**

Reading
Whole Group
Revisit the Question of the Week.

Group Time
Differentiated Instruction
Reread this week's Leveled Readers. See pp. 230h–230i for the small group lesson plan.

Whole Group
Use pp. 253b–253c.

Language Arts
Use pp. 253d–253l.

TONE OF VOICE

Fluency

DAY 1

Model Reread "Molly Pitcher" on p. 230m. Explain that you will use different tones of voice to show desperation, suspense, or other emotions. Model for students as you read.

DAY 2

Echo Reading Read aloud p. 236. Have students notice how your voice changes as the poem moves from narrative to dialogue to description. Have students practice as a class doing three echo readings of p. 236.

DAY 3

Model Read aloud p. 246. Have students notice how you pause at commas and how your voice changes as the conclusion begins with the line, "For, borne on the night-wind of the Past." Practice as a class by doing three echo readings.

DAY 4

Partner Reading Have partners practice reading p. 246, three times. Students should read with proper inflection and offer each other feedback.

Monitor Progress | Check Fluency WCPM

As students reread, monitor their progress toward their individual fluency goals. Current Goal: 110–116 words correct per minute. End-of-Year Goal: 140 words correct per minute.

If… students cannot read fluently at a rate of 110–116 words correct per minute,
then… make sure students practice with text at their independent level. Provide additional fluency practice, pairing nonfluent readers with fluent readers.

If… students already read at 140 words correct per minute,
then… they do not need to reread three to four times.

SUCCESS PREDICTOR

DAY 5

Assessment
Individual Reading Rate Use the Fluency Assessment Plan and do a one-minute timed reading of either selection from this week to assess students in Week 5. Pay special attention to this week's skill, tone of voice. Provide corrective feedback for each student.

RETEACH

⊚ Sequence

TEACH

Review the definition of *sequence* on p. 230. Students can complete Practice Book p. 98 on their own, or you can complete it as a class. Remind students to try to visualize a character or real person going from one event to the next. If they cannot picture the sequence from their time line, it may not be logical. For example, at the beginning of *The Midnight Ride of Paul Revere,* first Paul talks to his friend; second, says goodbye; and third, rows off. Any other order would not make sense.

ASSESS

Have partners sequence the actions of Paul Revere's friend on p. 239. *(First he wanders the streets listening for news; then he climbs the Old North Church; last, he stops to listen and look around.)*

For additional instruction on sequence, see DI·56.

EXTEND SKILLS

Personification

TEACH

Personification is giving human traits to animals, objects, forces of nature, and abstract ideas. These characteristics can be feelings, the ability to talk, intelligence, or personality. Writers use personification to:

• make fiction seem more real.

• make nonfiction more lively.

Point out the use of personification of wind on p. 239. Help them to see the human characteristics: intelligence *(watchful)*, action *(creeping)*, speech *("All is well").*

ASSESS

Have partners look for another example of personification in the first stanza on p. 245. Then have students write 3–4 examples of personification on their own.

OBJECTIVES

⊚ Identify sequence of events.

● Recognize personification.

Skills Trace ⊚ Sequence	
Introduce/Teach	TE: 5.1 90–91; 5.2 230–231; 5.6 726–727
Practice	Practice Book: 33, 37, 38, 66, 76, 93, 97, 98, 256, 266, 293, 297, 298
Reteach/Review	**TE: 5.1 111b, 121, DI•55; 5.2 173, 199, 253b, DI•56; 5.6 641, 655, 753b, DI•56**
Test	Selection Test: 13–16, 37–40, 117–120; Benchmark Test: Units 2, 6

ELL

Access Content Reteach the skill by reviewing the Picture It! lesson on sequence in the ELL Teaching Guide, pp. 64–65.

Sequence

- The **sequence** of events is the order in which they take place, from first to last.
- Clue words such as *first, next,* and *then* may show sequence in a story or article, but not always. Other clues are dates and times of day.
- Sometimes two events happen at the same time. Clue words that can show this are *meanwhile* and *in that same year.*

Directions Read the following passage and complete the time line below.

> Thomas Jefferson was the third president of the United States. After a close election, he took office in 1801. In 1803, Jefferson proposed an expedition to explore the West. This became the Lewis and Clark expedition. Meanwhile, he made an agreement with France called the Lousiana Purchase. Jefferson's re-election in 1804 was different from his first. This time he won every state except three. Lewis and Clark returned in 1806. They had traveled all the way to present-day Oregon. Jefferson was asked to run for president for a third term. He refused because he did not want the president to become like a king. In 1809, Jefferson returned to his much-loved home, Monticello.

Thomas Jefferson's Presidency

1801	1803		1804	1806	1809
Jefferson is elected president.	1. Jefferson proposes an expedition to explore the western part of the continent.	2. Jefferson arranges for the Louisiana Purchase.	3. Jefferson is elected president for the second time.	4. Lewis and Clark return.	Jefferson returns home to Monticello.

5. Which two events happened at nearly the same time? How can you tell?
Jefferson proposed exploration of the West and made the Louisiana
Purchase at about the same time; The word "meanwhile" is used.

School + Home Home Activity Your child read a short passage and identified the sequence of events in it. Read a historical story or article with your child and chart the sequence of events in the article.

▲ **Practice Book** p. 98

SUCCE
PREDICT

Vocabulary and Word Study

VOCABULARY STRATEGY

Word Structure

INFLECTED ENDINGS Remind students that when verbs contain inflected endings like -s, -ed, and -ing you can use the endings to help determine the verbs' meanings. Have students identify words that contain inflected endings from *The Midnight Ride of Paul Revere* and then write the endings and word meanings.

Word	Word Ending	Word Meaning
rowed	-ed	used oars to move a boat
watches		
moving		

Rhyming Words

Discuss the fact that *The Midnight Ride of Paul Revere* is a poem that contains rhyme. Have students work with partners to choose three words from the poem and brainstorm as many rhyming words as they can for each one.

1. **ride:** side, tied, hide, glide, pride, bride, died

2. **tower:** _____

3. **hill:** _____

BUILD CONCEPT VOCABULARY

Promoting Freedom

LOOKING BACK Remind students of the unit theme: Doing the Right Thing. Discuss the unit focus question: *What makes people want to do the right thing?* Ask students how the Concept Vocabulary from each week of this unit relates to the unit theme and unit focus question. Ask students if they have any words or categories to add. If time permits, create a Unit Concept Web.

Monitor Progress

Check Vocabulary

If... students suggest words or categories that are not related to the unit theme,	**then**... review the words and categories on the weekly Concept Webs and discuss how they relate to the unit theme.

SUCCESS PREDICTOR

Speaking and Listening

SPEAKING

Radio Feature Story

SET-UP Have students use the information from the biographical articles they wrote in Writing Workshop to do a biographical feature story for a radio broadcast. Emphasize they should not just read their articles to the class, but should retell the story from the subject's point of view to put a new spin on the story that will capture their audience's attention. Tell students they may focus their feature stories on one main event in the person's life.

ORGANIZATION Students should begin their feature stories with an interesting anecdote or fact. Then they should provide more detailed information about the person's life or the event. Remind them that a radio feature story is usually 1 to 2 minutes in length, so they may need to expand on some of the information in their articles. They should conclude with an interesting final statement about the person.

Delivery Tips
- Look up from your script as often as you can to make eye contact with people in the audience.
- Speak in a natural voice that is neither too loud nor too soft.
- Speak clearly with a purpose.
- Keep a constant tempo, except for emphasis.

LISTENING

Listen to a CD

Have students listen to the audio CD of *The Midnight Ride of Paul Revere.* In small groups, they can answer these questions orally or in writing.

1. **What mood does the speaker create?** *(Possible response: worry, excitement, suspense)*

2. **How do you feel listening to the speaker read the poem?** *(Possible response: excitement, interest, suspense)*

3. **Describe the rhythm of the poem.** *(Responses will vary but should include how the speaker uses pauses, tempo, and volume.)*

ELL

Support Vocabulary Use the following to review and extend vocabulary and to explore lesson concepts further:
- ELL Poster 10, Days 3–5 instruction
- Vocabulary Activities and Word Cards in ELL Teaching Guide, pp. 66–67

Assessment For information on assessing students' speaking and listening, see the ELL and Transition Handbook.

Grammar — Subject-Verb Agreement

Monitor Progress

Grammar

If... students have difficulty identifying subjects and verbs that agree,	then... provide additional instruction and practice in The Grammar and Writing Book pp. 104–107.

DAILY FIX-IT

This week use Daily Fix-It Transparency 10.

Spiral REVIEW

ELL

Support Grammar See the Grammar Transition lessons in the ELL and Transition Handbook.

▲ **The Grammar and Writing Book**
For more instruction and practice, use pp. 104–107.

DAY 1 — Teach and Model

DAILY FIX-IT

1. Mr. henry enjoy teaching U.S. history. *(Henry; enjoys)*
2. He is eager to teach we about the Revolutionary War. *(eager; us)*

READING-GRAMMAR CONNECTION

Write this sentence from *The Midnight Ride of Paul Revere* on the board:

> *A moment only he feels the spell/ Of the place and the hour . . . .*

Explain that the sentence subject *he* is singular, so it needs the singular form of the verb *feel*. This is why an *-s* is added to make *feels*.

Display Grammar Transparency 10. Read aloud the definitions and sample sentences. Work through the items.

Subject-Verb Agreement

The subject and verb in a sentence must **agree**, or work together. A singular subject needs a singular verb. A plural subject needs a plural verb.
Use the following rules for verbs that tell about the present time.
- If the subject is a singular noun or *he, she,* or *it,* add *-s* or *-es* to most verbs.
  A horse runs. A dog chases the horse. It barks loudly.
- If the subject is a plural noun or *I, you, we,* or *they,* do not add *-s* or *-es* to the verb.
  Horses run. Dogs chase the horse. They bark loudly.
- For the verb *be,* use *am* and *is* to agree with singular subjects and *are* to agree with plural subjects.
  I am afraid. Paul is fearless. The armies are here. We are surprised.
- A **collective noun** names a group, such as *family, team,* and *class.* A collective noun is singular if it refers to a group acting as one: The class *is going* on a field trip. A collective noun is plural if it refers to members of the group acting individually: The class *are debating* about which place to visit.

Directions Underline the subject of each sentence. Circle the verb in ( ) that agrees with the subject.

1. U.S. history (*is*, are) an interesting subject.
2. Our class (*is*, are) studying the American colonies.
3. Toby (ask, *asks*) to report on transportation in the colonies.
4. Williamsburg (*is*, are) a colonial community.
5. Actors (*play*, plays) the part of colonists.
6. A blacksmith (pound, *pounds*) metal at a forge.
7. He (make, *makes*) tools of all kinds.
8. Teams of horses (*pull*, pulls) wagons on dirt roads.
9. Women (*cook*, cooks) food on the hearth.
10. Winnie (hurry, *hurries*) up the stairs to the loft.
11. Husks of corn (*serve*, serves) as mattresses in these beds.
12. A colonial child (*has*, have) only a few toys.

Unit 2 The Midnight Ride of Paul Revere   Grammar **10**

▲ **Grammar Transparency** 10

DAY 2 — Develop the Concept

DAILY FIX-IT

3. Isnt that also called the War of Independence. *(Isn't; Independence?)*
4. Thirteen colonies was ruled by england until 1776. *(were; England)*

GUIDED PRACTICE

Review the concept of subject-verb agreement.

- The **subject** and **verb** of a sentence must work together, or **agree** in number.
- When a **singular subject** takes a present tense verb, that verb usually ends in *-s* or *-es*.
- When a **plural subject** takes a present tense verb, that verb usually does not end in *-s* or *-es*.

HOMEWORK Grammar and Writing Practice Book p. 37. Work through the first two items with the class.

Subject-Verb Agreement

The subject and verb in a sentence must **agree**, or work together. A singular subject needs a singular verb. A plural subject needs a plural verb.
Use the following rules for verbs that tell about the present time.
- If the subject is a singular noun or *he, she,* or *it,* add *-s* or *-es* to most verbs.
  The wagon creaks. It lurches along.
- If the subject is a plural noun or *I, you, we,* or *they,* do not add *-s* or *-es* to the verb.
  The oxen pull the wagon. They strain uphill.
- For the verb *be,* use *am* and *is* to agree with singular subjects and *are* to agree with plural subjects.
  I am hot. Thomas is happy. The patriots are loyal. We are late.
- A **collective noun** names a group, such as *family, team,* and *class.* A collective noun is singular if it refers to a group acting as one: The family *is taking* a vacation. A collective noun is plural if it refers to members of the group acting individually: The family *are arguing* about the destination.

Directions Match each subject with a verb that agrees. Write the letter of the correct verb on the line.

A or C	1. The colonists	A. are training.
D	2. The British king	B. is beginning.
B	3. A war	C. rebel.
A	4. Troops	D. sends his army.

Directions Underline the verb in ( ) that agrees with the subject of each sentence.

5. The American colonies (*trade*, trades) with England.
6. Two of the colonies' exports (is, *are*) cotton and indigo.
7. England (tax, *taxes*) the items imported into the colonies.
8. Tea (*is*, are) a popular drink in the colonies.
9. The Boston Tea Party (show, *shows*) the colonists' anger about taxes.
10. Today, Americans (*drink*, drinks) more coffee than tea.
11. Earlier conflicts (is, *are*) forgotten.
12. The two countries (*consider*, considers) themselves close allies.

Home Activity Your child learned about subject-verb agreement. Have your child make up sentences about clothes he or she wears, using both singular subjects (shirt, belt) and plural subjects (socks, shoes) and making sure verbs agree.

▲ **Grammar and Writing Practice Book** p. 37

DAY 3 Apply to Writing

DAILY FIX-IT

5. Paul revere watched for a glimmir of light in the tower. *(Revere; glimmer)*

6. Him horse was redy to run. *(His; ready)*

MAKE SUBJECTS/VERBS AGREE

Explain that errors in subject-verb agreement distract and confuse readers. Always match singular subjects with singular verb forms, and plural subjects with plural verb forms.

- Have students review something they have written to see if they can improve it by correcting errors in subject-verb agreement.

- Remind students that whether their sentences are simple, compound, or complex, subjects and verbs must agree.

HOMEWORK Grammar and Writing Practice Book p. 38.

Subject-Verb Agreement

Directions Add a verb to complete each sentence. Be sure to use the correct verb form.
Possible answers:
1. The Liberty Bell ____is____ a well-known American symbol.
2. It ____rests____ in the Liberty Bell Center in Philadelphia.
3. Many tourists ____visit____ this site.
4. ____Does____ the bell ever ring?
5. No. A crack ____runs____ up the side of the bell.
6. The main metals in the bell ____are____ copper and tin.
7. The bell ____weighs____ 2,080 pounds.
8. Philadelphia ____lies____ in southeastern Pennsylvania.
9. More than a million and a half people ____live____ there.
10. Tourists ____enjoy____ the many historic sites in Philadelphia.

Directions Circle the verb that agrees with each subject. Then write sentences using at least three of the subject-verb pairs.
11. class   (is studying)   are studying
12. historic site   inspire   (inspires)
13. teacher   tell   (tells)
14. some students   (sing)   sings
15. they   is   (are)
16. I   (feel)   feels

Possible answers: Our class is studying about the state capitol. This historic site inspires everyone. The teacher tells us many facts about our state's history. Some students sing the state anthem. They are doing a fine job. I feel a lump in my throat.

Home Activity Your child learned how to write subjects and verbs that agree. Ask your child to make up sentences in the present tense describing favorite animals, first using a singular subject, then a plural subject (dog/dogs, lion/lions, and so on).

▲ **Grammar and Writing Practice Book** p. 38

DAY 4 Test Preparation

DAILY FIX-IT

7. My family are visiting Boston on vakation. *(is visiting; vacation)*

8. Many heros lived hear. *(heroes; here)*

STANDARDIZED TEST PREP

Test Tip

Sometimes a prepositional phrase appears between a subject and verb. Be sure the verb agrees with the subject, not the object of the preposition.

No: The <u>battles</u> of that war <u>is</u> described in this book.

Yes: The <u>battles</u> of that war <u>are</u> described in this book.

HOMEWORK Grammar and Writing Practice Book p. 39.

Subject-Verb Agreement

Directions Mark the letter of the verb that agrees with the subject in the sentence.

1. Many poems ____
   (A) rhyme
   B rhymes
   C rhimes
   D rhiming

2. I ____ the poems of Longfellow.
   (A) enjoy
   B enjoys
   C enjoies
   D enjoying

3. His work ____ both rhyme and rhythm.
   A use
   (B) uses
   C using
   D user

4. "The Midnight Ride of Paul Revere" ____ a narrative poem.
   A be called
   B are called
   (C) is called
   D be

5. Narrative poems ____ a story.
   A telling
   B tells
   (C) tell
   D telled

6. Poetry ____ vivid word pictures.
   A paint
   B painting
   C painter
   (D) paints

7. Our class ____ in unison.
   A recite
   B reciting
   (C) recites
   D recities

8. We ____ to do choral readings.
   (A) like
   B likes
   C liking
   D be liking

9. It ____ like a song.
   A be
   B being
   C are
   (D) is

10. The rhyming words ____ good to me.
    (A) sound
    B sounding
    C sounds
    D soundies

Home Activity Your child prepared for taking tests on subject-verb agreement. Have your child copy some subject and verb pairs from a favorite book and explain why the subjects and verbs agree.

▲ **Grammar and Writing Practice Book** p. 39

DAY 5 Cumulative Review

DAILY FIX-IT

9. British Ships float in the harber. *(ships; harbor)*

10. They're sharp masts looks like dangerous weapons. *(Their; look)*

ADDITIONAL PRACTICE

Assign pp. 104–107 in The Grammar and Writing Book.

EXTRA PRACTICE Grammar and Writing Practice Book p. 131.

TEST PREPARATION Grammar and Writing Practice Book pp. 153–154.

ASSESSMENT

CUMULATIVE REVIEW Grammar and Writing Practice Book p. 40.

Subject-Verb Agreement

Directions Underline the subject of each sentence. Circle the verb in ( ) that agrees with the subject.
1. <u>Paul Revere</u> (is) are) a legendary figure of the Revolutionary War.
2. <u>Americans</u> (love) loves) hearing about his midnight ride.
3. <u>I</u> (imagine) imagines) that night.
4. <u>Three men</u> (ride) rides) from Boston to Concord.
5. <u>Danger</u> (lurk (lurks) around every bend.
6. An English <u>scout</u> (yell (yells) "Stop! Who goes there?"
7. His <u>companions</u> (stop) stops) one of the three riders.
8. One <u>man</u> (go (goes) no further that night.
9. <u>It</u> (is) are) Paul Revere.
10. Few <u>people</u> (know) knows) that fact.

Directions Add a present tense verb to complete each sentence. Be sure the verb agrees with the subject in number. **Possible answers:**
11. This portrait ____shows____ a serious man.
12. It ____is____ a portrait of Paul Revere.
13. Several objects ____lie____ on the table next to him.
14. They ____are____ a silversmith's tools.
15. The man's right hand ____frames____ his chin thoughtfully.
16. His left hand ____cradles____ a silver teapot.
17. Americans still ____treasure____ the silver work of Revere.
18. A silver piece by Paul Revere ____possesses____ great value today.

Home Activity Your child reviewed subject-verb agreement. Ask your child to read a newspaper or magazine article and point out singular and plural subjects. Have him or her explain why the verbs agree with those subjects.

▲ **Grammar and Writing Practice Book** p. 40

Writing for Tests Interview

Organization/Paragraphs Make sure English learners can decode words in the prompt. Work with students to complete a cloze sentence that addresses the prompt and could be used to launch writing (e.g., "A poem I know about a historical event is _____.").

Writing Traits

FOCUS/IDEAS Interview questions and answers address the key points of the event.

ORGANIZATION/PARAGRAPHS Responses trace events in a logical order and use sequence words as transitions.

VOICE The writer is involved with the subject. The writing is lively and interesting.

WORD CHOICE Vivid, precise details *(damp fog rose; lights glimmered)* help establish mood and recreate the event described.

SENTENCES Interview questions initiate thoughtful answers.

CONVENTIONS There is excellent control and accuracy. Subjects and verbs agree in number.

DAY 1 Model the Trait

READING-WRITING CONNECTION

- When you write a response for tests, remember that ordering parts logically and using transition words will strengthen your answer.

- Think about how Longfellow orders events in *The Midnight Ride of Paul Revere* and uses sequence phrases.

MODEL ORGANIZATION/ PARAGRAPHS

Discuss Writing Transparency 10A. Point out underlined words in the prompt. Then discuss the model and the writing trait of organization/paragraphs.

Think Aloud The person interviewed has organized responses in time order. The sequence of words and transition words show this: "for a long time," "at last," and "there would be." These transitions and verb tenses help me follow the action.

Interview

Prompt In an **interview**, a person answers questions about himself or herself. "Interview" a famous person from history that you have read about. Write questions and answers that are based on your reading. Try to make this person "come alive" for your audience.

A Night to Remember: A Conversation with Paul Revere

Question sets the scene and prepares interviewee to explain reasons.

Q: Why did you ride through the Middlesex countryside on the night of April 18, 1775?

A: We colonists knew that the British were going to attack. We had made up our minds to fight for freedom! What we didn't know was exactly when and how the redcoats would come. I was to warn the people in surrounding villages and farms so that they could take up arms.

Q: What do you remember about that night?

Sequence words highlight and clarify order of events.

A: The air was chill, and a damp fog rose. For a long time, my horse and I waited impatiently. It seemed the signal light would never appear in the Old North Church tower. At last, two lights glimmered! The British would travel by sea. Then I sprang into the saddle and away we flew!

Questions focus on how person thought and felt.

Q: How did you feel about the coming battle?

Details of description reinforce feeling of determination.

A: From this night, there would be no turning back. I felt certain we would fight bravely but sad that some soldiers would be killed. I felt as strong as steel for our cause.

Unit 2 The Midnight Ride of Paul Revere   **Writing Model 10A**

▲ **Writing Transparency** 10A

DAY 2 Improve Writing

WRITER'S CRAFT
Organization

Display Writing Transparency 10B. Read the directions and work together to put details in order and choose transitions to connect them.

Think Aloud **ORGANIZE INTERVIEW QUESTIONS LOGICALLY** Tomorrow we will write an interview. How should I order questions I'd ask Martin Luther King, Jr.? I'd first ask about his early life and why he became a minister. Then I could ask about how he came to lead a civil rights movement. Finally, I could ask what was most important about leading. This order is logical. It follows the course of his life.

GUIDED WRITING Some students may need more help writing transitions. Help them find sequence transitions in the selection, and brainstorm others for writing.

Organization

When **organizing** your writing about an event, use sequence words to make it clear when each action occurred. Some sequence words are at first, next, then, now, and finally.

Directions Number the events in the order in which they occurred. Then choose a sequence word or phrase from the box to begin each sentence. Write a paragraph putting the sentences in time order.

| Shortly before dawn | At last | At 12 midnight |
| As soon as darkness fell | Then | By 1 A.M. |

5 I made it to Lexington.
1 I parted from my friend and rowed to the Charlestown side of the river.
2 I waited for the signal to flash from the Old North Church.
6 My ride ended at Concord town, as birds began to sing.
4 My horse and I galloped into Medford town.
3 Two lights appeared in the belfry tower.

As soon as darkness fell, I parted from my friend and rowed to the Charlestown side of the river. Then I waited for the signal to flash from the Old North Church. At last, two lights appeared in the belfry tower. At 12 midnight my horse and I galloped into Medford town. By 1 A.M. I made it to Lexington. Shortly before dawn, my ride ended at Concord town, as birds began to sing.

Directions Write your own paragraph about something you have accomplished. Use sequence words to show the order of events. **Possible answer:**

The Smiths had asked me to take care of their dog for the weekend. First, I let myself in and greeted Lucky. Then I got the leash and took him for a walk. At the park, I threw the Frisbee for him. When we got back to the Smiths' house, I brushed Lucky. Finally, I gave him his food and water.

Unit 2 The Midnight Ride of Paul Revere   **Writer's Craft 10B**

▲ **Writing Transparency** 10B

DAY 3 Prewrite and Draft

READ THE WRITING PROMPT

on page 249 in the Student Edition.

The Midnight Ride of Paul Revere tells about a famous American.

Think about another famous American. Now write an interview with that person.

Writing Test Tips

1. **Read the prompt carefully.**
   - Find key words.
   - Consider the purpose and audience. How will they affect your writing?

2. **Develop a plan.** Think of what you want to say before writing. Fill out a simple graphic organizer. For example, for a story, think of a beginning, middle, and end. For a comparison/ contrast essay, fill out a T-chart or a Venn diagram.

3. **Support your ideas.** Use facts, examples, and details to strengthen your response. Avoid making general statements that are unsupported.

4. **Use a variety of sentence structures.** Include complex and compound sentences, and vary sentence beginnings, lengths, and types.

5. **Check your writing.** If this is a timed test, you may not have time to recopy your work. However, you can neatly add, delete, or change words and make corrections in spelling, punctuation, or grammar. Make sure your handwriting is legible. It pays to reread your work before handing it in.

DAY 4 Draft and Revise

EDITING/REVISING CHECKLIST

☑ **Focus** Do questions focus on the most important parts of the person's experience?

☑ **Organization** Are questions and answers clearly structured? Do transitions connect ideas clearly?

☑ **Support** Do sentence structures make the writing clear and interesting?

☑ **Conventions** Have I used verbs that agree with my subjects in number? Are words with the final syllables *or, er,* and *ar* spelled correctly?

See *The Grammar and Writing Book,* pp. 104–109.

Revising Tips

Organization/ Paragraphs

- Order questions logically, so that answers give readers a sense of what happened, why it happened, and how it happened.
- Use sequence words and phrases to connect steps in the event.
- Use vivid, concrete words that bring the action to life and show feelings.

ASSESSMENT Use the scoring rubric to evaluate students' work.

DAY 5 Connect to Unit Writing

How-to Report	
Week 1	Summary 161g–161h
Week 2	Story Review 185g–185h
Week 3	News Story 207g–207h
Week 4	Rules 229g–229h
Week 5	Interview 253g–253h

PREVIEW THE UNIT PROMPT

Write a report explaining how to make or do something that is familiar to you. Choose words that make your report interesting to read and easy to understand. Explain all the steps and materials needed.

APPLY

- A how-to report explains the steps for making or doing something.
- The writer of a how-to report uses sequence words to show the order of steps in the process.

Writing Trait Rubric

	4	3	2	1
Organization/ Paragraphs	Ideas well developed from beginning to end; strong attention-getter and closure	Ideas that progress from beginning to end; good attention-getter and closure	Some sense of movement from beginning to end; weak attention-getter and closure	No sense of movement from beginning to end; no closure
	Interview organized with helpful transitions	Interview organized with some logical order and some transitions	Interview not clearly organized; uses few transitions	Interview not organized; no transitions

Spelling & Phonics
Final Syllables *er, ar, or*

OBJECTIVE

● Spell words that end with *er, ar,* and *or.*

Generalization

Connect to Phonics Final syllables *er, ar,* and *or* often sound alike even when they are spelled differently: *danger, tractor, dollar.* Some sounds can be spelled in different ways.

Spelling Words

1. danger	11. locker
2. wander*	12. helicopter
3. tractor	13. pillar
4. dollar	14. refrigerator
5. harbor	15. caterpillar
6. eager*	16. rumor
7. eraser	17. glimmer
8. surrender	18. linger
9. solar	19. sensor
10. sticker	20. alligator

Challenge Words

21. numerator	24. counselor
22. collector	25. denominator
23. ancestor	

* Words from the selection

 ELL

Spelling/Phonics Support See the ELL and Transition Handbook for spelling support.

DAY 1 — Pretest and Sort

PRETEST

Use the Dictation Sentences from Day 5 to administer the pretest. Read the word, read the sentence, and then read the word again. Guide students in self-correcting their pretests and correcting any misspellings.

Monitor Progress
Spelling

If...	then...
If... students misspell more than 5 pretest words,	**then...** use words 1–10 for Strategic Intervention.
If... students misspell 1–5 pretest words,	**then...** use words 1–20 for On-Level practice.
If... students correctly spell all pretest words,	**then...** use words 1–25 for Advanced Learners.

HOMEWORK Spelling Practice Book, p. 37.

Final Syllables er, ar, or

Generalization Words with final syllables er, ar, and or often sound alike even when they are spelled differently: **danger, tractor, dollar.**

Word Sort Sort the list words by the spelling of the final syllable.

-er	-ar
1. danger	11. dollar
2. wander	12. solar
3. eager	13. pillar
4. eraser	14. caterpillar
5. surrender	**-or**
6. sticker	15. tractor
7. locker	16. harbor
8. helicopter	17. refrigerator
9. glimmer	18. rumor
10. linger	19. sensor
	20. alligator

Challenge Words

-or
21. numerator
22. collector
23. ancestor
24. counselor
25. denominator

Spelling Words
1. danger
2. wander
3. tractor
4. dollar
5. harbor
6. eager
7. eraser
8. surrender
9. solar
10. sticker
11. locker
12. helicopter
13. pillar
14. refrigerator
15. caterpillar
16. rumor
17. glimmer
18. linger
19. sensor
20. alligator

Challenge Words
21. numerator
22. collector
23. ancestor
24. counselor
25. denominator

School + Home **Home Activity** Your child is learning about final syllables that sound the same but are spelled differently. Ask your child to spell three list words with endings that sound alike but are spelled differently.

▲ **Spelling Practice Book** p. 37

DAY 2 — Think and Practice

TEACH

Since final syllables *er, ar,* and *or* often sound alike, words that end with these letters must be memorized. Write *locker, pillar,* and *harbor.* Underline *er, ar,* and *or* as you say the words. Have students repeat the words. Then have them spell the final syllable of each word.

> locker
> pillar
> harbor

COLOR CLUES Have students write the list words and highlight the final syllables, using one color for syllables with *er,* another color for syllables with *ar,* and a third color for syllables with *or.* If colors are not available, use geometric shapes, such as a square, a circle, and a triangle, for each ending.

HOMEWORK Spelling Practice Book, p. 38.

Final Syllables er, ar, or

Spelling Words				
danger	wander	tractor	dollar	harbor
eager	eraser	surrender	solar	sticker
locker	helicopter	pillar	refrigerator	caterpillar
rumor	glimmer	linger	sensor	alligator

Definitions Write a list word that means the same or almost the same as the word or phrase.

1. spark	1. glimmer		
2. port	2. harbor		
3. sun	3. solar		
4. gossip	4. rumor		
5. post	5. pillar		
6. peril	6. danger		
7. cooler	7. refrigerator		
8. excited	8. eager		
9. 100 cents	9. dollar		
10. roam	10. wander		

Missing Words Write the list word that completes the sentence.

11. I have a habit of chewing on my pencil ____.	11. eraser
12. Smart criminals ____ when spotted.	12. surrender
13. The farmer drove the ____ across the field.	13. tractor
14. I store my school books in my ____.	14. locker
15. The ____ floated silently across the swampy water.	15. alligator
16. The ____ became a beautiful butterfly.	16. caterpillar
17. She pulled the price ____ off the package.	17. sticker
18. The news ____ flew over the accident scene.	18. helicopter
19. I like to ____ in my room instead of watching television downstairs.	19. linger
20. The motion ____ turns on the light when anyone is near.	20. sensor

School + Home **Home Activity** Your child wrote words with final syllables er, ar, and or. Select three list words and ask your child to define them.

▲ **Spelling Practice Book** p. 38

DAY 3   Connect to Writing

WRITE ABOUT A HISTORIC PERSON

Ask students to use at least four spelling words to write facts about an historic person they admire.

Frequently Misspelled Words

another   *we're*

These words may seem easy to spell, but they are often misspelled by fifth-graders. Alert students to these frequently misspelled words. Point out that *another* ends with -*er* and is one word. Remind students that *we're* is the contraction for *we are*.

HOMEWORK Spelling Practice Book, p. 39.

Final Syllables er, ar, or

Proofread a Sign There are seven spelling errors and one capitalization error. Circle the errors and write the corrections on the lines.

(welcome) to the Wildlife and (Alligater) Preserve
- Admission is one dollar for an all-day parking pass.
- You can rent an all-day locker for your convenience.
- (Helicopter) rides are available to see the (harber) from the air.
- To preserve the ecology, stay on the path. Do not (wandar) off.
- There is no (dangor) Animals stay behind a motion (sensor) fence.
- Linger over lunch on our beautiful terrace.
- Do not forget to (surrendar) your parking pass at the gate when leaving.

Spelling Words
danger
wander
tractor
dollar
harbor
eager
eraser
surrender
solar
sticker
locker
helicopter
pillar
refrigerator
caterpillar
rumor
glimmer
linger
sensor
alligator

1. Welcome   2. Alligator
3. Helicopter   4. harbor
5. wander   6. danger
7. sensor   8. surrender

Frequently Misspelled Words
another
we're

Proofread Words Circle the word that is spelled correctly.

9. doller   (dollar)   dollor
10. erasor   (eraser)   erasar
11. stickar   (sticker)   stickor
12. soler   (solar)   solor
13. helicoptor   helicopter   (helicopter)
14. tracter   tractar   (tractor)
15. stickor   (sticker)   stickar

School + Home Home Activity Your child identified misspelled words with er, ar, and or endings. Select three list words and ask your child to spell them.

▲ **Spelling Practice Book** p. 39

DAY 4   Review

REVIEW WORDS WITH FINAL *er*, *ar*, AND *or*

Have students use ten list words to make a hidden word puzzle. Tell students to exchange papers and solve each other's puzzles.

Spelling Strategy
Steps for Spelling New Words

Step 1: Look at the word. Say it and listen to the sounds.

Step 2: Spell the word aloud.

Step 3: Think about its spelling. Is there anything special to remember?

Step 4: Picture the word with your eyes shut.

Step 5: Look at the word and write it.

Step 6: Cover the word. Picture it and write it again. Check its spelling.

HOMEWORK Spelling Practice Book, p. 40.

Final Syllables er, ar, or

Spelling Words				
danger	wander	tractor	dollar	harbor
eager	eraser	surrender	solar	sticker
locker	helicopter	pillar	refrigerator	caterpillar
rumor	glimmer	linger	sensor	alligator

Word Scramble Riddle Unscramble each list word and then write the numbered letters on the lines below to answer the riddle.

Riddle: What's the answer to "See you later, alligator!"?

1. RRNDSEURE   s u r r e n d e r
2. ARERSE   e r a s e r
3. EOERRIRRFAGT   r e f r i g e r a t o r
4. RAERPCTALIL   c a t e r p i l l a r
5. LEMMGRI   g l i m m e r
6. LOLDAR   d o l l a r
7. PALIRL   p i l l a r
8. EINGLR   l i n g e r
9. RLAITALGO   a l l i g a t o r
10. CISKTRE   s t i c k e r
11. OSRAL   s o l a r
12. LCERKO   l o c k e r
13. NGDREA   d a n g e r
14. UMRRO   r u m o r
15. RNEWAD   w a n d e r
16. ATOCRTR   t r a c t o r
17. HRRABO   h a r b o r
18. AGREE   e a g e r

n o t   f o r   a   w h i l e   c r o c o d i l e

School + Home Home Activity Your child has learned to spell words with final syllables er, ar, and or. Look through a book or magazine with your child and find four other words with the same endings.

▲ **Spelling Practice Book** p. 40

DAY 5   Posttest

DICTATION SENTENCES

1. The doctor said the patient was out of danger.
2. Deer wander in the forest.
3. The plow is attached to a tractor.
4. Whose picture is on a dollar bill?
5. The ship sailed out of the harbor.
6. Jerry was eager to join the team.
7. My pencil's eraser tore the paper.
8. He had to surrender his pass when he left the building.
9. That house uses solar heat.
10. I put the sticker on my notebook.
11. Hang your coat in your locker.
12. The helicopter took off.
13. The plant sits on top of a pillar.
14. Put the milk in the refrigerator.
15. A caterpillar crawled along a twig.
16. I heard the rumor, but it's not true.
17. Stars glimmer in the night sky.
18. I wanted to linger in the garden.
19. A sensor will trigger the alarm.
20. An alligator climbed out of the river.

CHALLENGE

21. The fraction's numerator is three.
22. Mom is an antique collector.
23. Do you have a famous ancestor?
24. The counselor can help with the problem.
25. The denominator is a fraction's bottom number.

OBJECTIVES

- Formulate an inquiry question that is connected to this week's lesson focus.

- Effectively and efficiently find, evaluate, and communicate information related to an inquiry question using electronic sources.

New Literacies

Day 1	Identify Questions
Day 2	Navigate/Search
Day 3	Analyze
Day 4	Synthesize
Day 5	Communicate

NEW LITERACIES

Internet Inquiry Activity

EXPLORE PROMOTING FREEDOM

Use the following 5-day plan to help students conduct this week's Internet inquiry activity on promoting freedom. Remind students to follow classroom rules when using the Internet.

DAY 1

Identify Questions Discuss the lesson focus question: *How can people promote freedom?* Brainstorm ideas for specific inquiry questions about promoting freedom. For example, students might want to explore freedom of speech and learn about places in the world where it is prohibited. Students can work individually, in pairs, or in small groups to identify their inquiry questions.

DAY 2

Navigate/Search Remind students to identify effective keywords to use in a student-friendly search engine. Point out that the keyword *freedom* would be too broad. Encourage them to be as specific as possible, with keywords like *freedom of speech* or *freedom of speech in China.* Encourage them to skim through Web site descriptions. If they think a site contains useful information, they can copy down the URL or bookmark the site words together.

DAY 3

Analyze Encourage students to skim and scan the Web sites identified from Day 2. Point out that some sites may provide links to other useful sites. When they find a useful site, encourage them to take notes from it, or if appropriate, print it out and highlight important information.

DAY 4

Synthesize Encourage students to synthesize information from Day 3. Remind them to avoid plagiarism by paraphrasing the information they find on the Web sites or by documenting the sources if they are lifting direct quotations. Have them think about the best approaches for sharing the information they gather.

DAY 5

Communicate Invite students to share their inquiry results in the form of oral reports, accompanied by charts or tables to summarize the important points.

RESEARCH/STUDY SKILLS
Illustration/Caption

TEACH

Show students a photo or illustration that includes a caption. You may use a photo or illustration from a newspaper, magazine, or textbook. Discuss with students the purpose of the illustration or photo, and how it helps explain the text. Then, discuss these terms.

- In fiction, **illustrations** are photos or drawings that can help readers understand characters and events by establishing mood, showing action, and giving insights or information about characters.

- In nonfiction, **illustrations** are photos or drawings that help explain the text.

- A **caption** explains an illustration, and usually appears below or to the side of the illustration.

Have students work in pairs. Provide each pair with a magazine or newspaper. Have pairs locate a photo or illustration with a caption. Have them discuss what their illustration shows, the context it is in, and its purpose. Then, as a class, discuss these questions:

1. **What does your illustration or photo show?** (Possible response: It shows astronauts about to board the space shuttle.)

2. **What is the purpose of the illustration or photo?** (Possible response: The purpose is to show who the astronauts are and to show their excitement as they begin their journey.)

3. **What additional information does the caption provide?** (Possible response: The caption explains that the astronauts have completed a 1-year training mission.)

ASSESS

As students examine photos and illustrations, check that they are able to identify events and actions, and the purposes of the illustrations and photos. Be sure that students use captions and illustrations to further their understanding of text.

For more practice or to assess students, use Practice Book pp. 99–100.

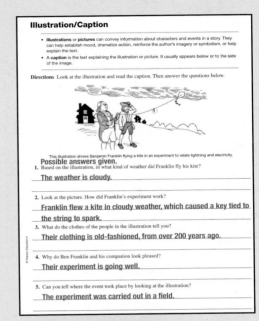

▲ **Practice Book** p. 99

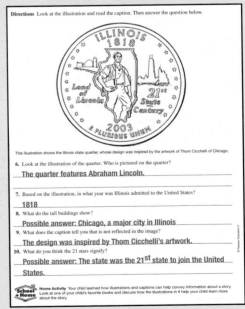

▲ **Practice Book** p. 100

Assessment Checkpoints *for the Week*

Selection Assessment

Use pp. 37–40 of Selection Tests to check:

 ☑ **Selection Understanding**

 ☑ **Comprehension Skill** *Sequence*

 ☑ **Selection Vocabulary**

fate	magnified
fearless	somber
glimmer	steed
lingers	

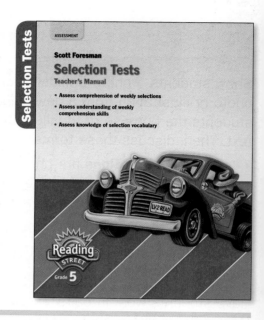

ASSESSMENT

Scott Foresman
Selection Tests
Teacher's Manual

- Assess comprehension of weekly selections
- Assess understanding of weekly comprehension skills
- Assess knowledge of selection vocabulary

Selection Tests

Reading STREET Grade 5

Leveled Assessment

On-Level

Strategic Intervention

Advanced

Use pp. 55–60 of Fresh Reads for Differentiated Test Practice to check:

 ☑ **Comprehension Skill** *Sequence*

 ☑ **REVIEW Comprehension Skill** *Setting and Theme*

 ☑ **Fluency** *Words Correct Per Minute*

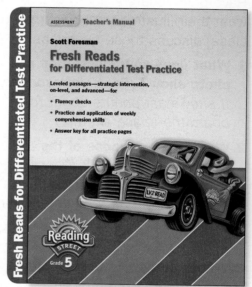

ASSESSMENT Teacher's Manual

Scott Foresman
Fresh Reads
for Differentiated Test Practice

Leveled passages—strategic intervention, on-level, and advanced—for

- Fluency checks
- Practice and application of weekly comprehension skills
- Answer key for all practice pages

Fresh Reads for Differentiated Test Practice

Reading STREET Grade 5

Managing Assessment

Use Assessment Handbook for:

 ☑ **Observation Checklists**

 ☑ **Record-Keeping Forms**

 ☑ **Portfolio Assessment**

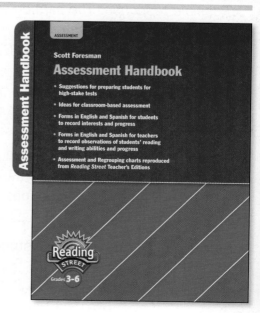

ASSESSMENT

Scott Foresman
Assessment Handbook

- Suggestions for preparing students for high-stake tests
- Ideas for classroom-based assessment
- Forms in English and Spanish for students to record interests and progress
- Forms in English and Spanish for teachers to record observations of students' reading and writing abilities and progress
- Assessment and Regrouping charts reproduced from *Reading Street* Teacher's Editions

Assessment Handbook

Reading STREET Grades 3–6

Unit 2
Concept Wrap-Up

CONCEPT QUESTION
What makes people want to do the right thing?

Students are ready to express their understanding of the unit concept question through discussion and wrap-up activities and to take the Unit 2 Benchmark Test.

Unit Poetry

Use the poetry on pp. 254-257 to help students appreciate poetry and further explore their understanding of the unit theme, Doing the Right Thing. It is suggested that you

- **read the poems aloud**
- **discuss and interpret the poems with students**
- **have students read the poems for fluency practice**
- **have students write interpretive responses**

Unit Wrap-Up

Use the Unit Wrap-Up on pp. 258-259 to discuss the unit theme, Doing the Right Thing, and to have students show their understanding of the theme through cross-curricular activities.

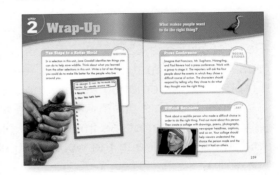

Unit Project

On p. 141, you assigned students a unit-long inquiry project, doing research for short speeches about local charities or service groups and how they help the community. Students have investigated, analyzed, and synthesized information during the course of the unit as they prepared their speeches. Schedule time for students to present their speeches. The project rubric can be found to the right.

Unit Inquiry Project Rubric

4	3	2	1
• Research is accurate and very detailed. Sources are reliable and relevant to inquiry question.	• Research is generally accurate and detailed. Most sources are reliable and relevant.	• Research includes inaccuracies, irrelevant information, or little detail. Some sources are unreliable.	• Research is not accurate, detailed, or relevant. Most sources are unreliable.
• Speech about a local charity or service group is well organized and clearly presented.	• Speech is organized and informative, but some parts could be presented more clearly.	• Speech gives some factual information, but ideas are not well organized or clearly presented.	• Speech is unclear and confusing. It shows little or no organization

Unit 2
Reading Poetry

OBJECTIVES

- Listen and respond to poems.
- Identify how meaning is conveyed through word choice.
- Read poetry fluently.
- Connect ideas and themes across texts.

Model Fluent Reading

Read "For Peace Sake" aloud. It is a lyric poem, or a poem that expresses feelings. Emphasize the emotion behind the poem. Tell students that this poem was written to convince the listener of the importance of peace. Listen for this plea in the words of the poem.

Discuss the Poem

 Generalize • Inferential

What generalizations does the speaker make?

Possible responses: The speaker makes generalizations, or broad statements, such as "it is never too late" and "we're all in this together."

 Repetition • Critical

Which phrases are repeated in the poem? What is the effect of this repetition?

Possible responses: The phrases *for peace sake, let's rid our lives of hate, let's do it,* and others are repeated. This repetition emphasizes key ideas and unifies the poem. The repetition of the whole section beginning with "I believe that we can . . ." acts like the refrain of a song, bringing a sense of unity and closure.

For Peace Sake
by Cedric McClester

For peace sake
we need to do our best.
For peace sake
let's put the hate to rest.
For peace sake
it never is too late.
For peace sake
let's rid our lives of hate.

I believe that we can
build a bridge to understand,
we're all in this together.
It never ever is too late,
together let's rid our lives of hate.
Let's do it for peace sake.

For peace sake
we need to do our best.
For peace sake
let's put love to the test.

Love is really what we need;
together we can plant the seed.
For peace sake let's work in harmo
For peace sake,
for love and happiness,
for peace sake
and for all the rest.

I believe that we can
build a bridge to understand,
we're all in this together.
It never ever is too late,
together let's rid our lives of hate.
Let's do it, let's do it
for peace sake.

For peace sake
we can make it right.
For peace sake
it can happen overnight.

254

Practice Fluent Reading

Have partners alternate reading verses of "For Peace Sake." Tell students to read slowly, with a serious tone, emphasizing the repeated phrases. Then have students listen to the AudioText of the poem and compare and contrast their readings with the CD recording.

Audio CD **AudioText**

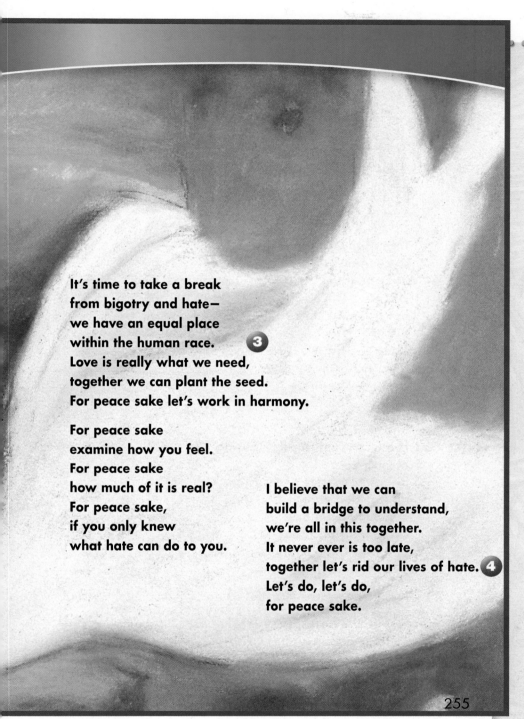

It's time to take a break
from bigotry and hate—
we have an equal place
within the human race. **③**
Love is really what we need,
together we can plant the seed.
For peace sake let's work in harmony.

For peace sake
examine how you feel.
For peace sake
how much of it is real?
For peace sake,
if you only knew
what hate can do to you.

I believe that we can
build a bridge to understand,
we're all in this together.
It never ever is too late,
together let's rid our lives of hate. **④**
Let's do, let's do,
for peace sake.

255

③ Draw Conclusions • Inferential

Why do you think the poet wrote this poem?

Possible response: The poet may want to tell readers how important it is to live in harmony with other people. He tells readers "to take a break from bigotry and hate."

④ Details and Facts • Inferential

What does the speaker ask readers to do and why?

Possible responses: The speaker urges readers to achieve peace, which is necessary for a life of love and enlightenment. The speaker says, "it can happen overnight," "it is never too late," and "we're all in this together."

WRITING POETRY

Have students write their own poems about peace. Encourage students to repeat key phrases or sections. Have them share their poems in pairs or small groups. If they wish, students can set their poems to music and perform them for the class.

Unit 2
Reading Poetry

Model Fluent Reading

Read "Two People I Want to Be Like" aloud twice—first pausing at the end of each line and then grouping words into phrases. Encourage students to see that the second reading better conveys the sense, or meaning, of the poem.

Discuss the Poem

1 **Alliteration • Literal**

What are some examples of alliteration in the poem?

Possible responses: Examples of alliteration are *slow steady* and *bagging bottles and...boxes.*

2 **Characters • Inferential**

Why does the speaker wish that the man and woman in the poem were married to each other?

Possible responses: The characters in the poem have a lot in common. Both stay calm in stressful situations and both are kind to others, spreading "sweet harmony."

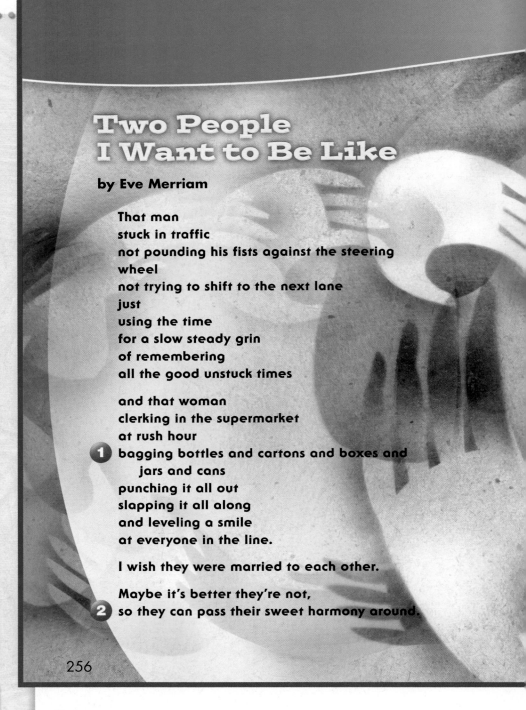

Two People I Want to Be Like

by Eve Merriam

That man
stuck in traffic
not pounding his fists against the steering
wheel
not trying to shift to the next lane
just
using the time
for a slow steady grin
of remembering
all the good unstuck times

and that woman
clerking in the supermarket
at rush hour
1 bagging bottles and cartons and boxes and
        jars and cans
punching it all out
slapping it all along
and leveling a smile
at everyone in the line.

I wish they were married to each other.

Maybe it's better they're not,
2 so they can pass their sweet harmony around.

256

EXTEND SKILLS

Author's Viewpoint/Bias

Explain that every author has a viewpoint when writing. Sometimes there is a clear bias in the writing toward one way of looking at things. In "Two People I Want to Be Like," the poet admires people who don't get angry or upset easily. They deal with the annoyances of everyday life with a smile. Discuss with students whether or not they agree with the viewpoint of the poet.

Practice Fluent Reading

Have partners read "Two People I Want to Be Like" aloud. Ask students to read the poem several times, experimenting with different ways to group words into phrases. Tell them to discuss which reading makes the poem easier to understand.

 **AudioText**

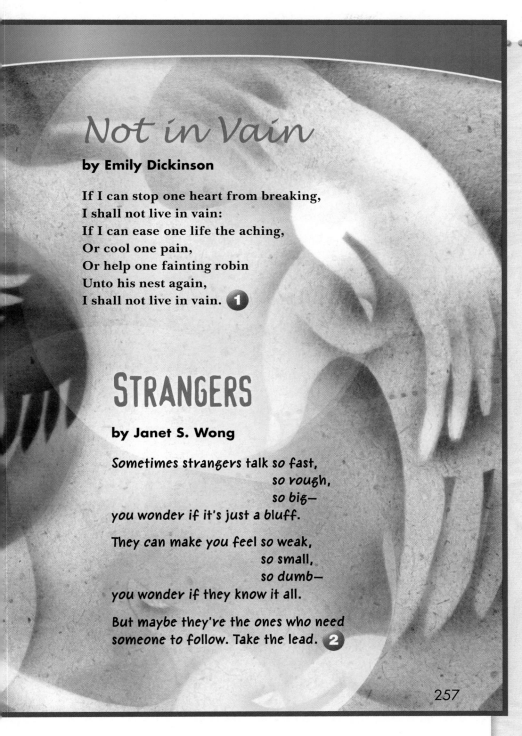

Not in Vain

by Emily Dickinson

If I can stop one heart from breaking,
I shall not live in vain:
If I can ease one life the aching,
Or cool one pain,
Or help one fainting robin
Unto his nest again,
I shall not live in vain. ❶

STRANGERS

by Janet S. Wong

Sometimes strangers talk so fast,
　　　　　so rough,
　　　　　so big—
you wonder if it's just a bluff.

They can make you feel so weak,
　　　　　so small,
　　　　　so dumb—
you wonder if they know it all.

But maybe they're the ones who need
someone to follow. Take the lead. ❷

257

WRITING POETRY

Ask students to write poems about a person they admire. Students might focus on a family member, friend, or acquaintance. Encourage students to include details that compliment qualities the person has and that show what makes this person admirable. Have students illustrate their poems in a cartoon style.

Most cartoons are drawings that are amusing because they show people or things in funny, exaggerated ways. However, many cartoons are serious, stretching or exaggerating the subject's real-life qualities. Students' cartoons should be serious and respectful.

Model Fluent Reading

Read "Strangers" aloud, emphasizing the rhythm of the words. Point out that the combination of short and long lines creates a varied rhythm.

Discuss the Poems

❶ **Theme • Inferential**
What might be the theme, or big idea, of "Not in Vain"?

Possible response: The theme might be stated: "Helping others makes life worthwhile."

❷ **Compare and Contrast • Inferential**
How are the two poems on this page similar? How are they different?

Possible responses: The poems give readers different advice about how to live their lives. "Not in Vain" suggests that people help others, while "Strangers" tells people to "take the lead" and be independent from others who make them feel inferior.

Connect Ideas and Themes

Remind students that this unit deals with doing the right thing. Ask students to discuss what the speaker in each poem is urging others to do. Then have students discuss what else it might mean to do the "right thing." Encourage them to share examples from real life, movies, or books.

Unit 2
Wrap-Up

OBJECTIVES

- Critically analyze unit theme.
- Connect content across selections.
- Combine content and skills in meaningful activities that build literacy.
- Respond to unit selections through a variety of modalities.

DOING THE RIGHT THING

Discuss the Big Idea

What makes people want to do the right thing?

Write the unit theme and Big Idea question on the board. Ask students to think about the selections they have read in the unit. Discuss how each selection and lesson concept can help them answer the Big Idea question from this unit.

Model this for students by choosing a selection and explaining how the selection and lesson concept address the Big Idea.

UNIT 2 Wrap-Up

Ten Steps to a Better World

connect to **WRITING**

In a selection in this unit, Jane Goodall identifies ten things you can do to help save wildlife. Think about what you learned from the other selections in this unit. Write a list of ten things you could do to make life better for the people who live around you.

10 things I can do to make life better for people around me.

1. Recycle
2. Mow Mrs. Lee's lawn
3.
5.
6.
7.
8.
9.
10.

258

What makes people want to do the right thing?

connect to
SOCIAL STUDIES

Press Conference

Imagine that Francisco, Mr. Sugihara, Hsiang-ling, and Paul Revere had a press conference. Work with a group to stage it. The reporters will ask the four people about the events in which they chose a difficult course of action. The characters should respond by telling why they chose to do what they thought was the right thing.

connect to
ART

Difficult Decisions

Think about a real-life person who made a difficult choice in order to do the right thing. Find out more about this person. Then create a collage with drawings, poems, photographs, newspaper headlines, captions, and so on. Your collage should help viewers understand the choice the person made and the impact it had on others.

259

ACTIVITIES

Ten Steps to a Better World

Make a List Model the activity using personal experiences. Then have students think about the lessons they have learned from the selections in the unit. Encourage them to think of ways they could use what they have learned to solve problems in their school or community.

Press Conference

Role-Play a Conference Have groups begin by jotting down notes on each character's actions and reasons why they did what they did. Then have students brainstorm likely interview questions and responses. Questions should require more than a *yes* or *no* response, and answers should reflect each character's personality. Groups can decide who will play the characters and the reporters.

Difficult Decisions

Make a Collage Help students create a list of people, like Mr. Sugihara, who have done the right thing in difficult situations. Then have each student choose a person and use print or online resources to find information about him or her. Discuss the types of text and visuals students could include in their collages, using Mr. Sugihara as a model.

Glossary

Glossary

How to Use This Glossary

This glossary can help you understand and pronounce some of the words in this book. The entries in this glossary are in alphabetical order. There are guide words at the top of each page to show you the first and last words on the page. A pronunciation key is at the bottom of every other page. Remember, if you can't find the word you are looking for, ask for help or check a dictionary.

The entry word is in dark type. It shows how the word is spelled and how the word is divided into syllables.

The pronunciation is in parentheses. It also shows which syllables are stressed.

Part-of-speech labels show the function or functions of an entry word and any listed form of that word.

ad·vise (ad vīz′), **1.** *V.* to give advice to; offer an opinion to; counsel: *I shall act as you advised.* **2.** *V.* to give notice; inform: *We were advised that a storm was approaching, so we didn't go sailing.* ❑ *V.* **ad·vised, ad·vis·ing.**

Sometimes, irregular and other special forms will be shown to help you use the word correctly.

The definition and example sentence show you what the word means and how it is used.

776

abdomen • advise

Aa

ab·do·men (ab′də mən), *N.* the part of the body containing the stomach, the intestines, and other important organs; belly.

ab·o·rig·i·ne (ab′ə rij′ə nē), *N.* one of the earliest known inhabitants of Australia. ❑ *N. PL.* **ab·o·rig·i·nes.**

ab·sence (ab′səns), *N.* condition of being without; lack: *Darkness is the absence of light.*

ac·com·plish·ment (ə kom′plish mənt), *N.* something that has been done with knowledge, skill, or ability; achievement: *The teachers were proud of the pupils' accomplishments.*

a·chieve (ə chēv′), *V.* to carry out to a successful end; accomplish; do: *Have you achieved your purpose?* ❑ *V.* **a·chieved, a·chiev·ing.**

ac·quaint (ə kwānt′), *V.* to make aware; let know; inform: *Let me acquaint you with your new duties.* ❑ *V.* **ac·quain·ted, ac·quain·ting.**

ad·mir·ing·ly (ad mīr′ing lē), *ADV.* With wonder, pleasure, and approval: *We gazed admiringly at the beautiful painting.*

a·dorn (ə dôrn′), *V.* to add beauty to; put ornaments on; decorate: *She adorned her hair with flowers.* ❑ *V.* **a·dorned, a·dorn·ing.**

ad·vice (ad vīs′), *N.* opinion about what should be done; suggestion: *My advice is that you study more.*

ad·vise (ad vīz′), **1.** *V.* to give advice to; offer an opinion to; counsel: *I shall act as you advised.* **2.** *V.* to give notice; inform: *We were advised that a storm was approaching, so we didn't go sailing.* ❑ *V.* **ad·vised, ad·vis·ing.**

agreement • belfry

a·gree·ment (ə grē′mənt), *N.* harmony in feeling or opinion: *The coaches are in complete agreement that she will be a superb gymnast.*

air·time (âr′tīm), *N.* specific amount of time in a television, radio, or any broadcast media program.

al·gae (al′jē), *N. PL.* group of related living things, mostly living in water.

Alz·heim·er's (älts′hī mərz), *N.* disease of the brain that causes confusion and gradual loss of memory.

a·nat·o·my (ə nat′ə mē), *N.* structure of a living thing: *the anatomy of an earthworm.*

ap·pre·ci·ate (ə prē′shē āt), *V.* to think highly of; recognize the worth or quality of; value; enjoy: *Almost everybody appreciates good food.* ❑ *V.* **ap·pre·ci·ated, ap·pre·ci·at·ing.**

ar·chi·tect (är′kə tekt), *N.* person who designs and makes plans for buildings. (*Architect* comes from two Greek words, *archi* meaning "chief" and *tekton* meaning "builder.")

ar·mor (är′mər), *N.* any kind of protective covering. The steel plates of a warship and the bony shell of an armadillo are armor.

armor

ar·ti·fi·cial (är′tə fish′əl), *ADJ.* made by human skill or labor; not natural: *Plastics are artificial substances that do not occur in nature.*

as·cent (ə sent′), *N.* act of going up; upward movement; rising: *The sudden ascent of the elevator made us dizzy.*

as·sign·ment (ə sīn′mənt), *N.* something assigned, especially a piece of work to be done: *Today's assignment in arithmetic consists of ten problems.*

as·ton·ish (ə ston′ish), *V.* to surprise greatly; amaze: *We were astonished by the child's remarkable memory.* ❑ *V.* **as·ton·ished, as·ton·ish·ing.**

au·da·cious (ö dā′shəs), *ADJ.* rudely bold; impudent: *The audacious waiter demanded a larger tip.*

Bb

back·flip (bak′ flip), *N.* backward somersault performed in the air. ❑ *N. PL.* **back·flips.**

back·ground (bak′ ground), *N.* the part of a picture or scene toward the back: *The cottage stands in the foreground with the mountains in the background.*

bar·ber (bär′bər), *N.* person whose business is cutting hair and shaving or trimming beards.

bass[1] (bās), **1.** *N.* the lowest male voice in music. **2.** *N.* the largest, lowest sounding stringed instrument in an orchestra or band.

bass[2] (bas), **1.** *N.* North American freshwater or saltwater fish with spiny fins, used for food.

be·hav·ior (bi hā′vyər), *N.* manner of behaving; way of acting: *Her sullen behavior showed that she was angry.*

bel·fry (bel′frē), *N.* space in a tower in which a bell or bells may be hung.

a	in hat	ō	in open	sh	in she
ā	in age	ò	in all	th	in thin
â	in care	ô	in order	ᴛʜ	in then
ä	in far	oi	in oil	zh	in measure
e	in let	ou	in out	ə	= a in about
ē	in equal	u	in cup	ə	= e in taken
ėr	in term	ů	in put	ə	= i in pencil
i	in it	ü	in rule	ə	= o in lemon
ī	in ice	ch	in child	ə	= u in circus
o	in hot	ng	in long		

777

benefactor • cavity

ben·e·fac·tor (ben′ə fak′tər), *N.* person who has given money or kindly help. (*Benefactor* comes from two Latin words, *bene* meaning "well" or "good" and *facere* meaning "do.")

be·queath (bi kwēth′), *V.* to give or leave by means of a will when a person dies: *He bequeathed his fortune to his children.* ❑ *V.* **be·queathed, be·queath·ing.**

bleach (blēch), *V.* to whiten by exposing to sunlight or by using chemicals: *animal skulls bleached by the desert sun.* ❑ *V.* **bleached, bleach·ing.**

blen·der (blen′dər), *N.* an electric kitchen appliance for grinding, mixing, or beating various foods.

blu·ish (blü′ish), *ADJ.* somewhat blue; somewhat like the color of the clear sky in daylight.

bluish

blun·der (blun′dər), *N.* a stupid mistake: *Misspelling the title of a book is a silly blunder to make in a book report.* ❑ *N. PL.* **blun·ders.**

bound·ar·y (boun′dər ē), *N.* a limiting line or thing; limit; border: *the boundary between Canada and the United States.* ❑ *N. PL.* **bound·aries.**

brack·ish (brak′ish), **1.** *ADJ.* slightly salty. Coastal marshes often have brackish waters. **2.** *ADJ.* bad-tasting.

brand (brand), **1.** *N.* a certain kind, grade, or make: *Do you like this brand of flour?* **2.** *V.* to mark by burning the skin with a hot iron: *The cowboys branded the cows.* ❑ *V.* **brand·ed, brand·ing.**

break·fast (brek′fəst), *V.* to eat the first meal of the day. ❑ *V.* **break·fast·ed, break·fast·ing.**

bronze (bronz), *N.* a dark yellow-brown alloy of copper and tin.

Cc

ca·ble (kā′bəl), *N.* a message sent through wires by electric current or electronic signals.

cal·cu·la·tion (kal′kyə lā′shən), *N.* careful thinking; deliberate planning: *The success of the expedition was the result of much calculation.* ❑ *N. PL.* **cal·cu·la·tions.**

cam·e·o (kam′ē ō), *N.* a semiprecious stone carved so that there is a raised design on a background, usually of a different color.

can·non (kan′ən), *N.* a big gun, especially one that is mounted on a base or wheels.

can·tan·ker·ous (kan tang′kər əs), *ADJ.* ready to make trouble; ill-natured; quarrelsome.

car·cass (kär′kəs), *N.* body of a dead animal. ❑ *N. PL.* **car·cass·es.**

cart·wheel (kärt′wēl′), *N.* a sideways handspring with the legs and arms kept straight. ❑ *N. PL.* **cart·wheels.**

cat·er·pil·lar (kat′ər pil′ər), *N.* the wormlike larvae of insects such as butterflies and moths.

cav·i·ty (kav′ə tē), *N.* hollow place; hole. Cavities in teeth are caused by decay. ❑ *N. PL.* **cav·i·ties.**

778

cerebral palsy • cramp

ce·re·bral pal·sy (ser′ə brəl pòl′zē), *N.* paralysis caused by damage to the brain before or at birth. Persons suffering from cerebral palsy have trouble coordinating their muscles.

choir (kwīr), *N.* group of singers who sing together, often in a church service.

cir·cum·stance (sėr′kəm stans), **1.** *N.* condition that accompanies an act or event: *Unfavorable circumstances such as fog and rain often delayed us in our trip to the mountains.* **2.** *N.* the existing condition or state of affairs: *He was forced by circumstances to resign.* ❑ *N. PL.* **cir·cum·stanc·es.**

civ·i·li·za·tion (siv′ə lə zā′shən), *N.* the ways of living of a people or nation: *The civilizations of ancient Egypt and ancient Greece had many contacts over the centuries.*

clar·i·net (klar′ə net′), *N.* a woodwind instrument, having a mouthpiece with a single reed and played by means of holes and keys.

cleanse (klenz), **1.** *V.* to make clean: *cleanse a wound before bandaging it.* **2.** *V.* to make pure: *cleanse the soul.* ❑ *V.* **cleansed, cleans·ing.**

close-up (klōs′up′), *N.* picture taken with a camera at close range.

close-up of chimpanzee

cock·le (kok′əl), *N.* any of several kinds of saltwater clams with two-ridged, heart-shaped shells. ❑ *N. PL.* **cock·les.**

co·coon (kə kün′), *N.* case of silky thread spun by the larvae of various insects, to live in while they are developing into adults. Most moth larvae form cocoons.

com·bi·na·tion (kom′bə nā′shən), *N.* series of numbers or letters dialed in opening a certain kind of lock: *Do you know the combination of the safe?*

com·plex (kom′pleks), *ADJ.* hard to understand: *The instructions for building the radio were complex.*

con·ceal (kən sēl′), *V.* to put out of sight; hide: *The murky water concealed the crabs.* ❑ *V.* **con·cealed, con·ceal·ing.**

con·fi·dence (kon′fə dəns), *N.* firm belief in yourself; self-confidence: *Years of experience at her work have given her great confidence.*

con·ser·va·tion (kon′sər vā′shən), *N.* preservation from harm or decay; protection from loss or from being used up: *Conservation of energy saves fuel.*

con·struct (kən strukt′), *V.* to put together; fit together; build: *construct a bridge.* ❑ *V.* **con·struct·ed, con·struct·ing.**

con·tri·bute (kən trib′yüt), *V.* to help bring about: *A poor diet contributed to the child's bad health.* ❑ *V.* **con·tri·but·ed, con·tri·but·ing.**

cove (kōv), *N.* a small, sheltered bay; inlet on the shore.

cramp (kramp), *V.* to shut into a small space; limit: *Living in only three rooms, the family was cramped.* ❑ *V.* **cramped, cramp·ing.**

a	in hat	ō	in open	sh	in she
ā	in age	ò	in all	th	in thin
â	in care	ô	in order	ᴛʜ	in then
ä	in far	oi	in oil	zh	in measure
e	in let	ou	in out	ə	= a in about
ē	in equal	u	in cup	ə	= e in taken
ėr	in term	ů	in put	ə	= i in pencil
i	in it	ü	in rule	ə	= o in lemon
ī	in ice	ch	in child	ə	= u in circus
o	in hot	ng	in long		

779

Glossary

cranny•distribution

cran·ny (kranʹē), *N.* a small, narrow opening; crack; crevice: *She looked in all the nooks and crannies of the house for the misplaced book.* ❑ *N. PL.* **cran·nies.**

crit·i·cal (kritʹə kəl), *ADJ.* being important to the outcome of a situation: *Help arrived at the critical moment.*

crit·i·cize (kritʹə sīz), *V.* to find fault with; disapprove of; blame: *Do not criticize him until you know all the circumstances.* ❑ *V.* **crit·i·cized, crit·i·ciz·ing.**

cruise (krüz), *V.* to travel in a car, airplane, boat, etc. at the speed at which the vehicle operates best. ❑ *V.* **cruised, cruis·ing.**

Dd

dain·ti·ly (dānʹti lē), *ADV.* with delicate beauty; freshly and prettily: *She daintily wiped her mouth with her napkin.*

deaf·en·ing (defʹən ing), *ADJ.* very loud; amazingly noisy.

de·bris (də brēʹ), *N.* scattered fragments; ruins; rubbish: *The street was covered with broken glass, stone, and other debris from the storm.*

debris in a landfill

de·cay (di kāʹ), *N.* process of rotting: *The decay in the tree trunk proceeded so rapidly that the tree fell over in a month.*

dem·on·strate (demʹən strāt), *V.* to show how a thing is done; explain by using examples. ❑ *V.* **dem·on·strates, dem·on·strat·ed, dem·on·strat·ing.**

de·pressed (di prestʹ), *ADJ.* gloomy; low-spirited; sad. (*Depressed* comes from the Latin word *depressum* meaning "pressed down.")

de·vas·ta·tion (devʹə stāʹshən), *N.* the act of laying waste, destroying.

die-off (dīʹ of), *N.* to die one after another until all are dead: *The entire herd experienced a die-off during the drought.*

dig·ni·tar·y (digʹnə terʹē), *N.* person who has a position of honor: *We saw several foreign dignitaries when we visited the United Nations.* ❑ *N. PL.* **dig·ni·tar·ies.**

di·gress (di gresʹ), *V.* to turn aside from the main subject in talking or writing: *I lost interest in the book because the author digressed too much.* ❑ *V.* **di·gressed, di·gres·sing.**

dip·lo·mat (dipʹlə mat), *N.* person whose work is to manage the relations between his or her nation and other nations.

dir·i·gi·ble (dirʹə jə bəl), *N.* an airship made with a rigid framework. It is filled with gas that is lighter than air.

dis·lodge (dis lojʹ), *V.* to drive or force out of a place, position, etc.: *She used a crowbar to dislodge a heavy stone.* ❑ *V.* **dis·lodged, dis·lodg·ing.**

dis·re·spect (disʹri spektʹ), *V.* to show a lack of respect; to be rude. ❑ *V.* **dis·re·spect·ed, dis·re·spect·ing.**

dis·tri·bu·tion (disʹtrə byüʹshən), *N.* the act of giving some of to each, of dividing and giving out in shares.

780

drench•explosion

drench (drench), *V.* to wet thoroughly; soak: *A sudden, heavy rain drenched us.* ❑ *V.* **drenched, drench·ing.**

drift·wood (driftʹwüdʹ), *N.* wood carried along by water or washed ashore from the water.

du·o (düʹō), *N.* pair.

Ee

e·co·nom·ic (ekʹə nomʹik), *ADJ.* of or about the management of the income, supplies, and expenses of a household, government, etc.

eer·ie (irʹē), *ADJ.* causing fear because of strangeness or weirdness: *a dark and eerie old house.*

el·bow (elʹbō), **1.** *N.* joint between the upper and lower arm. **2.** *V.* to push with the elbow; make your way by pushing: *Don't elbow me off the sidewalk.* ❑ *V.* **el·bow·ed, el·bow·ing.**

e·merge (i mėrjʹ), *V.* to come into view; come out; come up: *The sun emerged from behind a cloud.* ❑ *V.* **e·merged, e·mer·ging.**

em·phat·i·cal·ly (em fatʹi cal lē), *ADV.* said or done forcefully; strongly.

en·a·ble (en āʹbəl), *V.* to give ability, power, or means to; make able: *The airplane enables people to travel great distances rapidly.* ❑ *V.* **en·abled, en·a·bling.**

en·case (en kāsʹ), *V.* to cover completely; enclose: *A cocoon encased the caterpillar.* ❑ *V.* **en·cases, en·cased, en·cas·ing.**

en·thu·si·as·tic (en thüʹzē asʹtik), *ADJ.* full of enthusiasm; eagerly interested: *My little brother is very enthusiastic about going to kindergarten.*

en·vi·ron·ment (en vīʹrən mənt), *N.* condition of the air, water, soil, etc.: *working for a pollution-free environment.*

en·vy (enʹvē), *N.* feeling of discontent, dislike, or desire because another person has what you want: *The children were filled with envy when they saw her new bicycle.*

ep·i·sode (epʹə sōd), *N.* one part of a story that is published or broadcast in several parts, one at a time.

er·a (irʹə), *N.* a period of time or history: *We live in the era of space exploration.*

e·rect (i rektʹ), *V.* to put up; build: *That house was erected 40 years ago.* ❑ *V.* **e·rec·ted, e·rec·ting.**

es·sen·tial (ə senʹshəl), *ADJ.* absolutely necessary; very important: *Good food and enough rest are essential to good health.*

ex·pand (ek spandʹ), *V.* to make or grow larger; increase in size; enlarge: *The balloon expanded as it was filled with air.* ❑ *V.* **ex·pan·ded, ex·pan·ding.**

ex·plo·sion (ek splōʹzhən), *N.* act of bursting with a loud noise; a blowing up: *The explosions of the bombs shook the whole city.*

a	in hat	ò	in all	sh	in she
ā	in age	ô	in order	th	in thin
ä	in care			ᴛʜ	in then
ä	in far	oi	in oil	zh	in measure
e	in let	ou	in out	ə = a in about
ē	in equal	u	in cup	ə = e in taken
ėr	in term	ü	in put	ə = i in pencil
i	in it	ü	in rule	ə = o in lemon
ī	in ice	ch	in child	ə = u in circus
o	in hot	ng	in long	

781

exquisite•greenhorn

ex·qui·site (ekʹskwi zit, ek skwizʹit), *ADJ.* very lovely; delicate: *These violets are exquisite.*

ex·tinct (ek stingktʹ), *ADJ.* no longer existing.

ex·tra·ter·res·tri·al (ekʹstrə tə resʹtrē əl), *N.* a creature from outer space.

an **exquisite** pattern

Ff

fash·ion (fashʹən), *V.* to make, shape, or form: *He fashioned a whistle out of wood.* ❑ *V.* **fash·ioned, fash·ion·ing.**

fast·ball (fastʹbôlʹ), *N.* a pitch thrown at high speed with very little curve.

fate (fāt), *N.* what becomes of someone or something: *The Revolutionary War decided the fate of the United States.*

fear·less (firʹlis), *ADJ.* without fear; afraid of nothing; brave; daring.

fidg·et·y (fijʹi tē), *ADJ.* restless; uneasy: *That fidgety child keeps twisting and moving.*

flee (flē), *V.* to run away; get away by running: *The robbers were fleeing, but the police caught them.* ❑ *V.* **fled, flee·ing.**

fo·cus (fōʹkəs), **1.** *N.* the correct adjustment of a lens, the eye, etc., to make a clear image: *If the camera is not brought into focus, the photograph will be blurred.* **2.** *N.* the central point of attraction, attention, activity, etc.: *The new baby was the focus of attention.*

foot·man (fütʹmən), *N.* a uniformed male servant who answers the bell, waits on the table, goes with a car or carriage to open the door, etc. ❑ *N. PL.* **foot·men.**

for·get·ful (fər getʹfəl), *ADJ.* apt to forget; having a poor memory: *When I get too tired, I become forgetful.*

foun·da·tion (foun dāʹshən), *N.* part on which the other parts rest for support; base: *the foundation of a house.* ❑ *N. PL.* **foundations.**

Gg

gait (gāt), *N.* the kind of steps used in moving; manner of walking or running: *A gallop is one of the gaits of a horse.*

ges·ture (jesʹchər), *V.* to make a movement to help express an idea or feeling. ❑ *V.* **ges·tured, ges·tur·ing.**

glim·mer (glimʹər), *N.* a faint, unsteady light.

gnaw (nô), *V.* to bite at and wear away: *A mouse has gnawed the cover of this box.* ❑ *V.* **gnawed, gnaw·ing.**

gos·pel (gosʹpəl), *N.* religious music with much emotion and enthusiasm, including features of spirituals and jazz.

grat·i·tude (gratʹə tüd), *N.* kindly feeling because of a favor received; desire to do a favor in return; thankfulness. (*Gratitude* comes from the Latin word *gratia* meaning "favor.")

grav·i·ty (gravʹə tē), *N.* the natural force that causes objects to move or tend to move toward the center of the earth. Gravity causes objects to have weight.

green·horn (grēnʹhôrnʹ), *N.* person without training or experience.

782

grenadier•ichthyosaurus

gren·a·dier (grenʹə dirʹ), *N.* a member of a specially chosen unit of foot soldiers. ❑ *N. PL.* **gren·a·diers.**

guar·an·tee (garʹən tēʹ), *V.* to make certain that something will happen as a result: *Not studying for a test is a guaranteed way to make a poor grade.* ❑ *V.* **guar·an·teed, guar·an·tee·ing.**

gym·nas·tics (jim nasʹtiks), *N.* a sport in which very difficult exercises are performed.

girl doing **gymnastics**

Hh

ham·mock (hamʹək), *N.* a hanging bed or couch made of canvas, cord, etc. It has cords or ropes at each end for hanging it between two trees or posts. ❑ *N. PL.* **ham·mocks.**

hand·i·capped (hanʹdē kaptʹ), *ADJ.* having a physical or mental disability.

Ha·nuk·kah (häʹnə kə), *N.* a yearly Jewish festival that lasts eight days, mostly in December. It celebrates the rededication of the temple in Jerusalem after a victory over the Syrians in 165 B.C. Candles are lighted on each of the eight days of Hanukkah.

head·land (hedʹlənd), *N.* narrow ridge of high land jutting out into water; promontory.

hes·i·ta·tion (hezʹə tāʹshən), *N.* act of failing to act promptly; doubt; indecision.

hid·e·ous (hidʹē əs), *ADJ.* very ugly; frightful; horrible: *a hideous monster.*

hu·mane (hyü mānʹ), *ADJ.* not cruel or brutal; kind; merciful: *We believe in the humane treatment of animals.*

hus·tle (husʹəl), **1.** *V.* to push or shove roughly or hurriedly; jostle rudely: *Guards hustled the demonstrators away from the mayor's office.* **2.** *V.* to hurry along: *He had to hustle to get the lawn mowed before dinner.* **3.** *V. INFORMAL.* get or sell in a hurried or illegal way. ❑ *V.* **hus·tled, hus·tling.**

hy·dro·gen (hiʹdrə jən), *N.* a colorless, odorless gas that burns easily. Hydrogen is a chemical element that weighs less than any other element. It combines with oxygen to form water and is present in most organic compounds.

Ii

ich·thy·o·sau·rus (ikʹthē ə sôrʹəs), *N.* large, fishlike reptile, now extinct, that lived in the sea. It had a long beak, paddlelike flippers, and a tail with a large fin.

a	in hat	ò	in all	sh	in she
ā	in age	ô	in order	th	in thin
ä	in care			ᴛʜ	in then
ä	in far	oi	in oil	zh	in measure
e	in let	ou	in out	ə = a in about
ē	in equal	u	in cup	ə = e in taken
ėr	in term	ü	in put	ə = i in pencil
i	in it	ü	in rule	ə = o in lemon
ī	in ice	ch	in child	ə = u in circus
o	in hot	ng	in long	

783

Glossary **259b**

Glossary

im·mi·grant (im′ə grənt), *N.* someone who comes into a country or region to live there: *Canada has many immigrants from Europe.* ❑ *N. PL.* **im·mi·grants.**

in·con·ceiv·a·ble (in′kən sē′və bəl), *ADJ.* hard to imagine or believe; incredible: *It is inconceivable that two nations so friendly for centuries should now be at odds.*

in·con·ven·ience (in′kən vē′nyəns), *N.* something inconvenient; cause of trouble, difficulty, or bother.

in·de·pend·ence (in′di pen′dəns), *N.* freedom from the control, influence, support, or help of others: *The American colonies won independence from England.*

in·no·va·tion (in′ə vā′shən), *N.* change made in the established way of doing things: *The principal made many innovations.* ❑ *N. PL.* **in·no·va·tions.**

in·spire (in spīr′), *V.* to fill with a thought or feeling; influence: *A chance to try again inspired her with hope.* ❑ *V.* **in·spired, in·spir·ing.**

in·tact (in takt′), *ADJ.* with nothing missing or broken; whole; untouched; uninjured: *The missing money was found and returned to the bank intact.*

in·te·ri·or (in tir′ē ər), *N.* inner surface or part; inside: *The interior of the house was beautifully decorated.*

theater **interior**

in·ter·sec·tion (in′tər sek′shən), *N.* point, line, or place where one thing crosses another: *a dangerous intersection.*

in·ves·ti·ga·tion (in ves′tə gā′shən), *N.* a careful search; detailed or careful examination: *An investigation of the accident by the police put the blame on the drivers of both cars.*

i·ras·ci·ble (i ras′ə bəl), *ADJ.* easily made angry.

is·sue (ish′ü), *V.* to send out; put forth: *The government issues money and stamps.* ❑ *V.* **is·sued, is·su·ing.**

Jj

jam (jam), **1.** *V.* to press or squeeze tightly between two surfaces: *The ship was jammed between two rocks.* **2.** *V.* to make music with other musicians without having practiced (SLANG). ❑ *V.* **jammed, jamm·ing. 3.** *N.* preserve made by boiling fruit with sugar until thick: *strawberry jam.*

Kk

kelp (kelp), *N.* any of various large, tough, brown seaweeds.

Ll

lair (lâr), *N.* den or resting place of a wild animal.

la·ment (lə ment′), **1.** *V.* to feel or show grief for; mourn aloud for: *We lament the dead.* **2.** *V.* to say sadly, with grief: *She lamented his absence.* ❑ *V.* **la·ment·ed, la·ment·ing.**

land·scape (land′skāp), *N.* **1** view of scenery on land. **2** picture showing a land scene.

life·less (līf′lis), *ADJ.* without life: *a lifeless statue.*

lime·light (līm′līt′), *N.* center of public attention and interest: *Some people are never happy unless they are in the limelight.*

lin·ger (ling′gər), *V.* to stay on; go slowly, as if unwilling to leave: *He lingers after the others leave.* ❑ *V.* **ling·ered, ling·er·ing.**

---

log·ger (lò′gər), *N.* a person whose work is cutting down and removing trees. ❑ *N. PL.* **log·gers.**

lul·la·by (lul′ə bī), *N.* song for singing to a child in a cradle; soft song to lull a baby to sleep.

lux·u·ry (luk′shər ē), **1.** *N.* use of the best and most costly food, clothes, houses, furniture, and amusements: *The movie star was accustomed to luxury.* **2.** *N.* something pleasant but not necessary: *Candy is a luxury.*

Mm

mag·ni·fy (mag′nə fī), *V.* to cause something to look larger than it actually is; increase the apparent size of an object: *A microscope magnifies bacteria so that they can be seen and studied.* ❑ *V.* **mag·ni·fied, mag·ni·fy·ing.**

match·mak·er (mach′mā′kər), *N.* person who arranges, or tries to arrange, marriages for others.

mer·can·tile (mér′kən tīl), *ADJ.* of merchants or trade; commercial: *a mercantile company.*

midst (midst), *N.* in the middle of.

mi·grant (mī′ grənt), *ADJ.* migrating; roving: *a migrant worker.*

min·i·a·ture (min′ē ə chùr, min′ə chər), *ADJ.* a reduced image or likeness: *miniature furniture for a dollhouse.*

mock (mok), *V.* to laugh at; make fun of: *The student was punished for mocking the kindergartner.* ❑ *V.* **mocked, mock·ing.**

mold[1] (mōld), *N.* a hollow shape in which anything is formed, cast, or solidified, such as the mold into which melted metal is poured to harden into shape, or the mold in which gelatin is left to stiffen.

mold[2] (mōld), *N.* loose or broken earth.

mon·i·tor (mon′ə tər), **1.** *N.* a television set connected to a computer. **2.** *V.* to listen to and check radio or television transmissions, telephone messages, etc., by using a receiver. ❑ *V.* **mon·i·tored, mon·i·tor·ing.**

mon·u·men·tal (mon′yə men′tl), *ADJ.* very great: *monumental ignorance.*

mu·cus (myü′kəs), *N.* a slimy substance produced in the nose and throat to moisten and protect them.

Nn

nau·se·at·ing (nó′shē ā ting), *ADJ.* sickening; causing nausea.

Na·zi (nä′tsē *or* nat′sē), *N.* member of the National Socialist Party, a fascist political party in Germany, led by Adolf Hitler. ❑ *N. PL.* **Nazis.**

new·com·er (nü′kum′ər), *N.* person who has just come or who came not long ago.

news·reel (nüz rēl′), *N.* a short news story for a movie audience. ❑ *N. PL.* **news·reels.**

night·time (nīt′tīm′), *N.* time between evening and morning.

nu·tri·tious (nü trish′əs), *ADJ.* valuable as food; nourishing.

a in hat	ò in open	sh in she
ā in age	ò in all	th in thin
â in care	ô in order	ᴛʜ in then
ä in far	oi in oil	zh in measure
e in let	ou in out	ə = a in about
ē in equal	u in cup	ə = e in taken
ėr in term	ú in put	ə = i in pencil
i in it	ü in rule	ə = o in lemon
ī in ice	ch in child	ə = u in circus
o in hot	ng in long	

Oo

oc·ca·sion (ə kā′zhən), *N.* a special event: *The jewels were worn only on great occasions.*

on·stage (on′stāj′), *ADV.* on the part of a stage that the audience can see: *walk onstage.*

ooze (üz), *N.* a soft mud or slime, especially at the bottom of a pond or river or on the ocean bottom.

out·field (out′fēld′), **1.** *N.* the part of a baseball field beyond the diamond or infield. **2.** *N.* the three players in the outfield.

o·ver·run (ō′vər run′), *V.* to spread over: *Vines overran the wall.* ❑ *V.* **o·ver·ran, o·ver·run·ning.**

Pp

par·a·pet (par′ə pet), *N.* a low wall at the edge of a balcony, roof, or bridge.

par·a·site (par′ə sīt), *N.* any living thing that lives on or in another, from which it gets its food, often harming the other in the process. Lice and tapeworms are parasites. ❑ *N. PL.* **par·a·sites.**

parapet

pa·vil·ion (pə vil′yən), *N.* a light building, usually somewhat open, used for shelter, pleasure, etc.: *The swimmers took shelter from the sudden storm in the beach pavilion.*

ped·dler (ped′lər), *N.* person who travels about selling things carried in a pack or in a truck, wagon, or cart.

per·mit (pər mit′), **1.** *V.* to let; allow: *My parents will not permit me to stay up late.* ❑ *V.* **per·mit·ted, per·mit·ting. 2.** *N.* license or written order giving permission to do something: *Do you have a permit to fish in this lake?*

phi·los·o·pher (fə los′ə fər), *N.* a person who attempts to discover and understand the basic nature of knowledge and reality. (*Philosopher* comes from a Greek word *philosophia* meaning "love of wisdom.")

pitch (pich), **1.** *V.* to throw or fling; hurl; toss: *They were pitching horseshoes.* ❑ *V.* **pitched, pitch·ing. 2.** *N.* thick, black, sticky substance made from tar or turpentine, used to fill the seams of wooden ships, to cover roofs, to make pavements, etc.

ple·si·o·saur·us (plē′sē ə sôr′əs), *N.* any of several large sea reptiles that lived about 200 million years ago. They had long necks and flippers instead of legs.

plesiosaurus

plunge (plunj), *V.* to fall or move suddenly downward or forward: *The sea turtle plunged into the water.* ❑ *V.* **plunged, plung·ing.**

pon·der (pon′dər), *V.* to consider carefully; think over: *ponder a problem.* ❑ *V.* **pon·dered, pon·der·ing.** (*Ponder* comes from a Latin word *pondus* meaning "weight.")

---

post·hu·mous·ly (pos′chə məs lē), *ADV.* happening after death: *The author was honored posthumously.*

pot·hole (pot′hōl′), *N.* a deep hole in the surface of a street or road. ❑ *N. PL.* **pot·holes.**

pre·cious (presh′əs), *ADJ.* having great value; worth much; valuable. Gold, platinum, and silver are often called the precious metals. Diamonds, rubies, and sapphires are precious stones.

pred·a·tor (pred′ə tər), *N.* animal or person that lives by killing and eating other animals.

pre·his·tor·ic (prē′hi stôr′ik), *ADJ.* Of or belonging to periods before recorded history: *Some prehistoric people lived in caves.*

pro·ce·dure (prə sē′jər), *N.* way of proceeding; method of doing things: *What is your procedure in making bread?* ❑ *N. PL.* **pro·ce·dures.**

pro·ces·sion (prə sesh′ən), *N.* something that moves forward; persons marching or riding: *The opening procession started at noon.*

pro·file (prō′fīl), **1.** *N.* a side view, especially of the human face. **2.** *N.* low profile; moderate attitude or position, deliberately chosen in order to avoid notice (IDIOMATIC).

pro·por·tion (prə pôr′shən), *N.* a proper relation among parts: *The dog's short legs were not in proportion to its long body.*

pros·per·i·ty (prə sper′ə tē), *N.* prosperous condition; good fortune; success: *a time of peace and prosperity.*

pro·to·type (prō′tə tīp), *N.* the first or primary type of anything: *A modern ship has its prototype in the hollowed log used by primitive peoples.*

push·cart (push′kärt′), *N.* a light cart pushed by hand. ❑ *N. PL.* **push·carts.**

Rr

ra·vine (rə vēn′), *N.* a long, deep, narrow valley eroded by running water.

realm (relm), *N.* kingdom.

re·as·sem·ble (rē′ə sem′ bəl), *V.* come or bring together again. ❑ *V.* **re·as·sem·bled, re·as·sem·bling.**

rec·om·mend (rek′ə mend′), *V.* to speak in favor of; suggest favorably: *The teacher recommended him for the job.* ❑ *V.* **rec·om·men·ded, rec·om·men·ding.**

ref·u·gee (ref′yə jē′ *or* ref′yə jē′), *N.* person who flees for refuge or safety, especially to a foreign country, in time of persecution, war, or disaster: *Refugees from the war were cared for in neighboring countries.* ❑ *N. PL.* **refugees.**

re·lease (ri lēs′), *V.* to permit to be published, shown, sold, etc. ❑ *V.* **re·leased, re·leas·ing.**

re·li·gious (ri lij′əs), *ADJ.* much interested in the belief, study, and worship of God or gods; devoted to religion: *He is very religious and prays often.*

a in hat	ò in open	sh in she
ā in age	ò in all	th in thin
â in care	ô in order	ᴛʜ in then
ä in far	oi in oil	zh in measure
e in let	ou in out	ə = a in about
ē in equal	u in cup	ə = e in taken
ėr in term	ú in put	ə = i in pencil
i in it	ü in rule	ə = o in lemon
ī in ice	ch in child	ə = u in circus
o in hot	ng in long	

Renaissance • severe

Ren·ais·sance (ren′ə säns′ *or* ren′ə säns), *N.* the great revival of art and learning in Europe during the 1300s, 1400s, and 1500s; the period of time when this revival occurred.

rep·re·sent·a·tive (rep′ri zen′tə tiv), *N.* person appointed or elected to act or speak for others: *She is the club's representative at the convention.* ❑ *N. PL.* **rep·re·sent·a·tives.**

re·proach·ful·ly (ri prōch′fəl lē), *ADV.* with disapproval.

rep·u·ta·tion (rep′yə tā′shən), *N.* what people think and say the character of someone or something is; character in the opinion of others; name; repute: *This store has an excellent reputation for fair dealing.*

re·source·ful (ri sôrs′fəl), *ADJ.* good at thinking of ways to do things; quick-witted: *The resourceful children mowed lawns to earn enough money to buy new bicycles.*

ri·val (rī′vəl), *N.* person who wants and tries to get the same thing as another or who tries to equal or do better than another; competitor: *The two girls were rivals for the same class office.*

ro·bo·tic (rō bot′ik), *ADJ.* of or for a machine with moving parts and sensing devices controlled by a computer: *robotic design.*

role (rōl), **1.** *N.* an actor's part in a play, movie, etc.: *She played the leading role in the school play.* **2.** *N.* role model, a person whose patterns of behavior influence someone else's actions and beliefs: *Parents are important role models for children.*

rus·tle (rus′əl), *V.* to make or cause to make a light, soft sound of things gently rubbing together: *The leaves were rustling in the breeze.* ❑ *V.* **rus·tled, rus·tling.**

Ss

sa·cred (sā′krid), **1.** *ADJ.* worthy of reverence: *the sacred memory of a dead hero.* **2.** *ADJ.* not to be violated or disregarded: *a sacred promise.* (*Sacred* comes from a Latin word *sacrare* meaning "holy.")

scarce (skârs), *ADJ.* hard to get; rare: *Water is becoming scarce.*

scin·til·late (sin′tl āt), *V.* to sparkle; flash: *Her brilliant wit scintillates.* ❑ *V.* **scin·til·lat·ed, scin·til·lat·ing.**

scoun·drel (skoun′drəl), *N.* an evil, dishonorable person; villain; rascal: *The scoundrels who set fire to the barn have been caught.*

scrawl (skrȯl), *V.* to write or draw poorly or carelessly. ❑ *V.* **scrawled, scrawl·ing.**

scraw·ny (skrȯ′nē), *ADJ.* having little flesh; lean; thin; skinny: *Turkeys have scrawny necks.*

sea ur·chins (sē′ ėr′chəns), *N.* any of numerous small, round sea animals with spiny shells.

sec·ond·hand (sek′ənd hand′), **1.** *ADJ.* not new; used already by someone else: *secondhand clothes.* **2.** *ADV.* from other than the original source; not firsthand: *The information came to us secondhand.*

sed·i·ment (sed′ə mənt), *N.* material that settles to the bottom of a liquid: *A film of sediment covered the underwater wreck.*

seed·ling (sēd′ling), *N.* a young plant grown from a seed. ❑ *N. PL.* **seed·lings.**

sem·i·pro (sem′ī prō′), *N.* a part-time professional athlete.

ser·pent (sėr′pənt), *N.* snake, especially a big snake.

se·vere (sə vir′), *ADJ.* serious; grave: *a severe illness.*

788

shellfish • spiritual

shell·fish (shel′fish′), *N.* a water animal with a shell. Oysters, clams, crabs, and lobsters are shellfish.

shut·down (shut′doun′), **1.** *N.* act of closing of a factory, or the like, for a time: *The factory had a partial shutdown last week to fix some faulty equipment.* **2.** *N.* a stopping; a checking of (*INFORMAL*): *His reply was a real shutdown to her negative comment.*

side·track (sīd′trak′), *V.* to draw someone's attention away from something: *Don't sidetrack me with pointless questions.* ❑ *V.* **side·tracked, side·track·ing.**

sin·ew (sin′yü), *N.* tendon.

sketch (skech), *V.* to draw roughly and quickly. ❑ *V.* **sketched, sketch·ing.**

skid (skid), *V.* to slip or slide sideways while moving: *The car skidded on the slippery road.* ❑ *V.* **skid·ded, skid·ding.**

slav·er·y (slā′vər ē), *N.* the condition of being owned by another person and being made to work without wages.

sol·i·tar·y (sol′ə ter′ē), *ADJ.* without companions; away from people; lonely.

som·ber (som′bər), **1.** *ADJ.* having deep shadows; dark; gloomy: *A cloudy winter day is somber.* **2.** *ADJ.* sad; gloomy; dismal: *His losses made him somber.*

a **somber** picture (def. 2)

som·er·sault (sum′ər sȯlt), *V.* to run or jump, turning the heels over the head. ❑ *V.* **som·er·saul·ted, som·er·saul·ting.**

so·nar (sō′när), *N.* device for finding the depth of water or for detecting and locating underwater objects. Sonar sends sound waves into water, and they are reflected back when they strike the bottom or any object.

So·vi·et (sō′vē et), *N.* a person belonging to or fighting for the former Soviet Union. ❑ *N. PL.* **So·vi·ets.**

spe·cial·ize (spesh′ə līz), *V.* to develop in a special way: *Animals and plants are specialized to fit their surroundings.* ❑ *V.* **spe·cial·ized, spe·cial·iz·ing.**

spe·cif·ic (spi sif′ik), *ADJ.* definite; precise; particular: *There was no specific reason for the party.*

spec·ta·cles (spek′tə kəlz), *N. PL.* eyeglasses. (*Spectacles* comes from a Latin word *spectare* meaning "to watch.")

spec·tac·u·lar (spek tak′ yə lər), *ADJ.* making a great display or show; very striking or imposing to the eye: *a spectacular storm.*

spin·dly (spind′lē), *ADJ.* very long and slender; too tall and thin: *a spindly plant.*

spir·i·tu·al (spir′ə chü əl), *N.* a religious song which originated among African Americans of the southern United States. ❑ *N. PL.* **spir·i·tu·als.**

a	in hat	ō	in open	sh	in she
ā	in age	ȯ	in all	th	in thin
â	in care	ô	in order	ᴛʜ	in then
ä	in far	oi	in oil	zh	in measure
e	in let	ou	in out	ə	= a in about
ē	in equal	u	in cup	ə	= e in taken
ėr	in term	u̇	in put	ə	= i in pencil
i	in it	ü	in rule	ə	= o in lemon
ī	in ice	ch	in child	ə	= u in circus
o	in hot	ng	in long		

789

spoonful • unique

spoon·ful (spün′fu̇l), *N.* as much as a spoon can hold.

star·va·tion (stär vā′shən), *N.* suffering from extreme hunger; being starved: *Starvation caused his death.*

stealth·y (stel′thē), *ADJ.* done in a secret manner; secret; sly: *The cat crept in a stealthy way toward the bird.*

steed (stēd), *N.* horse, especially a riding horse.

ster·ile (ster′əl), *ADJ.* free from germs: *Bandages should always be kept sterile.*

stern·ly (stėrn′ lē), *ADV.* strictly; firmly: *The teacher frowned sternly.*

strat·e·gy (strat′ə jē), *N.* the skillful planning and management of anything.

strict (strict), *ADJ.* very careful in following a rule or in making others follow it: *The teacher was strict but fair.*

stroke (strōk), *N.* a sudden attack of illness, especially one caused by a blood clot or bleeding in the brain; apoplexy.

sub·ject (sub′jikt), **1.** *N.* something that is thought about, discussed, investigated, etc.; topic: *The subject for our composition was "An Exciting Moment."* **2.** *N.* person under the power, control, or influence of another: *subjects of the king.*

su·per·i·or (sə pir′ē ər), *N.* person who is higher in rank, position, or ability: *A captain is a lieutenant's superior.* ❑ *N. PL.* **su·per·i·ors.**

sus·pend·ers (sə spen′dərz), *N. PL.* straps worn over the shoulders to hold up the trousers.

sus·pi·cion (sə spish′ən), *N.* belief; feeling; thought: *I have a suspicion that the weather will be very hot today.* ❑ *N. PL.* **sus·pi·cions.**

Tt

tape·worm (tāp′wėrm′), *N.* any of the numerous long, flat worms that live during their adult stage as parasites in the intestines of human beings and other animals. ❑ *N. PL.* **tape·worms.**

teen·ag·er (tēn′ā′jər), *N.* person in his or her teens.

ther·a·pist (ther′ə pist), *N.* person who specializes in the treatment of diseases, injuries, or disorders.

thieve (thēv), *V.* to steal. ❑ *V.* **thieved, thiev·ing.**

throb (throb), *V.* to beat rapidly or strongly: *My injured foot throbbed.* ❑ *V.* **throb·bed, throb·bing.**

ti·dy (tī′dē), *V.* to put in order; make neat: *I tidied the room.* ❑ *V.* **ti·died, ti·dy·ing.**

to·ga (tō′gə), *N.* a loose, outer garment worn in public. ❑ *N. PL.* **to·gas.**

tra·di·tion (trə dish′ən), *N.* custom or belief handed down from generation to generation: *According to tradition, Betsy Ross made the first American flag.* ❑ *N. PL.* **tra·di·tions.**

trans·at·lan·tic (tran′sət lan′tik), *ADJ.* crossing the Atlantic: *a transatlantic liner.*

tum·ble·down (tum′bəl doun′), *ADJ.* ready to fall down; not in good condition; dilapidated: *a tumbledown shack in the mountains.*

tun·dra (tun′drə), *N.* a vast, level, treeless plain in the arctic regions. The ground beneath its surface is frozen even in summer.

tweez·ers (twē′zərz), *N.* small pincers for pulling out hairs, picking up small objects, etc.

Uu

u·nique (yü nēk′), *ADJ.* having no like or equal; being the only one of its kind: *a unique specimen of rock, a unique experience.*

790

unscrew • worthless

un·screw (un skrü′), *V.* to loosen or take off by turning: *Can you help me unscrew this tight lid?* ❑ *V.* **un·screwed, un·screw·ing.**

Vv

va·cant (vā′kənt), *ADJ.* not occupied: *a vacant chair, a vacant house.*

var·mint (vär′mənt), *N.*.an objectionable animal or person (*DIALECT*).

vein (vān), *N.* **1.** membranous tubes forming part of the system of vessels that carry blood to the heart. **2.** a small natural channel within the earth through which water trickles or flows. ❑ *N. PL.* **veins.**

vi·bra·phone (vī′brə fōn), *N.* musical instrument similar to the xylophone, with metal bars and artificially increased vibration; vibraharp.

view·port (vyü′pôrt), *N.* small window in a small vessel, such as a space capsule or mini-submarine.

vi·sa (vē′zə), *N.* an official signature or endorsement upon a passport, showing that it has been examined and approved. A visa is granted by the consul or other representative of the country to which a person wishes to travel.

Ww

wai·tress (wā′tris), *N.* woman who serves or brings food to people in a restaurant.

weak·ness (wēk′nis), *N.* a weak point; slight fault: *Putting things off is her weakness.*

weight·less·ness (wāt′lis nis), *N.* the condition of being free from the pull of gravity: *weightless travelers in space.*

wheel·chair (wēl′châr′), *N.* chair on wheels, used especially by people who are sick or unable to walk. It can be moved by the person who is sitting in the chair.

wince (wins), *V.* to draw back suddenly; flinch slightly: *I winced when the dentist's drill touched my tooth.* ❑ *V.* **winced, winc·ing.**

wind·up (wīnd′up′), *N.* (in baseball), a swinging movement of the arms while twisting the body just before pitching the ball.

with·er (wiᴛʜ′ər), *V.* to lose or cause to lose freshness; make or become dry and lifeless; dry up; fade; shrivel: *Age had withered the old woman's face.* ❑ *V.* **with·ered, with·er·ing.**

work·shop (wėrk′shop′), *N.* space or building where work is done.

wor·ship (wėr′ship), *V.* to pay great honor and reverence to: *to worship God.* ❑ *V.* **wor·shipped, wor·ship·ping.**

worth·less (wėrth′lis), *ADJ.* without value; good-for-nothing; useless: *Throw those worthless, broken toys away.*

a	in hat	ō	in open	sh	in she
ā	in age	ȯ	in all	th	in thin
â	in care	ô	in order	ᴛʜ	in then
ä	in far	oi	in oil	zh	in measure
e	in let	ou	in out	ə	= a in about
ē	in equal	u	in cup	ə	= e in taken
ėr	in term	u̇	in put	ə	= i in pencil
i	in it	ü	in rule	ə	= o in lemon
ī	in ice	ch	in child	ə	= u in circus
o	in hot	ng	in long		

791

English/Spanish Selection Vocabulary List

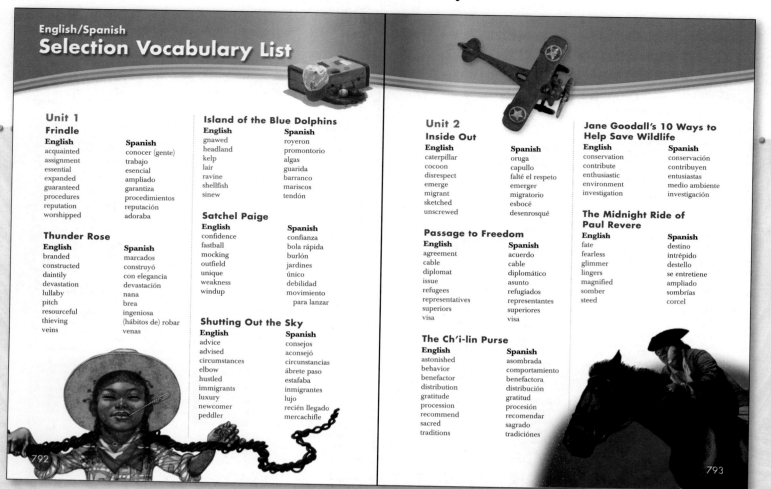

English/Spanish
Selection Vocabulary List

Unit 1
Frindle

English	Spanish
acquainted	conocer (gente)
assignment	trabajo
essential	esencial
expanded	ampliado
guaranteed	garantiza
procedures	procedimientos
reputation	reputación
worshipped	adoraba

Thunder Rose

English	Spanish
branded	marcados
constructed	construyó
daintily	con elegancia
devastation	devastación
lullaby	nana
pitch	brea
resourceful	ingeniosa
thieving	(hábitos de) robar
veins	venas

Island of the Blue Dolphins

English	Spanish
gnawed	royeron
headland	promontorio
kelp	algas
lair	guarida
ravine	barranco
shellfish	mariscos
sinew	tendón

Satchel Paige

English	Spanish
confidence	confianza
fastball	bola rápida
mocking	burlón
outfield	jardines
unique	único
weakness	debilidad
windup	movimiento para lanzar

Shutting Out the Sky

English	Spanish
advice	consejos
advised	aconsejó
circumstances	circunstancias
elbow	ábrete paso
hustled	estafaba
immigrants	inmigrantes
luxury	lujo
newcomer	recién llegado
peddler	mercachifle

Unit 2
Inside Out

English	Spanish
caterpillar	oruga
cocoon	capullo
disrespect	falté el respeto
emerge	emerger
migrant	migratorio
sketched	esbocé
unscrewed	desenrosqué

Passage to Freedom

English	Spanish
agreement	acuerdo
cable	cable
diplomat	diplomático
issue	asunto
refugees	refugiados
representatives	representantes
superiors	superiores
visa	visa

The Ch'i-lin Purse

English	Spanish
astonished	asombrada
behavior	comportamiento
benefactor	benefactora
distribution	distribución
gratitude	gratitud
procession	procesión
recommend	recomendar
sacred	sagrado
traditions	tradiciónes

Jane Goodall's 10 Ways to Help Save Wildlife

English	Spanish
conservation	conservación
contribute	contribuyen
enthusiastic	entusiastas
environment	medio ambiente
investigation	investigación

The Midnight Ride of Paul Revere

English	Spanish
fate	destino
fearless	intrépido
glimmer	destello
lingers	se entretiene
magnified	ampliado
somber	sombrías
steed	corcel

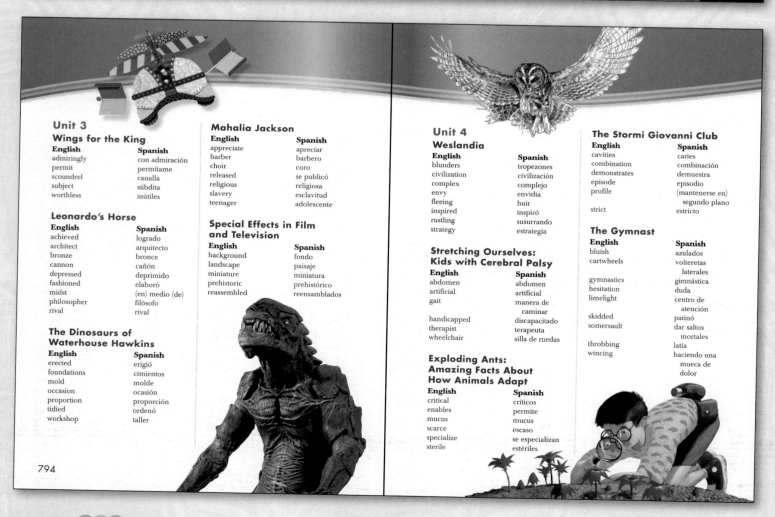

Unit 3
Wings for the King

English	Spanish
admiringly	con admiración
permit	permítame
scoundrel	canalla
subject	súbdita
worthless	inútiles

Leonardo's Horse

English	Spanish
achieved	logrado
architect	arquitecto
bronze	bronce
cannon	cañón
depressed	deprimido
fashioned	elaboró
midst	(en) medio (de)
philosopher	filósofo
rival	rival

The Dinosaurs of Waterhouse Hawkins

English	Spanish
erected	erigió
foundations	cimientos
mold	molde
occasion	ocasión
proportion	proporción
tidied	ordenó
workshop	taller

Mahalia Jackson

English	Spanish
appreciate	apreciar
barber	barbero
choir	coro
released	se publicó
religious	religiosa
slavery	esclavitud
teenager	adolescente

Special Effects in Film and Television

English	Spanish
background	fondo
landscape	paisaje
miniature	miniatura
prehistoric	prehistórico
reassembled	reensamblados

Unit 4
Weslandia

English	Spanish
blunders	tropezones
civilization	civilización
complex	complejo
envy	envidia
fleeing	huir
inspired	inspiró
rustling	susurrando
strategy	estrategia

Stretching Ourselves: Kids with Cerebral Palsy

English	Spanish
abdomen	abdomen
artificial	artificial
gait	manera de caminar
handicapped	discapacitado
therapist	terapeuta
wheelchair	silla de ruedas

Exploding Ants: Amazing Facts About How Animals Adapt

English	Spanish
critical	críticos
enables	permite
mucus	mucus
scarce	escaso
specialize	se especializan
sterile	estériles

The Stormi Giovanni Club

English	Spanish
cavities	caries
combination	combinación
demonstrates	demuestra
episode	episodio
profile	(mantenerse en) segundo plano
strict	estricto

The Gymnast

English	Spanish
bluish	azulados
cartwheels	volteretas laterales
gymnastics	gimnástica
hesitation	duda
limelight	centro de atención
skidded	patinó
somersault	dar saltos mortales
throbbing	latía
wincing	haciendo una mueca de dolor

English/Spanish Selection Vocabulary List

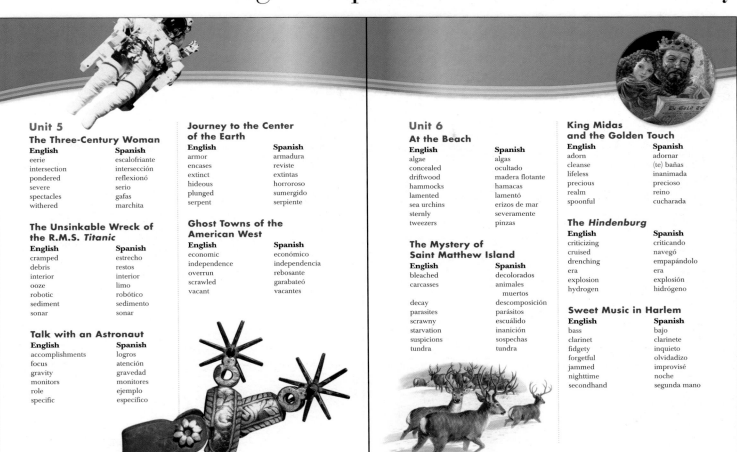

Unit 5

The Three-Century Woman

English	Spanish
eerie	escalofriante
intersection	intersección
pondered	reflexionó
severe	serio
spectacles	gafas
withered	marchita

The Unsinkable Wreck of the R.M.S. *Titanic*

English	Spanish
cramped	estrecho
debris	restos
interior	interior
ooze	limo
robotic	robótico
sediment	sedimento
sonar	sonar

Talk with an Astronaut

English	Spanish
accomplishments	logros
focus	atención
gravity	gravedad
monitors	monitores
role	ejemplo
specific	específico

Journey to the Center of the Earth

English	Spanish
armor	armadura
encases	reviste
extinct	extintas
hideous	horroroso
plunged	sumergido
serpent	serpiente

Ghost Towns of the American West

English	Spanish
economic	económico
independence	independencia
overrun	rebosante
scrawled	garabateó
vacant	vacantes

Unit 6

At the Beach

English	Spanish
algae	algas
concealed	ocultado
driftwood	madera flotante
hammocks	hamacas
lamented	lamentó
sea urchins	erizos de mar
sternly	severamente
tweezers	pinzas

The Mystery of Saint Matthew Island

English	Spanish
bleached	decolorados
carcasses	animales muertos
decay	descomposición
parasites	parásitos
scrawny	escuálido
starvation	inanición
suspicions	sospechas
tundra	tundra

King Midas and the Golden Touch

English	Spanish
adorn	adornar
cleanse	(te) bañas
lifeless	inanimada
precious	precioso
realm	reino
spoonful	cucharada

The *Hindenburg*

English	Spanish
criticizing	criticando
cruised	navegó
drenching	empapándolo
era	era
explosion	explosión
hydrogen	hidrógeno

Sweet Music in Harlem

English	Spanish
bass	bajo
clarinet	clarinete
fidgety	inquieto
forgetful	olvidadizo
jammed	improvisé
nighttime	noche
secondhand	segunda mano

796

797

Writing Traits

- **Focus/Ideas** refers to the main purpose for writing and the details that make the subject clear and interesting. It includes development of ideas through support and elaboration.

- **Organization/Paragraphs** refers to the overall structure of a piece of writing that guides readers. Within that structure, transitions show how ideas, sentences, and paragraphs are connected.

- **Voice** shows the writer's unique personality and establishes a connection between writer and reader. Voice, which contributes to style, should be suited to the audience and the purpose for writing.

- **Word Choice** is the use of precise, vivid words to communicate effectively and naturally. It helps create style through the use of specific nouns, lively verbs and adjectives, and accurate, well-placed modifiers.

- **Sentences** covers strong, well-built sentences that vary in length and type. Skillfully written sentences have pleasing rhythms and flow fluently.

- **Conventions** refers to mechanical correctness and includes grammar, usage, spelling, punctuation, capitalization, and paragraphing.

Rubric
4 | 3 | 2 | 1

- Focus/Ideas
- Organization/ Paragraphs
- Voice
- Word Choice
- Sentences
- Conventions

Writing Workshop

How-to Report

Writing Prompt: Doing the Right Thing
Write a report explaining how to make or do something that is familiar to you. Choose words that make your report interesting to read and easy to understand. Explain all the steps and materials needed.
Purpose: Describe a familiar task
Audience: A friend or classmate

READ LIKE A WRITER

Look back at "Jane Goodall's 10 Ways to Help Save Wildlife." Point out that Goodall gives general outlines for how to observe animals. In four simple steps, she tells young people to set out food, sit quietly a short distance away, take notes, and imagine the animal's life. Tell students that they will sequence steps as they write a **how-to report.**

EXAMINE THE MODEL AND RUBRIC

GUIDED WRITING Read the model aloud. Point out time-order words such as *first, next,* and *then* that the writer uses to signal the steps of the process. Also, point out that the writer uses a colon to introduce a list. Discuss how the model reflects traits of good writing.

How to Build a Fort with Recyclables

So your kid brother is in the basement, and your room is a mess. Where can you go and what can you do with your friends? Build your own fort outdoors.

Follow these instructions to create the best fort. First, choose a good place, such as the corner of the backyard or the side of your house.

Second, find good building materials. Building a fort is a great way to recycle materials: cardboard boxes, wood scraps, plastic tarp, old sheets and blankets. Once you find your place and your building materials, you are ready to begin construction.

Start by breaking down the boxes. Make holes for windows in the cardboard. Then build walls by resting the cardboard against a tree or the side of the house. Use the wood to hold the cardboard in place. Next, cover the windows with old sheets or blankets so you can open or close them.

Finally, construct the roof. An old plastic tarp makes a good roof. If your walls are made of wood, you can use cardboard for a roof. Cover the floor of your fort with the rest of the sheets and blankets, and you're all set. Invite your friends in for lunch, card games, and fun!

Unit 2 How-to Report • PREWRITE   Writing Process **8**

▲ **Writing Transparency** WP8

Traits of a Good How-to Report

Focus/Ideas	The report is focused on one activity, and the steps explain the task clearly.
Organization/ Paragraphs	The writer has organized the report into paragraphs, using time-order words to show the sequence of steps.
Voice	The voice is conversational. The writer explains the activity as though describing the steps to a friend.
Word Choice	The writer has used strong verbs such as *create, choose, build, cover,* and *construct* to tell readers what to do.
Sentences	Sentences are clear and concise. Sentence length is varied.
Conventions	Correct spelling, punctuation, and grammar are used throughout the report.

Unit 2 How-to Report • PREWRITE   Writing Process **9**

▲ **Writing Transparency** WP9

FINDING A TOPIC

- Ask students to list activities they do at home, at school, or for fun. Have students circle the activities they could describe step by step.
- Initiate a discussion of worthwhile activities that students have participated in, such as making donations to a food drive or recycling materials at home. Have students consider writing about one of these topics in their report.
- Have students think about step-by-step instructions that people use regularly. Ask them to provide some examples, which might include directions for a school project, game instructions, or a recipe.

NARROW A TOPIC

How to Change a Light Bulb This is too simple.
How to Ride a Bike This may be too complicated.
How to Organize a Bake Sale This can be explained in steps.

PREWRITING STRATEGY

GUIDED WRITING Display Writing Transparency WP10. Model how to complete a how-to chart.

 MODEL This student has decided to explain how to organize a bake sale. She has thought about the steps in the process. When she writes the report, she will use time-order words to organize the steps. The student has also planned an introduction and conclusion.

PREWRITING ACTIVITIES

- Have students use Grammar and Writing Practice Book p. 164 to help them organize information.
- Students can add details and time-order words for each step in the process they are describing.

First, ask parents in your neighborhood or school if they would like to participate.

Then, decide on a place for your bake sale.

Monitor Progress

Differentiated Instruction

If... students	then...
have trouble writing all the steps of the process,	suggest that they explain the steps to a partner orally.

How-To Chart
Directions Fill in the how-to chart with information about your project.

Explain task   how to organize a bake sale

Materials   goods to sell, table, sign

Introduction   A bake sale is a great fundraising idea.

Steps   Get volunteers to bake.
Have them drop off baked goods.
Find good location.
Make sign to advertise sale.
Set up table.
Sell!

Conclusion   You'll be glad you made the effort.

Unit 2 How-to Report • PREWRITE   Writing Process **10**

▲ **Writing Transparency** WP10

How-to Chart
Directions Fill in the graphic organizer with information about your project.
Explain Task   Answers should include details about each part of the how-to report.

Materials

Introduction

Steps

Conclusion

▲ **Grammar and Writing Practice Book** p. 164

Writing Workshop

1 PREWRITE 2 DRAFT 3 REVISE 4 EDIT 5 PUBLISH

Think Like a Writer

Visualize the Steps Before you write, close your eyes and visualize the steps for your task, from beginning to end. Think of a verb to tell what is done in each step.

Support Writing If students include home-language words in their drafts, help them find replacement words in English.
Resources can include
- conversations with you
- other home-language speakers
- bilingual dictionaries, if available
- online translation sources

Time-Order Words

Directions Add a time-order word to each of the five steps below. Write each sentence. Then add a final sentence using a time-order word. Tell what would happen in the last step.
Possible answers:
1. Grab a soccer ball and head to the field.
   First, grab a soccer ball and head to the field.
2. Stand about five feet in front of the goal posts.
   Next, stand about five feet in front of the goal posts.
3. Take five steps back and two large steps to the left.
   Then take five steps back and two large steps to the left.
4. Drop the ball to the ground in front of you.
   Now drop the ball to the ground in front of you.
5. Wind up and kick that soccer ball as hard as you can toward the goal.
   Finally, wind up and kick that soccer ball as hard as you can toward the goal.
6. That's how to successfully score a goal in soccer.

▲ **Grammar and Writing Practice Book** p. 165

WRITING THE FIRST DRAFT

GUIDED WRITING Use Writing Transparency WP11 to practice using time-order words.

- Ask students to read the sentences and think about each step of the process. Have them add a word that makes each step in the sequence clear.
- Point out that time-order words are especially necessary in a how-to report because readers must follow the steps in an exact order.

Think Aloud **MODEL** The sentences here are missing time-order words. As a result, the reader won't know the sequence of steps. Using time-order words such as *first* and *next* will allow the reader to follow the directions correctly.

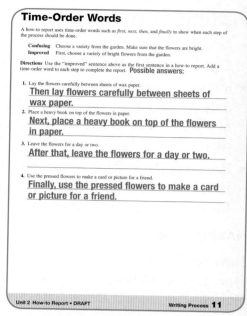

Time-Order Words

A how-to report uses time-order words such as *first, next, then,* and *finally* to show when each step of the process should be done.

Confusing Choose a variety from the garden. Make sure that the flowers are bright.
Improved First, choose a variety of bright flowers from the garden.

Directions Use the "improved" sentence above as the first sentence in a how-to report. Add a time-order word to each step to complete the report. **Possible answers:**

1. Lay the flowers carefully between sheets of wax paper.
   Then lay flowers carefully between sheets of wax paper.
2. Place a heavy book on top of the flowers in paper.
   Next, place a heavy book on top of the flowers in paper.
3. Leave the flowers for a day or two.
   After that, leave the flowers for a day or two.
4. Use the pressed flowers to make a card or picture for a friend.
   Finally, use the pressed flowers to make a card or picture for a friend.

Unit 2 How-to Report • DRAFT   Writing Process **11**

▲ **Writing Transparency** WP11

WRITER'S CRAFT Know Your Purpose

Here are some ways to check the purpose of your how-to report:
- Do you instruct the reader?
- Do you explain a task or activity?
- Do you give clear directions?

DRAFTING STRATEGIES

- Have students review their how-to chart before they write.
- Students should make sure they use time-order words to show the sequence of steps.
- Remind students to keep their audience and purpose in mind.
- Students should review their report and identify the purpose.
- Have students use Grammar and Writing Practice Book p. 165 to choose time-order words.

WRITER'S CRAFT Elaboration

STRONG VERBS Explain that one way to elaborate is to use strong action verbs. Action verbs make the writing more precise.

Vague   When you try to _make_ a goal, _go_ down the field.

Specific   When you attempt to _score_ a goal, _charge_ down the field.

Use Grammar and Writing Practice Book p. 166 to practice elaboration by using strong action verbs.

REVISING STRATEGIES

GUIDED WRITING Use Writing Transparency WP12 to model revising. Point out the Revising Marks, which students should use when they revise their work.

Think Aloud

MODEL This how-to report makes a good start by asking two questions. Asking questions draws the reader into the text. Then the writer states the topic of the report: organizing a bake sale. She deletes the words _I recommend,_ which aren't necessary. She changes several vague words to more specific words: _doing_ to _organize, guys_ to _volunteers, help_ to _participate._ Each change makes her writing more precise.

PEER REVISION Write the Revising Checklist on the board or make copies to distribute. Students can use this checklist to revise their how-to reports. Have partners read each other's first drafts. Remind them to be courteous and specific with suggestions.

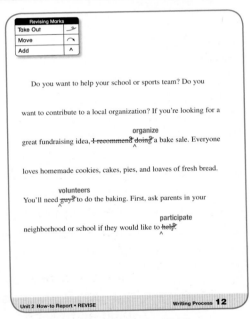

Revising Marks	
Take Out	⌐
Move	⌒
Add	∧

Do you want to help your school or sports team? Do you want to contribute to a local organization? If you're looking for a

                        organize
great fundraising idea, I recommend doing a bake sale. Everyone loves homemade cookies, cakes, pies, and loaves of fresh bread.

         volunteers
You'll need guys to do the baking. First, ask parents in your

                                    participate
neighborhood or school if they would like to help.

Unit 2 How-to Report • REVISE   Writing Process **12**

▲ **Writing Transparency** WP12

Trait Checklist

REVISING

Focus/Ideas
✔ Is the how-to report focused?
✔ Is the purpose clear?

Organization/Paragraphs
✔ Does the report have a brief introduction and conclusion?

Voice
✔ Are the steps of the process explained clearly?

Word Choice
✔ Do time-order words help make the sequence of steps clear?
✔ Did I use action verbs to improve my writing?

Sentences
✔ Are sentences concise? Are there any run-on sentences?

Elaboration
Strong Action Verbs

When you write, you can elaborate by using strong action verbs. The right action verbs make your writing more vivid and interesting to readers.
 Vague   Last night, snow _fell in_ our city.
 Specific   Last night, snow _blanketed_ our city.

Directions Replace each underlined word with an action verb. Write each sentence.
Possible answers:
1. After a heavy snowfall, I love to _make_ a snowman.
   After a heavy snowfall, I love to build a snowman.

2. Begin by _getting_ the largest snowball you can.
   Begin by packing the largest snowball you can.

3. Then _move_ the snowball through the snow.
   Then roll the snowball through the snow.

4. Next, _put_ three of these giant snowballs one on top of the other.
   Next, stack three of these giant snowballs one on top of the other.

5. Finally, _put_ your snowman in clothes, a scarf, or a hat.
   Finally, dress your snowman in clothes, a scarf, or a hat.

▲ **Grammar and Writing Practice Book** p. 166

Doing the Right Thing   **WA5**

Writing Workshop

1 PREWRITE 2 DRAFT 3 REVISE 4 EDIT 5 PUBLISH

Editing Checklist

✔ Did I spell all plural nouns correctly?

✔ Did I use the correct forms for singular and plural possessives?

✔ Did I check for subject-verb agreement?

✔ Did I avoid run-on sentences?

Support Writing Invite students to read their drafts aloud to you. Observe whether they seem to note any spelling or grammatical errors by stumbling or self-correcting. Return to those errors and explain how to correct them. Use the appropriate Grammar Transition Lessons in the ELL Resource Handbook to explicitly teach the English conventions.

EDITING STRATEGY

KEEP A DICTIONARY HANDY Suggest that students use an editing strategy. They can check their spelling by looking up words they are unsure of in a dictionary.

GUIDED WRITING Use Writing Transparency WP13 to model the process of keeping a dictionary handy. Indicate the Proofreading Marks, which students should use when they edit their work. Write the Editing Checklist on the board or make copies to distribute. Students can use this checklist to edit their work.

 MODEL The writer was uncertain about the spelling of a word in the second sentence, so she looked up the word in a dictionary to find the correct spelling, *prepare*. In the third sentence, she substituted the pronoun *it* for the noun phrase *the sign* to eliminate wordiness. She also fixed a run-on sentence by dividing it into two sentences. In the second paragraph, she added a comma after a dependent clause. She took out the *s* in *makes* to make that verb agree with its subject, *customers*.

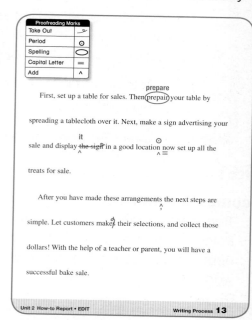

Proofreading Marks	
Take Out	
Period	
Spelling	
Capital Letter	
Add	

prepare
First, set up a table for sales. Then prepare your table by
spreading a tablecloth over it. Next, make a sign advertising your
it
sale and display the sign in a good location now set up all the
treats for sale.

After you have made these arrangements the next steps are
simple. Let customers make their selections, and collect those
dollars! With the help of a teacher or parent, you will have a
successful bake sale.

Unit 2 How-to Report • EDIT   Writing Process **13**

▲ **Writing Transparency** WP13

 USING TECHNOLOGY Students who have written or revised their how-to reports on computers should keep these points in mind as they edit:

- If your computer has spell check, you may use it to check your work, but it may miss homophone errors. Pay close attention to easily confused words and spellings.

- If your program has a print preview or a page layout feature, you may wish to use it when you are done typing your work. It will show you how your final draft will appear on the page.

- Using a print preview or page layout feature can show you how your work will appear before it is printed.

SELF-EVALUATION

Prepare students to fill out a Self-Evaluation Guide. Display Writing Transparency WP14 to model the self-evaluation process.

Think Aloud

MODEL I would give the how-to report a *4*.

Focus/Ideas Report shows steps to organize a bake sale.

Organization/Paragraphs The report is written in paragraphs using time-order words to show sequence.

Voice The writer describes a task that is familiar.

Word Choice The writer has used action verbs where appropriate.

Sentences Sentences are clear.

Conventions Grammar, capitalization, and spelling are excellent.

EVALUATION Assign Grammar and Writing Practice Book p. 167. Tell students that when they evaluate their own how-to reports, assigning a score of 3, 2, or even 1 does not necessarily indicate a bad paper. The ability to identify areas for improvement in future writing is a valuable skill.

How to Organize a Bake Sale

Do you want to help your school or sports team? Do you want to contribute to a local organization? If you're looking for a great fundraising idea, organize a bake sale. Everyone loves homemade cookies, cakes, pies, and loaves of fresh bread. You'll need volunteers to do the baking. First, ask parents in your neighborhood or school if they would like to participate.

Once you have a list of bakers, decide on a place for your bake sale. A neighborhood bake sale can be held outside a friend's home. A sale for your school could be held at lunchtime, right in the hallway. Ask volunteers to drop off their baked goods at the school or neighborhood location.

First, set up a table for sales. Then prepare your table by spreading a tablecloth over it. Next, make a sign advertising your sale and display it in a good location. Now set up all the treats for sale.

After you have made these arrangements, the next steps are simple. Let customers make their selections, and collect those dollars! With the help of a teacher or parent, you will have a successful bake sale.

Finally, count up all the money you've earned and make your donation to your school or sports team or that organization you wanted to support. You'll be glad you made the effort.

Unit 2 How-to Report • PUBLISH   Writing Process **14**

▲ **Writing Transparency** WP14

Ideas for Publishing

Oral Reports Ask volunteers to share their reports orally and demonstrate directions, if possible, either reading aloud or from memory.

How-to Display Create a classroom or hallway bulletin board display of student reports. Group them by subject.

Self-Evaluation Guide
How-to Report

Directions Think about the final draft of your how-to report. Then rate yourself on a scale of from 4 to 1 (4 is the highest) on each writing trait. After you fill out the chart, answer the questions.

Writing Traits	4	3	2	1
Focus/Ideas				
Organization/Paragraphs				
Voice				
Word Choice				
Sentences				
Conventions				

1. What is the best part of your how-to report?
   Students' responses should show that they have given thought to the how-to reports they have written.

2. Write one thing you would change about this how-to report if you had the chance to write it again.
   Students' responses should show that they have given thought to the how-to reports they have written.

▲ **Grammar and Writing Practice Book** p. 167

Scoring Rubric How-to Report

Rubric 4 3 2 1	4	3	2	1
Focus/Ideas	How-to report well focused with complete steps; clear purpose	How-to report generally focused with most steps; stated purpose	How-to report with incomplete steps, unclear purpose	How-to report without sufficient information or purpose
Organization/ Paragraphs	Clear sequence of events with time-order words	Reasonably clear sequence with some time-order words	Confused sequence of events; few time-order words	No attempt to put events into sequence
Voice	Conversational tone, knowledgeable writer	Engaging voice but lacks expertise	Uncertain voice	Dull writing with no clear voice
Word Choice	Uses action verbs correctly	Uses some action verbs	Uses few action verbs	No attempt to use action verbs
Sentences	Clear sentences; no run-ons	Mostly clear sentences	Some sentences unclear; too many steps in some sentences	Incoherent sentences or short, choppy sentences
Conventions	Few, if any, errors	Several minor errors	Errors that detract from writing and may interfere with understanding	Errors that hamper understanding

For 6-, 5-, and 3-point Scoring Rubrics, see pp. WA11–WA14.

Writing Workshop

How-to Report
Differentiated Instruction

WRITING PROMPT: Doing the Right Thing

Write a report explaining how to make or do something that is familiar to you. Choose words that make your report interesting to read and easy to understand. Explain all the steps and materials needed.

Purpose: Describe a familiar task

Audience: A friend or classmate

MODIFY INSTRUCTION

Pick One

ALTERNATIVE PROMPTS

ALTERNATIVE PROMPTS: Expository Writing

Strategic Intervention Think of familiar playground games, such as tag, jump rope, and hopscotch. Write the steps you follow when playing this game. Add simple diagrams or illustrations if you want.

On-Level Think of a favorite snack or meal that you know how to prepare. Make a numbered list. Describe the steps you take when you make the snack or meal. Compile your how-to and those of classmates in a booklet titled *Quick Meals for Kids*.

Advanced Do you know how to fix a flat tire on your bike? Weave a lanyard bracelet? Think of a challenging task you can do that involves several steps. Write about this task in your how-to report. Demonstrate this task to the class, if possible, or show pictures or the finished product.

Strategic Intervention

MODIFY THE PROMPT

Help emerging writers choose a simple task to explain in their how-to report. Encourage collaborative writing: pair emerging writers with able writers and allow students to brainstorm and list steps together.

PREWRITING SUPPORT

- Celebrate how-to success stories. Initiate a discussion in which students can share highlights from activities, games, or sports at which they excel.

- Encourage students to use their how-to charts to set up their reports. Make sure they list the steps before describing them in sentences with time-order words.

- Discuss with students the steps of their how-to reports. Guide their decision-making process by suggesting a task that can be explained in a manageable number of steps.

OPTIONS

- Give students the option of writing a group how-to report under your supervision.

CHECK PROGRESS Segment the assignment into manageable pieces. Check work at intervals, such as graphic organizers and first drafts, to make sure writing is on track.

Advanced

MODIFY THE PROMPT

Expect advanced writers to explain a more complicated task in their how-to report. Set a minimum number of steps that they must include. Advanced writers should use strong verbs, correct grammar, and good sentence structure throughout their report.

APPLY SKILLS

- As students revise their work, have them consider some ways to improve it.

  Use a thesaurus to find strong verbs that make the writing more interesting.

  Read their report aloud to see if they have included any unnecessary information.

  Make sure they have written an introduction that clearly identifies the process and draws readers in.

OPTIONS

- Students can follow these steps to create their own class rubrics.

  1. Read examples of class how-to reports and rank them 1–4, with 4 the highest.

  2. Discuss how they arrived at each rank.

  3. Isolate the six traits and make a rubric based on them.

CHECK PROGRESS Discuss the students' Self-Evaluation Guides. Work with students to monitor their growth and identify their strengths and weaknesses as writers.

ELL

MODIFY THE PROMPT

Allow beginning speakers to work with a partner, dictating the steps of their how-to report as their partner records them as a list. In the revising step, have students rewrite the list, adding time-order words.

BUILD BACKGROUND

- Display directions from a board game, a recipe, and an instruction manual to students. Have students explain what these items have in common. (They all inform the reader how to do something.) Tell students the purpose of a how-to report is the same; it explains how to do something. Discuss the list of Key Features of a how-to report that appears in the left column of p. WA2.

OPTIONS

- As students write their how-to reports, guide them toward books, magazines, or Web sites that provide comprehension support through features such as the following:

    step-by-step instructions

    illustrated game directions

    text in the home-language

- For more suggestions on scaffolding the Writing Workshop, see the ELL and Transition Handbook.

CHECK PROGRESS You may need to explain certain traits and help students fill out their Self-Evaluation Guides. Downplay conventions and focus more on ideas. Recognize examples of vocabulary growth and efforts to use language in more complex ways.

LOOK BACK AND WRITE RUBRICS

Scoring Rubric — Look Back and Write

2 points The response indicates that the student has a complete understanding of the reading concept embodied in the task. The response is accurate, complete, and fulfills all the requirements of the task. Necessary support and/or examples are included, and the information given is clearly text-based.

1 point The response indicates that the student has a partial understanding of the reading concept embodied in the task. The response includes information that is essentially correct and text-based, but the information is too general or too simplistic. Some of the support and/or examples may be incomplete or omitted.

0 points The response indicates that the student does not demonstrate an understanding of the reading concept embodied in the task. The student has either failed to respond or has provided a response that is inaccurate or has insufficient information.

Scoring Rubric — Look Back and Write

4 points The response indicates that the student has a thorough understanding of the reading concept embodied in the task. The response is accurate, complete, and fulfills all the requirements of the task. Necessary support and/or examples are included, and the information is clearly text-based.

3 points The response indicates that the student has an understanding of the reading concept embodied in the task. The response is accurate and fulfills all the requirements of the task, but the required support and/or details are not complete or clearly text-based.

2 points The response indicates that the student has a partial understanding of the reading concept embodied in the task. The response that includes information is essentially correct and text-based, but the information is too general or too simplistic. Some of the support and/or examples and requirements of the task may be incomplete or omitted.

1 point The response indicates that the student has a very limited understanding of the reading concept embodied in the task. The response is incomplete, may exhibit many flaws, and may not address all requirements of the task.

0 points The response indicates that the student does not demonstrate an understanding of the reading concept embodied in the task. The student has either failed to respond or has provided a response that is inaccurate or has insufficient information.

Scoring Rubric — Narrative Writing

Rubric 4 3 2 1	6	5	4	3	2	1
Focus/Ideas	Excellent, focused narrative; well elaborated with quality details	Good, focused narrative; elaborated with telling details	Narrative focused; adequate elaboration	Generally focused narrative; some supporting details	Sometimes unfocused narrative; needs more supporting details	Rambling narrative; lacks development and detail
Organization/Paragraphs	Strong beginning, middle, and end; appropriate order words	Coherent beginning, middle, and end; some order words	Beginning, middle, and end easily identifiable	Recognizable beginning, middle, and end; some order words	Little direction from beginning to end; few order words	Lacks beginning, middle, end; incorrect or no order words
Voice	Writer closely involved; engaging personality	Reveals personality	Pleasant but not compelling voice	Sincere voice but not fully engaged	Little writer involvement, personality	Careless writing with no feeling
Word Choice	Vivid, precise words that bring story to life	Clear words to bring story to life	Some specific word pictures	Language adequate but lacks color	Generally limited or redundant language	Vague, dull, or misused words
Sentences	Excellent variety of sentences; natural rhythm	Varied lengths, styles; generally smooth	Correct sentences with some variations in style	Correctly constructed sentences; some variety	May have simple, awkward, or wordy sentences; little variety	Choppy; many incomplete or run-on sentences
Conventions	Excellent control; few or no errors	No serious errors to affect understanding	General mastery of conventions but some errors	Reasonable control; few distracting errors	Weak control; enough errors to affect understanding	Many errors that prevent understanding

Scoring Rubric — Narrative Writing

Rubric 4 3 2 1	5	4	3	2	1
Focus/Ideas	Excellent, focused narrative; well elaborated with quality details	Good, focused narrative; elaborated with telling details	Generally focused narrative; some supporting details	Sometimes unfocused narrative; needs more supporting details	Rambling narrative; lacks development and detail
Organization/Paragraphs	Strong beginning, middle, and end; appropriate order words	Coherent beginning, middle, and end; some order words	Recognizable beginning, middle, and end; some order words	Little direction from beginning to end; few order words	Lacks beginning, middle, end; incorrect or no order words
Voice	Writer closely involved; engaging personality	Reveals personality	Sincere voice but not fully engaged	Little writer involvement, personality	Careless writing with no feeling
Word Choice	Vivid, precise words that bring story to life	Clear words to bring story to life	Language adequate but lacks color	Generally limited or redundant language	Vague, dull, or misused words
Sentences	Excellent variety of sentences; natural rhythm	Varied lengths, styles; generally smooth	Correctly constructed sentences; some variety	May have simple, awkward, or wordy sentences; little variety	Choppy; many incomplete or run-on sentences
Conventions	Excellent control; few or no errors	No serious errors to affect understanding	Reasonable control; few distracting errors	Weak control; enough errors to affect understanding	Many errors that prevent understanding

Scoring Rubric — Narrative Writing

Rubric 4 3 2 1	3	2	1
Focus/Ideas	Excellent, focused narrative; well elaborated with quality details	Generally focused narrative; some supporting details	Rambling narrative; lacks development and detail
Organization/Paragraphs	Strong beginning, middle, and end; appropriate order words	Recognizable beginning, middle, and end; some order words	Lacks beginning, middle, end; incorrect or no order words
Voice	Writer closely involved; engaging personality	Sincere voice but not fully engaged	Careless writing with no feeling
Word Choice	Vivid, precise words that bring story to life	Language adequate but lacks color	Vague, dull, or misused words
Sentences	Excellent variety of sentences; natural rhythm	Correctly constructed sentences; some variety	Choppy; many incomplete or run-on sentences
Conventions	Excellent control; few or no errors	Reasonable control; few distracting errors	Many errors that prevent understanding

Scoring Rubric — Descriptive Writing

Rubric 4 3 2 1

	6	5	4	3	2	1
Focus/Ideas	Excellent, focused description; well elaborated with quality details	Good, focused description; elaborated with telling details	Description focused; good elaboration	Generally focused description; some supporting details	Sometimes unfocused description; needs more supporting details	Rambling description; lacks development and detail
Organization/ Paragraphs	Compelling ideas enhanced by order, structure, and transitions	Appealing order, structure, and transitions	Structure identifiable and suitable; transitions used	Adequate order, structure, and transitions to guide reader	Little direction from beginning to end; few transitions	Lacks direction and identifiable structure; no transitions
Voice	Writer closely involved; engaging personality	Reveals personality	Pleasant but not compelling voice	Sincere voice but not fully engaged	Little writer involvement, personality	Careless writing with no feeling
Word Choice	Vivid, precise words that create memorable pictures	Clear, interesting words to bring description to life	Some specific word pictures	Language adequate; appeals to senses	Generally limited or redundant language	Vague, dull, or misused words
Sentences	Excellent variety of sentences; natural rhythm	Varied lengths, styles; generally smooth	Correct sentences with variations in style	Correctly constructed sentences; some variety	May have simple, awkward, or wordy sentences; little variety	Choppy; many incomplete run-on sentences
Conventions	Excellent control; few or no errors	No serious errors to affect understanding	General mastery of conventions but some errors	Reasonable control; few distracting errors	Weak control; enough errors to affect understanding	Many errors that prevent understanding

Scoring Rubric — Descriptive Writing

Rubric 4 3 2 1

	5	4	3	2	1
Focus/Ideas	Excellent, focused description; well elaborated with quality details	Good, focused description; elaborated with telling details	Generally focused description; some supporting details	Sometimes unfocused description; needs more supporting details	Rambling description; lacks development and detail
Organization/ Paragraphs	Compelling ideas enhanced by order, structure, and transitions	Appealing order, structure, and transitions	Adequate order, structure, and some transitions to guide reader	Little direction from beginning to end; few transitions	Lacks direction and identifiable structure; no transitions
Voice	Writer closely involved; engaging personality	Reveals personality	Sincere voice but not fully engaged	Little writer involvement, personality	Careless writing with no feeling
Word Choice	Vivid, precise words that create memorable pictures	Clear, interesting words to bring description to life	Language adequate; appeals to senses	Generally limited or redundant language	Vague, dull, or misused words
Sentences	Excellent variety of sentences; natural rhythm	Varied lengths, styles; generally smooth	Correctly constructed sentences; some variety	May have simple, awkward, or wordy sentences; little variety	Choppy; many incomplete or run-on sentences
Conventions	Excellent control; few or no errors	No serious errors to affect understanding	Reasonable control; few distracting errors	Weak control; enough errors to affect understanding	Many errors that prevent understanding

Scoring Rubric — Descriptive Writing

Rubric 4 3 2 1

	3	2	1
Focus/Ideas	Excellent, focused description; well elaborated with quality details	Generally focused description; some supporting details	Rambling description; lacks development and detail
Organization/ Paragraphs	Compelling ideas enhanced by order, structure, and transitions	Adequate order, structure, and some transitions to guide reader	Lacks direction and identifiable structure; no transitions
Voice	Writer closely involved; engaging personality	Sincere voice but not fully engaged	Careless writing with no feeling
Word Choice	Vivid, precise words that create memorable pictures	Language adequate; appeals to senses	Vague, dull, or misused words
Sentences	Excellent variety of sentences; natural rhythm	Correctly constructed sentences; some variety	Choppy; many incomplete or run-on sentences
Conventions	Excellent control; few or no errors	Reasonable control; few distracting errors	Many errors that prevent understanding

Scoring Rubric — Persuasive Writing

Rubric 4 3 2 1	6	5	4	3	2	1
Focus/Ideas	Persuasive argument carefully built with quality details	Persuasive argument well supported with details	Persuasive argument focused; good elaboration	Persuasive argument with one or two convincing details	Persuasive piece sometimes unfocused; needs more support	Rambling persuasive argument; lacks development and detail
Organization/ Paragraphs	Information chosen and arranged for maximum effect	Evident progression of persuasive ideas	Progression and structure evident	Information arranged in a logical way with some lapses	Little structure or direction	No identifiable structure
Voice	Writer closely involved; persuasive but not overbearing	Maintains persuasive tone	Persuasive but not compelling voice	Sometimes uses persuasive voice	Little writer involvement, personality	Shows little conviction
Word Choice	Persuasive words carefully chosen for impact	Argument supported by persuasive language	Uses some persuasive words	Occasional persuasive language	Generally limited or redundant language	Vague, dull, or misused words; no persuasive words
Sentences	Excellent variety of sentences; natural rhythm	Varied lengths, styles; generally smooth	Correct sentences with variations in style	Carefully constructed sentences; some variety	Simple, awkward, or wordy sentences; little variety	Choppy; many incomplete or run-on sentences
Conventions	Excellent control; few or no errors	No serious errors to affect understanding	General mastery of conventions but some errors	Reasonable control; few distracting errors	Weak control; enough errors to affect understanding	Many errors that prevent understanding

Scoring Rubric — Persuasive Writing

Rubric 4 3 2 1	5	4	3	2	1
Focus/Ideas	Persuasive argument carefully built with quality details	Persuasive argument well supported with details	Persuasive argument with one or two convincing details	Persuasive piece sometimes unfocused; needs more support	Rambling persuasive argument; lacks development and detail
Organization/ Paragraphs	Information chosen and arranged for maximum effect	Evident progression of persuasive ideas	Information arranged in a logical way with some lapses	Little structure or direction	No identifiable structure
Voice	Writer closely involved; persuasive but not overbearing	Maintains persuasive tone	Sometimes uses persuasive voice	Little writer involvement, personality	Shows little conviction
Word Choice	Persuasive words carefully chosen for impact	Argument supported by persuasive language	Occasional persuasive language	Generally limited or redundant language	Vague, dull, or misused words; no persuasive words
Sentences	Excellent variety of sentences; natural rhythm	Varied lengths, styles; generally smooth	Carefully constructed sentences; some variety	Simple, awkward, or wordy sentences; little variety	Choppy; many incomplete or run-on sentences
Conventions	Excellent control; few or no errors	No serious errors to affect understanding	Reasonable control; few distracting errors	Weak control; enough errors to affect understanding	Many errors that prevent understanding

Scoring Rubric — Persuasive Writing

Rubric 4 3 2 1	3	2	1
Focus/Ideas	Persuasive argument carefully built with quality details	Persuasive argument with one or two convincing details	Rambling persuasive argument; lacks development and detail
Organization/ Paragraphs	Information chosen and arranged for maximum effect	Information arranged in a logical way with some lapses	No identifiable structure
Voice	Writer closely involved; persuasive but not overbearing	Sometimes uses persuasive voice	Shows little conviction
Word Choice	Persuasive words carefully chosen for impact	Occasional persuasive language	Vague, dull, or misused words; no persuasive words
Sentences	Excellent variety of sentences; natural rhythm	Carefully constructed sentences; some variety	Choppy; many incomplete or run-on sentences
Conventions	Excellent control; few or no errors	Reasonable control; few distracting errors	Many errors that prevent understanding

Scoring Rubric — Expository Writing

Rubric 4 3 2 1

	6	5	4	3	2	1
Focus/Ideas	Insightful, focused exposition; well elaborated with quality details	Informed, focused exposition; elaborated with telling details	Exposition focused, good elaboration	Generally focused exposition; some supporting details	Sometimes unfocused exposition needs more supporting details	Rambling exposition; lack development and detail
Organization/ Paragraphs	Logical, consistent flow of ideas; good transitions	Logical sequencing of ideas; uses transitions	Ideas sequenced with some transitions	Sequenced ideas with some transitions	Little direction from beginning to end; few order words	Lacks structure and transitions
Voice	Writer closely involved; informative voice well suited to topic	Reveals personality; voice suited to topic	Pleasant but not compelling voice	Sincere voice suited to topic	Little writer involvement, personality	Careless writing with no feeling
Word Choice	Vivid, precise words to express ideas	Clear words to express ideas	Words correct and adequate	Language adequate but may lack precision	Generally limited or redundant language	Vague, dull, or misused words
Sentences	Strong topic sentence; fluent, varied structures	Good topic sentence; smooth sentence structure	Correct sentences that are sometimes fluent	Topic sentence correctly constructed; some sentence variety	Topic sentence unclear or missing; wordy, awkward sentences	No topic sentence; many incomplete or run-on sentences
Conventions	Excellent control; few or no errors	No serious errors to affect understanding	General mastery of conventions but some errors	Reasonable control; few distracting errors	Weak control; enough errors to affect understanding	Many errors that prevent understanding

Scoring Rubric — Expository Writing

Rubric 4 3 2 1

	5	4	3	2	1
Focus/Ideas	Insightful, focused exposition; well elaborated with quality details	Informed, focused exposition; elaborated with telling details	Generally focused exposition; some supporting details	Sometimes unfocused exposition needs more supporting details	Rambling exposition; lacks development and detail
Organization/ Paragraphs	Logical, consistent flow of ideas; good transitions	Logical sequencing of ideas; uses transitions	Sequenced ideas with some transitions	Little direction from beginning to end; few order words	Lacks structure and transitions
Voice	Writer closely involved; informative voice well suited to topic	Reveals personality; voice suited to topic	Language adequate but may lack precision	Little writer involvement, personality	Careless writing with no feeling
Word Choice	Vivid, precise words to express ideas	Clear words to express ideas	Topic sentence correctly constructed; some sentence variety	Generally limited or redundant language	Vague, dull, or misused words
Sentences	Strong topic sentence; fluent, varied structures	Good topic sentence; smooth sentence structure	Sincere voice suited to topic	Topic sentence unclear or missing; wordy, awkward sentences	No topic sentence; many incomplete or run-on sentences
Conventions	Excellent control; few or no errors	No serious errors to affect understanding	Reasonable control; few distracting errors	Weak control; enough errors to affect understanding	Many errors that prevent understanding

Scoring Rubric — Expository Writing

Rubric 4 3 2 1

	3	2	1
Focus/Ideas	Insightful, focused exposition; well elaborated with quality details	Generally focused exposition; some supporting details	Rambling exposition; lacks development and detail
Organization/ Paragraphs	Logical, consistent flow of ideas; good transitions	Sequenced ideas with some transitions	Lacks structure and transitions
Voice	Writer closely involved; informative voice well suited to topic	Sincere voice suited to topic	Careless writing with no feeling
Word Choice	Vivid, precise words to express ideas	Language adequate but may lack precision	Vague, dull, or misused words
Sentences	Strong topic sentence; fluent, varied structures	Topic sentence correctly constructed; some sentence variety	No topic sentence; many incomplete or run-on sentences
Conventions	Excellent control; few or no errors	Reasonable control; few distracting errors	Many errors that prevent understanding

Monitoring Fluency

Ongoing assessment of student reading fluency is one of the most valuable measures we have of students' reading skills. One of the most effective ways to assess fluency is taking timed samples of students' oral reading and measuring the number of words correct per minute (WCPM).

How to Measure Words Correct Per Minute—WCPM

Choose a Text

Start by choosing a text for the student to read. The text should be:

• narrative

• unfamiliar

• on grade level

Make a copy of the text for yourself and have one for the student.

Timed Reading of the Text

Tell the student: As you read this aloud, I want you to do your best reading and to read as quickly as you can. That doesn't mean it's a race. Just do your best, fast reading. When I say begin, start reading.

As the student reads, follow along in your copy. Mark words that are read incorrectly.

Incorrect	Correct
• omissions	• self-corrections within 3 seconds
• substitutions	• repeated words
• mispronunciations	
• reversals	

After One Minute

At the end of one minute, draw a line after the last word that was read. Have the student finish reading but don't count any words beyond one minute. Arrive at the words correct per minute—WCPM—by counting the total number of words that the student read correctly in one minute.

Fluency Goals

Grade 5 End-of-Year Goal = 140 WCPM

Target goals by unit

Unit 1 105 to 110 WCPM	Unit 4 120 to 128 WCPM
Unit 2 110 to 116 WCPM	Unit 5 125 to 134 WCPM
Unit 3 115 to 122 WCPM	Unit 6 130 to 140 WCPM

More Frequent Monitoring

You may want to monitor some students more frequently because they are falling far below grade-level benchmarks or they have a result that doesn't seem to align with their previous performance. Follow the same steps above, but choose 2 or 3 additional texts.

Fluency Progress Chart Copy the chart on the next page. Use it to record each student's progress across the year.

Fluency Progress Chart, Grade 5

Name _____

WCPM

	1	2	3	4	5	6	7	8	9	10	11	12	13	14	15	16	17	18	19	20	21	22	23	24	25	26	27	28	29	30
150																														
145																														
140																														
135																														
130																														
125																														
120																														
115																														
110																														
105																														
100																														
95																														
90																														
85																														
80																														
75																														
70																														
65																														
55																														
50																														

Timed Reading

See also Assessment Handbook, p. 174.

© Pearson Education, Inc.

Name _____ Date _____

Assessment and Regrouping Chart

Unit 2

	Day 3 Retelling Assessment		Day 5 Fluency Assessment		Reteach	Teacher's Comments	Grouping
The assessed group is highlighted for each week.	Benchmark Score	Actual Score	The assessed group is highlighted for each week.	Benchmark WCPM	Actual Score			

WEEK 1

Inside Out — Compare and Contrast						✓		
Strategic	1–2		Strategic	Less than 110				
On-Level	3		On-Level	110–116				
Advanced	4		Advanced*	110–116				

WEEK 2

Passage to Freedom — Author's Purpose								
Strategic	1–2		Strategic	Less than 110				
On-Level	3		On-Level	110–116				
Advanced	4		Advanced*	110–116				

WEEK 3

The Ch'i-lin Purse — Compare and Contrast								
Strategic	1–2		Strategic	Less than 110				
On-Level	3		On-Level	110–116				
Advanced	4		Advanced*	110–116				

WEEK 4

Jane Goodall's 10 Ways — Fact and Opinion								
Strategic	1–2		Strategic	Less than 110				
On-Level	3		On-Level	110–116				
Advanced	4		Advanced*	110–116				

WEEK 5

The Midnight Ride — Sequence								
Strategic	1–2		Strategic	Less than 110				
On-Level	3		On-Level	110–116				
Advanced	4		Advanced*	110–116				

Unit 2 Benchmark Test Score

* **RECORD SCORES** Use this chart to record scores for the Day 3 Retelling, Day 5 Fluency, and Unit Benchmark Test Assessments.

* **REGROUPING** Compare the student's actual score to the benchmark score for each group level and review the *Questions to Consider*. Students may move to a higher or lower group level, or they may remain in the same group.

* **RETEACH** If a student is unable to complete any part of the assessment process, use the weekly Reteach lessons for additional support. Record the lesson information in the space provided on the chart. After reteaching, you may want to reassess using the Unit Benchmark Test.

*Students in the advanced group should read above-grade-level materials.

See also *Assessment Handbook*, p. 176

Unit 2
Assess and Regroup

FYI In Grade 5 there are opportunities for regrouping every five weeks—at the end of Units 2, 3, 4, and 5. These options offer sensitivity to each student's progress, although some teachers may prefer to regroup less frequently.

Regroup for Unit 3

To make regrouping decisions at the end of Unit 2, consider students' end-of-unit scores for

- Unit 2 Retelling
- Fluency (WCPM)
- Unit 2 Benchmark Test

Group Time

On-Level

To continue On-Level or to move into the On-Level group, students should

- score 3 or better on their cumulative unit rubric scores for Retelling
- meet the current benchmark for fluency (110–116 WCPM), reading On-Level text such as Student Edition selections
- score 80% or better on the Unit 2 Benchmark Tests
- be capable of working in the On-Level group based on teacher judgment

Strategic Intervention

Students would benefit from Strategic Intervention if they

- score 2 or lower on their cumulative unit rubric scores for Retelling
- do not meet the current benchmark for fluency (110–116 WCPM)
- score below 60% on the Unit 2 Benchmark Tests
- are struggling to keep up with the On-Level group based on teacher judgment

Advanced

To move to the Advanced group, students should

- score 4 on their cumulative unit rubric scores for Retelling and demonstrate expansive vocabulary and ease of language in their retellings
- score 95% on the Unit 2 Benchmark Test
- read above-grade-level material fluently (110–116 WCPM)
- be capable of handling the problem solving and investigative work of the Advanced group based on teacher judgment

QUESTIONS TO CONSIDER

- What types of test questions did the student miss? Are they specific to a particular skill or strategy?
- Does the student have adequate background knowledge to understand the test passages or selections for retelling?

- Has the student's performance met expectations for daily lessons and assessments with little or no reteaching?
- Is the student performing more like students in another group?
- Does the student read for enjoyment, different purposes, and varied interests?

Benchmark Fluency Scores

Current Goal: **110–116** WCPM

End-of-Year Goal: **140** WCPM

Vocabulary

Directions Find and circle the following words. All words go from left to right.

Check the Words You Know

___caterpillar ___cocoon ___disrespect ___emerge
___migrant ___sketched ___unscrewed

```
C  O  C  O  O  N  A  T  Y  L  J  M  K  R  T
L  Y  M  C  E  M  E  R  G  E  T  C  A  T  P
M  T  I  E  N  Y  E  G  R  L  P  U  F  L  T
O  D  I  S  R  E  S  P  E  C  T  K  A  I  L
M  I  G  R  A  N  T  K  N  W  J  S  S  R  G
T  E  N  A  R  G  E  L  K  M  I  G  A  R  T
A  K  T  S  K  E  T  C  H  E  D  Y  T  C  M
C  O  C  O  R  U  N  S  C  R  E  W  E  D  Y
A  J  T  S  K  E  A  T  C  H  E  D  Y  L  O
D  I  T  C  A  T  E  R  P  I  L  L  A  R  T
```

Directions Use each vocabulary word in a sentence.

1. _____

2. _____

3. _____

4. _____

5. _____

6. _____

7. _____

35

Using Special Talents

Using Special Talents
by Sharon Franklin

Unit 2 Week 1

⦿ **COMPARE AND CONTRAST**

⦿ **ANSWER QUESTIONS**

LESSON VOCABULARY caterpillar, cocoon, disrespect, emerge, migrant, sketched, unscrewed

---

SUMMARY This book follows the action of several children who want to help others. It also gives useful information on ways that readers can help their communities.

INTRODUCE THE BOOK

BUILD BACKGROUND Ask students to discuss personal experiences with fundraising or volunteer work.

PREVIEW/USE TEXT FEATURES As students preview the book, draw their attention to the charts on pages 11 and 18. How do the charts present information on ways to help others? Note that the captions throughout the book give additional information on the topic.

TEACH/REVIEW VOCABULARY Have pairs of students create vocabulary word cards. Then instruct one partner to hold up a card while the other partner gives the definition. Students can use the glossary to check the definitions. Pairs should keep playing until both partners have correctly defined all words.

ELL Use illustrations from the book, visual aids in the classroom, drawings, and gestures to explain words that students do not understand.

TARGET SKILL AND STRATEGY

⦿ **COMPARE AND CONTRAST** Remind students that to *compare* is to tell how two or more things are alike. To *contrast* is to tell how two or more things are different. Tell students that as they read *Using Special Talents,* they should think about the many ways that kids can help others. After reading, compare the different opportunities.

⦿ **ANSWER QUESTIONS** Remind students that there are four ways to find answers to questions: the answers can come from one sentence, from several sentences throughout the text, from the text and by the use of prior knowledge, and by the use of prior knowledge alone. As students answer the following comprehension questions, have them tell you how they came up with the answers.

READ THE BOOK

Use the following questions to support comprehension.

PAGE 11 Compare the different categories. Which one interests you most? Why? *(Response will vary.)*

PAGE 13 What does Annie do to raise money? Where did you find the answer? *(She bakes. I used text plus prior knowledge.)*

PAGES 20–22 What did Hallanah do to find out more information for her Web site? *(did online research, called and talked to many people)*

TALK ABOUT THE BOOK

READER RESPONSE
1. Alike: worked directly with people; Different: one helped a family, other helped a scientist
2. Responses will vary.
3. *Disrespect* contains the prefix *dis–. Unscrewed* contains the prefix *un–.*
4. Responses will vary.

RESPONSE OPTIONS

SPEAKING Have students pick one of the children in the book to role-play. Staying in character, students should explain how they help others and why.

CONTENT CONNECTIONS

Time for SOCIAL STUDIES

SOCIAL STUDIES Using the information found in the book and in online sources, encourage students to research volunteer opportunities and different volunteer organizations.

Name_____

Compare and Contrast

- To **compare** is to tell how two or more things are alike.
- To **contrast** is to tell how two or more things are different.

Directions Read the following sentence from *Using Special Talents*.

> In contrast to Annie, Miguel, and Lee, Hallanah is an experienced volunteer.

1. Think about all the different children you read about in *Using Special Talents*. What is one thing they all have in common?

_____

2. How does Hallanah differ from Annie, Miguel, and Lee?

_____

3. What clue words tell that Hallanah is being compared to Annie, Miguel, and Lee?

_____

4. Make a list of your own interests and talents.

_____

_____

_____

_____

5. Compare your list to the activities on the chart on page 11 of *Using Special Talents*. Based on your comparison, which activity would you like to do most. Why?

_____

_____

_____

_____

_____

_____

© Pearson Education 5

34

Vocabulary

Directions Choose the word from the box that best matches each definition. Write the word on the line.

> ## Check the Words You Know
>
> ___caterpillar   ___cocoon   ___disrespect   ___emerge
> ___migrant   ___sketched   ___unscrewed

1. _____ to come out of

2. _____ the opposite of respect

3. _____ an insect

4. _____ where a caterpillar turns into a butterfly

5. _____ traveling from one place to another

6. _____ past tense of twisting something off

7. _____ something an artist might have done to make a quick drawing

Directions Write three sentences using one vocabulary word in each.

8. _____

_____

9. _____

_____

10. _____

_____

35

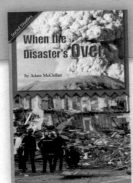

When the Disaster's Over

by Adam McClellan

🎯 **COMPARE AND CONTRAST**

🎯 **ANSWER QUESTIONS**

LESSON VOCABULARY aftermath, chaos, debris, dehydration, evacuate, impassable, infrastructure, insurance, psychological, rubble

SUMMARY This book tells of the damage caused by natural disasters and the ways that people aid in disaster relief efforts.

INTRODUCE THE BOOK

BUILD BACKGROUND Ask students to define what a natural disaster is. Identify various kinds of natural disasters, such as earthquakes, floods, mudslides, and tsunamis. Discuss the damage that these disasters cause and what students think can be done to help relief efforts.

PREVIEW/USE TEXT FEATURES Before reading, have students look through the book. Do they think it is fiction or nonfiction? Why? Point out the headings and captions. Ask students how they help. *(organize and give more information)* Ask: What do you think you might learn about natural disasters from this book?

TEACH/REVIEW VOCABULARY Review the meanings for vocabulary words that might not be familiar to students. Then preview the pages with highlighted words to make sure students understand how these words could be used in a text on natural disasters.

ELL Use the photographs in the book to help students better understand the vocabulary words.

TARGET SKILL AND STRATEGY

🎯 **COMPARE AND CONTRAST** In this book, students will learn about the effects of various natural disasters. Comparing the disasters and relief efforts will help students better understand the text. Point out that students will later complete the Venn Diagram in the back of the book.

🎯 **ANSWER QUESTIONS** *Answering questions* about a text is one way to monitor comprehension and better remember what was learned. As students read, they should come up with one or two questions to be answered by a classmate. The questions should be text-based and not rely on outside knowledge.

READ THE BOOK

Use the following questions to support comprehension.

PAGE 4 What is one of the most important things that happens right after a disaster? *(People look for survivors.)*

PAGES 16–17 What happened in the 1906 San Francisco earthquake that did not happen in the 1989 earthquake? *(The city was destroyed by fire.)*

PAGE 19 What did the people of Valmeyer do to make sure their town would not get flooded again? *(They moved to higher ground.)*

TALK ABOUT THE BOOK

READER RESPONSE
1. Both: disaster caused by volcanoes; widespread damage occurred; Armero: helicopters used to rescue survivors; Goma: plastic sheeting used to create temporary shelters
2. Answers will vary but should reflect understanding of FEMA.
3. *Rubble* is a type of *debris*. Possible synonyms: *remains, ruins, rubbish, trash, refuse, truck, litter*
4. Headings arrange text in chronological order of events connected with disaster relief.

RESPONSE OPTIONS

WRITING Invite students to think about how looking at the pictures and reading the text in *When the Disaster's Over* made them feel. Have them write a brief paragraph on what they felt and why.

CONTENT CONNECTIONS

SOCIAL STUDIES Have students make a list of natural disasters and research more about what causes them.

Time for **SOCIAL STUDIES**

Compare and Contrast

- To **compare** is to tell how two or more things are alike or different.
- To **contrast** is to tell how two or more things are different.

Directions Refer to the selection and answer the questions below.

1. Make a list of things that are commonly needed by many survivors of natural disasters.

_____

_____

_____

2. How can the water supply after a disaster be different from before the disaster? Why?

_____

_____

_____

3. When it comes to natural disasters, what are some differences between the National Guard and Doctors Without Borders?

_____

_____

_____

4. In areas where earthquakes happen, why is it better to build with wood and steel than with brick?

_____

_____

_____

5. Did using the skill Compare and Contrast help you better understand the information in this book? Why or why not?

_____

_____

_____

34

Name_____

Vocabulary

Directions Use the glossary at the back of the book *When the Disaster's Over* to review the meaning of the vocabulary words. Then choose eight of the words to use in sentences that relate to natural disasters.

Example: When the rivers started to flood the land, the police helped the people to evacuate the area safely.

Check the Words You Know

___aftermath	___chaos	___debris
___dehydration	___evacuate	___impassable
___infrastructure	___insurance	___psychological
___rubble		

---

1. _____
   _____

2. _____
   _____

3. _____
   _____

4. _____
   _____

5. _____
   _____

6. _____
   _____

7. _____
   _____

8. _____
   _____

35

A Day in the Life of Peter and Eve
by Gretchen McBride
illustrated by Ralph Canaday

A Day in the Life of Peter and Eve

◎ **AUTHOR'S PURPOSE**

◎ **MONITOR AND FIX UP**

LESSON VOCABULARY agreement, cable, diplomat, issue, refugees, representatives, superiors, visa

SUMMARY This fictional book tells the story of Peter and Eve Kissel and their family, living in Germany during World War II. The story describes a day in their lives and their discovery of the Nazi Party policies against Jewish people.

INTRODUCE THE BOOK

BUILD BACKGROUND Discuss what students know about World War II and the Nazi Party. Briefly describe the Nazis' policies toward Jews and the events of the Holocaust. Ask students what they think life may have been like for children living in Germany during the war.

PREVIEW/USE TEXT FEATURES Have students skim the text and the pictures. Ask if the book is fiction or nonfiction. Guide students to notice the dialogue, drawings, and lack of tables or other informational graphics. Ask why the author might have written a work of fiction about Germany during World War II.

TEACH/REVIEW VOCABULARY Have students work in groups to define each vocabulary word using a dictionary. Ask groups to write their words in sentences that will help their classmates understand the meanings.

ELL Have students use translation dictionaries in their own languages to define vocabulary words.

TARGET SKILL AND STRATEGY

◎ **AUTHOR'S PURPOSE** Remind students that authors may have more than one *purpose* for writing—to persuade, inform, entertain, or express a mood or feeling. As students read, have them think about the following questions: Why did the author write this story? Is this the same reason you predicted before you read the book?

◎ **MONITOR AND FIX UP** Tell students that one important reason for figuring out the author's purpose is to adjust the way they read the book. Students may read quickly if they think the author's purpose is to entertain or slowly if the purpose is to inform.

READ THE BOOK

Use the following questions to support comprehension.

PAGE 3 Why are Peter, his mother, and his sister sleeping in the cellar? *(to stay safe from enemy bombers)*

PAGE 8 Why do you think Fräulein Mann is uncomfortable repeating the salute to Hitler? *(She is not a Nazi and does not support Hitler.)*

PAGES 16–17 Why do you think the author has Peter and his mother talk kindly about the Karps? *(She wants the reader to know that not all Germans agreed with the Nazis' belief that Jewish people were bad.)*

TALK ABOUT THE BOOK

READER RESPONSE
1. Possible response: The author's purpose was to inform of the struggles of life in Nazi Germany.
2. left Germany; got a visa; disappeared; entered England
3. a type of message or communication
4. Answers will vary.

RESPONSE OPTIONS

WRITING Have students write a new ending to the story in which Peter presents the jar of apple butter to his teacher.

CONTENT CONNECTIONS

SOCIAL STUDIES Present students with some other stories about how non-Jewish people helped Jewish friends and neighbors escape the Holocaust. *The Diary of Anne Frank* is one example. Have students write a paragraph summarizing the risks people took.

Time for SOCIAL STUDIES

Author's Purpose

- An **author's purpose** is the reason an author writes something. Some purposes an author may have are to persuade, to inform, to entertain, and to express a mood or feeling.
- An author may have more than one purpose in writing a particular selection.

Directions Refer to *A Day in the Life of Peter and Eve* and answer the questions below. Use complete sentences.

1. What is the author's purpose in describing what it was like for Peter, Eve, and their mother to sleep in the basement?

_____

_____

_____

2. What are some of the ways the author lets the reader know that Fräulein Mann does not agree with Hitler and the Nazis?

_____

_____

_____

3. What images of the war does the author demonstrate through Carl's letter?

_____

_____

_____

4. Why does the author have their mother wait until they are in the cellar before she tells Peter and Eve her feelings about the Nazis?

_____

_____

_____

© Pearson Education 5

38

Name_____

Vocabulary

Directions Draw a line from the vocabulary word to its correct definition.

Check the Words You Know

___agreement	___cable	___diplomat	___issue
___refugees	___representative	___superiors	___visa

1. agreement   **a.** a message sent through wires by electric current or electronic signals

2. cable   **b.** an official signature or endorsement upon a passport that gives someone permission to enter a foreign country

3. issue   **c.** an understanding reached by two or more persons or groups

4. superiors   **d.** people of higher position, rank, or ability

5. visa   **e.** to send out; put forth

Directions For each of the following characters from the story, write the vocabulary word from the box that best describes him or her.

6. Herr Karp _____

7. Herr Meitzel _____

8. Fräulein Mann's cousin Thomas _____

9. Peter's friend Hans Karp _____

10. Herr Lutz _____

Directions Choose three of the vocabulary words and write a sentence for each word.

11. _____

_____

12. _____

_____

13. _____

_____

39

Holocaust Rescuers

Unit 2 Week 2

🔘 **AUTHOR'S PURPOSE**

🔘 **MONITOR AND FIX UP**

LESSON VOCABULARY agreement, cable, diplomat, issue, refugees, representatives, superiors, visa

---

SUMMARY This informational book describes the efforts to save Jewish people across Europe from certain death at the hands of the Nazis during World War II. The book supports and extends the lesson concept of the risks people took to help others during World War II.

INTRODUCE THE BOOK

BUILD BACKGROUND Examine with students the title and the author of *Holocaust Rescuers.* Discuss with students what they expect the book will be about based on its genre (nonfiction), its cover photographs, and its title, even if they don't know the meaning of the word *Holocaust.*

PREVIEW/USE TEXT FEATURES Have students preview the book by skimming the headings and text, looking at the photographs, and reading the captions. Ask what students expect to learn from reading this book.

TEACH/REVIEW VOCABULARY Write the vocabulary words on the board and read them aloud. Ask: Which words are unfamiliar to you? Where might you find the meanings of those words?

ELL Have students put the vocabulary words and their meanings on separate index cards and play a matching game with them.

TARGET SKILL AND STRATEGY

🔘 **AUTHOR'S PURPOSE** Remind students that an author may write for different purposes—to inform, to persuade, to entertain, or to express feelings. Based on their previews, ask students what they think the author's purpose was for writing *Holocaust Rescuers.*

🔘 **MONITOR AND FIX UP** Tell students that one way to *fix up* their comprehension is to make a quick summary of the details they have just read. Suggest that understanding what they read will help them determine the author's purpose in writing all or part of the selection.

READ THE BOOK

Use the following questions to support comprehension.

PAGES 10–11 What did Britain do to help Jewish children during World War II? *(It gave visas to thousands of children so that they could live in England.)*

PAGES 12–13 What is the author's purpose in telling the story of Varian Fry? *(Possible response: to show that individuals and groups helped the Jews)*

PAGES 14–15 Make a generalization about the villagers in Le Chambon-sur-Lignon. *(Possible response: They helped many Jews escape the Holocaust but did not expect praise for their actions.)*

TALK ABOUT THE BOOK

READER RESPONSE

1. Possible responses: The Kindertransport played an important role in saving Jewish children's lives.
2. He created "Swedish houses" where Jews were safe. He handed out protective passes on trains. What he was doing was not allowed. Descriptive words may include *journey, foster, families, sad, safety.*
3. Sentences should show understanding of the definitions.
4. Responses will vary.

RESPONSE OPTIONS

WRITING Provide students with an excerpt from *The Diary of Anne Frank.* Have them write a personal response to Anne's descriptions of life while hiding from the Nazis.

CONTENT CONNECTIONS

SOCIAL STUDIES Have students research other people or groups that helped Jews survive the Holocaust.

Author's Purpose

- An **author's purpose** is the reason an author writes something. Some purposes an author may have are to persuade, to inform, to entertain, and to express a mood or feeling.
- An author may have more than one purpose in writing a particular selection.

Directions Refer to the selection and answer the questions below.

1. What do you think is the author's purpose for writing *Holocaust Rescuers?*

_____

_____

_____

2. Why do you think the author includes the section entitled "Did people know?" (pages 5–7)?

_____

_____

_____

_____

3. The author starts page 16 with this sentence: "More than anyone else, Raoul Wallenberg is remembered for saving Jewish people from the Holocaust." Why does she write this about Wallenberg? Use details from the selection to explain your answer.

_____

_____

_____

_____

4. How does the last section entitled "Remembering: Yad Vashem" support the author's purpose?

_____

_____

_____

© Pearson Education 5

38

Name_____

Vocabulary

Directions Use the vocabulary words above to complete the following sentences. Not all words will be used.

Check the Words You Know

___agreement   ___cable   ___diplomat   ___issue
___refugees   ___representatives   ___superiors   ___visa

1. Many _____ from the Holocaust fled to foreign countries and became citizens in their new lands.

2. My friend and I are in _____ that the Holocaust was a terrible time in history.

3. The work of a _____ must be interesting and exciting, since you travel and meet people from many other countries.

4. Without a _____, it is difficult to enter some foreign countries.

5. When she was growing up, Grandma says, people feared to receive a

   _____ because it almost always meant bad news.

Directions For each word below, use a thesaurus to find as many synonyms as you can that relate to the meaning of the word as it is used in *Holocaust Rescuers*.

6. issue _____

7. representatives _____

8. superiors _____

Directions Write two sentences using the words *diplomat* and *refugees*.

9. _____

   _____

10. _____

    _____

A Safe Haven
by Lara Bove

Unit 2 Week 2

- **AUTHOR'S PURPOSE**
- **MONITOR AND FIX UP**

LESSON VOCABULARY concentration camps, customs agents, Holocaust, kosher, quarantine, quotas, tours of duty, translator

A Safe Haven

SUMMARY This informational book describes how the United States set up a shelter for more than nine-hundred World War II refugees at a former army base in Oswego, New York.

INTRODUCE THE BOOK

BUILD BACKGROUND Ask students to tell what they know about the term *refugee.* Explain that refugees are people who have to flee their homes to find safety or refuge. Tell them that World War II created many European refugees who left their homes for safer places.

ELL If applicable, have students whose families fled difficult situations in their home countries describe their experiences leaving their native lands and coming to the United States.

PREVIEW/USE TEXT FEATURES Have students preview the book by skimming the headings and text, looking at the photos, and reading the captions. Ask students what they expect to learn from reading the book.

TEACH/REVIEW VOCABULARY To reinforce the importance of using a dictionary or glossary to define unfamiliar words, ask students questions such as, "Which words are unfamiliar to you? Where might you find the meanings of those words?"

TARGET SKILL AND STRATEGY

AUTHOR'S PURPOSE Based on their previews, ask students what they think the *author's purpose* was for writing *A Safe Haven*—to inform, to persuade, to entertain, or to express feelings?

MONITOR AND FIX UP Remind students to *monitor,* or check, whether or not they understand what they read. Tell them that if they do not understand something, one way to *fix up* their comprehension is to quickly summarize the details they have just read.

READ THE BOOK

Use the following questions to support comprehension.

PAGE 6 What did Ruth Gruber do for the refugees onboard the *Henry Gibbins*? *(Gruber acted as a translator for the refugees and wrote down their stories.)*

PAGES 12–13 How did the townspeople of Oswego try to help the refugees at the shelter? *(They gave them clothing, bedspreads, and toys.)*

PAGES 20–21 How did the United States help the refugees after the war ended? *(The government gave visas to the refugees so they could live in the United States.)*

TALK ABOUT THE BOOK

READER RESPONSE
1. The author wanted to document what happened to the *Henry Gibbins* refugees. page 21, paragraph 2
2. Learned: how the refugees interacted with the soldiers, were well-fed, and experienced mild discomforts; Want to Know: Answers will vary.
3. Possible response: The store sold kosher meats.
4. Possible response: Hitler taking power was the most important event because the events that followed would not have occurred without him.

RESPONSE OPTIONS

WRITING Have students imagine that they are refugees living in the Oswego shelter in 1944. Ask them to write diary entries in which they describe what life is like at the shelter.

CONTENT CONNECTIONS

Time for
SOCIAL STUDIES

SOCIAL STUDIES Have students research first-hand accounts of European refugees who settled in the United States during or after World War II. Students can prepare reports on the refugees and describe what their lives were like in America.

Name_____

Author's Purpose

- An **author's purpose** is the reason an author writes something. Some purposes an author may have are to persuade, to inform, to entertain, or to express a mood or feeling.
- An author may have more than one purpose in writing a particular selection.

Directions Refer to the selection and answer the questions below.

1. Reread your answer to the first question in Reader Response. What other purpose do you think the author had for writing *A Safe Haven?*

_____

_____

_____

2. On pages 4 and 5, the author describes some ways in which the U.S. government failed to help war refugees before it set up the shelter at Oswego. Why do you think the author describes these failures?

_____

_____

_____

3. Why does the author describe the many ways that Ruth Gruber helped the refugees aboard the *Henry Gibbins* and at the Oswego shelter?

_____

_____

_____

4. On pages 17 and 19, the author includes questions in her descriptions of life at Oswego. What do you think is the purpose of the questions in these sections?

_____

_____

_____

38

Vocabulary

Directions Use the vocabulary words to complete the crossword puzzle below.

Check the Words You Know

_____concentration camps   _____customs agents   _____Holocaust
_____kosher   _____quarantine   _____quotas
_____tours of duty   _____translator

Down

1. places used by the Nazis to imprison and kill people they thought were inferior, especially Jewish people
2. the term given to the Nazis' systematic killing of six million Jews during World War II
3. numbers that tell how many people can emigrate from different countries
4. someone who helps people communicate with each other and is able to speak more than one language

Across

4. the amounts of time soldiers serve their countries
5. rule that keeps people from having contact with other people for a period of time
6. people who inspect materials that travelers bring into countries
7. made according to Jewish religious rules for preparing food

39

© Pearson Education 5

China: Now and Then

China: Now and Then *by Kelly Kong*

🎯 **COMPARE AND CONTRAST**

🎯 **PREDICT**

LESSON VOCABULARY astonished, behavior, benefactor, distribution, gratitude, procession, recommend, sacred, traditions

SUMMARY The author compares the government, culture, writing, and educational systems of China, past and present. The title enables students to predict the text structure before reading.

INTRODUCE THE BOOK

BUILD BACKGROUND Point to China on a map of the world. Encourage students to share what they already know about China, such as the Great Wall, Chinese New Year, and Chinese cuisine.

PREVIEW/USE TEXT FEATURES As they preview, encourage students to share their comments and predictions about what the book will be about. Remind them to look carefully at the photographs for support for their ideas.

TEACH/REVIEW VOCABULARY Group students in pairs to play vocabulary charades. Assign each pair of students one or two words. Give students time to decide how they will act out the words for their classmates to guess.

ELL Discuss word endings. Call attention to the difference between the words *sacred* and *astonished*. *(-ed does not always signal verbs in the past tense)* Also review how the suffix *-tion* signals a noun.

TARGET SKILL AND STRATEGY

🎯 **COMPARE AND CONTRAST** Prompt students to explain in their own words that a *comparison* tells how things are alike and different, while a *contrast* only tells how things are different. After reading the book, form small groups and assign them one of the following sections: *Government, Arts and Entertainment, Sports.* Have groups complete Venn Diagrams about their sections and present them to the class.

🎯 **PREDICT** Before reading, call attention to the title of the book. Ask students to *predict* how the information in the text will be organized. During reading, pause and confirm students' predictions. Encourage them to share comments and questions about the strategy.

READ THE BOOK

Use the following questions to support comprehension.

PAGE 5 What is one of the biggest differences between communist and democratic governments? *(Officials aren't elected in communist countries.)*

PAGE 11 What can you conclude about the people of China based on what you just read? *(Athletic ability is respected in China.)*

PAGE 16 What do you predict the author will write about education? *(The author will probably compare and contrast education in the past and the present.)*

TALK ABOUT THE BOOK

READER RESPONSE
1. Possible response: Similarities—People travel by bus, car, and bicycle. Differences—Fewer Chinese own cars.
2. Possible response: It will be more difficult because of China's growing population.
3. *benediction, beneficial, beneficiary, benefit, benevolent.* Answers will vary.
4. Responses will vary.

RESPONSE OPTIONS

WRITING Have students practice writing using the text structure Comparison and Contrast.

CONTENT CONNECTIONS

SOCIAL STUDIES Students can learn on the Internet or at the library about how Western cultures have borrowed aspects of Chinese culture.

Time for **SOCIAL STUDIES**

Compare and Contrast

- To **compare** is to tell how two or more things are alike or different.
- To **contrast** is to tell only how two or more things are different.

Directions Use *China: Now and Then* to help you complete this page.

1. In the past China was ruled by _____; China's government today is

   _____.

2. In contrast to a democratic country, people in a communist country _____

   _____.

3. The ancient Chinese did activities such as _____

   _____, and _____. In addition

   to doing many of these same activities, modern Chinese _____.

4. In ancient times, the sports popular in China were _____,

   _____, and _____. Today, the athletic

   activities that are popular in China are _____,

   and _____.

5. How are Chinese bicycles different from American bicycles? _____

   _____

   _____

6. How does Chinese writing differ from English writing? _____

   _____

   _____

42

Name _____

Vocabulary

Directions Fill in each blank with a word from the box that matches the definition.

Check the Words You Know

____astonished   ____behavior   ____benefactor
____distribution   ____gratitude   ____procession
____recommend   ____sacred   ____traditions

1. holy _____

2. thankfulness _____

3. a line or sequence of people or things _____

4. way of acting _____

5. the act of giving out _____

6. very surprised _____

7. person who gives money or kindly help _____

8. to suggest _____

9. customs _____

Directions Write a paragraph about *China: Now and Then* using as many vocabulary words as you can.

_____

_____

_____

_____

_____

_____

_____

_____

43

The Gift

Unit 2 Week 3

The Gift
by Isabel Sendao

illustrated by Dunja Bernhard

◉ **COMPARE AND CONTRAST**

◉ **PREDICT**

LESSON VOCABULARY astonished, behavior, benefactor, distribution, gratitude, procession, recommend, sacred, traditions

SUMMARY In *The Gift,* a young girl experiences the joy of both giving and receiving family-oriented gifts.

INTRODUCE THE BOOK

BUILD BACKGROUND Ask students if they have ever made, or would like to make, gifts for members of their families. Discuss meaningful types of gifts that family members could make for each other.

PREVIEW/USE ILLUSTRATIONS Before reading the text, invite students to look at the illustrations in *The Gift.* Have them use the illustrations to predict the setting and characters of the story.

TEACH/REVIEW VOCABULARY Challenge students to use vocabulary words in sentences that relate to food.

TARGET SKILL AND STRATEGY

◉ **COMPARE AND CONTRAST** Review with students that *comparing and contrasting* means finding what is alike and what is different between objects and ideas. As students read, invite them to take notes on how Lupe's gift and her grandmother's gift are similar and how they are different.

◉ **PREDICT** Remind students that to *predict* means to tell what might happen next in a story based on what has already happened. Invite students to choose places as they read to stop and write their predictions of what might happen next. After students have finished the book, discuss their predictions and whether they were correct.

READ THE BOOK

Use the following questions to support comprehension.

PAGE 5 Why does Lupe decide to make a recipe book for her grandmother? *(to thank her)*

PAGE 16 Why does Lupe like hearing stories about the women in her family making Rosca de Reyes? *(It makes her feel like an important part of a family tradition.)*

TALK ABOUT THE BOOK

READER RESPONSE
1. Abuelas: all sorts of family information; Lupés: recipes; Both: show family traditions
2. Answers will vary.
3. Possible response: *benefit, beneficial, benevolent; bene–* means "good."
4. Answers will vary.

RESPONSE OPTIONS

WRITING Have students think of their favorite foods that they eat at home. Invite them to make a list of dishes they would like to learn how to cook. Ask them whether certain dishes are special within their families; if so, suggest they write a paragraph describing why.

ELL Have students complete the writing activity above. Ask them to describe or draw the foods so that you can help them translate ingredients into English.

CONTENT CONNECTIONS

Time for **SOCIAL STUDIES**

SOCIAL STUDIES Review with students that celebrating the Three Kings is an important tradition in Lupe's family. Ask students to research and report on an important tradition that their own families celebrate.

Name _____

Compare and Contrast

- To **compare** is to tell how two or more things are alike or different.
- To **contrast** is to tell only how two or more things are different.

Directions Use *The Gift* to help you answer the following questions.

1. Contrast the language Lupe speaks in America with the one she speaks in Mexico.

_____

_____

2. Why does Lupe feel sad when she thinks about the Three Kings and her friends at home?

_____

_____

3. Lupe's mother tells Lupe that her mother taught her to make Rosca de Reyes. How is that different from Lupe's experience?

_____

_____

_____

4. What are some things that are typical of the Christmas celebrations at Abuela's house?

_____

_____

_____

5. Did using the reading skill of comparison and contrast help you to understand this story better? Why or why not?

_____

_____

_____

42

Vocabulary

Directions In each of the following sentences, the vocabulary words are italicized. Underline the sentences in which the vocabulary words are used correctly. Do nothing with the sentences in which the vocabulary words are used incorrectly.

Check the Words You Know

___astonished   ___behavior   ___benefactor
___distribution   ___gratitude   ___procession
___recommend   ___sacred   ___traditions

1. Abuela's ability to bake a great pastry is *astonished*.

2. Lupe wanted to help, so she was on her best *behavior*.

3. Helping each other cook was very *benefactor* for the family.

4. The pieces of pastry were *distribution* equally among the people at the table.

5. Lupe was filled with *gratitude* at the chance to be part of a family tradition.

6. They watched the *procession* of the Three Kings wind through the streets.

7. The *recommend* is to use three cups of flour in the recipe.

8. The recipes were *sacred* to Lupe's family.

9. *Traditions*, the Lupe's family eats a special pastry to celebrate Christmas.

Directions Select three vocabulary words and use each in a sentence.

10. _____

_____

11. _____

_____

12. _____

_____

© Pearson Education 5

43

Making Friends in Mali

◉ **COMPARE AND CONTRAST**

◉ **PREDICT**

LESSON VOCABULARY ambition, efficiency, moped, rummaging, simplicity, thriving, volunteer

---

SUMMARY A young woman joins the Peace Corps, leaving her rural home in Maine for a village in Africa. While helping others, she learns to see both the similarities and the differences between her old life and her new life.

INTRODUCE THE BOOK

BUILD BACKGROUND Inform students that the Peace Corps is an organization that sends Americans to other countries to provide assistance. Discuss the kind of help people in other countries might need. Ask students if they think it would be interesting to join the Peace Corps when they are older. Discuss where they might want to go and what kind of help they might want to offer.

PREVIEW/USE TEXT FEATURES Have students skim the chapter headings and illustrations. Ask them to use these features to predict what the story will be about.

TEACH/REVIEW VOCABULARY Discuss the vocabulary words, using a Word Knowledge Rating Chart. Write each word on the board and ask students to rate it: *Know, Have Seen, Don't Know*. Then write each word under the appropriate head. After reading the book, review the ratings and make changes based on revised understandings.

TARGET SKILL AND STRATEGY

◉ **COMPARE AND CONTRAST** Review with students that *comparing and contrasting* means finding what is alike and what is different between objects and ideas. Point out that although much in the main character's life will change, some things will still be familiar to her. As students read the story, have them take notes comparing Georgia's life in Mali with her former life in Maine.

◉ **PREDICT** Before reading the last chapter, suggest that students write a sentence *predicting* how the story will end. After reading the story, have students share their predictions and discuss whether they were correct.

READ THE BOOK

Use the following questions to support comprehension.

PAGE 7 How does Georgia convince her father that it is okay for her to join the Peace Corps? *(She reminds him that she is just like him and wishes to help people.)*

PAGE 18 How do you think Georgia will feel during her first few days in Mali? *(Responses will vary.)*

PAGE 29 Why does Moussa give Georgia the piece of fabric? *(The gift is to thank her for helping him.)*

TALK ABOUT THE BOOK

READER RESPONSE
1. Information on graphic organizer might include the weather, experiences with chickens, friendship with an eleven-year-old boy, and motivated people.
2. Responses will vary.
3. You can pedal or use the motor. *Pedem* means "foot." Words include *biped, pedestal, pedestrian, pedicure, pedometer, quadruped*.
4. Answers will vary.

RESPONSE OPTIONS

ELL Have students create vocabulary word cards and then take turns asking each other riddles like *This word ends with the letter _____.*

WRITING Invite students to imagine that they are Georgia in Mali. Have them write a diary entry that she might write after spending a day with Moussa.

CONTENT CONNECTIONS

Time for **SOCIAL STUDIES**

SOCIAL STUDIES Ask students to brainstorm a list of ways they can help others in their own communities. Help them use the Internet or library to find organizations that welcome student volunteers.

Compare and Contrast

- To **compare** is to tell how two or more things are alike or different.
- To **contrast** is to tell only how two or more things are different.

Directions Use *Making Friends in Mali* to help you answer the questions below.

1–2. Compare Georgia and her father. How is Georgia like her father? How is she different?

_____

_____

_____

3. Contrast Georgia's home in Mali with her home in Maine.

_____

_____

4–5. Contrast the Zeroulias' garden center when they first bought it with the way it is now.

_____

_____

_____

6–7. Compare Moussa and Georgia.

_____

_____

8. How are Ibrahim and Charlie alike?

_____

_____

42

Name _____

Vocabulary

Directions Use a word from the box to complete each sentence below.

Check the Words You Know
___ambition   ___efficiency   ___moped   ___rummaging
___simplicity   ___thriving   ___volunteer

1. Georgia started _____ through the photographs looking for her favorite picture of Charlie crowing.

2. Many people love the _____ of life in developing countries.

3. Georgia was impressed with the _____ with which Ibrahim made the bricks.

4. A characteristic that both Moussa and Georgia's father had in common was

_____.

5. Costa had built an old barn and greenhouse into a popular, _____ business.

6. Georgia had become a _____ worker for the Peace Corps.

7. Georgia hopped on the _____ behind Moussa.

Directions Underline the word does not belong in each set.

8. volunteer, tradesperson, professional

9. waste, effectiveness, efficiency

10. rummaging, selling, searching

11. book, moped, magazine

12. simplicity, difficulty, complexity

13. ambition, laziness, drive

14. prospering, failing, thriving

43

Endangered Animals

Endangered Animals by Beth Parlikar

⊚ **FACT AND OPINION**

⊚ **ASK QUESTIONS**

LESSON VOCABULARY conservation, contribute, enthusiastic, environment, investigation

---

SUMMARY Though animal extinction is a part of nature, human actions can cause animals to become extinct faster than they naturally would. The book shows how this happens and what people have done to prevent it.

INTRODUCE THE BOOK

BUILD BACKGROUND Ask students to think about the roles that animals play in their everyday lives. Discuss what would happen if these animals disappeared forever. How would people's food, clothing, and other aspects of daily life change?

PREVIEW/USE TEXT FEATURES Ask students to flip through the book, glancing only at the photographs. Then have them preview it again, taking time to study the images and read the captions. How does this second read-through help?

TEACH/REVIEW VOCABULARY Invite volunteers to make up sentences, each of which includes and helps define a vocabulary word from the glossary.

ELL Have students compare English terminology such as *conservation, environment,* and *investigation* with related words in their home language.

TARGET SKILL AND STRATEGY

⊚ **FACT AND OPINION** Explain that a *statement of fact* can be proven true or false. A *statement of opinion* is a judgment or belief that cannot be proven true or false. Create a two-column chart on the board, heading one column *Statements of Fact* and the other *Statements of Opinion.* Read aloud statements from the book. Challenge students to identify what types of statements they are. Write each statement in the appropriate column.

⊚ **ASK QUESTIONS** Remind students that using this strategy properly means *asking good questions* about important text information. Asking questions before, during, and after reading helps students activate prior knowledge, clarify confusion, engage with the text, and remember important ideas.

READ THE BOOK

Use the following questions to support comprehension.

PAGE 5 What are endangered species? *(animals that are in danger of becoming extinct)*

PAGE 6 What U.S. law protects endangered species? *(the Endangered Species Act)*

PAGES 8–11 Why are the giant panda, spotted owl, and Karner blue butterfly all endangered or threatened? *(Widespread loss of their natural habitats leaves them with fewer places to live.)*

TALK ABOUT THE BOOK
READER RESPONSE
1. The first part is opinion, and the second part is fact.
2. Possible responses: Which animals suffer most from poaching? What are governments doing to stop poaching? Is there anything I can do?
3. *Contribute* can change to *contribution.* Sample sentence: He made a strong contribution to the project.
4. The map shows a huge shrinkage of panda habitat.

RESPONSE OPTIONS

WRITING Invite students to create endangered and threatened animal trading cards based on what they have learned. They should include facts about why the animal is endangered.

CONTENT CONNECTIONS

SCIENCE Students can learn more about endangered animals by visiting zoos and/or their Web sites.

TIME FOR Science

Fact and Opinion

- A statement of **fact** can be proven true or false by reading, observing, or asking an expert.
- A statement of **opinion** is a judgment or belief. It cannot be proven true or false but can be supported or explained.

Directions Read the following passage. Decide which sentences are facts and which sentences are opinions. Then complete the chart below.

A law called the Endangered Species Act protects endangered and threatened species. It is one of the most important laws in America. Under the Endangered Species Act, endangered species of animals are listed by the government. Then plans are made to keep the species from becoming extinct. The government must try to protect the animal habitats from being destroyed and may breed young animals in captivity for release in the wild. Hunting and fishing for endangered animals might be limited by the government.

Some people's jobs or businesses are affected by these rules. But saving endangered species is worth the sacrifice. Without protection, many animals will disappear from the Earth forever.

Statements of Fact	**Statements of Opinion**

46

Vocabulary

Directions Write the word from the box that best completes each sentence.

Check the Words You Know
___conservation   ___contribute   ___enthusiastic
___environment   ___investigation

1. Our class will _____ cupcakes to the school bake sale.

2. The police are conducting an _____ of the robbery.

3. A hot, dry desert is the perfect _____ for a camel.

4. I love animals, so I am _____ about my job at the pet store.

5. The _____ of habitats will help save endangered animals.

Directions Circle the word that has the same meaning as the vocabulary word.

6. **contribute**	neglect	harm	help
7. **conservation**	waste	guarding	destruction
8. **enthusiastic**	excited	disinterested	uncaring
9. **environment**	people	object	setting
10. **investigation**	examination	test	routine

Directions Write a sentence of your own for each vocabulary word.

11. _____

_____

12. _____

_____

13. _____

_____

14. _____

_____

15. _____

_____

47

Habitats in Need of Help

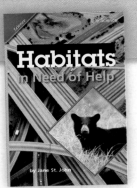

◉ **FACT AND OPINION**

◉ **ASK QUESTIONS**

LESSON VOCABULARY conservation, contribute, enthusiastic, environment, investigation

---

SUMMARY The growth of human populations often results in greater demand for limited natural resources and the clearing of land to meet people's needs. The author explains how this trend contributes to the alarming loss of animal habitats.

INTRODUCE THE BOOK

BUILD BACKGROUND Tell students that a habitat is a place where living things can find food, water, shelter, and nesting places. Ask students to think about their own habitats and those of different animals. Discuss how these places meet the needs of living things.

PREVIEW/USE TEXT FEATURES Ask students to flip through the book, glancing only at the photos. Then have them preview it again, taking time to study the images and accompanying captions. Discuss how this second read-through changes their understanding of the book's subject.

TEACH/REVIEW VOCABULARY Help students decipher the meanings of vocabulary words such as *investigation* (page 15) and *conservation* (page 23). Read aloud the sentences in which these words appear along with the sentences that precede and/or follow them. What contextual clues help define the words?

TARGET SKILL AND STRATEGY

◉ **FACT AND OPINION** Help students make distinctions between *statements of facts* and *statements of opinion* by reading aloud sentences about animal habitats and asking students to identify their types.

◉ **ASK QUESTIONS** *Asking questions* properly means asking good questions about important text information. Skilled readers ask questions before, during, and after reading to activate prior knowledge and clarify confusion.

ⒺⓁⓁ Invite less proficient speakers to ask questions such as, "What is this?" and "What is happening here?" while more proficient speakers answer the questions in detail.

READ THE BOOK

Use the following questions to support comprehension.

PAGE 3 What are some examples of animal habitats around the world? *(oceans, rivers, lakes, forests, deserts, and prairies)*

PAGES 3, 7 How does the destruction of habitats hurt animals? *(It prevents animals from thriving by harming their sources of food, water, shelter, and nesting places.)*

TALK ABOUT THE BOOK

READER RESPONSE
1. Possible response: Fact: Forest-clearing has resulted in a loss of Asian elephants' natural habitat. Opinion: The habitat of Asian elephants deserves more protection than other animals' homes.
2. Answers will vary but may include forests, swamps, and marshes; runoff from factories and air pollution; recycling, conserving water.
3. Articles will vary.
4. Responses will vary.

RESPONSE OPTIONS

WRITING Invite students to create an oversized postcard that features an animal habitat of their choice.

CONTENT CONNECTIONS

SCIENCE Invite students to consult other reference materials for more information on animal habitats. Then have them use art materials to re-create one of these habitats.

Fact and Opinion

- A statement of **fact** can be proven true or false by reading, observing, or asking an expert.
- A statement of **opinion** is a judgment or belief. It cannot be proven true or false but can be supported or explained.

Directions Read the following passage. Decide which sentences are facts and which sentences are opinions. Then complete the chart below by listing three statements of fact and two statements of opinion.

> The habitat of orangutans is at risk of disappearing. Orangutans are large, funny-looking apes. They live on the island of Borneo and the neighboring Indonesian island of Sumatra. An orangutan can weigh from sixty to three hundred pounds and requires large areas of forest in which to roam. But today, due to humans having taken over land for mining, logging, and various types of farming, less than 20 percent of the orangutans' original habitat remains. Some researchers estimate that there are fewer than thirty thousand orangutans on the islands today. Losing even one of these amazing apes would be a big tragedy.

Statements of Fact	Statements of Opinion

46

© Pearson Education 5

Name_____

Vocabulary

Directions Choose a word from the box that belongs with each group of words below.

> ## Check the Words You Know
>
> ___conservation   ___contribute   ___enthusiastic
> ___environment   ___investigation

1. surroundings   background   setting   _____

2. examination   exploration   probe   _____

3. donate   add   enrich   _____

4. interested   eager   excited   _____

5. care   saving   guarding   _____

Directions Circle the word that has the opposite meaning of the vocabulary word.

6. **contribute**   add   harm   enrich

7. **conservation**   attention   guarding   destruction

8. **enthusiastic**   uncaring   interested   excited

Directions Write two sentences about the loss of endangered animals' habitats. Use as many vocabulary words as you can.

9. _____

_____

_____

10. _____

_____

_____

_____

47

Endangered Species

Life Science

Saving Endangered Species

by Catherine Podojil

◎ **FACT AND OPINION**

◎ **ASK QUESTIONS**

LESSON VOCABULARY conservationists, endangered, extinct, habitats, population, scavenger, species, threatened

SUMMARY Many animals are in danger of extinction due to overhunting, pollution, and other human actions. The author explains what people are doing today to ensure that California condors, Bengal tigers, and other endangered animals will not disappear from the Earth forever.

INTRODUCE THE BOOK

BUILD BACKGROUND Have students discuss their knowledge of animals that became extinct due to natural events or human activities. Then ask them to share what they know about animals that are in danger of extinction today and why it is so.

PREVIEW/USE TEXT FEATURES Ask students how pairing photographs of animals with images of their natural habitats can enhance one's understanding of endangered animals.

ELL Use visual aids such as maps or globes to show students where animals such as the California condor, Andean condor, and grizzly bear live.

TEACH/REVIEW VOCABULARY Ask each volunteer to take a vocabulary word and point out how it is used in the reader.

TARGET SKILL AND STRATEGY

◎ **FACT AND OPINION** Draw a T-chart on the board and label one column *Statements of Fact* and the other *Statements of Opinion*. Ask students to discuss what they know about endangered animals, and then point out which of their statements belongs in which column and why. What sources would they use to check statements of fact?

◎ **ASK QUESTIONS** *Asking questions* helps readers actively engage with text and remember important ideas. Tell students that a good question often asks about an important detail of the story and can be answered in the reading. Ask students to record questions they have while reading about endangered animals.

READ THE BOOK

Use the following questions to support comprehension.

PAGE 5 Why do some species of animals and plants become extinct? *(They become extinct because of human actions.)*

PAGE 8 How does the Endangered Species Act help certain animals? *(It protects them from hunting, collecting, and other dangers.)*

PAGE 16 How does the saving of wild lands help save animals? *(Wild lands provide a home where animals can survive and thrive.)*

TALK ABOUT THE BOOK

READER RESPONSE

1. Possible response: An asteroid caused the extinction of plants and dinosaurs.

2. Answers will vary but might include questions about how much land the corridors take up, how close they are to cities, and how they're guarded.

3. Possible responses: conserving water; learning about endangered species; cleaning up a beach, park, or yard

4. Possible response: The grizzly bear's habitat has shrunk a great deal over time.

RESPONSE OPTIONS

WRITING Have students adopt an endangered animal's point of view and write a journal entry detailing its hopes, fears, and daily life.

CONTENT CONNECTIONS

SCIENCE Discuss how saving endangered animals and their habitats can support life for all living creatures on Earth.

TIME FOR Science

Fact and Opinion

- A statement of **fact** can be proven true or false by reading, observing, or asking an expert.
- A statement of **opinion** is a judgment or belief. It cannot be proven true or false but can be supported or explained.

Directions Read the following passage. Decide which sentences are statements of fact and which sentences are statements of opinion. Then complete the chart below.

> One animal that desperately needs its wild lands to be saved is the grizzly bear. The grizzly bear is one of the largest animals in North America. Male grizzlies can stand on their hind legs to a height of seven feet! They have been known to attack hikers, but that happens rarely. Grizzlies probably have more reasons to fear people. Humans have destroyed much of their habitat. Building roads through forests destroys grizzlies' territory. Many bears are also killed on these roads.

Statements of Fact	Statements of Opinion

46

© Pearson Education 5

Vocabulary

Directions Choose the vocabulary word that best matches each definition. Write the word on the line.

Check the Words You Know

____conservationists   ____endangered   ____extinct
____habitats   ____population   ____scavenger
____species   ____threatened

---

1. a group of organisms with common characteristics

    _____

2. no longer existing

    _____

3. all the living things of one kind in a single place

    _____

4. at risk of becoming endangered

    _____

5. an organism that eats dead animal matter

    _____

6. people who work to preserve natural resources

    _____

7. places where an animal or plant lives or grows naturally

    _____

8. in danger of becoming extinct

    _____

Directions Write a paragraph about endangered species using as many vocabulary words as you can.

_____

_____

_____

_____

_____

_____

_____

_____

_____

_____

_____

47

Paul Revere's Midnight Ride

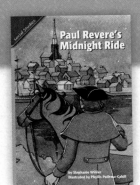

- SEQUENCE
- GRAPHIC ORGANIZERS

LESSON VOCABULARY fate, fearless, glimmer, lingers, magnified, somber, steed

SUMMARY The book tells the story of Paul Revere's ride at the beginning of the American Revolution. It explains how Revere and others warned colonial leaders to be prepared to fight the British.

INTRODUCE THE BOOK

BUILD BACKGROUND Discuss with students what they know about the beginnings of the American Revolution. Ask: In what part of the nation did the American Revolution begin? Discuss what students have heard about the role of Paul Revere. Explain the difference between a legend and a historical fact.

PREVIEW/USE TEXT FEATURES Encourage students to look at the illustrations in the book. Ask them to think about how they can distinguish between the American colonists and the British soldiers. Discuss how the illustrated map on the title page is helpful in giving a visual picture of Paul Revere's travels.

TEACH/REVIEW VOCABULARY Explain that the word *serious* is a synonym for the word *somber*. Discuss other possible synonyms for *somber* and explain that the context in which a word is used determines which synonym fits best. Repeat with the other vocabulary words.

ELL Show students a few maps that trace the growth of America from its colonial period to the days of the American Revolution. Discuss how the growth of America threatened Great Britain. Ask: Were there people who came to your home country to gain their freedom?

TARGET SKILL AND STRATEGY

SEQUENCE Remind students that when they read about historical events, it is helpful to put events in *sequence* to improve understanding. Select important story events and suggest that students put them in sequence.

GRAPHIC ORGANIZERS Ask students what kinds of *graphic organizers* might be most effective with historical narratives. (*time lines or sequence charts*)

READ THE BOOK

Use the following questions to support comprehension.

PAGE 4 What event came before Paul Revere's boat trip to Lexington? (*Robert Newman hung two lanterns in the bell tower.*)

PAGE 8 Why did it make sense for William Dawes to travel to Lexington when Paul Revere was already headed there? (*If one were stopped, the other could warn the colonists.*)

PAGE 13 Why did Paul Revere tell the British that they should flee Lexington? (*He tricked them into worrying more about the Americans' strength at Lexington rather than at Concord.*)

TALK ABOUT THE BOOK

READER RESPONSE
1. Possible responses: Revere met with Dawes; they rode to Concord; they were stopped; Revere was arrested and freed; Revere helped warn leaders.
2. Possible responses: Who fought at Lexington? Who was killed there? Internet or library
3. Possible responses: *homeless:* "without a home"; *tasteless:* "without taste"; sentences will vary.
4. Possible response: They left in the middle of the night.

RESPONSE OPTIONS

WRITING Suggest that students write a few paragraphs to express their opinions about Paul Revere's role in the American Revolution.

CONTENT CONNECTIONS

SOCIAL STUDIES Encourage students to use the library or the Internet to find out more about people who worked for freedom during Revolutionary times. Suggest that students find information about people who are not well-known and share it with their classmates.

Time for SOCIAL STUDIES

Sequence

- **Sequence** refers to the order of events in both fiction and nonfiction.
- Sequence can also refer to steps in a process.

Directions Reread the following paragraphs from *Paul Revere's Midnight Ride*. Then put the bulleted events in sequence.

> Revere woke Adams and Hancock and told them about the British. Hearing the news, the two men planned to return to Boston within a few hours.
>
> Then Revere met with William Dawes to decide what to do next. They both would ride on to Concord. There they would be able to help in the fight against the British.
>
> Along the way, Revere and Dawes met Dr. Samuel Prescott. Dr. Prescott joined them, and the three men rode on together.

- Adams and Hancock decided to go to Boston.
- Dawes and Revere started their trip to Concord.
- Revere woke Adams and Hancock.
- Revere met with William Dawes.
- Dr. Prescott met Dawes and Revere on their way.

1. _____

_____

2. _____

_____

3. _____

_____

4. _____

_____

5. _____

_____

50

Vocabulary

Directions Draw a line from each word to its definition.

Check the Words You Know
___fate ___fearless ___glimmer ___lingers
___magnified ___somber ___steed

1. fate   lasts; stays around or near

2. fearless   solemn or serious; sad

3. glimmer   something that cannot be controlled

4. lingers   made to appear larger

5. magnified   shine with a faint light

6. somber   not afraid; brave

7. steed   horse or other riding animal

Directions Write a paragraph about Paul Revere's ride. Use as many vocabulary words as you can.

_____

_____

_____

_____

_____

_____

_____

_____

_____

_____

_____

_____

51

PAUL REVERE AND THE
AMERICAN REVOLUTION
BY PATRICIA WEST

Paul Revere . . .

SEQUENCE

GRAPHIC ORGANIZERS

LESSON VOCABULARY fate, fearless, glimmer, lingers, magnified, somber, steed

SUMMARY The author describes the activities of Paul Revere before the early battles of the American Revolution. In addition, she sets the stage for the conflict behind the American Revolution by reviewing the disagreements between the American Colonists and the British—particularly the feeling among the British that the Colonists should bear some of the cost of the French and Indian War and the resentment of the Colonists that they were taxed without having any official power.

INTRODUCE THE BOOK

BUILD BACKGROUND Discuss with students what they know about situations in which someone's rights are not respected. Ask: What are some basic American freedoms? What action would you take to protect your freedoms if someone tried to take them away?

PREVIEW/USE ILLUSTRATIONS Encourage students to look at the illustrations in the book. Ask them to choose one and explain what it seems to tell about the book. Suggest that they check after their reading to see if their prediction was correct.

ELL Remind students that a noun is the name of a person, place, or thing. Point to objects around the classroom and identify them as nouns. Ask students to name additional nouns.

TEACH/REVIEW VOCABULARY Ask students to identify the nouns among the vocabulary words. (*fate, steed, glimmer*) Discuss the other parts of speech that are used (adjectives and verbs) and identify them.

TARGET SKILL AND STRATEGY

SEQUENCE Remind students that when we read, we put information in *sequence,* or order, to help us understand it. Discuss some of the events in this book that could be put in sequence.

GRAPHIC ORGANIZERS To put historical events in order, students might use a numbered list or *graphic organizer* such as a time line or sequence chart.

READ THE BOOK

Use the following questions to support comprehension.

PAGE 4 What was the purpose of a liberty tree? (*Colonists posted complaints and gathered there to discuss their problems with the British.*)

PAGES 5–6 What event came before the American Revolution that caused the British to go deeply into debt? (*The French and Indian War*)

PAGE 7 Why did the colonists oppose taxation so fiercely? (*They had no voice in the British government.*)

TALK ABOUT THE BOOK

READER RESPONSE
1. Possible response: B, A, C
2. Possible response: What was it like to be a dentist during the Revolution? in an encyclopedia
3. Possible response: In the *glimmer* of the candle, I saw a *steed* go by my window. He had a *somber* tread, as though he knew his master's *fate.* But as the danger *magnified,* his master became even more *fearless,* and the two easily jumped over the high fence. The memory of their brave leap still *lingers* in my mind.
4. Possible response: White pants were hard to keep clean.

RESPONSE OPTIONS

WRITING Ask students to write a few paragraphs explaining why they would nominate Paul Revere as a great American hero. Encourage them to include details from the book to support their nomination.

CONTENT CONNECTIONS

SOCIAL STUDIES Encourage students to find out information about the Boston Tea Party that describes the drama of the event. Suggest that they check the Internet or the library to see whether any short stories, poems, or plays have been written about it.

Time for
SOCIAL
STUDIES

Name_____

Sequence

- **Sequence** refers to the order of events in both fiction and nonfiction.
- Sequence can also refer to the steps in a process.

Directions Reread the following paragraphs from *Paul Revere and the American Revolution*. Then put the bulleted events in sequence.

> One law, passed in 1764, was called the Sugar Act. It taxed sugar, molasses, and other products shipped to the colonies. Colonists who ignored the act were punished as smugglers.
>
> A year later, the Stamp Act was passed by the British. This law required all legal and business documents in the colonies to carry a stamp showing that a tax had been paid . . . The colonists were very angry. They wondered what tax the British would decide on next . . . They claimed the British were taxing them without representation.

Put the following events in sequence.
- The Stamp Act was passed by the British government.
- The colonists disliked being taxed without having a voice in the government.
- The Sugar Act was passed by the British government.
- Colonists who did not pay taxes on molasses were punished.
- Colonists had to stamp all business documents.

1. _____

2. _____

3. _____

4. _____

5. _____

_____

© Pearson Education 5

50

Vocabulary

Directions Draw a line from each word to its synonym.

Check the Words You Know

___fate	___fearless	___glimmer	___lingers
___magnified	___somber	___steed	

1. fate   increased

2. fearless   unafraid

3. glimmer   uncontrolled event

4. lingers   horse

5. magnified   faint light

6. somber   stays

7. steed   solemn

Directions Write a paragraph about the beginning of the American Revolution. Use as many vocabulary words as you can.

_____

_____

_____

_____

_____

_____

_____

_____

_____

_____

_____

_____

51

The National Guard

The National Guard:
Modern Minutemen

by Patricia Walsh

Unit 2 Week 5

🎯 **SEQUENCE**

🎯 **GRAPHIC ORGANIZERS**

LESSON VOCABULARY citizen-soldiers, defending, mobilize, National Guard, relief, riot, steed, troops, volunteers

SUMMARY The book gives the historical background that led to the creation of the National Guard. It traces the activities of the Minutemen during Colonial times as well as the decision to maintain a National Guard for national emergencies. The author also discusses the twentieth-century activities of the U.S. National Guard, including civil rights protection, riot protection, disaster relief, and international defense.

INTRODUCE THE BOOK

BUILD BACKGROUND Discuss what students know about Colonial times and why colonists needed to be ready to fight at any time. Discuss today's National Guard and activities they are involved in.

PREVIEW/USE TEXT FEATURES Have students preview the cover illustration and the subtitles. Ask: What do you think this book will be about? Encourage them to study the time line on pages 20–21. Ask: What information on the time line is most unfamiliar?

ELL Using clothing as props, act out the role of a person taking off his or her everyday farmer's coat or hat and donning military garb. Discuss the concept of a *citizen-soldier.* Ask: Would you have been interested in being a citizen-soldier during Colonial times?

TEACH/REVIEW VOCABULARY Define the term *National Guard* for students. Describe how the National Guard is like and unlike the other United States armed forces. Discuss possible synonyms for the term and for the rest of the vocabulary words.

TARGET SKILL AND STRATEGY

🎯 **SEQUENCE** Remind students that we put events or ideas in *sequence* so that we can better understand what we have read and the order in which events happen. Discuss the sequence of events in America that led to the formation of the National Guard.

🎯 **GRAPHIC ORGANIZERS** Ask students what kinds of *graphic organizers* might be most useful in putting historical events in chronological order.

READ THE BOOK

Use the following questions to support comprehension.

PAGE 3 What question might you ask about the Minutemen before reading this page? *(Why were they called Minutemen?)*

PAGE 5 Who are the people who served as the Minutemen? *(They were farmers.)*

PAGE 6 What was the earliest evidence of a group of fighting volunteers in the United States? *(The earliest group was the Ancient and Honorable Artillery Company, which was formed in 1638 in Boston.)*

TALK ABOUT THE BOOK

READER RESPONSE
1. Possible responses: World War I (1917); World War II (1941); Korean War (1950); Gulf War (1991); Iraq War (2003)
2. Possible responses: How does one join the National Guard? How long do people serve? the Internet
3. *defend, defended, defending; mobilize, mobilized, mobilizing*
4. Possible response: Maine was part of Massachusetts.

RESPONSE OPTIONS

WRITING Encourage students to write a few paragraphs about why they think people decide to join the National Guard. Ask them to write about whether they would want to join.

CONTENT CONNECTIONS

SOCIAL STUDIES Suggest to students that they may wish to do additional research on the Minutemen. Ask: What questions do you have about the Minutemen that were not answered by this book?

Time for **SOCIAL STUDIES**

Sequence

- **Sequence** refers to the order of events in both fiction and nonfiction.
- Sequence can also refer to the steps in a process.

Directions Put the following events into sequence.

- The National Guard protected the civil rights of people who fought for integration of schools.
- The volunteer militia made up much of the army during the American Revolution.
- A colonial volunteer group set up the Ancient and Honorable Artillery Company in 1638.
- After the Civil War, many states renamed their militias to be called the National Guard.

1. _____

_____

2. _____

_____

3. _____

_____

4. _____

_____

Directions Draw lines from the left column to the right column to show the order in which these events occurred.

5. American Civil War fought   First

6. Iraq War   Second

7. Minutemen fought   Third
   in Massachusetts

8. Riots in American Cities   Fourth

50

Name_____

Vocabulary

Directions Write each word in the appropriate column to show whether it is a noun or a verb. Use a dictionary if necessary.

Check the Words You Know

___citizen-soldiers	___defending	___mobilize
___National Guard	___relief	___riot
___steed	___troops	___volunteers

Nouns	Verbs

Directions Use each vocabulary word in a sentence that shows its meaning.

1. _____

2. _____

3. _____

4. _____

5. _____

6. _____

7. _____

8. _____

9. _____

51

Answer Key for Below-Level Reader Practice

Juan's Journey
LR1

Compare and Contrast, LR2
Possible responses given. **What Juan Wants:** to stay in one place; to have a big house for his parents; to have a big house next to his parents; to buy his parents a new red car; (circled) a dog **What Juan Has:** a life where he moves around; lives in a tent, trailer, or small houses; old station wagon; (circled) gets a dog

Vocabulary, LR3
cocoon, emerge, disrespect, migrant, sketched, unscrewed, caterpillar
1–7. Sentences will vary.

Peter and Eve
LR10

Author's Purpose, LR11
1. Possible response: She wants the reader to imagine the sacrifices that Peter's family, and maybe other families, had to make to survive the war. **2.** Possible responses: She is uncomfortable repeating the salute to Hitler; she bows her head during the presentation by the councilmen; she has a cousin and knows other people who helped Jews. **3.** Possible responses: The food eaten by German soldiers is often spoiled, the fighting is terrible; soldiers don't often get to visit families back home. **4.** Possible response: She doesn't want anyone to overhear her say bad things about the Nazis. Not all people agree with her, and she might be punished for her opinions.

Vocabulary, LR12
1. agreement—c **2.** cable—a **3.** issue—e **4.** superiors—d **5.** visa—b
6. refugee **7.** diplomat **8.** representative **9.** refugee **10.** representative
11–13. Sentences will vary.

China: Now and Then
LR19

Compare and Contrast, LR20
1. emperors / communist **2.** do not elect their officials **3.** paper cutting, painting, writing poetry / going to the Peking Opera / go to the movies **4.** hunting, horseback riding, archery / soccer, basketball, swimming / diving **5.** They are designed for transportation, not for sport. They have a rack behind the seat for carrying things. **6.** In Chinese, each word is a picture. In English, words are made up of letters.

Vocabulary, LR21
1. sacred **2.** gratitude **3.** procession **4.** behavior **5.** distribution
6. astonished **7.** benefactor **8.** recommend **9.** traditions
Responses will vary.

Endangered Animals
LR28

Fact and Opinion, LR29
Possible response given. **Statements of Fact: 1.** A law called the Endangered Species Act protects endangered and threatened species. **2.** Under the Endangered Species Act, endangered species of animals are listed by the government. **3.** Some people's jobs or businesses are affected because of the Endangered Species Act. **Statements of Opinion: 4.** The Endangered Species Act is one of the most important laws in America. **5.** Saving endangered species is worth the sacrifice.

Vocabulary, LR30
1. contribute **2.** investigation **3.** environment **4.** enthusiastic
5. conservation **6.** help **7.** guarding **8.** excited **9.** setting
10. examination **11–15.** Sentences will vary.

Paul Revere's Midnight Ride
LR37

Sequence, LR38
1. Revere woke Adams and Hancock. **2.** Adams and Hancock decided to go to Boston. **3.** Revere met with William Dawes. **4.** Dawes and Revere started their trip to Concord. **5.** Dr. Prescott met Dawes and Revere on their way.

Vocabulary, LR39
1. fate—an event that seems meant to happen **2.** fearless—not afraid; brave **3.** glimmer—shine with a faint light **4.** lingers—lasts; stays around or near **5.** magnified—made to appear larger **6.** somber—solemn or serious; sad **7.** steed—horse or other riding animal
Possible response given. It was Paul Revere's *fate* to end up riding his way into the history books. He took his responsibility to help our nation with a *somber* attitude, realizing that the *glimmer* of liberty rested partly on his shoulders. With a *fearless* manner, he rode into the night to warn American leaders. Riding on his *steed,* he spread the word that the British were on their way. Although his legend has been *magnified* by the passing of time, the importance of his ride *lingers* even today.

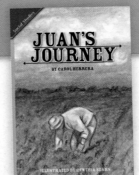

COMPARE AND CONTRAST

ANSWER QUESTIONS

LESSON VOCABULARY caterpillar, cocoon, disrespect, emerge, migrant, sketched, unscrewed

Juan's Journey

SUMMARY Juan, a child in a migrant worker family, longs for a permanent home as he deals with the realities of migrant worker life.

INTRODUCE THE BOOK

BUILD BACKGROUND Explain that migrant workers are people who travel around the country harvesting crops. Discuss with students what they know about the lives of migrant workers.

PREVIEW/USE TEXT FEATURES As students preview the book, draw their attention to the map on page 3. Discuss the route migrant workers travel as they look for work. Ask: What do you expect to learn about migrant workers?

ELL Compare the map on page 3 to a United States map. Point out the states mentioned on the page.

TEACH/REVIEW VOCABULARY Review the meaning of the words. Then give students word cards. Have students sort the words by parts of speech (noun, verb, adjective). Students can play a quick game of charades using the verbs (*sketched, unscrewed, emerged*). To give an answer, students should hold up the correct card.

TARGET SKILL AND STRATEGY

COMPARE AND CONTRAST Students should not only *compare* things within a text, but also compare what they are learning to what they already know. During reading, students should compare Juan's life and feelings to their own experiences.

ANSWER QUESTIONS Tell students that after reading, they will be asked to develop questions that compare what is happening in Juan's life to what he wants to happen. They should choose questions with answers that can be found either in one sentence in the text, several different sentences in the text, or by using prior knowledge. Students should then answer each other's questions.

READ THE BOOK

Use the following questions to support comprehension.

PAGE 8 Why would Juan buy his mom a red car? *(because it was her favorite color)*

PAGE 13 Where can you find the answer to the question: "What was the weather like the week that Juan picked strawberries?" *(first sentence, second paragraph)*

PAGE 17 Were you surprised that Manuel quit working for Spike? Why or why not? *(Responses will vary.)*

TALK ABOUT THE BOOK

READER RESPONSE

1. Advantages: The crew leader arranged work, housing, and car rides. Disadvantages: A farm worker had to give money to the crew leader.
2. Responses will vary, but they should relate to text.
3. Responses will vary.
4. Responses will vary, but they should be based on the realities and powerlessness of Manuel's life.

RESPONSE OPTIONS

SPEAKING Have students work in small groups and discuss whether or not children Juan's age should be migrant workers. Students should create a list of reasons supporting their decision or decisions. Afterwards, have the groups share their decisions and supporting reasons.

CONTENT CONNECTIONS

SOCIAL STUDIES Encourage students to find out more about migrant workers and their lives, such as reading biographies of César Chávez and other books about migrant workers. They might be especially interested in information about children who were migrant workers. Information can be found on the Internet and at the library.

Time for SOCIAL STUDIES

Compare and Contrast

- To **compare** is to tell how two or more things are alike.
- To **contrast** is to tell how two or more things are different.

Directions Fill in the following chart to compare what Juan wants to what Juan has.
Circle the one thing Juan wanted and then got.

What Juan Wants	What Juan Has

Directions Look at your chart. Draw a picture of Juan leading the kind of life he would like to have.

34

Answer Key for On-Level Reader Practice

Using Special Talents — LR4

⦿ Compare and Contrast, LR5
Possible responses given. **1.** They all want to help others. **2.** She has volunteered before. **3.** in contrast to **4.** Answers will vary. **5.** Answers will vary but should show understanding of how talents and interests relate to the chosen volunteering activity.

Vocabulary, LR6
1. emerge **2.** disrespect **3.** caterpillar **4.** cocoon **5.** migrant **6.** unscrewed **7.** sketched **8–10.** Sentences will vary.

Holocaust Rescuers — LR13

⦿ Author's Purpose, LR14
Possible responses given. **1.** She wants to inform the reader about some of the people who took risks to help Jews escape the Nazi Holocaust. **2.** She wants the reader to understand why Hitler was able to kill so many Jews during the Holocaust and why more people did not step forward to help Jews and stop the Nazis. **3.** She wants to persuade the reader that Wallenberg was a great hero. She supports her argument by telling how he saved thousands of Jews by having them live in "Swedish houses"; how he climbed on train cars to hand out protective passes to Jews; and how he threatened a German general. **4.** It informs the reader of one way that Holocaust rescuers have been recognized for the risks they took.

Vocabulary, LR15
1. refugees **2.** agreement **3.** diplomat **4.** visa **5.** cable
Possible responses given: **6.** provide, distribute, allot **7.** legislators, elected officials **8.** bosses, managers, chiefs **9–10.** Responses will vary.

The Gift — LR22

⦿ Compare and Contrast, LR23
1. In America Lupe speaks English. In Mexico she speaks Spanish. **2.** Lupe's friends at home don't celebrate the Three Kings. **3.** It is Lupe's grandmother, not Lupe's mother, who teaches Lupe to make the pastry. **4.** smell of hot chocolate, smell of wood stove, lots of cooking, family together **5.** Answers will vary.

Vocabulary, LR24
Underline sentences 2, 5, 6, 8. **10–12.** Responses will vary.

Habitats In Need of Help — LR31

⦿ Fact and Opinion, LR32
Possible responses given. **Statements of Fact: 1.** Orangutans live on the island of Borneo and the neighboring Indonesian island of Sumatra. **2.** An orangutan can weigh from sixty to three hundred pounds and requires large areas of forest in which to roam. **3.** Due to humans having taken over land for mining, logging, and various types of farming, less than 20 percent of the orangutan's original habitat remains. **Statements of Opinion: 4.** Orangutans are large, funny-looking apes. **5.** Losing even one of these amazing apes would be a big tragedy.

Vocabulary, LR33
1. environment **2.** investigation **3.** contribute **4.** enthusiastic **5.** conservation **6.** harm **7.** destruction **8.** uncaring **9–10.** Answers will vary.

Paul Revere and the American Revolution — LR40

⦿ Sequence, LR41
1. The Sugar Act was passed by the British government. **2.** Colonists who did not pay taxes on molasses were punished. **3.** The Stamp Act was passed by the British government. **4.** Colonists had to stamp all business documents. **5.** The colonists disliked being taxed without having a voice in the government.

Vocabulary, LR42
1. fate—uncontrolled event **2.** fearless—unafraid **3.** glimmer—faint light **4.** lingers—stays **5.** magnified—increased **6.** somber—solemn **7.** steed—horse Possible response: Maybe it was *fate* that led the colonists and the British to fight against one another. Their early battles over taxation ended up being *magnified* to the point where one *fearless* soldier was pitted against the other—the British on his *steed*, and the colonist often on foot. The colonists took the *somber* news of taxation badly, because they did not even have the *glimmer* of a voice in the British government. The memory of their hard-won battle *lingers*, as we remember their contribution.

Answer Key for Advanced-Level Reader Practice

When the Disaster's Over — LR7

🎯 Compare and Contrast, LR8

Possible responses given. **1.** shelter, food, medical attention, psychological support **2.** The water might be unsafe after a storm due to damaged sewer systems. **3.** The doctors provide medical relief. The National Guard tries to restore order. **4.** Wood and steel can absorb the shaking of an earthquake better than brick. **5.** Answers will vary.

Vocabulary, LR9

1–8. Answers will vary.

A Safe Haven — LR16

🎯 Author's Purpose, LR17

Possible responses given. **1.** She wanted to give the reader an idea of what it was like for many World War II refugees to leave their homes and move to new lands. **2.** By describing the government's early failures, the author shows a contrast with the success of the Oswego shelter. **3.** She wants to persuade the reader that Ruth Gruber was a heroic person because she helped the refugees even when there were obstacles. **4.** The author wants to describe for the reader the uncertainty the refugees felt about their future and the questions they might have been asking themselves.

Vocabulary, LR18

Down: 1. concentration camps **2.** Holocaust **3.** quotas **4.** translator
Across: 4. tours of duty **5.** quarantine **6.** customs agents **7.** kosher

Making Friends in Mali — LR25

🎯 Compare and Contrast, LR26

1–2. Both are ambitious; both like to improve things; both like working with chickens and agriculture. Georgia wants to improve things in a place that needs it more than where she lives. **3.** Unlike her home in Maine, Georgia's home in Mali is made out of mud, is very small, and has no electricity. **4–5.** When they bought it, the garden center had been a tumbledown place with a sagging greenhouse and a barn with a hole in the roof. Now, customers come from all over to buy their flowers. **6–7.** Both are go-getters; both have big plans. Moussa is Muslim; Georgia is not. **8.** Both are the same age; both notice things around them.

Vocabulary, LR27

1. rummaging **2.** simplicity **3.** efficiency **4.** ambition **5.** thriving **6.** volunteer **7.** moped **8.** volunteer **9.** waste **10.** selling **11.** moped **12.** simplicity **13.** laziness **14.** failing

Saving Endangered Species — LR34

🎯 Fact and Opinion, LR35

Statements of Fact: 1. Male grizzlies can stand on their hind legs to a height of seven feet! **2.** They have been known to attack hikers, but that happens rarely. **3.** Building roads through forests destroys grizzlies' territory. **Statements of Opinion: 4.** One animal that desperately needs its wild lands to be saved is the grizzly bear. **5.** Grizzlies probably have more reasons to fear people.

Vocabulary, LR36

1. species **2.** extinct **3.** population **4.** threatened **5.** scavenger **6.** conservationists **7.** habitat **8.** endangered. Paragraphs will vary.

The National Guard: Modern Minutemen — LR43

🎯 Sequence, LR44

Possible responses given. **1.** A colonial volunteer group set up the Ancient and Honorable Artillery Company in 1638. **2.** The volunteer militia made up much of the army during the American Revolution. **3.** After the Civil War, many states renamed their militias to be called the National Guard. **4.** The National Guard protected the civil rights of people who fought for integration of schools. **5.** American Civil War fought—Second **6.** Iraq War—Fourth **7.** Minutemen fought in Massachusetts—First **8.** Riots in American Cities—Third

Vocabulary, LR45

Nouns: citizen-soldiers, National Guard, relief, riot, steed, troops, volunteers

Verbs: defending, mobilize (also accept riot)

Possible responses given. **1.** *Citizen-soldiers* were often farmers who fought during wartime. **2.** The soldiers were responsible for *defending* the fort. **3.** It was time to *mobilize* the troops to head south to fight. **4.** The *National Guard* has been serving the nation for many years. **5.** The end of the battle brought *relief* to the soldiers' families. **6.** The crowd pushed so that police feared a *riot*. **7.** A Minuteman would jump upon his *steed* to ride off to war. **8.** Thousands of *troops* were sent abroad to fight the war. **9.** I needed several *volunteers* to help with this charity.

Routine Cards

Multisyllabic Word Routine

Teach students this Routine to read long words with meaningful parts.

1 Teach Tell students to look for meaningful parts and to think about the meaning of each part. They should use the parts to read the word and determine meaning.

2 Model Think aloud to analyze a long word for the base word, ending, prefix, and/or suffix and to identify the word and determine its meaning.

3 Guide Practice Provide examples of long words with endings (-ing, -ed, -s), prefixes (un-, re-, dis-, mis-, non-), and/or suffixes (-ly, -ness, -less, -ful, and so on). Help students analyze base words and parts.

4 Provide Feedback Encourage students to circle parts of the words to help identify parts and determine meaning.

Picture Walk Routine

To build concepts and vocabulary, conduct a structured picture walk before reading.

1 Prepare Preview the selection and list key concepts and vocabulary you wish to develop.

2 Discuss As students look at the pages, discuss illustrations, have students point to pictured items, and/or ask questions that target key concepts and vocabulary.

3 Elaborate Elaborate on students' responses to reinforce correct use of the vocabulary and to provide additional exposure to key concepts.

4 Practice For more practice with key concepts, have each student turn to a partner and do the picture walk using the key concept vocabulary.

Multisyllabic Word Routine

Teach students this Routine to chunk words with no recognizable parts.

1 Teach Tell students to look for chunks in words with no meaningful parts. They should say each chunk slowly and then say the chunks fast to make a whole word.

2 Model Think aloud to demonstrate breaking a word into chunks, saying each chunk slowly, and then saying the chunks fast to make a word.

3 Guide Practice Provide examples of long words with no meaningful parts. Help students chunk the words.

4 Provide Feedback If necessary, reteach by modeling how to break words into chunks.

Concept Vocabulary

Use this Routine to teach concept vocabulary.

1 Introduce the Word Relate the word to the week's concept. Supply a student-friendly definition.

2 Demonstrate Provide several familiar examples to demonstrate meaning.

3 Apply Have students demonstrate understanding with a simple activity.

4 Display the Word Relate the word to the concept by displaying it on a concept web. Have students identify word parts and practice reading the word.

5 Use the Word Often Encourage students to use the word often in their writing and speaking. Ask questions that require students to use the word.

© Pearson Education, Inc.

ONLINE

PearsonSuccessNet.com

Monitor Progress

Selection Reading and Comprehension

If... students have difficulty reading the selection with a partner,	**then...** have them follow along as they listen to the Online Leveled Reader Audio.
If... students have trouble understanding the role of migrant workers in farming,	**then...** reread p. 3 and discuss the map together.

Strategic Intervention

ROUTINE

1 Build Background

REINFORCE CONCEPTS Display the Kindness Concept Web. This week's concept is *kindness.* Kindness is thinking of and doing for others to show that you care. Discuss the meaning of each word on the web, using the definitions on p. 142l and the Concept Vocabulary routine on p. DI·1.

CONNECT TO READING This week you will read about ways people have showed kindness to others. Some people show kindness to people they know. Others show kindness to complete strangers. Recall the Read Aloud "Dwaina Brooks." Do you think that Dwaina's classmates were helping her, or helping strangers? Explain your answer. *(Both, because they helped Dwaina and her mother make the meals, but the meals were for strangers who were hungry.)*

2 Read Leveled Reader *Juan's Journey*

BEFORE READING Using the Picture Walk routine on p. DI·1, guide students through the text focusing on key concepts and vocabulary. Ask questions such as:

pp. 3–5 The story talks about the way that Juan and his family live. What does this picture tell you about their lives? *(They might be going on a trip or moving.)*

pp. 8–9 The picture on p. 8 shows what Juan wishes for. What does this tell you about Juan? *(He cares about his family and wishes they could have a home and a new car.)* Migrant farmers travel from farm to farm, picking crops in fields. Where do you think Juan and his family are headed next? *(to pick strawberries)*

DURING READING Read pp. 3–5 aloud while students track the print. Do a choral reading of pp. 6–9. If students are capable, have them read and discuss the remainder of the book with a partner. Ask: Who works in Juan's family? When do the children go to school? *(Everyone works except the youngest child. They go to school when the growing season is over.)*

AFTER READING Encourage pairs of students to discuss the hardships of making a living as a migrant farmer. We read *Juan's Journey* to understand Juan's feelings and how he deals with his problems. Understanding Juan will help you relate to the character in "Inside Out."

For alternate Leveled Reader lesson plans that teach
🔄 **Compare and Contrast,** 🔄 **Answer Questions,**
and **Lesson Vocabulary,** see pp. LR10–LR18.

On-Level

1 Build Background

DEVELOP VOCABULARY Write the word *volunteered* and ask students to define it in their own words. *(when someone says they will do something for free or without obligation.)* What are some things you have volunteered to do? Repeat this activity with the words *permanent, emerge,* and other words from the Leveled Reader *Using Special Talents.* Use the Concept Vocabulary routine on p. DI·1 as needed.

2 Read Leveled Reader *Using Special Talents*

BEFORE READING Have students create a two-column chart with the heads *Similar* and *Different* to complete as they read. This book tells a lot about ways that young people reach out to help others. As you read, look at what is the same and what is different about the ways people help. Record the information on your chart.

DURING READING Have students follow along as you read pp. 3–7. Then let them complete the book on their own. Remind students to add similarities and differences on their chart as they read.

AFTER READING Have students share the entries in their charts. Point out that understanding acts of kindness toward others will help as they read tomorrow's selection, "Inside Out."

Advanced

1 Read Leveled Reader *When the Disaster's Over*

BEFORE READING Recall the Read Aloud "Dwaina Brooks." Why did Dwaina recruit friends from class to help her? *(She would be able to prepare more meals with more volunteers.)* Today you will read about Americans who help others after disasters such as earthquakes and hurricanes.

PROBLEM SOLVING Have students read the leveled reader independently. Encourage them to think of the problems that groups like FEMA and the Red Cross face, and how they would solve them. For example, ask:

- How do rescue groups get fresh water for survivors when the water supply is not safe?
- How would a group such as FEMA decide what should get rebuilt first in a community?
- Are news stories helpful or hurtful when a disaster strikes? Explain your answer.

AFTER READING Have students review the selection to find five or more unfamiliar words and determine their meanings. Then ask them to compose a summary of a disaster using the words they chose. Have students meet with you to discuss the selection and the summary they wrote.

2 Independent Extension Activity

NOW TRY THIS Assign "Now Try This" on pp. 22–23 of *When the Disaster's Over* for students to work on throughout the week.

Inside Out
Group Time

DAY 2

Audio CD   AudioText

Monitor Progress

Word and Story Reading

If... students have difficulty reading multisyllabic words in the selection,	**then...** have them look for and read meaningful parts in the words or have them chunk words with no recognizable parts.
If... students need practice reading words fluently,	**then...** use the Fluent Word Reading Routine on the DI tab.
If... students have difficulty reading along with the group,	**then...** have them follow along as they listen to the AudioText.

Strategic Intervention

ROUTINE

1 Word Study/Phonics

LESSON VOCABULARY Use p. 144b to review the meanings of *caterpillar, cocoon, disrespect, emerge, migrant, sketched,* and *unscrewed.* Students can blend all of the words. Have individuals practice reading the words from word cards.

DECODING MULTISYLLABIC WORDS Write *yellowish,* saying the word as you write it. Then model how to decode when there are meaningful word parts. This is a three-syllable word formed from the base word *yellow* and the suffix *-ish.* First I cover the suffix and say the base word: *yellow.* Then I add the suffix to read the whole word: *yellow ish, yellowish.* The suffix *-ish* means "a bit," so *yellowish* means "a bit yellow."

Use the Multisyllabic Word routine on p. DI·1 to help students read these other words from "Inside Out": *discovered, rippling, interesting, intrigued, wondered,* and *beautiful.* Be sure students understand the meanings of words such as *rippling* and *intrigued.*

Use *Strategies for Word Analysis,* Lesson 6, with students who have difficulty mastering word analysis and need practice with decodable text.

2 Read "Inside Out," pp. 146–153

BEFORE READING Yesterday we read about a family of migrant farmers. Today we will read about another child in a family of migrant workers and how he deals with a new school.

Using the Picture Walk routine on p. DI·1, guide students through the text, asking questions such as those listed below. Then read the question on p. 147. Together, set a purpose for reading.

pp. 148–149 Francisco is on p. 149. What does the picture tell you about Francisco and his classmates? *(He's standing outside the group. He doesn't fit in.)* We'll read why Francisco feels different.

p. 155 What is on Francisco's shirt? *(a blue ribbon)* As we read, let's see how Francisco wins the ribbon.

DURING READING Follow the Guiding Comprehension routine on pp. 148–153. Have students read along with you while tracking the print or do a choral reading of the selection. Stop every two pages to ask what students have learned so far. Prompt as necessary.

- What does Francisco do at recess? Why?
- Why does Curtis fight with Francisco?

AFTER READING What has happened in the story so far? What do you think will happen next? Reread passages as needed.

Advanced

DAY 2

1 Extend Vocabulary

⊙ **WORD STRUCTURE** Choose and read a sentence or passage containing a difficult word with identifiable word parts, such as this sentence from p. 151 of "Inside Out": "I liked it because it was green and it hid my suspenders." What does the word suspenders mean? *(straps that hold up someone's pants)* How did you figure out the word's meaning? *(I looked at the word's parts. Suspend means "to hang or hold up." Suspenders hold something up.)* Remind students to use the strategy as they read "Inside Out."

2 Read "Inside Out," pp. 146–153

BEFORE READING In "When the Disaster's Over," you read about how people show kindness by helping others when a disaster strikes. Today you will read a selection about a child who is kind to another child for no particular reason. As you read, think about how the types of kindness are the same and how they are different.

Have students write a description of a time when they were the new kid in a group in their Strategy Response Logs (p. 146).

CRITICAL THINKING Have students read pp. 146–153 independently. Encourage them to think critically. For example, ask:

• What experiences have you had that are similar to Francisco's?

AFTER READING Have partners discuss the selection and share their Strategy Response Log entries. Have them record their experiences that are similar to Francisco's in their Strategy Response Logs (p. 153). Then have students come up with ways they could help new students like Francisco. Have students compile the information as a "New Student's Survival Guide." Give students an opportunity to share their ideas with you.

Audio CD AudioText

Inside Out
Group Time

DAY 3

Audio CD **AudioText**

ROUTINE

1 Reinforce Comprehension

SKILL COMPARE AND CONTRAST Have students explain what it means to compare and contrast *(to name similarities and differences)* and list clue words that signal similarities and differences *(like, as, similar; unlike, as opposed to, while).* If necessary, review the meanings and provide a model. You compare to show how things are alike. *Francisco and Juan were both sons of migrant farmers* tells how the two characters are the same. You contrast to show how two things are different. *Juan's Journey* tells about Juan's experience on a farm, while *Inside Out* tells about Francisco's experience in school.

Have students find what is compared and contrasted by reading the questions below. Ask them to explain their reasoning.

How are Curtis and Francisco different? *(Possible answer: Curtis was the biggest kid in class, and Francisco was the smallest.)*

What did Francisco and Arthur have in common? *(They speak the same language.)*

Why were Francisco's art lessons different from those of the rest of the class? *(Since he couldn't understand the teacher's instructions, he drew whatever he wanted.)*

2 Read "Inside Out," pp. 154–157

BBEFORE READING Have students retell what happened in the story so far. Ask: What questions do you have about what will happen in the story? Reread p. 150. Model how to ask questions. As I read, I wonder what Francisco can do during school when he doesn't understand the teacher. The story tells me he looks at books and draws. Remind students to ask questions and try to find the answers as they read the rest of "Inside Out." **STRATEGY Ask Questions**

DURING READING Follow the Guiding Comprehension routine on pp. 154–157. Have students read along with you while tracking print or do a choral reading. Stop every two pages to ask students what has happened so far. Prompt as necessary.

- What did the letter to Francisco's parents probably say?
- What did Francisco do to earn a blue ribbon?
- How does the title relate to the story?

AFTER READING Why did Francisco give Curtis the drawing? Reread with students for comprehension as needed. Tell them that tomorrow they will read "Random Acts of Kindness," a collection of short articles on how people have shown kindness to others.

Monitor Progress

Word and Story Reading

If... students have difficulty reading multisyllabic words in the selection,	**then...** have them look for and read meaningful parts in the words or have them chunk words with no recognizable parts.
If... students have difficulty reading along with the group,	**then...** have them follow along as they listen to the AudioText.

Advanced

DAY 3

1 Extend Comprehension

SKILL COMPARE AND CONTRAST Ask students to look at the story to find examples of Francisco telling how he is like or unlike others in his class. Ask students to name words or phrases that help them recognize comparisons or contrasting information or words.

STRATEGY ANSWER QUESTIONS Have students think about the experiences the author of "Inside Out" wants to share. Have students think not just about the main ideas but also about the details the author includes.

• What questions did the author want you to think about, and how were they answered in the story?

2 Read "Inside Out," pp. 154–157

BEFORE READING Have students recall what has happened in the story so far. Remind them to look for information to compare and contrast and to ask and answer questions as they read the remainder of "Inside Out."

CRITICAL THINKING Have students read pp. 154–157 independently. Encourage them to think critically. For example, ask students if they agree or disagree with this statement and why:

• Francisco gave Curtis the drawing because Francisco felt bad about the fight.

AFTER READING Have students complete the Strategy Response Log activity (p. 156). Then have them find out about teaching students who don't speak English. Tell students to write what parts of Francisco's experience were related to not speaking English in the story "Inside Out." Give students an opportunity to meet with you as they plan their response.

Audio CD AudioText

Group Time

DAY 4

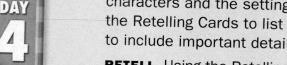

1 Practice Retelling

REVIEW STORY ELEMENTS Help students identify the main characters and the setting of "Inside Out." Then guide them in using the Retelling Cards to list story events in sequence. Prompt students to include important details.

RETELL Using the Retelling Cards, have students work in pairs to retell "Inside Out." Monitor retelling and prompt students as needed. For example, ask:

Grade 5
Retelling Cards
PEARSON
Scott Foresman

- Tell me what this story is about in a few sentences.
- What is the main character in the story like?
- Has anything like this happened to you?

If students struggle, model a fluent retelling.

2 Read "Random Acts of Kindness," pp. 160–161

BEFORE READING Read the genre information on p. 160. Point out that people use e-mail to communicate at work and at home. As we read "Random Acts of Kindness," look for ways that people show kindness to one another.

Read the rest of the panel on p. 160. Have students read the title and identify the topic of this selection. *(how people practice kindness)* Ask: Who are these e-mails written to? *(people who visit a Web site)* Random means "by chance." As you read, think about how these acts are considered random.

DURING READING Have students read along with you while tracking the print or do a choral reading of the selection. Stop to discuss difficult vocabulary, such as *generously, inspiration,* and *statement.*

AFTER READING Have students share their reactions to the selection. Then guide them through the Reading Across Texts and Writing Across Texts activities, prompting if necessary.

- Were there other acts of kindness in "Inside Out"?
- Have you ever done a random act of kindness?

Audio CD AudioText

Monitor Progress

Word and Selection Reading

If... students have difficulty reading multisyllabic words in the selection,	**then...** have them look for and read meaningful parts in the words or have them chunk words with no recognizable parts.
If... students have difficulty reading along with the group,	**then...** have them follow along as they listen to the AudioText.

Advanced

ROUTINE

1 Read "Random Acts of Kindness"

CREATIVE THINKING Have students read pp. 160–161 independently. Encourage them to think creatively. For example, ask:

- If you could perform a random act of kindness for someone, who would it be?
- What act of kindness do you think this person would value and appreciate?

AFTER READING Have students meet with you to discuss the selection and Reading Across Texts. Have students do Writing Across Texts independently.

2 Extend Genre Study

RESEARCH Have students use the Internet to locate information about e-mail etiquette. Have students create a public service message teaching others how to correctly write e-mail messages.

WRITE Have students write an e-mail to an official at school or in the community encouraging people to participate in random acts of kindness. Students can include anecdotes and examples to make a convincing letter.

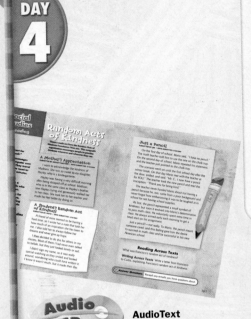

Audio CD AudioText

Inside Out

Group Time

DAY 5

Leveled Reader Database
ONLINE
PearsonSuccessNet.com

Strategic Intervention — ROUTINE

1 Reread for Fluency

MODEL Tell students that good readers read the words and ideas of different characters clearly to tell the characters apart. Readers also pause between sections of dialogue to help the listener tell the characters apart. Then model reading aloud p. 9 of the Leveled Reader *Juan's Journey.* Use a different tone of voice for Juan's mother than you use for Juan as you read the dialogue. Discuss how reading dialogue well will help students understand and remember what they read.

PRACTICE Have students reread passages from *Juan's Journey* individually. Encourage students to self-correct. Then have partners reread passages aloud. For optimal fluency, they should reread three or four times. As students read, monitor fluency and provide corrective feedback. Students in this group are assessed in Weeks 2 and 4.

2 Retell Leveled Reader *Juan's Journey*

Model how to use skimming to retell the events on pp. 3–6. Then ask students to retell *Juan's Journey,* skimming the story. Prompt them as needed.

- What is the story mostly about?
- What happens when the family gets to Mr. Spike's farm?

Monitor Progress

Fluency

If... students have difficulty reading fluently,	**then...** provide additional fluency practice by pairing nonfluent readers with fluent ones.

For alternate Leveled Reader lesson plans that teach **Compare and Contrast,** **Answer Questions,** and **Lesson Vocabulary,** see pp. LR10–LR18.

On-Level

DAY 5

1 Reread for Fluency ROUTINE

MODEL Tell students that good silent readers read at a speed that is appropriate for the material. Point out that in *Inside Out,* the genre is fiction, so they can read this material fairly quickly. In the nonfiction book *Using Special Talents,* however, there is much information they need to remember, so they should read more slowly. Then model pacing, reading p. 3 of the Leveled Reader *Using Special Talents.* Discuss how knowing how fast to read will help them understand and remember what they read.

PRACTICE Have individuals silently reread passages from *Using Special Talents.* Remind them to self-correct if they misread or skip a word. Then have partners reread passages aloud. For optimal fluency, students should reread three or four times. As students read, monitor fluency and provide corrective feedback. Students in this group are assessed in Week 3.

2 Retell Leveled Reader *Using Special Talents*

Have students use subheads as a guide to summarize important facts they learned from each section of the book. Prompt as needed.

- What was this section mostly about?
- What did you learn from reading this selection?
- What was the author trying to teach us?

Advanced

DAY 5

1 Reread for Fluency ROUTINE

PRACTICE Have students silently reread passages from the Leveled Reader *When the Disaster's Over.* Then have them reread aloud with a partner or individually. As students read, monitor fluency and provide corrective feedback. If students read fluently on the first reading, they do not need to reread three to four times. Assess the fluency of students in this group using p. 161a.

2 Revisit Leveled Reader *When the Disaster's Over*

RETELL Have students retell the Leveled Reader *When the Disaster's Over.*

NOW TRY THIS Have students complete their news broadcasts. You may wish to review the information and script that students plan to follow. Have them share their broadcasts with classmates.

Group Time

DAY **1**

❶ Build Background

REINFORCE CONCEPTS Display the Taking Risks Concept Web. This week's concept is *taking risks*. Taking risks can mean putting yourself in danger to help others. Discuss the meaning of each word on the web, using the definitions on p. 162I and the Concept Vocabulary routine on p. DI·1.

CONNECT TO READING This week you will read about ways people take risks to help others. During World War II, there were many people who were in danger because of their religion or culture. In *Number the Stars,* what risks were the Johansens taking? *(The Nazis would probably punish them as well as take Ellen away.)*

❷ Read Leveled Reader *A Day in the Life of Peter and Eve*

BEFORE READING Using the Picture Walk routine on p. DI·1, guide students through the text focusing on key concepts and vocabulary. Ask questions such as:

p. 7 This is Peter's teacher. What can you tell about her from the picture? *(She looks tired. Her dress is patched.)* Yes, Fräulein Mann is introducing the class to town council members who are Nazis and supporters of Adolf Hitler. Peter suspects that she is uncomfortable with them being there.

p. 10 On p. 10 Peter is remembering what happened to his friend's house. His friend, Hans Karp, is Jewish. What do you think may have happened to the Karp's house? *(People threw rocks at the window and broke it.)* Yes, the Nazis blamed Jewish people for Germany's problems and encouraged German people to dislike Jewish people.

DURING READING Read pp. 4–5 aloud while students track the print. Do a choral reading of pp. 6–9. If students are capable, have them read and discuss the remainder of the book with a partner. Ask: Why does Peter and Eve's mother talk about the Nazis only when they are in the cellar?

AFTER READING Encourage pairs of students to discuss the risks Peter and Eve's family took. We read *A Day in the Life of Peter and Eve* to understand what life was like for people living in Nazi Germany. Understanding Peter and Eve's life will help you relate to the characters in *Passage to Freedom: The Sugihara Story.*

A Day in the Life of Peter and Eve
by Gretchen McBride
Illustrated by Ralph Canaday

Leveled Reader Database
ONLINE
PearsonSuccessNet.com

Monitor Progress

Story Reading and Comprehension

If...	then...
If... students have difficulty reading the selection with a partner,	**then...** have them follow along as they listen to the Online Leveled Reader Audio.
If... students have trouble understanding the conditions in the cellar where Peter and Eve sleep,	**then...** have them reread p. 16 and look at the picture on the page. Have students describe where the cellar would be and what it would look like.

For alternate Leveled Reader lesson plans that teach
🔊 **Author's Purpose,** 🔊 **Monitor and Fix Up,**
and **Lesson Vocabulary,** see pp. LR10–LR18.

On-Level

DAY 1

1 Build Background

DEVELOP VOCABULARY Write the word *officers* and ask students to define it and give examples. *(members of the military or other organizations who command others)* How do people usually treat officers? *(They usually treat them with respect.)* Repeat this activity with the word *identity* and other words from the Leveled Reader *Holocaust Rescuers*. Use the Concept Vocabulary routine on p. DI·1 as needed.

2 Read Leveled Reader *Holocaust Rescuers*

BEFORE READING Have students create a KWL chart to complete as they read. This book gives information about the Holocaust during World War II. Complete the KWL chart with what you know about the Holocaust now as well as things you want to know. As you find answers during your reading, complete the chart.

DURING READING Have students follow along as you read pp. 3–7. Then let them complete the book on their own. Remind students to add answers to their questions on their KWL chart as they read.

AFTER READING Have students share the entries in their charts. Point out that understanding the risks people took to save others from the Nazis will help as they read tomorrow's selection, *Passage to Freedom: The Sugihara Story.*

Advanced

DAY 1

1 Read Leveled Reader *A Safe Haven*

BEFORE READING Recall the Read Aloud *Number the Stars.* Why was Ellen posing as Annemarie's sister? *(Ellen was hiding from the Nazis because she was Jewish, and Annemarie's family was not.)* Today you will read about more people who were targets of the Nazis and how people worked to rescue them.

PROBLEM SOLVING Have students read the Leveled Reader independently. Encourage them to think of the problems faced by World War II refugees. For example, ask:

• Why would traveling on the *Henry Gibbons* be difficult?
• How would the U.S. government decide which refugees to allow into the country?
• Why didn't the refugees want to return to Europe?

AFTER READING Have students review the selection to list five or more unfamiliar words and look up their meanings. Then have partners ask and answer questions of each other using the words. Have students meet with you to discuss the selection and the questions and answers they developed.

2 Independent Extension Activity

NOW TRY THIS Assign "Now Try This" on pp. 22–23 of *A Safe Haven* for students to work on throughout the week.

Group Time

Audio CD **AudioText**

ROUTINE

DAY 2

1 Word Study/Phonics

LESSON VOCABULARY Use p. 164b to review the meanings of *agreement, cable, diplomat, issue, refugees, representatives, superiors,* and *visa.* Students can blend all of the words. Have individuals practice reading the words from word cards.

DECODING MULTISYLLABIC WORDS Write *encouraged* and model how to decode when there are meaningful word parts. First I look for parts I know. I see the ending *-ed.* This tells me it happened in the past. I also see that the prefix *en-* is part of the word. I know that *en-* means "to give." Next I look at the base word, *courage.* So, when I combine all three parts, I know it means "gave courage."

Use the Multisyllabic Word routine on p. DI·1 to help read these other words from *Passage to Freedom: The Sugihara Story: forever, translated,* and *exhausted.* Be sure students understand the meanings of words such as *translated* and *exhausted.*

Use *Strategies for Word Analysis,* Lesson 7, with students who have difficulty mastering word analysis and need practice with decodable text.

2 Read *Passage to Freedom: The Sugihara Story,* pp. 166–173

BEFORE READING Yesterday we read about a family in Germany during World War II. Today we will read about another family who helped refugees to flee from the Nazis.

Using the Picture Walk routine on p. DI·1, guide students through the text, asking questions such as those listed below. Then read the question on p. 167. Together, set a purpose for reading.

pp. 170–171 Where do you think these people are? What do you think they are doing?

p. 172 Hiroki's father is having a family meeting to decide whether or not to help the refugees. What do you think they will decide?

DURING READING Follow the Guiding Comprehension routine on pp. 168–173. Have students read along with you while tracking the print or do a choral reading of the selection. Stop every two pages to ask what students have learned so far. Prompt as necessary.

• Why didn't the father give visas to everyone right away?
• Why do you think the father asked the family's opinion of his plan?
• What did the visas do for the refugees?

AFTER READING What has happened so far? What do you think will happen next? Reread passages for comprehension as needed.

Monitor Progress

Word and Story Reading

If...	then...
If... students have difficulty reading multisyllabic words in the selection,	**then...** have them look for and read meaningful parts in the words or have them chunk words with no recognizable parts.
If... students need practice reading words fluently,	**then...** use the Fluent Word Reading Routine on the DI tab.
If... students have difficulty reading along with the group,	**then...** have them follow along as they listen to the AudioText.

1 Extend Vocabulary

DICTIONARY/GLOSSARY Choose and read a sentence or passage with a word that students may not know, such as this sentence from p. 172 of *Passage to Freedom: The Sugihara Story:* "My father sent his message by cable." When I think of the word *cable,* I think of cable television. The word means something different here. How could I figure out its meaning? If needed, demonstrate finding the word's meaning in a dictionary. Reread the sentence with the meaning in place. Tell students that as they read *Passage to Freedom: The Sugihara Story,* to use the strategy of using a dictionary or glossary if they are unable to figure out the meaning of the word from context.

2 Read *Passage to Freedom: The Sugihara Story,* pp. 166–173

BEFORE READING In *A Safe Haven,* you read about the risks people took to get World War II refugees to safety in the United States. Today you will read a selection about a family who decides to help other refugees of the same war. As you read, think about how both groups took risks to get the refugees to safety.

Have students write two questions about the passage in their Strategy Response Logs (p. 166). Tell them to look for answers during reading and to record other questions as they arise.

CRITICAL/CREATIVE THINKING Have students read pp. 166–173 independently. Encourage them to think critically while reading. Then ask them to answer questions such as the following:

- Why would Japan have a diplomat in Lithuania in 1940?
- What did the father mean when he said that if he didn't help the refugees he would be disobeying his conscience?
- If you were Mr. Sugihara would you have taken the risks he took? Why or why not?

AFTER READING Have partners discuss the selection and share their Strategy Response Log entries. Then have students discuss their questions and the history of the Nazi regime in World War II. Allow students to briefly research using history books, encyclopedias, and the Internet. Give students an opportunity to share their findings with you and the group.

AudioText

Passage to Freedom: The Sugihara Story
Group Time

Audio
CD AudioText

1 Reinforce Comprehension

⊙ SKILL AUTHOR'S PURPOSE Have students explain what the word *purpose* means. *(the reason for doing something)* Explain that every author has a purpose for writing. When you understand the author's purpose, you have a better idea of what is important in the passage. *A Safe Haven* gives a lot of facts and information. Although the author of *Passage to Freedom: The Sugihara Story* was a child in the passage, he also gives many facts and much information. Both of these selections were written to inform, but authors also write to entertain, to express opinions, or to persuade. Have students tell the author's purpose in the statements below. Ask students to explain their answers.

The Japanese government was wrong in not granting visas to all of the refugees as soon as they were asked. *(Express an opinion; "wrong" is not a statement of fact but a statement of opinion.)*

The United Nations should work to be sure that refugees of war always have a safe place. *(Persuade; "should" sounds like a word that would convince me of something.)*

Adolf Hitler brought the Nazi party to power in Germany in 1933. *(Inform; this sentence states a fact.)*

2 Read *Passage to Freedom: The Sugihara Story, pp. 174–177*

BEFORE READING Have students retell what happened in the selection so far. Ask: What questions do you have about what will happen in the selection? Reread p. 171. Model how to monitor and fix up. Remind students to monitor their reading and fix up any problems they encounter as they continue reading *Passage to Freedom: The Sugihara Story.*

⊙ STRATEGY Monitor and Fix up

DURING READING Follow the Guiding Comprehension routine on pp. 174–177. Have students read along with you while tracking print or do a choral reading. Stop every two pages to ask students what has happened so far. Prompt as necessary.
- How many people do you think were waiting for visas?
- How did the author's feelings about his father change as he became an adult?

AFTER READING Reread with students for comprehension as needed. Ask: How did the author's father respect life? Tell them that tomorrow they will read "I Wanted My Mother," an autobiography of a Jewish girl during World War II.

Monitor Progress

Word and Story Reading

If... students have difficulty reading multisyllabic words in the selection,	then... have them look for and read meaningful parts in the words or have them chunk words with no recognizable parts.
If... students have difficulty reading along with the group,	then... have them follow along as they listen to the AudioText.

Advanced

ROUTINE

① Extend Comprehension

◎ **SKILL AUTHOR'S PURPOSE** Ask students to look at the story to find examples that show that the passage was written to inform. Ask students to give examples from the passage that help them recognize the author's purpose.

◎ **STRATEGY MONITOR AND FIX UP** Have students think about the information included in *Passage to Freedom: The Sugihara Story*. Ask students what they will do if they encounter a passage with many details that they find confusing. *(reread; read more slowly)*

- What parts of the passage require you to slow down to read them well?

② Read *Passage to Freedom: The Sugihara Story*, pp. 174–177

BEFORE READING Have students recall what has happened in the story so far. Remind them to keep in mind the author's purpose and to monitor and fix up as they read the remainder of *Passage to Freedom: The Sugihara Story*.

CRITICAL THINKING Have students read pp. 174–177 independently. Encourage them to think critically. For example, ask students if they agree or disagree with this statement and why:

- The author's father should have let his wife help write the visas when she offered.

AFTER READING Have students complete the Strategy Response Log activity (p. 176). Then have them write a brief description about Japan's role during World War II to see why its acceptance of the refugees is so ironic. Give students an opportunity to meet with you as they plan their response.

DAY **3**

 AudioText

Group Time

DAY 4

1 Practice Retelling

REVIEW STORY ELEMENTS Help students identify the main characters and the setting of *Passage to Freedom: The Sugihara Story.* Then guide them in using the Retelling Cards to list story events in sequence. Prompt students to include important details.

RETELL Using the Retelling Cards, have students work in pairs to retell *Passage to Freedom: The Sugihara Story.* Show partners how to summarize in as few words as possible. Monitor retelling and prompt students as needed. For example, ask:

* Tell me about the major events in order.
* What did you learn from reading this selection?
* What was the author trying to teach us?

If students struggle, model a fluent retelling.

2 Read "I Wanted My Mother"

BEFORE READING Read the genre information on p. 180. Point out that autobiographies can be entertaining or interesting to read even when they are informing us. As we read "I Wanted My Mother," pay attention to the risks involved in hiding from the Nazis.

Read the rest of the panel on p. 180. Have students read the title and the introduction on p. 180 and identify the topic of this selection. *(how a girl hid from the Nazis in Lithuania)* Ask: How is this similar to *Passage to Freedom: The Sugihara Story?* *(they both talk about the Jews in Lithuania)* Who is in danger in both selections? *(refugees, the Sugiharas, the Karashkas family)*

DURING READING Have students read along with you while tracking the print or do a choral reading of the selection. Stop to discuss difficult vocabulary, such as *closing in, bunker,* and *trap door.*

AFTER READING Have students share their reactions to the selection. Then guide them through the Reading Across Texts and Writing Across Texts activities, prompting if necessary.

* Think about the reasons that people in the selections helped others. Add your own ideas to the list.
* Read through the list and put a * by the reasons that you think are most important. Write about why each reason is important as you create your list.

AudioText

Monitor Progress

Word and Selection Reading

If...	then...
If... students have difficulty reading multisyllabic words in the selection,	**then...** have them look for and read meaningful parts in the words or have them chunk words with no recognizable parts.
If... students have difficulty reading along with the group,	**then...** have them follow along as they listen to the AudioText.

Advanced

ROUTINE

1 Read "I Wanted My Mother"

⊙ **CREATIVE THINKING** Have students read pp. 180–185 independently. Encourage them to think creatively. For example, ask:

- What could you do to your home that would make it possible to hide an entire family?
- Whom do you know that has taken risks for the benefit of another person?

AFTER READING Have students meet with you to discuss the selection and Reading Across Texts. Have students do Writing Across Texts independently.

2 Extend Genre Study

RESEARCH Have students use the library to find autobiographical information written by a World War II survivor, soldier, or leader.

WRITE Have students write a one-page biographical summary of the person's life and his or her experiences in the war.

AudioText

Group Time

DAY 5

Strategic Intervention

ROUTINE

① Reread for Fluency

MODEL Tell students that good readers read with different tones to show emotion in the reading. Listeners should be able to detect fear, anger, and other emotions from the reader's tone. Then model, reading aloud p. 3 of the Leveled Reader *A Day in the Life of Peter and Eve.* Use a clear tone of voice to show Peter's sad feelings for his sister as well as his longing for sausages. Then read p. 4 word-by-word in a monotone voice. Have students tell which model sounded better. Discuss how reading with different tones of voice makes reading more interesting and easy to understand.

PRACTICE Have partners reread passages from *A Day in the Life of Peter and Eve.* For optimal fluency, they should reread three or four times. As students read, monitor fluency and provide corrective feedback. Assess the fluency of students in this group using p. 185a.

② Retell Leveled Reader
A Day in the Life of Peter and Eve

Model how to use skimming to retell the events on pp. 3–6. Then ask students to retell *A Day in the Life of Peter and Eve,* skimming the story. Prompt them as needed.

- What are the characters in the story like?
- Tell me what this story is about in a few sentences.

Monitor Progress

Fluency

If... students have difficulty reading fluently,	then... provide additional fluency practice by pairing nonfluent readers with fluent ones.

For alternate Leveled Reader lesson plans that teach
◎ **Author's Purpose,** ◎ **Monitor and Fix Up,**
and **Lesson Vocabulary,** see pp. LR10–LR18.

On-Level

DAY 5

1 Reread for Fluency ROUTINE

MODEL Tell students that good readers use tone of voice to communicate the emotion in the passage. Point out that in *Passage to Freedom: The Sugihara Story,* the genre is a biography, and the author is the son of the subject. The son shows many emotions in his writing, all of which can be illustrated with tone of voice. In *Holocaust Rescuers,* the reader's tone of voice can help listeners understand the danger and fear felt by so many people. Then model reading p. 4 of the Leveled Reader *Holocaust Rescuers.* Discuss how tone of voice makes reading more interesting and meaningful to listeners.

PRACTICE Have students reread passages from *Holocaust Rescuers* with a partner or individually. For optimal fluency, students should reread three or four times. As students read, monitor fluency and provide corrective feedback. Students in this group are assessed in Week 3.

2 Retell Leveled Reader
Holocaust Rescuers

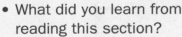

Have students use heads as a guide to summarize important facts they learned from each section of the book. Prompt as needed.

- What did you learn from reading this section?
- What was the author trying to tell us?

Advanced

1 Reread for Fluency ROUTINE

PRACTICE Have students reread passages from the Leveled Reader *A Safe Haven* with a partner or individually. As students read, monitor fluency and provide corrective feedback. If students read fluently on the first reading, they do not need to reread three to four times. Students in this group were assessed in Week 1.

2 Revisit Leveled Reader
A Safe Haven

NOW TRY THIS Have students complete their research project. You may wish to review the resources that students used. Have them share their charts and findings.

The Ch'i-lin Purse

Group Time

ONLINE
PearsonSuccessNet.com

DAY
1

1 Build Background

REINFORCE CONCEPTS Display the Helping Others Concept Web. This week's concept is *helping others*. Helping others can be as small as loaning a friend a pencil, or as large as changing a person's life. Discuss the meaning of each word on the web, using the definitions on p. 186l and the Concept Vocabulary routine on p. DI·1.

CONNECT TO READING This week you will read about people helping other people. Sometimes helping someone is a one-time gesture. Recall the Read Aloud "The Call of the Sea." Why do you think Joseph helped the mermaid when he knew mermaids sometimes lured men to their death? *(He couldn't bear to see the mermaid die.)*

2 Read Leveled Reader *China: Now and Then*

BEFORE READING Using the Picture Walk routine on p. DI·1, guide students through the text focusing on key concepts and vocabulary. Ask questions such as:

pp. 4–5 The pictures show the leaders of China as well as the common workers in China long ago. What can you tell about the people? *(The leaders seem to have many comforts; the workers had a harder life.)*

pp. 10–11 The pictures represent different types of recreation in China. What do people in China do for fun? *(games, basketball)* The Chinese enjoy many ancient and modern forms of recreation and participate in international sports and competitions.

DURING READING Read pp. 3–5 aloud, while students track the print. Do a choral reading of pp. 6–9. If students are capable, have them read and discuss the remainder of the book with a partner. Ask: How is life in China different from your life? How is it the same?

AFTER READING Encourage pairs of students to discuss the life of people in China today. We read *China: Now and Then* to understand the life of people, past and present, in China. Understanding Chinese culture will help you relate to the characters in "The Ch'i-lin Purse."

Monitor Progress

Selection Reading and Comprehension

If... students have difficulty reading the selection with a partner,	**then...** have them follow along as they listen to the Online Leveled Reader Audio.
If... students have trouble visualizing the location of China,	**then...** reread p. 3 and discuss the map in relation to the continents and countries with which students are familiar.

For alternate Leveled Reader lesson plans that teach
⊙**Compare and Contrast,** ⊙**Predict,** and
Lesson Vocabulary, see pp. LR19–LR27.

On-Level

DAY 1

❶ Build Background

DEVELOP VOCABULARY Write the word *panic* and ask students to define it in their own words. *(being very frightened or terrified)* What might cause people to panic? *(accidents, explosions, vicious animals, and so on)* Repeat this activity with the word *cherished* and other words from the Leveled Reader *The Gift.* Use the Concept Vocabulary routine on p. DI·1 as needed.

❷ Read Leveled Reader *The Gift*

BEFORE READING Have students create a three-column chart with heads *Similarities Between Lupe and Abuela, Differences Between Lupe and Abuela,* and *Comparisons with My Life.* Have students *complete* it as they read. This book tells the story of a girl who spends Christmas with her grandmother. As you read, look at what is the same about the way the girl and the grandmother live and what is different. Include how the book compares to your life. Record the information on your chart.

DURING READING Have students follow along as you read pp. 3–7. Then let them complete the book on their own. Remind students to add similarities and differences to their chart as they read.

AFTER READING Have students share the entries on their charts. Point out that understanding how people help others will be important as they read tomorrow's selection "The Ch'i-lin Purse."

Advanced

DAY 1

❶ Read Leveled Reader *Making Friends in Mali*

BEFORE READING Recall the Read Aloud "The Call of the Sea." How did the mermaid repay Joseph for his help? *(She rescued the sailors.)* Today you will read about a woman who helps a family in Africa and how they repay her.

CREATIVE THINKING Have students read the Leveled Reader independently. Encourage them to think of ways that they can show gratitude when people help them. For example, ask:

- When has someone helped you?
- What is an unusual way to show your gratitude other than with words?
- How has someone shown you gratitude in an unusual way?

AFTER READING Have students review the selection to find five or more unfamiliar words and determine their meanings. Then ask them to create flash cards with the word on one side and the definition on the other. Students can then quiz each other to learn the words' meanings. Have students meet with you to discuss the selection and the words they chose.

❷ Independent Extension Activity

DESIGN A MUD CLOTH Have students read the article on page 32. Then have them find online or print resources to find examples of Mali mud cloths. Throughout the week, have students use the examples they found to design their own pattern for a mud cloth.

Group Time

Audio CD AudioText

Monitor Progress

Word and Story Reading

If... students have difficulty reading multisyllabic words in the selection,	then... have them look for and read meaningful parts in the words or have them chunk words with no recognizable parts.
If... students need practice reading words fluently,	then... use the Fluent Word Reading Routine on the DI tab.
If... students have difficulty reading along with the group,	then... have them follow along as they listen to the AudioText.

Strategic Intervention

ROUTINE

1 Word Study/Phonics

LESSON VOCABULARY Use p. 188b to review the meanings of *astonished, behavior, benefactor, distribution, gratitude, procession, recommend, sacred,* and *traditions.* Students can practice saying all of the words. Have individuals read the words from word cards.

DECODING MULTISYLLABIC WORDS Write *intelligent,* saying the word as you write it. Then model how to decode when there are no meaningful word parts. I see a chunk at the beginning of the word: *in.* I see a part in the middle: *tel.* The next chunk is *li.* I see a chunk at the end of the word: *gent.* I say each chunk slowly: *in tel li gent.* I say the chunks smoothly to make a whole word: *intelligent.* Is it a real word? Yes, I know the word *intelligent.*

Use the Multisyllabic Word routine on p. DI·1 to help students read these other words from "The Ch'i-lin Purse": *engaged, neighboring, satisfied, lunar,* and *mention.* Be sure students understand the meanings of words such as *lunar* and *mention.*

Use *Strategies for Word Analysis,* Lesson 8, with students who have difficulty mastering word analysis and need practice with decodable text.

2 Read "The Ch'i-lin Purse," pp. 190–197

BEFORE READING Yesterday we read about life in China. Today we will read a folk tale about a young woman in China many years ago. She learns to help others and finds she needs the help of others.

Using the Picture Walk routine on p. DI·1, guide students through the text, asking questions such as those listed below. Then read the question on p. 191. Together, set a purpose for reading.

p. 192 How do the young woman and the old man seem to be relating to each other?

pp. 194–195 The illustration shows two *hua-chiaos,* small carriages carried by servants, used to take brides to their weddings. How do they compare? Why might this be?

DURING READING Follow the Guiding Comprehension routine on pp. 192–197. Have students read along with you while tracking the print or do a choral reading of the selection. Stop every two pages to ask students what they have learned so far. Prompt as necessary.

• Why did Hsiang-ling's mother want her to have the purse?
• How do you feel about Hsiang-ling giving away her mother's gift?

AFTER READING What has happened in the story so far? What do you think will happen next? Reread passages as needed.

Advanced

ROUTINE

1 Extend Vocabulary

⊙ **WORD STRUCTURE** Choose and read a sentence or passage containing a difficult word with identifiable word parts, such as this sentence from p. 192 of "The Ch'i-lin Purse": "It was the Ch'i-lin Purse, a red satin bag embroidered on both sides with a *ch'i-lin*, a *legendary* animal from ancient times . . ." What does the word *legendary* mean? *(something from the past that might be real, but no one can ever be sure is real)* How did you figure out the word's meaning? (Legendary *contains the word* legend, *which is a story about things that people think happened in the past, but might not be true.)* Remind students to use the strategy as they read "The Ch'i-lin Purse."

2 Read "The Ch'i-lin Purse," pp. 190–197

BEFORE READING In "Making Friends in Mali," you read about a woman who helped a family learn to grow and store food. Today you will read a selection about a young woman who helped another woman and later on needed help. As you read, think about the potential real results and potential results of helping others.

Have students write two questions about ancient China in their Strategy Response Logs (p. 190). Have them look for answers as they read or through research.

CRITICAL THINKING Have students read pp. 190–197 independently. Encourage them to think critically. For example, ask:

• How can someone be both spoiled and helpful?

AFTER READING Have partners discuss the selection and share their Strategy Response Log questions and answers. Give students an opportunity to discuss the selection and share their information about ancient China with you.

DAY **2**

AudioText

The Ch'i-lin Purse

Group Time

Audio CD AudioText

1 Reinforce Comprehension

🔵 **SKILL COMPARE AND CONTRAST** Have students explain what it means to compare and contrast *(to name similarities and differences)* and list clue words that signal similarities and differences. *(like, as, similar; unlike, as opposed to, while)* If necessary, review the meanings and provide a model. You compare to show how things are alike. *The two girls had similar types of wedding ceremony* tells how the two characters are the same. You contrast to show how two things are different. *China: Now and Then* is nonfiction, while "The Ch'i-lin Purse" is fiction.

Have students find what is compared and contrasted by reading the statements below. Ask them to explain their reasoning.

How are Mrs. Hsueh and the servant similar? *(They both try to please Hsiang-ling.)*

How was Hsiang-ling different after she had a son than she was when she was younger? *(She was not as selfish.)*

How did the Chinese culture see men and women differently? *(When women married, they left their home and families, but men did not.)*

2 Read "The Ch'i-lin Purse," pp. 198–203

BEFORE READING Have students retell what has happened in the story so far. Ask: What questions do you have about what will happen in the story? Reread p. 197. Model how to predict. As I read, I try to think about what could happen next. I think the family she meets will know where her husband and son are. I think meeting the family will be important to Hsiang-ling. Remind students to make predictions as they read the rest of "The Ch'i-lin Purse."

🔵 **STRATEGY Predict**

DURING READING Follow the Guiding Comprehension routine on pp. 198–203. Have students read along with you while tracking print or do a choral reading. Stop every two pages to ask students what has happened so far. Prompt as necessary.

- What is important about the Pearl Hall?
- How do the two women know each other?
- How did the purse help Mrs. Lu?

AFTER READING Why did Mrs. Lu put the purse at the altar? Reread with students for comprehension as needed. Tell them that tomorrow they will read "The Lion and the Mouse," a different type of folk tale that also tells about helping others.

Monitor Progress

Word and Story Reading

If... students have difficulty reading multisyllabic words in the selection,	**then...** have them look for and read meaningful parts in the words or have them chunk words with no recognizable parts.
If... students have difficulty reading along with the group,	**then...** have them follow along as they listen to the AudioText.

Advanced

DAY 3

1 Extend Comprehension

⊙ SKILL COMPARE AND CONTRAST Ask students to look at the story to find examples of how Hsiang-ling and the bride in the other *hua-chiao* are alike and examples of how they are different. Ask students to use words or phrases that help identify comparisons or contrasting information.

⊙ STRATEGY PREDICT Have students think about the story of "The Ch'i-lin Purse" and what has happened so far. Have students think about what would make sense to happen next.

- What do you think could happen next? Why do you think this?

2 Read "The Ch'i-lin Purse," pp. 198–203

BEFORE READING Have students recall what has happened in the story. Remind them to look for information to compare and contrast and to make predictions as they read the remainder of "The Ch'i-lin Purse."

CRITICAL THINKING Have students read pp. 198–203 independently. Encourage them to think critically. For example, ask students if they agree or disagree with this statement and why:

- Hsiang-ling went into the Pearl Hall because she didn't like the little boy's crying.

AFTER READING Have students complete the Strategy Response Log activity (p. 202). Have students meet with you to discuss the story. Then have them find out about the traditions of modern Chinese weddings and compare them to "The Ch'i-lin Purse." Give students an opportunity to meet with you as they plan their response.

Audio CD   AudioText

Group Time

DAY 4

Audio CD **AudioText**

ROUTINE

1 Practice Retelling

REVIEW STORY ELEMENTS Help students identify the main characters and the setting of "The Ch'i-lin Purse." Then guide them in using the Retelling Cards to list story events in sequence. Prompt students to include important details.

RETELL Using the Retelling Cards, have students work in pairs to retell "The Ch'i-lin Purse." Monitor retelling and prompt students as needed. For example, ask:

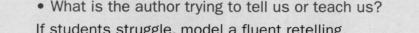

Grade 5
Retelling Cards
PEARSON
Scott Foresman

- Where and when does the story take place?
- What is the main character in the story like?
- What is the author trying to tell us or teach us?

If students struggle, model a fluent retelling.

2 Read "The Lion and the Mouse," pp. 206–207

BEFORE READING Read the genre information on p. 206. Explain that fables are short stories that teach a lesson or have a moral. As we read "The Lion and the Mouse," look for the reward that comes from helping others.

Read the rest of the panel on p. 206. Have students read the title and identify what makes the story a fable. *(It is brief, has animals as the characters, and probably has a moral at the end.)* Ask: What relationship would you expect between a lion and a mouse? *(Since lions eat meat and hunt, I would think the lion might eat the mouse.)*

DURING READING Have students read along with you while tracking the print or do a choral reading of the selection. Stop to discuss difficult vocabulary, such as *spare*, *suspended*, and *gnaw*.

AFTER READING Have students share their reactions to the selection. Then guide them through the Reading Across Texts and Writing Across Texts activities, prompting if necessary.

- What characters would you say were alike in "The Lion and the Mouse" and "The Ch'i-lin Purse"?
- Is "The Ch'i-lin Purse" a fable as well?

Monitor Progress

Word and Story Reading

If... students have difficulty reading multisyllabic words in the selection,	**then...** have them look for and read meaningful parts in the words or have them chunk words with no recognizable parts.
If... students have difficulty reading along with the group,	**then...** have them follow along as they listen to the AudioText.

1 Read "The Lion and the Mouse"

CREATIVE THINKING Have students read pp. 206–207 independently. Encourage them to think creatively. For example, ask:

- What other reasons could the mouse have given for the lion not to eat him?
- The moral does not discuss helping. How does the fable fit in with the theme?

AFTER READING Have students meet with you to discuss this fable and Reading Across Texts. Have students do Writing Across Texts independently.

DAY 4

2 Extend Genre Study

RESEARCH Have students use the Internet to locate information about Aesop. Have students create a list of common stories that can be credited to Aesop.

WRITE Have students use one of Aesop's fables to write a modern-day fable. Students can then share their modern fables with classmates.

AudioText

The Ch'i-lin Purse
Group Time

ONLINE

PearsonSuccessNet.com

Strategic Intervention

1 Reread for Fluency

MODEL Tell students that good readers read aloud using different pitches. Pitch is the high or low quality of your voice. Readers can use higher and lower pitch to distinguish between characters in a story. Pitch can also help show emotion. Then model, reading aloud p. 4 of the Leveled Reader *China: Now and Then.* Use a deeper pitch as you describe the powerful and sacred emperors. Discuss how reading with pitch makes listeners pay better attention.

PRACTICE Have individuals silently reread passages from *China: Now and Then.* Encourage students to self-correct. Then have partners reread passages aloud. For optimal fluency, they should reread three or four times. As students read, monitor fluency and provide corrective feedback. Students in this group are assessed in Weeks 2 and 4.

2 Retell Leveled Reader *China: Now and Then*

Model how to use skimming to retell the information on pp. 3–9. Then ask students to retell *China: Now and Then,* skimming the selection. Prompt them as needed.

- What have been some of the biggest changes in China?
- What are some things that are the same about ancient and modern China?

Monitor Progress

Fluency

If... students have difficulty reading fluently,	then... provide additional fluency practice by pairing nonfluent readers with fluent ones.

For alternate Leveled Reader lesson plans that teach
◎ **Compare and Contrast,** ◎ **Predict,** and
Lesson Vocabulary, see pp. LR19–LR27.

On-Level

ROUTINE

1 Reread for Fluency

MODEL Tell students that good readers use the pitch of their voice to show emotion as well as to distinguish between characters. Point out that in "The Ch'i-lin Purse" and *The Gift,* there are many different characters and exciting events that would have a reader changing pitch as he or she reads. Then model changing pitch, reading p. 15 of the Leveled Reader *The Gift.* Discuss how changing pitch helps listeners recognize excitement as well as different characters speaking.

PRACTICE Have individuals silently reread passages from *The Gift.* Remind them to self-correct if they misread or skip a word. Then have partners reread passages aloud. For optimal fluency, students should reread three or four times. As students read, monitor fluency and provide corrective feedback. Assess the fluency of students in this group using p. 207a.

2 Retell Leveled Reader *The Gift*

Have students retell *The Gift* using illustrations as a guide. Prompt as needed.

- Tell me what this story is about in a few sentences.
- What else happens in this story?
- How does this story remind you of other stories?

Advanced

ROUTINE

DAY 5

1 Reread for Fluency

PRACTICE Have students silently reread passages from the Leveled Reader *Making Friends in Mali.* Then have them reread aloud with a partner or individually. As students read, monitor fluency and provide corrective feedback. If students read fluently on the first reading, they do not need to reread three to four times. Students in this group were assessed in Week 1.

2 Revisit Leveled Reader *Making Friends in Mali*

RETELL Have students retell the Leveled Reader *Making Friends in Mali.*

DESIGN A MUD CLOTH Have students complete their Mali mud cloths. You may wish to review the design that students have created. Have them share their designs with classmates.

Group Time

Leveled Reader Database ONLINE

PearsonSuccessNet.com

Monitor Progress

Selection Reading and Comprehension

If... students have difficulty reading the selection with a partner,	**then...** have them follow along as they listen to the Online Leveled Reader Audio.
If... students have trouble understanding the relationship between protecting endangered species and loss of habitat,	**then...** reread p. 7 and discuss the idea that, although development does not hurt animals directly, it hurts animals by destroying their homes.

Strategic Intervention

ROUTINE

① Build Background

REINFORCE CONCEPTS Display the Protecting Animals Concept Web. This week's concept is *protecting animals*. Animals need protection when they are no longer able to survive in their environment. Discuss the meaning of each word on the web, using the definitions on p. 208l and the Concept Vocabulary routine on p. DI·1.

CONNECT TO READING This week you will read about endangered animals and how conservationists work to protect those animals. Humans must sometimes put their needs and desires below the needs of animals and plants. Recall the Read Aloud "Jane Goodall." What does Jane's method for observing nature tell about her? *(She doesn't want humans disturbing animals' natural environments.)*

② Read Leveled Reader *Endangered Animals*

BEFORE READING Using the Picture Walk routine on p. DI·1, guide students through the text focusing on key concepts and vocabulary. Ask questions such as:

p. 3 What do the plants and animals on this page have in common? *(They are all living things.)*

pp. 8–9 The map on p. 8 shows where the giant panda once lived and where it lives now. What does the map tell you? *(The giant panda is living in a much smaller area than it used to.)* What do you think that means for the giant panda? *(It is in danger of having nowhere to live and might become extinct.)*

DURING READING Read pp. 3–5 aloud while students track the print. Do a choral reading of pp. 6–9. If students are capable, have them read and discuss the remainder of the book with a partner. Ask: Why are many species becoming endangered? Why is losing one animal species a problem?

AFTER READING Encourage pairs of students to discuss the things that people can do to protect endangered animals. We read *Endangered Animals* to understand how people have caused animal populations to decline. Understanding how animals become endangered will help you relate to the problems in "Jane Goodall's 10 Ways to Help Save Wildlife."

For alternate Leveled Reader lesson plans that teach
Fact and Opinion, **Ask Questions,** and
Lesson Vocabulary, see pp. LR28–LR36.

On-Level

ROUTINE

1 Build Background

DEVELOP VOCABULARY Write the word *naturalist* and ask students to define it in their own words. *(a person who studies living things)* How could a naturalist help people protect animals? *(Naturalists study animals, so they know what animals need to survive.)* Repeat this activity with the word *dependent* and other words from the Leveled Reader *Habitats in Need of Help.* Use the Concept Vocabulary routine on p. DI·1 as needed.

2 Read Leveled Reader *Habitats in Need of Help*

BBEFORE READING Have students create a KWL chart to complete as they read. This book gives information about animal habitats that need to change if the animals are to survive. Complete the KWL chart with information you know now about the endangered animal habitats as well as things you want to know. As you find answers during your reading, complete the chart.

DURING READING Have students follow along as you read pp. 3–11. Then let them complete the book on their own. Remind students to add information that they find and answers to their questions on their chart as they read.

AFTER READING Have students share the entries in their charts. Point out that understanding problems with animal habitats will help as they read tomorrow's selection, "Jane Goodall's 10 Ways to Help Save Wildlife."

Advanced

ROUTINE

1 Read Leveled Reader *Saving Endangered Species*

BEFORE READING Recall the Read Aloud "Jane Goodall." What qualities did Jane Goodall have that would make her a great naturalist one day? *(She loved animals, she enjoyed observing them, and she was patient when she watched them.)* Today you will read about conservationists trying to save endangered species of animals.

PROBLEM SOLVING Have students read the leveled reader independently. Encourage them to think of the problems that conservationists face in trying to save endangered animals. For example, ask:

- How would you convince a hunter to stop hunting an endangered species of animal?
- How can we get oil from the earth without harming animals and their habitats?
- What would you do to explain the importance of protecting the Andean Condor?

AFTER READING Have students review the selection to find five or more unfamiliar words and determine their meanings. Then ask them to create an illustration that uses the words as labels. Have students meet with you to discuss the selection and the illustration they created.

2 Independent Extension Activity

NOW TRY THIS Assign "Now Try This" on pp. 22–23 of *Saving Endangered Species* for students to work on throughout the week.

Jane Goodall's 10 Ways to Help Save Wildlife

Group Time

DAY 2

Audio CD **AudioText**

ROUTINE

1 Word Study/Phonics

LESSON VOCABULARY Use p. 210b to review the meanings of *conservation, contribute, enthusiastic, environment,* and *investigation.* Students can practice saying all of the words. Have individuals read the words from word cards.

DECODING MULTISYLLABIC WORDS Write *marvelous* and model how to decode when there are meaningful word parts. This is a three-syllable word formed from the base word *marvel* and the suffix *-ous.* First I cover the suffix and say the base word: *marvel.* Then I blend the suffix to read the whole word: *marvel ous, marvelous.* The suffix *-ous* means "having the quality of," so *marvelous* means "having the quality of marvel or wonder and amazement."

Use the Multisyllabic Word routine on p. DI·1 to help students read these other words from "Jane Goodall's 10 Ways to Help Save Wildlife": *realize, distance, mysterious, informational,* and *production.* Be sure students understand the meanings of words such as *production.*

Use *Strategies for Word Analysis,* Lesson 9, with students who have difficulty mastering word analysis and need practice with decodable text.

2 Read "Jane Goodall's 10 Ways to Help Save Wildlife," pp. 212–219

BFORE READING Yesterday we read about endangered animals. Today we will read about a conservationist and how she suggests we can protect animals in the wild.

Using the Picture Walk routine on p. DI·1, guide students through the text, asking questions such as those listed below. Then read the question on p. 213. Together, set a purpose for reading.

pp. 216–217 What do the chimpanzees on p. 217 remind you of? *(a human mother and child)*

p. 218 What do you see in this photograph? *(a child with a lizard)*

DURING READING Follow the Guiding Comprehension routine on pp. 214–219. Have students read along with you while tracking the print or do a choral reading of the selection. Stop every two pages to ask what students have learned so far. Prompt as necessary.

• Why do you think Jane Goodall's suggestions are good advice?
• Which suggestions were most interesting to you so far?
• Why is it so important that we protect wildlife?

AFTER READING What have you learned so far? What do you think you will learn next? Reread passages with students as needed.

Monitor Progress

Word and Story Reading

If... students have difficulty reading multisyllabic words in the selection,	**then...** have them look for and read meaningful parts in the words or have them chunk words with no recognizable parts.
If... students need practice reading words fluently,	**then...** use the Fluent Word Reading Routine on the DI tab.
If... students have difficulty reading along with the group,	**then...** have them follow along as they listen to the AudioText.

Advanced

ROUTINE

1 Extend Vocabulary

🎯 **CONTEXT CLUES** Choose and read a sentence or passage containing a difficult word that can be defined from context, such as this sentence from p. 8 of *Saving Endangered Species:* "Conservationists began to call for protections to preserve species that were at risk." *How could you figure out the meaning of* preserve? *(By using the word* protections *in this sentence and the next two sentences about the Endangered Species Act, I know that the word* preserve *means "save.")* Point out that context clues might be in the same sentence as an unknown word, but clues could also be in a sentence before or after the unknown word. Remind students to use the strategy as they read "Jane Goodall's 10 Ways to Help Save Wildlife."

2 Read "Jane Goodall's 10 Ways to Help Save Wildlife," pp. 212–219

Audio CD AudioText

BEFORE READING In *Saving Endangered Species,* you read about how conservationists protect species that are shrinking in number. Today you will read a list of suggestions by a famous conservationist. As you read, think about how the selections are related.

Have students write two questions about Jane Goodall's suggestions in their Strategy Response Logs (p. 212). Have them think about the answers to their questions as they read and record any additional questions that arise.

CRITICAL/CREATIVE THINKING Have students read pp. 212–219 independently. Encourage them to think critically. For example, ask:

- What can you learn from familiar animals such as dogs and cats?
- Describe a pet you have or know of that can do an amazing or special thing.

AFTER READING Have partners discuss the selection and share their Strategy Response Log entries. Then have students come up with two more suggestions that they have for protecting wildlife. Give students an opportunity to share their ideas with you.

Group Time

DAY 3

AudioText

1 Reinforce Comprehension

🎯 **SKILL FACT AND OPINION** Have students explain the difference between a fact and an opinion *(A fact is something you can prove true or false; an opinion is one person's thoughts and feelings and can't be proved.)* Have students list clue words that signal an opinion *(I think, I believe, in my opinion).* If necessary, provide a model. Facts are statements that you can prove. *It's true that bees sting and sharks bite* is a fact because you can prove it by researching. *My dog felt guilty* is an opinion. There is no way to prove how a dog feels.

Have students read the statements below and tell whether each tells a statement of fact or a statement of opinion. Ask them to explain their reasoning.

Jane named the chimpanzees Flo and David Greybeard. *(fact; You can read her books or ask her to find out if these are the names she gave them.)*

Most animals can be taught to trust people. *(opinion; There is no way to prove this statement with most animals.)*

2 Read "Jane Goodall's 10 Ways to Help Save Wildlife," pp. 220–223

BEFORE READING Have students retell what happened in the selection so far. Ask: How does Jane Goodall suggest getting to know animals? Reread p. 219. Model how to ask questions. As I read, I wonder how scientists can track how far butterflies can travel. Remind students to ask questions and try to find the answers as they read the rest of "Jane Goodall's 10 Ways to Help Save Wildlife."

🎯 **STRATEGY Ask Questions**

DURING READING Follow the Guiding Comprehension routine on pp. 220–223. Have students read along with you while tracking the print or do a choral reading. Stop every two pages to ask students what has happened so far. Prompt as necessary.

- How can speaking up for what you believe in make a difference?
- How does eating less red meat save forests?
- Which suggestion would you like to start doing?

AFTER READING Are there any problems in our community that you could speak up against that will help protect wildlife? Reread with students for comprehension as needed. Tell them that tomorrow they will read "Why Some Animals Are Considered Bad or Scary," an article that describes how some animals got their reputations.

Monitor Progress

Word and Selection Reading

If... students have difficulty reading multisyllabic words in the selection,	then... have them look for and read meaningful parts in the words or have them chunk words with no recognizable parts.
If... students have difficulty reading along with the group,	then... have them follow along as they listen to the AudioText.

Advanced

1 **Extend Comprehension**

⊙ **SKILL** **FACT AND OPINION** Ask students to look at the selection to find examples of facts and opinions. Ask students to name words or phrases that help them recognize whether the statements are facts or opinions.

⊙ **STRATEGY** **ASK QUESTIONS** Have students think about the experiences the author of "Jane Goodall's 10 Ways to Help Save Wildlife" shares in the book. Have students think not just about Goodall's experiences, but those of others that the author shares.

• What questions would you ask some of the people described in the selection?

DAY 3

Audio CD   AudioText

2 **Read** "Jane Goodall's 10 Ways to Help Save Wildlife," pp. 220–223

BEFORE READING Have students recall the selection so far. Remind them to look for facts and opinions and to ask and answer questions as they read the remainder of "Jane Goodall's 10 Ways to Help Save Wildlife."

CRITICAL THINKING Have students read pp. 220–223 independently. Encourage them to think critically. For example, ask students if they agree or disagree with this statement and why:

• Jane Goodall suggests that we become vegetarians.

AFTER READING Have students complete the Strategy Response Log activity (p. 222). Then have them write letters to editors of local and regional newspapers supporting conservationist actions. Tell students to summarize the ten suggestions that Jane Goodall offers in "Jane Goodall's 10 Ways to Help Save Wildlife." Give students an opportunity to meet with you as they write their summaries.

Group Time

DAY **4**

Audio CD AudioText

Strategic Intervention

ROUTINE

1 Practice Retelling

REVIEW STORY ELEMENTS Help students identify the main ideas in "Jane Goodall's 10 Ways to Help Save Wildlife." List the ideas that students mention. Then ask questions to help students differentiate between important and not so important information.

RETELL Using the Retelling Cards, have students work in pairs to retell "Jane Goodall's 10 Ways to Help Save Wildlife." Monitor retelling and prompt students as needed. For example, ask:

Grade 5
Retelling Cards
PEARSON
Scott Foresman

- What was this selection mostly about?
- What did you learn from reading this selection?
- Why do you think the author wrote this selection?

If students struggle, model a fluent retelling.

2 Read "Why Some Animals Are Considered Bad or Scary"

BEFORE READING Read the genre information on p. 226. Point out that many magazines are filled with expository nonfiction articles. As we read "Why Some Animals Are Considered Bad or Scary," look for facts and opinions the author included.

Read the rest of the panel on p. 226. Have students read the title and identify the topic of this selection. *(how some animals got the reputation of being bad or scary)* Ask: Who might read an article like this? *(someone interested in animals)* What animals would you expect to read about? *(lions, bears, snakes)*

DURING READING Have students read along with you while tracking the print or do a choral reading of the selection. Stop to discuss difficult vocabulary, such as *deliberately, superstitions,* and *aggressive.*

AFTER READING Have students share their reactions to the selection. Then guide them through the Reading Across Texts and Writing Across Texts activities, prompting if necessary.

- What is the point of this article? In what ways do you think Jane Goodall would agree with the author of this article?
- How would you summarize the point of this article to teach your readers another lesson about animals?

Monitor Progress

Word and Selection Reading

If... students have difficulty reading multisyllabic words in the selection,	**then...** have them look for and read meaningful parts in the words or have them chunk words with no recognizable parts.
If... students have difficulty reading along with the group,	**then...** have them follow along as they listen to the AudioText.

Advanced

1 Read "Why Some Animals Are Considered Bad or Scary"

CREATIVE THINKING Have students read pp. 226–229 independently. Encourage them to think creatively. For example, ask:

- What other myths can you recall about animals?
- How do you think these myths originated?

AFTER READING Have students meet with you to discuss the selection and Reading Across Texts. Have students do Writing Across Texts independently.

2 Extend Genre Study

RESEARCH Have students use the Internet to locate information about scary animals.

WRITE Have students create a "Fact and Opinion" chart describing what people think about the animals compared with the truth about them.

AudioText

Group Time

DAY 5

ONLINE

PearsonSuccessNet.com

Strategic Intervention

ROUTINE

1 Reread for Fluency

MODEL Tell students that good readers use appropriate phrasing to read in a smooth and natural way. Good phrasing makes a reader sound like he or she is talking, not reading. Model, reading aloud p. 9 of the Leveled Reader *Endangered Animals.* Use phrasing to show students how you pause in places that make the reading sound more natural. Then read p. 10 without grouping related words or using appropriate phrasing. Ask students which model sounded better. Discuss how good phrasing will help students better understand and enjoy what they read.

PRACTICE Have partners reread passages from *Endangered Animals.* For optimal fluency, they should reread three or four times. As students read, monitor fluency and provide corrective feedback. Assess the fluency of students in this group using p. 229a.

2 Retell Leveled Reader *Endangered Animals*

Model how to use skimming to retell the passage on pp. 3–6. Then ask students to retell *Endangered Animals,* skimming the selection. Prompt them as needed.

• How are Northern spotted owls threatened?
• What is poaching?

Monitor Progress

Fluency

If... students have difficulty reading fluently,	then... provide additional fluency practice by pairing nonfluent readers with fluent ones.

For alternate Leveled Reader lesson plans that teach 🔄 **Fact and Opinion,** 🔄 **Ask Questions,** and **Lesson Vocabulary,** see pp. LR28–LR36.

On-Level

ROUTINE

1 Reread for Fluency

MODEL Tell students that good readers use appropriate phrasing to sound natural. Point out that "Jane Goodall's 10 Ways to Help Save Wildlife" is written as if she is talking, so phrasing appropriately is not too difficult. In *Habitats in Need of Help,* however, the writing is more formal, so the reader may need to focus more on phrasing to make it sound natural. Then model phrasing, reading p. 3 of the Leveled Reader *Habitats in Need of Help.* Discuss how pausing at commas and other punctuation will help them better understand and enjoy what they read.

PRACTICE Have students reread passages from *Habitats in Need of Help* with a partner or individually. For optimal fluency, students should reread three or four times. As students read, monitor fluency and provide corrective feedback. Students in this group were assessed in Week 3.

2 Retell Leveled Reader *Habitats in Need of Help*

Have students use subheads as a guide to summarize important facts they learned from each section of the book. Prompt as needed.

- What was this selection mostly about?
- What did you learn from reading this selection?
- Why do you think the author wrote this selection?

Advanced

ROUTINE

1 Reread for Fluency

PRACTICE Have students reread passages from the Leveled Reader *Saving Endangered Species* with a partner or individually. As students read, monitor fluency and provide corrective feedback. If students read fluently on the first reading, they do not need to reread three to four times. Students in this group were assessed in Week 1.

2 Revisit Leveled Reader *Saving Endangered Species*

RETELL Have students retell the Leveled Reader *Saving Endangered Species.*

NOW TRY THIS Have students complete their endangered species report. You may wish to review the information on which students plan to report. Have them share their reports with classmates.

Group Time

DAY 1

Leveled Reader
Database

ONLINE

PearsonSuccessNet.com

Strategic Intervention

ROUTINE

1 Build Background

REINFORCE CONCEPTS Display the Promoting Freedom Concept Web. This week's concept is *promoting freedom*. A few hundred years ago, men and women in the American colonies were struggling to earn their independence, or freedom, from the British. Discuss the meaning of each word on the web, using the definitions on p. 230l and the Concept Vocabulary routine on p. DI·1.

CONNECT TO READING This week you will read about ways Americans worked to gain their freedom. Some people fought in the American Revolution. Others helped in different ways. Recall the Read Aloud "Molly Pitcher." What do you think would have happened if Molly did not provide water to the soldiers? *(The soldiers could have become overheated, or sick.)*

2 Read Leveled Reader *Paul Revere's Midnight Ride*

BEFORE READING Using the Picture Walk routine on p. DI·1, guide students through the text focusing on key concepts and vocabulary. Ask questions such as:

p. 5 This illustration shows Paul Revere waiting and watching for a signal. What kind of signal do you think he might receive? *(smoke, fire, a bell ringing, or a cannon firing)* He was watching the bell tower in the Old North Church for the lanterns that would tell him whether the British were coming by land or by sea.

p. 11 What do the clothes the men are wearing tell you? *(They were probably asleep or it is late at night.)* Yes, they were awakened in the middle of the night to hear of the coming of the British.

DURING READING Read pp. 3–6 aloud while students track the print. Do a choral reading of pp. 7–9. If students are capable, have them read and discuss the remainder of the book with a partner. Ask: What message does Paul Revere need to deliver?

AFTER READING Encourage pairs of students to discuss the importance of Paul Revere's ride. We read *Paul Revere's Midnight Ride* to understand how important Paul Revere was to the early part of the Revolutionary War. Understanding Paul Revere's actions will help you understand the poem *The Midnight Ride of Paul Revere*.

Monitor Progress

Selection Reading and Comprehension

If... students have difficulty reading the selection with a partner,	then... have them follow along as they listen to the Online Leveled Reader Audio.
If... students have trouble understanding the difficulty of Paul Revere's ride,	then... reread p. 7 and discuss the map on the title page together.

For alternate Leveled Reader lesson plans that teach
🎯 **Sequence,** 🎯 **Graphic Organizers,** and **Lesson Vocabulary,** see pp. LR37–LR45.

On-Level

ROUTINE

DAY 1

❶ Build Background

DEVELOP VOCABULARY Write the word *freedom* and ask students to define it in their own words. *(the power to do something you want to do)* What kinds of freedoms do you have? *(the freedom to wear the clothes I want to wear to school, the freedom to ask questions about our government)* Repeat this activity with the word *colonial* and other words from the Leveled Reader *Paul Revere and the American Revolution.* Use the Concept Vocabulary routine on p. DI·1 as needed.

❷ Read Leveled Reader
Paul Revere and the American Revolution

BEFORE READING Have students create a time line to complete as they read. This book tells the events that Paul Revere was a part of in the American Revolution. As you read, look at the events and when they happen. Record the information on your time line.

DURING READING Have students follow along as you read pp. 3–7. Then let them complete the book on their own. Remind students to add events to their time lines as they read.

AFTER READING Have students share the entries on their time lines. Point out that understanding the events of the Revolutionary War will help as they read tomorrow's selection, *The Midnight Ride of Paul Revere.*

Advanced

ROUTINE

DAY 1

❶ Read Leveled Reader
The National Guard: Modern Minutemen

BEFORE READING Recall the Read Aloud "Molly Pitcher." What were the battles like between the American and British soldiers? *(dangerous, difficult)* Today you will read about modern-day Americans who are ready to protect the United States at a moment's notice, much like the soldiers during the American Revolution.

CRITICAL THINKING Have students read the leveled reader independently. Have them consider the role of the National Guard in emergencies. For example, ask:

• If you were the President, in what instances would you decide to call up the National Guard?

• At what times do you think it would be necessary to send the National Guard to serve outside of the United States?

• How is serving in the National Guard different from serving in the other branches of the military?

AFTER READING Have students review the selection to find five or more unfamiliar words and determine their meanings. Then ask them to compose a letter to a National Guard member using the words so that their meanings are evident. Have students meet with you to discuss the selection and the letters they wrote.

❷ Independent Extension Activity

NOW TRY THIS Assign "Now Try This" on pp. 22–23 of *The National Guard: Modern Minutemen* for students to work on throughout the week.

Group Time

DAY 2

Audio CD — AudioText

ROUTINE

1 Word Study/Phonics

LESSON VOCABULARY Use p. 232b to review the meanings of *fate, fearless, glimmer, lingers, magnified, somber,* and *steed.* Students can practice saying all of the words. Have individuals practice reading the words from word cards.

DECODING MULTISYLLABIC WORDS Write *phantom* and model how to decode when there are no meaningful word parts. I see a chunk at the beginning: *phan,* and I know the letters *ph* probably sound like an *f.* I see a chunk at the end of the word: *tom.* I say each chunk slowly: *phan tom.* I say the chunks smoothly to make a whole word: *phantom.* Do you know what a *phantom* is?

Use the Multisyllabic Word routine on p. DI·1 to help students read these other words from *The Midnight Ride of Paul Revere: moorings, sentinel, kindled, bleating* and *peril.* Be sure students understand the meanings of words such as *sentinel* and *peril.*

Use *Strategies for Word Analysis,* Lesson 10, with students who have difficulty mastering word analysis and need practice with decodable text.

2 Read *The Midnight Ride of Paul Revere,* pp. 234–241

BEFORE READING Yesterday we read a selection about Paul Revere. Today we will read a poem that also tells the story of Paul Revere's ride.

Using the Picture Walk routine on p. DI·1, guide students through the text, asking questions such as those listed below. Then read the question on p. 234. Together, set a purpose for reading.

pp. 238–239 There is a man on the left page. What does he seem to be doing? *(spying on the soldiers)* Yes, it's Paul Revere's friend watching to see what the British soldiers will do so that he can hang the lanterns in the church tower as a signal to Paul Revere.

pp. 242–243 Look at Paul Revere's face. What does his face tell you about how he feels? *(He looks determined.)*

DURING READING Follow the Guiding Comprehension routine on pp. 236–241. Have students read along with you while tracking the print or do a choral reading of the selection. Stop every two pages to ask what students have learned so far. Prompt as necessary.

• What signal did Paul Revere see?
• What does the poet mean by "the secret dread" on p. 239?

AFTER READING What has happened in the poem so far? What do you think will happen next? Reread passages as needed.

Monitor Progress

Word and Story Reading

If... students have difficulty reading multisyllabic words in the selection,	**then...** have them look for and read meaningful parts in the words or have them chunk words with no recognizable parts.
If... students need practice reading words fluently,	**then...** use the Fluent Word Reading Routine on the DI tab.
If... students have difficulty reading along with the group,	**then...** have them follow along as they listen to the AudioText.

Advanced

DAY 2

1 Extend Vocabulary

🎯 **WORD STRUCTURE** Choose and read a sentence or passage containing a difficult word with identifiable word parts, such as this sentence from p. 240 of *The Midnight Ride of Paul Revere:* "Booted and spurred, with a heavy stride . . ." What does the word *spurred* mean? *(to be wearing spurs)* How did you figure out the word's meaning? *(I looked at the word parts. In the past people who rode horses often wore spurs on their boots. Since Paul Revere is riding a horse,* spurred *must mean that he is wearing spurs to get the horse to run.)* Remind students to use the strategy as they read *The Midnight Ride of Paul Revere.*

2 Read *The Midnight Ride of Paul Revere,* pp. 234–241

Audio CD   AudioText

BEFORE READING In *The National Guard: Modern Minutemen,* you read about militias from the Revolutionary War and how they evolved into the National Guard. Today you will read a poem that describes how Paul Revere alerted the Minutemen in the Revolutionary War to help them prepare for battle against the British. As you read, think about how important freedom from British rule must have been to Paul Revere and the Minutemen.

Have students write two questions about Paul Revere's ride in their Strategy Response Logs (p. 234). Remind them to think about the answers to their questions as they read. They can record their answers and any additional questions they have.

CREATIVE THINKING Have students read pp. 234–241 independently. Encourage them to think creatively. For example, ask:

• What are some other methods Paul Revere could have used to warn the Minutemen that the British were coming?

AFTER READING Have partners discuss the selection and share their Strategy Response Log entries. Then have students work with partners to write their own poems about Paul Revere's ride.

Group Time

Audio CD — **AudioText**

ROUTINE

DAY 3

1 Reinforce Comprehension

SKILL SEQUENCE Have students explain what the word *sequence* means *(the order of events)* and list clue words that signal sequence *(first, second, next, then, later)*. If necessary, review the meaning and provide a model. Sequence is very helpful when you are reading a selection about history. It also helps with reading and understanding directions. In the sentence *Paul Revere waited to see the lanterns, and then he rode off,* the word *then* tells about the order of events. The lanterns came first. Riding was second.

Have students tell which event is first in the statements below.

The birds flew off after I climbed the belfry. *(I climbed the belfry.)*

The clock struck midnight, then he crossed the bridge. *(The clock struck midnight.)*

First he traveled to Medford; second he rode through Concord. *(He traveled to Medford.)*

2 Read *The Midnight Ride of Paul Revere,* pp. 242–247

BEFORE READING Have students retell what happened in the poem so far. Ask: What questions do you have about what you think will happen next in the poem? Reread p. 240. Model how to use graphic organizers. As I read, I can write the events mentioned on a time line. This will help me understand and remember the events that happened. Remind students that they can use a graphic organizer as they read the rest of *The Midnight Ride of Paul Revere.*

STRATEGY Graphic Organizers

DURING READING Follow the Guiding Comprehension routine on pp. 242–247. Have students read along with you while tracking the print or do a choral reading. Stop every two pages to ask students what has happened so far. Prompt as necessary.

- What happened first?
- What does the poet compare the windows of the houses to on p. 245?
- Why do you think the author wrote this poem?

AFTER READING How does the poem compare to a history book? Reread with students for comprehension as needed. Tell them that tomorrow they will read "Women of the Revolutionary War," a collection of Internet articles.

Monitor Progress

Word and Selection Reading

If...	then...
If... students have difficulty reading multisyllabic words in the selection,	**then...** have them look for and read meaningful parts in the words or have them chunk words with no recognizable parts.
If... students have difficulty reading along with the group,	**then...** have them follow along as they listen to the AudioText.

Advanced

1 **Extend Comprehension**

◎ **SKILL** **SEQUENCE** Ask students to find examples in the poem of how the poet shows the sequence of events. Ask students to name words or phrases that help them recognize sequence in the poem.

◎ **STRATEGY** **GRAPHIC ORGANIZERS** Have students consider the events in *The Midnight Ride of Paul Revere.* Have them think about graphic organizers that might display the events in a meaningful way.

• What other graphic organizers could you use instead of a time line?

2 **Read** *The Midnight Ride of Paul Revere,* **pp. 242–247**

BEFORE READING Have students recall what has happened in the poem so far. Remind them to look for words that help with sequence and to use their graphic organizer as they read the remainder of *The Midnight Ride of Paul Revere.*

CRITICAL THINKING Have students read pp. 242–247 independently. Encourage them to think critically. For example, ask students if they agree or disagree with this statement and why:

• The Minutemen would have been defeated if Paul Revere had not told them which way the British soldiers were traveling.

AFTER READING Have students complete the Strategy Response Log activity (p. 246). Then ask students to add details that were not included in *The Midnight Ride of Paul Revere.* Give students an opportunity to meet with you as they plan their response.

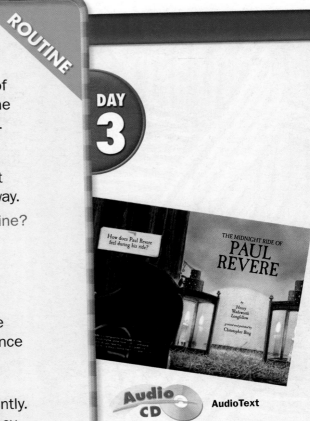

Audio CD   AudioText

Group Time

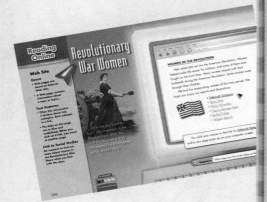

DAY
4

Audio
CD   AudioText

Strategic Intervention

1 Practice Retelling

REVIEW STORY ELEMENTS Help students identify the main characters and the setting of *The Midnight Ride of Paul Revere.* Then guide them in using the Retelling Cards to list the poem events in sequence. Prompt students to include important details.

RETELL Using the Retelling Cards, have students work in pairs to retell *The Midnight Ride of Paul Revere.* Monitor retelling and prompt students as needed. For example, ask:

Grade 5
Retelling
Cards
PEARSON
Scott
Foresman

- Tell me what this poem is about in a few sentences.
- What is Paul Revere like?
- Why do you think the poet wrote this poem?

If students struggle, model a fluent retelling.

2 Read "Revolutionary War Women"

BEFORE READING Read the genre information on p. 250. Point out that people use the Internet for research just as we use reference books in the library. Other Web sites are for entertainment and persuasion. As we read "Revolutionary War Women," look for features that are specific to Web pages.

Read the rest of the panel on p. 250. Have students read the title and identify the topic of this selection. *(women who helped in the Revolutionary War)* Ask: Who might want to go to a Web site like this? *(students researching women in the past or people interested in history)* How are these women's actions similar to the actions of the Minutemen?

DURING READING Have students read along with you while tracking the print or do a choral reading of the selection. Stop to discuss difficult vocabulary, such as *disguise, enlisted,* and *skirmish.*

AFTER READING Have students share their reactions to the selection. Then guide them through the Reading Across Texts and Writing Across Texts activities, prompting if necessary.

- Why did Deborah Sampson disguise herself as a man? Why did she expect to be punished when her commanding officer found out the truth? How would you feel if you wanted to fight for your country but weren't allowed to?
- Why did Paul Revere risk his life to ride through the countryside at night? Why did the actions of Paul Revere and Deborah Sampson cause others to respect them?

Monitor Progress

Word and Selection Reading

If... students have difficulty reading multisyllabic words in the selection,	**then...** have them look for and read meaningful parts in the words or have them chunk words with no recognizable parts.
If... students have difficulty reading along with the group,	**then...** have them follow along as they listen to the AudioText.

Advanced

ROUTINE

1 Read "Revolutionary War Women"

CREATIVE THINKING Have students read pp. 250–253 independently. Encourage them to think creatively. For example, ask:

- Is there a time when you would be willing to break the rules like Deborah Sampson did? Explain your answer.
- Who else have you heard or read about that took the same kinds of risks as Deborah Sampson took? Why do you think people have taken these kinds of risks for freedom by putting themselves in danger? Do you think the danger is worth it? Why or why not?

AFTER READING Have students meet with you to discuss the selection and Reading Across Texts. Have students do Writing Across Texts independently.

2 Extend Genre Study

RESEARCH Have students use the Internet to locate information about other women who served during the Revolutionary War, as well as women who served in other American wars.

WRITE Have students create a time line of women who served or participated in wars in which the United States was involved.

AudioText

The Midnight Ride of Paul Revere

Group Time

ONLINE

PearsonSuccessNet.com

Strategic Intervention

ROUTINE

1 Reread for Fluency

MODEL Tell students that good readers read the words using different tones of voice. Readers can communicate suspense, action, excitement, and other feelings. Then model, reading aloud p. 9 of the Leveled Reader *Paul Revere's Midnight Ride.* For a first reading, read the sentences without showing emotion in a monotone voice. Then reread, using emotion and different tones of voice for sentences that are urgent and suspenseful. Ask students which reading helped them understand the text. Discuss how reading with various tones of voice will help students understand, remember, and enjoy what they read.

PRACTICE Have students reread passages from *Paul Revere's Midnight Ride* with a partner or individually. For optimal fluency, they should reread three or four times. As students read, monitor fluency and provide corrective feedback. Assess any students you have not yet checked during this unit.

2 Retell Leveled Reader *Paul Revere's Midnight Ride*

Model how to use skimming to retell the events on pp. 3–6. Then ask students to retell *Paul Revere's Midnight Ride,* skimming the story. Prompt them as needed.

- What are the major events in order?
- Why do you think the poet wrote this poem?

Monitor Progress

Fluency

If... students have difficulty reading fluently,	then... provide additional fluency practice by pairing nonfluent readers with fluent ones.

For alternate Leveled Reader lesson plans that teach ◎ **Sequence,** ◎ **Graphic Organizers,** and **Lesson Vocabulary,** see pp. LR37–LR45.

On-Level

ROUTINE

① Reread for Fluency

MODEL Tell students that good readers read using an appropriate tone of voice. Point out that in *The Midnight Ride of Paul Revere,* the poet uses many words that lead you to read with excitement, suspense, and even fear. In *Paul Revere and the American Revolution,* the language isn't as descriptive, but tone of voice can get emotions across to listeners, too. Then model an appropriate tone of voice, reading p. 3 of the Leveled Reader *Paul Revere and the American Revolution.* Discuss how reading with different tones of voice will help them better understand and enjoy what they read.

PRACTICE Have partners reread passages from *Paul Revere and the American Revolution.* For optimal fluency, students should reread three or four times. As students read, monitor fluency and provide corrective feedback. Assess any students you have not yet checked during this unit.

② Retell Leveled Reader *Paul Revere and the American Revolution*

Have students use subheads as a guide to summarize important facts they learned from each section of the book. Prompt as needed.

- What was this section mostly about?
- Tell me about the major events in order.
- What did you learn from reading this section?

Advanced

ROUTINE

① Reread for Fluency

PRACTICE Have students reread passages from the Leveled Reader *The National Guard: Modern Minutemen* with a partner or individually. As students read, monitor fluency and provide corrective feedback. If students read fluently on the first reading, they do not need to reread three to four times. Assess any students you have not yet checked during this unit.

② Revisit Leveled Reader *The National Guard: Modern Minutemen*

RETELL Have students retell the Leveled Reader *The National Guard: Modern Minutemen.*

NOW TRY THIS Have students complete their displays about their state's National Guard. You may wish to review the information that students plan to use. Have them share their presentations with classmates.

Compare and Contrast

Noticing, understanding, and making comparisons and contrasts can clarify for students what they read. Use this routine to teach comparing and contrasting.

1 DEFINE THE TERMS

Explain that when you compare and contrast, you tell how two things are alike and different. Point out that in some contexts, questions asking students to compare may be asking students to describe both similarities and differences.

2 GIVE AN EXAMPLE

Provide a simple example, such as comparing a dog and a chameleon.

- Alike: Both are animals; both have four legs and a tail; both can be pets.
- Different: One is a mammal, the other is a reptile; one has fur, the other does not.

3 DISCUSS CLUE WORDS

Students should look for clue words that signal comparisons and contrasts as they read. List some examples on the board:

Compare	Contrast
like	unlike
alike	on the other hand
similarly	however

4 USE A VENN DIAGRAM

Students can use a Venn diagram to record comparisons and contrasts.

5 PROVIDE PRACTICE

- Ask students to compare and contrast two characters in a story or two characters in different stories.
- Ask students to compare and contrast information in a nonfiction article.

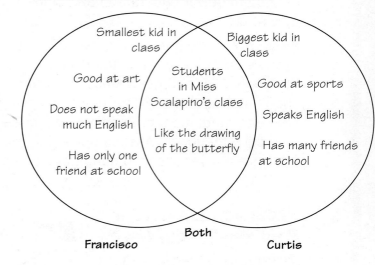

Smallest kid in class
Good at art
Does not speak much English
Has only one friend at school

Students in Miss Scalapino's class
Like the drawing of the butterfly

Biggest kid in class
Good at sports
Speaks English
Has many friends at school

Francisco   Both   Curtis

▲ **Graphic Organizer** 18

Research on Compare and Contrast

"Comparisons are one means of making concepts clear to the reader, and some writers use comparisons simply and effectively."

Rebecca J. Lukens,
A Critical Handbook of Children's Literature

Lukens, Rebecca J. *A Critical Handbook of Children's Literature.* Pearson Education, 2003, p. 286.

Author's Purpose

Evaluating the author's purpose for writing helps students decide how quickly or slowly and carefully to read. Use this routine to teach author's purpose.

1 DISCUSS AUTHOR'S PURPOSE

Explain that the author's purpose is the author's reason or reasons for writing. Four common reasons for writing are to persuade, to inform, to entertain, or to express ideas or feelings.

2 EXPLAIN ITS USE

Tell students that one reason they need to consider the author's purpose is to adjust their reading rate. If a story is meant to be fun, they may decide to read quickly. If the author wants to explain how something works, they may need to read slowly and carefully.

3 ASK QUESTIONS

Authors don't usually state their purposes for writing, and they often have more than one purpose. Before, during, and after reading a selection, ask questions to help students draw conclusions about the author's purposes: *Why do you think the author wrote this story? What reasons might the author have for writing it the story this way? What is the author trying to tell you? Why is the author telling you that?*

4 USE A GRAPHIC ORGANIZER

Have students predict the author's purpose before reading by previewing the title, illustrations, and graphics. During and after reading, students should check and confirm their predictions. Have them record ideas and evidence in a three-column chart.

	Author's Purpose	Why Do You Think So?
Before you read: What do you think it will be?	To tell about people trying to escape a dangerous place	The pictures show people who look tired and hungry. The title talks about freedom.
As you read: What do you think it is?	To show how difficult it was for Jewish refugees in Lithuania during the war	The story talks about how the people are trying to escape Nazi soldiers, and how they will be killed if they do not leave the country.
After you read: What was it?	To tell the story of how one man's courage and compassion saved the lives of hundreds of refugees	The author describes how Mr. Sugihara risked his own family's safety, and went against his governments wishes in order to help hundreds of Jewish refugees escape the Nazis.

▲ **Graphic Organizer** 26

Research on Author's Purpose

"Younger and less proficient readers are unlikely to differentiate between 'study' reading and 'fun' reading."

Ruth Garner,
"Metacognition and Self-Monitoring Strategies"

Garner, Ruth. "Metacognition and Self-Monitoring Strategies." In *What Research Has to Say About Reading Instruction*, edited by S. J. Samuels and A. E. Farstrup. Second Edition. International Reading Association, 1992, p. 238.

Compare and Contrast

Noticing, understanding, and making comparisons and contrasts can clarify for students what they read. Use this routine to teach comparing and contrasting.

1 DEFINE THE TERMS

Explain that when you compare and contrast, you tell how two things are alike and different. Point out that in some contexts, questions asking students to compare may be asking students to describe both similarities and differences.

2 GIVE AN EXAMPLE

Provide a simple example, such as comparing a dog and a chameleon.

- Alike: Both are animals; both have four legs and a tail; both can be pets.
- Different: One is a mammal, the other is a reptile; one has fur, the other does not.

3 DISCUSS CLUE WORDS

Students should look for clue words that signal comparisons and contrasts as they read. List some examples on the board:

Compare	Contrast
like	unlike
alike	on the other hand
similarly	however

4 USE A VENN DIAGRAM

Students can use a Venn diagram to record comparisons and contrasts.

5 PROVIDE PRACTICE

- Ask students to compare and contrast two characters in a story or two characters in different stories.
- Ask students to compare and contrast information in a nonfiction article.

Hsüeh Hsiang-ling	Mrs. Lu
1. Spoiled growing up	1. Poor growing up
2. Happily married	2. Happily married
3. Mother of little boy	3. Mother of little boy
4. Grateful for what she once had	4. Grateful for what she has
5. Separated from family	5. Living with family on large estate
6. Puts needs of others ahead of hers after flood	6. Admires generosity of stranger

▲ **Graphic Organizer** 25

Research on Compare and Contrast

"Comparisons are one means of making concepts clear to the reader, and some writers use comparisons simply and effectively."

Rebecca J. Lukens,
A Critical Handbook of Children's Literature

Lukens, Rebecca J. *A Critical Handbook of Children's Literature*. Pearson Education, 2003, p. 286.

Fact and Opinion

When students can identify statements of fact and opinion, they are able to make critical judgments concerning what they hear, read, and write. Use this routine to help students recognize statements of fact and statements of opinion and distinguish between them.

1 DEFINE FACT AND OPINION

Explain that a statement of fact can be proved true or false. A statement of opinion is someone's judgment, belief, or way of thinking about something. It cannot be proved true or false, but it can be supported or explained.

2 GIVE EXAMPLES

Write three statements on the board:

Charlotte's Web *was published in 1952. E. B. White wrote* Charlotte's Web. *You should read* Charlotte's Web.

Ask: *Which sentences are statements of fact? (the first two) How can you tell?* Elicit ways the facts could be verified, such as looking at the book or asking the school librarian. Talk about other ways to check statements of fact (observing, weighing, measuring, asking an expert).

Ask: *Which sentence is a statement of opinion? (the third one)* Point out the judgment word *should.* Explain opinions often contain judgment words such as *should, I think, cute,* and *best.*

3 PROVIDE PRACTICE

- Partners can read nonfiction selections and use a T-chart to list statements of fact and opinion.

- Have small groups read newspaper editorials. Students can list opinions and their supporting arguments.

Facts	Opinions
1. Bees sting and sharks bite.	1. We don't need to love a creature to respect it.
2. Jane Goodall referred to the animals she studied by name.	2. Naming animals makes them special.
3. Reusing, recycling, and using less paper will help to conserve trees.	3. Using less paper, gasoline, and red meat is easy to do.
4. Jane Goodall started a program for young people called Roots and Shoots.	4. Roots and Shoots has accomplished wonderful things.

▲ **Graphic Organizer** 25

Research on Fact and Opinion

"Students will—and should—argue about the difference between fact and opinion . . .; they will often dispute one another about inferences . . . . The point of such discussions is to help students sensitize themselves to the kinds of statements they encounter and make them aware of the inferences of others."

Thomas G. Devine,
Teaching Reading Comprehension

Devine, Thomas G. *Teaching Reading Comprehension.* Allyn and Bacon, Inc., 1986; 1992, p. 238.

Sequence

Keeping track of the sequence of events helps students understand what they read. Use this routine to help students develop sequence skills.

1 DISCUSS SEQUENCE

Tell students it is important to keep track of the sequence, or order, of events to understand some stories and articles. Discuss a story recently read in which the sequence of events was crucial to a correct understanding of the story.

2 TEACH CLUE WORDS

Write clue words on the board that can signal sequence, such as *first, next, then,* and *finally.* Explain that these words show the order in which things happen. Also teach that dates and times of the day also signal sequence.

3 SEQUENCE SENTENCE STRIPS

Write a clear sequence of events on sentence strips. Partners can work together to place the strips in the correct order. They can retell the events, inserting clue words to show the sequence.

4 RECORD A SEQUENCE ON A CHART

- After reading a story, students can work in pairs to create story sequence charts to show the order of events.

- For a nonfiction selection, partners can create time lines to show the chronological sequence of events.

Title
The Midnight Ride of Paul Revere

Characters
Paul Revere, his friend, British soldiers

Settings
Massachusetts, 1775, midnight

Problem
Someone must warn the people of Massachusetts the British are about to attack.

Events

1. Paul Revere tells a friend to hang a lantern in the Old North Church if the British march that night.
2. The friend sees the British soldiers marching down to their boats, and he signals Revere that the British are going to attack.
3. Paul Revere sets out on horseback to warn the people that the British are coming.
4. Paul Revere rides through Medford, Lexington, and Concord warning the people.

▲ **Graphic Organizer** 9

Research on Sequence

"Classes that read widely will encounter all sorts of ways authors play with time; recognizing flashbacks and attending to words and phrases denoting the passage of time or the sequential order of events are crucial to comprehension."

Sharon Kane,
"Teaching Skills Within Meaningful Contexts"

Kane, Sharon. "Teaching Skills Within Meaningful Contexts." *The Reading Teacher,* vol. 52, no. 2 (October 1998), pp. 182–184.

Providing students with reading materials they can and want to read is an important step toward developing fluent readers. A running record allows you to determine each student's instructional and independent reading level. Information on how to take a running record is provided on pp. DI•59–DI•60.

Instructional Reading Level

Only approximately 1 in 10 words will be difficult when reading a selection from the Student Edition for students who are at grade level. (A typical fifth-grader reads approximately 120–140 words correct per minute.)

- Students reading at grade level should read regularly from the Student Edition and On-Level Leveled Readers, with teacher support as suggested in the Teacher's Editions.
- Students reading below grade level can read the Strategic Intervention Leveled Readers. Instructional plans can be found in the Teacher's Edition and the Leveled Reader Teaching Guide.
- Students who are reading above grade level can read the Advanced Leveled Readers. Instructional plans can be found in the Teacher's Edition and the Leveled Reader Teaching Guide.

Independent Reading Level

Students should read regularly in independent-level texts in which no more than approximately 1 in 20 words is difficult for the reader. Other factors that make a book easy to read include the student's interest in the topic, the amount of text on a page, how well illustrations support meaning, and the complexity and familiarity of the concepts. Suggested books for self-selected reading are provided for each lesson on p. TR14 in this Teacher's Edition.

Guide students in learning how to self-select books at their independent reading level. As you talk about a book with students, discuss the challenging concepts in it, list new words students find in sampling the book, and ask students about their familiarity with the topic. A blackline master to help students evaluate books for independent reading is provided on p. DI•58.

Self-Selected/Independent Reading

While oral reading allows you to assess students' reading level and fluency, independent reading is of crucial importance to students' futures as readers and learners. Students need to develop their ability to read independently for increasing amounts of time.

- Schedule a regular time for sustained independent reading in your classroom. During the year, gradually increase the amount of time devoted to independent reading.
- Encourage students to track the amount of time they read independently and the number of pages they read in a given amount of time. Tracking will help motivate them to gradually increase their duration and speed. Blackline masters for tracking independent reading are provided on pp. DI•58 and TR15.

Choosing a Book for Independent Reading

When choosing a book, story, or article for independent reading, consider these questions:

_____ 1. Do I know something about this topic?

_____ 2. Am I interested in this topic?

_____ 3. Do I like reading this kind of book (fiction, fantasy, biography, or whatever)?

_____ 4. Have I read other things by this author? Do I like this author?

If you say "yes" to at least one of the questions above, continue:

_____ 5. In reading the first page, was only about 1 of every 20 words hard?

If you say "yes," continue:

_____ 6. Does the number of words on a page look about right to me?

If you say "yes," the book or article is probably at the right level for you.

Silent Reading

Record the date, the title of the book or article you read, the amount of time you spent reading, and the number of pages you read during that time.

Date	Title	Minutes	Pages

Taking a Running Record

A running record is an assessment of a student's oral reading accuracy and oral reading fluency. Reading accuracy is based on the number of words read correctly. Reading fluency is based on the reading rate (the number of words correct per minute) and the degree to which a student reads with a "natural flow."

How to Measure Reading Accuracy

1. Choose a grade-level text of about 80 to 120 words that is unfamiliar to the student.
2. Make a copy of the text for yourself. Make a copy for the student or have the student read aloud from a book.
3. Give the student the text and have the student read aloud. (You may wish to record the student's reading for later evaluation.)
4. On your copy of the text, mark any miscues or errors the student makes while reading. See the running record sample on page DI·60, which shows how to identify and mark miscues.
5. Count the total number of words in the text and the total number of errors made by the student. Note: If a student makes the same error more than once, such as mispronouncing the same word multiple times, count it as one error. Self-corrections do not count as actual errors. Use the following formula to calculate the percentage score, or accuracy rate:

$$\frac{\text{Total Number of Words} - \text{Total Number of Errors}}{\text{Total Number of Words}} \times 100 = \text{percentage score}$$

Interpreting the Results

- A student who reads **95–100%** of the words correctly is reading at an **independent level** and may need more challenging text.
- A student who reads **90–94%** of the words correctly is reading at an **instructional level** and will likely benefit from guided instruction.
- A student who reads **89%** or fewer of the words correctly is reading at a **frustrational level** and may benefit most from targeted instruction with lower-level texts and intervention.

How to Measure Reading Rate (wcpm)

1. Follow Steps 1–3 above.
2. Note the exact times when the student begins and finishes reading.
3. Use the following formula to calculate the number of words correct per minute (wcpm):

$$\frac{\text{Total Number of Words Read Correctly}}{\text{Total Number of Seconds}} \times 60 = \text{words correct per minute}$$

Interpreting the Results

An appropriate reading rate for a fifth-grader is 120–140 (wcpm).

Running Record Sample

Running Record Sample

Did you know that every day in cities across the United States, students like you are helping others?

Each year in Louisiana, a young student and her younger brother have gone around collecting stuffed animals for the children who live in a homeless shelter.

In New York City, seventy-six students from Harlem teamed up with four Olympic athletes to transform a run-down park into a playground featuring a daffodil garden.

And each year in Indiana, a young student has gone around collecting hundreds of bundles of baby clothes and other baby items. In the fall she delivers them to a home for mothers who are having tough times.

—From *Using Special Talents*
On-Level Reader 5.2.1

Symbols

Accurate Reading
The student reads a word correctly.

Hesitation
The student hesitates over a word, and the teacher provides the word. Wait several seconds before telling the student what the word is.

Insertion
The student inserts words or parts of words that are not in the text.

Omission
The student omits words or word parts.

Substitution
The student substitutes words or parts of words for the words in the text.

Self-Correction
The student reads a word incorrectly but then corrects the error. Do not count self-corrections as actual errors. However, noting self-corrections will help you identify words the student finds difficult.

Mispronunciation/Misreading
The student pronounces or reads a word incorrectly.

Running Record Results	Reading Accuracy	Reading Rate—WCPM
Total Number of Words: **107**	$\frac{107-5}{107}$ x 100 = 95.327 = 95%	$\frac{102}{51}$ x 60 = 120 = 120 words correct per minute
Number of Errors: **5**		
Reading Time: **51 seconds**	Accuracy Percentage Score: **95%**	Reading Rate: **120** WCPM

Number the Stars
from p. 162m

"Lise Margrete," he read finally, and stared at Ellen for a long, unwavering moment. In her mind, Annemarie pictured the photograph that he held: the baby, wide-eyed, propped against a pillow, her tiny hand holding a silver teething ring, her bare feet visible below the hem of an embroidered dress. The wispy curls. Dark.

The officer tore the photograph in half and dropped the pieces on the floor. Then he turned, the heels of his shiny boots grinding into the pictures, and left the apartment. Without a word, the other two officers followed. Papa stepped forward and closed the door behind him.

WORD LIST

Unit 1

Title	Vocabulary Words	Spelling Words

Frindle — Vocabulary: acquainted, assignment, essential, expanded, guaranteed, procedures, reputation, worshipped

Short vowel VCCV, VCV: distance, method, anger, problem, butter, petals, enjoy, perhaps, figure, channel, admire, comedy, husband, tissue, mustard, shuttle, advance, drummer, regular, denim

Thunder Rose — Vocabulary: branded, constructed, daintily, devastation, lullaby, pitch, resourceful, thieving, veins

Long vowel VCV: fever, broken, climate, hotel, basic, vocal, native, silent, labor, spider, label, icon, agent, motive, vital, acorn, item, aroma, legal, solo

Island of the Blue Dolphins — Vocabulary: gnawed, headland, kelp, lair, ravine, shellfish, sinew

Long vowel digraphs: coast, feast, speech, wheat, Spain, paint, arrow, needle, charcoal, praise, faint, maintain, crease, groan, breeze, willow, appeal, bowling, complain, sneeze

Satchel Paige — Vocabulary: confidence, fastball, mocking, outfield, unique, weakness, windup

Adding -ed, -ing: supplied, supplying, denied, denying, decided, deciding, included, including, admitted, admitting, occurred, occurring, qualified, qualifying, identified, identifying, delayed, delaying, satisfied, satisfying

Shutting Out the Sky — Vocabulary: advice, advised, circumstances, elbow, hustled, immigrants, luxury, newcomer, peddler

Contractions: they're, you've, weren't, needn't, there'd, they've, mustn't, what'll, doesn't, hadn't, could've, would've, should've, might've, wouldn't, who've, shouldn't, who'd, this'll, couldn't

Unit 2	Vocabulary Words	Spelling Words

Inside Out

Vocabulary Words: caterpillar, cocoon, disrespect, emerge, migrant, sketched, unscrewed

Digraphs *th, sh, ch, ph*

shovel	establish	shatter	attach
southern	although	ethnic	ostrich
northern	challenge	shiver	
chapter	approach	pharmacy	
hyphen	astonish	charity	
chosen	python	china	

Passage to Freedom

Vocabulary Words: agreement, cable, diplomat, issue, refugees, representatives, superiors, visa

Irregular plurals

staffs	chiefs	quizzes	chefs
ourselves	buffaloes	sheriffs	pianos
pants	flamingos	dominoes	
scissors	beliefs	thieves	
loaves	echoes	measles	
volcanoes	shelves	avocados	

The Ch'i-lin Purse

Vocabulary Words: astonished, behavior, benefactor, distribution, gratitude, procession, recommend, sacred, traditions

Vowel sounds with *r*

snore	report	repair	volunteer
tornado	prepare	sword	declare
spare	pioneer	ignore	
appear	chair	order	
career	beware	engineer	
square	smear	resort	

Jane Goodall's 10 Ways to Help Save Wildlife

Vocabulary Words: conservation, contribute, enthusiastic, environment, investigation

Final Syllables *-en, -an, -el, -le, -il*

example	oxygen	fossil	sudden
level	wooden	toboggan	beagle
human	double	veteran	
quarrel	travel	chisel	
scramble	cancel	suburban	
evil	chuckle	single	

The Midnight Ride of Paul Revere

Vocabulary Words: fate, fearless, glimmer, lingers, magnified, somber, steed

Final Syllables *-er, -ar, -or*

danger	surrender	caterpillar
wander	solar	rumor
tractor	sticker	glimmer
dollar	locker	linger
harbor	helicopter	sensor
eager	pillar	alligator
eraser	refrigerator	

Unit 3

Unit 3	Vocabulary Words		Spelling Words			
Wings for the King	admiringly permit scoundrel	subject worthless	**Schwas**			
			jewel kingdom gasoline factory garage tropical	pajamas estimate tomorrow humidity Chicago bulletin	carnival illustrate elegant census terrific celebrate	operate celery
Leonardo's Horse	achieved architect bronze cannon depressed	fashioned midst philosopher rival	**Compound words**			
			waterproof teaspoon grasshopper homesick barefoot courthouse	earthquake rowboat scrapbook countryside lightweight fishhook	spotlight blindfold whirlpool tablespoon greenhouse	postcard humming-bird thumbtack
The Dinosaurs of Waterhouse Hawkins	erected foundations mold occasion	proportion tidied workshop	**Consonant sounds /j/, /ks/, /sk/, and /s/**			
			excuse scene muscle explore pledge journal	science schedule gigantic scheme Japan excellent	exclaim fascinate ginger scholar scent dodge	smudge schooner
Mahalia Jackson	appreciate barber choir released	religious slavery teenager	**One consonant or two**			
			address college mirror recess committee collect	Mississippi immediate command appreciate announce possess	Tennessee gallop opponent barricade broccoli accomplish	allowance zucchini
Special Effects in Film and Television	background landscape miniature prehistoric reassembled		**Prefixes un-, de-, dis**			
			uncover defrost uncomfortable discourage disadvantage unfortunate unfamiliar	disability discomfort deodorant unemployed deflate disbelief	unpredict-able disapprove disappoint unpleasant dehydrated	disqualify undecided

Unit 4	Vocabulary Words		Spelling Words

Words from many cultures

Weslandia	blunders	fleeing	
	civilization	inspired	
	complex	rustling	
	envy	strategy	

khaki	vanilla	cobra	karate
hula	canyon	koala	kiosk
banana	yogurt	barbecue	
ballet	banquet	safari	
waltz	macaroni	buffet	
tomato	polka	stampede	

Prefixes over-, under-, sub-, super-, out-

Stretching Ourselves: Kids With Cerebral Palsy	abdomen
	artificial
	gait
	handicapped
	therapist
	wheelchair

overlook	underground	submarine	subdivision
underline	overboard	undercover	subhead
subway	undercurrent	overcast	
subset	superstar	outfield	
supermarket	overtime	output	
outlet	supersonic	supernatural	

Homophones

Exploding Ants: Amazing Facts About How Animals Adapt	critical
	enables
	mucus
	scarce
	specialize
	sterile

cent	whether	tide	course
sent	their	tied	coarse
scent	there	pale	
threw	they're	pail	
through	chili	aloud	
weather	chilly	allowed	

Suffixes -ible, -able

The Stormi Giovanni Club	cavities
	combination
	demonstrates
	episode
	profile
	strict

sensible	flexible	laughable	responsible
washable	reasonable	sociable	tolerable
available	favorable	allowable	
agreeable	breakable	divisible	
fashionable	convertible	hospitable	
valuable	forgettable	reversible	

Negative prefixes

The Gymnast	bluish	skidded
	cartwheels	somersault
	gymnastics	throbbing
	hesitation	wincing
	limelight	

invisible	impatient	illogical
illiterate	independent	indefinite
irregular	incorrect	imperfect
irresistible	inactive	immobile
impossible	imperfect	irresponsible
informal	impolite	
illegal	immature	inexpensive

Unit 5 | Vocabulary Words | Spelling Words

The Three-Century Woman

Vocabulary Words: eerie, intersection, pondered, severe, spectacles, withered

Spelling Words — Multisyllabic words:

elementary	variety	mosaic	centennial
vehicle	literature	tuxedo	curiosity
miniature	elevator	meteorite	
probability	Pennsylvania	fascination	
definition	ravioli	cylinder	
substitute	cafeteria	intermediate	

The Unsinkable Wreck of the R.M.S. *Titanic*

Vocabulary Words: cramped, debris, interior, ooze, robotic, sediment, sonar

Spelling Words — Unusual spellings:

league	blood	intrigue	subtle
sergeant	vague	villain	disguise
yacht	anxious	cantaloupe	
doubt	foreign	flood	
fatigue	bargain	depot	
debt	condemn	cordial	

Talk with an Astronaut

Vocabulary Words: accomplishments, focus, gravity, monitors, role, specific

Spelling Words — Greek word parts:

geology	disaster	biosphere	ecology
thermometer	meteorology	thermos	mythology
astronaut	technology	asterisk	
atmosphere	hemisphere	thermostat	
biology	zoology	astronomy	
thermal	sociology	spherical	

Journey to the Center of the Earth

Vocabulary Words: armor, encases, extinct, hideous, plunged, serpent

Spelling Words — Latin roots:

project	decimal	audit	dejected
audience	injection	decimeter	terrain
decade	December	audition	
territory	reject	audible	
auditorium	eject	decathlon	
terrier	terrace	terrarium	

Ghost Towns of the American West

Vocabulary Words: economic, independence, overrun, scrawled, vacant

Spelling Words — Related words:

politics	signature	clean
political	arrive	cleanse
major	arrival	resign
majority	inspire	resignation
equal	inspiration	unite
equation	human	unity
sign	humanity	

Unit 6 — Vocabulary Words — Spelling Words

At the Beach

Vocabulary Words

algae	lamented
concealed	sea urchins
driftwood	sternly
hammocks	tweezers

Spelling Words

Suffixes -ous, -sion, -ion, -ation

famous	nervous	tension	occupation
invention	explanation	humorous	destination
election	various	exhibition	
furious	decision	attraction	
imagination	relaxation	invasion	
education	conversation	creation	

The Mystery of Saint Matthew Island

Vocabulary Words

bleached	scrawny
carcasses	starvation
decay	suspicions
parasites	tundra

Spelling Words

Final Syllable -ant, -ent, -ance, -ence

important	absence	confidence	excellence
experience	appearance	conference	persistent
ignorant	intelligent	insurance	
entrance	evidence	ambulance	
difference	pollutant	hesitant	
instance	clearance	consistent	

King Midas and the Golden Touch

Vocabulary Words

adorn	precious
cleanse	realm
lifeless	spoonful

Spelling Words

Words with ei and ie

brief	seize	yield	shield
believe	ceiling	deceive	conceited
receive	field	achieve	
leisure	neither	grief	
piece	apiece	niece	
relief	receipt	protein	

The Hindenburg

Vocabulary Words

criticizing	era
cruised	explosion
drenching	hydrogen

Spelling Words

Compound words

ice cream	textbook	dead end	cartwheel
a lot	guidelines	password	root beer
keyboard	newspaper	teenager	fingerprint
fairy tale	space shuttle	skateboard	
horseshoe	hay fever	everything	
piggy bank		barbed wire	

Sweet Music in Harlem

Vocabulary Words

bass
clarinet
fidgety
forgetful
jammed
nighttime
secondhand

Spelling Words

Easily confused words

quiet	than	from	medal
quite	then	form	metal
finely	since	later	
finally	sense	latter	
except	affect	adapt	
accept	effect	adopt	

Grade 4 Vocabulary

Use this list of fourth grade tested vocabulary words for review and leveled activities.

A
aboard
affords
amazed
amphibians
ancestors
ancient
anticipation
appeared
aquarium
astronauts
atlas
aviator
avoided
awkward

B
bargain
bawling
bewildered
biologist
bluff
boarding school
bow
brilliant
brisk
bustling

C
canopy
capable
capsule
cargo
celestial
chant
chorus
cockpit
colonel
conducted
Constitution
continent
convergence
cord

coward
coyote
cradle
crime
crumbled
curiosity

D
dangle
dappled
daring
depart
destruction
dignified
dismay
docks
dolphins
dormitory
draft
drag
dudes
duke
dungeon

E
elegant
enchanted
endurance
escape
etched
exhibit
expected

F
fascinated
favor
flex
flexible
forbidding
forecasts
fouled
fragrant

frost
furiously

G
generations
genius
glacier
gleamed
glider
glimpses
glint
glorious
grand
granite
grizzly

H
hangars
hatch
heaves
homeland
hoop
horizon
howling
humble

I
icebergs
immense
impressive
inland

J
jersey

L
lagoon
lassoed
link
lizard
longed
loomed

lunar
lurking

M
magician
majesty
manual
marveled
massive
mechanical
memorial
migrating
minister
miracle
module
monument

N
naturalist
navigation
noble
numerous

O
offended
outspoken

P
palettes
parlor
payroll
peasant
peculiar
politics
pollen
pollinate
porridge
positive
prairie
preserve
prideful
pulpit
pulses

Q
quaint
quarantine
quivered

R
recalls
reference
reptiles
reseats
resemblance
reservation
responsibility
rille
rim
riverbed
roundup
rudder
ruins
rumbling
runt

S
salamander
scan
scent
scholars
sculptures
seeker
selecting
shatter
shielding
shimmering
shrieked
slithered
slopes
society
solemnly
solo
species
speechless
spurs

staggered
stalled
stern
still
stumped
summoning
surface
surge
swatted

T
taunted
temple
terraced
terror
thickets
timid
torrent
towering
trench
triumph
tropical
trudged

U
unbelievable
uncover

V
vain
vanished
vehicle

W
wharf
wilderness
wondrous

Y
yearned

Grade 6 Vocabulary

Use this list of sixth grade tested vocabulary words for leveled activities.

A
absurd
abundant
access
accustomed
aggressive
aliens
apparently
application
architecture
artifacts
astronomers
authority

B
barge
basin
beacon
behalf
benefits
bondage
burden

C
campaigns
candidate
captive
caravans
characteristic
charities
collapse
collide
combustion
commissioned
compact
companionship
comrades
confidently
conformed
conquer
converts
corridors
corrode

counselor
customary

D
dean
decline
decrees
delirious
democracy
densest
destination
destiny
detect
devise
dingy
diploma
disgraced
dismounted
distressed
dramatic
dubiously

E
earthen
eaves
efficiency
emphasized
empire
encounter
engulfed
enraged
enrich
equator
erosion
eternity
evaporates
existence
expanse
expedition
exploit
exported
extract

F
fixtures
flimsy
flourish
foreigners
formal
former
fragile
frantic
frustration
fulfill

G
galaxy
generated
groping

H
hatchet
hoard
homesteaders
hospitable
hovers

I
ideal
identity
ignite
immortal
imprinted
incident
industrial
insulated
invaders
isolation

L
lance
legacy
leisure
lunging
lush

M
maintenance
manuscripts
materialize
medieval
menacing
migration
misfortune
moisture
molten
momentous
mongrel
mythology

N
navigator
negotiate
nub

O
obedient
observatory
obstacle
opera
ordeal
ore

P
painstaking
particles
patron
percentage
permission
persisted
physical
pleas
poisonous
prejudice
presence
prey
primitive
privileged
proclaimed

progress
promoted
provisions

Q
quests
quill

R
receded
recital
recycled
refrain
registered
reigned
reject
relish
renewed
renowned
repay
reproduce
resound
retreat
revolting
romping
rowdy
rural

S
sanctuaries
secretive
settlement
sluggish
slung
smoldered
specimens
speckled
squire
stiffened
stimulating
stunned
subscribe
sufficient

surplus
survive

T
technology
tolerated
toll
torment
transmitted
traversed
treacherous
treaded
tropics

U
unaccompanied
unison
universal
urban

V
ventured
verify
version
vigorously
volcanic

W
waft
waning
wilt

Legibility

When handwriting is legible, letters, words and numbers can be read easily. Handwriting that is not legible can cause problems for the reader and make communication difficult. Legibility can be improved if students are able to identify what is causing legibility problems in their handwriting. Focus instruction on the following five elements of legible handwriting.

Size

Letters need to be a consistent size. Students should focus on three things related to size: letters that reach to the top line, letters that reach halfway between the top and bottom line, and letters that extend below the bottom line. Writing letters the correct size can improve legibility. Often the letters that sit halfway between the top and bottom line cause the most problems. When students are writing on notebook paper, there is no middle line to help them size letters such as *m, a, i,* and *r* correctly. If students are having trouble, have them draw middle lines on their notebook paper.

Shape

Some of the most common handwriting problems are caused by forming letters incorrectly. These are the most common types of handwriting problems:

- round letters such as *a, o,* and *g* are not closed
- looped letters such as *i, e,* and *b* have no loops
- letters such as *i, t,* and *d* have loops that shouldn't be there

Have students examine one another's writing to indicate which words are hard to read, and then discuss which letters aren't formed correctly. They can then practice those particular letters.

Spacing

Letters within words should be evenly spaced. Too much or too little space can make writing difficult to read. A consistent amount of space should also be used between words in a sentence and between sentences. Suggest that students use the tip of their pencil to check the spacing between words and the width of their pencil to check the spacing between sentences.

Slant

Correct writing slant can be to the right or to the left, or there may be no slant at all. Slant becomes a legibility problem when letters are slanted in different directions. Suggest that students use a ruler to draw lines to determine if their slant is consistent.

Smoothness

Written letters should be produced with a line weight that is not too dark and not too light. The line should be smooth without any shaky or jagged edges. If students' writing is too dark, they are pressing too hard. If the writing is too light, they are not pressing hard enough. Usually shaky or jagged lines occur if students are unsure of how to form letters or if they are trying to draw letters rather than using a flowing motion.

D'Nealian™ Cursive Alphabet

a b c d e f g
h i j k l m n
o p q r s t u
v w x y z

A B C D E F G
H I J K L M N
O P Q R S T U
V W X Y Z . , ' ?

1 2 3 4 5 6
7 8 9 10

D'Nealian™ Alphabet

a b c d e f g h i

j k l m n o p q r s t

u v w x y z

A B C D E F G

H I J K L M N O

P Q R S T U V

W X Y Z . , ' ?

1 2 3 4 5 6

7 8 9 10

Manuscript Alphabet

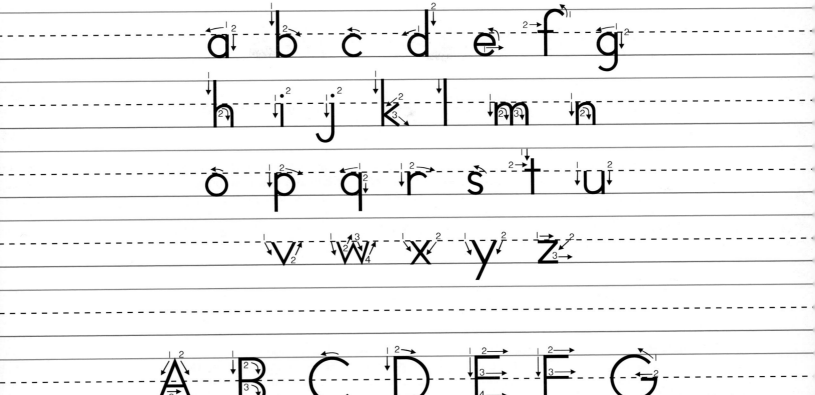

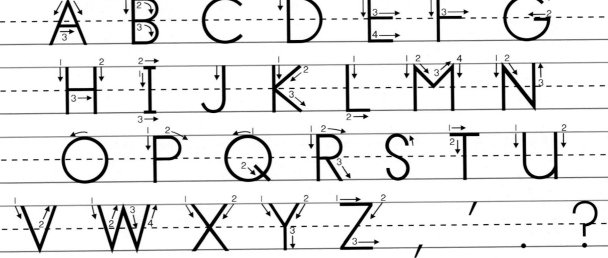

Unit 2 *Doing the Right Thing*

	Below-Level	On-Level	Advanced

Inside Out

To Read Aloud!
In the Year of the Boar and Jackie Robinson
by Betty Bao Lord (Harper, 1984) In 1947, the Brooklyn Dodgers play a crucial role in a Chinese girl's adjustment to life in the United States.

Eagle Song
by Joseph Bruchac (Dial, 1997) Danny Bigtree, an Iroquois boy living in Brooklyn, is teased because of his heritage and needs to find a way to stand up for himself.

Yolanda's Genius
by Carol Fenner (McElderly, 1995) Life in a new town brings out all of Yolanda's protective instincts for her younger brother, whom she believes to be a musical genius.

Dragonwings
by Laurence Yep (HarperCollins, 1975) Eight-year-old Moonshadow leaves China to join his father in America and endures loss and hardship to make his dream come true.

Passage to Freedom

To Read Aloud!
A Time to Fight Back
by Jayne Pettit (Houghton, 1996) This moving book shares the wartime experiences of eight children from eight different countries.

The Lily Cupboard
by Shulamith Levey Oppenheim (Harper Trophy, 1995) In this moving tale, a young Jewish girl hides in the country house of strangers during the German occupation of Holland.

Number the Stars
by Lois Lowry (Dell Yearling, 1989) This Newbery-Award winner is set in Denmark during the German occupation in 1943 and tells of a family's courageous efforts to help a Jewish family escape the country.

Hana's Suitcase: A True Story
by Karen Levine (Whitman, 2003) In 2000, the curator of Japan's Holocaust museum began a suspenseful journey across Europe to discover the fate of a girl whose suitcase was sent to the museum.

The Ch'i-lin Purse

To Read Aloud!
The Magic Tapestry: A Chinese Folktale
by Demi (Henry Holt & Company, 1994) The youngest of three sons must overcome frightening obstacles to win back his mother's heavenly tapestry, stolen by the fairies of Sun Mountain.

The Talking Eggs
by Robert San Souci (Dial, 1989) A beautifully illustrated adaptation of a Creole Cinderella folk tale in which a girl's kindness is rewarded.

The Fairy's Mistake
by Gail Carson Levine (HarperCollins, 1999) In this funny, spirited variation of a classic fairy tale, a fairy rewards a kind sister and punishes a cruel one, but all does not go according to plan.

A Single Shard
by Linda Sue Park (Clarion, 2001) A 12th-century Korean orphan wants to become a master potter and learns the value of perseverance and selflessness as he goes further than he ever dreamed possible.

Jane Goodall's 10 Ways to Help Save Wildlife

To Read Aloud!
Bug Watching with Charles Henry Turner
by Michael Elsohn Ross (Carolrhoda, 1997) This is the compelling story of a little-known naturalist who made amazing discoveries about bees, ants, and other creatures.

Nature's Green Umbrella: The Tropical Rain Forests
by Gail Gibbons (Harper Trophy, 1997) This beautifully illustrated book explains the importance of tropical rain forests and why we need to preserve and protect them.

Jane Goodall, Living with the Chimps
by Julie Fromer (Twenty-First Century Books, 1992) Goodall's life and her dedication to observing animals changed the way we think about nature and ourselves.

The Incredible Journey: A Tale of Three Animals
by Sheila Burnford (Little, Brown, 1960) This classic tale examines a long trek through the wilderness and the devotion of three animals.

The Midnight Ride of Paul Revere

To Read Aloud!
Yankee Doodle Boy: A Young Soldier's Adventures in the American Revolution
told by Joseph Plumb Martin, edited by George F. Scheer (Holiday House, 1995) This is the complete account of one soldier's experiences, told with vivid detail and a strong sense of immediacy.

The Liberty Tree: The Beginning of the American Revolution
by Lucille Recht Penner (Random, 1998) This easy-to-read account of the Stamp Act, the Boston Massacre, Paul Revere's ride, and the first shot fired at Lexington makes United States history accessible.

Sarah Bishop
by Scott O'Dell (Scholastic, 1991) After her brother and father are killed fighting on opposite sides in the American Revolution, Sara flees the British and begins a new life in the American wilderness.

The Fifth of March: A Story of Boston Massacre
by Ann Rinaldi (Gulliver Books, 1993) This book tells the story of the Boston Massacre from the perspective of Rachel Marsh, a 14-year-old indentured servant in the household of John and Abigail Adams.

See also Assessment Handbook, p. 119

Unit 1 Reading Log

Name _____

Dates Read	Title and Author	What is it about?	How would you rate it?	Explain your rating.
From _____ to _____			Great 5 4 3 2 1 Awful	
From _____ to _____			Great 5 4 3 2 1 Awful	
From _____ to _____			Great 5 4 3 2 1 Awful	
From _____ to _____			Great 5 4 3 2 1 Awful	
From _____ to _____			Great 5 4 3 2 1 Awful	

See also *Assessment Handbook*, p. 111

Unit 2 Narrative Retelling Chart

Selection Title ______________________ **Name** ______________________ **Date** __________

Retelling Criteria/Teacher Prompt	**Teacher-Aided Response**	**Student-Generated Response**	**Rubric Score** (Circle one.)
Connections Has anything like this happened to you? How does this story remind you of other stories?			4 3 2 1
Author's Purpose Why do you think the author wrote this story? What was the author trying to tell us?			4 3 2 1
Characters Describe ________ (character's name) at the beginning and end of the story.			4 3 2 1
Setting Where and when did the story happen?			4 3 2 1
Plot Tell me what the story was about in a few sentences.			4 3 2 1

Summative Retelling Score 4 3 2 1

Comments ____

See also Assessment Handbook, p. 112

Unit 2 Expository Retelling Chart

Name _____ Date _____

Selection Title _____

Retelling Criteria/Teacher Prompt	Teacher-Aided Response	Student-Generated Response	Rubric Score (Circle one.)		
Connections Did this selection make you think about something else you have read? What did you learn about as you read this selection?			4	3	2	1
Author's Purpose Why do you think the author wrote this selection?			4	3	2	1
Topic What was the selection mostly about?			4	3	2	1
Important Ideas What is important for me to know about _____ (topic)?			4	3	2	1
Conclusions What did you learn from reading this selection?			4	3	2	1

Summative Retelling Score   4   3   2   1

Comments _____

_____

Reading

Concepts of Print and Print Awareness	Pre-K	K	1	2	3	4	5	6
Develop awareness that print represents spoken language and conveys and preserves meaning	•	•	•					
Recognize familiar books by their covers; hold book right side up	•	•						
Identify parts of a book and their functions (front cover, title page/title, back cover, page numbers)	•	•	•					
Understand the concepts of letter, word, sentence, paragraph, and story	•	•	•					
Track print (front to back of book, top to bottom of page, left to right on line, sweep back left for next line)	•	•	•					
Match spoken to printed words	•	•	•					
Know capital and lowercase letter names and match them	•	• T	•					
Know the order of the alphabet	•	•	•					
Recognize first name in print	•	•	•					
Recognize the uses of capitalization and punctuation		•	•					
Value print as a means of gaining information	•	•	•					

Phonological and Phonemic Awareness	Pre-K	K	1	2	3	4	5	6
Phonological Awareness								
Recognize and produce rhyming words	•	•	•					
Track and count each word in a spoken sentence and each syllable in a spoken word	•	•	•					
Segment and blend syllables in spoken words			•					
Segment and blend onset and rime in one-syllable words		•	•					
Recognize and produce words beginning with the same sound	•	•	•					
Identify beginning, middle, and/or ending sounds that are the same or different	•	•	•					
Understand that spoken words are made of sequences of sounds	•	•	•					
Phonemic Awareness								
Identify the position of sounds in words		•	•					
Identify and isolate initial, final, and medial sounds in spoken words	•	•	•					
Blend sounds orally to make words or syllables		•	•					
Segment a word or syllable into sounds; count phonemes in spoken words or syllables		•	•					
Manipulate sounds in words (add, delete, and/or substitute phonemes)	•	•	•					

Phonics and Decoding	Pre-K	K	1	2	3	4	5	6
Phonics								
Understand and apply the *alphabetic principle* that spoken words are composed of sounds that are represented by letters	•	•	•					
Know letter-sound relationships	•	• T	• T	• T				
Blend sounds of letters to decode		•	• T	• T	• T			
Consonants, consonant blends, and consonant digraphs		•	• T	• T	• T			
Short, long, and r-controlled vowels; vowel digraphs; diphthongs; common vowel patterns			• T	• T	• T			
Phonograms/word families		•	•	•	•			
Word Structure								
Decode words with common word parts		•	• T	• T	• T	•	•	•
Base words and inflected endings			• T	• T	•	•	•	
Contractions and compound words			• T	• T	• T	•	•	
Suffixes and prefixes			• T	• T	• T	•	•	
Greek and Latin roots						•	•	
Blend syllables to decode words			• T	• T	• T	•	•	
Decoding Strategies								
Blending strategy: Apply knowledge of letter-sound relationships to decode unfamiliar words		•	•	•	•			
Apply knowledge of word structure to decode unfamiliar words		•	•	•	•	•	•	
Use context and syntax along with letter-sound relationships and word structure to decode		•	•	•	•	•	•	
Self-correct				•	•	•	•	

Fluency	Pre-K	K	1	2	3	4	5	6
Read aloud fluently with accuracy, comprehension, appropriate pace/rate; with expression/intonation (prosody); with attention to punctuation and appropriate phrasing			• T	• T	• T	• T	• T	
Practice fluency in a variety of ways, including choral reading, partner/paired reading, Readers' Theater, repeated oral reading, and tape-assisted reading		•	•	•	•	•	•	

• instructional opportunity   T tested in standardized test fo

	Pre-K	K	1	2	3	4	5	6
...ork toward appropriate fluency goals by the end of each grade			•T	•T	•T	•T	•T	•T
...ead regularly in independent-level material			•	•	•	•	•	•
...ead silently for increasing periods of time			•	•	•	•	•	•

Vocabulary (Oral and Written)

	Pre-K	K	1	2	3	4	5	6
Word Recognition								
...ecognize regular and irregular high-frequency words	•	•	•T	•T				
...ecognize and understand selection vocabulary		•	•	•T	•	•	•	•
...nderstand content-area vocabulary and specialized, technical, or topical words			•	•	•	•	•	•
Word Learning Strategies								
...evelop vocabulary through direct instruction, concrete experiences, reading, listening to text read aloud	•	•	•	•	•	•	•	•
...se knowledge of word structure to figure out meanings of words			•	•T	•T	•T	•T	•T
...se context clues for meanings of unfamiliar words, multiple-meaning words, homonyms, homographs			•	•T	•T	•T	•T	•T
...se grade-appropriate reference sources to learn word meanings	•	•	•	•	•T	•T	•T	•T
...se picture clues to help determine word meanings	•	•	•	•	•	•		
...se new words in a variety of contexts	•	•	•	•	•	•	•	•
...xamine word usage and effectiveness		•	•	•	•	•	•	•
...reate and use graphic organizers to group, study, and retain vocabulary		•	•	•	•	•	•	•
Extend Concepts and Word Knowledge								
...cademic language	•	•	•	•	•	•	•	•
...lassify and categorize	•	•	•	•	•	•	•	•
...ntonyms and synonyms			•	•T	•T	•T	•T	•T
...omographs, homonyms, and homophones				•	•T	•T	•T	•T
...ultiple-meaning words			•	•	•T	•T	•T	•T
...elated words and derivations					•	•	•	•
...nalogies					•		•	
...onnotation/denotation						•	•	•
...igurative language and idioms			•	•	•	•	•	•
...escriptive words (location, size, color, shape, number, ideas, feelings)	•	•	•	•	•	•	•	•
...igh-utility words (shapes, colors, question words, position/directional words, and so on)	•	•	•	•	•	•	•	•
...ime and order words	•	•	•	•	•	•	•	•
...ransition words						•	•	•
...ord origins: Etymologies/word histories; words from other languages, regions, or cultures						•	•	•
...hortened forms: abbreviations, acronyms, clipped words			•	•	•	•	•T	•

Text Comprehension

	Pre-K	K	1	2	3	4	5	6
Comprehension Strategies								
Preview the text and formulate questions		•	•	•	•	•	•	•
Set and monitor purpose for reading and listening		•	•	•	•	•	•	•
Activate and use prior knowledge		•	•	•	•	•	•	•
Make predictions		•	•	•	•	•	•	•
Monitor comprehension and use fix-up strategies to resolve difficulties in meaning: adjust reading rate, reread and read on, seek help from reference sources and/or other people, skim and scan, summarize, use text features				•	•	•	•	•
Create and use graphic and semantic organizers			•	•	•	•	•	•
Answer questions (text explicit, text implicit, scriptal), including *who, what, when, where, why, what if, how*	•	•	•	•	•	•	•	•
Look back in text for answers				•	•	•	•	•
Answer test-like questions			•	•	•	•	•	•
Generate clarifying questions, including *who, what, where, when, how, why,* and *what if*	•	•	•	•	•	•	•	•
Recognize text structure: story and informational (cause/effect, chronological, compare/contrast, description, problem/solution, propostion/support)	•	•	•	•	•	•	•	•
Summarize text			•	•	•	•	•	•
Recall and retell stories		•	•	•	•	•	•	•
Identify and retell important/main ideas (nonfiction)			•	•	•	•	•	•
Identify and retell new information			•	•	•	•	•	•
Visualize; use mental imagery			•	•	•	•	•	•
Use strategies flexibly and in combination			•	•	•	•	•	•

Comprehension Skills

Skill	Pre-K	K	1	2	3	4	5	6
Author's purpose			•T	•T	•T	•T	•T	•T
Author's viewpoint/bias/perspective					•	•	•	•T
Categorize and classify	•	•	•	•				
Cause and effect		•	•T	•T	•T	•T	•T	•T
Compare and contrast		•	•T	•T	•T	•T	•T	•T
Details and facts		•	•	•	•	•	•	•
Draw conclusions		•	•T	•T	•T	•T	•T	•T
Fact and opinion				•T	•T	•T	•T	•T
Follow directions/steps in a process	•	•	•	•	•	•	•	•
Generalize					•T	•T	•T	•T
Graphic sources		•	•	•		•T	•T	•T
Main idea and supporting details		•T	•T	•T	•T	•T	•T	•T
Paraphrase			•	•	•	•	•	•
Persuasive devices and propaganda			•	•	•	•	•	•
Realism/fantasy		•	•T	•T	•T			
Sequence of events		•T	•T	•T	•T	•T	•T	•T

Higher Order Thinking Skills

Skill	Pre-K	K	1	2	3	4	5	6
Analyze				•	•	•	•	•
Describe and connect the essential ideas, arguments, and perspectives of a text			•	•	•	•	•	•
Draw inferences, conclusions, or generalizations, support them with textual evidence and prior knowledge	•		•	•	•	•	•	•
Evaluate and critique ideas and text			•	•	•	•	•	•
Hypothesize						•	•	•
Make judgments about ideas and text			•	•	•	•	•	•
Organize and synthesize ideas and information			•			•	•	•

Literary Analysis, Response, & Appreciation

	Pre-K	K	1	2	3	4	5	6
Genre and Its Characteristics								
Recognize characteristics of a variety of genre	•	•	•	•	•	•	•	•
Distinguish fiction from nonfiction		•	•	•	•	•	•	•
Identify characteristics of literary texts, including drama, fantasy, traditional tales		•	•	•	•	•	•	•
Identify characteristics of nonfiction texts, including biography, interviews, newspaper articles		•	•	•	•	•	•	•
Identify characteristics of poetry and song, including nursery rhymes, limericks, blank verse	•	•	•	•	•	•	•	•

Literary Elements and Story Structure

	Pre-K	K	1	2	3	4	5	6
Character	•	•T	•T	•T	•T	•T	•T	
Recognize and describe traits, actions, feelings, and motives of characters		•	•	•	•	•	•	•
Analyze characters' relationships, changes, and points of view		•	•	•	•	•	•	•
Analyze characters' conflicts				•		•	•	•
Plot and plot structure	•	•T	•T	•T	•T	•T	•T	
Beginning, middle, end	•	•	•	•	•			
Goal and outcome or problem and solution/resolution		•		•	•	•	•	•
Rising action, climax, and falling action/denouement; setbacks						•	•	•
Setting	•	•T	•T	•T	•T	•T	•	•
Relate setting to problem/solution						•	•	•
Explain ways setting contributes to mood						•	•	•
Theme		•	•T	•T	•	•	•	•
Use Literary Elements and Story Structure	•	•	•	•	•	•	•	•
Analyze and evaluate author's use of setting, plot, character				•	•	•	•	•
Identify similarities and differences of characters, events, and settings within or across selections/cultures	•	•	•	•	•	•	•	•

Literary Devices

	Pre-K	K	1	2	3	4	5	6
Allusion								•
Dialect						•	•	•
Dialogue and narration	•	•	•	•	•	•	•	•
Exaggeration/hyperbole						•	•	•
Figurative language: idiom, jargon, metaphor, simile, slang			•	•	•	•	•	•

• instructional opportunity   **T** tested in standardized test for

	Pre-K	K	1	2	3	4	5	6
nback						•	•	•
shadowing							•	•
al and informal language				•	•	•	•	•
or					•	•	•	•
gery and sensory words				•	•	•	•	•
d				•	•		•	•
onification				•	•	•	•	•
t of view (first person, third person, omniscient)					•	•	•	•
s and word play				•	•	•	•	•
nd devices and poetic elements	•	•	•	•	•	•	•	•
iteration, assonance, onomatopoeia	•	•	•	•	•	•	•	•
yme, rhythm, repetition, and cadence	•	•	•	•	•	•	•	•
rd choice				•	•	•	•	•
bolism				•	•	•	•	•
e							•	•

thor's and Illustrator's Craft

	Pre-K	K	1	2	3	4	5	6
nguish the roles of author and illustrator		•	•	•				
ognize/analyze author's and illustrator's craft or style		•	•	•	•	•	•	•

erary Response

	Pre-K	K	1	2	3	4	5	6
ollect, talk, and write about books	•	•	•	•	•	•	•	•
ect on reading and respond (through talk, movement, art, and so on)	•	•	•	•	•	•	•	•
sk and answer questions about text	•	•	•	•	•	•	•	•
rite about what is read	•	•	•	•	•	•	•	•
se evidence from the text to support opinions, interpretations, or conclusions				•	•	•	•	•
upport ideas through reference to other texts and personal knowledge				•	•	•	•	•
cate materials on related topic, theme, or idea				•	•	•	•	•
enerate alternative endings to plots and identify the reason for, and the impact of, the alternatives	•	•	•	•	•	•	•	•
thesize and extend the literary experience through creative responses	•	•	•	•	•	•	•	•
e connections: text to self, text to text, text to world	•	•	•	•	•	•	•	•
uate and critique the quality of the literary experience				•	•	•	•	•
r observations, react, speculate in response to text				•	•	•	•	•

erary Appreciation/Motivation

	Pre-K	K	1	2	3	4	5	6
w an interest in books and reading; engage voluntarily in social interaction about books	•	•	•	•	•	•	•	•
ose text by drawing on personal interests, relying on knowledge of authors and genres, estimating text culty, and using recommendations of others	•	•	•	•	•	•	•	•
d a variety of grade-level appropriate narrative and expository texts		•	•	•	•	•	•	•
d from a wide variety of genres for a variety of purposes	•	•	•	•	•	•	•	•
d independently		•	•	•	•	•	•	•
ablish familiarity with a topic		•	•	•	•	•	•	•

ltural Awareness

	Pre-K	K	1	2	3	4	5	6
elop attitudes and abilities to interact with diverse groups and cultures	•	•	•	•	•	•	•	•
nnect experiences and ideas with those from a variety of languages, cultures, customs, perspectives	•	•	•	•	•	•	•	•
derstand how attitudes and values in a culture or during a period in time affect the writing from that ure or time period						•	•	•
npare language and oral traditions (family stories) that reflect customs, regions, and cultures		•	•	•	•	•	•	•
ognize themes that cross cultures and bind them together in their common humanness						•	•	•

nguage Arts

riting	Pre-K	K	1	2	3	4	5	6

ncepts of Print for Writing

	Pre-K	K	1	2	3	4	5	6
velop gross and fine motor skills and hand/eye coordination	•	•	•					
t own name and other important words	•	•	•					
te using pictures, some letters, and transitional spelling to convey meaning	•	•	•					
tate messages or stories for others to write	•	•	•					

	Pre-K	K	1	2	3	4	5	6
Create own written texts for others to read; write left to right on a line and top to bottom on a page	•	•	•					
Participate in shared and interactive writing	•	•	•					

Traits of Writing

Focus/Ideas

	Pre-K	K	1	2	3	4	5	6
Maintain focus and sharpen ideas		•	•	•	•	•	•	
Use sensory details and concrete examples; elaborate		•	•	•	•	•	•	
Delete extraneous information			•	•	•	•	•	
Rearrange words and sentences to improve meaning and focus				•	•	•	•	
Use strategies, such as tone, style, consistent point of view, to achieve a sense of completeness						•	•	

Organization/Paragraphs

	Pre-K	K	1	2	3	4	5	6
Use graphic organizers to group ideas		•	•	•	•	•	•	
Write coherent paragraphs that develop a central idea			•	•	•	•	•	
Use transitions to connect sentences and paragraphs			•	•	•	•	•	
Select an organizational structure based on purpose, audience, length						•	•	
Organize ideas in a logical progression, such as chronological order or by order of importance		•	•	•	•	•	•	
Write introductory, supporting, and concluding paragraphs					•	•	•	
Write a multi-paragraph paper				•	•	•	•	

Voice

	Pre-K	K	1	2	3	4	5	6
Develop personal, identifiable voice and an individual tone/style			•	•	•	•	•	
Maintain consistent voice and point of view						•	•	
Use voice appropriate to audience, message, and purpose						•	•	

Word Choice

	Pre-K	K	1	2	3	4	5	6
Use clear, precise, appropriate language		•	•	•	•	•	•	
Use figurative language and vivid words				•	•	•	•	
Select effective vocabulary using word walls, dictionary, or thesaurus		•	•	•	•	•	•	

Sentences

	Pre-K	K	1	2	3	4	5	6
Combine, elaborate, and vary sentences		•	•	•	•	•	•	
Write topic sentence, supporting sentences with facts and details, and concluding sentence			•	•	•	•	•	
Use correct word order				•	•	•	•	
Use parallel structure in a sentence							•	

Conventions

	Pre-K	K	1	2	3	4	5	6
Use correct spelling and grammar; capitalize and punctuate correctly		•	•	•	•	•	•	
Correct sentence fragments and run-ons					•	•	•	
Use correct paragraph indention				•	•	•	•	

The Writing Process

	Pre-K	K	1	2	3	4	5	6
Prewrite using various strategies	•	•	•	•	•	•	•	
Develop first drafts of single- and multiple-paragraph compositions		•	•	•	•	•	•	
Revise drafts for varied purposes, including to clarify and to achieve purpose, sense of audience, precise word choice, vivid images, and elaboration		•	•	•	•	•	•	
Edit and proofread for correct spelling, grammar, usage, and mechanics		•	•	•	•	•	•	
Publish own work	•	•	•	•	•	•	•	

Types of Writing

	Pre-K	K	1	2	3	4	5	6
Narrative writing (such as personal narratives, stories, biographies, autobiographies)	•	•	• T	• T	• T	• T	• T	•
Expository writing (such as essays, directions, explanations, news stories, research reports, summaries)		•	• T	• T	• T	• T	• T	•
Descriptive writing (such as labels, captions, lists, plays, poems, response logs, songs)	•	•	• T	• T	• T	• T	• T	•
Persuasive writing (such as ads, editorials, essays, letters to the editor, opinions, posters)		•	• T	• T	• T	• T	• T	•

Writing Habits and Practices

	Pre-K	K	1	2	3	4	5	6
Write on a daily basis	•	•	•	•	•	•	•	
Use writing as a tool for learning and self-discovery				•	•	•	•	
Write independently for extended periods of time			•	•	•	•	•	

ENGLISH LANGUAGE CONVENTIONS in WRITING and SPEAKING	Pre-K	K	1	2	3	4	5	

Grammar and Usage in Speaking and Writing

Sentences

	Pre-K	K	1	2	3	4	5	6
Types (declarative, interrogative, exclamatory, imperative)	•	•	• T	• T	• T	• T	• T	
Structure (simple, compound, complex, compound-complex)	•	•	•	•	•	• T	• T	

• instructional opportunity   **T** tested in standardized test f

	Pre-K	K	1	2	3	4	5	6
rts (subjects/predicates: complete, simple, compound; phrases; clauses)			•T	•	•T	•T	•T	•T
agments and run-on sentences		•	•	•	•	•	•	•
ombine sentences, elaborate				•	•	•	•	•
s of speech: nouns, verbs and verb tenses, adjectives, adverbs, pronouns and antecedents, unctions, prepositions, interjections		•	•T	•T	•T	•T	•T	•T
ge								
bject-verb agreement		•	•T	•	•	•T	•T	•T
onoun agreement/referents			•T	•	•	•T	•T	•T
splaced modifiers						•	•T	•T
sused words					•	•	•	•T
egatives; avoid double negatives					•	•	•	•

chanics in Writing

	Pre-K	K	1	2	3	4	5	6
talization (first word in sentence, proper nouns and adjectives, pronoun *I*, titles, and so on)	•	•	•T	•T	•T	•T	•T	•T
ctuation (apostrophe, comma, period, question mark, exclamation mark, quotation marks, and so on)		•	•T	•T	•T	•T	•T	•T

elling

	Pre-K	K	1	2	3	4	5	6
ll independently by using pre-phonetic knowledge, knowledge of letter names, sound-letter knowledge	•	•	•	•	•	•	•	•
sound-letter knowledge to spell	•	•	•	•	•	•	•	•
onsonants: single, double, blends, digraphs, silent letters, and unusual consonant spellings		•	•	•	•	•	•	•
wels: short, long, *r*-controlled, digraphs, diphthongs, less common vowel patterns, schwa		•	•	•	•	•	•	•
knowledge of word structure to spell			•	•	•	•	•	•
se words and affixes (inflections, prefixes, suffixes), possessives, contractions and compound words			•	•	•	•	•	•
eek and Latin roots, syllable patterns, multisyllabic words			•	•	•	•	•	•
ll high-frequency, irregular words		•	•	•	•	•	•	•
ll frequently misspelled words correctly, including homophones or homonyms			•	•	•	•	•	•
meaning relationships to spell					•	•	•	•

ndwriting

	Pre-K	K	1	2	3	4	5	6
n increasing control of penmanship, including pencil grip, paper position, posture, stroke	•	•	•	•				
e legibly, with control over letter size and form; letter slant; and letter, word, and sentence spacing		•	•	•	•	•		•
e lowercase and capital letters	•	•	•	•				
anuscript	•	•	•	•	•	•	•	•
ursive				•	•	•	•	•
e numerals	•	•	•					

stening and Speaking

	Pre-K	K	1	2	3	4	5	6
tening Skills and Strategies								
en to a variety of presentations attentively and politely	•	•	•	•	•	•	•	•
-monitor comprehension while listening, using a variety of skills and strategies	•	•	•	•	•	•	•	•
en for a purpose								
r enjoyment and appreciation	•	•	•	•	•	•	•	•
expand vocabulary and concepts	•	•	•	•	•	•	•	•
obtain information and ideas	•	•	•	•	•	•	•	•
follow oral directions	•	•	•	•	•	•	•	•
answer questions and solve problems	•	•	•	•	•	•	•	•
participate in group discussions	•	•	•	•	•	•	•	•
identify and analyze the musical elements of literary language	•	•	•	•	•	•	•	•
gain knowledge of one's own culture, the culture of others, and the common elements of cultures	•	•	•	•	•	•	•	•
ognize formal and informal language				•	•	•	•	•
en critically to distinguish fact from opinion and to analyze and evaluate ideas, information, experiences		•						
luate a speaker's delivery				•	•	•	•	•
rpret a speaker's purpose, perspective, persuasive techniques, verbal and nonverbal messages, and of rhetorical devices					•	•	•	•
eaking Skills and Strategies								
ak clearly, accurately, and fluently, using appropriate delivery for a variety of audiences, and purposes	•	•	•	•	•	•	•	•
proper intonation, volume, pitch, modulation, and phrasing		•	•	•	•	•	•	•
ak with a command of standard English conventions	•	•	•	•	•	•	•	•
appropriate language for formal and informal settings	•	•	•	•	•	•	•	•

	Pre-K	K	1	2	3	4	5
Speak for a purpose							
To ask and answer questions	•	•	•	•	•	•	•
To give directions and instructions	•	•	•	•	•	•	•
To retell, paraphrase, or explain information		•	•	•	•	•	•
To communicate needs and share ideas and experiences	•	•	•	•	•	•	•
To participate in conversations and discussions	•	•	•	•	•	•	•
To express an opinion	•	•	•	•	•	•	•
To deliver dramatic recitations, interpretations, or performances	•	•	•	•	•	•	•
To deliver presentations or oral reports (narrative, descriptive, persuasive, and informational)	•	•	•	•	•	•	•
Stay on topic	•	•	•	•	•		
Use appropriate verbal and nonverbal elements (such as facial expression, gestures, eye contact, posture)	•	•	•	•	•	•	•
Identify and/or demonstrate methods to manage or overcome communication anxiety						•	•

Viewing/Media	Pre-K	K	1	2	3	4	5
Interact with and respond to a variety of print and non-print media for a range of purposes	•	•	•	•	•	•	•
Compare and contrast print, visual, and electronic media					•	•	•
Analyze and evaluate media			•	•	•	•	•
Recognize purpose, bias, propaganda, and persuasive techniques in media messages			•	•	•	•	•

Research and Study Skills

Understand and Use Graphic Sources	Pre-K	K	1	2	3	4	5
Advertisement			•	•	•	•	•
Chart/table	•	•	•	•	•	•	•
Diagram/scale drawing			•	•	•	•	•
Graph (bar, circle, line, picture)			•	•	•	•	•
Illustration, photograph, caption, label	•	•	•	•	•	•	•
Map/globe	•	•	•	•	•	•	•
Order form/application						•	•
Poster/announcement	•	•	•	•	•	•	•
Schedule						•	•
Sign	•	•	•	•		•	
Time line				•	•	•	•

Understand and Use Reference Sources	Pre-K	K	1	2	3	4	5
Know and use parts of a book to locate information	•	•	•	•	•	•	•
Use alphabetical order			•	•	•	•	
Understand purpose, structure, and organization of reference sources (print, electronic, media, Internet)	•	•	•	•	•	•	•
Almanac						•	•
Atlas		•		•	•	•	•
Card catalog/library database				•	•	•	•
Dictionary/glossary		•	•	•	• T	• T	• T
Encyclopedia			•	•	•	•	•
Magazine/periodical				•	•	•	•
Newspaper and Newsletter			•	•	•	•	•
Readers' Guide to Periodical Literature						•	•
Technology (computer and non-computer electronic media)		•	•	•	•	•	•
Thesaurus				•	•	•	•

Study Skills and Strategies	Pre-K	K	1	2	3	4	5
Adjust reading rate			•	•	•	•	•
Clarify directions	•	•	•	•	•	•	•
Outline				•	•	•	•
Skim and scan			•	•	•	•	•
SQP3R						•	•
Summarize		•	•	•	•	•	•
Take notes, paraphrase, and synthesize			•	•	•	•	•
Use graphic and semantic organizers to organize information		•	•	•	•	•	•

• instructional opportunity   **T** tested in standardized test fo

st-Taking Skills and Strategies	Pre-K	K	1	2	3	4	5	6
...erstand the question, the vocabulary of tests, and key words			•	•	•	•	•	•
...wer the question; use information from the text (stated or inferred)		•	•	•	•	•	•	•
...e across texts			•	•	•	•	•	•
...plete the sentence			•	•	•	•	•	•

chnology/New Literacies	Pre-K	K	1	2	3	4	5	6
n-Computer Electronic Media								
...o tapes/CDs, video tapes/DVDs	•	•	•	•	•	•	•	
..., television, and radio		•	•	•	•	•	•	•
mputer Programs and Services: Basic Operations and Concepts								
...accurate computer terminology	•	•	•	•	•	•	•	•
...ate, name, locate, open, save, delete, and organize files		•	•	•	•	•	•	•
...input and output devices (such as mouse, keyboard, monitor, printer, touch screen)	•	•	•	•	•	•	•	•
...basic keyboarding skills		•	•	•		•	•	•
ponsible Use of Technology Systems and Software								
...k cooperatively and collaboratively with others; follow acceptable use policies	•	•	•	•	•	•	•	•
...ognize hazards of Internet searches		•	•	•	•	•	•	•
...pect intellectual property					•	•	•	•
ormation and Communication Technologies: Information Acquisition								
...electronic web (non-linear) navigation, online resources, databases, keyword searches			•	•	•	•	•	•
...visual and non-textual features of online resources	•	•	•	•	•	•	•	•
...rnet inquiry			•	•	•	•	•	•
...entify questions			•	•	•	•	•	•
...ocate, select, and collect information			•	•	•	•	•	•
...alyze information			•	•	•	•	•	•
...Evaluate electronic information sources for accuracy, relevance, bias					•	•	•	•
...Understand bias/subjectivity of electronic content (about this site, author search, date created)						•	•	•
...nthesize information						•	•	•
...ommunicate findings			•	•	•	•	•	•
...fix-up strategies (such as clicking *Back, Forward,* or *Undo;* redoing a search; trimming the URL)			•	•	•	•	•	•
nmunication								
...aborate, publish, present, and interact with others		•	•	•	•	•	•	•
...online resources (e-mail, bulletin boards, newsgroups)			•	•	•	•	•	•
...a variety of multimedia formats			•	•	•	•	•	•
blem Solving								
...ect the appropriate software for the task	•	•	•	•	•	•	•	•
...technology resources for solving problems and making informed decisions			•	•	•	•	•	•
...ermine when technology is useful					•	•	•	•

e Research Process	Pre-K	K	1	2	3	4	5	6
...ose and narrow the topic; frame and revise questions for inquiry		•	•	•	•	•	•	•
...ose and evaluate appropriate reference sources		•	•	•	•	•	•	•
...ate and collect information	•	•	•	•	•	•	•	•
...e notes/record findings				•	•	•	•	•
...nbine and compare information				•	•	•	•	•
...luate, interpret, and draw conclusions about key information		•	•	•	•	•	•	•
...nmarize information		•	•	•	•	•	•	•
...ke an outline				•	•	•	•	•
...anize content systematically		•	•	•	•	•	•	•
...nmunicate information			•	•	•	•	•	•
...rite and present a report			•	•	•	•	•	•
...Include citations						•	•	•
...Respect intellectual property/plagiarism						•	•	•
...elect and organize visual aids		•	•	•	•	•	•	•

A

Abbreviations. *See* **Vocabulary strategies.**

Accountability. *See* **Adequate yearly progress.**

Achieving English proficiency. *See* **ELL (English Language Learners) suggestions.**

Acronyms. *See* **Vocabulary strategies.**

Activate prior knowledge. *See* **Prereading strategies.**

Adequate yearly progress (AYP), 5.1 16g–16h, 5.2 140g–140h, 5.3 260g–260h, 5.4 390g–390h, 5.5 510g–540h, 5.6 632g–632h

Adjectives, 5.5 559e–559f, 581e–581f, 5.6 653e–653f

articles, 5.5 559e–559f

comparative and superlative, 5.5 603e–603f

Advanced learners

group time, 5.1 18f–18g, 42f–42g, 68f–68g, 90f–90g, 112f–112g, DI·3, DI·5, DI·7, DI·9, DI·11, DI·13, DI·15, DI·17, DI·19, DI·21, DI·23, DI·25, DI·27, DI·29, DI·31, DI·33, DI·35, DI·37, DI·39, DI·41, DI·43, DI·45, DI·47, DI·49, DI·51, 5.2 142f–142g, 162f–162g, 186f–186g, 208f–208g, 230f–230g, DI·3, DI·5, DI·7, DI·9, DI·11, DI·13, DI·15, DI·17, DI·19, DI·21, DI·23, DI·25, DI·27, DI·29, DI·31, DI·33, DI·35, DI·37, DI·39, DI·41, DI·43, DI·45, DI·47, DI·49, DI·51, 5.3 262f–262g, 288f–288g, 316f–316g, 346f–346g, 364f–364g, DI·3, DI·5, DI·7, DI·9, DI·11, DI·13, DI·15, DI·17, DI·19, DI·21, DI·23, DI·25, DI·27, DI·29, DI·31, DI·33, DI·35, DI·37, DI·39, DI·41, DI·43, DI·45, DI·47, DI·49, DI·51, 5.4 392f–392g, 412f–412g, 436f–436g, 458f–458g, 484f–484g, DI·3, DI·5, DI·7, DI·9, DI·11, DI·13, DI·15, DI·17, DI·19, DI·21, DI·23, DI·25, DI·27, DI·29, DI·31, DI·33, DI·35, DI·37, DI·39, DI·41, DI·43, DI·45, DI·47, DI·49, DI·51, 5.5 512f–512g, 536f–536g, 560f–560g, 582f–582g, 604f–604g, DI·3, DI·5, DI·7, DI·9, DI·11, DI·13, DI·15, DI·17, DI·19, DI·21, DI·23, DI·25, DI·27, DI·29, DI·31, DI·33, DI·35, DI·37, DI·39, DI·41, DI·43, DI·45, DI·47, DI·49, DI·51, 5.6 634f–634g, 654f–654g, 674f–674g, 700f–700g, 726f–726g, DI·3, DI·5, DI·7, DI·9, DI·11, DI·13, DI·15, DI·17, DI·19, DI·21, DI·23, DI·25, DI·27, DI·29, DI·31, DI·33, DI·35, DI·37, DI·39, DI·41, DI·43, DI·45, DI·47, DI·49, DI·51. *See also* **Grouping students for instruction.**

leveled readers, 5.1 LR7–LR9, LR16–LR18, LR25–LR27, LR34–LR36, LR43–LR45, 5.2 LR7–LR9, LR16–LR18, LR25–LR27, LR34–LR36, LR43–LR45, 5.3 LR7–LR9, LR16–LR18, LR25–LR27, LR34–LR36, LR43–LR45, 5.4 LR7–LR9, LR16–LR18, LR25–LR27, LR34–LR36, LR43–LR45, 5.5 LR7–LR9, LR16–LR18, LR25–LR27, LR34–LR36, LR43–LR45, 5.6 LR7–LR9, LR16–LR18, LR25–LR27, LR34–LR36, LR43–LR45

resources, 5.1 18g, 42g, 68g, 90g, 112g, 5.2 142g, 162g, 186g, 208g, 230g, 5.3 262g, 288g, 316g, 346g, 364g, 5.4 392g, 412g, 436g, 458g, 484g, 5.5 512g, 536g, 560g, 582g, 604g, 5.6 634g, 654g, 674g, 700g, 726g

writing, 5.1 WA9, 5.2 WA9, 5.3 WA9, 5.4 WA9, 5.5 WA9, 5.6 WA9

Adventure fiction. *See* **Genres.**

Adverbs, 5.5 625e–625f, 5.6 653e–653f

Advertisement. *See* **Graphic sources.**

Affective domain. *See* **Habits and attitudes, Literary response and appreciation.**

Affixes. *See* **Spelling,** word structure; **Word structure,** prefixes, suffixes.

Almanac. *See* **Reference sources.**

Alphabetical order, 5.1 70, 5.2 162–163, 5.5 536–537, 549, 5.6 634–635, 645

Analyzing. *See* **Reading across texts.** In addition, analytical thinking questions are raised throughout Guiding Comprehension and Reader Response.

Analogy. *See* **Vocabulary strategies.**

Answering questions. *See* **Questions, answering.**

Antonyms, 5.1 20b, 92–93, 5.3 348b, 348–349, 363c, 5.4 394b, 5.5 514b, 584b. *See also* **Vocabulary strategies.**

Apostrophe, 5.2 185e–185f, 5.5 535e–535f

Appreciating literature. *See* **Literary response and appreciation.**

Appropriate word meaning, 5.1 114–115, 133c, 5.2 164b, 5.3 264–265, 275, 287, 348b, 5.4 414b, 460b, 5.5 514b, 562–563, 581c

Art activities. *See* **Cross-curricular activities.**

Art, interpreting. *See* **Literary craft,** illustrator's craft/style.

Asking questions. *See* **Questions, asking.**

Assessment

classroom-based. "If/then" assessment occurs throughout lessons and Guiding Comprehension.

formal, 5.1 35, 41h, 41j, 65, 67h, 67j, 85, 89h, 89j, 109, 111h, 111j, 129, 133h, 133j, 134a, WA7, WA10–WA14, 5.2 159, 161h, 161j, 179, 185h, 185j, 205, 207h, 207j, 225, 229h, 229j, 249, 253h, 253j, 254a, WA7, WA10–WA14, 5.3 281, 287h, 287j, 311, 315h, 315j, 339, 345h, 345j, 359, 363h, 363j, 379, 383h, 383j, 384a, WA7, WA10–WA14, 5.4 409, 411h, 411j, 433, 435h, 435j, 453, 457h, 457j, 479, 483h, 483j, 499, 503h, 503j, 504a, WA7, WA10–WA14, 5.5 531, 535h, 535j, 553, 559h, 559j, 577, 581h, 581j, 599, 603h, 603j, 621, 625h, 625j, 626a, WA7, WA10–WA14, 5.6 651, 653h, 653j, 669, 673h, 673j, 697, 699h, 699j, 721, 725h, 725j, 749, 753h, 753j, 754a, WA7, WA10–WA14,

fluency, 5.1 41a, 67a, 89a, 111a, 133a, WA15–WA16, DI·59–DI·60, 5.2 161a, 185a, 207a, 229a, 253a, WA15–WA16, DI·59–DI·60, 5.3 287a, 315a, 345a, 363a, 383a, WA15–WA16, DI·59–DI·60, 5.4 411a, 435a, 457a, 483a, 503a, WA15–WA16, DI·59–DI·60, 5.5 535a, 559a, 581a, 603a, 625a, WA15–WA16, DI·59–DI·60, 5.6 653a, 673a, 699a, 725a, 753a, WA15–WA16, DI·59–DI·60

scoring guide (rubric), 5.1 34, 35, 41h, 64, 65, 67h, 84, 85, 89h, 108, 109, 111h, 128, 129, 133h, 134a, WA7, WA10–WA14, 5.2 158, 159, 161h, 178, 179, 185h, 204, 205, 207h,

224, 225, 229h, 248, 249, 253h, 254a, WA7, WA10–WA14, 5.3 280, 281, 287h, 310, 311, 315h, 338, 339, 345h, 358, 359, 363h, 378, 379, 383h, 384a, WA7, WA10–WA14, 5.4 408, 409, 411h, 432, 433, 435h, 452, 453, 457h, 478, 479, 483h, 498, 499, 503h, 504a, WA7, WA10–WA14, 5.5 530, 531, 535h, 552, 553, 559h, 576, 577, 581h, 598, 599, 603h, 620, 621, 625h, 626a, WA7, WA10–WA14, 5.6 650, 651, 653h, 668, 669, 673h, 696, 697, 699h, 720, 721, 725h, 748, 749, 753h, 754a, WA7, WA10–WA14

self-assessment, 5.1 41h, 67h, 89h, 111h, 133h, WA7, 5.2 161h, 185h, 207h, 229h, 253h, WA7, 5.3 287h, 315h, 345h, 363h, 383h, WA7, 5.4 411h, 435h, 457h, 483h, 503h, WA7, 5.5 535h, 559h, 581h, 603h, 625h, WA7, 5.6 653h, 673h, 699h, 725h, 753h, WA7

spelling, 5.1 41j, 67j, 89j, 111j, 133j, 5.2 161j, 185j, 207j, 229j, 253j, 5.3 287j, 315j, 345j, 363j, 383j, 5.4 411j, 435j, 457j, 483j, 503j, 5.5 535j, 559j, 581j, 603j, 625j, 5.6 653j, 673j, 699j, 725j, 753j

test-taking strategies, 5.1 34, 64, 84, 108, 128, 133h, 5.2 158, 178, 204, 224, 248, 253h, 5.3 280, 310, 338, 358, 378, 383h, 5.4 408, 432, 452, 478, 498, 503h, 5.5 530, 552, 576, 598, 620, 5.6 650, 668, 696, 720, 748

writing, 5.1 WA7, WA10–WA14, 5.2 WA7, WA10–WA14, 5.3 WA7, WA10–WA14, 5.4 WA7, WA10–WA14, 5.5 WA7, WA10–WA14, 5.6 WA7, WA10–WA14

Atlas. *See* **Reference sources.**

Attitudes, personal. *See* **Habits and attitudes.**

Authors (of reading selections)

Aesop, 5.2 206–207

Alexander, Sally Hobart, 5.4 434–435

Archbold, Rich, 5.5 540–551

Asch, Frank, 5.6 755

Ballard, Robert D., 5.1 139f, 5.5 540–551

Baylor, Byrd, 5.4 506

Bial, Raymond, 5.5 608–619

Biron, Debora, 5.2 180–185

Brooks, Gwendolyn, 5.4 411

Buckley, Susan, 5.5 622–625

Carter, Alden, 5.4 416–431

Clements, Andrew, 5.1 22–33

Cline-Ransome, Lena, 5.1 94–107

Craft, Charlotte, 5.6 678–695

Delacre, Lulu, 5.4 638–649

Diamond, Lydia R., 5.4 462–477

Dickenson, Emily, 5.2 257

Fang, Linda, 5.1 139f, 5.2 190–203

Fisher, Lillian M., 5.4 507

Fleischman, Paul, 5.4 396–407

Floriatt, Douglas, 5.3 386

Fritz, Jean, 5.1 139d, 5.3 292–309

George, Kristine O'Connell, 5.4 504

Giovanni, Nikki, 5.4 505

Goodall, Jane, 5.2 212–223

Hamilton, Jake, 5.3 368–377

Hamilton, Virginia, 5.4 410

Herford, Oliver, 5.3 387

Hill, Donna, 5.5 554–559

Hopkinson, Deborah, 5.1 116–127, 139h

Jiménez, Francisco, 5.1 139j, 5.2 146–157

Johnson, Georgia Douglas, 5.5 626

Kerley, Barbara, 5.1 139d, 5.3 320–337

Klages, Ellen, 5.1 110–111

Independent reading, 5.1 18f–18g, 18j, 42f–42g, 42j, 68f–68g, 68j, 90f–90g, 90j, 112f–112g, 112j, TR14, 5.2 142f–142g, 142j, 162f–162g, 162j, 186f–186g, 186j, 208f–208g, 208j, 230f–230g, 230j, TR14, 5.3 262f–262g, 262j, 288f–288g, 288j, 316f–316g, 316j, 346f–346g, 346j, 364f–364g, 364j, TR14, 5.4 392f–392g, 392j, 412f–412g, 412j, 436f–436g, 436j, 458f–458g, 458j, 484f–484g, 484j, TR14, 5.5 512f–512g, 512j, 536f–536g, 536j, 560f–560g, 560j, 582f–582g, 582j, 604f–604g, 604j, TR14, 5.6 634f–634g, 634j, 654f–654g, 654j, 674f–674g, 674j, 700f–700g, 700j, 726f–726g, 726j, TR14. See also **Bibliography,** self-selected reading.

Inductive reasoning, 5.6 662. See also **Critical thinking.**

Inferences. See **Author's purpose; Cause and effect; Comparing and contrasting; Conclusions, drawing; Fact and opinion, statements of; Generalizations, making; Predicting; Summarizing.** In addition, inferential thinking questions appear throughout Guiding Comprehension in each lesson.

Inflected endings. See **Spelling,** word structure; **Word structure.**

Informal assessment. See **Assessment.**

Informational article. See **Genres.**

Integrated curriculum. See **Cross-curricular activities.**

Interjections, 5.1 41e

Internet (as reference source). See **New literacies (for student reading), Reference sources, Technology.**

Internet article. See **Genres.**

Intervention
  author's purpose, 5.2 162, 5.3 262, 5.5 560
  cause and effect, 5.1 42, 112 5.5 582
  character, 5.1 18, 5.5 512
  compare and contrast, 5.2 142, 186, 5.6 674
  conclusions, draw, 5.4 392, 484, 5.6 634
  context clues, 5.1 44, 92, 114, 5.2 210, 5.3 264, 318, 348, 5.4 414, 438, 460, 5.5 562, 5.6 702, 728
  dictionary/glossary, 5.1 70, 5.2 164, 5.5 538, 5.6 636
  English language learners. See **ELL (English language learners) suggestions.**
  fact and opinion, 5.2 208, 5.3 316, 5.6 700
  generalize, 5.4 412, 458, 5.5 604
  graphic sources, 5.3 364, 5.4 436, 5.5 536
  Greek and Latin roots, 5.5 514
  group time, 5.1 18f–18g, 42f–42g, 68f–68g, 90f–90g, 112f–112g, DI·2, DI·4, DI·6, DI·8, DI·10, DI·12, DI·14, DI·16, DI·18, DI·20, DI·22, DI·24, DI·26, DI·28, DI·30, DI·32, DI·34, DI·36, DI·38, DI·40, DI·42, DI·44, DI·46, DI·48, DI·50, 5.2 142f–142g, 162f–162g, 186f–186g, 208f–208g, 230f–230g, DI·2, DI·4, DI·6, DI·8, DI·10, DI·12, DI·14, DI·16, DI·18, DI·20, DI·22, DI·24, DI·26, DI·28, DI·30,

DI·32, DI·34, DI·36, DI·38, DI·40, DI·42, DI·44, DI·46, DI·48, DI·50, 5.3 262f–262g, 288f–288g, 316f–316g, 346f–346g, 364f–364g, DI·2, DI·4, DI·6, DI·8, DI·10, DI·12, DI·14, DI·16, DI·18, DI·20, DI·22, DI·24, DI·26, DI·28, DI·30, DI·32, DI·34, DI·36, DI·38, DI·40, DI·42, DI·44, DI·46, DI·48, DI·50, 5.4 392f–392g, 412f–412g, 436f–436g, 458f–458g, 484f–484g, DI·2, DI·4, DI·6, DI·8, DI·10, DI·12, DI·14, DI·16, DI·18, DI·20, DI·22, DI·24, DI·26, DI·28, DI·30, DI·32, DI·34, DI·36, DI·38, DI·40, DI·42, DI·44, DI·46, DI·48, DI·50, 5.5 512f–512g,536f–536g, 560f–560g, 582f–582g, 604f–604g, DI·2, DI·4, DI·6, DI·8, DI·10, DI·12, DI·14, DI·16, DI·18, DI·20, DI·22, DI·24, DI·26, DI·28, DI·30, DI·32, DI·34, DI·36, DI·38, DI·40, DI·42, DI·44, DI·46, DI·48, DI·50, 5.6 634f–634g, 654f–654g, 674f–674g, 700f–700g, 726f–726g, DI·2, DI·4, DI·6, DI·8, DI·10, DI·12, DI·14, DI·16, DI·18, DI·20, DI·22, DI·24, DI·26, DI·28, DI·30, DI·32, DI·34, DI·36, DI·38, DI·40, DI·42, DI·44, DI·46, DI·48, DI·50. See also **Grouping students for instruction.**
  leveled readers, 5.1 LR1–LR3, LR10–LR12, LR19–LR21, LR28–LR30, LR38–LR39, 5.2 LR1–LR3, LR10–LR12, LR19–LR21, LR28–LR30, LR38– LR39, 5.3 LR1–LR3, LR10–LR12, LR19–LR21, LR28–LR30, LR38–LR39, 5.4 LR1–LR3, LR10–LR12, LR19–LR21, LR28–LR30, LR38– LR39, 5.5 LR1–LR3, LR10–LR12, LR19–LR21, LR28–LR30, LR38–LR39, 5.6 LR1–LR3, LR10–LR12, LR19–LR21, LR28–LR30, LR38– LR39
  main idea, 5.3 288, 346, 5.6 654
  plot, 5.1 18, 5.5 512
  resources for, 5.1 18f, 42f, 68f, 90f, 112f, 5.2 142f, 162f, 186f, 208f, 230f, 5.3 262f, 288f, 316f, 346f, 364f, 5.4 392f, 412f, 436f, 458f, 484f, 5.5 512f, 536f, 560f, 582f, 604f, 5.6 634f, 654f, 674f, 700f, 726f
  sequence, 5.1 90 5.2 230, 5.6 726
  setting, 5.1 68
  theme, 5.1 68
  word structure, 5.1 20, 5.2 144, 188, 232, 5.3 290, 366, 5.4 394, 486, 5.5 606, 5.6 656, 676
  writing support, 5.1 WA8, 5.2 WA8, 5.3 WA8, 5.4 WA8, 5.5 WA8, 5.6 WA8

Interview. See **Genres; Speaking,** activities.

Italics, 5.6 753e–753f

J

Jargon. See **Literary devices.**

Journal. See **Genres; Logs, strategy response; Writing forms/products.**

Judgments, making. See **Author's purpose; Conclusions, drawing; Fact and opinion, statements of; Generalizations, making; Predicting.**

K

KWL reading strategy, 5.1 92a, 5.2 164a, 210a, 5.3 264a, 290a, 316a, 348a, 5.4 414a, 486a, 5.5 538a, 562a, 5.6 656a, 728a, WA3

L

Language arts. See **Capitalization, Creative/dramatic activities, Cross-curricular activities, Grammar and usage, Listening, Punctuation, Speaking, Spelling,** all **Writing** categories.

Language, oral. See **Fluency, reading; Listening; Oral reading ability; Speaking.**

Latin and Greek roots. See **Word structure.**

Learning centers. See **Cross-curricular activities.**

Legend. See **Genres.**

Less-able readers. See **Intervention.**

Leveled readers, 5.1 18c, 42c, 68c, 90c, 112c, LR1–LR48, 5.2 142c, 162c, 186c, 208c, 230c, LR1–LR48, 5.3 262c, 288c, 316c, 346c, 364c, LR1–LR48, 5.4 392c, 412c, 436c, 458c, 484c, LR1–LR48, 5.5 512c, 536c, 560c, 582c, 604c, LR1–LR48, 5.6 634c, 654c, 674c, 700c, 726c, LR1–LR48

Levels of thinking. See **Critical thinking.**

Limited English proficient students. See **ELL (English Language Learners) suggestions.**

Listening
  activities
    advertisement, 5.3 383d
    advice, 5.4 483d
    audio products, 5.1 20a, 44a, 70a, 92a, 114a, 5.2 144a, 164a, 188a, 210a, 232a, 5.3 264a, 290a, 318a, 348a, 366a, 5.4 394a, 414a, 438a, 460a, 486a, 5.5 514a, 538a, 562a, 584a, 606a, 5.6 636a, 656a, 676a, 702a, 728a
    debate, 5.2 229d, 5.5 625d
    demonstration, 5.4 411d
    description, 5.4 457f
    discussion, 5.1 34, 41d, 64, 84, 108, 111d, 5.2 158, 178, 204, 224, 248, 5.3 280, 310, 338, 345d, 358, 378, 5.4 408, 432, 452, 457d, 478, 498, 5.5 530, 552, 576, 598, 620, 5.6 650, 668, 696, 720, 748, 753d
    dramatization, 5.1 41d
    informational speech, 5.4 503d, 5.5 581d
    introductions, 5.3 345d, 5.5 535d
    multimedia presentation, 5.3 383d, 5.4 503d
    music, 5.3 363d
    oral presentation/report, 5.4 435d
    persuasive speech, 5.2 161d
    poetry reading, 5.4 457d
    read-alouds, 5.1 18m, 42m, 68m, 90m, 112m, 5.2 142m, 162m, 186m, 208m, 230m, 5.3 262m, 288m, 316m, 346m, 364m, 5.4 392m, 412m, 436m, 458m, 484m, 5.5 512m, 536m, 560m, 582m, 604m, 5.6 634m, 654m, 674m, 700m, 726m
    review, 5.1 89d, 5.3 287d
    sportscast, 5.1 111d

W

Teacher's Edition

Text

KWL Strategy: The KWL Interactive Reading Strategy was developed and is used by permission of Donna Ogle, National-Louis University, Evanston, Illinois, co-author of *Reading Today and Tomorrow*, Holt, Rinehart & Winston Publishers, 1988. (See also *The Reading Teacher*, February 1986, pp. 564–570.)

Page 142m: From "Dwaina Brooks" from *It's Our World, Too!* by Phillip Hoose. Copyright © 2002 by Phillip Hoose. Reprinted by permission of Farrar, Strauss, and Giroux, LLC.

Page 162m: From *Number the Stars* by Lois Lowry. Copyright © 1989 by Lois Lowry. Reprinted by permission of Houghton Mifflin Company. All rights reserved.

Page 186m: From "The Call of the Sea" from *The Crystal Pool* by Geraldine McCaughrean. Text copyright © 1998 by Geraldine McCaughrean. Reprinted by permission of Margaret K. McElderry Books, an imprint of Simon & Schuster Children's Publishing Division and Orion Children's Books, a division of The Orion Publishing Group.

Page 208m: From "Jane Goodall: The Dream," *Girls Who Looked Under Rocks* by Jeannine Atkins. Copyright © 2000 by Jeannine Atkins. Reprinted by permission of DAWN Publications.

Page 230m: From *Molly Pitcher* by Jan Gleiter and Kathleen Thompson, Steck-Vaughn Company, 1991.

Artists

Greg Newbold: cover, page i